Computerized Accounting with
Sage 50® 2017

Jim Mazza PhD, MBA
DeVry University

Gary Chavez, MBA
DeVry University

PARADIGM
EDUCATION SOLUTIONS

St. Paul

Senior Vice President	Linda Hein
Editor in Chief	Christine Hurney
Managing Editor	Cheryl Drivdahl
Assistant Developmental Editor	Katie Werdick
Testers	Crystal Hootman, Jeff Johnson
Director of Production	Timothy W. Larson
Production Editor	Carrie Rogers
Cover Designers	Sara Schmidt Boldon, Jaana Bykonich
Text Designer	Sara Schmidt Boldon
Senior Design and Production Specialist	Jack Ross
Proofreader	Traci J. H. Post
Indexer	Terry Casey
Digital Projects Manager	Tom Modl
Director of Marketing	Lara McLellan

Care has been taken to verify the accuracy of information presented in this book. However, the authors, editors, and publisher cannot accept responsibility for Web, e-mail, newsgroup, or chat room subject matter or content, or for consequences from application of the information in this book, and make no warranty, expressed or implied, with respect to its content.

Trademarks: Some of the product names and company names included in this book have been used for identification purposes only and may be trademarks or registered trade names of their respective manufacturers and sellers. The authors, editors, and publisher disclaim any affiliation, association, or connection with, or sponsorship or endorsement by, such owners.

We have made every effort to trace the ownership of all copyrighted material and to secure permission from copyright holders. In the event of any question arising as to the use of any material, we will be pleased to make the necessary corrections in future printings. Thanks are due to the aforementioned authors, publishers, and agents for permission to use the materials indicated.

ISBN 978-0-76387-601-2 (print)
ISBN 978-0-76387-602-9 (digital)

© 2018 by Paradigm Publishing, Inc.

875 Montreal Way
St. Paul, MN 55102
Email: educate@emcp.com
Website: ParadigmEducation.com

Printed in the United States of America

25 24 23 22 21 20 19 18 17 16   1 2 3 4 5 6 7 8 9 10

Brief Contents

Contents

Preface

Computerized Accounting with Sage 50® 2017 teaches all of the key accounting software skills supported in Sage 50® Accounting, Release 2017. In addition, it covers the accounting concepts associated with each chapter in that release. Detailed, step-by-step explanations followed by hands-on exercises provide the opportunity to practice with program features immediately after learning about them. A variety of end-of-chapter exercises help ensure mastery of the key course content.

As you complete the *Computerized Accounting with Sage 50® 2017* text and work problems using Sage 50 software, you will

- learn software procedures through step-by-step instructions while examining screen captures;
- gain insight into processes through hints and identified key phrases, which are included in the textbook margins;
- assess your comprehension with Checkpoint features that appear at the end of each chapter section;
- experience working with others, which is essential for success in a workplace setting, through Cooperative Learning team activities;
- sharpen your critical-thinking skills while completing end-of-chapter Writing and Decision Making problems that relate to chapter learning objectives; and
- test your knowledge of learning objectives through practice exercises and two sets of comprehensive Case Problems.

Course Objectives

Computerized Accounting with Sage 50® 2017 is designed to be used in a one-semester or one-quarter beginning accounting and Sage 50 course. After completion of a course that uses *Computerized Accounting with Sage 50® 2017*, you will be able to do the following:

- Identify and apply terms, concepts, principles, and procedures used in accounting for service and merchandising businesses
- Create a company using Sage 50
- Know the difference between the cash and accrual methods of accounting
- Record transactions and manipulate data in Sage 50
- Demonstrate a working knowledge of accounts receivable and accounts payable, including treatment of taxes and discounts
- Demonstrate and apply Sage 50 skills for managing inventory and inventory-related accounts
- Demonstrate and apply a working knowledge of the concepts associated with payroll and their application using Sage 50
- Demonstrate and apply a working knowledge of costing concepts and their application using Sage 50
- Understand fixed assets and the depreciation of fixed assets
- Differentiate between a partnership and a corporation and know how Sage 50 deals with each

Textbook Features

This textbook allows you to practice all of the basic accounting activities of operating a business of small to intermediate size. Chapters 1–7 progress through setting up a new company, building a chart of accounts, entering beginning balances in the general ledger, processing transactions (accounts payable, accounts receivable, cash, etc.) in both the general journal and special journals, preparing financial statements, and reconciling accounts for a service business. Chapters 8 and 9 focus on inventory transactions for a merchandise business and discuss the various inventory valuation methods.

Chapters 10–12 address processing payroll and job costing transactions. These chapters also discuss the advantages and disadvantages of the different forms of business organizations (sole proprietorship, partnership, and corporation). Because the Student Version of Sage 50 does not contain the Fixed Assets Module (available only in the Commercial Version of the software), the Appendix covers the purchase, depreciation, and sale of fixed assets using the general journal.

The topics presented in each chapter build on the topics covered in previous chapters. *Computerized Accounting with Sage 50® 2017* is designed around features that support student mastery of skills and concepts while providing flexibility in its approach for instructors.

Chapter Features

Chapter features introduce accounting principles, lead you through Sage 50 procedures, and provide periodic checks of comprehension. These features include the following:

- Learning objectives that focus the instruction for each chapter
- Explanations of accounting concepts before practice using Sage 50 features
- Chapter sections that are aligned to learning objectives, with a combination of tutorial and problem solving
- Step-by-step instruction of software features
- Detailed screen captures that illustrate software features and steps taken throughout the exercise
- Checkpoint features, such as the one shown below, appearing at the end of each chapter section and providing an opportunity to check comprehension of key concepts and to reinforce learned skills, with answers provided in the Chapter Review and Assessment section at the end of each chapter
- Objective practice exercises aligned to each learning objective, offering an opportunity to practice Sage 50 procedures

Checkpoint

1. Why do some businesses impose finance charges on customer accounts?
2. What account is used to record finance charges?

- Two methods of negotiating the Sage 50 environment, which are applied intermittently throughout the text: using Menu bar drop-down menus or navigation aids and toolbars to work through the problems.

Margin Features

The following margin features (examples shown to the left) provide helpful definitions and hints:

- Definitions of key accounting terms, which can be used as convenient review tools
- Hints, which offer suggestions and reminders about Sage 50 features

End-of-Chapter Features

The elements in the Chapter Review and Assessment section summarize chapter content and test comprehension of Sage 50 procedures. The Chapter Review and Assessment features include the following:

- Software Command Summary – a succinct summary of the Sage 50 commands presented in the chapter
- Checkpoint Answers – answers to the Checkpoint questions offered at the end of each chapter section
- Study Quiz – an online quiz that can be taken multiple times, accessed through a link in the ebook
- Content Check – multiple-choice questions that review key concepts
- Short Essay Response – short essay questions that require written responses
- Cooperative Learning – problems that focus on specific chapter issues and promote collaborative learning
- Writing and Decision Making – a problem that encourages creative problem solving
- Case Problems – problems designed to reinforce the chapter learning objectives and allow you to demonstrate mastery of the chapter topics by applying accounting concepts and Sage 50 software procedures; the four problems in each chapter are paired, so the A set can be used for practice and the B set can be used for assessment

Appendix – Fixed Assets

The appendix discusses the concepts of depreciation and fixed assets valuation. The most widely accepted depreciation methods are demonstrated in manual form. In the appendix, you will learn to use Sage 50 to create the individual fixed asset accounts and to create the appropriate supporting accounts, including the accumulated depreciation accounts. Transactions for the purchase, monthly depreciation, and disposal of assets are explained, demonstrated, and practiced.

Sage 50 2017 Software

To complete chapter work, you must access and download the Student Version or Educational Version of Sage 50 2017. The version of Sage 50 available for download on the Sage website is known as the Student Version; the version preinstalled at some institutions is known as the Educational Version. The institutional Educational Version and the downloaded Student Version are identical and compatible.

System Requirements

To install and run Sage 50 Accounting Release 2017, Student or Educational Version successfully, you will need at a minimum the following hardware and software:

- 2.0 GHz processor for single user and multiple users (2.4 GHz recommended)
- 1 GB of RAM for single user and multiple users (2 GB recommended for multiple users)
- Windows Vista SP2, Windows 7, Windows 8, or Windows 10, with the latest updates from Microsoft installed
- 1 GB of disk space for installation
- Internet Explorer 9.0, 10.0, and 11.0 supported
- Microsoft .NET Framework 4.5.2; requires an additional 280 MB to 850 MB
- At least high-color (16-bit) SVGA video; supports 1024 × 768 resolution with small fonts required
- All online features/services require Internet access
- Excel, Outlook, and Word integration requires Microsoft Excel, Outlook, and Word 2007, 2010, 2013, or 2017 (32-bit)
- Printers supported by Microsoft Vista, Windows 7, Windows 8, or Windows 10
- In-product demos require Adobe Flash Player 11 or greater
- Adobe Reader 11.0 required

Installing Sage 50 2017

Before you begin the installation process, check with your instructor to see if Sage 50 Accounting and/or the company files have already been loaded in a designated location for you. If you need to install Sage 50 on your workstation or you are using this book at home, you must register your student version with Sage 50 Software by visiting http://sage50-2017.ParadigmEducation .com/sagedownloadpage.

As part of the registration process, you will receive via email a serial number (it may be referred to in the email as an activation code) that is required for installation. Once registered, you can download the Sage 50 2017 software from the Sage website.

To download the software from the Sage website:

1. Visit http://sage50-2017.ParadigmEducation.com/sagedownloadpage.
2. Note that you are given options to download the 2013, 2015, 2016, and 2017 versions of Sage. Select the 2017 option.
3. Follow the installation instructions. The installation process takes approximately 30 minutes.

Student eBook

The student ebook, available online at ParadigmEducation.com/ebooks, provides access to *Computerized Accouting with Sage 50® 2017* from any device (desktop, tablet, and smartphone) anywhere, through a live Internet connection. The versatile ebook platform features dynamic navigation tools including a linked table of contents and the ability to jump to specific pages, search for terms, bookmark, highlight, and take notes. The ebook offers live links to the resources that support the print textbook, including the student data files (company files), study quizzes, a glossary of key terms, and two comprehensive problems (at the end of Chapters 7 and 11). You can download all of the company files at the beginning of the chapter or when you see the icon shown to the left on an ebook page.

You will need an access code for the student ebook, available on the card packaged with this textbook. Replacement cards are available for purchase from Paradigm Education Solutions at educate@emcp.com or 800-535-6865.

Downloading Company Files from the eBook

If you are using a computer in a lab setting, we suggest that you create a separate folder, either on your hard drive or in a designated network directory, in which to save the Sage 50 company files that you create, open, and add to while working through this book. Your instructor may have already set up a designated location for your files. Once you have either created that folder or been told where your folder is, download the company files from your *Computerized Accounting with Sage 50® 2017* ebook to your folder.

To download company files, first launch the ebook by following the instructions on the card packaged with this textbook and then download the company files by accessing the links menu or the navigation pane in the ebook. Chapter folders can be downloaded individually or as a group by right-clicking on the desired folder and selecting *Download* from the drop-down menu. Note that there are no company files for Chapters 1 and 2.

If you are using a computer at home, and you are the only student who is going to use that computer for the course, create a folder called Sage 50 2017 Student Data (Company Files) at the following location, and then download the company files to this folder.

C:\Program Files\Sage\Peachtree\Sage 50 2017 Student Data (Company Files)

Creating and Naming Company Files

As you work through the exercises in this textbook, you will also create, open, and name Sage 50 company files. You will learn the procedures for opening, creating, and backing up company files in Chapters 1 and 2.

Company files created in Sage 50 use a lot of computer memory. Typically, you will save your files to a computer hard drive or a designated network directory. You may also back up and restore the files to a flash drive. Be aware that if you use a flash drive or email to transfer company files between two computers, you will need to back up your files at the end of each session and then restore them at the beginning of the next session. See your instructor to determine where exactly you should save your company files.

When you create a company file, or use one of the company files that are provided, you may want to customize the name so that it is readily identifiable. You can do this by adding alphanumeric (letter or number) characters to the end of the company name. The additional alphanumeric characters could be your last name and first initial. For example, if your name is John Jones, when naming or saving the Acme Laundry Company file, you would use the file name **Acme Laundry Company – JONESJ**. This is only a suggestion—ask your instructor for specific instructions on how to name and save files.

To customize the name of a company as you create it, key the customized company name in the *Company Name* field of the New Company Setup – Company Information dialog box.

To customize the names of the provided company files, complete the following steps:

1. At the Sage 50 Accounting Start Window, click *Open an existing company.*
2. Find and open the company file on which you will be working.
3. Click Maintain and then click *Company Information.*
4. At the Maintain Company Information window, click in the *Company Name* field and then change the company name as needed.
5. Click the OK button at the top of the window.

The next time you open the company file, its name will reflect the changes you made.

 ## Instructor eResources eBook

The *Sage 50® 2017 Instructor eResources* ebook includes access to the following materials:

- Objectives and Overview
- Syllabus Suggestions
- Lecture Notes
- Backup Files showing completed intra-chapter work
- Content Check and Case Problems Answer Keys
- Chapter Tests
- Comprehensive Problems with Model Answers
  - Comprehensive Problem One covers Chapters 1–7
  - Comprehensive Problem Two covers Chapters 8–11
- Objective Midterm and Final Exams (in RTF format and cartridges, including Blackboard, Canvas, D2L, and Common Cartridge 1.1)

About the Authors

Jim Mazza is a Senior Professor of Business at the Keller Graduate School of Management, DeVry University, Sacramento, California. He received a BA in Business and Human Resource Management from California State University-Stanislaus, an MBA from California State University-Stanislaus, and a PhD in Organizational Behavior from Capella University. Mazza began his teaching career in 1994 and has taught accounting, accounting application, business, and economic courses at the undergraduate and graduate level. He was selected as an Instructor of Instructors at the Conference on Accounting Education in 2004, 2005, and 2006. Mazza is co-author of *Computerized Accounting with Peachtree® 2000, 2002, 2005, 2007, 2008, 2009, 2010, 2011,* and *2012* and *Computerized Accounting with Sage 50® 2013, 2015, 2016,* and *2017,* published by Paradigm Education Solutions. He previously owned and managed his own retail and wholesale businesses in the Northern California Bay Area before they were sold to a national retailer.

Gary Chavez is a Professor of Accounting at the Keller Graduate School of Management, DeVry University, Sacramento, California. Chavez is also an accounting instructor at the University of the Pacific, Stockton, California. He earned a BS in Business Administration with an emphasis in International Business from San Francisco State University, an MBA from University of the Pacific, and a Master of Accounting and Financial Management (MAFM) from Keller Graduate School of Management, DeVry University. He has been teaching accounting and other business courses since 1990. Chavez is co-author of *Computerized Accounting with Peachtree® 2000, 2002, 2005, 2007, 2008, 2009, 2010, 2011,* and *2012* and *Computerized Accounting with Sage 50® 2013, 2015, 2016,* and *2017,* published by Paradigm Education Solutions and has served as a contributor to other college accounting textbooks. His main emphasis is helping students achieve their dream of an education. He strongly believes that education is the key to creating more opportunities in life for not only students, but also the students' families. Chavez was selected as Teacher of the Year and has also received Leadership Awards for his community service. He is also a former US Marine.

Acknowledgements

The authors and editors are grateful to Crystal Hootman, Jeff Johnson, and Traci J. H. Post for reviewing chapters, testing exercises, and providing many helpful suggestions.

CHAPTER 1

Getting Started

Objectives

1–1 Understand the differences between computerized and manual accounting

1–2 Open Sage 50 Accounting

1–3 Use the basic Sage 50 window, Navigation Aids toolbar, and Menu bar

1–4 Use the Help feature

1–5 Open, back up, and restore company files

Understand the Differences between Computerized and Manual Accounting

accounting The process of recording, summarizing, analyzing, and interpreting financial activities.

Accounting is the process of recording, summarizing, analyzing, and interpreting financial activities—activities that involve money. The purpose of accounting is to provide financial information that owners, managers, and other interested parties can use to make decisions about a business.

Every accounting system—simple or complex, manual or computerized—must produce a complete, ongoing record of the financial events that take place in a business, and must provide periodic reports showing the results of operations and the financial condition of the business. The steps of the accounting process are recording, summarizing, analyzing, and interpreting.

- *Recording* involves preparing a written record of financial events.
- *Summarizing* involves organizing the financial data into reports at regular intervals.
- *Analyzing* involves examining the reports to determine financial success or failure.
- *Interpreting* involves using financial data to make decisions.

Accounting is often called "the language of business" because it is used to communicate information about the financial results and financial condition of businesses. Is a firm profitable? Can it pay its debts? Does it have the resources to expand? This is the kind of information that accounting provides. Users of such information include owners, managers, current and potential investors, banks and other lending institutions, tax authorities, government agencies that regulate business activities, and potential suppliers and customers.

Manual and Computerized Accounting Systems

Whether an accounting system is manual or computerized, the underlying principles of accounting are the same. What does change when using a computerized system is the method of recording data and preparing reports. Once data about financial events is entered into a computerized accounting system, the system can be used to perform many tasks automatically: print a journal, post to the ledger accounts, prepare a trial balance, and print reports and financial statements.

Sage 50 Accounting is designed for small- and medium-sized businesses. One of the advantages of this software is that it produces records that are similar to those found in a manual accounting system. For example, Sage 50 allows you to work with special journals for sales, purchases, cash receipts, and cash disbursements as well as a general journal. Some other computerized accounting systems permit the use of just a single journal.

Special journals are an efficient means of recording financial data, and they make it easier to locate information that may be needed later. It is much quicker to look for a particular sale on credit in the sales journal than it is to trace through all the different transactions recorded in a single journal.

Computerized accounting systems like Sage 50 save an enormous amount of time and effort for you because they do so many tasks automatically. Just as important, computerized accounting systems greatly reduce the number of errors that can occur with a manual accounting system.

A manual accounting system offers many opportunities for making errors. Data must be transferred by hand from the journals to the ledger accounts, then to the trial balance, and finally to the financial statements. Throughout this process, many calculations must be made.

With a computerized accounting system, there is still the possibility of making an error when a financial event is entered into the system. However, many computerized accounting systems have built-in checks that help you avoid errors. For example, when an entry is being made in the general journal, Sage 50 alerts you if the entry contains unequal debits and credits.

Computerized accounting systems also reduce errors because they make all calculations automatically. For example, they compute the balances of the ledger accounts, the totals of the trial balance, and the subtotals and totals of the financial statements.

Note that computerized accounting systems like Sage 50 do more than just the traditional tasks of journalizing, posting, preparing a trial balance, and preparing financial statements. These systems also handle many other financial activities, such as doing payroll and tax calculations, keeping records of the time and costs involved in projects, billing customers, processing credit card transactions, keeping records of fixed assets such as equipment, and keeping track of prospective customers.

Checkpoint 1-1

1. What is the purpose of accounting?
2. What are two major advantages of computerized accounting systems over manual accounting systems?

OBJECTIVE 1-2

Open Sage 50 Accounting

Sage 50 Accounting includes two sample companies: Stone Arbor Landscaping and Bellwether Garden Supply. These sample companies are provided to help you become familiar with the basic functions of the software. In this chapter, we will work with Bellwether Garden Supply, a retail firm that sells goods and services.

The Sage 50 software is available in either the institutional Educational version, which is available on many school workstations, or the Student version, which can be downloaded via the Sage website. The two versions are identical and compatible. This text assumes you will use Sage 50 Accounting as you work through the book. To be more concise, from this point on, the software will be referred to as "Sage 50 Accounting" or "Sage 50."

See the preface of this book for information on registering your copy of Sage 50. You must register before you can install and use the software.

Follow the steps outlined on the following pages to begin the opening process for Sage 50 Accounting.

Step 1:

Double-click the *Sage 50 Accounting* icon from the desktop or click *Start, All Programs, Sage 50 Accounting,* and again *Sage 50 Accounting* from the Start menu lists that pop up. (See Figure 1–1.)

FIGURE 1–1
Sage 50 Startup Menus

Step 2:

Click *Explore a sample company* from the Startup window, as shown in Figure 1–2.

FIGURE 1–2
Sage 50 Accounting Startup Window

Step 3:

At the Explore a Sample Company window, click *Bellwether Garden Supply,* as shown in Figure 1–3. Then click OK.

FIGURE 1–3
Bellwether Garden Supply Selected

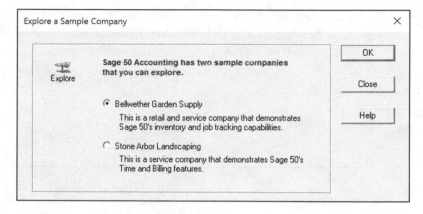

The Sage 50 window that appears allows you to access many helpful options to analyze several business aspects. From these options, you can obtain information about Sage 50 and your accounts. Sage 50 also offers a number of services that can be obtained by clicking the tab headings labeled Business Status, Customers & Sales, Vendors & Purchases, Inventory & Services, Employees & Payroll, Banking, Payment Center, Services, and System on the Navigation Aids toolbar.

For example, the Business Status tab provides an instant view of a firm's overall financial performance within specified areas. This view can be reached by clicking the Business Status tab that appears in the Sage 50 opening window.

Step 4:

Close the What's New in Sage 50 window. Select *Do not display this message again,* click Close, and click OK.

Click the Business Status tab on the Navigation Aids toolbar, as shown in Figure 1–4.

FIGURE 1–4
Business Status Tab Selected

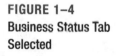

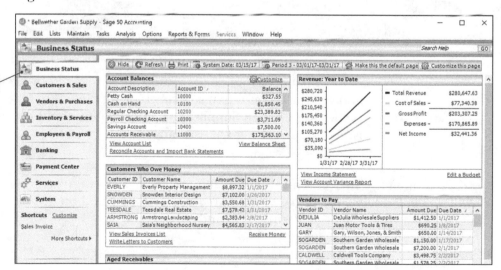

Follow steps 5 through 8 to explore a few of the valuable reports and graphs available in the Business Status tab. The information shown is for Bellwether Garden Supply.

Step 5:

Scroll down to view the Aged Receivables and Aged Payables pie charts, as shown in Figure 1–5.

FIGURE 1–5
Summary Reports and Graphs from the Business Status Tab

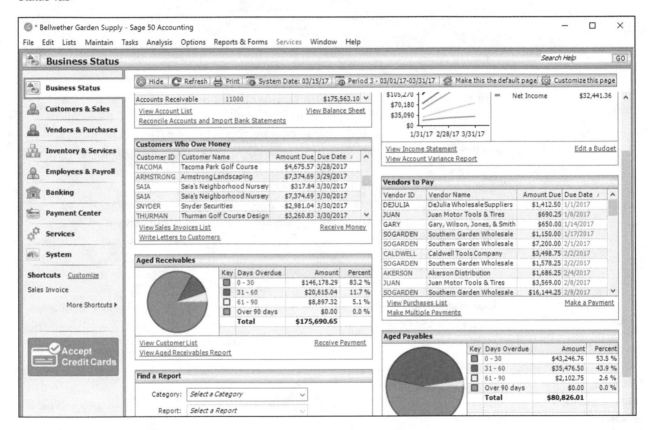

Information about any account can be reached by clicking the customer and vendor account name or any blue text line. For example, suppose that Bellwether Garden Supply wants information about the sales invoice that it issued to Armstrong Landscaping.

Step 6:

To access information about sales invoices to Armstrong Landscaping, scroll up to *Customers Who Owe Money* located on the Business Status tab of the Sage 50 opening window.

Step 7:

Click *ARMSTRONG* in the Customer ID column, as shown in Figure 1–6.

FIGURE 1–6
Armstrong Landscaping
Selected from the
Business Status Window

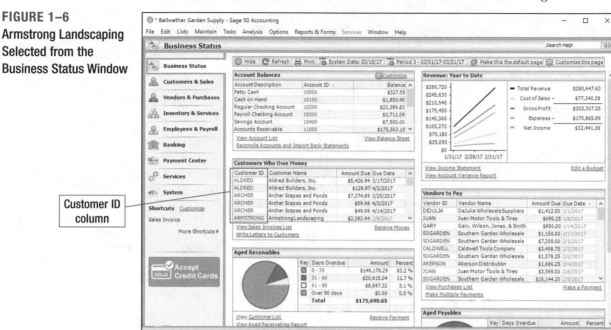

Step 8:

Review the latest invoice for Armstrong Landscaping in the Sales/Invoicing window. (See Figure 1–7.) Then click *Close* on the Sales/Invoicing toolbar.

FIGURE 1–7
Armstrong Landscaping
Sales/Invoicing Window

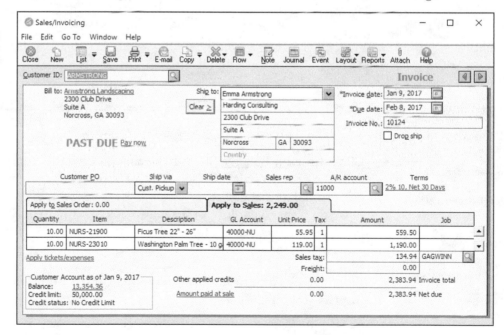

Step 9:

Hover the mouse over the <u>View Balance Sheet</u> hyperlink, as shown in Figure 1–8. This is one example of the helpful features that are available to users on the Business Status tab of the opening window.

FIGURE 1–8
View Balance Sheet
Hyperlink

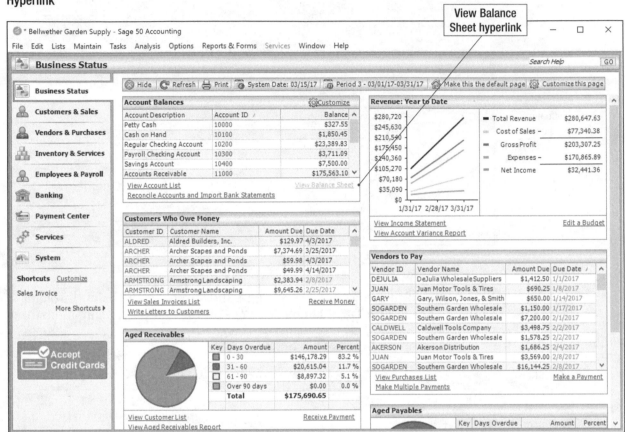

Step 10:

Click the <u>View Balance Sheet</u> hyperlink to view the Report or Form window with the current balance sheet. Click Close after you have reviewed the current balance sheet.

If you want to explore other features, click the hyperlinks to move between the sections of the window.

Step 11:

Exit Sage 50 Accounting by clicking *File* on the Menu bar, and then clicking *Exit.* (See Figure 1–9.)

HINT

The Sage 50 Business Status tab or any other tab listed with a tab heading can be minimized by clicking *Hide* on the Business Status Menu toolbar and maximized by clicking *Show* on the same toolbar.

FIGURE 1–9

Exit Selected from the File Drop-Down List

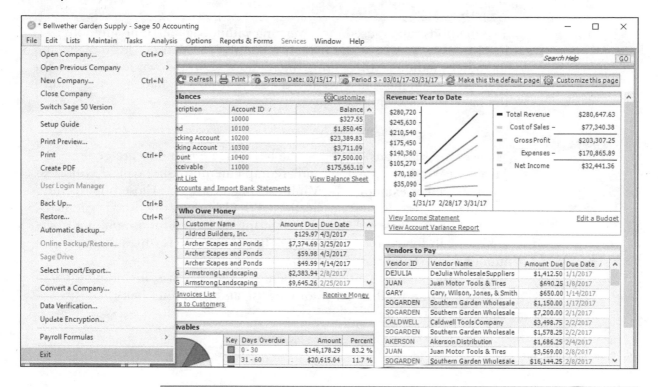

Checkpoint 1–2

1. What is the major purpose of the Business Status window?
2. What are the nine service tabs on the Navigation Aids toolbar?

Objective 1–2 Practice

1. Open Sage 50 Accounting.
2. Click *Explore a sample company* and then *Bellwether Garden Supply*. Click OK.
3. Click the Business Status tab on the Sage 50 opening window.
4. Access *Snowden Interior Design* from the *Customers Who Owe Money* section, review the account information, and then close the Snowden Interior Design Sales/Invoicing window.
5. Click the <u>View Income Statement</u> hyperlink from the Revenue: Year to Date section, review the financial statement, and then close the <Standard> Income Stmnt window.
6. Exit Sage 50 Accounting.

Use the Basic Sage 50 Window, Navigation Aids Toolbar, and Menu Bar

Two methods can be used for navigating within Sage 50. One method involves using the icons and hyperlinks on the Navigation Aids toolbar, and the other method involves using the traditional drop-down menus from the Menu bar. Both methods produce the same results and are accessed from the basic Sage 50 window.

Basic Sage 50 Window

Many of the functions located in the basic Sage 50 window are general Microsoft Windows functions and are implemented using typical Windows commands. For example, the Minimize, Maximize, and Close buttons function the same way for any application of the Windows operating system.

In addition, the scroll bar, window sizing tools, and mouse pointer operate normally for Windows. There are, however, some features that are unique to the basic Sage 50 window.

The basic Sage 50 window is made up of several parts, including the Navigation Aids toolbar, the Shortcuts list, and the Menu bar. (See Figure 1–10.)

FIGURE 1–10
Basic Sage 50 Window with System Tab Selected

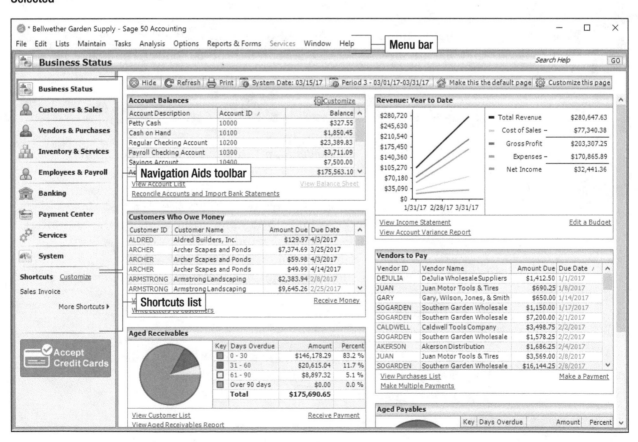

Shortcuts List on the Navigation Aids Toolbar

The Navigation Aids toolbar helps you move through the Sage 50 accounting system. The Shortcuts List, located at the bottom of the Navigation Aids toolbar, can be fully accessed by the <u>More Shortcuts</u> hyperlink below the Shortcuts heading. This allows the user to view and access several functions used on a daily basis, as shown in Figure 1–11.

FIGURE 1–11
More Shortcuts Selected on the Navigation Aids Toolbar

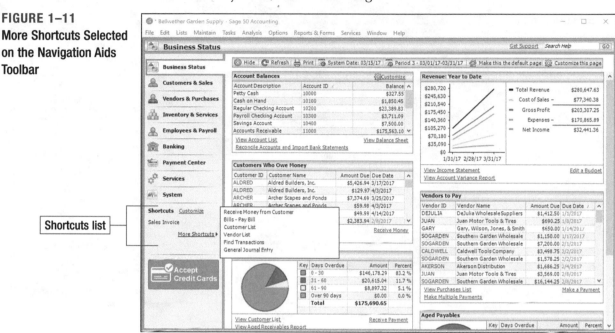

There are seven preprogrammed shortcuts, providing for rapid access to vital business functions.

- Sales Invoice
- Receive Money from Customer
- Bills – Pay Bill
- Customer List
- Vendor List
- Find Transactions
- General Journal Entry

To customize the Shortcuts List, click the <u>Customize</u> hyperlink and add, organize, or delete shortcuts at the Customize Shortcuts dialog box. After adding the desired functions to the Shortcuts List, you can click any of these general business functions and the corresponding Sage 50 work area, such as Sales/Invoicing, will appear.

To view other available functions accessed by clicking icons, follow the steps outlined below.

Step 1:

Open Sage 50 Accounting, and then open Bellwether Garden Supply, if not already open, by clicking *Explore a sample company.*

Step 2:

Click the Customers & Sales tab on the Navigation Aids toolbar. You will now see the options available on the Customers & Sales tab, as shown in Figure 1–12. For each tab, you will get a similar collection of icons directing you to the various parts and functions of the program.

FIGURE 1–12
Options Available on the Customers & Sales Tab

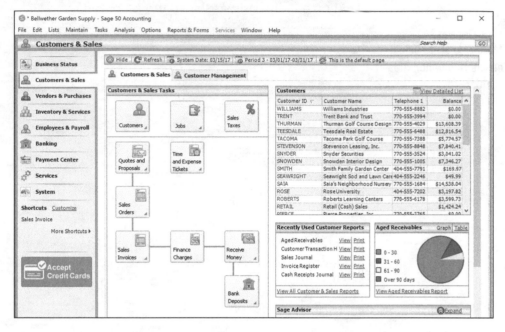

Menu Bar

The Menu bar, located at the top of the basic Sage 50 window, can be used to move through Sage 50 in the same way that the icons on the tabs are used. However, the Menu bar has 11 different general areas that can be accessed. These areas serve the following functions:

- File – Open, create, back up, and restore companies.
- Edit – Make changes and locate transactions.
- Lists – Create lists of various accounting aspects such as Customers & Sales, Vendors & Purchases, Chart of Accounts, and others.
- Maintain – Create and update the chart of accounts and accounts for customers, vendors, and inventory items.
- Tasks – Enter transactions of all types in the general journal and the special journals.
- Analysis – Access the cash, collection, payment, and financial management features.
- Options – Open, close, and customize toolbars. Use to change global options and to change the system date.
- Reports & Forms – Generate various reports.
- Services – Order checks, forms, and various customer support services.
- Window – Arrange the window.
- Help – Access help, a tutorial, technical support, and information about Sage 50 products.

The File menu, shown in Figure 1–13, is a typical Menu bar drop-down list. Click anywhere on the screen to close the drop-down list.

FIGURE 1–13
File Menu Drop-Down
List

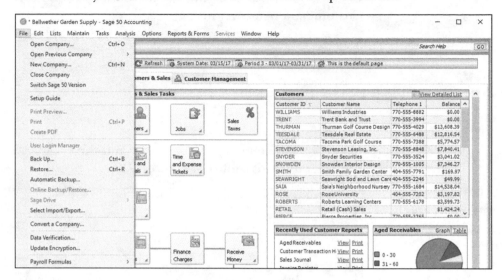

A Comparison of the Two Navigation Methods

To understand the differences between the two navigation methods, we will assume that Bellwether Garden Supply provides a service to a customer on credit.

Navigation Aids Toolbar

Step 1:

Click the Customers & Sales tab from the left side of the basic Sage 50 window.

Step 2:

Click the *Customers* icon at the top of the Customers & Sales Tasks section. (See Figure 1–14.)

FIGURE 1–14
Customers Selected
from Customers
& Sales Tasks Section

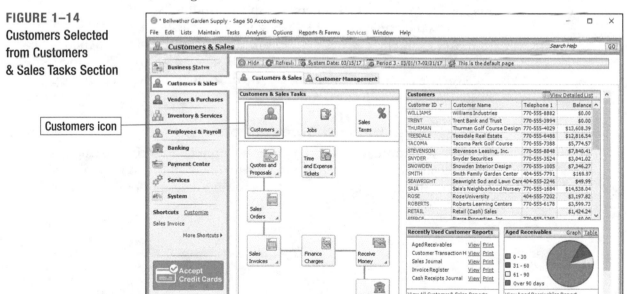

Step 3:

Click *New Customer* from the submenu list and then review the Maintain Customers/Prospects window.

Step 4:

Click the Close button from the toolbar at the top of the Maintain Customers/Prospects window.

Menu Bar

Step 1:

Now click Maintain on the Menu bar and then *Customers/Prospects* from the drop-down list, as shown in Figure 1–15.

FIGURE 1–15
Customers/Prospects
Selected from Maintain
Drop-Down List

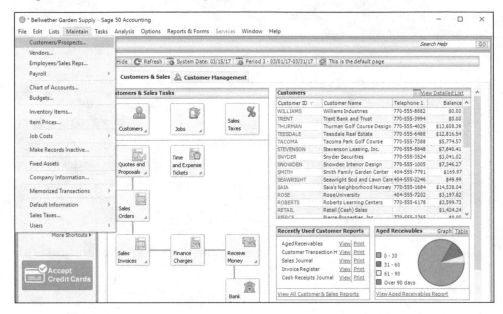

Step 2:

Review the Maintain Customers/Prospects window. Note that it is the same window as the one you reached using the *Customers* icon.

In this example, there is no difference in the destination reached. The only difference is the route taken through Sage 50 Accounting. One route involves use of the Sage 50 icons on the different tabs, whereas the other route involves use of the Menu bar.

General Window and Screen Options

Sage 50 Accounting uses certain terms in connection with its particular windows and screens. These terms are explained on the following page, using the Maintain Customers/Prospects window as a reference. (See Figure 1–16.)

FIGURE 1–16
**Maintain Customers/
Prospects Window with
Parts Labeled**

FIGURE 1–16
Maintain Customers/
Prospects Window with
Parts Labeled

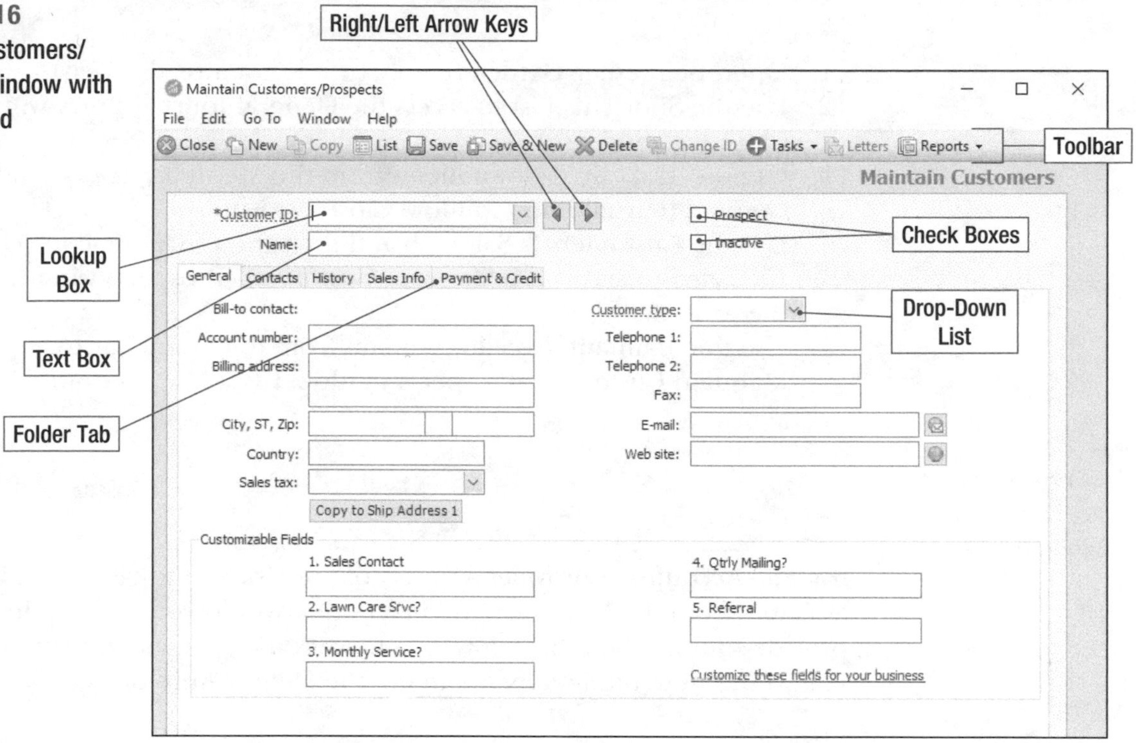

- Toolbar – Use to access the command buttons, including the Help feature.
- Lookup Box – Use the drop-down arrow in this type of field to access additional records and use the Sort and Find buttons.
- Right/Left Arrow Keys – Use to move to previous or next record.
- Check Box – Select by clicking inside the box.
- Folder Tab – Use to access the information in a file folder within the system.
- Text Box – Use to enter information.
- Drop-Down List – Click the arrow to display a list of options.
- Date Box – Use the *calendar* icon in this type of field to change dates (not shown).

Examine the Maintain Customers/Prospects window to see examples of a toolbar, lookup boxes, right/left arrow keys, check boxes, folder tabs, text boxes, and drop-down list arrows. Then click the Close button to close the window.

Checkpoint 1–3

1. What are the two methods of navigating through Sage 50?
2. Will the results differ when different navigation methods are used?

Objective 1-3 Practice

1. Open Bellwether Garden Supply (if it is not already open).
2. Use the Shortcuts List to access the General Journal Entry window. Close the window.
3. Use the Tasks drop-down menu from the Menu bar to access the General Journal Entry window. Close the window.
4. Use the Customers & Sales tab and then the *Customers* icon (click *New Customer*) to access the Maintain Customers/Prospects window. Close the window.
5. Use the Maintain drop-down menu from the Menu bar to access the Maintain Customers/Prospects window. Close the window.

OBJECTIVE 1-4

Use the Help Feature

Sage 50 Accounting provides a variety of ways for you to get help. Help is available from the Menu bar and in all other windows. The Help feature provides information that allows you to work more efficiently with Sage 50. Follow the steps outlined below to use the Help feature of Sage 50.

Step 1:

Click Help from the Menu bar, as shown in Figure 1–17.

FIGURE 1–17
Sage 50 Accounting Help Selected

Help options

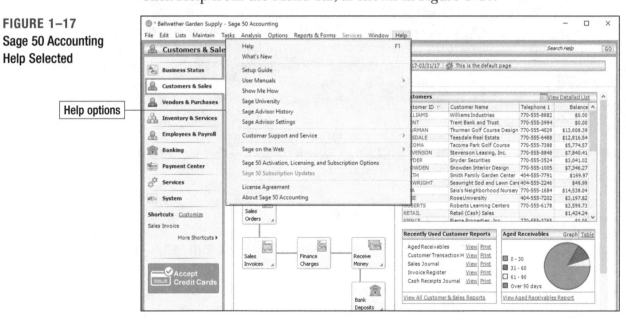

Step 2:

Click the *Help* option from the Help drop-down list.

Step 3:

Select and review the <u>C</u>ontents tab of the Help window, as shown in Figure 1–18.

FIGURE 1–18
Contents Tab of Help Window

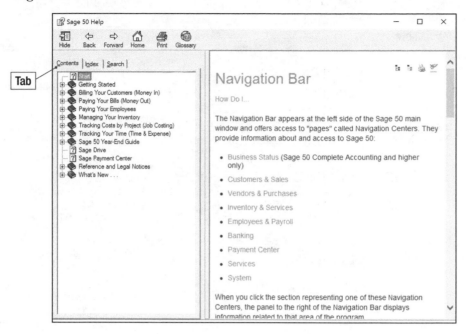

Step 4:

Click the <u>S</u>earch tab in the Sage 50 Help window to view the search options, as shown in Figure 1–19.

FIGURE 1–19
Search Tab of Help Window

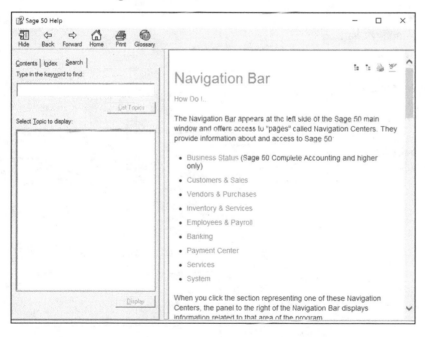

Step 5:

Key **Accounts Receivable** in the *Type in the keyword to find* text box.

Step 6:

Click the List Topics button to reveal a partial list of related topics, as shown in Figure 1–20.

FIGURE 1–20
Accounts Receivable Topic List

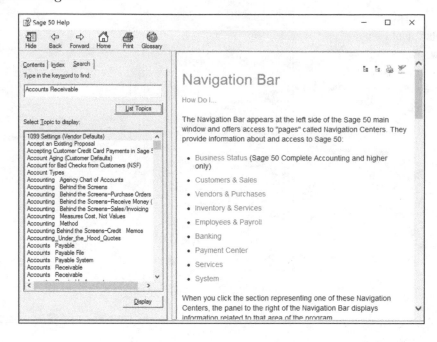

Step 7:

Use the scroll bar to find and then click to select *Service Company Chart of Accounts,* as shown in Figure 1–21.

FIGURE 1–21
Service Company Chart of Accounts Selected from the Accounts Receivable Topics List

HINT
Select means to click a word or choice once with the mouse.

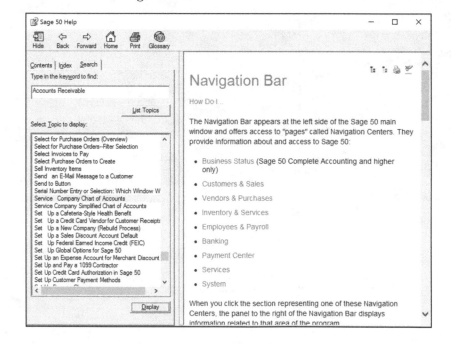

Step 8:

Double-click *Service Company Chart of Accounts* or click the Display button to reveal the topic information on the right side of the Sage 50 Help window, as shown in Figure 1–22.

FIGURE 1–22
Service Company Chart of Accounts Information Displayed in the Help Window

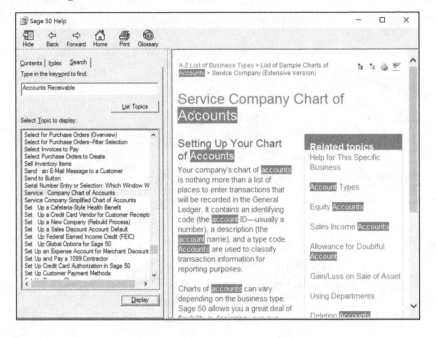

Step 9:

Scroll down the right side of the window to reveal additional topic suggestions.

Step 10:

Click *Account Types* to obtain information about establishing the chart of accounts.

Step 11:

Click the I_ndex tab in the Help window.

Step 12:

Key the words **Accounts Receivable** to reveal general related topics, as shown in Figure 1–23.

FIGURE 1–23
Index Topics Selected

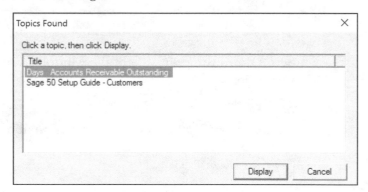

Step 13:

Click the Display button at the bottom of the Help window to reveal all of the directly related topics. This information appears in the Topics Found window, as shown in Figure 1–24.

FIGURE 1–24
Accounts Receivable in
Topics Found Window

Step 14:

Click Display and view the Accounts Receivable information on the right side of the window.

Step 15:

Close the Sage 50 Help window by clicking the Close button (X) in the upper right corner of the active window.

Note: Do not click the Close button (X) on the main Sage 50 window because you will be closed out of Sage 50 and will have to restart the program.

In addition to the Help feature on screen, there is an Internet Help feature called Sage 50 on the Web. By going online, you can review product news, get answers to frequently asked questions, obtain online support, and send feedback about Sage 50 features. You can access this resource by

clicking Help on the Menu bar, clicking Sage 50 on the Web, and then clicking *Product Community* from the submenu.

Checkpoint 1–4

1. How can the on-screen Help feature of Sage 50 be accessed?
2. How can the Internet Help feature of Sage 50 be accessed?

Objective 1-4 Practice

1. Open Bellwether Garden Supply (if it is not already open).
2. Open the Help feature by using the Menu bar.
3. Locate the following information under the Index tab:
   a. Accounts Payable
   b. Maintain Vendors
   c. Maintain Customers/Prospects
   d. Chart of Accounts
4. Close the Help window and close Sage 50.

OBJECTIVE 1–5

Open, Back Up, and Restore Company Files

To this point, we have opened the sample company by using the Explore
a sample company option from the Sage 50 Accounting startup window.
Normally, however, a company is opened by using the *Open an existing
company* option from the startup window or by clicking File from the Menu
bar and then clicking *Open Company*.

In most working environments, it is necessary to save and back up
computer files. This practice reduces the risk of lost data. Anyone who
works with computers and disks is aware of the potential for data loss and
the problems that it can cause. The loss of financial data can be especially
troublesome. For example, suppose a computer error results in the loss of
the data needed to bill customers for goods sold to them. This can result in
the loss of thousands of dollars of potential cash receipts. Because so much
of the data you enter into an accounting system is vital, it is important that
you save and back up data.

Fortunately, Sage 50 makes it easy to save data. Once posted, all transactions are saved. Data that does not require posting is automatically saved
when you exit Sage 50.

The backup process saves a copy of the company data that can be used to
restore a company to a previous condition. This procedure usually requires
saving to a hard disk, flash drive, or CD-ROM.

Opening an Existing Company

Follow the steps outlined below to open an existing company.

Step 1:

Start Sage 50 Accounting.

Step 2:

Click *Open an existing company* from the Sage 50 Accounting Startup window, as shown in Figure 1–25.

FIGURE 1–25
Startup Window with Open an Existing Company Option Selected

Sage 50 Complete Accounting—Educational **sage**

> Open an existing company

> Create a new company

Other Tasks:
- Explore a sample company
- Convert from another accounting program

Step 3:

Click OK at the Open an Existing Company dialog box to open Bellwether Garden Supply, as shown in Figure 1–26.

FIGURE 1–26
Open an Existing Company Dialog Box

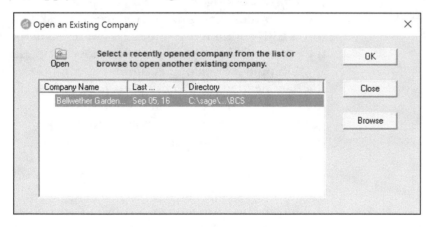

Open an Existing Company ✕

Open · Select a recently opened company from the list or browse to open another existing company.

Company Name	Last...	Directory
Bellwether Garden...	Sep 05, 16	C:\sage\...\BCS

OK · Close · Browse

HINT

If a company has recently been opened, it will appear in the list. The company can then be opened by highlighting its name and clicking OK. The dialog box may also list other companies.

To open an existing company through the File option of the Menu bar, use the following steps.

Step 4:

Click File from the Menu bar.

HINT

Sage 50 allows the user to keep several companies open at one time.

Step 5:

Click *Open Company* from the drop-down list and then click No at the Sage 50 Accounting message "Do you want to keep Bellwether Garden Supply open?"

Step 6:

Select *Bellwether Garden Supply* and click OK in the Open Company dialog box, as shown in Figure 1–27.

FIGURE 1–27
Open Company Dialog Box

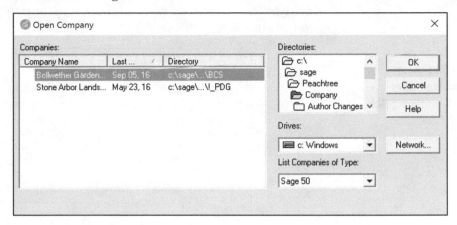

Backing Up Data

Frequently, a user of Sage 50 must back up work. Follow the steps outlined below to back up data.

Step 1:

Click File from the Menu bar.

Step 2:

Click *Back Up* from the drop-down list. The Back Up Company dialog box appears and offers you the option to be reminded to back up data. It also offers the option to include the company name in the name of the backup files.

Step 3:

If necessary, click the check box to insert a check mark next to *Include company name in the backup file name.*

Step 4:

Click Back Up, as shown in Figure 1–28.

FIGURE 1–28
Back Up Company Window

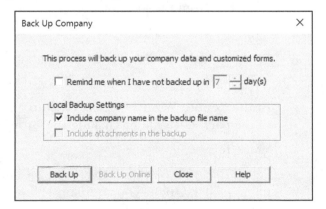

Step 5:

The Save Backup for Bellwether Garden Supply as dialog box will appear, as shown in Figure 1–29. If you will be backing up your company files on a flash drive, insert the flash drive into the appropriate drive. (For most computers this is the E drive.)

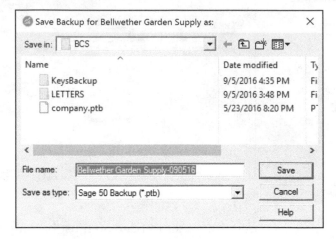

Click the down arrow next to the *Save in* box to select the destination where the backup will be stored. The file name has already been entered. It consists of the company name and the date the file is being saved.

Step 6:

Click Save to save the backup file to the destination.

Step 7:

Click OK at the Sage 50 Accounting window that indicates the file size. The progress of the backup is displayed until it is complete.

Restoring Data to Its Original Condition

If it is necessary to restore data you have backed up, the process is not difficult. It can be accomplished by completing the following steps.

Step 1:

Click File from the Menu bar.

Step 2:

Click *Restore.*

Step 3:

At the Restore Wizard – Select Backup File dialog box, select the location of the backed-up file by clicking the Browse button.

Step 4:

Select *Bellwether Garden Supply.* (Various dates will appear as part of the file name.) Click Open. The company will now appear in the *Location* text box, as shown in Figure 1–30.

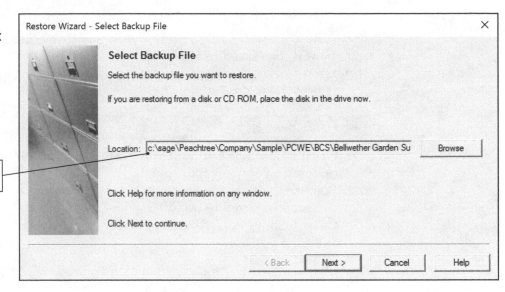

Notice the
full path.

Step 5:

Click Next.

Step 6:

At the Restore Wizard – Select Company dialog box, click *Overwrite Existing Company Data* and then Browse to select the company, Bellwether Garden Supply, to restore to a previous condition. Click Next.

Step 7:

At the Restore Wizard – Restore Options dialog box, click to insert a check mark in the box next to *Company Data*, as shown in Figure 1–31, and click Next.

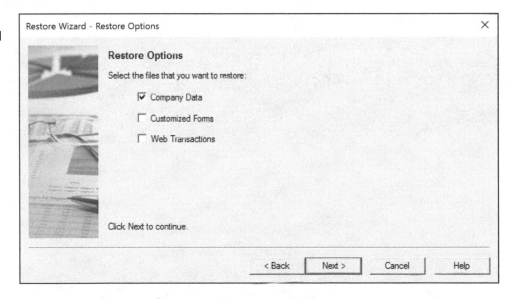

Step 8:

At the Restore Wizard – Confirmation dialog box, click Finish.

Step 9:

At the dialog box that says "This process will overwrite and replace existing data permanently. Do you want to continue?," click Yes.

Checkpoint 1-5

1. How is data saved in Sage 50?
2. What is the purpose of the restore process?

Objective 1-5 Practice

1. Open Bellwether Garden Supply using each of the two methods for opening a company file.
2. Practice the Back Up feature. (However, do not save any work unless you are instructed to do so.)
3. Close Bellwether Garden Supply.

Chapter Review and Assessment

Software Command Summary

Open Start Window	Start, All Programs, Sage 50 Accounting 2017, Sage 50 Accounting 2017
Open Company	File, Open Company
	or
	Open an existing company, "Company Name," OK
Help	The Help button from any menu toolbar
Back Up	File, Back Up
Restore	File, Restore

Checkpoint Answers

Checkpoint 1–1
1. The purpose of accounting is to provide financial information that owners, managers, and other interested parties can use to make decisions about a business.
2. Computerized accounting systems save time and effort because they do many tasks automatically, and they also reduce errors because they make all calculations automatically.

Checkpoint 1–2
1. The Business Status tab provides an instant view of a firm's overall financial performance within specified areas.
2. The nine service tabs are Business Status, Customers & Sales, Vendors & Purchases, Inventory & Services, Employees & Payroll, Banking, Payment Center, Services, and System.

Checkpoint 1–3
1. The two methods are Sage 50 icons and the Menu bar.
2. No, the results of the two navigation methods are the same.

Checkpoint 1–4
1. The on-screen Help feature of Sage 50 can be accessed from the Menu bar or by clicking the Help button in any window.
2. The Internet Help feature of Sage 50 can be accessed by clicking Help from the Menu bar, clicking Sage on the Web, and then clicking *Product Community* from the submenu.

Study Quizzes

Take the study quiz online to check your understanding of chapter concepts. The quiz can be taken multiple times.

Content Check

Multiple Choice: Choose only one response for each question.

1. Select _____ from the Menu bar to enter transactions of all types in the general journal and the special journals.
   A. File
   B. Lists
   C. Maintain
   D. Tasks
   E. None of the above

2. Accounting is the process of
   A. recording, summarizing, analyzing, and interpreting financial activities.
   B. journalizing, posting, and preparing financial statements.
   C. recording, adjusting, and closing entries.
   D. transferring data to the computer.
   E. None of the above

3. The users of accounting information include
   A. managers.
   B. investors.
   C. lenders.
   D. government agencies.
   E. All of the above

4. Sage 50 Accounting allows users to record financial events in
   A. just a general journal.
   B. just special journals.
   C. special journals and a general journal.
   D. a single combined journal.
   E. None of the above

5. Computerized accounting systems
   A. improve accuracy and efficiency.
   B. save time and effort.
   C. perform many tasks automatically.
   D. handle many different types of financial activities.
   E. All of the above

Short Essay Response

Provide a detailed answer for each question.

1. What is the difference between manual and computerized accounting systems?
2. Name some of the various tasks and financial activities that Sage 50 Accounting can perform. Explain how these might help you in operating a business.
3. Explain two ways to open Sage 50.
4. Describe the processes of back up and restore.
5. Explain the two generally accepted methods of navigating through Sage 50. Is one superior to the other?
6. What benefits do you see from the Help feature of Sage 50?

Cooperative Learning

1. Form into pairs and write a one-page paper comparing and contrasting manual and computerized accounting systems. Indicate which type of system you would prefer to use and why.
2. In groups of three or four students, research some local businesses or other entities that use computerized accounting programs. List the names of the programs. How are the programs used in the daily operation of the business?
3. In groups of three or four students, search the Internet for a review of accounting software. List the names, prices, and main features of the most popular accounting software packages.

Writing and Decision Making

Your employer has announced that the company will be switching from a manual accounting system to a computerized accounting system. Sage 50 Accounting is considered to be the favored accounting software because of all of its accounting and financial capabilities. However, the owner would still like to know what types of products and solutions would be available once the decision has been made to switch. Therefore, you have been asked to visit the Sage 50 website at http://sage.com and prepare a summary of products and solutions available.

Case Problems

Demonstrate your knowledge of the Sage 50 Accounting features discussed in this chapter by completing the following case problems.

Case Problem 1–1A

1. Start Sage 50 Accounting.
2. Open Bellwether Garden Supply.
3. Click the Customers & Sales tab.
4. Click the *Sales Invoices* icon and then *New Sales Invoice*.
5. On a separate piece of paper, list the names of the buttons on the toolbar of the Sales/Invoicing tab. Then close the tab.

6. Click Tasks from the Menu bar.
7. Click *General Journal Entry* from the drop-down list.
8. On a separate piece of paper, list the names of the buttons on the toolbar of the General Journal Entry window. Then close the window.

Case Problem 1–2A

1. Using Bellwether Garden Supply, open the Help feature by using the Menu bar.
2. Click *Help* from the drop-down list.
3. Click the Index tab and key **Accounts Receivable**.
4. Click the Display button.
5. Click the Display button again, and note the definition of *Days Accounts Receivable Outstanding* and how it is determined.
6. Key **Payroll** in the Index tab.
7. Scroll down and double-click *setup wizard*.
8. On a separate piece of paper, list the payroll items that the Payroll Setup Wizard establishes.
9. Close the Sage 50 Help window.

Case Problem 1–1B

1. Open Stone Arbor Landscaping.
2. Click the Business Status tab.
3. Click the View Account List hyperlink and then click *New* from the Account List window.
4. On a separate piece of paper, list the names of the buttons on the toolbar of the Maintain Chart of Accounts section. Then close the two open tabs.
5. Click Reports & Forms from the Menu bar.
6. Click *Financial Statements* from the drop-down list.
7. On a separate piece of paper, list the names of the buttons on the toolbar of the Select a Report or Form window. Then close the window.

Case Problem 1–2B

1. Using Stone Arbor Landscaping, open the Help feature by using the Menu bar.
2. Click *Help* from the drop-down list.
3. Click the Index tab and key **Payroll**.
4. Click the Display button.
5. Click the Display button again, and note the information regarding Fringe Benefits.
6. Key **Accounts Payable** in the Index tab.
7. Scroll down and double-click *using Payments Manager* under Accounts Payable.
8. On a separate piece of paper, list the information that the payment manager provides.
9. Close the Sage 50 Help window.

CHAPTER 2

Setting Up a Company

Objectives

2–1 Review organization types and company information

2–2 Set up a new company in Sage 50

2–3 Create a chart of accounts

2–4 Enter beginning account balances

Software Features

- Create function

- Edit function

- Print function for the chart of accounts and general ledger

An individual company must set up its books before any transactions can be entered. Regardless of whether the company uses a manual or computerized accounting system, the procedure is basically the same. The business setup process involves several steps:

1. Enter company information
2. Select a business organization type
3. Create a chart of accounts
4. Select an accounting method
5. Select a posting method
6. Select an accounting period

OBJECTIVE 2–1

Review Organization Types and Company Information

Businesses can operate as merchandising, service, or manufacturing organizations. *Merchandising businesses* purchase goods from wholesalers and resell them to consumers for a profit. Examples include department stores, grocery stores, and sporting goods stores.

Service businesses, including law offices, medical offices, and accounting firms, provide services to consumers for a profit. Note, however, that some service businesses also sell merchandise. A beauty shop, for example, might sell hair care products. However, its main business of styling hair generates the vast majority of its revenue.

Manufacturing businesses produce products from raw materials and sell those products to consumers for a profit. Their customers might be wholesalers or end users. Airplane manufacturers, construction companies, and furniture makers would be considered manufacturing businesses.

Some companies are difficult to classify because of their mix of revenue from service, merchandising, and manufacturing activities. For example, restaurants provide a service, sell products, and manufacture products using raw materials. So, what type of business is a restaurant?

Each business takes on one of three basic organization types: sole proprietorship, partnership, or corporation. The organization type, or structure, that a business decides on is a result of various factors. How many owners the company will have is one factor. Another factor is expertise. Will one owner have the knowledge required to run a specific business? If yes, then the sole proprietorship form of business might be sufficient. However, if more expertise is needed to own and operate the company, then perhaps a partnership will provide better results.

Before an owner decides on a business organization type, liability, capital formation, and tax issues must be considered. For example, some business types provide less liability protection for their owners than others. Sole proprietorships and partnerships, for example, have unlimited liability. This means that the owners are personally liable for the debts of the business. The owners can lose their personal as well as their business assets if the business does poorly or is the guilty party in a lawsuit. Liability is just one of the important issues to consider in determining which type of organization is best for a specific business.

merchandising businesses Firms that purchase merchandise from vendors and resell merchandise to consumers.

service businesses Firms that provide services to consumers.

manufacturing businesses Firms that produce products from raw materials and sell those products to wholesalers or end users.

Sole Proprietorships

sole proprietorship A business owned by one person.

A *sole proprietorship* is a business owned by one person who makes the decisions, takes all the risks, and earns all the profits. Unfortunately, the sole proprietor suffers all the losses, too. A sole proprietorship is easy to form. One owner with a limited amount of capital can open a business. In most states, all that is needed is a business license and a mailing address. The sole proprietor is free to make all the management decisions. Small local businesses such as barbershops, hardware stores, and dry cleaning stores are examples of firms that might be sole proprietorships. In recent years, many individuals have set up small sole proprietorship firms that provide computer consulting and management consulting services.

One drawback to the sole proprietorship type of organization is that a single owner often does not have all the expertise needed to run a particular business. Individuals with specific technical skills open businesses and then realize later that those skills are not sufficient. For example, suppose a ski instructor decides to open a ski equipment shop. The ski instructor may know all about skiing and can discuss skiing with potential buyers. In other words, the ski instructor has a lot of technical knowledge about skiing and ski equipment. However, what does the ski instructor know about advertising, accounting, or finance? Frequently, a sole proprietor knows very little about basic business procedures.

Financing and capital formation also may be difficult for the sole proprietor. Because the asset base and creditworthiness of the business rests with one individual, banks and other potential lenders might be leery of lending to that person. This can be especially true in the early years of a business when there is little credit history for potential lenders to evaluate.

The freedom to make all the decisions that a sole proprietor enjoys comes with a price—unlimited liability for the debts of the business. The owner's personal and business assets are accessible to creditors in the case of a business failure. Table 2–1 lists the advantages and disadvantages of the sole proprietorship type of business.

TABLE 2–1
Sole Proprietorships

Advantages	Disadvantages
1. Complete management control by owner	1. Limited level of expertise
2. Ease of formation	2. Limited amount of capital
3. Few government restrictions	3. Unlimited liability

Partnerships

partnership A business owned by two or more people.

A *partnership* is a group of two or more people who enter into a business arrangement for the purpose of making a profit. The benefits of a partnership can be great. Because there are more people involved as owners, the amount of expertise brought to the business is increased. This can lead to a synergistic relationship that can help the business grow. In the United States today, 10 percent of all businesses are partnerships. These businesses include small local firms as well as large national firms. In fact, some large multinational accounting firms are partnerships.

Because a partnership has more than one owner, it usually has more capital and capital formation potential than a sole proprietorship. Often, businesses do not start with enough capital to succeed. The owners must borrow money so that the firm can survive and grow. Generally, the more partners involved in a business, the easier it is to borrow money.

As with a sole proprietorship, in a partnership the owners are subject to unlimited liability. Creditors can go after the personal and business assets of all partners to satisfy the debts of the firm. This can be costly if a business experiences financial difficulties.

One of the biggest drawbacks to the partnership business type is the mutual agency rule. This rule provides that each partner can bind all the other partners to an agreement. For example, suppose partner X goes to a car dealer to buy a new car in the name of the partnership and, before the purchase, does not tell the other partners about the purchase. The result is that all partners are liable for the purchase even though they had no prior knowledge of it. Also, even if partner X leaves the business, the remaining partners are still required to pay for the car.

Partnerships have a limited life. Any time an old partner leaves or a new partner is added, a new partnership must be formed. This creates accounting as well as relationship problems. Assets, for example, must be revalued when a new partner is added or an old partner leaves. Table 2–2 lists advantages and disadvantages of partnerships.

TABLE 2–2
Partnerships

Advantages	Disadvantages
1. Ease of formation	1. Unlimited liability
2. Greater amount of expertise	2. Possible disagreements about management decisions
3. Greater potential for raising capital	3. Mutual agency rule
4. Synergistic relationship	4. Limited life

Corporations

corporation A business owned by stockholders or shareholders.

The ownership of a corporation is divided into shares of stock. Therefore, a *corporation* is a business owned by stockholders or shareholders. A large corporation usually has many stockholders. A small corporation may have just a few stockholders. Unlike a sole proprietorship or a partnership, a corporation is considered a legal entity in and of itself. It acts as its own "person" when it comes to business transactions and holdings. In other words, the corporation acts on its own behalf. Large, well-known companies such as Ford, Sears, IBM, and Microsoft are examples of corporations that operate in the United States. The corporation type is so dominant in our economy that even though corporations make up only 20 percent of the businesses in the country, they receive more than 90 percent of the revenue. The stockholders, or owners, of a corporation are not personally liable for its actions or debts. Stockholders can only lose what they have invested in the corporation's stock. This is known as *limited liability*. By issuing or selling stock, a corporation can raise needed capital more easily than can a sole proprietorship or partnership.

Stockholders elect a board of directors for a corporation, which in turn hires the management. Ordinary stockholders are not directly involved in the day-to-day operations of the business. They must rely on management to work in their best interest. However, one of the duties of the board of directors is to periodically evaluate the performance of management and make changes if necessary. Management must also consult with the board of directors about financial policies.

Because a corporation is considered a separate legal entity, it is taxed like an individual. This tax reduces the amount of income available for stockholders, who are, after all, owners. Stockholders share in the earnings of the corporation by receiving dividends or by selling their stock for a profit, or capital gain. The stockholders then pay personal income tax on these dividends and capital gains. The result is double taxation: the earnings of the corporation are taxed once at the corporate level and again at the individual level when stockholders receive dividends or realize capital gains. Table 2–3 lists the advantages and disadvantages of a corporation.

TABLE 2–3
Corporations

Advantages	Disadvantages
1. Ease of raising capital	1. More difficult and expensive to form
2. Limited liability	2. Subject to more government regulation
3. Continuous life	3. Double taxation
4. No mutual agency rule	

Checkpoint 2–1

1. What are the three main types of business organizations?
2. In what two types of business organizations do the owners have unlimited liability?

OBJECTIVE 2–2

Set Up a New Company in Sage 50

Several steps are necessary when setting up a new company in Sage 50. Each step must be read carefully and evaluated before you select a particular system, date, or accounting method. Follow the steps below to begin the business setup process for Wildwood Medical Services.

Step 1:
Start Sage 50 Accounting.

Step 2:

At the Sage 50 Accounting Startup window, click *Create a new company*. (See Figure 2–1.)

FIGURE 2–1
Sage 50 Accounting
Startup Window

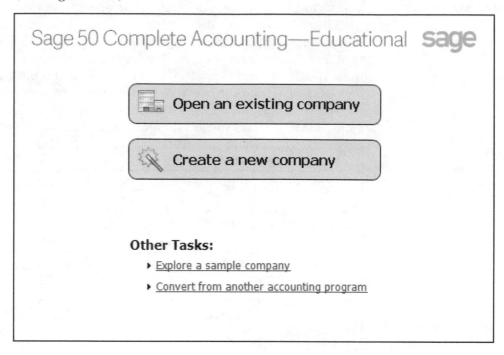

Step 3:

After reading the screen, click Next at the Create a New Company – Introduction dialog box. (See Figure 2–2.)

FIGURE 2–2
Create a New Company –
Introduction Dialog Box

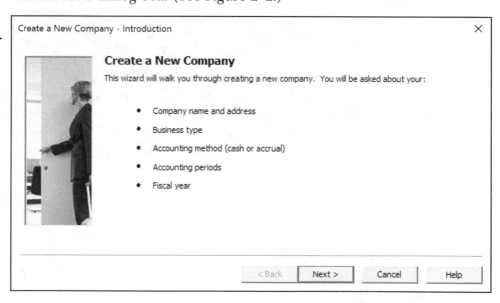

The Create a New Company – Company Information dialog box appears, as shown in Figure 2–3.

FIGURE 2–3
Create a New Company –
Company Information
Dialog Box

Create a New Company - Company Information ✕

Enter your company information * Required field

* Company Name: |

Address Line 1:

Address Line 2:

City, State, Zip:

Country:

Telephone:

Fax:

Business Type: Corporation ▼

Federal Employer ID:

State Employer ID:

St. Unemployment ID:

Web Site:

E-mail:

Note: You can edit this information after your company is created.

< Back   Next >   Cancel   Help

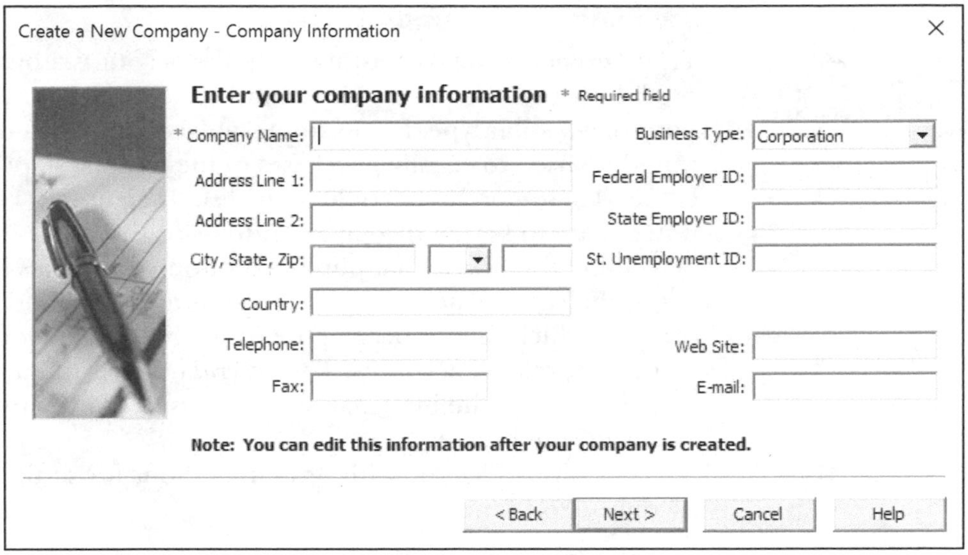

Step 4:

Complete the Create a New Company – Company Information dialog box using the following information:

Company Name:	**Wildwood Medical Services**
Address Line 1:	**2345 Highland Drive**
Address Line 2:	
City, State, Zip:	**Merced, CA 95555**
Country:	**USA**
Telephone:	**877-555-9902**
Fax:	**877-555-9900**
Business Type:	**Sole Proprietorship**
Federal Employer ID:	**45-789987**
State Employer ID:	**06-009-01**
St. Unemployment ID:	**00566-08**

Press the Tab or Enter key after you complete each entry. Compare your entries with Figure 2–4, and correct any errors before continuing. Click Next at the bottom of the dialog box when all entries are correct.

FIGURE 2–4
Completed Create a New
Company – Company
Information Dialog Box

Create a New Company - Company Information ✕

Enter your company information * Required field

* Company Name: Wildwood Medical Services

Address Line 1: 2345 Highland Drive

Address Line 2:

City, State, Zip: Merced   CA ▼   95555

Country: USA

Telephone: 877-555-9902

Fax: 877-555-9900

Business Type: Sole Proprietorship ▼

Federal Employer ID: 45-789987

State Employer ID: 06-009-01

St. Unemployment ID: 00566-08

Web Site:

E-mail:

Note: You can edit this information after your company is created.

< Back   Next >   Cancel   Help

The Chart of Accounts

chart of accounts A listing of all the accounts used by a business.

The *chart of accounts* is a listing of all the accounts a business uses. Accounts provide a record of transactions in which each account groups all transactions of a similar type. For example, an account labeled Office Supplies would be used to classify purchases of file folders, staples, and rubber bands. These purchases could all be listed separately, but that would make it necessary to search through hundreds or thousands of transactions to determine the firm's total purchases of office supplies in any period.

ledger A group of related accounts.

general ledger The main ledger of a business.

On the chart of accounts, all accounts are listed and numbered in the order in which they appear in the firm's general ledger. A *ledger* is simply a group of related accounts. The *general ledger* is the main ledger of a business. It contains the information that is used to prepare financial statements for the business.

Sage 50 provides you with several methods for setting up a chart of accounts. You can:

- Use the chart of accounts of a sample company from the list provided. Several companies are included in the list. Once a particular company's chart of accounts is selected, accounts can be added, edited, or deleted.
- Copy a chart of accounts from an existing Sage 50 Accounting company.
- Import a company's chart of accounts from another accounting program. QuickBooks files, for example, convert easily.
- Build the chart of accounts from scratch.

Step 5:

Click the *Use a sample business type that closely matches your company* option in the Create a New Company – Setup dialog box, as shown in Figure 2–5, and then click Next.

A Create a New Company – Business Type dialog box appears. Within the *Select a business type* text box, Service Company is highlighted. (See Figure 2–6.)

FIGURE 2–5
Create a New Company – Setup Dialog Box

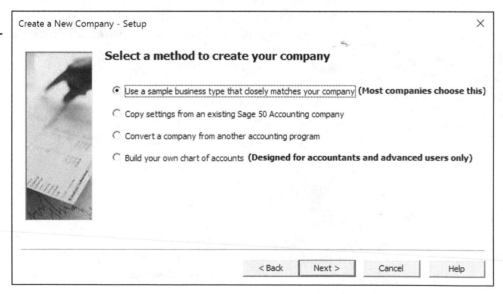

FIGURE 2–6
Create a New Company –
Business Type Dialog Box
with Service Company
Highlighted

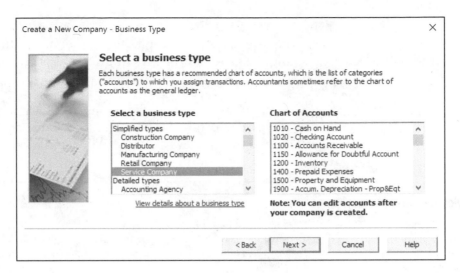

FIGURE 2–6
Create a New Company –
Business Type Dialog Box
with Service Company
Highlighted

Step 6:

Click the <u>View details about a business type</u> hyperlink below the dialog box to view the help area. This area provides a brief overview of the service industry. (See Figure 2–7.)

FIGURE 2–7
Service Company with
Simplified Chart of
Accounts Overview and
Related Topics

Explore the related topics listed in the Sage 50 Help for Your Business window by selecting the desired topic.

Step 7:

After reviewing the related topics for the service industry, close the window by clicking the Close button (X) in the upper right corner of the window.

Step 8:

Now view the Chart of Accounts options in the Create a New Company – Business Type dialog box. Scroll up and down to see the accounts that will be established for the newly created Wildwood Medical Services. Figure 2–8 illustrates a portion of the chart of accounts.

FIGURE 2–8
Service Business (Partial) Chart of Accounts

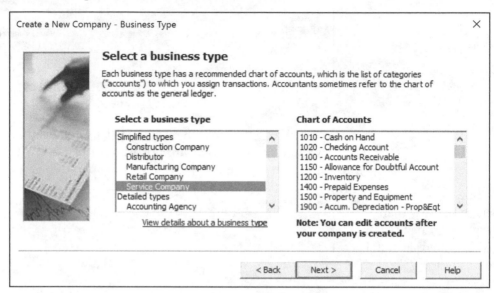

The chart of accounts selected from the sample company list will be incorporated into the accounting system being set up for Wildwood Medical Services. Some of the accounts will not be used, and some will be renamed. However, modifying an existing chart of accounts saves time and effort. If you want to build all new accounts, you would click the *Build your own chart of accounts* option in the previous Create a New Company – Setup dialog box. (See Figure 2–9.)

FIGURE 2–9
Build Your Own Chart of Accounts Option Selected

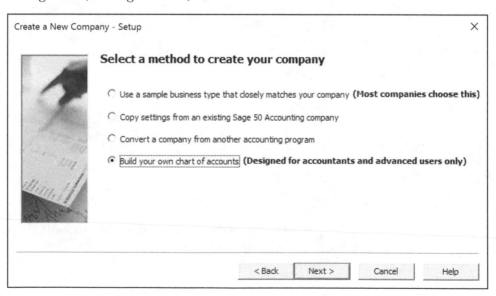

Step 9:

Click Next in the Create a New Company – Business Type dialog box with *Service Company (Simplified Types)* selected to establish the chart of accounts and move to the next step in the company setup process.

Accounting Methods

Every business must decide on an accounting method. Some firms use the cash basis, others use the accrual basis, and still others use a hybrid of cash and accrual accounting. Sage 50 allows businesses to use either cash or accrual accounting.

The *cash basis* requires a business to recognize (record) revenue when the related cash is received and recognize (record) expenses when the related cash is paid. Small companies with no inventory, no accounts receivable, and no accounts payable can use the cash basis. Thus, this basis is limited to small service businesses such as law offices, consulting firms, and bookkeeping firms.

Generally accepted accounting principles (GAAP) require the use of the accrual basis by merchandising and manufacturing businesses. Under the *accrual basis*, a firm recognizes (records) revenue when it is earned, even if the related cash has not yet been received. Similarly, the firm recognizes (records) expenses when they are incurred, even if the related cash has not yet been paid. For example, if a customer purchases merchandise or receives services on account, generally, this transaction would be recorded using an accrual accounting method. Similarly, if a business purchases supplies on account, it would use an accrual accounting method. In addition to merchandising and manufacturing businesses, service businesses that make sales on credit must use the accrual basis.

cash basis An accounting method in which a firm recognizes revenue when cash is received and recognizes expenses when cash is paid.

accrual basis An accounting method in which a firm recognizes revenue when it is earned and recognizes expenses when they are incurred.

Step 10:

At the Create a New Company – Accounting Method dialog box (Figure 2–10), click *Cash*. This is the accounting method that Wildwood Medical Services will use. ***Caution: After you choose an accounting method, you cannot change it.*** Click Next.

FIGURE 2–10
Create a New Company –
Accounting Method
Dialog Box with Cash
Selected

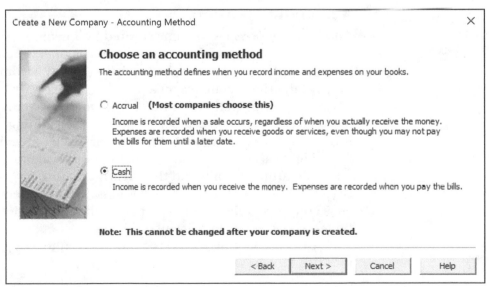

Posting Methods

After entries are made for transactions, the information must be transferred to the appropriate ledger accounts. This process is known as *posting*. Sage 50 offers two alternative posting methods: real-time and batch processing.

posting The transfer of information about transactions to ledger accounts.

Real-time processing results in instant account updates. For example, when a customer in a bank makes a deposit, the teller enters the transaction and the customer generally has immediate access to those funds. However, suppose a customer sends a check to a department store, and the department store waits until the end of the day to post that payment; this would be an example of batch posting.

Step 11:

Most companies select real time as their posting method so that their accounts will be updated as each transaction is entered and saved. Click *Real Time* at the Create a New Company – Posting Method dialog box. (See Figure 2–11.) Then click Next.

FIGURE 2–11
Create a New Company – Posting Method Dialog Box with Real Time Selected

Accounting Periods

An *accounting period* is the time covered by a firm's financial statements. It is the period for which the firm reports its operating results—its net income or net loss. Most businesses have a yearly accounting period but prepare interim statements on a monthly or quarterly basis.

accounting period The period of time covered by a firm's financial statements.

An accounting period cannot exceed one year. Many firms use the calendar year (January 1–December 31) as their accounting period. However, it is not necessary to do so. Some firms have legitimate business reasons for using an accounting period other than the calendar year. For example, many department stores end their yearly accounting period on January 31. Because so much of their yearly business occurs in December, it would be an accounting nightmare to compile all the information needed for the financial statements by December 31.

A yearly accounting period is often referred to as a *fiscal year*. Sage 50 uses this term as well.

fiscal year An accounting period of one year.

Step 12:

Wildwood Medical Services will use the calendar year as its accounting period. Therefore, click *12 monthly accounting periods per year* at the Create a New Company – Accounting Periods dialog box, as shown in Figure 2–12, and then click Next.

FIGURE 2–12
Create a New Company –
Accounting Periods
Dialog Box

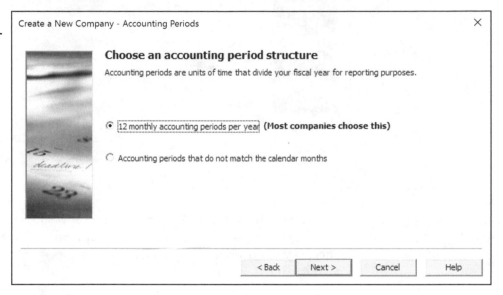

Step 13:

At the Create a New Company – Fiscal Year dialog box, follow the procedures listed below.

1. Select *January* from the drop-down list.
2. Select *2017* from the drop-down list.

Compare your entries with Figure 2–13 before continuing, and then click Next.

FIGURE 2–13
Create a New Company –
Fiscal Year Dialog Box

Step 14:

The Create a New Company – Finish dialog box indicates that your setup of Wildwood Medical Services is complete. (See Figure 2–14.) Click Finish.

FIGURE 2–14
Create a New Company –
Finish Dialog Box

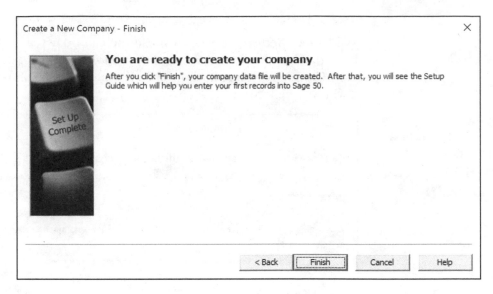

Step 15:

If the Sage 50 Accounting Warning window appears, click OK.

The Sage 50 Setup Guide window now appears. (See Figure 2–15.) You can access various areas of your business setup procedure by clicking the hyperlinks at this window.

Note: If the Setup Guide does not appear, click File and then Setup Guide. Insert a check mark next to "Don't show this screen at startup."

FIGURE 2–15
Sage 50 Setup Guide
Window

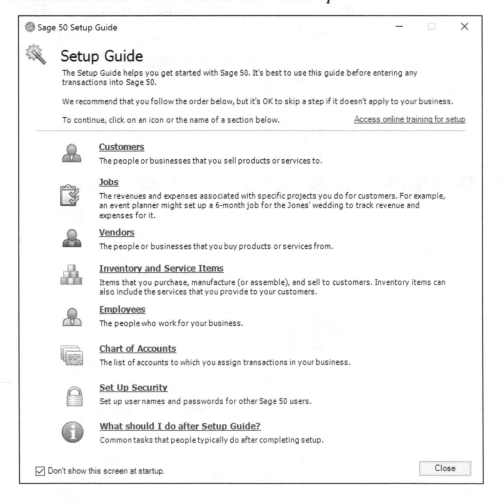

To review a specific area of the window, follow these steps:

1. Click the item you want to view, for example, *Chart of Accounts*.
2. Hover the mouse over the <u>general ledger</u> hyperlink to get more detailed information about the general ledger.
3. Click the Close button (X) in the upper right corner of the Sage 50 Setup Guide – Chart of Accounts window.
4. Close the Sage 50 Setup Guide window and Sage Adviser dialog box.

Note: Sage 50 automatically creates the new company in the program folder on the hard drive. You may therefore open, work on, and save the company from and to the hard drive. However, in the unique circumstance you are unable to save any data to the hard drive because of your institution's policy, simply use the back-up feature to save a copy of the company to an external drive such as a flash drive.

When you need to open the company from the external drive, use the restore feature and it will place a copy of the company back on the hard drive. In this situation, you will need to back up at the end of each session and restore at the beginning of each session. The only difference with the restore process given in Chapter 1 is that you will click the *A New Company* option at the Restore Wizard – Select Company window.

An alternative method is available if you are unable to save to the hard drive. This process requires cutting and pasting the newly created company folder from the hard drive to the flash drive. For example, the company folder for Wildwood Medical Services will most likely be located under the following directory: C:\Program Files\Sage Software\Sage 50\Company \wilmedse. After locating the company folder, cut and paste it to the flash drive. This will allow you to open and close directly from the flash drive without having to use the back-up and restore features.

Checkpoint 2–2

1. Name one aspect of the company setup process that cannot be changed after it is selected.
2. When does posting occur if you select the real-time posting process?

Note: You can keep Wildwood Medical Services open while completing steps in the activity.

Set up the following company using the procedures outlined in Objective 2-2. Note that Maslow's Financial Services will use the accrual accounting method and will build its own chart of accounts.

Company Name:	**Maslow's Financial Services**
Address Line 1:	**329 Smith Ave.**
Address Line 2:	
City, State, Zip:	**Ceres, CA 95101**
Country:	**USA**
Telephone:	**209-555-2222**
Fax:	**209-555-6666**
Business Type:	**Sole Proprietorship**
Federal Employer ID:	**95-343434**
State Employer ID:	**06-3333-01**
St. Unemployment ID:	**00221-78**
Chart of Accounts:	**Build your own chart of accounts**
Accounting Method:	**Accrual**
Posting Method:	**Real Time**
Accounting Periods:	**12 monthly accounting periods**
Fiscal Year to Start:	**January 2017**

Click OK at the Sage 50 Accounting window. Close the Sage 50 Setup Guide and click OK at the Sage 50 Setup Guide dialog box. Close the Sage Advisor Getting Started window.

OBJECTIVE 2–3

Create a Chart of Accounts

In Objective 2–2, you learned the company setup process. Now you will review the setup process and explore some variations to it. For example, you set up Wildwood Medical Services with cash basis as its accounting method. The company setup you will do in this section will use the accrual basis as the accounting method. Follow the steps below to set up a new company.

Step 1:
Click File from the Menu bar.

Step 2:
Select *New Company* from the drop-down list, as shown in Figure 2–16.

Note: You can keep Maslow's Financial Services open while completing steps in this objective.

FIGURE 2–16
New Company Selected
from the File Drop-Down
List

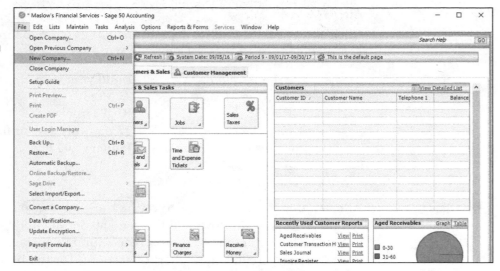

Step 3:

Click Next at the Create a New Company – Introduction window. Then carefully enter the information shown below in the Create a New Company – Company Information dialog box. Compare your entries with Figure 2–17 before continuing.

Company Name:	**Tile Installation by Ramirez**
Address Line 1:	**2110 West Avenue**
City, State, Zip:	**Fremont, CA 95700**
Country:	**USA**
Telephone:	**209-555-1111**
Fax:	**209-555-5555**
Business Type:	**Sole Proprietorship**
Federal Employer ID:	**95-3458767**
State Employer ID:	**06-3363-01**
St. Unemployment ID:	**00321-78**

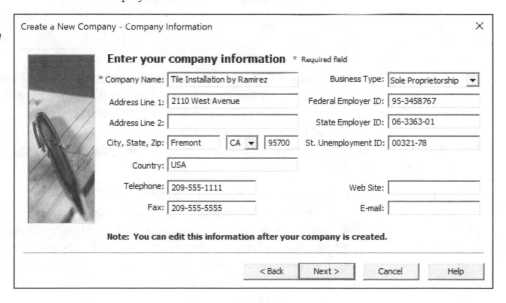

Step 4:

Click Next. Enter the following information in the remaining dialog boxes to complete the Create a New Company Setup process, and then click Finish:

Chart of Accounts:	**Build your own chart of accounts**
Accounting Method:	**Accrual**
Posting Method:	**Real Time**
Accounting Periods:	**12 monthly accounting periods**
Fiscal Year to Start:	**January 2017**

Step 5:

After waiting for the software to create the company data files, close the Action Items and windows and the Sage 50 Setup Guide window, if open.

You have completed the setup process for Tile Installation by Ramirez. Now you must create a new chart of accounts for the business because you selected the *Build your own chart of accounts* option at the Chart of Accounts setup dialog box. You will need to create all of the accounts using information that includes account ID, account description, and account type.

Account ID

Every general ledger account must have a separate number for identification purposes. In Sage 50, this number is called the *account ID*. Sage 50 specifies a numeric range for each account classification. For example, all asset accounts must fall within the range of 100–199, 1000–1999, or 10000–19999. The starting point for each numeric range is shown in Table 2–4.

TABLE 2–4
Sage 50 Starting Numbers for Account Classification

Account Classification	Starting Number for Account ID
Assets	100, 1000, 10000
Liabilities	200, 2000, 20000
Equity	300, 3000, 30000
Revenue	400, 4000, 40000
Expenses	500, 5000, 50000

A small business might use 100 for its Cash account and 102 for its Petty Cash account. A larger business that needs many accounts might assign 1000 or 10000 to Cash and 1020 or 10200 to Petty Cash.

All of the general ledger accounts used in Sage 50 fall into the five broad classifications listed in Table 2–4. The meaning of these classifications is as follows:

- *Assets* are the things a business owns.
- *Liabilities* are the debts a business owes.
- *Equity* is the difference between what a business owns and what it owes.
- *Revenue* is what a business earns when it sells goods or provides a service.
- *Expenses* are the costs a business incurs to produce revenue.

Account Description

In Sage 50, every general ledger account must have an account description as well as an account ID. The account description indicates the nature of the transactions that will be recorded in the account. For example, Cash is the account description for the account that will be used to record all transactions involving the receipt and payment of cash. Other examples of account descriptions are Office Supplies, Accounts Receivable, Office Equipment, and Accounts Payable.

Account Type

When creating a chart of accounts in Sage 50, it is necessary to assign an account type to each general ledger account as well as an ID and a description. The account type indicates to which group of accounts on the financial statements a particular account belongs. Having this information in the chart of accounts makes it possible for Sage 50 to prepare automated financial statements at the end of each accounting period.

Sage 50 uses the following 16 account types:

- **Cash**

  This account type is used for any accounts that involve cash. In business, cash consists of funds on hand in the firm and funds on deposit in banks. The funds on hand include not only currency and coin but also cash equivalents such as checks and money orders received from customers. Some firms maintain just one cash account, but others have a variety of cash accounts such as Cash on Hand, Petty Cash, Regular Checking Account, Payroll Checking Account, and Money Market Savings.

- **Accounts Receivable**

  The *accounts receivable* of a business are the amounts owed by its customers for goods or services sold to them on credit or on account.

- **Inventory**

  Inventory is the stock of goods on hand. In a merchandising business, inventory is the stock of goods that the firm has purchased for resale to customers. A manufacturing business has three kinds of inventory— raw materials, work in process, and finished goods. The inventory accounts that a business uses depend on its operations.

- **Other Current Assets**

  Accounts receivable and inventory are considered *current assets*—that is, assets that will be used up or turned into cash within one year. There are also other kinds of current assets that involve much smaller amounts of money, such as office supplies and prepaid insurance. In Sage 50, any current assets besides cash, accounts receivable, and inventory are classified as other current assets.

- **Fixed Assets**

  Physical assets that will be used by a business for more than a year are called *fixed assets*. Examples of fixed assets are equipment, trucks, buildings, and land. Fixed assets are also known as plant assets, long-term assets, and property, plant, and equipment.

- **Accumulated Depreciation**

  Part of the cost of a fixed asset is allocated, or expensed, to operations during each accounting period of its useful life. This process is known as *depreciation*. Depreciation allows a business to match the cost of fixed assets against the revenue those assets help to produce. The accumulated depreciation represents the total depreciation expense taken in past accounting periods.

accounts receivable The amounts owed to a business by its customers for goods or services sold on credit.

current assets Assets that will be used up or turned into cash within one year.

fixed assets Physical assets that will be used by a business for more than a year.

accounts payable
The amounts that a business owes to its creditors for goods or services purchased on credit.

current liabilities
Debts due for payment within one year.

long-term liabilities
Debts that extend for more than one year.

- **Other Assets**

  In Sage 50, assets that are not current assets or fixed assets are classified as other assets. This category includes intangible assets such as goodwill, patents, trademarks, copyrights, and franchises. Intangible assets are assets that have no physical substance.

- **Accounts Payable**

  The *accounts payable* of a business are the amounts that it owes to creditors for goods and services that it purchased on credit.

- **Other Current Liabilities**

  Current liabilities are debts that are due within one year. Accounts payable are one type of current liability. In Sage 50, all current liabilities besides accounts payable are classified as other current liabilities. This category includes items such as salaries payable, taxes payable, short-term notes payable, and interest payable.

- **Long-Term Liabilities**

  Long-term liabilities are debts that extend for more than one year. This category includes mortgages payable and long-term notes payable.

- **Equity—Doesn't Close**

  In Sage 50, there are three types of equity accounts. The first type consists of accounts that do not close. These are the capital accounts of a sole proprietorship and a partnership and the capital stock accounts of a corporation.

- **Equity—Retained Earnings**

  This category consists of the Retained Earnings account. At the end of each accounting period, the revenue and expense accounts are closed into Retained Earnings. The difference between the balances of the revenue and expense accounts is the net income or net loss for the period.

- **Equity—Gets Closed**

  The last category of equity accounts contains the accounts that are used to record owner contributions and distributions of earnings to owners (drawings in sole proprietorships and partnerships and dividends in corporations). These equity accounts are closed at the end of the accounting period.

- **Income**

  In Sage 50, the income accounts include all accounts used to record the revenue from sales of goods or services and all accounts used to record other types of revenue, such as interest income.

- **Cost of Sales**

  The accounts in this category apply to merchandising and manufacturing businesses but not to service businesses. The cost of sales is the cost of purchasing or making the goods that were sold during an accounting period. Cost of sales is also known as cost of goods sold. In a merchandising business, accounts for purchases, purchase returns and allowance, purchase discounts, and transportation charges would be categorized as cost of sales.

- **Expenses**

  In Sage 50, the expense accounts include all operating expenses incurred to earn revenue such as rent and salaries and other expenses such as interest.

Step 6:

Click Maintain from the Menu bar and then click *Chart of Accounts.*

For the following steps, use Tile Installation by Ramirez's chart of accounts, as shown in Table 2–5. Complete the account ID, account description, and account type for all of Ramirez's accounts.

TABLE 2–5
Tile Installation by Ramirez Chart of Accounts

Account ID	Description	Account Type
100	Cash	Cash
102	Petty Cash	Cash
104	Accounts Receivable	Accounts Receivable
106	Office Supplies	Other Current Assets
108	Equipment	Fixed Assets
108.5	Accum. Depreciation-Equipment	Accumulated Depreciation
200	Accounts Payable	Accounts Payable
300	J. Ramirez, Capital	Equity-doesn't close
301	J. Ramirez, Equity	Equity-Retained Earnings
301.5	J. Ramirez, Drawing	Equity-gets closed
400	Revenue	Income
500	Rent Expense	Expenses
502	Utilities Expense	Expenses
504	Telephone Expense	Expenses
506	Office Supplies Expense	Expenses
508	Repairs Expense	Expenses
510	Depreciation Expense-Equipment	Expenses
512	Wages and Salaries Expense	Expenses
514	Miscellaneous Expense	Expenses

Step 7:

Enter **100** in the *Account ID* field at the Maintain Chart of Accounts window to create Tile Installation by Ramirez's first account—the Cash account. After entering the value 100, click the drop-down arrow and this will prompt the lookup box to appear, as shown in Figure 2–18.

FIGURE 2–18
Account ID Lookup Box

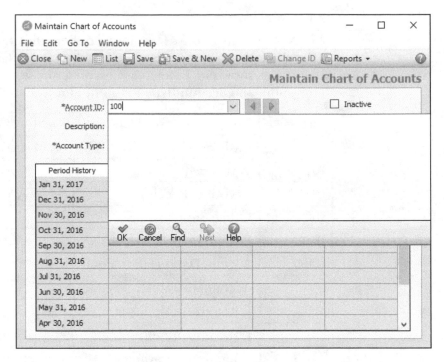

Step 8:
Click the OK button to accept 100 as the Account ID.

Step 9:
Key **Cash** in the *Description* field.

Step 10:
Select *Cash* from the Account Type drop-down list if it is not already showing.

HINT
Press the Tab or Enter key to move from one box to the next. Holding down the Shift key while pressing the Tab key moves the cursor to the previous box.

Step 11:
Click the Save button on the toolbar to save the account if the information is accurate. Compare the newly created account with Figure 2–19.

FIGURE 2–19
Completed Cash Account

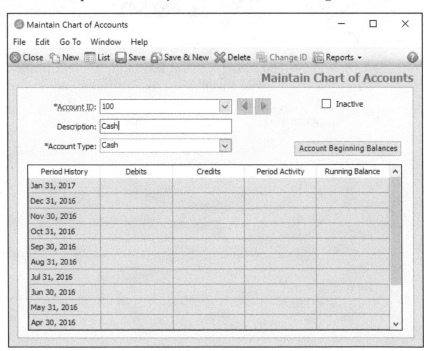

HINT

Be sure to click the Save button or Alt S after each account is created.

Step 12:

Repeat steps 7 through 11 until you have created all the accounts listed on Tile Installation by Ramirez's chart of accounts, as shown in Table 2–5 (page 51).

Step 13:

Click the drop-down arrow or the Previous Record or Next Record buttons (left- and right-pointing arrows) next to the *Account ID* field to view a list of the accounts created. Use the scroll bar to view all the accounts.

HINT

You can create an account at any time by clicking Maintain and then *Chart of Accounts*. Then, follow steps 7 through 11 to create accounts.

Editing Accounts

In Sage 50, an account can be viewed, edited, or deleted at any time.

Step 1:

At the Maintain Chart of Accounts window, click the drop-down arrow next to the *Account ID* field, use the down arrow on the keyboard to highlight *Revenue* (ID# 400), and then click the OK button on the toolbar at the bottom of the drop-down list, as shown in Figure 2–20.

FIGURE 2–20
Account ID Drop-Down List with Revenue Selected

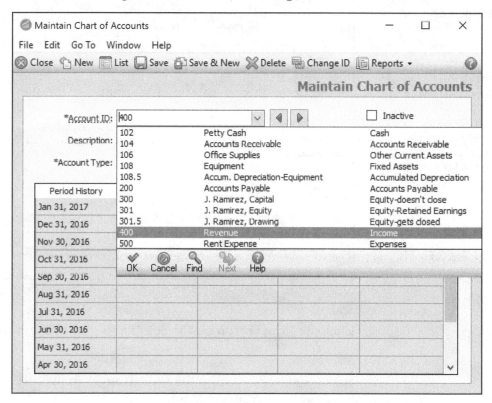

Step 2:

HINT

The account ID and account type can also be edited during this process.

Any necessary changes can be made to an account by entering those changes and then clicking the Save button on the toolbar. Change the account description to *Installation Fees Earned* and then click Save. You can also delete an account by clicking the account and then clicking the Delete button on the toolbar.

Step 3:

Review and edit any accounts as necessary, and then click the Close button on the toolbar.

Printing the Chart of Accounts

It may be necessary to review the chart of accounts. If a company's chart of accounts is extensive, it may be impractical to view all of it on a computer screen. To print a chart of accounts, follow these steps.

Step 1:

Open Wildwood Medical Services. Close the Action Items, Setup Guide, and Sage Advisor Getting Started windows, if open.

Step 2:

Click Reports & Forms from the Menu bar and then click *General Ledger*.

Step 3:

Click the <u>R</u>eports folder tab and select *Chart of Accounts*, as shown in Figure 2–21.

FIGURE 2–21
Select a Report or Form Window with Chart of Accounts Selected

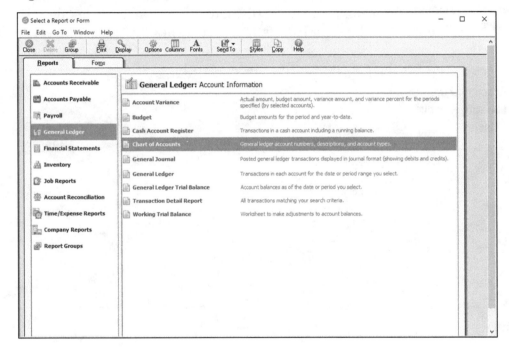

Step 4:

Click the <u>P</u>rint button on the Select a Report or Form toolbar.

Step 5:

Select *Specific Period* from the Date drop-down list and *Period 1, (1/31/17)* from the As of drop-down list.

Step 6:

Click *GL Account ID* from the Sort by drop-down list (it may already be selected by default). Select GL Account ID from the *Select a filter:* list.

Step 7:

Click to insert a check mark in the box next to *Include accounts with zero amounts.* Compare your entries with Figure 2–22. If they are correct, click OK.

FIGURE 2–22
Modify Report –
Chart of Accounts
Window

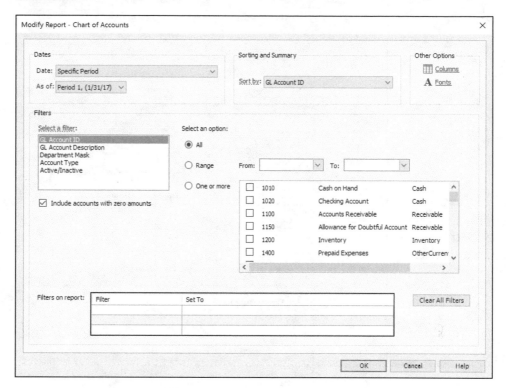

Step 8:

At the Print dialog box, click *All* in the Print range section. (Any pages, or combination of pages, may be printed by clicking the Pages option and entering the desired page range.) Click the number of copies desired from the *Number of copies* box, and then click OK.

Step 9:

Compare your printcd chart of accounts with Figure 2–23.

FIGURE 2–23
Wildwood Medical
Services Chart of
Accounts

9/5/16 at 17:22:14.49   *****EDUCATIONAL VERSION ONLY*****   Page: 1

Wildwood Medical Services
Chart of Accounts
As of Jan 31, 2017

Filter Criteria includes: Report order is by ID. Report is printed with Accounts having Zero Amounts and in Detail Format.

Account ID	Account Description	Active?	Account Type
1010	Cash on Hand	Yes	Cash
1020	Checking Account	Yes	Cash
1100	Accounts Receivable	Yes	Accounts Receivable
1150	Allowance for Doubtful Acc	Yes	Accounts Receivable
1200	Inventory	Yes	Inventory
1400	Prepaid Expenses	Yes	Other Current Assets
1500	Property and Equipment	Yes	Fixed Assets
1900	Accum. Depreciation - Prop	Yes	Accumulated Depreciation
2000	Accounts Payable	Yes	Accounts Payable
2310	Sales Tax Payable	Yes	Other Current Liabilities
2320	Deductions Payable	Yes	Other Current Liabilities
2330	Federal Payroll Taxes Paya	Yes	Other Current Liabilities
2340	FUTA Payable	Yes	Other Current Liabilities
2350	State Payroll Taxes Payabl	Yes	Other Current Liabilities
2360	SUTA Payable	Yes	Other Current Liabilities
2370	Local Taxes Payable	Yes	Other Current Liabilities
2380	Income Taxes Payable	Yes	Other Current Liabilities
2400	Customer Deposits	Yes	Other Current Liabilities
2500	Current Portion Long-Term	Yes	Other Current Liabilities
2700	Long Term Debt-Noncurren	Yes	Long Term Liabilities
3910	Retained Earnings	Yes	Equity-Retained Earnings
3920	Owner's Contribution	Yes	Equity-gets closed
3930	Owner's Draw	Yes	Equity-gets closed
4000	Professional Fees	Yes	Income
4050	Sales of Materials	Yes	Income
4100	Interest Income	Yes	Income
4200	Finance Charge Income	Yes	Income
4300	Other Income	Yes	Income
4900	Sales/Fees Discounts	Yes	Income
5000	Cost of Sales	Yes	Cost of Sales
5400	Cost of Sales-Salary & Wa	Yes	Cost of Sales
5900	Inventory Adjustments	Yes	Cost of Sales
6000	Wages Expense	Yes	Expenses
6050	Employee Benefit Program	Yes	Expenses
6100	Payroll Tax Expense	Yes	Expenses
6150	Bad Debt Expense	Yes	Expenses
6200	Income Tax Expense	Yes	Expenses
6250	Other Taxes Expense	Yes	Expenses
6300	Rent or Lease Expense	Yes	Expenses
6350	Maintenance & Repairs Ex	Yes	Expenses
6400	Utilities Expense	Yes	Expenses
6450	Office Supplies Expense	Yes	Expenses
6500	Telephone Expense	Yes	Expenses
6550	Other Office Expense	Yes	Expenses
6600	Advertising Expense	Yes	Expenses
6650	Commissions and Fees Ex	Yes	Expenses
6800	Freight Expense	Yes	Expenses
6850	Service Charge Expense	Yes	Expenses
6900	Purchase Disc-Expense Ite	Yes	Expenses
6950	Insurance Expense	Yes	Expenses
7050	Depreciation Expense	Yes	Expenses
7100	Gain/Loss - Sale of Assets	Yes	Expenses

Step 10:

Click the Close button to close the Select a Report or Form window.

HINT

The Sage 50 Setup
Guide can be prevented
from appearing each
time the company is
opened by inserting a
check mark in the box
next to *Don't show this
screen at startup* and
then clicking Close.

Step 11:

Open Tile Installation by Ramirez and close the Action Items & Sage 50
Setup Guide windows, if open.

Step 12:

Print a copy of the chart of accounts for Tile Installation by Ramirez by
repeating steps 2 through 8. Compare your chart of accounts to the one
shown in Figure 2–24.

FIGURE 2–24
Tile Installation by Ramirez Chart of Accounts

9/5/16 at 17:22:56.18 *****EDUCATIONAL VERSION ONLY***** Page: 1

Tile Installation by Ramirez
Chart of Accounts
As of Jan 31, 2017

Filter Criteria includes: Report order is by ID. Report is printed with Accounts having Zero Amounts and in Detail Format.

Account ID	Account Description	Active?	Account Type
100	Cash	Yes	Cash
102	Petty Cash	Yes	Cash
104	Accounts Receivable	Yes	Accounts Receivable
106	Office Supplies	Yes	Other Current Assets
108	Equipment	Yes	Fixed Assets
108.5	Accum. Depreciation-Equip	Yes	Accumulated Depreciation
200	Accounts Payable	Yes	Accounts Payable
300	J. Ramirez, Capital	Yes	Equity-doesn't close
301	J. Ramirez, Equity	Yes	Equity-Retained Earnings
301.5	J. Ramirez, Drawing	Yes	Equity-gets closed
400	Installation Fees Earned	Yes	Income
500	Rent Expense	Yes	Expenses
502	Utilities Expense	Yes	Expenses
504	Telephone Expense	Yes	Expenses
506	Office Supplies Expense	Yes	Expenses
508	Repairs Expense	Yes	Expenses
510	Depreciation Expense-Equi	Yes	Expenses
512	Wages and Salaries Expen	Yes	Expenses
514	Miscellaneous Expense	Yes	Expenses

Step 13:

Click the Close button to close the Select a Report or Form window.

Checkpoint 2–3

1. What are the three pieces of information needed to create an account in Sage 50?
2. How many account types does Sage 50 support?

Open Maslow's Financial Services and create the accounts listed in Table 2–6.

**TABLE 2–6
Maslow's Financial
Services Chart of
Accounts**

Account ID	Description	Account Type
100	Cash	Cash
102	Petty Cash	Cash
104	Accounts Receivable	Accounts Receivable
106	Maintenance Supplies	Other Current Assets
108	Office Supplies	Other Current Assets
110	Prepaid Insurance	Other Current Assets
112	Equipment	Fixed Assets
112.5	Accum. Depreciation-Equipment	Accumulated Depreciation
200	Accounts Payable	Accounts Payable
300	H. Maslow, Capital	Equity-doesn't close
301	H. Maslow, Equity	Equity-Retained Earnings
301.5	H. Maslow, Drawing	Equity-gets closed
400	Revenue	Income
500	Rent Expense	Expenses
502	Utilities Expense	Expenses
504	Maintenance Supplies Expense	Expenses
506	Office Supplies Expense	Expenses
508	Insurance Expense	Expenses
510	Depreciation Expense-Equipment	Expenses
512	Wages and Salaries Expense	Expenses
514	Miscellaneous Expense	Expenses

Your chart of accounts should look like Figure 2–25. Print and then close the chart of accounts.

FIGURE 2–25
Maslow's Financial
Services Chart of
Accounts

Maslow's Financial Services
Chart of Accounts
As of Sep 30, 2017

Filter Criteria includes: Report order is by ID. Report is printed with Accounts having Zero Amounts and in Detail Format.

Account ID	Account Description	Active?	Account Type
100	Cash	Yes	Cash
102	Petty Cash	Yes	Cash
104	Accounts Receivable	Yes	Accounts Receivable
106	Maintenance Supplies	Yes	Other Current Assets
108	Office Supplies	Yes	Other Current Assets
110	Prepaid Insurance	Yes	Other Current Assets
112	Equipment	Yes	Fixed Assets
112.5	Accum. Depreciation-Equip	Yes	Accumulated Depreciation
200	Accounts Payable	Yes	Accounts Payable
300	H. Maslow, Capital	Yes	Equity-doesn't close
301	H. Maslow, Equity	Yes	Equity-Retained Earnings
301.5	H. Maslow, Drawing	Yes	Equity-gets closed
400	Revenue	Yes	Income
500	Rent Expense	Yes	Expenses
502	Utilities Expense	Yes	Expenses
504	Maintenance Supplies Exp	Yes	Expenses
506	Office Supplies Expense	Yes	Expenses
508	Insurance Expense	Yes	Expenses
510	Depreciation Expense-Equi	Yes	Expenses
512	Wages and Salaries Expen	Yes	Expenses
514	Miscellaneous Expense	Yes	Expenses

OBJECTIVE 2–4

Enter Beginning Account Balances

Once you have created the general ledger accounts for your company, it is time to enter the beginning balances. If a company is converting to Sage 50 from a manual accounting system, the normal practice is to use the ending balances from the previous month, which appear on the trial balance. For example, if a company wants to convert to Sage 50 on July 1, the balances from the June 30 trial balance are used. Thus, the ending balances of the general ledger accounts as of June 30 become the beginning balances as of July 1. The *trial balance* is a listing of the general ledger accounts and their balances. It is used to prove that the general ledger is in balance.

trial balance A proof that the general ledger is in balance.

Entering the Beginning Account Balances

To enter beginning balances, follow these steps:

Step 1:
Open Tile Installation by Ramirez.

Step 2:
Click Maintain and then click *Chart of Accounts*.

Step 3:
Click the Account Beginning Balances button in the Maintain Chart of Accounts window. (See Figure 2–26.)

FIGURE 2–26
Maintain Chart of
Accounts Window

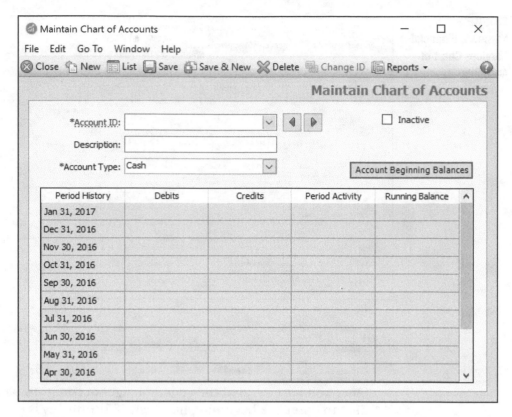

Step 4:

Use the scroll bar on the right side of the Select Period dialog box, click *From 1/1/17 through 1/31/17*, as shown in Figure 2–27, and then click OK. Tile Installation by Ramirez will now start its fiscal year on January 1, 2017.

FIGURE 2–27
Select Period Dialog Box

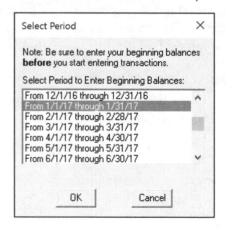

Step 5:

Enter the beginning balances, as indicated in Table 2–7, in the Chart of Accounts Beginning Balances window. (See Figure 2–28 on page 62.) Press the Enter or Tab key to move between accounts. Remember to enter the decimal points as needed. *Note: You do not need to key the dollar sign ($)— Sage 50 will not accept an entry with that character.*

TABLE 2–7
Tile Installation by
Ramirez Beginning
Balances, January 1,
2017

Account ID	Account Description	Account Type	Assets, Expenses	Liabilities, Equity, Income
100	Cash	Cash	$12,000.00	
102	Petty Cash	Cash	250.00	
104	Accounts Receivable	Accounts Receivable	13,000.00	
106	Office Supplies	Other Current Assets	590.00	
108	Equipment	Fixed Assets	112,000.00	
108.5	Accum. Depreciation Equipment	Accumulated Depreciation		$12,000.00
200	Accounts Payable	Accounts Payable		2,300.00
300	J. Ramirez, Capital	Equity-doesn't close		123,540.00
301	J. Ramirez, Equity	Equity-Retained Earnings		
301.5	J. Ramirez, Drawing	Equity-gets closed		
400	Installation Fees Earned	Income		
500	Rent Expense	Expenses		
502	Utilities Expense	Expenses		
504	Telephone Expense	Expenses		
506	Office Supplies Expense	Expenses		
508	Repairs Expense	Expenses		
510	Depreciation Expense-Eq.	Expenses		
512	Wages and Salaries Expense	Expenses		
514	Miscellaneous Expense	Expenses		

FIGURE 2–28
Chart of Accounts
Beginning Balances
Window

Chart of Accounts Beginning Balances   ✕

Cancel   OK   New   Find   Next   Help

Beginning Balances as of January 31, 2017   How do I enter these beginning balances?

Account ID	Account Description	Account Type	Assets, Expenses	Liabilities, Equity, Income
100	Cash	Cash		
102	Petty Cash	Cash		
104	Accounts Receivable	Accounts Receivable		
106	Office Supplies	Other Current Assets		
108	Equipment	Fixed Assets		
108.5	Accum. Depreciation-Equipme	Accumulated Deprecia		
200	Accounts Payable	Accounts Payable		

The Trial Balance is made up of the balances of all accounts. In order for the Trial Balance to be in balance, the sum of Assets and Expenses should equal the sum of Liabilities, Equity, and Income.

Total:	0.00	0.00
Trial Balance: (Difference posts to Beg Bal Equity)	0.00	

Net Income is the difference of Income and Expense account values. The Income and Expense values making up Net Income are already included in the total.

Income - Expenses:	0.00	0.00
Net Income:	0.00	

HINT

A new account may be added at any time while entering beginning balances by clicking the New button at the top of the Chart of Accounts Beginning Balances window.

HINT

Sage 50 will not allow the Beginning Balances window to close unless the general ledger accounts are in balance. The trial balance at the bottom of the Chart of Accounts Beginning Balances window must show a zero (0) difference.

Step 6:

When you have finished entering the balances, click the OK button to save the entries and return to the Maintain Chart of Accounts window.

Step 7:

Close the Maintain Chart of Accounts window.

Displaying the General Ledger with the Beginning Balances

The best way to check the accuracy of the general ledger is to display a copy. You can then check the newly created accounts and their balances. Follow these steps to print a copy of the general ledger.

Step 1:

Click the Business Status tab on the Sage 50 opening window to reveal the Find a Report section (bottom of the screen).

Step 2:

Select *General Ledger* from the Category drop-down list and *General Ledger* from the Report drop-down list. (See Figure 2–29.)

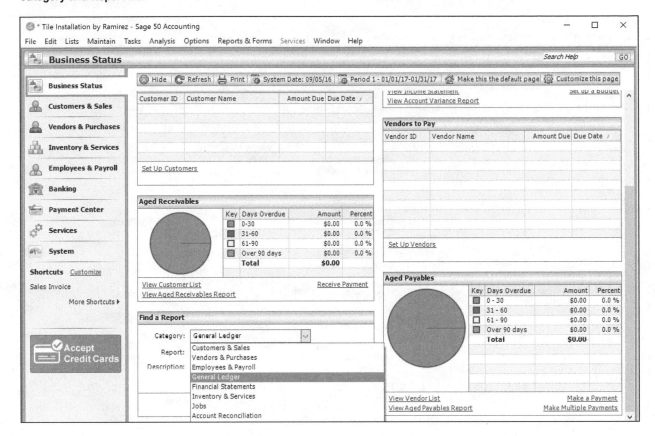

Step 3:

Click Display at the bottom of the window to display the report. To modify the report, click *Options* on the toolbar.

The General Ledger report will include all transactions that occurred between January 1 and January 31, 2017. Compare your printout of the general ledger with Figure 2–30.

FIGURE 2–30
Tile Installation by
Ramirez General
Ledger Report

9/5/16 at 17:43:20.00   *****EDUCATIONAL VERSION ONLY*****   Page: 1

Tile Installation by Ramirez
General Ledger
For the Period From Jan 1, 2017 to Jan 31, 2017

Filter Criteria includes: Report order is by ID. Report is printed with shortened descriptions and in Detail Format.

Account ID Account Description	Date	Reference	Jrnl	Trans Description	Debit Amt	Credit Amt	Balance
100 Cash	1/1/17			Beginning Balance			
	1/1/17	BEGBAL	GEN		12,000.00		
				Current Period Cha	12,000.00		12,000.00
	1/31/17			**Ending Balance**			**12,000.00**
102 Petty Cash	1/1/17			Beginning Balance			
	1/1/17	BEGBAL	GEN		250.00		
				Current Period Cha	250.00		250.00
	1/31/17			**Ending Balance**			**250.00**
104 Accounts Receivable	1/1/17			Beginning Balance			
	1/1/17	BEGBAL	GEN		13,000.00		
				Current Period Cha	13,000.00		13,000.00
	1/31/17			**Ending Balance**			**13,000.00**
106 Office Supplies	1/1/17			Beginning Balance			
	1/1/17	BEGBAL	GEN		590.00		
				Current Period Cha	590.00		590.00
	1/31/17			**Ending Balance**			**590.00**
108 Equipment	1/1/17			Beginning Balance			
	1/1/17	BEGBAL	GEN		112,000.00		
				Current Period Cha	112,000.00		112,000.00
	1/31/17			**Ending Balance**			**112,000.00**
108.5 Accum. Depreciation-	1/1/17			Beginning Balance			
	1/1/17	BEGBAL	GEN			12,000.00	
				Current Period Cha		12,000.00	-12,000.00
	1/31/17			**Ending Balance**			**-12,000.00**
200 Accounts Payable	1/1/17			Beginning Balance			
	1/1/17	BEGBAL	GEN			2,300.00	
				Current Period Cha		2,300.00	-2,300.00
	1/31/17			**Ending Balance**			**-2,300.00**
300 J. Ramirez, Capital	1/1/17			Beginning Balance			
	1/1/17	BEGBAL	GEN			123,540.00	
				Current Period Cha		123,540.00	-123,540.00
	1/31/17			**Ending Balance**			**-123,540.00**

Checkpoint 2–4

1. What accounting period is usually used to enter beginning balances?

2. As with any accounting system, the trial balance must be in balance. What does Sage 50 do to ensure the trial balance is in balance?

Open Maslow's Financial Services and enter the beginning balances of the general ledger accounts. Use the information given in Table 2–8. Use the period 1/1/17 through 1/31/17 for beginning balances.

TABLE 2–8
Maslow's Financial Services Beginning Balances, January 1, 2017

Account ID	Account Description	Account Type	Assets, Expenses	Liabilities, Equity, Income
100	Cash	Cash	$14,400	
102	Petty Cash	Cash	100	
104	Accounts Receivable	Accounts Receivable		
106	Maintenance Supplies	Other Current Assets	2,300	
108	Office Supplies	Other Current Assets	490	
110	Prepaid Insurance	Other Current Assets	1,000	
112	Equipment	Fixed Assets	42,000	
112.5	Accum. Depr.-Equipment	Accumulated Depreciation		$10,000
200	Accounts Payable	Accounts Payable		
300	H. Maslow, Capital	Equity-doesn't close		50,290
301	H. Maslow, Equity	Equity-Retained Earnings		
301.5	H. Maslow, Drawing	Equity-gets closed		
400	Revenue	Income		
500	Rent Expense	Expenses		
502	Utilities Expense	Expenses		
504	Maintenance Supplies Expense	Expenses		
508	Insurance Expense	Expenses		
510	Depreciation Expense-Eq.	Expenses		
512	Wages and Salaries Expense	Expenses		
514	Miscellaneous Expense	Expenses		

Your general ledger should look like Figure 2–31.

FIGURE 2–31
Maslow's Financial Services General Ledger

9/5/16 at 17:45:45.77 *****EDUCATIONAL VERSION ONLY***** Page: 1

Maslow's Financial Services
General Ledger
For the Period From Jan 1, 2017 to Jan 31, 2017

Filter Criteria includes: Report order is by ID. Report is printed with shortened descriptions and in Detail Format.

Account ID Account Description	Date	Reference	Jrnl	Trans Description	Debit Amt	Credit Amt	Balance
100	1/1/17			Beginning Balance			
Cash	1/1/17	BEGBAL	GEN		14,400.00		
				Current Period Cha	14,400.00		14,400.00
	1/31/17			**Ending Balance**			**14,400.00**
102	1/1/17			Beginning Balance			
Petty Cash	1/1/17	BEGBAL	GEN		100.00		
				Current Period Cha	100.00		100.00
	1/31/17			**Ending Balance**			**100.00**
106	1/1/17			Beginning Balance			
Maintenance Supplies	1/1/17	BEGBAL	GEN		2,300.00		
				Current Period Cha	2,300.00		2,300.00
	1/31/17			**Ending Balance**			**2,300.00**
108	1/1/17			Beginning Balance			
Office Supplies	1/1/17	BEGBAL	GEN		490.00		
				Current Period Cha	490.00		490.00
	1/31/17			**Ending Balance**			**490.00**
110	1/1/17			Beginning Balance			
Prepaid Insurance	1/1/17	BEGBAL	GEN		1,000.00		
				Current Period Cha	1,000.00		1,000.00
	1/31/17			**Ending Balance**			**1,000.00**
112	1/1/17			Beginning Balance			
Equipment	1/1/17	BEGBAL	GEN		42,000.00		
				Current Period Cha	42,000.00		42,000.00
	1/31/17			**Ending Balance**			**42,000.00**
112.5	1/1/17			Beginning Balance			
Accum. Depreciation-	1/1/17	BEGBAL	GEN			10,000.00	
				Current Period Cha		10,000.00	-10,000.00
	1/31/17			**Ending Balance**			**-10,000.00**
300	1/1/17			Beginning Balance			
H. Maslow, Capital	1/1/17	BEGBAL	GEN			50,290.00	
				Current Period Cha		50,290.00	-50,290.00
	1/31/17			**Ending Balance**			**-50,290.00**

Chapter Review and Assessment

Software Command Summary

Set Up Company	Create a New Company or File, New Company, Enter Company Information, Select Chart of Accounts Option, Select Accounting Method, Select Posting Method, Set Accounting Periods, Finish
Create Chart of Accounts	Maintain, Chart of Accounts, Account ID, Description, Account Type
Enter Account Balances	Maintain, Chart of Accounts, Account Beginning Balances, Select Period, Enter Balances

Checkpoint Answers

Checkpoint 2–1
1. The three main types of business organizations are sole proprietorships, partnerships, and corporations.
2. Owners have unlimited liability in sole proprietorships and partnerships.

Checkpoint 2–2
1. The accounting method, either cash or accrual, cannot be changed after its selection.
2. Posting occurs immediately when each transaction is entered and saved.

Checkpoint 2–3
1. The account ID, account description, and account type are required.
2. Sage 50 supports 16 account types (See pp. 49–50).

Checkpoint 2–4
1. Either the current accounting period or the accounting period prior to the first period in which transactions will be entered.
2. Sage 50 will not allow the trial balance to be saved unless it is in balance.

Study Quizzes

Take the study quiz online to check your understanding of chapter concepts. The quiz can be taken multiple times.

Content Check

Multiple Choice: Choose only one response for each question.

1. After graduating from college, a fellow student started a payroll processing business. He handles payroll work for small firms in your area. This is an example of what type of business?
   A. manufacturing business
   B. merchandising business
   C. service business
   D. a combined merchandising and service business
   E. None of the above

2. Which of the following is *not* an advantage of a sole proprietorship?
   A. complete management control by owner
   B. ease of formation
   C. few government restrictions
   D. unlimited liability
   E. None of the above

3. Revenue accounts would use which set of account IDs in Sage 50?
   A. 100, 1000, 10000
   B. 200, 2000, 20000
   C. 300, 3000, 30000
   D. 400, 4000, 40000
   E. 500, 5000, 50000

4. The amounts owed to a business by its customers for goods or services sold to them on credit are called
   A. accounts payable.
   B. accounts receivable.
   C. equity – retained earnings.
   D. notes payable.
   E. None of the above

5. The financial report that lists all of a company's accounts and their balances is the
   A. general journal.
   B. general ledger.
   C. chart of accounts.
   D. account ID.
   E. None of the above

Short Essay Response

Provide a detailed answer for each question.

1. Describe the three basic forms of business organizations. List the advantages and disadvantages of each.
2. What is the difference between the cash basis and accrual basis of accounting?
3. What are the steps required for entering beginning balances in Sage 50?

4. When setting up a new business in Sage 50, what are the main steps in the setup process?
5. What is the difference between the two posting methods in Sage 50—real time and batch?
6. What are the three items necessary to create a new account in Sage 50? Define each.

Cooperative Learning

1. Form into groups of three or four students, and create your own hypothetical service business. Decide on the information needed for the business setup. Summarize your ideas on paper.
2. Using Sage 50 and the newly formed company from Cooperative Learning Exercise 1, create the chart of accounts that will be needed. Print the chart of accounts.
3. Using Sage 50 and the newly created accounts from Cooperative Learning Exercise 2, enter beginning balances that you consider reasonable for the new business. Print the general ledger.

Writing and Decision Making

The owner of the company for which you work, Maria Richardson, believes in cross-training employees. Therefore, she has informed you that next week an employee from the purchasing department will spend a day with you and observe some of the reports you work with in the accounting department. She especially wants you to explain to this employee the significance of both the chart of accounts and the general ledger and how they relate to each other. Ms. Richardson would like you to give her a memo with the information that you plan to share with the employee from the purchasing department.

Case Problems

Demonstrate your knowledge of the Sage 50 Accounting features discussed in this chapter by completing the following case problems.

Case Problem 2–1A

1. Set up a new company for GJ Professional Accounting. Use the information given below.

Company Name:	**GJ Professional Accounting**
Address Line 1:	**1506 East March Lane**
City, State, Zip:	**Stockton, CA 95207**
Country:	**USA**
Telephone:	**209-555-2112**
Fax:	**209-555-1221**
Business Type:	**Sole Proprietorship**
Federal Employer ID:	**95-2962962**
State Employer ID:	**06-556-02**
St. Unemployment ID:	**00546-76**

Chart of Accounts:	**Use a sample business type that closely matches your company**
Available Charts of Accounts:	**Accounting Agency**
Accounting Method:	**Accrual**
Posting Method:	**Real Time**
Accounting Periods:	**12 monthly accounting periods**
Fiscal Year to Start:	**January 2017**

2. Edit the following accounts to reflect the information given:

Account ID	Account Description	Account Type
12000	Office Supplies	Other Current Assets
15100	Computer Equipment	Fixed Assets
39006	Garret Johnson, Capital	Equity-doesn't close
39007	Garret Johnson, Drawing	Equity-gets closed
40200	Tax Preparation Fees	Income
67500	Office Cleaning Expense	Expenses
75500	Equipment Repair Expense	Expenses

3. Enter the following beginning balances for the period from 1/1/17 through 1/31/17:

GJ Professional Accounting Beginning Balances

Account ID	Account Description	Account Type	Assets, Expenses	Liabilities, Equity, Income
10200	Regular Checking Account	Cash	$23,000	
11000	Accounts Receivable	Accounts Receivable	5,600	
12000	Office Supplies	Other Current Assets	1,120	
15100	Computer Equipment	Fixed Assets	4,700	
20000	Accounts Payable	Accounts Payable		$4,920
39006	Garret Johnson, Capital	Equity-doesn't close		29,500

4. Delete the following accounts:

Account ID	Account Description	Account Type
10000	Petty Cash	Cash
10500	Special Account	Cash
14100	Employee Advances	Other Current Assets
48000	Fee Refunds	Income
63000	Commissions and Fees Exp	Expenses

5. Print a Chart of Accounts report and a General Ledger report for the period 1/1/17 to 1/31/17.

Case Problem 2–2A

1. Set up a new company for the Olsen Construction Company. Use the information given below.

Company Name:	**Olsen Construction Company**
Address Line 1:	**1308 Madison Avenue**
City, State, Zip:	**Tracy, CA 95376**
Country:	**USA**
Telephone:	**209-555-7695**
Fax:	**209-555-7698**
Business Type:	**Sole Proprietorship**
Federal Employer ID:	**95-2862978**
State Employer ID:	**06-556-05**
St. Unemployment ID:	**00546-79**
Chart of Accounts:	**Build your own chart of accounts**
Accounting Method:	**Accrual**
Posting Method:	**Real Time**
Accounting Periods:	**12 monthly accounting periods**
Fiscal Year to Start:	**January 2017**

2. Create the following chart of accounts, and then enter the beginning balances for the period from 1/1/17 through 1/31/17:

Olsen Construction Company Chart of Accounts

Account ID	Account Description	Account Type	Assets, Expenses	Liabilities, Equity, Income
100	Cash	Cash	$27,340	
104	Accounts Receivable	Accounts Receivable	13,250	
106	Office Supplies	Other Current Assets	365	
108	Construction Equipment	Fixed Assets	11,300	
108.5	Accum. Depr.-Equipment	Accumulated Depreciation		$1,800
200	Accounts Payable	Accounts Payable		2,455
300	Dave Olsen, Capital	Equity-doesn't close		48,000
301	Dave Olsen, Equity	Equity-Retained Earnings		
301.5	Dave Olsen, Drawing	Equity-gets closed		
400	Revenue	Income		
500	Rent Expense	Expenses		

Account ID	Account Description	Account Type	Assets, Expenses	Liabilities, Equity, Income
502	Utilities Expense	Expenses		
504	Telephone Expense	Expenses		
506	Office Supplies Expense	Expenses		
508	Repairs Expense	Expenses		
510	Depreciation Expense-Eq.	Expenses		
512	Wages and Salaries Expense	Expenses		
514	Miscellaneous Expense	Expenses		

3. Print a Chart of Accounts report and a General Ledger report for the period 1/1/17 to 1/31/17.

Case Problem 2–1B

1. Set up a new company for Finite Graphics. Use the information given below.

Company Name:	**Finite Graphics**
Address Line 1:	**6051 East Sycamore Avenue**
City, State, Zip:	**Stockton, CA 95207**
Country:	**USA**
Telephone:	**209-555-3113**
Fax:	**209-555-1331**
Business Type:	**Sole Proprietorship**
Federal Employer ID:	**95-2962984**
State Employer ID:	**06-557-03**
St. Unemployment ID:	**00546-68**
Chart of Accounts:	**Use a sample business type that closely matches your company**
Available Charts of Accounts:	**Graphic Artist**
Accounting Method:	**Accrual**
Posting Method:	**Real Time**
Accounting Periods:	**12 monthly accounting periods**
Fiscal Year to Start:	**January 2017**

2. Edit the following accounts to reflect the information given:

Account ID	Account Description	Account Type
12000	Graphing Supplies	Other Current Assets
15100	Graphing Equipment	Fixed Assets
39006	Ana Rosario, Capital	Equity-doesn't close
39007	Ana Rosario, Drawing	Equity-gets closed

3. Enter the following beginning balances for the period from 1/1/17 to 1/31/17.

Finite Graphics
Beginning Balances

Account ID	Account Description	Account Type	Assets, Expenses	Liabilities, Equity, Income
10200	Regular Checking Account	Cash	$13,000	
11000	Accounts Receivable	Accounts Receivable	2,600	
12000	Graphing Supplies	Other Current Assets	750	
15100	Graphing Equipment	Fixed Assets	7,700	
20000	Accounts Payable	Accounts Payable		$3,290
39006	Ana Rosario, Capital	Equity-doesn't close		20,760

4. Delete the following accounts:

Account ID	Account Description	Account Type
10000	Petty Cash	Cash
15500	Building	Fixed Assets
15600	Building Improvements	Fixed Assets
19100	Organization Costs	Other Assets
58500	Inventory Adjustments	Cost of Sales

5. Print a Chart of Accounts report and a General Ledger report for the period 1/1/17 to 1/31/17.

Case Problem 2–2B

1. Set up a new company for Robinson Brothers Builders. Use the information given below.

Company Name:	**Robinson Brothers Builders**
Address Line 1:	**732 Alhambra Way**
City, State, Zip:	**Tracy, CA 95376**
Country:	**USA**
Telephone:	**209-555-9567**
Fax:	**209-555-5679**
Business Type:	**Sole Proprietorship**
Federal Employer ID:	**95-2862879**
State Employer ID:	**06-566-15**
St. Unemployment ID:	**00564-97**
Chart of Accounts:	**Build your own chart of accounts**
Accounting Method:	**Accrual**
Posting Method:	**Real Time**
Accounting Periods:	**12 monthly accounting periods**
Fiscal Year to Start:	**January 2017**

2. Create the following chart of accounts, and then enter the beginning balances for the period from 1/1/17 through 1/31/17:

Robinson Brothers Builders Chart of Accounts

Account ID	Account Description	Account Type	Assets, Expenses	Liabilities, Equity, Income
100	Cash	Cash	$18,470	
104	Accounts Receivable	Accounts Receivable	4,320	
106	Construction Supplies	Other Current Assets	3,560	
108	Construction Equipment	Fixed Assets	5,300	
108.5	Accum. Depr.-Equipment	Accumulated Depreciation		$2,400
200	Accounts Payable	Accounts Payable		2,350
300	Randy Robinson, Capital	Equity-doesn't close		26,900
301	Randy Robinson, Equity	Equity-Retained Earnings		
301.5	Randy Robinson, Drawing	Equity-gets closed		
400	Revenue	Income		
500	Rent Expense	Expenses		
502	Utilities Expense	Expenses		
504	Telephone Expense	Expenses		
506	Construction Supplies Expense	Expenses		
508	Repairs Expense	Expenses		
510	Depreciation Expense-Eq.	Expenses		
512	Wages and Salaries Expense	Expenses		
514	Miscellaneous Expense	Expenses		

3. Print a Chart of Accounts report and a General Ledger report for the period 1/1/17 to 1/31/17.

Entering Transactions for a Cash Business

Objectives

3–1 Review transactions and the general journal

3–2 Create new accounts and enter beginning balances for a simple cash business

3–3 Record transactions in the general journal

3–4 Edit selected transactions in the general journal

3–5 Print the general journal and financial statements

Software Features

- General journal toolbar buttons

- General journal edit function

- General journal delete function

- General journal recurring transaction function

- General journal memorized transaction function

- Report filter and print procedures

Company Files

Before beginning chapter work, access the links menu to download company files.

transactions Financial events that change a firm's assets, liabilities, or owner's equity.

Transactions are financial events that change a firm's assets, liabilities, or owner's equity. Examples of transactions are selling goods on credit, purchasing office supplies with cash, paying salaries to employees, and paying an amount owed to a creditor. Every firm must record the financial effects of its transactions. Generally, the first record of a business transaction is entered in a journal.

OBJECTIVE 3–1

Review Transactions and the General Journal

journal A record in which transactions are listed in order by date.

A *journal* is simply a chronological record of transactions—a listing of transactions in order by date. There are various types of journals, but the most basic type is the *general journal*, which can be used to record all kinds of financial transactions.

general journal A journal in which all kinds of financial transactions can be recorded.

Sage 50's General Journal Entry window, shown in Figure 3–1, is similar to a manual general journal. In both manual and computerized accounting systems, the information needed for general journal entries normally comes from business papers such as invoices, check stubs, cash register tapes, bills, and receipts, which provide evidence of the transactions. These business papers are known as *source documents*.

source documents Business papers that provide evidence of transactions.

FIGURE 3–1
General Journal Entry Window

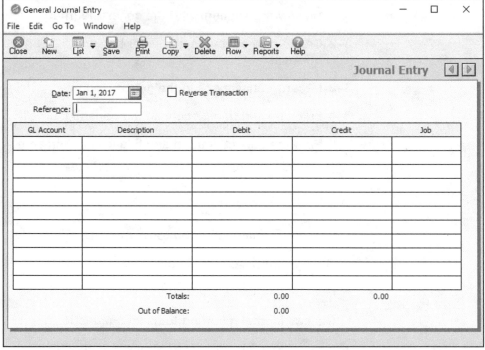

Debits and Credits

double-entry accounting A method of accounting in which equal debits and credits are recorded for each transaction.

Debits and credits are at the heart of *double-entry accounting*. Every transaction is recorded by debiting one or more accounts and crediting one or more accounts. The total of the debits and the total of the credits recorded for the transaction must be equal.

Using source documents, the accountant analyzes each transaction to determine what accounts must be debited and credited and the amounts involved. The accountant follows the rules of debit and credit, which can be summarized as follows:

- *Asset, drawing, dividend, and expense accounts* record increases as debits and decreases as credits.

- *Liability, capital, and revenue accounts* record increases as credits and decreases as debits.

HINT

To learn more about the general ledger, select Help from the Menu bar and *Sage 50 Accounting Help* from the drop-down list. Key *General Ledger* at the prompt.

One of the great advantages of a computerized accounting system like Sage 50 is that it has features that alert the accountant to unbalanced journal entries and prevent the posting of such entries to the general ledger. In a manual accounting system, entries with unequal debits and credits often go unnoticed in the general journal and are posted to the general ledger. The presence of errors is not revealed until the trial balance is prepared at the end of the accounting period. At this point, much time and effort must be spent tracing the individual errors through the journal and ledger and recording correct entries.

Figure 3–2 illustrates a general journal entry in Sage 50 that has unequal debits and credits. A notice at the bottom of the screen indicates that the journal is out of balance and shows the difference between the debit and credit totals $90. Sage 50 will not allow an unbalanced entry such as this one to be posted.

FIGURE 3–2
General Journal Entry with Unequal Debits and Credits

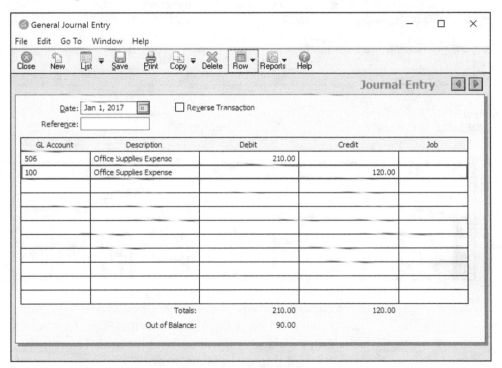

Journalizing and Posting a Sample Transaction

Suppose that a business purchases office supplies for $250 in cash. The accountant's analysis of this transaction reveals that an expense (Office Supplies Expense) has increased by $250 and an asset (Cash) has decreased by $250. The accountant records this transaction by debiting Office Supplies Expense for $250 and crediting Cash for $250. (In this example, the business operates on a pure cash basis and therefore treats purchases of supplies as an expense.)

If the business has a manual accounting system, the accountant will make the necessary entry in the general journal, as shown in Figure 3–3.

FIGURE 3–3
General Journal Entry

	Date		Account Title	P.R.	Debit	Credit
1	Feb.	1	Office Supplies Expense	508	250 00	
2			Cash	100		250 00
3			Purchased office supplies.			

General Journal — Page 1

HINT
It is a good practice to provide a brief explanation.

After the general journal entry is made, the accountant posts to the appropriate general ledger accounts and records the account numbers in the posting reference (P.R.) column of the general journal. (See Figures 3–4 and 3–5.) In the Cash account, as shown in Figure 3–4, the credit entry of $250 is subtracted from the beginning debit balance of $6,500 to find the new debit balance of $6,250.

FIGURE 3–4
Cash Account

Account Cash — Account No. 100

	Date		Item	P.R.	Debit	Credit	Balance Debit	Balance Credit
1	Feb.	1	Beginning balance	✔			6500 00	
2		1		GJ1		250 00	6250 00	
3								

FIGURE 3–5
Office Supplies Expense Account

Account Office Supplies Expense — Account No. 508

	Date		Item	P.R.	Debit	Credit	Balance Debit	Balance Credit
1	Feb.	1		GJ1	250 00		250 00	
2								
3								

Once an entry is posted to the ledger accounts, a P.R. is recorded in the accounts to identify the source of the entry. In this example, the source of the entry is page 1 of the general journal. Therefore, GJ1 is recorded in the P.R. column of each account.

In computerized accounting systems like Sage 50, posting is done automatically by the system. Once the chart of accounts has been set up, as described in Chapter 2, Sage 50 can automatically transfer information from journal entries to the general ledger accounts. This feature eliminates much repetitive work and prevents many of the errors that occur in manual posting.

The General Journal and Special Journals

special journal A journal that is used to record a single type of transaction.

A very small business may record all of its transactions in the general journal, but a larger business would probably use special journals as well as the general journal. A *special journal* is a journal that is used to record a single type of transaction. Sage 50 allows you to use special journals for sales, purchases, cash receipts, and cash payments. These journals increase efficiency by grouping like transactions in their own journals.

The sales journal is used to record sales of goods or services on credit. The purchases journal is used to record purchases of goods or services on credit. The cash receipts journal is used to record all cash receipts. The cash disbursements journal is used to record all cash payments.

The use of special journals does not eliminate the need for a general journal. Some transactions still require a general journal entry. For example, in Sage 50, it is necessary to use the general journal for correcting and adjusting entries.

In the rest of this chapter, you will establish an accounting system for a small business in Sage 50 and then use the general journal functions of Sage 50. The business that you will work with—Forward Thinking Graphic Design—is a small service business that operates on a cash basis.

Checkpoint 3–1

1. Each journal entry for a transaction must be in balance. What does that mean?
2. How does Sage 50 treat a general journal entry that is not in balance?
3. What is the advantage of using the special journals provided by Sage 50?
4. What are the four basic types of special journals?

OBJECTIVE 3-2

Create New Accounts and Enter Beginning Balances for a Simple Cash Business

In Chapter 2, you learned how to set up a company in Sage 50, create a chart of accounts, and enter the beginning balances of the general ledger accounts. You will now use this knowledge to establish a computerized accounting system for Forward Thinking Graphic Design.

Setting Up a Simple Cash Business in Sage 50

Follow the steps outlined below to begin the setup process.

Step 1:
Start Sage 50 Accounting.

Step 2:
At the Sage 50 Accounting opening window, click *Create a new company*.

Step 3:
Click Next at the bottom of the Create a New Company – Introduction dialog box.

Step 4:

Enter the information for Forward Thinking Graphic Design in the Create a New Company – Company Information dialog box. Use the information shown in Figure 3–6.

FIGURE 3–6
Create a New Company –
Company Information
Dialog Box

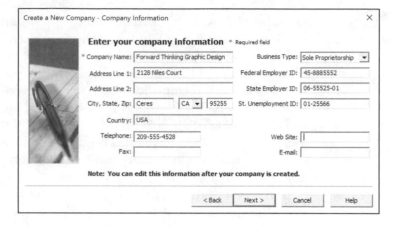

Step 5:

Click Next to reveal the Create a New Company – Setup dialog box. Click the *Build your own chart of accounts* option.

Step 6:

Click Next to move to the Create a New Company – Accounting Method dialog box, and then click *Cash*.

Step 7:

Click Next to move to the Create a New Company – Posting Method dialog box, and then click *Real Time*.

Step 8:

Click Next to move to the Create a New Company – Accounting Periods dialog box, and click the *12 monthly accounting periods per year* option.

Step 9:

Click Next to move to the Create a New Company – Fiscal Year dialog box. Forward Thinking Graphic Design will use the calendar year as its fiscal year. Choose *January 2017* as the starting date of the fiscal year. (See Figure 3–7.)

FIGURE 3–7
Create a New Company –
Fiscal Year Dialog Box

Step 10:

Click Next to move to the Create a New Company – Finish dialog box.

Step 11:

Click Finish. Wait for Sage 50 to finish creating files. Then close the Action Items and Sage 50 Setup Guide windows.

Creating New Accounts and Entering Beginning Balances

In Chapter 2, you learned about the procedures for creating general ledger accounts and entering their beginning balances. You will now use these procedures for Forward Thinking Graphic Design. Follow the steps outlined below to create new accounts and enter the beginning balances for Forward Thinking Graphic Design.

Step 1:

Click Maintain on the Menu bar and then click *Chart of Accounts.*

Step 2:

Create the Cash account by keying **100** in the *Account ID* field.

Step 3:

Click OK to accept account number 100. Then key **Cash** in the *Description* field.

Step 4:

At the Account Type drop-down list, click *Cash* (if it is not already selected). Compare your entries with those shown in Figure 3–8. Then click Save.

FIGURE 3–8
Completed Cash Account

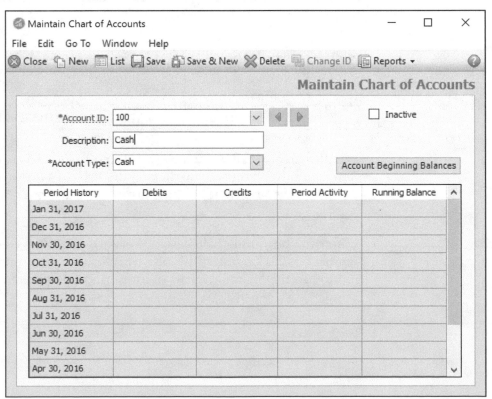

Step 5:

Click New to set up another account. Create the remainder of the general ledger accounts for Forward Thinking Graphic Design. Use the account IDs, account descriptions, and account types shown in Table 3–1.

TABLE 3–1
Forward Thinking Graphic Design Accounts and Beginning Balances as of January 1, 2017

Account ID	Account Description	Account Type	Assets, Expenses	Liabilities, Equity, Income
100	Cash	Cash	$107,650.00	
102	Petty Cash	Cash	400.00	
300	Y. Lopez, Capital	Equity-doesn't close		$108,050.00
301	Y. Lopez, Equity	Equity-Retained Earnings		
301.5	Y. Lopez, Drawing	Equity-gets closed		
400	Design Fees	Income		
500	Independent Contractor Expense	Expenses		
502	Rent Expense	Expenses		
504	Utilities Expense	Expenses		
506	Office Supplies Expense	Expenses		
508	Telephone Expense	Expenses		
510	Design Expense	Expenses		
512	Professional Expense	Expenses		
		TOTALS	$108,050.00	$108,050.00

After creating all of the accounts listed in Table 3–1, view your accounts to ensure their accuracy by clicking the Previous Record or Next Record buttons (left- and right-pointing arrows) to the right of the *Account ID* field.

Step 6:

Enter the beginning balances for Forward Thinking Graphic Design as of January 1, 2017. To start this process, click the Account Beginning Balances button in the Maintain Chart of Accounts dialog box.

Step 7:

Select *From 1/1/17 through 1/31/17* from the Select Period dialog box, as shown in Figure 3–9, and then click OK.

FIGURE 3–9
Select Period Dialog Box

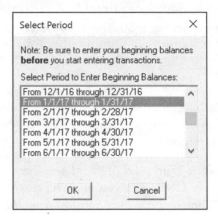

Step 8:

Enter the balances for Forward Thinking Graphic Design from Table 3–1. The completed Chart of Accounts Beginning Balances window is shown in Figure 3–10. Press the Tab key to move from account to account.

FIGURE 3–10
Completed Chart of Accounts Beginning Balances Window

Account ID	Account Description	Account Type	Assets, Expenses	Liabilities, Equity, Income
100	Cash	Cash	107,650.00	
102	Petty Cash	Cash	400.00	
300	Y. Lopez, Capital	Equity-doesn't close		108,050.00
301	Y. Lopez, Equity	Equity-Retained Earnir		
301.5	Y. Lopez, Drawing	Equity-gets closed		
400	Design Fees	Income		
500	Independent Contractor Exper	Expenses		

Chart of Accounts Beginning Balances

Cancel   OK   New   Find   Next   Help

Beginning Balances as of January 31, 2017   How do I enter these beginning balances?

The Trial Balance is made up of the balances of all accounts. In order for the Trial Balance to be in balance, the sum of Assets and Expenses should equal the sum of Liabilities, Equity, and Income.

Total: 108,050.00   108,050.00
Trial Balance: 0.00
(Difference posts to Beg Bal Equity)

Net Income is the difference of Income and Expense account values. The Income and Expense values making up Net Income are already included in the total.

Income - Expenses: 0.00   0.00
Net Income: 0.00

Step 9:

The totals at the bottom of the window should be equal, and the trial balance difference should be zero. This indicates that the general ledger accounts are in balance. Click the OK button after reviewing the Chart of Accounts Beginning Balances window.

Step 10:

Close the Maintain Chart of Accounts window.

Objective 3–2 Practice

Create a new account and enter beginning balances for Wildwood Medical Services.

Note: Wildwood Medical Services was created in Chapter 2. If you did not complete Chapter 2, you may still complete this chapter's tasks by opening Chapter 3 Wildwood Medical Services from the student data files.

Step 1:

Open Wildwood Medical Services from the previous chapter, or Chapter 3 Wildwood Medical Services from the student data files if you failed to complete the previous chapter's tasks.

Step 2:

Create the following account:

Account ID:	**3904**
Description:	**James, Capital**
Account Type:	**Equity-doesn't close**

Step 3:

Enter the beginning balances for the accounts listed in Table 3–2 for the period January 1, 2017 to January 31, 2017.

TABLE 3–2
Wildwood Medical Services, January 1, 2017 to January 31, 2017

Account ID	Account Description	Account Type	Assets, Expenses	Liabilities, Equity, Income
1010	Cash on Hand	Cash	$250.00	
1020	Checking Account	Cash	15,000.00	
3904	James, Capital	Equity-doesn't close		$15,250.00

Step 4:

Preview the general ledger for the period January 1, 2017 to January 31, 2017 and compare it with Figure 3–11.

FIGURE 3–11
Wildwood Medical
Services General
Ledger

9/10/16 at 16:38:46.90   *****EDUCATIONAL VERSION ONLY*****   Page: 1

Chapter 3 - Wildwood Medical Services
General Ledger
For the Period From Jan 1, 2017 to Jan 31, 2017

Filter Criteria includes: Report order is by ID. Report is printed with shortened descriptions and in Detail Format.

Account ID Account Description	Date	Reference	Jrnl	Trans Description	Debit Amt	Credit Amt	Balance
1010	1/1/17			Beginning Balance			
Cash on Hand	1/1/17	BEGBAL	GEN		250.00		
				Current Period Cha	250.00		250.00
	1/31/17			**Ending Balance**			**250.00**
1020	1/1/17			Beginning Balance			
Checking Account	1/1/17	BEGBAL	GEN		15,000.00		
				Current Period Cha	15,000.00		15,000.00
	1/31/17			**Ending Balance**			**15,000.00**
3904	1/1/17			Beginning Balance			
James, Capital	1/1/17	BEGBAL	GEN			15,250.00	
				Current Period Cha		15,250.00	-15,250.00
	1/31/17			**Ending Balance**			**-15,250.00**

Record Transactions in the General Journal

Once you have established the general ledger accounts and their balances, you can enter transactions. The transactions presented in this section are for Forward Thinking Graphic Design, a simple cash business. The company has no accounts receivable or accounts payable and owns no fixed assets. It rents a furnished office suite.

You will use the general journal entry function of Sage 50 to record these transactions. Follow the steps listed below to journalize the January transactions of Forward Thinking Graphic Design.

Step 1:

Open Forward Thinking Graphic Design, which you created previously in the chapter. Close the Action Items and Setup Guide windows.

Step 2:

Analyze the following transaction:

- On January 4, 2017, Forward Thinking Graphic Design purchased office supplies for $1,200 in cash from a local store.

  Analysis: An expense (Office Supplies Expense) has increased by $1,200 and an asset (Cash) has decreased by $1,200. Therefore, debit Office Supplies Expense for $1,200 and credit Cash for $1,200.

The manual general journal entry needed to record this transaction is shown in Figure 3–12.

FIGURE 3–12
General Journal Entry

	Date		General Journal	P.R.	Debit	Credit	Page 1
			Account Title				
1	Jan.	4	Office Supplies Expense	506	1 2 0 0 00		
2			Cash	100		1 2 0 0 00	
3			Purchased office supplies.				

FIGURE 3–12
General Journal Entry

Step 3:

Use Sage 50 to record the above transaction in the general journal of Forward Thinking Graphic Design. Click Tasks, and then click *General Journal Entry.*

You can also access the general journal by clicking General Journal Entry in the More Shortcuts pop-up menu at the lower left of the Sage 50 screen, as shown in Figure 3–13. The general journal entry window appears.

FIGURE 3–13
General Journal Entry
Shortcut

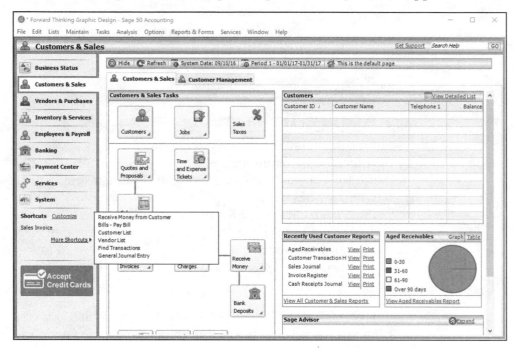

Step 4:

Enter the date of the transaction, January 4, 2017, by clicking the *calendar* icon to the right of the *Date* field. Choose *January* as the month, *4* as the day, and *2017* as the year.

Step 5:

Enter the account to be debited. Click the cell under *GL Account* and then click the *magnifying glass* icon to the right of the *GL Account* field. Scroll down to and select the account *506, Office Supplies Expense.* Compare your screen with Figure 3–14 and then click OK.

FIGURE 3–14
Account 506 Selected

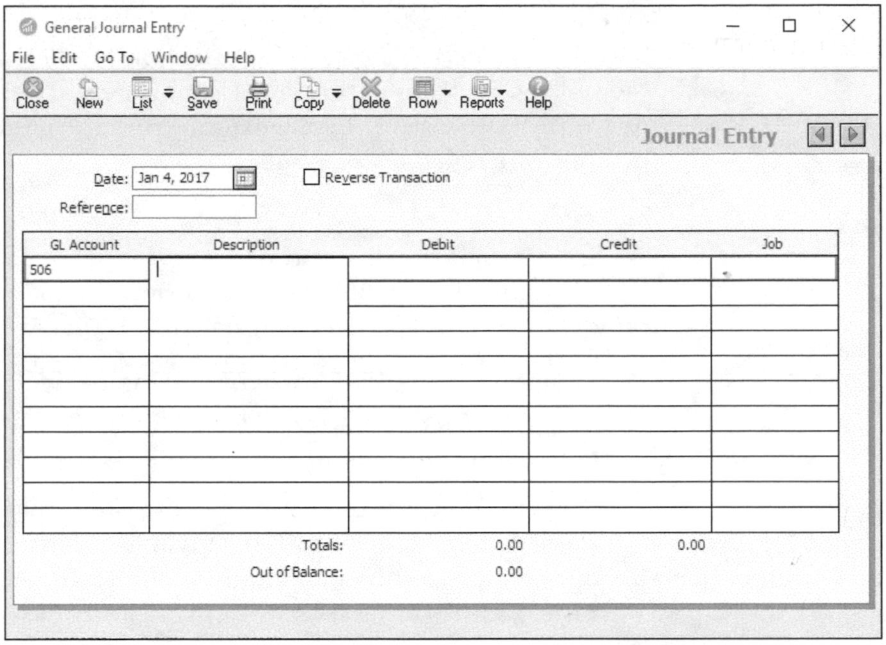

Step 6:

Key **Purchased Office Supplies** in the *Description* field. Press the Tab key and key **1,200.00** in the *Debit* field. Then tab down to the second row.

Step 7:

Enter the account to be credited. Click the *magnifying glass* icon to the right of the *GL Account* field in the second row, highlight or click the account *100, Cash,* and then click OK.

Step 8:

Sage 50 will automatically enter the same description, *Purchased Office Supplies,* in the *Description* field. Press the Tab key two times and key **1,200.00** in the *Credit* field. Compare your completed general journal entry with Figure 3–15.

FIGURE 3–15
Completed General
Journal Entry – Office
Supplies

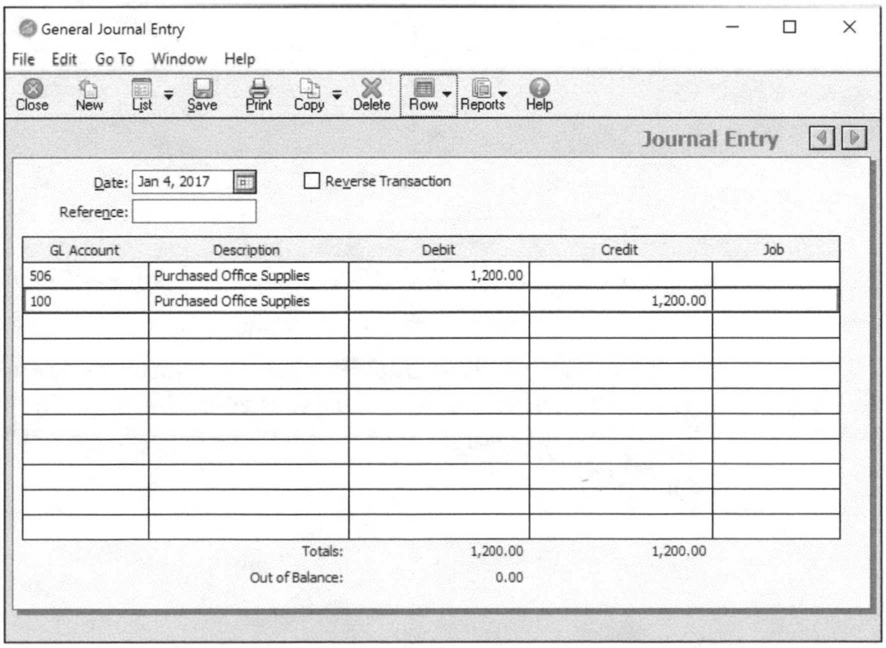

Step 9:

Complete the recording of the transaction by clicking the Save button on the toolbar. Click Yes at the Sage Current Period warning window. Sage 50 then transfers (posts) the information from the general journal entry to the appropriate ledger accounts.

Step 10:

Use Sage 50 to journalize and post the rest of the January transactions for Forward Thinking Graphic Design. Review the following analysis of these transactions and the general journal entries that are shown.

- On January 5, 2017, Forward Thinking decided to increase the petty cash fund from $400 to $500. The owner writes a check for $100 to petty cash, cashes the check, and puts the money in the petty cash box.

   Analysis: This transaction produces a shift in assets. One asset (Petty Cash) has increased by $100, and another asset (Cash) has decreased by $100. Therefore, debit Petty Cash for $100 and credit Cash for $100. (See Figure 3–16.)

FIGURE 3–16
Completed General Journal Entry – Petty Cash

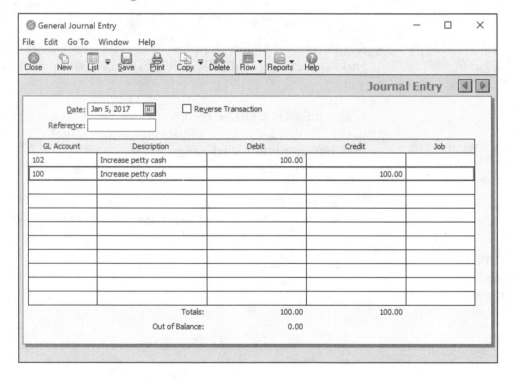

- On January 7, 2017, Forward Thinking collected fees of $9,200 for a completed design job.

   Analysis: Revenue (Design Fees) has increased by $9,200, and an asset (Cash) has increased by $9,200. Therefore, debit Cash for $9,200 and credit Design Fees for $9,200. (See Figure 3–17.)

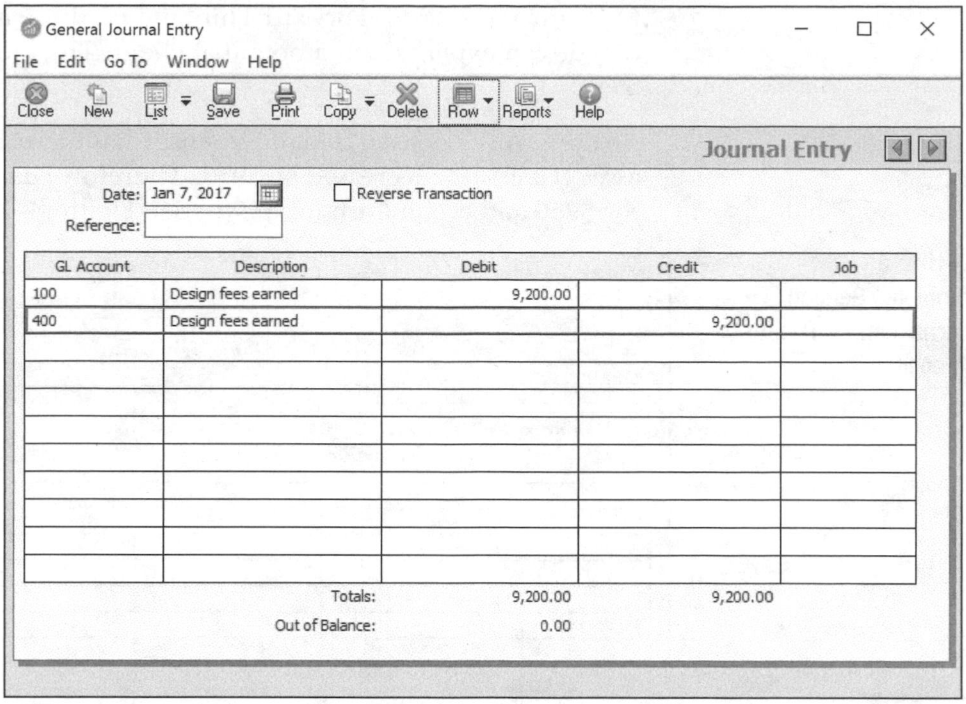

FIGURE 3–17

Completed General
Journal Entry – Design
Fees

General Journal Entry

File Edit Go To Window Help

Close New List Save Print Copy Delete Row Reports Help

Journal Entry

| Date: | Jan 7, 2017 | | Reverse Transaction | | |
| Reference: | | | | | |

GL Account	Description	Debit	Credit	Job
100	Design fees earned	9,200.00		
400	Design fees earned		9,200.00	

| | Totals: | 9,200.00 | 9,200.00 | |
| | Out of Balance: | 0.00 | | |

- On January 9, 2017, Forward Thinking paid the electric bill of $675.

   Analysis: An expense (Utilities Expense) has increased by $675, and an asset (Cash) has decreased by $675. Therefore, debit Utilities Expense for $675 and credit Cash for $675. (See Figure 3–18.)

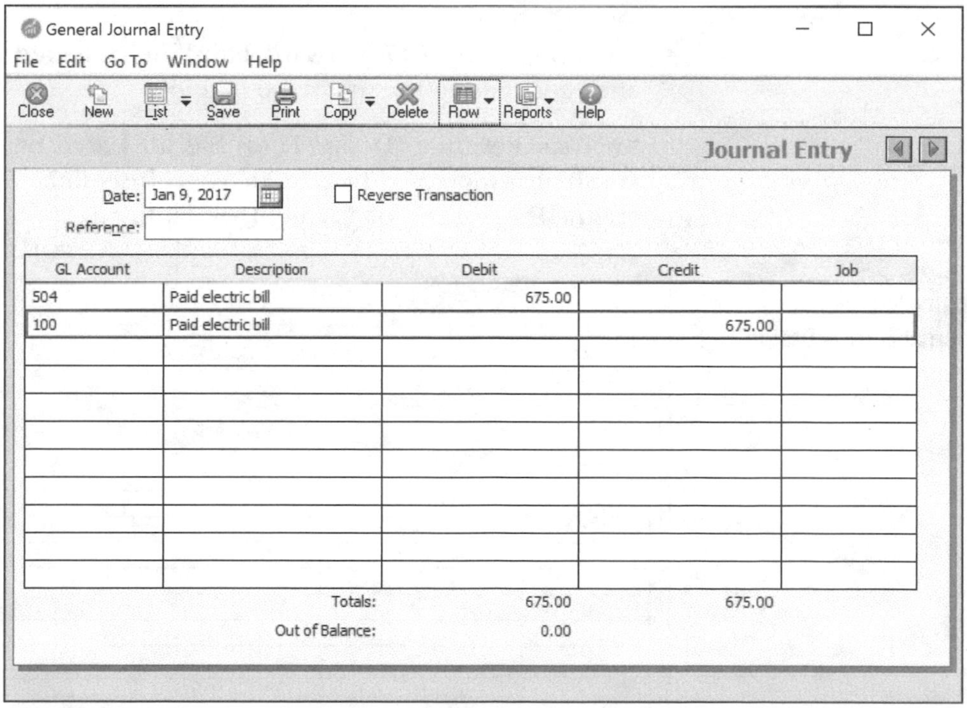

FIGURE 3–18

Completed General
Journal Entry – Electric
Bill

General Journal Entry

File Edit Go To Window Help

Close New List Save Print Copy Delete Row Reports Help

Journal Entry

| Date: | Jan 9, 2017 | | Reverse Transaction | | |
| Reference: | | | | | |

GL Account	Description	Debit	Credit	Job
504	Paid electric bill	675.00		
100	Paid electric bill		675.00	

| | Totals: | 675.00 | 675.00 | |
| | Out of Balance: | 0.00 | | |

- On January 12, 2017, Forward Thinking used the consulting services of a design expert about a potential client. The fee for that service was $950.

  Analysis: An expense (Design Expense) has increased by $950, and an asset (Cash) has decreased by $950. Therefore, debit Design Expense for $950 and credit Cash for $950. (See Figure 3–19.)

FIGURE 3–19
Completed General Journal Entry – Design Expense

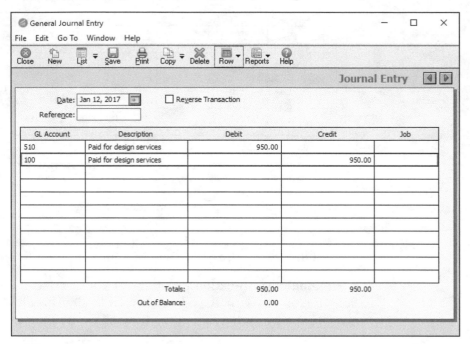

- On January 20, 2017, Forward Thinking collected fees of $2,200 after completing the first stage of a job.

  Analysis: Revenue (Design Fees) has increased by $2,200, and an asset (Cash) has increased by $2,200. Therefore, debit Cash for $2,200 and credit Design Fees for $2,200. (See Figure 3–20.)

FIGURE 3–20
Completed General Journal Entry – Design Fees

General Journal Entry — File Edit Go To Window Help

Close New List Save Print Copy Delete Row Reports Help

Journal Entry

Date: Jan 20, 2017   ☐ Reverse Transaction
Reference:

GL Account	Description	Debit	Credit	Job
100	Design fees earned	2,200.00		
400	Design fees earned		2,200.00	
	Totals:	2,200.00	2,200.00	
	Out of Balance:	0.00		

- On January 23, 2017, Forward Thinking paid $2,600 to an independent contractor who did work for the business. (An independent contractor is someone who is not an employee and does not receive a salary. Instead, this person works for a fee on a project-by-project basis.)

  Analysis: An expense (Independent Contractor Expense) has increased by $2,600, and an asset (Cash) has decreased by $2,600. Therefore, debit Independent Contractor Expense for $2,600 and credit Cash for $2,600. (See Figure 3–21.)

FIGURE 3–21
Completed General Journal Entry – Contractor's Fee

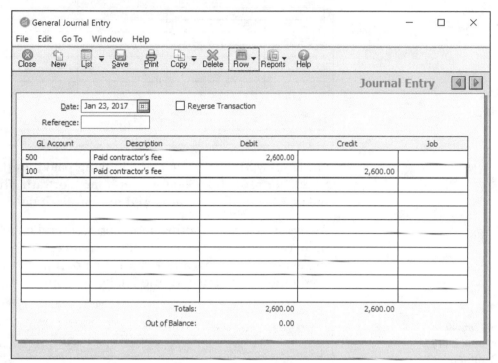

- On January 24, 2017, Forward Thinking paid $850 to a local newspaper for advertising.

  Analysis: An expense (Advertising Expense) has increased by $850, and an asset (Cash) has decreased by $850. Therefore, debit Advertising Expense for $850 and credit Cash for $850. (See Figure 3–22.) Forward Thinking has no Advertising Expense account, and you must create one. Use the following information to create the account:

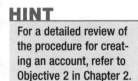

HINT
For a detailed review of the procedure for creating an account, refer to Objective 2 in Chapter 2.

Account ID:	**514**
Description:	**Advertising Expense**
Account Type:	**Expenses**

FIGURE 3-22
Completed General
Journal Entry –
Newspaper Ads

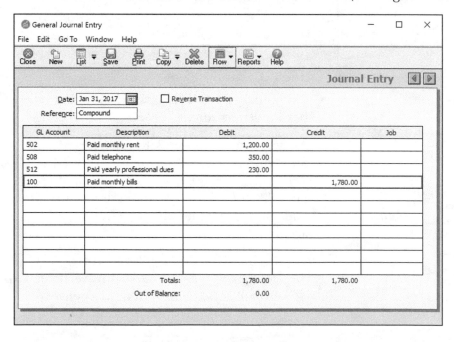

- On January 31, 2017, Forward Thinking paid month-end bills of $1,200 for rent and $350 for telephone. Forward Thinking also paid a bill of $230 for yearly dues owed to a professional organization.

  Analysis: As a result of this transaction, several expenses have increased, and the asset Cash has decreased. Therefore, debit each of the expense accounts affected for the appropriate amount and then credit Cash all at once for the total of the amounts. (See Figure 3–23.)

FIGURE 3-23
Completed General
Journal Entry –
Month-End Bills

Notice that this transaction requires a compound entry in the general journal. A *compound entry* involves more than two accounts. In Sage 50, such entries can be tracked most easily if the word *Compound* is recorded in either the Reference or Description section of the General Journal Entry window. In the Reference section of this entry, key the word **Compound**.

compound entry A journal entry that involves more than two accounts.

Step 11:

Click Save. Then close the General Journal Entry window.

Checkpoint 3–3

1. What are two methods for accessing the general journal in Sage 50?
2. Why is it necessary to analyze a transaction before journalizing it?

Objective 3–3 Practice

Several transactions for Wildwood Medical Services are listed below. Record these transactions in the general journal for the month of January 2017.

Step 1:

Open Wildwood Medical Services (Chapter 3 - Wildwood Medical Services in the student data files).

HINT

Remember that Wildwood Medical Services uses the cash basis accounting method and will not use Accounts Receivable, Other Current Assets, Fixed Assets, and Accounts Payable type accounts.

Step 2:

Change the description of Account 4000 from Professional Fees to Medical Services.

Step 3:

Journalize the following transactions. *Note: For all cash transactions, use Account 1020, Checking Account.*

- On January 2, Wildwood purchased $2,400 of office supplies. (Because Wildwood uses the cash basis, it records purchases of supplies in an expense account.) Use Account 6450, Office Supplies Expense.
- On January 4, Wildwood provided medical services for $5,200 in cash.
- On January 12, Wildwood paid $1,235 for maintenance and repair services (Account 6350).
- On January 20, Wildwood paid for an employee's retirement dinner (Account 6550) for $450.
- On January 24, Wildwood paid advertising costs of $750. Use Account 6600, Advertising Expense.
- On January 31, Wildwood paid the following month-end bills (compound entry):

Utilities	$300
Telephone	$245

Step 4:

Review your journal entries for accuracy.

Step 5:

Close the General Journal Entry window.

Edit Selected Transactions in the General Journal

Occasionally it is necessary to alter a general journal entry that contains an error. For example, if you have used the wrong date or selected a wrong account, the entry must be corrected. Sage 50 has an edit function that can be used to accomplish this task.

Editing a General Journal Entry

The steps outlined below illustrate the procedures for editing a general journal entry.

Step 1:

Open Forward Thinking Graphic Design. Close the Setup Guide and Action Items windows, if open. Change the period by clicking the Period button below the Menu bar, selecting *01 - Jan 01, 2017 to Jan 31, 2017* at the Change Accounting Period window, and clicking <u>O</u>K.

Step 2:

Click Tasks and then click *General Journal Entry*.

Step 3:

Click the L<u>i</u>st button at the top of the General Journal Entry toolbar. The General Journal List window will appear.

Step 4:

At the General Journal List window, click the entry that shows the purchase of office supplies for $1,200. Compare your screen with Figure 3–24. Click Open when the correct journal entry is highlighted.

FIGURE 3–24
General Journal List Window

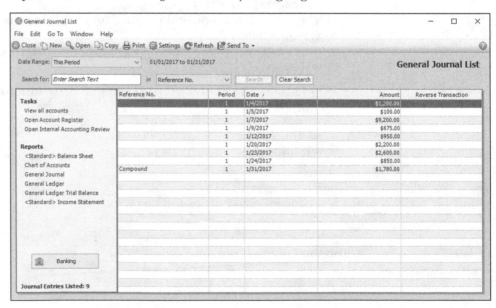

The general journal entry selected for editing is now in the active window, as shown in Figure 3–25, and can be changed.

FIGURE 3-25

Selected General Journal Entry

General Journal Entry

File   Edit   Go To   Window   Help

Close   New   List   Save   Print   Copy   Delete   Row   Reports   Help

Journal Entry

Date: Jan 4, 2017   ☐ Reverse Transaction

Reference: |

GL Account	Description	Debit	Credit	Job
506	Purchased Office Supplies	1,200.00		
100	Purchased Office Supplies		1,200.00	
	Totals:	1,200.00	1,200.00	
	Out of Balance:	0.00		

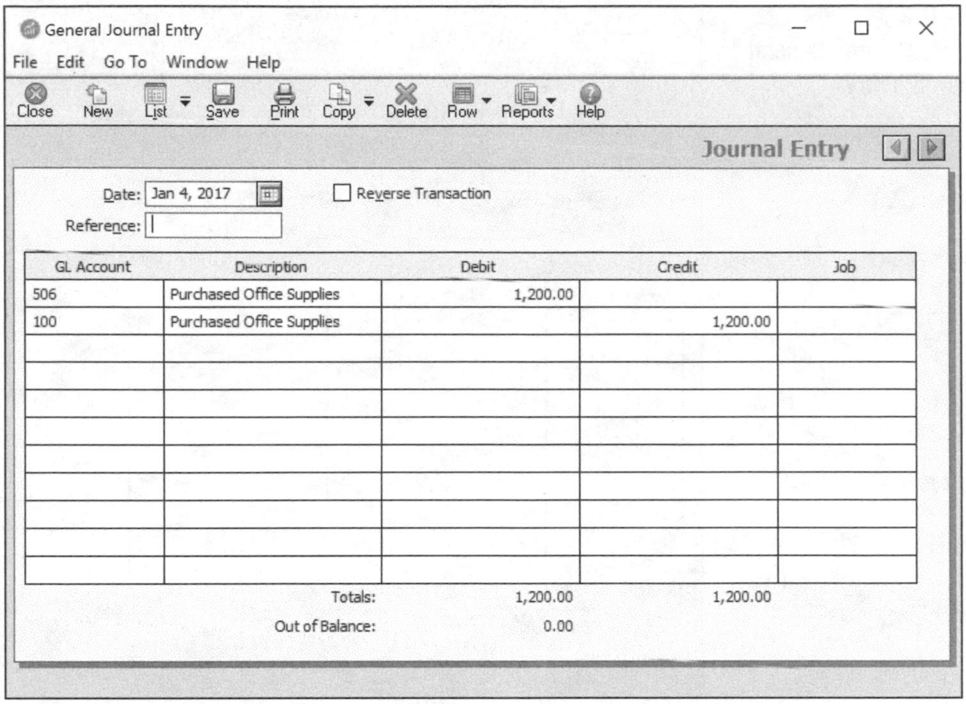

Step 5:

Assume that the accountant for Forward Thinking Graphic Design has entered the wrong date for the purchase of office supplies. Change the date from January 4, 2017, to January 5, 2017. Click the *calendar* icon, and then click *5* at the drop-down calendar.

Step 6:

Click Save and then Close to complete the editing process.

Step 7:

Use the List function or the Previous Transaction or Next Transaction buttons (left- and right-pointing arrows) at the top right of the General Journal Entry window to review the other transactions you posted for Objective 2. Make any necessary changes.

Deleting a General Journal Entry

It may be necessary to delete an entire general journal entry. Sage 50 has a function that makes this process simple.

Step 1:

Open Forward Thinking Graphic Design, if it is not currently open.

Step 2:

Create the following general journal entry for Forward Thinking Graphic Design:

- On January 23, 2017, purchased office supplies for $230 in cash.

Compare the newly completed general journal entry with Figure 3–26.

FIGURE 3–26
Newly Created General
Journal Entry

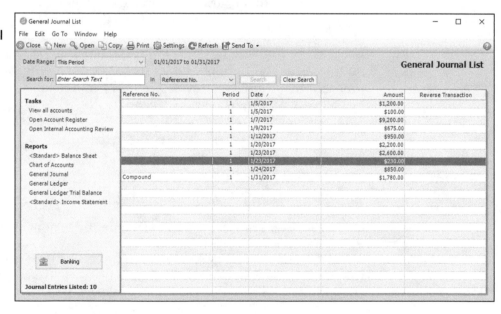

Step 3:

Click Save.

Step 4:

Retrieve the general journal entry just posted by clicking the List button on the toolbar and highlighting the desired entry, as shown in Figure 3–27. Then click Open (on the General Journal List toolbar).

FIGURE 3–27
Selected General Journal
Entry Highlighted

Step 5:

Assume that the accountant for Forward Thinking Graphic Design wants to delete the entire general journal entry created in step 2. Click the Delete button on the General Journal Entry toolbar. Sage 50 will ask, "Are you sure you want to delete this transaction?" Click Yes and the general journal entry is deleted. Close the General Journal List window.

Adding a Recurring Transaction

Most businesses have certain transactions that recur regularly. For example, payment of rent may be due on a specified day each month. Sage 50 has a recurring transaction function that makes it possible to journalize and post such transactions automatically on a predetermined schedule. This feature of Sage 50 greatly increases efficiency and reduces errors. The following steps demonstrate how to establish a recurring transaction.

Step 1:

Create the following general journal entry for Forward Thinking Graphic Design:

- On January 31, 2017, paid the monthly rent of $1,200. (See Figure 3–28.)

FIGURE 3–28
Completed General Journal Entry

Copy button drop-down arrow

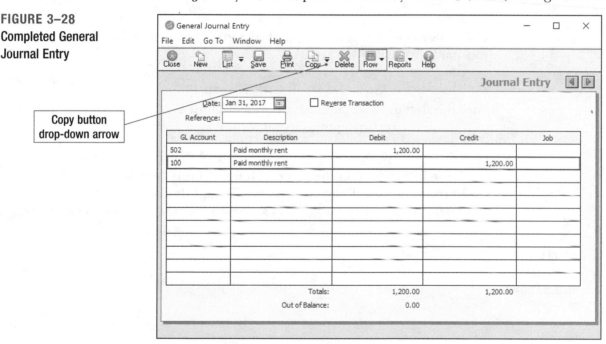

Step 2:

Because the rent payment occurs at the same time and for the same amount each month, the transaction can be saved and automatically recalled at specific intervals by Sage 50. Click the Copy button drop-down arrow at the top of the General journal Entry window, as shown in Figure 3–28. Then select *Create Recurring* from the drop-down list.

Step 3:

You can now save the journal entry for the payment of rent and designate how often it should recur. Select *Monthly* to answer "How often do you want to recur this transaction?"

Step 4:

Select *Jan 31, 2017* as "First transaction date." Select *End after* and key **12** for occurrences, as shown in Figure 3–29.

FIGURE 3–29
Create Recurring Journal Entries Dialog Box

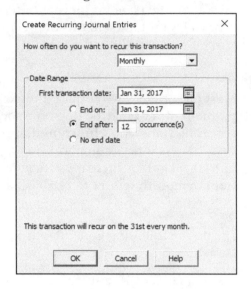

Step 5:

Click OK to save the recurring transaction and return to the General Journal Entry dialog box.

Removing a Recurring Transaction

Suppose that the accountant for Forward Thinking Graphic Design wants to remove the recurring transaction for the rent payment.

Step 1:

Click the List button on the General Journal Entry toolbar. Select *This Period* from the Date Range drop-down list and then choose the entry for $1,200.00 (rent) on 1/31/2017, as shown in Figure 3–30, and click Open.

FIGURE 3–30
General Journal List Window with Recurring Rent Transaction Chosen

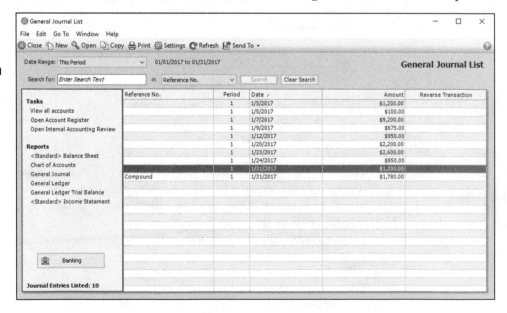

Step 2:

Click the Delete button on the General Journal Entry toolbar.

Step 3:

At the Delete Recurring Journal Entries dialog box, click the button next to *This transaction and all remaining,* as shown in Figure 3–31, and click OK. This selection eliminates both the current journal entry for the rent payment and all recurring entries.

FIGURE 3–31
Delete Recurring Journal Entries Dialog Box

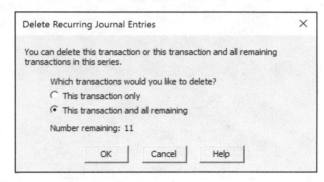

Step 4:

Close the General Journal Entry window.

Step 5:

Close the General Journal List.

Adding a Memorized Transaction

Sage 50 allows users to store in its memory transactions that occur often and recall such transactions as they are needed. These transactions are known as memorized transactions.

Memorized transactions differ from recurring transactions because you must recall memorized transactions, whereas Sage 50 makes recurring transactions automatically once they are established. The following steps demonstrate how to create, edit, and delete a memorized transaction.

Step 1:

Open Forward Thinking Graphic Design, if it is not already open.

Step 2:

Click Maintain, and then select *Memorized Transactions.*

Step 3:

At the Memorized Transactions submenu, click *General Journal Entries.*

Create a general journal entry for the following transaction, which Forward Thinking Graphic Design wants to establish as a memorized transaction. The actual date of this transaction will vary from month to month.

- Paid a monthly fee of $250 to the bookkeeper, who is an independent contractor.

Step 4:

Every memorized transaction requires an identification name or number. Key **BOOKKEEPER** in the *Transaction ID* lookup box, as shown in Figure 3–32. Then press Tab or Enter to move to the *Description* field.

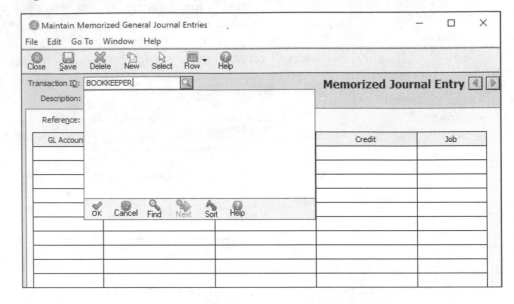

Step 5:

Key **Bookkeeper's Fee** in the *Description* field.

Step 6:

Record the remaining data as you would a regular general journal entry. Debit Independent Contractor Expense (Account 500) for $250 and credit Cash (Account 100) for $250. The completed entry for the memorized transaction is shown in Figure 3–33.

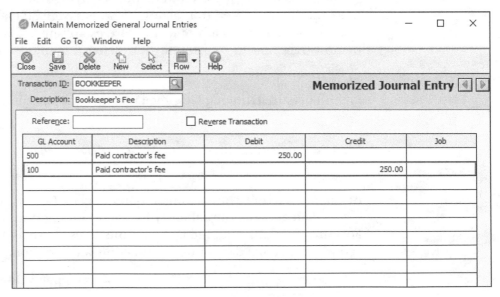

Step 7:

Click Save and Close. The memorized transaction is now available for recall whenever it is needed.

Recalling a Memorized Transaction

HINT
Transactions can be memorized and saved directly from the General Journal Entry window by clicking the down arrow key to the right of the *Copy* icon and selecting *Memorize for future use* option.

Suppose that Forward Thinking Graphic Design pays the bookkeeper's fee on January 31, 2017, and wants to recall the memorized transaction.

Step 1:

Click Maintain and then select *Memorized Transactions*.

Step 2:

At the Memorized Transactions submenu, click *General Journal Entries*.

Step 3:

Click the *magnifying glass* icon next to the *Transaction ID* lookup box, and then click *BOOKKEEPER*. The general journal entry for the memorized transaction appears.

Step 4:

Click the Select button on the Maintain Memorized General Journal Entries toolbar. This places the memorized transaction in the general journal entry window.

Step 5:

HINT
The date of the transaction is not memorized. It is necessary to enter the date each time the memorized transaction is used.

Key **1/31/17** in the *Date* field and press the Enter key. Jan 31, 2017 will appear as the date. Save the completed entry and close the general journal entry window. Close the Maintain Memorized General Journal Entries window.

Editing or Deleting a Memorized Transaction

It is possible to edit or delete existing memorized transactions by completing the following steps.

Step 1:

Click Maintain, select *Memorized Transactions*, and then click *General Journal Entries*.

Step 2:

Click the magnifying glass and select *BOOKKEEPER* from the *Transaction ID* lookup box and edit it as desired. For example, the description could be changed and then saved.

Step 3:

To delete an entire memorized transaction, click Delete and click <u>Y</u>es when prompted with the "Are you sure you want to delete this record?" message. Do not delete the BOOKKEEPER memorized transaction.

Step 4:

Close the active window.

Checkpoint 3–4

1. What is the difference between a memorized transaction and a recurring transaction?
2. What is the purpose of the edit function for general journal entries?

Use the general journal entries that you previously recorded for Wildwood Medical Services to practice the edit function. Then record recurring and memorized transactions for Wildwood.

Step 1:

Open Wildwood Medical Services (Chapter 3 - Wildwood Medical Services in the student data files).

Step 2:

Edit the journal entry for the January 4, 2017, transaction. Change the date to January 5, 2017.

Step 3:

Create a recurring transaction for the payment of rent on January 31, 2017, for $900. (Use Account 6300, Rent or Lease Expense.) This transaction should recur monthly for 12 months.

Step 4:

Create a memorized transaction for maintenance costs of $750 and name it **Maintenance Expense**. (Use Account 6350, Maintenance and Repairs Expense.)

Step 5:

Review your work for accuracy. If any changes are necessary, use the edit function.

Step 6:

Close the active window.

Print the General Journal and Financial Statements

Sage 50 allows you to review and print the general journal and financial statements by using the Reports function. There are two methods for accessing the Select a Report or Form dialog box. The first method is by clicking Reports & Forms on the Menu bar and then selecting *General Ledger*. The second method for accessing the Select a Report or Form dialog box is to select the Business Status tab from the Navigation Aids toolbar and then *General Ledger* from the Category drop-down list and *General Journal* from the Report drop-down list, as shown in Figure 3–34.

FIGURE 3–34
Find a Report with General Journal Selected

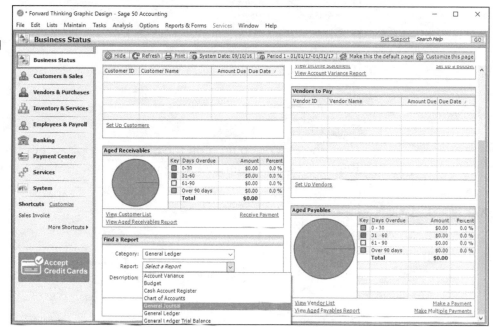

Viewing the General Journal

Follow the steps outlined below to view and filter the general journal.

Step 1:

Open Forward Thinking Graphic Design.

Step 2:

Click Reports & Forms on the Menu bar and select *General Ledger*, and then click *General Journal* in the General Ledger: Account Information section, as shown in Figure 3–35.

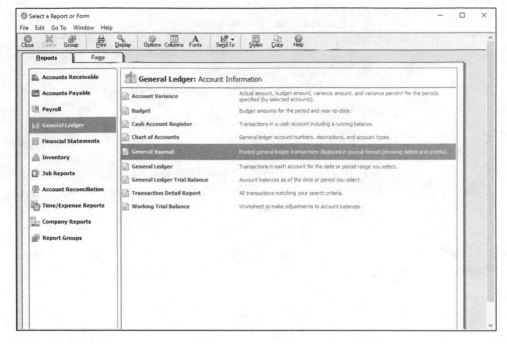

Step 3:

Click the Options button on the Select a Report or Form toolbar. The Modify Report – General Journal dialog box appears, as shown in Figure 3–36.

FIGURE 3–36
Modify Report – General
Journal Dialog Box

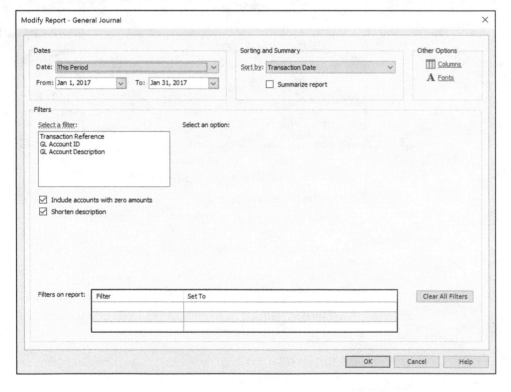

Step 4:

Click *Range* at the Date drop-down list. In addition to the current monthly period, several other options, including quarterly and annual periods, are available.

Step 5:

Select the first date of the period when transactions were entered, *Jan. 1, 2017*, in the From drop-down calendar, and *Jan. 31, 2017* in the To drop-down calendar.

Step 6:

Deselect (or uncheck) the check mark in the box next to *Include accounts with zero amounts.* This feature is a toggle function. It is like an on/off switch. The check mark in this box indicates that all accounts, even those with zero balances, will be listed in the report. Also, deselect the *Shorten description* box.

Step 7:

Check your selections against Figure 3–37. Then click OK.

FIGURE 3–37
Completed Modify Report – General Journal Dialog Box

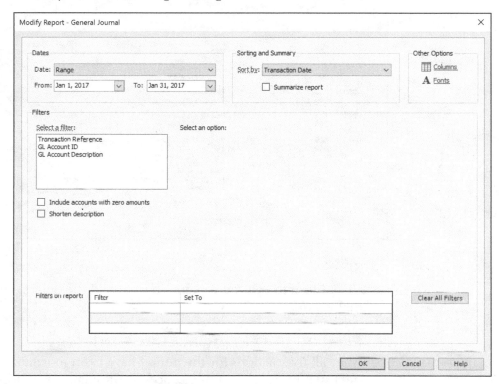

Step 8:

Review the general journal entries of Forward Thinking Graphic Design. Then click Close. Close the Select a Report or Form window.

Printing the General Journal

To print the general journal, follow the same procedure as you did to view the journal entries, but in step 3, click the Print button on the toolbar. Remember to use the same selection criteria in the Modify Report – General Journal dialog box. This will result in a printed copy. However, also take the following additional steps.

Step 1:

Make sure that the printer is on. Then click OK.

Step 2:

Compare your printout with the one shown in Figure 3–38. If you find any errors, correct them by using the edit function as described in Objective 3.

FIGURE 3–38
Printout of General Journal Entries

Page: 1

Forward Thinking Graphic Design
General Journal
For the Period From Jan 1, 2017 to Jan 31, 2017

Filter Criteria includes: Report order is by Date. Report is printed in Detail Format.

Date	Account ID	Reference	Trans Description	Debit Amt	Credit Amt
1/1/17	100	BEGBAL		107,650.00	
	102			400.00	
	300				108,050.00
1/5/17	506		Purchased Office Supplies	1,200.00	
	100		Purchased Office Supplies		1,200.00
	102		Increase petty cash	100.00	
	100		Increase petty cash		100.00
1/7/17	100		Design fees earned	9,200.00	
	400		Design fees earned		9,200.00
1/9/17	504		Paid electric bill	675.00	
	100		Paid electric bill		675.00
1/12/17	510		Paid for design services	950.00	
	100		Paid for design services		950.00
1/20/17	100		Design fees earned	2,200.00	
	400		Design fees earned		2,200.00
1/23/17	500		Paid contractor's fee	2,600.00	
	100		Paid contractor's fee		2,600.00
1/24/17	514		Paid for newspaper ads	850.00	
	100		Paid for newspaper ads		850.00
1/31/17	500		Paid contractor's fee	250.00	
	100		Paid contractor's fee		250.00
1/31/17	502	Compound	Paid monthly rent	1,200.00	
	508		Paid telephone	350.00	
	512		Paid yearly professional dues	230.00	
	100		Paid monthly bills		1,780.00
		Total		**127,855.00**	**127,855.00**

Step 3:

Click Close to exit the General Journal and the Select a Report or Form dialog box.

Printing the Financial Statements

After all transactions for the period have been journalized and posted, the next step in the accounting process for a small cash business like Forward Thinking Graphic Design is to produce financial statements. For example, on January 31, 2017, the accountant for Forward Thinking used Sage 50 to print an income statement, a statement of changes in financial position, and a balance sheet.

An *income statement* reports the results of operations for the period—the revenue, expenses, and net income or net loss. The *net income* or *net loss* is the difference between the revenue and expenses.

A *statement of changes in financial position* shows the sources and uses of working capital for the period. *Working capital* is the excess of current assets over current liabilities.

A *balance sheet* reports the financial condition of a business on a specific date. It shows the assets, liabilities, and owner's equity of the business. A cash firm like Forward Thinking Graphic Design has a simple balance sheet because it has no accounts receivable and accounts payable and no fixed assets (property and equipment).

You can view/display the financial statements for any given period by using the Reports & Forms function of Sage 50, as outlined below.

Step 1:
Click Reports & Forms on the Menu bar.

Step 2:
Click *Financial Statements*.

Step 3:
Click *<Standard> Income Stmnt* in the Financial Statements: Balance Sheets and Income Statements section, as shown in Figure 3–39.

FIGURE 3–39
<Standard> Income Stmnt Chosen at Select a Report or Form Dialog Box

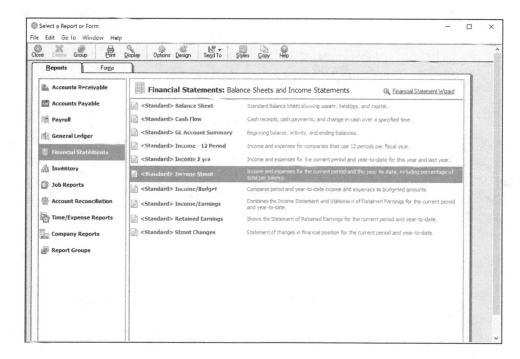

Step 4:
Click the Options button on the Select a Report or Form toolbar.

Step 5:

Select the following in the Options folder tab for the predefined income statement:

- *Range* in the *Time Frame* field.
- *Period 1, (1/1/17)* in the *From* field and *Period 1, (1/31/17)* in the *To* field. (Only one month will be covered.)
- No check mark in the box next to *Show Zero Amounts*.

Compare your screen to the Options folder tab shown in Figure 3–40.

FIGURE 3–40
Completed Options Folder Tab for <Standard> Income Stmnt

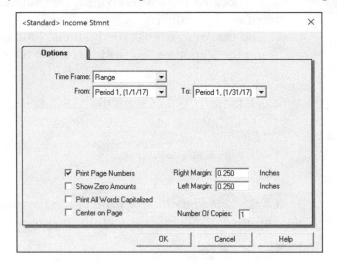

Step 6:

Click OK.

Step 7:

Compare your income statement with the one shown in Figure 3–41.

FIGURE 3–41
Income Statement for Forward Thinking Graphic Design, January 31, 2017

Page: 1

Forward Thinking Graphic Design
Income Statement
For the One Month Ending January 31, 2017

	Current Month		Year to Date	
Revenues				
Design Fees	$ 11,400.00	100.00	$ 11,400.00	100.00
Total Revenues	11,400.00	100.00	11,400.00	100.00
Cost of Sales				
Total Cost of Sales	0.00	0.00	0.00	0.00
Gross Profit	11,400.00	100.00	11,400.00	100.00
Expenses				
Independent Contractor Expense	2,850.00	25.00	2,850.00	25.00
Rent Expense	1,200.00	10.53	1,200.00	10.53
Utilities Expense	675.00	5.92	675.00	5.92
Office Supplies Expense	1,200.00	10.53	1,200.00	10.53
Telephone Expense	350.00	3.07	350.00	3.07
Design Expense	950.00	8.33	950.00	8.33
Professional Expense	230.00	2.02	230.00	2.02
Advertising Expense	850.00	7.46	850.00	7.46
Total Expenses	8,305.00	72.85	8,305.00	72.85
Net Income	$ 3,095.00	27.15	$ 3,095.00	27.15

Step 8:

Close the income statement for Forward Thinking Graphic Design.

Step 9:

Click *<Standard> Stmnt Changes* in the Financial Statements: Balance Sheets and Income Statements section, as shown in Figure 3–42.

FIGURE 3–42
<Standard> Stmnt Changes
Chosen at Select a Report
or Form Dialog Box

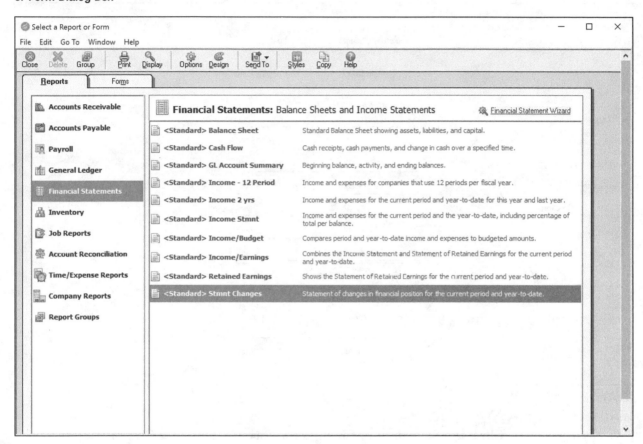

Step 10:

Repeat the procedures from step 5 to complete the Options folder tab for the predefined statement of changes in financial position.

Step 11:

Click OK when the Options folder tab for the predefined statement of changes in financial position is complete.

Step 11:

Compare your statement of changes in financial position with the one shown in Figure 3–43.

FIGURE 3–43
Statement of Changes in Financial Position for Forward Thinking Graphic Design, January 31, 2017

		Page: 1
Forward Thinking Graphic Design		
Statement of Changes in Financial Position		
For the one month ended January 31, 2017		

	Current Month	Year To Date
Sources of Working Capital		
Net Income	$ 3,095.00	$ 3,095.00
Add back items not requiring working capital		
Working capital from operations	3,095.00	3,095.00
Other sources		
Y. Lopez, Capital	108,050.00	108,050.00
Total sources	111,145.00	111,145.00
Uses of working capital		
Total uses	0.00	0.00
Net change	$ 111,145.00	$ 111,145.00
Analysis of componants of changes		
Increase <Decrease> in Current Assets		
Cash	$ 110,645.00	$ 110,645.00
Petty Cash	500.00	500.00
<Increase> Decrease in Current Liabilities		
Net change	$ 111,145.00	$ 111,145.00

Step 12:

Close the Statement of Changes for Forward Thinking Graphic Design.

Step 13:

Click *<Standard> Balance Sheet* in the Financial Statements: Balance Sheets and Income Statements section.

Step 14:

Repeat the procedures from step 5 to complete the Options folder tab for the predefined balance sheet.

Step 15:

Click OK when the Options folder tab for the predefined balance sheet is complete.

Step 16:

Compare your balance sheet with the one shown in Figure 3–44.

FIGURE 3–44
Balance Sheet for
Forward Thinking
Graphic Design,
January 31, 2017
(Partial View)

Forward Thinking Graphic Design
Balance Sheet
January 31, 2017

ASSETS

Current Assets
Cash $ 110,645.00
Petty Cash   500.00

Total Current Assets   111,145.00

Property and Equipment

Total Property and Equipment   0.00

Other Assets

Total Other Assets   0.00

Total Assets $ 111,145.00

LIABILITIES AND CAPITAL

Current Liabilities

Total Current Liabilities   0.00

Step 16:

Close the Balance Sheet. Then click the Close button on the Select a Report or Form toolbar.

Checkpoint 3–5

1. What are the two methods used to access the General Ledger report from the Reports menu?
2. What three financial statements were prepared for Forward Thinking Graphic Design?

Objective 3–5 Practice

Print the general journal and the financial statements for Wildwood Medical Services.

Step 1:

Open Wildwood Medical Services (Chapter 3 - Wildwood Medical Services in the student data files).

Step 2:

Display the general journal entries for January 1–31, 2017. Compare your printout to Figure 3–45.

9/10/16 at 17:45:27.24	*****EDUCATIONAL VERSION ONLY*****				Page: 1

Chapter 3 - Wildwood Medical Services
General Journal
For the Period From Jan 1, 2017 to Jan 31, 2017

Filter Criteria includes: Report order is by Date. Report is printed with Accounts having Zero Amounts and with shortened descriptions and in Detail Format.

Date	Account ID	Reference	Trans Description	Debit Amt	Credit Amt
1/1/17	1010	BEGBAL		250.00	
	1020			15,000.00	
	3904				15,250.00
	3910				
1/2/17	6450		Purchased office supplies	2,400.00	
	1020		Purchased office supplies		2,400.00
1/5/17	1020		Provided medical services	5,200.00	
	4000		Provided medical services		5,200.00
1/12/17	6350		Paid for maintenance and repairs	1,235.00	
	1020		Paid for maintenance and repairs		1,235.00
1/20/17	6550		Paid for employee's retirement dinne	450.00	
	1020		Paid for employee's retirement dinne		450.00
1/24/17	6600		Paid for advertising costs	750.00	
	1020		Paid for advertising costs		750.00
1/31/17	6300		Paid monthly rent	900.00	
	1020		Paid monthly rent		900.00
1/31/17	6400	Compound	Paid utility bill	300.00	
	6500		Paid telephone bill	245.00	
	1020		Paid monthly bills		545.00
		Total		26,730.00	26,730.00

Step 3:

Display the income statement for the month of January 2017. Compare your printout to Figure 3–46.

Page: 1

Chapter 3 - Wildwood Medical Services
Income Statement
For the One Month Ending January 31, 2017

	Current Month			Year to Date	
Revenues					
Medical Services	$ 5,200.00	100.00	$	5,200.00	100.00
Total Revenues	5,200.00	100.00		5,200.00	100.00
Cost of Sales					
Total Cost of Sales	0.00	0.00		0.00	0.00
Gross Profit	5,200.00	100.00		5,200.00	100.00
Expenses					
Rent or Lease Expense	900.00	17.31		900.00	17.31
Maintenance & Repairs Expense	1,235.00	23.75		1,235.00	23.75
Utilities Expense	300.00	5.77		300.00	5.77
Office Supplies Expense	2,400.00	46.15		2,400.00	46.15
Telephone Expense	245.00	4.71		245.00	4.71
Other Office Expense	450.00	8.65		450.00	8.65
Advertising Expense	750.00	14.42		750.00	14.42
Total Expenses	6,280.00	120.77		6,280.00	120.77
Net Income	$ (1,080.00)	(20.77)	$	(1,080.00)	(20.77)

Step 4:

Display the statement of changes in financial position for the month of January 2017. Compare your printout to Figure 3–47.

FIGURE 3–47
Statement of Changes in Financial Position for Wildwood Medical Services

Page: 1

Chapter 3 - Wildwood Medical Services
Statement of Changes in Financial Position
For the one month ended January 31, 2017

		Current Month		Year To Date
Sources of Working Capital				
Net Income	$	(1,080.00)	$	(1,080.00)
Add back items not requiring working capital				
Working capital from operations		(1,080.00)		(1,080.00)
Other sources				
James, Capital		15,250.00		15,250.00
Total sources		14,170.00		14,170.00
Uses of working capital				
Total uses		0.00		0.00
Net change	$	14,170.00	$	14,170.00
Analysis of componants of changes				
Increase <Decrease> in Current Assets				
Cash on Hand	$	250.00	$	250.00
Checking Account		13,920.00		13,920.00
<Increase> Decrease in Current Liabilities				
Net change	$	14,170.00	$	14,170.00

Step 5:

Display the balance sheet for January 31, 2017. Compare your printout to Figure 3–48.

FIGURE 3–48
Balance Sheet for Wildwood Medical Services (Partial View)

Chapter 3 - Wildwood Medical Services
Balance Sheet
January 31, 2017

ASSETS

Current Assets				
Cash on Hand	$	250.00		
Checking Account		13,920.00		
Total Current Assets				14,170.00
Property and Equipment				
Total Property and Equipment				0.00
Other Assets				
Total Other Assets				0.00
Total Assets			$	14,170.00

LIABILITIES AND CAPITAL

Current Liabilities				
Total Current Liabilities				0.00

Step 6:

Review the general journal and financial statements for accuracy.

Step 7:

Close the Select a Report or Form dialog box.

Chapter Review and Assessment

Software Command Summary

Create New Account	Maintain, Chart of Accounts, Account ID, Description, Account Type
Enter Beginning Balances	Maintain, Chart of Accounts, Account Beginning Balances, Select Period, Enter Balances
Journalize	Tasks, General Journal Entry, Save
Edit a Selected Transaction	Tasks, General Journal Entry, List, Select Desired Transaction, Open, Make Necessary Changes, Save
Delete a Selected Transaction	Tasks, General Journal Entry, List, Select Desired Transaction, Open, Delete
Print or Preview Reports	Reports & Forms, Select Category of Reports, Highlight Specific Report, Print or Options Screen

Checkpoint Answers

Checkpoint 3–1
1. The total of the debits must equal the total of the credits.
2. Sage 50 will not allow an unbalanced general journal entry to be posted.
3. The special journals increase efficiency by grouping similar transactions.
4. The four basic types of special journals are the sales journal, purchases journal, cash receipts journal, and cash disbursements journal.

Checkpoint 3–2
1. If the totals of the balances are equal and the trial balance difference is zero, the general ledger accounts are in balance.
2. The account ID, description, account type, and balance for each account appear in the completed Chart of Accounts Beginning Balances window.

Checkpoint 3–3
1. The general journal can be accessed by using the Menu bar or the Shortcuts list.
2. It is necessary to analyze a transaction to determine the appropriate accounts and amounts to debit and credit in the journal entry for that transaction.

Study Quizzes

Take the study quiz online to check your understanding of chapter concepts. The quiz can be taken multiple times.

Content Check

Multiple Choice: Choose only one response for each question.

1. A record in which transactions are listed in order by date is a
   A. chart of accounts.
   B. journal.
   C. income statement.
   D. trial balance.
   E. None of the above

2. The financial statement that reports assets, liabilities, and owner's equity as of a specific date is the
   A. statement of changes in financial position.
   B. chart of accounts.
   C. balance sheet.
   D. income statement.
   E. None of the above

3. The financial statement that shows the revenues, expenses, and net income or net loss for a period of time is known as the
   A. balance sheet.
   B. general journal.
   C. general ledger.
   D. income statement.
   E. None of the above

4. Suppose that an accountant has recorded the wrong date in a journal entry. In Sage 50, the best way to correct the error is to
   A. use the delete function and then record the entire entry again.
   B. use the list function and then open transaction.
   C. use the memorized transaction function.
   D. use the recurring transaction function.
   E. None of the above

5. Which of the following functions is used to set up a journal entry that will automatically repeat in future accounting periods?
   A. add a row function
   B. open function
   C. memorized transaction function
   D. recurring transaction function
   E. None of the above

Short Essay Response

Provide a detailed answer for each question.

1. What is the purpose of the general journal?
2. What are the steps necessary to add a new account to the chart of accounts?
3. What steps are necessary to ensure accurate posting of journal entries?
4. Under what circumstances can a business use the cash basis of accounting?
5. What is the purpose of the general ledger?
6. What information must be recorded in the general journal entry window before a transaction can be posted?

Cooperative Learning

1. Form groups of three or four students and create your own retail business. Decide on the business setup criteria.
2. Create 10 transactions for the newly formed business from Cooperative Learning Exercise 1. Use Sage 50 to enter the transactions in the general journal. Create any new accounts as needed. Print the general ledger, general journal, income statement, and balance sheet.

Writing and Decision Making

The company for which you work, MH Design Consulting, is converting from a manual accounting system to a computerized system. You are responsible for the conversion. The owner of the company, Maria Holtzman, wants to know how you plan to use Sage 50 to ensure that an accurate conversion to a computerized accounting system occurs. Therefore, in memo format, list in detail what information is needed and what decisions must be made for each screen of the New Company Setup procedure.

Case Problems

Demonstrate your knowledge of the Sage 50 Accounting features discussed in this chapter by completing the following case problems.

Case Problem 3–1A

Open Johnson & Associates Accounting from the student data files.
The following transactions occurred during the month of January 2017.

Date	Transaction
Jan. 4	Paid rent of $2,500 for January. Because this payment must be made each month, set it up as a recurring transaction. Use 12 as the number of times the transaction will recur.
4	Purchased computer equipment for $3,500 in cash. (Because this business is using the accrual basis of accounting, it records purchases of equipment in an Asset account.)
4	Purchased office supplies for $375 in cash. (Because this business is on the accrual basis, it records purchases of supplies in an Asset account.)
5	Paid a $240 insurance premium for the month. This is also a recurring monthly transaction. Use 12 as the number of times that it will recur. (Because this insurance covers just one month, treat it as an expense.)
6	Purchased furniture and fixtures for $3,100 on account. (*Use Account 20000, Accounts Payable.*)
10	Paid $600 for a newspaper ad that will run during the month of January. The business may run more ads in the future. Thus, create this transaction using the memorization feature. You will need to create a new account for this transaction: *60200, Advertising Expense, Expenses.*
12	Performed accounting services for Monroe Construction and received $2,400 in cash.
14	Performed accounting services for Ramirez Consultants and received $2,250 in cash.
18	The owner withdrew $500 for his personal use. (Use *Account 39007, Richard Johnson, Drawing.*)
24	Performed accounting services for Steve's Landscaping and received $1,575 in cash.
28	Paid automobile expenses of $350 in cash.
29	Paid utilities of $325.
29	Paid the telephone bill of $135.
30	Performed accounting services for Mary's Daycare for $160 in cash.

1. Enter each of the transactions for January in the general journal. Create new accounts as needed. For all cash transactions, use *Account 10200, Regular Checking Account.*

2. Print the following reports for the month of January: General Journal, Income Statement, and Balance Sheet.

Case Problem 3–2A

1. Set up a new company for Ruben's Auto Detailing. Use the information given below:

Company Name:	**Ruben's Auto Detailing**
Address Line 1:	**1480 East Madison Avenue**
City, State, Zip:	**Stockton, CA 95207**
Country:	**USA**
Telephone:	**209-555-4358**
Fax:	**209-555-2332**
Business Type:	**Sole Proprietorship**
Federal Employer ID:	**09-6776754**
State Employer ID:	**098-8743-09**
St. Unemployment ID:	**00441-98**
Chart of Accounts:	**Build your own chart of accounts**
Accounting Method:	**Cash**
Posting Method:	**Real Time**
Accounting Periods:	**12 monthly accounting periods**
Fiscal Year to Start:	**January 2017**

2. Enter the following in the chart of accounts:

Account ID	Description	Account Type
10200	Regular Checking Account	Cash
39004	Ruben Sanchez, Capital	Equity-doesn't close
39005	Ruben Sanchez, Equity	Equity-Retained Earnings
39006	Ruben Sanchez, Drawing	Equity-gets closed
40000	Detailing Fees	Income
60000	Advertising Expense	Expenses
60010	Laundry Expense	Expenses
60020	Telephone Expense	Expenses
60030	Utilities Expense	Expenses
60040	Rent Expense	Expenses
60050	Detailing Supplies Expense	Expenses

3. The following transactions occurred during the month of January 2017. Enter each of the transactions in the general journal. Create new accounts as needed.

Date	Transaction
Jan. 3	The owner invested $12,500 of his personal funds in the business. (*Ruben Sanchez, Capital*)
3	Paid rent of $1,250 for January. Because this payment must be made each month, set it up as a recurring transaction. Use 12 as the number of times the transaction will recur.
3	Purchased detailing supplies for $850 in cash.
5	Set up a petty cash fund of $200. You will need to create a new account for this transaction: *10100, Petty Cash, Cash.*
5	Detailed a fleet of cars for Mavis Car Rentals and received $725 in cash. This is a recurring biweekly transaction. The number of times it will recur is 26.
11	Paid $180 for advertising flyers. Create this transaction using the memorization feature.
15	Detailing fees for the week amounted to $1,220 in cash.
19	The owner withdrew $525 for his personal use. (Use *Ruben Sanchez, Drawing.*)
19	Detailed a fleet of trucks for Blackmun Trucking and received $625 in cash. This is a recurring monthly transaction. The number of times it will recur is 12.
20	Paid the telephone bill of $145.
23	Detailing fees for the week amounted to $860 in cash.
25	Paid automobile expenses of $475 in cash. You will need to create a new account for this transaction: *60060, Automobile Expense, Expenses.*
25	Paid utilities bill of $320.
31	Detailing fees for the week amounted to $760 in cash.

4. Print the following reports for the month of January: General Ledger Trial Balance, General Journal, Income Statement, and Balance Sheet.

Case Problem 3–1B

Open Katie's Graphic Designs from the student data files. The following transactions occurred during the month of January 2017.

Date	Transaction
Jan. 3	Paid office rent of $650 for January. Because this payment must be made each month, set it up as a recurring transaction. Use 12 as the number of times the transaction will recur.
4	Purchased graphing equipment for $2,750 on account. (Because this business is using the accrual basis of accounting, it records purchases of equipment in an Asset account. Use *Account 20000, Accounts Payable.*)
4	Purchased graphing supplies for $265 in cash. (Because this business is using the accrual basis of accounting, it records purchases of supplies in an Asset account.)
5	Paid a $110 insurance premium for the month. This is also a recurring monthly transaction. Use 12 as the number of times that it will recur. (Because this insurance covers just one month, treat it as an expense.)
6	Purchased furniture and fixtures for $2,210 on account.
11	Paid $195 for a newspaper ad that will run during the month of January. The business may run more ads in the future. Thus, create this transaction using the memorization feature.
12	Created a business logo (*Graphic Design Income*) for the ABC Nursery School and received $420 in cash.
13	Performed printing services for Gomez Consultants and received $2,100 in cash.
15	The owner withdrew $300 for her personal use. (*Katie Rosario, Drawing*)
18	Retouched photos for an advertising campaign and received $1,800 in cash.
26	Performed photo services for the *Daily News* and received $1,090 in cash.
28	Paid automobile expenses of $328 in cash.
28	Paid utilities bill of $183.
29	Paid the telephone bill of $122.
30	Performed illustration services for J and K Architects and received $1,725 in cash.

1. Enter each of the transactions for January in the general journal. Create new accounts as needed. For all cash transactions, use *Account 10200, Regular Checking Account.*

2. Print the following reports for the month of January: General Journal, Income Statement, and Balance Sheet.

Case Problem 3-2B

1. Set up a new company for Cindy's Office Cleaning. Use the information given below:

Company Name:	**Cindy's Office Cleaning**
Address Line 1:	**64 West Bessie Avenue**
City, State, Zip:	**Stockton, CA 95207**
Country:	**USA**
Telephone:	**209-555-3536**
Fax:	**209-555-3537**
Business Type:	**Sole Proprietorship**
Federal Employer ID:	**09-6776457**
State Employer ID:	**098-8734-08**
St. Unemployment ID:	**00221-87**
Chart of Accounts:	**Build your own chart of accounts**
Accounting Method:	**Cash**
Posting Method:	**Real Time**
Accounting Periods:	**12 monthly accounting periods**
Fiscal Year to Start:	**January 2017**

2. Enter the following in the chart of accounts:

Account ID	Description	Account Type
10200	Regular Checking Account	Cash
39004	Cindy Robinson, Capital	Equity-doesn't close
39005	Cindy Robinson, Equity	Equity-Retained Earnings
39006	Cindy Robinson, Drawing	Equity-gets closed
40000	Cleaning Fees	Income
60000	Advertising Expense	Expenses
60010	Laundry Expense	Expenses
60020	Telephone Expense	Expenses
60030	Utilities Expense	Expenses
60040	Rent Expense	Expenses
60050	Cleaning Supplies Expense	Expenses

3. The following transactions occurred during the month of January 2017. Enter each of the transactions in the general journal. Create new accounts as needed.

Date	Transaction
Jan. 3	The owner invested $3,400 of her personal funds in the business. (*Cindy Robinson, Capital*)
3	Paid $250 in cash for a bonding fee. You will need to create a new account for this transaction: *60060, Bond Fee Expense, Expenses.*
3	Purchased cleaning supplies for $375 in cash.
4	Established a petty cash fund of $125. You will need to create a new account for this transaction: *10100, Petty Cash, Cash.*
4	Cleaned the offices of O'Brien Car Rentals and received $420 in cash. Set this up as a recurring biweekly transaction. The number of times it will recur is 26.
5	Purchased an ad in the local newspaper for $120.
7	Performed cleaning services for the Delta Insurance Agency and received $145 in cash. Set this up as a recurring weekly transaction. The number of times it will recur is 52.
15	Cleaning fees for the week amounted to $760 in cash.
19	The owner withdrew $450 for her personal use.
21	Cleaned the offices of Baxter Trucking and received $200 in cash. Set this up as a recurring monthly transaction. The number of times it will recur is 12.
24	Paid utilities bill of $158.
27	Paid automobile expenses of $650 in cash. You will need to create a new account for this transaction: *60070, Auto Expense, Expenses.*
28	Paid the telephone bill of $110.
30	Cleaning fees for the week amounted to $1,290 in cash.

4. Print the following reports for the month of January: General Ledger Trial Balance, General Journal, Income Statement, and Balance Sheet.

CHAPTER 4

Accounts Receivable and Sales for a Business

Objectives

4–1 Review recording accounts receivable

4–2 Create subsidiary ledger accounts for customers and enter the beginning balances

4–3 Process accounts receivable and sales transactions

4–4 Create action items and event logs

4–5 Adjust the accounts receivable for uncollectible accounts and print reports

Software Features

- Maintain Customer Prospects toolbar buttons
- Customer defaults
- Sales and Invoicing toolbar
- Action items
- Alerts
- Accounting Behind the Screens function

Company Files

Before beginning chapter work, access the links menu to download company files.

Many firms sell goods and services on credit. In fact, it is often said that credit is the lifeblood of American business. Credit makes it possible for customers to obtain goods and services immediately and pay for them in the future. This arrangement is convenient for customers and usually produces higher sales for the firms that offer credit.

OBJECTIVE 4–1

Review Recording Accounts Receivable

The amounts owed by customers to a business for goods or services sold to them on credit are called *accounts receivable*. Firms that sell on credit set up an asset account called Accounts Receivable in their general ledger.

When these firms make a sale on credit, they debit the amount to Accounts Receivable and credit the appropriate revenue account. Later, when they collect the amount owed by the customer, they debit (increase) Cash and credit (decrease) Accounts Receivable.

The Accounts Receivable Subsidiary Ledger

In addition to the Accounts Receivable account in the general ledger, most businesses that sell on credit maintain a subsidiary ledger with individual accounts for their customers. This subsidiary ledger is known as the *accounts receivable ledger* or customer ledger.

A *subsidiary ledger* contains detailed information for a single general ledger account. Remember that the general ledger is a firm's main ledger. It includes the accounts that are used to prepare the financial statements. Subsidiary ledgers supplement the information in the general ledger.

The advantage of having an accounts receivable subsidiary ledger is that it provides detailed information about the transactions with credit customers and shows the balances they owe. Sage 50 updates these accounts automatically when transactions are recorded and posted. As a result, management can closely monitor the status of the firm's accounts receivable.

Being able to collect its accounts receivable on time is critical to the success of a business that sells on credit. The cash from accounts receivable is needed to pay debts and operating expenses such as rent and salaries. A business may have rising sales but experience cash flow problems if it does not manage its accounts receivable properly.

Sage 50 improves the efficiency of accounts receivable procedures because it allows for:

- Quick preparation of invoices (bills)
- Automatic posting of accounts receivable transactions, which eliminates the time and effort required by manual posting
- Quick preparation of a wide variety of reports, which show management the current status of the accounts receivable
- An action item feature that can be programmed to alert users to high balances, past-due amounts, and other problems with a specific customer account
- Quick preparation of contact letters and past-due notices

accounts receivable The amounts owed to a business by its customers for goods or services sold on credit.

accounts receivable ledger A subsidiary ledger that contains accounts for credit customers.

subsidiary ledger A ledger that contains detailed information for a single general ledger account.

The Controlling Account in the General Ledger

When there is an accounts receivable subsidiary ledger, the Accounts Receivable account in the general ledger becomes a *controlling account*. It provides a link between the general ledger and the accounts receivable subsidiary ledger because its balance is equal to the total of all the balances of the individual accounts in the subsidiary ledger.

Every subsidiary ledger must have a controlling account in the general ledger.

controlling account
A general ledger account that summarizes the balances of all the accounts in a subsidiary ledger.

Uncollectible Accounts

No matter how careful management is in granting credit to customers, monitoring the status of the accounts receivable, and making efforts to collect overdue balances, some accounts will become uncollectible. Events occur that are beyond the control of the seller. For example, companies may go bankrupt or have disasters occur that prevent them from paying their accounts. In those cases, the accounts must be written off or discharged. When accounts are written off, it is considered an expense of doing business.

Two methods are used to account for uncollectible accounts: the allowance method and the direct write-off method. Both will be discussed later in this chapter.

Checkpoint 4–1

1. What is the advantage of having an accounts receivable subsidiary ledger?
2. Which accounts are debited and credited when a firm makes a sale on credit?

OBJECTIVE 4–2

Create Subsidiary Ledger Accounts for Customers and Enter the Beginning Balances

In Chapters 2 and 3, you learned how to set up general ledger accounts and enter the beginning balances. The procedure for establishing customer accounts in the accounts receivable ledger is similar. In this chapter, you will use Sage 50 to handle the accounts receivable of Superior Carpet and Tile.

The Maintain Customers/Prospects Window

In Sage 50, certain information is needed to create an account for each customer in the accounts receivable subsidiary ledger. This information is entered into the following fields of the Maintain Customers/Prospects window. To view this window, open Chp. 4 – Superior Carpet and Tile, click Maintain and then *Customers/Prospects*. Review the following fields:

- **Customer ID**
  Sage 50 requires an alphanumeric identifier for each customer's account. For example, Superior Carpet and Tile uses Norman-01 as the identifier for the first account in its accounts receivable subsidiary ledger. This account is for Norman Construction Company.

- **Name**

  The name given to a customer's account may be the name of the business, such as Norman Construction Company, or the name of an individual.

- **Prospect**

  Sage 50 allows a firm to open accounts for potential customers as well as current customers. This feature helps salespeople keep track of potential customers. When an order is placed, Sage 50 automatically activates the account of the potential customer and changes it to a current customer. A check mark is entered in the *Prospect* box to indicate a potential customer.

- **Inactive**

  Sometimes customers stop doing business with a company. A check mark is entered in the *Inactive* box to indicate this type of customer. Sage 50 automatically removes the accounts of inactive customers when the fiscal year closes.

General Tab

- **Account Number**

  Enter the customer's identifying account number.

- **Billing Address**

  Sage 50 permits the entry of separate billing and shipping addresses for a customer. In fact, Sage 50 allows for several shipping addresses. If a customer has a single address for both billing and shipping, you need only enter the billing address.

- **Sales Tax**

  Retail businesses in most states and some cities and counties must charge their customers a sales tax on goods. In some areas, this tax is also levied on services. Wholesale businesses that sell to retailers do not charge sales tax because the retailers have resale certificates that exempt them from paying sales tax. If sales tax does apply, you enter the type when creating each customer's account.

- **Customer Type**

  Sage 50 allows you to classify customers by type. For example, some companies have both retail and wholesale customers.

- **Telephone/Fax Numbers and E-Mail Addresses**

  Sage 50 provides space for recording two telephone numbers, a fax number, and an email address in each customer's account. You can email a customer directly by clicking on the E-mail button to the right of the *E-mail address* field.

- **Web Site**

  Enter the customer's web address. The customer's website can be displayed by clicking the Internet button to the right of the *Web Site* field.

- **Customizable Fields**

  Sage 50 provides additional space for second contact information, references, and other customized business-related fields.

Contacts Tab

- **Contact**

  The contact is the person whom the business calls or writes in connection with questions about orders.

- **Edit Addresses**
  This allows the Sage 50 user to select different billing addresses to be set up for any individual client. The default address is Address 1.

History Tab

- **Customer Since**
  Some businesses enter the date of the customer's first order in the customer's account.
- **Last Invoice Date**
  Some businesses enter the date of the last invoice sent to the customer.
- **Last Invoice Amount**
  Some businesses enter the amount of the last invoice sent to the customer.
- **Last Payment Date**
  Some businesses enter the date of the last payment the customer made.
- **Last Payment Amount**
  Some businesses enter the amount of the last payment the customer made.
- **Last Statement Date**
  Some businesses enter the date of the last statement sent to the customer.
- **Customer Beginning Balances**
  When a business creates accounts for its customers, there may be some outstanding (unpaid) invoices. Information about these invoices is needed to enter the beginning balances in the accounts.

Sales Info Tab

- **Sales Rep**
  Some businesses assign a sales representative to each customer. The name of the sales representative is entered in the customer's account. (Sage 50's accounts receivable procedures allow a business to organize information about its sales staff and to maintain an up-to-date list of sales representatives.)
- **GL Sales Account**
  GL Sales Account refers to the revenue account in the general ledger that is credited when a sale is made to the customer. The number of the appropriate general ledger account is entered in the customer's account.
- **Open PO Number**
  When a customer's account is created, it may have an open purchase order. The number of this purchase order is entered in the account.
- **Ship Via**
  Some businesses allow their customers to select a shipping method. The method chosen is entered in the customer's account.
- **Resale Number**
  Sales tax authorities issue certificates to retailers that exempt them from paying sales tax on goods they buy for resale. If a customer is a retailer, the resale certificate number must be entered here.

- **Pricing Level**

  Some businesses have several different pricing levels for merchandise. For example, if a firm sells to both retailers and wholesalers, it will charge them different prices. The pricing level is entered in the customer's account.

- **Form Options**

  Businesses today use differing methods for delivering invoices. This option allows the user to check for delivery via Paper Form or E-mail, including a choice to forward invoices or statements to the sales representative when sending customers emails.

Payment & Credit Tab

- **Cardholder's Name and Address**

  A business may want to create account information for credit card users. The cardholder's information is entered in this section.

- **City, State, Zip and Country**

  The customer's or prospective customer's city, state, zip, and country information are entered here.

- **Credit Card Number and Expiration Date**

  The credit card information is entered and stored here.

- **Receipt Settings**

  The payment method and the account to be debited are selected in this section. All major credit cards, as well as cash, are supported. The system's default settings are used by Sage 50 if the *Use payment method and cash account from last saved receipt* box is selected.

- **Terms and Credit**

  Many companies use Default (Standard) credit terms, and this is an option that can be selected. Other terms as well as specified discount periods, credit periods, discount percentages, credit limits, credit status, and finance changes can be selected.

Click the Close button when you have finished reviewing the fields of the Maintain Customers/Prospects window.

Creating Subsidiary Ledger Accounts for Customers

In this section, you will create subsidiary ledger accounts for four customers of Superior Carpet and Tile.

Follow the steps outlined below to create subsidiary ledger accounts for the customers.

Step 1:

Open Superior Carpet and Tile (Chp. 4 – Superior Carpet and Tile if student data files are used).

Step 2:

Click Maintain, and then click *Customers/Prospects.*

Step 3:

Click the General folder tab, if it is not already selected. (See Figure 4–1.)

FIGURE 4–1
Maintain Customers/Prospects Window with General Tab Selected

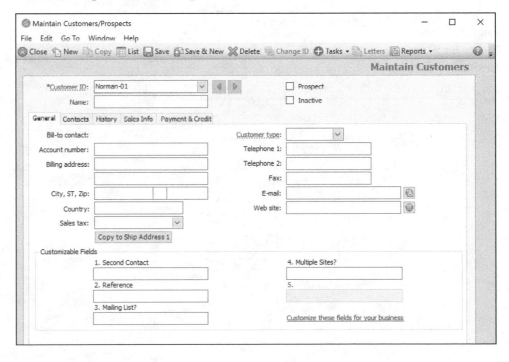

Set up the account information listed below for Norman Construction Company, the first customer of Superior Carpet and Tile.

Step 4:

Key **Norman-01** in the *Customer ID* field. Verify that your screen appears as in the example shown in Figure 4–2.

FIGURE 4–2
Customer ID Field with Norman-01 Entered

Step 5:

Key **Norman Construction Company** in the *Name* field.

Step 6:

Key **12021** in the *Account Number* field.

Step 7:

Key **2890 Washington Ave.** in the *Billing Address* field.

Step 8:

Key **Kelsey, CA 95556** in the *City, ST, Zip* field.

Step 9:

Key **USA** in the *Country* field and click the Copy to Ship Address 1 button.

Step 10:

Key **General** in the *Customer Type* field.

Step 11:

Key **916-555-1947** in the *Telephone 1* field.

Step 12:

Key **916-555-4653** in the *Fax* field.

Step 13:

Click the Contacts tab and key **John Norman** in the *Contact name* field.

Step 14:

Click the General tab and compare your completed window with Figure 4–3. Make any necessary corrections by selecting the erroneous items and re-entering the information.

FIGURE 4–3
Completed General Window for Norman Construction Company

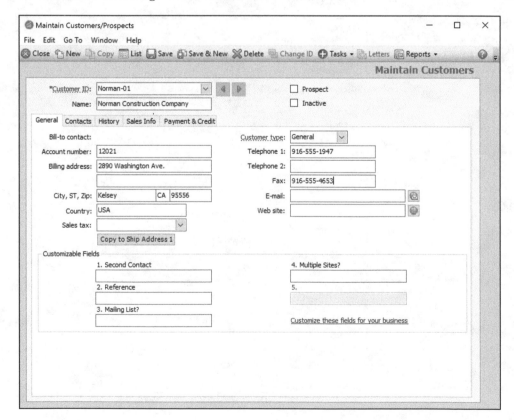

Sales Info Tab

Whenever you create a customer's account, you need to establish sales defaults.

Step 1:

Click the Sales Info tab as shown in Figure 4–4.

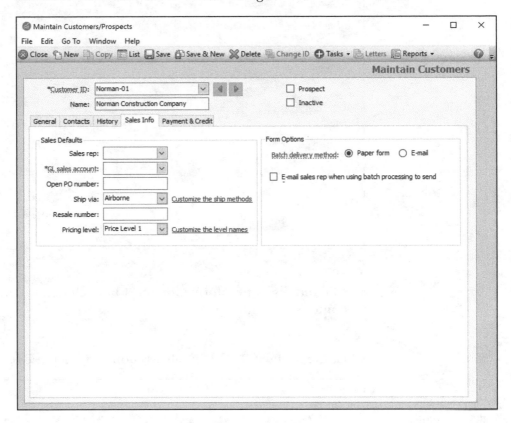

Step 2:

Click the drop-down arrow next to GL Sales Account, and then click *Account 400, Installation Services* (Income).

Step 3:

Click *Fed-EX* in the Ship Via drop-down list.

Step 4:

Accept the default (*Price Level 1*) in the Pricing Level drop-down list.

Step 5:

Accept the default in the Form Options box. Compare your entries for Norman Construction Company with the entries shown in Figure 4–5. Make any necessary changes.

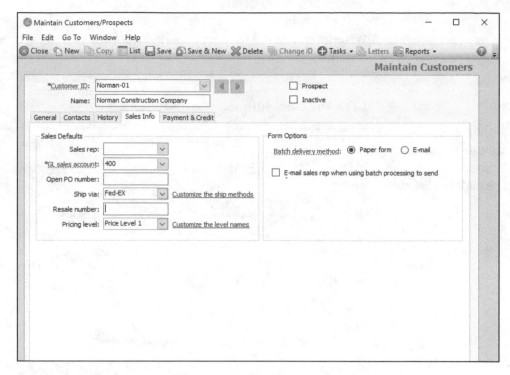

Payment & Credit Tab

Credit and discount information must be included when you create a customer's account.

Step 1:

Click the Payment & Credit tab, as shown in Figure 4–6.

FIGURE 4–6
Payment & Credit
Window for Norman
Construction Company

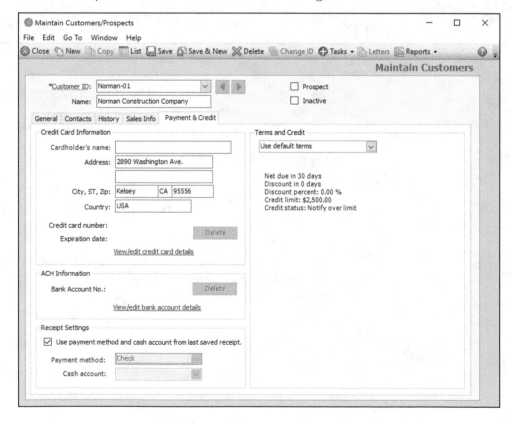

The default for the credit terms is currently set at Net 30 days. Superior offers terms set at 2% 10 days, net 30 days. These terms mean that the customer can pay in 10 days and receive a 2% discount or pay the net (full) amount in 30 days.

The pricing level and the credit terms relate mostly to merchandising businesses and will be explained in future chapters. The credit terms can be changed by selecting *Customize terms for this customer* from the Terms and Credit drop-down list. Make the following changes to reflect Superior's credit terms.

Step 2:

Select *Customize terms for this customer* from the Terms and Credit drop-down list.

Step 3:

Select *Due in number of days* and key **30** in the Net due in days box.

Step 4:

Select *Use discounts* and key **10** in the Discount in days box.

Step 5:

Key **2.00** in the Discount Percent box.

There is also a default for a credit limit, which is currently set at $2,500. Whenever the recording of a sale takes a customer's balance over this limit, Sage 50 sends a warning message.

Step 6:

Click the Save button at the top of the Maintain Customers/Prospects window.

Beginning Balances

The final phase in creating the customer account involves the entry of the beginning balances.

Step 1:

Click the History folder tab in the Maintain Customers/Prospects window.

Step 2:

Click the Customer Beginning Balances button at the bottom of the window.

Step 3:

Key **Beginning Balance** in the *Invoice Number* field.

Step 4:

Key **01/01/17** in the *Date* field. (Sage 50 will convert this to *Jan 1, 2017*.)

Step 5:

Key **5,000.00** in the *Amount* field.

Step 6:

Click *Account 104 (Accounts Receivable)* at the A/R Account drop-down list.

Step 7:

Click the Save button and then the Close button.

Create the remaining three customer accounts for Superior Carpet and Tile by clicking the Save & New button at the top of the Maintain Customers/Prospects window and enter the beginning balances as of 01/01/17 using the information listed below. Use the steps that you followed for the Norman Construction Company account. When you complete your work, save and exit Superior Carpet and Tile.

Customer

Customer ID:	**Calif-02**
Name:	**State of California**

General Tab

Account Number:	**120202**
Billing Address:	**2356 State Street**
City, ST, Zip:	**Sacramento, CA 95670**
Country:	**USA**
Customer Type:	**General**
Telephone 1:	**916-555-2122**
Fax:	**916-555-2887**

Contacts Tab

Contact:	**Lisa Jones**

Sales Info Tab

GL Sales Account:	**400**
Ship Via:	**Fed-EX**
Pricing Level:	**Default**
Form Options:	**Default**

Payment & Credit Tab

Terms and Credit:	**2% 10 days, net 30 days**

History Tab

Beginning Balance:	**4,000.00**

Customer

Customer ID:	**Parker-03**
Name:	**Parker's Construction**

General Tab

Account Number:	**120203**
Billing Address:	**326 Henry Ave.**
City, ST, Zip:	**Sacramento, CA 95665**
Country:	**USA**
Customer Type:	**General**
Telephone 1:	**916-555-9147**
Fax:	**916-555-5536**

Contact Tab

Contact:	**George Parker**

Sales Info Tab

GL Sales Account:	**400**
Ship Via:	**Fed-EX**
Pricing Level:	**Default**
Form Options:	**Default**

Payment & Credit Tab

Terms and Credit:	**2% 10 days, net 30 days**

History Tab

Beginning Balance:	**2,000.00**

Customer

Customer ID:	**Running-04**
Name:	**Running Water Tile**

General Tab

Account Number:	**120204**
Billing Address:	**3234 Flying Spur Road**
City, ST, Zip:	**Roseville, CA 95660**
Country:	**USA**
Customer Type:	**General**
Telephone 1:	**916-555-2556**
Fax:	**916-555-9998**

Contact Tab

Contact:	**Joyce Holman**

Sales Info Tab

GL Sales Account:	**400**
Ship Via:	**Fed-EX**
Pricing Level:	**Default**
Form Options:	**Default**

Payment & Credit Tab

Terms and Credit:	**2% 10 days, net 30 days**

History Tab

Beginning Balance:	**4,000.00**

Checkpoint 4–2

1. What is the purpose of the customer accounts in the accounts receivable subsidiary ledger?
2. Why is the Accounts Receivable account in the general ledger known as a controlling account?

Create subsidiary ledger accounts for the customers of Meadowland Healthcare Services.

Step 1:

Open Chp. 4 – Meadowland Healthcare Services from the student data files. This company has been created for you.

Step 2:

Create the following customer accounts. There are no beginning balances.

Customer

Customer ID:	**Doctor's-10**
Name:	**Doctor's Medical Center**

General Tab

Account Number:	**120210**
Billing Address:	**2122 Mercy Street**
City, ST, Zip:	**Sacramento, CA 95661**
Country:	**USA**
Customer Type:	**General**
Telephone 1:	**916-555-4934**
Fax:	**916-555-3122**

Contact Tab

Contact:	**Jim Conway, MD**

Sales Info Tab

GL Sales Account:	**40000**
Ship Via:	**Fed-EX**
Pricing Level:	**Default**
Form Delivery Options:	**Default**

Payments & Credit Tab

Terms and Credit:	**2% 10 days, net 30 days**

History Tab

Beginning Balance:	**0**

Customer

Customer ID:	**Good-20**
Name:	**Good Samaritan Hospital**

General Tab

Account Number:	**120220**
Billing Address:	**2415 10th Street**
City, ST, Zip:	**Sacramento, CA 95671**
Country:	**USA**
Customer Type:	**General**
Telephone 1:	**916-555-6780**
Fax:	**916-555-8987**

Contact Tab

Contact:	**Jane Campbell, RN**

Sales Info Tab

GL Sales Account:	**40000**
Ship Via:	**Fed-EX**
Pricing Level:	**Default**
Form Delivery Options:	**Default**

Payments & Credit Tab

Terms and Credit:	**2% 10 days, net 30 days**

History Tab

Beginning Balance:	**0**

Customer

Customer ID:	**Rapid-30**
Name:	**Rapid Medical Response**

General Tab

Account Number:	**120230**
Billing Address:	**2516 Main Street**
City, ST, Zip:	**Sacramento, CA 95671**
Country:	**USA**
Customer Type:	**General**
Telephone 1:	**916-555-4719**
Fax:	**916-555-2166**

Contact Tab

Contact:	**Kim Smith, RN**

Sales Info Tab

GL Sales Account:	**40000**
Ship Via:	**Fed-EX**
Pricing Level:	**Default**
Form Delivery Options:	**Default**

Payments & Credit Tab

Terms and Credit:	**2% 10 days, net 30 days**

History Tab

Beginning Balance:	**0**

Customer

Customer ID:	**Valley-40**
Name:	**Valley Response**

General Tab

Account Number:	**120240**
Billing Address:	**3211 Main Street**
City, ST, Zip:	**Sacramento, CA 95761**
Country:	**USA**
Customer Type:	**General**
Telephone 1:	**916-555-5678**
Fax:	**916-555-7812**

Contact Tab
  Contact: **Robert Romero, PA**

Sales Info Tab
  GL Sales Account: **40000**
  Ship Via: **Fed-EX**
  Pricing Level: **Default**
  Form Delivery Options: **Default**

Payments & Credit Tab
  Terms and Credit: **2% 10 days, net 30 days**

History Tab
  Beginning Balances: **0**

Step 3:
Close the Maintain Customers/Prospects window.

OBJECTIVE 4–3

Process Accounts Receivable and Sales Transactions

Once the customer accounts have been established, you can use Sage 50 to record transactions with credit customers and post them automatically to the accounts receivable subsidiary ledger. Remember that you record a sale on credit by debiting Accounts Receivable and crediting the appropriate revenue account. You record cash collected from a credit customer by debiting Cash and crediting Accounts Receivable.

When there is an accounts receivable ledger, each sale on credit requires a debit to both the Accounts Receivable controlling account in the general ledger and the customer's account in the subsidiary ledger. Similarly, each collection of cash from a credit customer requires a credit to both the Accounts Receivable controlling account in the general ledger and the customer's account in the subsidiary ledger.

In Chapter 3, you recorded all transactions in the general journal. However, the general journal function of Sage 50 does not permit the automatic posting of entries to the customer accounts. Therefore, in this chapter, you will use the sales and invoicing function of Sage 50 to record credit sales and cash received on account. The sales and invoicing function, which is part of the accounts receivable module of Sage 50, permits automatic posting to both the general ledger and the accounts receivable subsidiary ledger.

Recording Sales on Credit

A sale on credit may involve goods or services. Superior Carpet and Tile is a small firm that provides construction services to local businesses and individuals. Almost all of its sales to businesses are made on credit.

On January 4, 2017, Superior Carpet and Tile did a small job for Norman Construction Company. The job involved 10 hours of installation work at $125 per hour. Norman issued a purchase order (PO 4567) before the job began. After it was completed, Superior issued Invoice 1001 to bill Norman Construction Company for $1,250. Superior's invoice has default terms of 2% 10 days, net 30 days.

An analysis of this transaction reveals that an asset (Accounts Receivable) has increased by $1,250 and revenue has increased by $1,250. The account for Norman Construction Company has also increased by $1,250. The accountant records this transaction by debiting Accounts Receivable for $1,250 and crediting Revenue for $1,250.

When this transaction is posted, the debit part of the entry must be posted to both the Accounts Receivable controlling account in the general ledger and the Norman Construction Company account in the accounts receivable subsidiary ledger.

Use the steps outlined below to record the sale on credit that Superior Carpet and Tile made to Norman Construction Company.

Step 1:

Open Chp. 4 – Superior Carpet and Tile from the student data files.

Step 2:

Click Tasks and then click *Sales/Invoicing*.

Step 3:

The Sales/Invoicing window will appear, as shown in Figure 4–7. Enter the information for the sale on credit that occurred on January 4, 2017, using the steps outlined below.

FIGURE 4–7
Sales/Invoicing Window

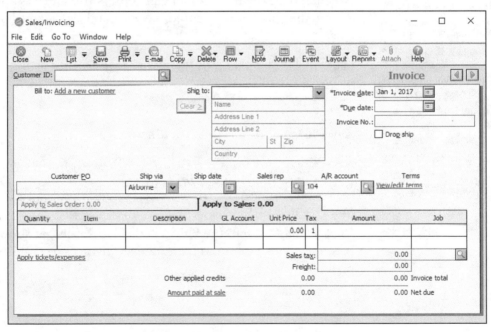

HINT

If the *GL Account* field does not display, as shown in Figure 4–7, click Options, and then click *Global*. The Maintain Global Options dialog box will appear. Remove the check mark from the box next to Accounts Receivable (Quotes, Sales Orders, Invoicing, Credit Memos, Receipts). Click OK. Then close and reopen the Sales/Invoicing window.

Step 4:

Click the *magnifying glass* icon next to the Customer ID drop-down list.

Step 5:

Highlight *Norman-01* in the drop-down list of customers, as shown in Figure 4–8.

FIGURE 4–8
Customer ID Drop-Down List with Norman-01 Selected

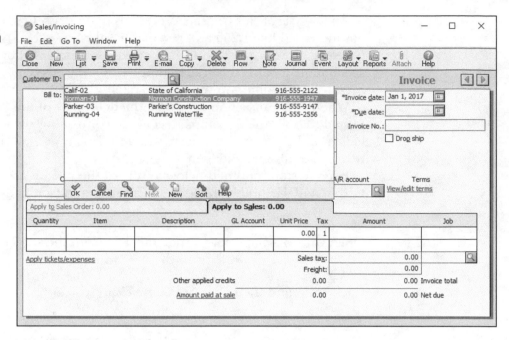

HINT

A warning stating that the customer's balance will exceed a predetermined credit limit may appear. Click OK to continue. The default for the credit limit is set at $2,500. Sage 50 is programmed to show a warning message in the event that a customer's balance goes over the credit limit.

Step 6:

Click OK at the bottom of the drop-down list of customers to accept Norman-01. Sage 50 automatically enters the address and billing information. (Alternatively, you could have clicked Norman-01.)

Step 7:

Click the *calendar* icon to the right of the *Invoice Date* field and choose *Jan 4, 2017.*

Step 8:

Key **1001** in the *Invoice No.* field.

Step 9:

Key **4567** in the *Customer PO* field.

Step 10:

Click *Hand Deliver* in the Ship Via drop-down list, as shown in Figure 4–9. It is Superior's custom to hand deliver invoices to customers whenever possible.

FIGURE 4–9
Ship Via Drop-Down
List with Hand Deliver
Selected

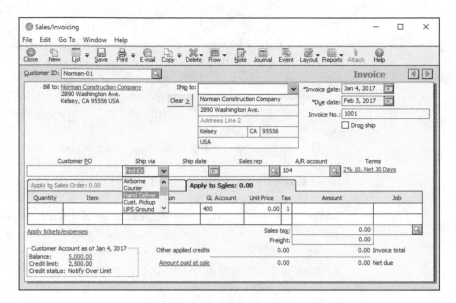

Step 11:

Key **10.00** (10 hours) in the *Quantity* field.

HINT

In some cases, you may want to omit the quantity and unit price and enter only a total amount.

Step 12:

Key **10 Hours of Installation** in the *Description* field.

Step 13:

Key **125.00** in the *Unit Price* field. The total of $1,250 is automatically calculated. Leave the *Tax* field at 1.

Step 14:

Review the completed Sales/Invoicing window for Norman Construction Company, as shown in Figure 4–10. If your entries contain any errors, correct them.

FIGURE 4–10
Completed Sales/Invoicing
Window for Norman
Construction Company

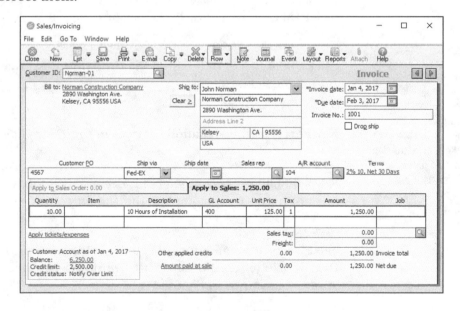

Step 15:

Click the **S**ave button to save the entry of the sale on credit.

Recording a Sale on Credit and a Partial Collection

On occasion, a business will present an invoice for a sale on credit to a customer and immediately collect part of the amount owed. For example, Superior Carpet and Tile did a job for Parker's Construction for a fixed fee of $5,000. The job was completed on January 14, 2017, and Invoice 1002 was hand delivered. Parker immediately issued a check for one-half of the total due ($2,500).

The analysis of this transaction reveals that revenue has increased by $5,000, the asset Accounts Receivable has increased by $2,500, and the asset Cash has increased by $2,500. The account for Parker's Construction has also increased by $2,500.

You would record this transaction by debiting Accounts Receivable for $2,500, debiting Cash for $2,500, and crediting Revenue for $5,000. The debit of $2,500 to Accounts Receivable must be posted to both the controlling account in the general ledger and the Parker's Construction account in the accounts receivable subsidiary ledger.

Use the steps outlined below to record the sale on credit and the partial collection involving Parker's Construction.

Step 1:

Click the *magnifying glass* icon next to the *Customer ID* field at the Sales/Invoicing window.

Step 2:

Click *Parker-03* in the drop-down list of customers.

Step 3:

Use the *calendar* icon next to the *Invoice Date* field and choose *Jan 14, 2017*.

Step 4:

Key **2356** in the *Customer PO* field. This is the number of the purchase order that was issued by Parker's Construction.

Step 5:

Click *Hand Deliver* in the Ship Via drop-down list. Key **1002** in the *Invoice No.* field.

Step 6:

Key **Performed installation services** in the *Description* field.

Step 7:

Key **5,000.00** in the *Amount* field. Because this job was done for a fixed fee, it is not necessary to complete the *Quantity* and *Unit Price* fields.

Step 8:

Next, record the amount collected from the customer. Click Amount Paid at Sale (at the bottom of the window). The Receive Money window appears, as shown in Figure 4–11.

HINT

Sage 50 will automatically assign invoice numbers in sequence. For example, 1002 is assigned to the invoice for Parker's Construction because the previous invoice for Norman Construction Company was 1001.

FIGURE 4–11
Receive Money Window

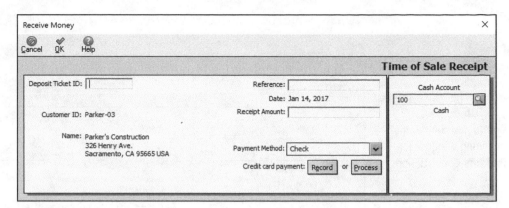

Step 9:

Key **01/14/17** in the *Deposit Ticket ID* field. This is the date of the probable bank deposit.

Step 10:

Key **1002** in the *Reference* field. This is the invoice number.

Step 11:

Key **2,500.00** in the *Receipt Amount* field.

Step 12:

At the Payment Method drop-down list, click *Check*. (It should be already selected as a default.)

Step 13:

At the Cash Account drop-down list, double-click *Cash* if it is not already selected.

Step 14:

Compare your work with the completed Receive Money window, as shown in Figure 4–12.

FIGURE 4–12
Completed Receive
Money Window

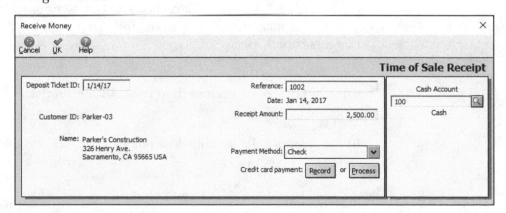

Step 15:

Click OK. Sage 50 will automatically transfer the information about the amount collected to the Sales/Invoicing window and will calculate the net amount that is now due.

Step 16:

Review the completed Sales/Invoicing window for Parker's Construction, as shown in Figure 4–13.

FIGURE 4–13
Completed Sales/
Invoicing Window for
Parker's Construction

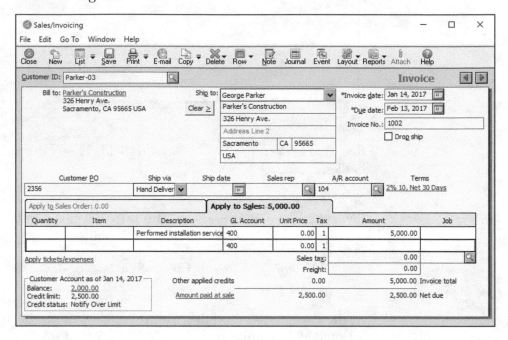

Step 17:

Click Save, and then Yes (at the credit warning message) to save the transaction, then close the Sales/Invoicing window.

Displaying Customer Ledger Reports

Sage 50 produces a wide variety of accounts receivable reports. The Customer Ledgers report is probably the most important of the accounts receivable reports. This report shows all transactions with credit customers and the balances they owe. Use the following steps to view the Customer Ledgers report.

Step 1:

Click Reports & Forms and then click *Accounts Receivable.*

Step 2:

In the Accounts Receivable: Customers and Sales section, click *Customer Ledgers,* as shown in Figure 4–14.

FIGURE 4–14
Accounts Receivable Report List with Customer Ledgers Selected

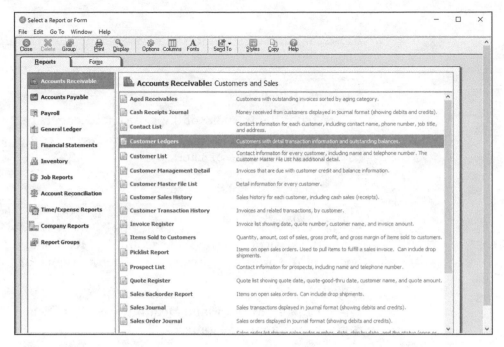

Step 3:

Click the Options button on the Select a Report or Form toolbar.

Step 4:

At the Modify Report – Customer Ledgers window, click *Range* in the Date drop-down list, and then *Jan 1, 2017* to *Jan 31, 2017* as the range date. Then click OK.

Step 5:

Examine the Customer Ledgers report shown in Figure 4–15. (The abbreviation SJ in the report stands for *sales journal.* The abbreviation CRJ stands for *cash receipts journal.*)

FIGURE 4–15
Customer Ledgers Report

9/11/16 at 07:20:05.61   *****EDUCATIONAL VERSION ONLY*****   Page: 1

Chp. 4 - Superior Carpet and Tile
Customer Ledgers
For the Period From Jan 1, 2017 to Jan 31, 2017
Filter Criteria includes: Report order is by ID. Report is printed in Detail Format.

Customer ID Customer	Date	Trans No	Type	Debit Amt	Credit Amt	Balance
Calif-02 State of California	1/1/17	Beginning Balan	SJ	4,000.00		4,000.00
Norman-01 Norman Construction Co	1/1/17 1/4/17	Beginning Bala 1001	SJ SJ	5,000.00 1,250.00		5,000.00 6,250.00
Parker-03 Parker's Construction	1/1/17 1/14/17 1/14/17	Beginning Bala 1002 1002	SJ SJ CRJ	2,000.00 5,000.00	 2,500.00	2,000.00 7,000.00 4,500.00
Running-04 Running WaterTile	1/1/17	Beginning Bala	SJ	4,000.00		4,000.00
Report Total				**21,250.00**	**2,500.00**	**18,750.00**

Step 6:

Close the Customer Ledgers window and the Select a Report or Form dialog box.

Checkpoint 4–3

1. What is the purpose of the Customer Ledgers report?
2. What function of Sage 50 is used to record credit sales and partial payment at time of sale?

Objective 4–3 Practice

Enter the services provided on account by Meadowland Healthcare Services. You previously created customer accounts for this firm.

Step 1:

Open Chp. 4 – Meadowland Healthcare Services, which you updated previously with customer accounts.

Step 2:

Record the following transactions using the Sales/Invoicing window. All cash must be entered into the Regular Checking Account (10200) account.

- On January 2, 2017, Meadowland Healthcare Services issued Invoice 1101 to Doctor's Medical Center for 100 hours of professional fees at a rate of $120 per hour. The invoice was sent by US mail.
- On January 8, 2017, Meadowland Healthcare Services issued Invoice 1102 to Good Samaritan Hospital for a fixed professional fee of $2,420, which covers monthly services. The invoice was hand delivered.
- On January 19, 2017, Meadowland Healthcare Services issued Invoice 1103 to Rapid Medical Response for 48 hours of professional fees at a rate of $120 per hour. The invoice was sent by US mail.
- On January 29, 2017, Meadowland Healthcare Services issued Invoice 1104 to Valley Response for a fixed fee of $1,650, which covers monthly professional fees and services. The invoice was hand delivered, and the customer immediately wrote a check for one-half of the amount due.

Step 3:

Display the Customer Ledgers report. Check the accuracy of your work by comparing your report with Figure 4–16.

FIGURE 4–16
Meadowland
Healthcare
Services
Customer
Ledgers Report

Chp. 4 - Meadowland Healthcare Services
Customer Ledgers
For the Period From Jan 1, 2017 to Jan 31, 2017
Filter Criteria includes: Report order is by ID. Report is printed in Detail Format.

Customer ID Customer	Date	Trans No	Type	Debit Amt	Credit Amt	Balance
Doctor's-10 Doctor's Medical Center	1/2/17	1101	SJ	12,000.00		12,000.00
Good-20 Good Samaritan Hospital	1/8/17	1102	SJ	2,420.00		2,420.00
Rapid-30 Rapid Medical Response	1/19/17	1103	SJ	5,760.00		5,760.00
Valley-40 Valley Response	1/29/17 1/29/17	1104 1104	SJ CRJ	1,650.00	825.00	1,650.00 825.00
Report Total				**21,830.00**	**825.00**	**21,005.00**

Step 4:

Close the Customer Ledgers window and the Select a Report or Form dialog box.

OBJECTIVE 4–4

Create Action Items and Event Logs

Having reliable, up-to-date information about customer accounts is one of the keys to collecting balances on time and minimizing losses from bad debts. Management must keep a close watch on the status of customer accounts and take prompt action to collect overdue amounts. The longer an amount remains overdue, the more likely it is that the account will eventually become uncollectible.

Sage 50 has certain features that help management track problem customer accounts. One of these features has already been mentioned: the warning message that the system produces whenever a customer's balance exceeds the credit limit. Other features provided by Sage 50 are action items and event logs.

Accessing the Action Items and Event Log Options

Action items and event logs allow you to create a list of actions to be taken, as well as program the system to display alerts on your screen before these events occur. For example, you might want to schedule meetings, telephone calls, or letters in connection with overdue balances, and you might want to be alerted to these events two days ahead of time. Action items and event logs can be used for other purposes besides managing customer accounts. They can also be used to schedule actions related to the vendor (creditor) accounts and to employees.

Follow the steps listed below to access the Action Items/Event Log Options.

Step 1:

Open Chp. 4 – Superior Carpet and Tile.

Step 2:

Click Tasks on the Menu bar and then *Action Items* in the drop-down list.

Step 3:

Click Options on the Action Items toolbar. The Action Items and Event Log Options window appears.

Using the Activities and Transactions Tabs

Events can be set up as defaults so that they can later be displayed as action items. For example, the managers of Superior Carpet and Tile want to be advised one day before any meeting and two days before any telephone call is to be made. Use the following steps to establish the necessary defaults.

Step 1:

Click the Activities tab in the Action Items and Event Log Options window.

Step 2:

Place a check mark for *Call To* in the *Display in Action Items* field. Key **2** in the *# of Days* field. Then place a check mark for *Meeting* in the *Display in Action Items* field. Key **1** in the *# of Days* field if it is not already entered. Compare the window with Figure 4–17.

FIGURE 4–17
Activities Tab

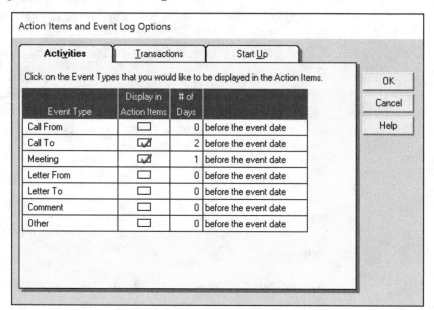

Sage 50 can be programmed to generate alerts for a variety of events. For example, Superior Carpet and Tile wants to create events for all possible event types specified by Sage 50. Superior also wants an advance warning for customer invoices that are due for payment. They want this warning to appear as an action item two days before payment due dates. Use the following steps to generate an alert to Superior two days before a customer's invoice is due.

Step 1:

Click the Transactions tab in the Action Items and Event Log Options window.

Step 2:

For *Customer Invoices Due,* key **2** in the *# of Days* field, as shown in Figure 4–18.

FIGURE 4–18
Transactions Tab

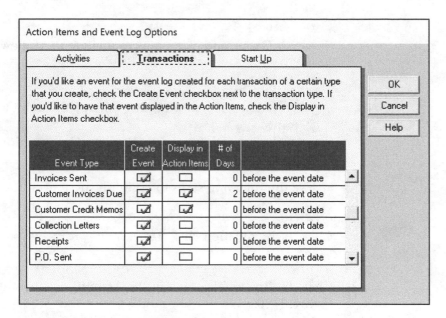

FIGURE 4–19
Start Up Tab

Using the Start Up Tab

You can have the action items displayed whenever you open a new company, or you can have the items displayed on top of the screen.

Step 1:

Click the Start Up tab in the Action Items and Event Log Options window.

Step 2:

Place a check mark next to *Display Action Items each time a new company is opened* if it is not already checked. (See Figure 4–19.)

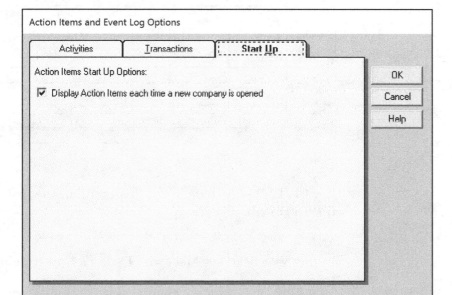

Step 3:

Click OK to accept all of the defaults that you have established and then close Action Items.

Because the process of setting up the defaults is complete, you can now create and access events that are action items.

Recording Action Items on the To Do List

Superior Carpet and Tile wants to include the following events as action items:

- On January 12, meet with Parker's Construction at 2:00 p.m.
- On January 13, call Running Water Tile about an increase in its credit limit.
- On January 13, meet with Norman Construction Company for lunch at 12:30 p.m.

Use the following steps to establish these events as action items.

Step 1:

Click Tasks and then click *Action Items.*

Step 2:

Click the To Do folder tab in the Action Items window, as shown in Figure 4–20.

FIGURE 4–20
To Do Tab Selected from Action Items Window

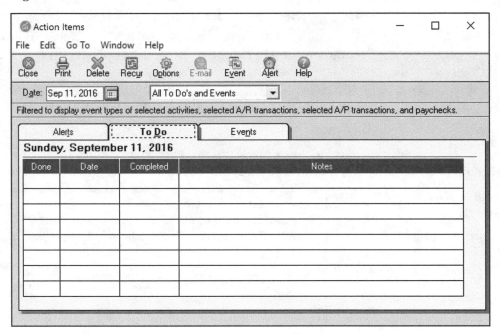

Step 3:

Key **01/12/17**, the date of the first event, in the first cell of the *Date* field in the To Do tab.

Step 4:

In the *Notes* field, key **Meet with Parker's Construction at 2:00 p.m.**

Step 5:

Key **01/13/17**, the date of the second event, in the second cell of the *Date* field in the To Do tab.

Step 6:

In the *Notes* field, key **Call Running Water Tile about an increase in its credit limit.**

Step 7:

Key **01/13/17**, the date of the third event, in the next cell of the *Date* field.

Step 8:

In the *Notes* field, key **Meet with Norman Construction Company for lunch at 12:30 p.m.**

Step 9:

Compare your completed To Do list with the one shown in Figure 4–21.

FIGURE 4–21
Completed To Do List

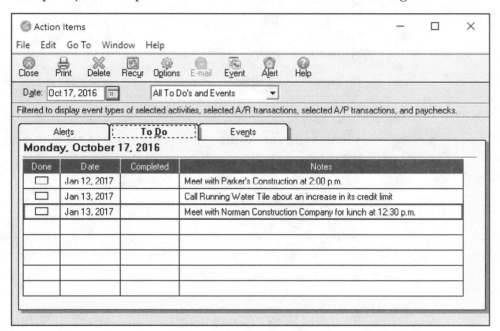

Recording Events on the Action List

Some events have been programmed to appear as action items. For example, customer invoices that are due for payment will be listed as action items two days before their due dates. The programming of this item was accomplished when the defaults were set up. However, a business might want to add other events to its action list.

Assume that Superior Carpet and Tile wants to place the following additional event on its action list: Set up a meeting with Parker's Construction for January 18, 2017. Advise two days ahead of time.

Step 1:

Click the Events tab, as shown in Figure 4–22.

FIGURE 4–22
Events Tab Selected from
Action Items Window

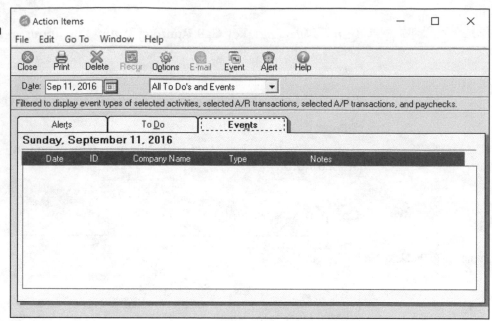

Step 2:

Click the Event button on the Action Items toolbar. The Create Event window appears.

Step 3:

At the Type drop-down list, click *Customer/Prospect.*

Step 4:

At the ID drop-down list, click the *magnifying glass* icon and then click *Parker-03.*

Step 5:

To the right of the *Date* field, click the *calendar* icon and choose *Jan 18, 2017.*

Step 6:

At the Event Type section, click *Meeting.*

Step 7:

In the *Note* field, key **Set up meeting.**

Step 8:

Place a check mark next to *Display in Action Items.*

Step 9:

Key **2** as the number of days. Then click *Before* in the "_____ the event date" drop-down list. (These may already be selected by default.)

Step 10:

Compare your work with the completed Create Event window shown in Figure 4–23.

FIGURE 4–23
Completed Create Event
Window

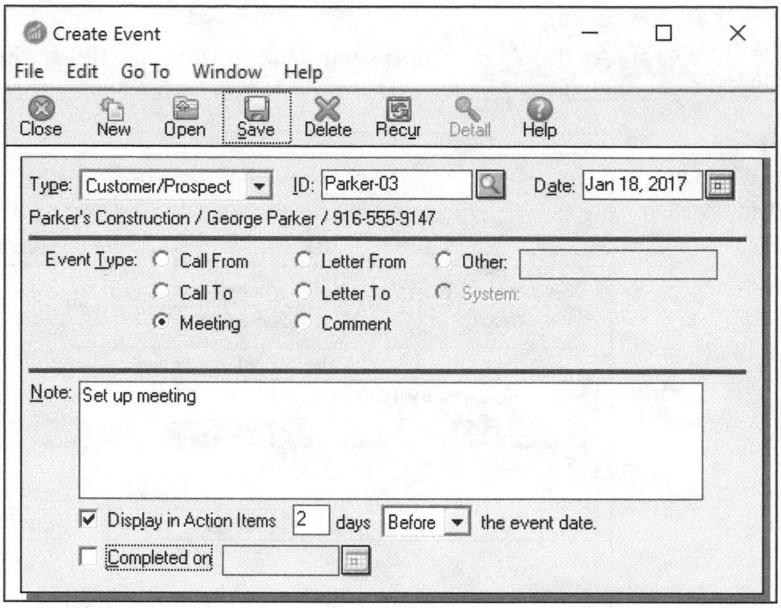

Step 11:

Click the Save button on the Create Event window toolbar, and then click Close.

Step 12:

Superior Carpet and Tile wants to add the following two events to its action list. Add them using steps 1 through 11:

- Call Norman Construction Company three days before a meeting set for January 19, 2017.
- Send a letter to Running Water Tile advising it of a change in credit terms that will take effect on January 31, 2017. Send the letter five days before (on January 26).

Step 13:

Click the Close button and then close the Action Items window.

Displaying the Events

Each of the events placed on the action list is scheduled to appear according to the number of days set before the event. For example, the first event for Superior Carpet and Tile—the meeting with Parker's Construction on January 18—will automatically appear two days before the event in the Action Items window as the system date changes to January 16. Follow the steps outlined below to check the events listed for any date. In this case, the date to be checked is January 16, 2017.

Step 1:

Click Tasks and then *Action Items.*

Step 2:

Click the Events tab.

Step 3:

At the Action Items window, in the *Date* field, click the *calendar* icon to choose *Jan 16, 2017*. (See Figure 4–24.)

FIGURE 4–24
Action Items Window
with Date Field Showing
Jan 16, 2017

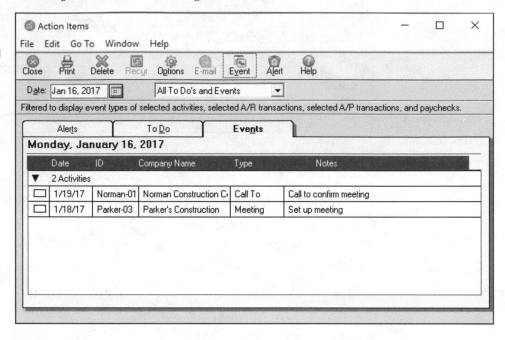

The events that are scheduled will appear in the Action Items window when Sage 50 is started on January 16, 2017.

Setting Alerts

The Action Items window has an Alerts tab that allows you to select certain conditions for notification. For example, an alert can be set to notify you when a particular customer's balance is too high. Assume that Superior Carpet and Tile wants to be notified when the balance owed by Norman Construction Company, the State of California, or Parker's Construction reaches $4,000. Follow the steps outlined below to set the alert.

Step 1:

Click the Alerts tab in the Action Items window.

Step 2:

Click the Alert button on the Action Items toolbar. The Set Company Alerts window appears, as shown in Figure 4–25.

FIGURE 4–25
Set Company Alerts
Window

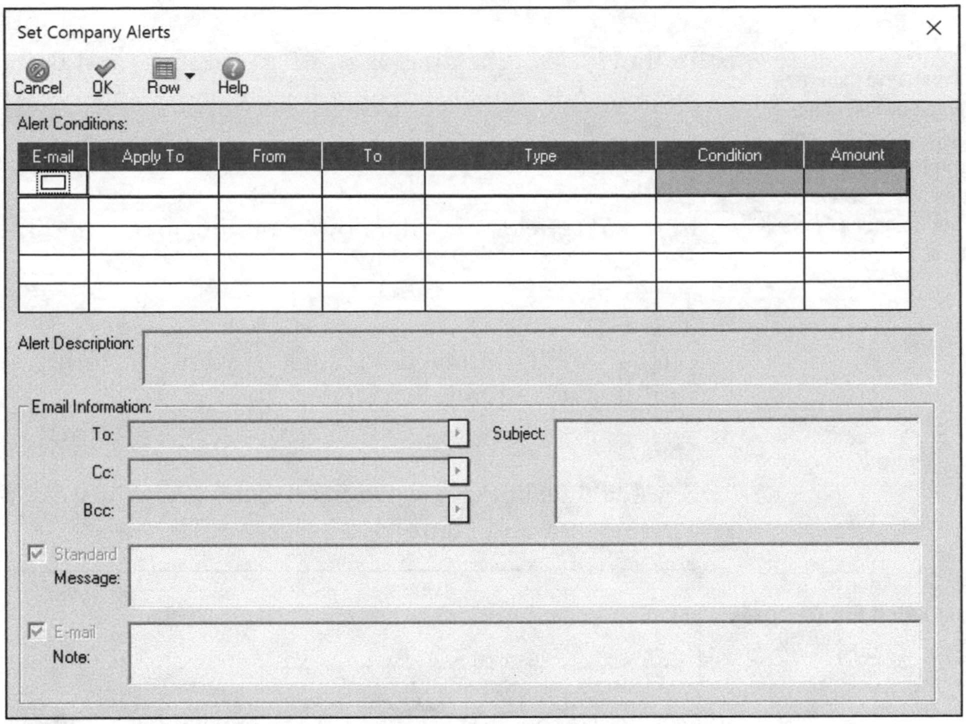

Setting an alert requires entry of information using the following steps:

Step 3:

Click inside the *Apply To* field, click the down-pointing arrow that appears, and then click *Customer.*

Step 4:

Click in the *From* field, click the *magnifying glass* icon, and then click *Calif-02.* (See Figurc 4–26.)

FIGURE 4–26
Set Company Alerts
Window – From Field

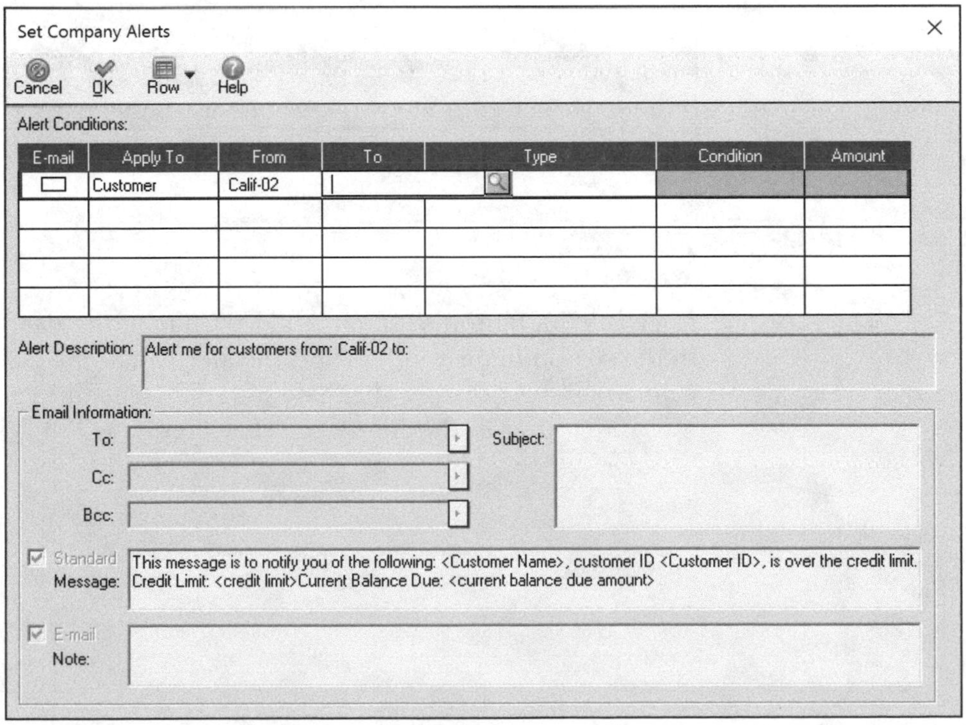

HINT

You can alert customers via email by selecting the *E-mail* box and completing the email information at the bottom of the Set Company Alerts window.

Step 5:

In the *To* field, click the *magnifying glass* icon, and then click *Parker-03*. Steps 4 and 5 establish a filter for the customer who is the subject of the alert.

Step 6:

In the *Type* field, click the down-pointing arrow, and then click *Current Balance*.

Step 7:

Click in the *Condition* field, click the down-pointing arrow, and then click >= if it is not already selected.

Step 8:

Key **4,000.00** in the *Amount* field. Compare your work with the completed window shown in Figure 4–27.

FIGURE 4–27
Completed Set Company Alerts Window

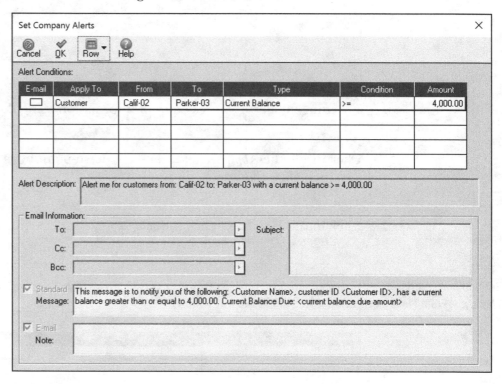

Step 9:

Click the OK button to save the alert. Change the date to January 16, 2017, in the Action Items window, and the alerts that were set up for Norman Construction Company, the State of California, and Parker's Construction will now appear in the Alerts tab. (See Figure 4–28.)

FIGURE 4–28
Alerts Tab with Alerts for
Customers' Balances

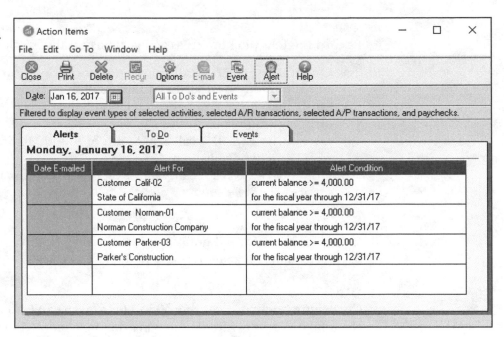

Step 10:

Close the Action Items window.

Checkpoint 4–4

1. What is the purpose of the action items and event log options of Sage 50?
2. What is the purpose of the alert function of Sage 50?

Objective 4-4 Practice

You previously established customer accounts for Meadowland Healthcare Services. Now you will set up action items and alerts for this firm.

Step 1:

Open Chp. 4 – Meadowland Healthcare Services.

Step 2:

Click the Start Up tab at the Action Items and Event Log Options window and then insert a check mark in the *Display Action Items each time a new company is opened* box.

Step 3:

Record the following events as action items on the To Do list:

- On January 12, 2017, call Doctor's Medical Center to discuss professional monthly services for its new facility.
- On January 18, 2017, meet with Good Samaritan Hospital to explain our new pricing policy.
- On January 23, 2017, call Kim Smith of Rapid Medical Response to wish her a happy birthday.
- On January 24, 2017, call Valley Response to set up a new professional service schedule.

Step 4:

Create an alert that will notify you when the current balance owed by any of the customers reaches or exceeds $1,500.

Step 5:

Create an event in which Sage 50 will tell you to call Good Samaritan Hospital two days before the meeting that is scheduled for January 18, 2017.

Step 6:

Close the Action Items window.

OBJECTIVE 4–5

Adjust the Accounts Receivable for Uncollectible Accounts and Print Reports

A well-run business is careful about extending credit, closely monitors the status of its customer accounts, and makes strong efforts to collect overdue balances. However, no matter how diligent a business is in managing its accounts receivable, some customer accounts will become uncollectible. Bad economic conditions in an area, bad management decisions, or new competition may cause a previously sound customer to go bankrupt.

Methods for Recording Uncollectible Accounts

Two methods are available for recording uncollectible accounts. The first and simpler approach is the *direct write-off method*. With this method, the expense from an uncollectible account is recorded when the customer's account actually becomes a bad debt. At that time, you debit the loss to Uncollectible Accounts Expense and credit it to Accounts Receivable. The credit part of this entry is posted to both the Accounts Receivable controlling account in the general ledger and the customer's account in the subsidiary ledger.

The second approach to recording uncollectible accounts is the *allowance method*. At the end of each accounting period, the accountant makes an estimate of the bad debts loss that will result from the period's sales. This amount is recorded by means of an adjusting entry. You debit Uncollectible Accounts Expense and credit Allowance for Doubtful Accounts. Figure 4–29 illustrates the adjusting entry for an estimated bad debts loss of $45,000.

direct write-off method A method in which the expense from uncollectible accounts is recorded when the accounts actually become bad debts.

allowance method A method in which the expense from uncollectible accounts is estimated at the end of each accounting period and recorded by means of an adjusting entry.

FIGURE 4–29
Initial Adjustment for Estimation of Bad Debt Loss Using the Allowance Method

General Journal Entry — □ ×

File   Edit   Go To   Window   Help

Close   New   List   Save   Print   Copy   Delete   Row   Reports   Help

Journal Entry ◄ ►

Date: Jan 31, 2017   ☐ Reverse Transaction
Reference:

GL Account	Description	Debit	Credit	Job
62000	Adjustment for bad debt loss	45,000.00		
11500	Adjustment for bad debt loss		45,000.00	
	Totals:	45,000.00	45,000.00	
	Out of Balance:	0.00		

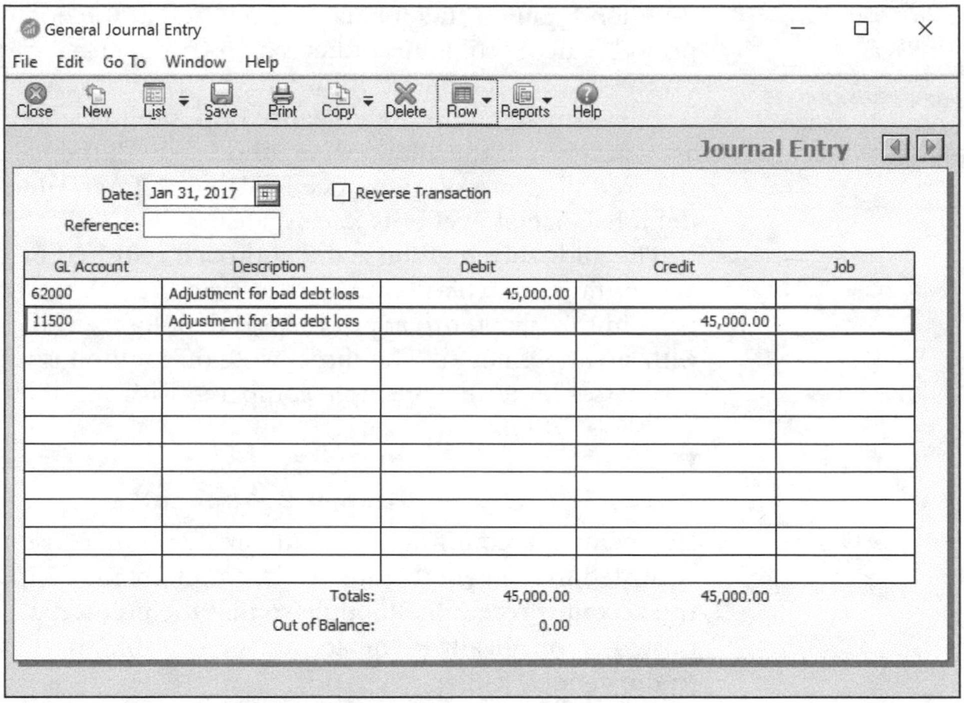

With the allowance method, when a customer's account actually becomes uncollectible, you write it off by debiting Allowance for Doubtful Accounts and crediting Accounts Receivable, as shown in Figure 4–30. The credit part of this entry is posted to both the Accounts Receivable controlling account in the general ledger and the customer's account in the subsidiary ledger.

FIGURE 4–30
Write-off of Bad Debt Loss against a Specific Customer Account Using the Allowance Method

General Journal Entry — □ ×

File   Edit   Go To   Window   Help

Close   New   List   Save   Print   Copy   Delete   Row   Reports   Help

Journal Entry ◄ ►

Date: Jan 31, 2017   ☐ Reverse Transaction
Reference:

GL Account	Description	Debit	Credit	Job
11500	Write-off customer's account	45,000.00		
11000	Write-off customer's account		45,000.00	
	Totals:	45,000.00	45,000.00	
	Out of Balance:	0.00		

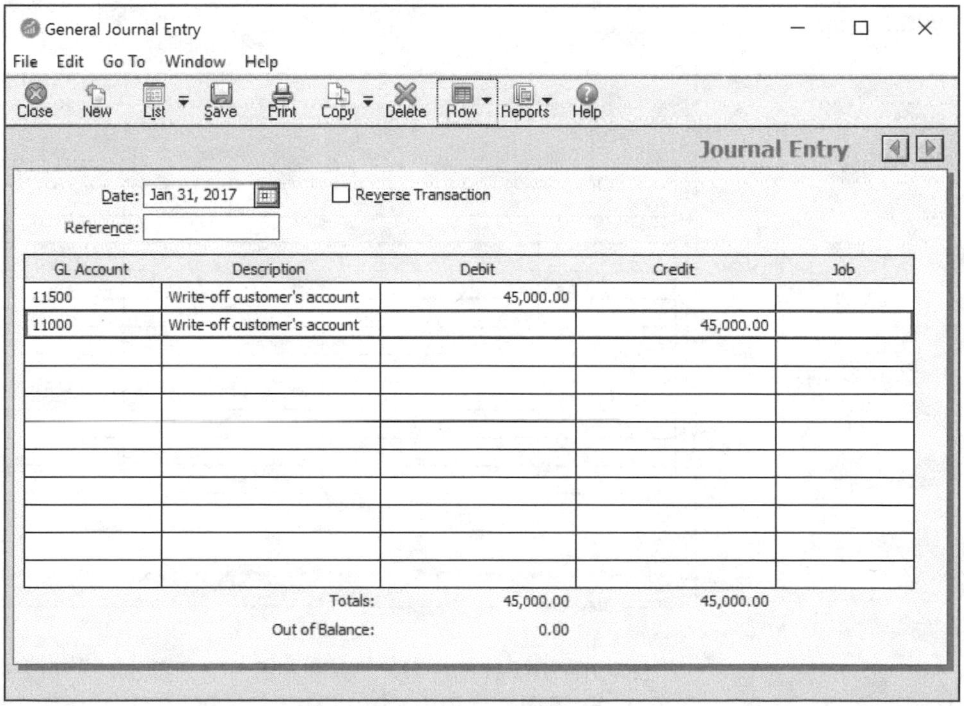

contra asset account An account with a balance opposite to the normal balance of an asset account.

When financial statements are prepared at the end of an accounting period, Uncollectible Accounts Expense appears as an operating expense on the income statement. Allowance for Doubtful Accounts is a *contra asset account*—an account with a balance opposite to the normal balance of an asset account. If the allowance method is used, the balance sheet will show the credit balance of Allowance for Doubtful Accounts deducted from the debit balance of Accounts Receivable.

The allowance method is the approach required by generally accepted accounting principles (GAAP). However, the direct write-off method will be used in this chapter to adjust for bad debt loss because this chapter deals with small businesses. The direct write-off method is used by many small businesses because it is simple compared with the allowance method.

Using the Direct Write-Off Method to Record the Write-Off of a Customer's Account

In a manual accounting system, the write-off of a customer's account is recorded in the general journal. However, in Sage 50, it is necessary to use the accounts receivable module so that the credit part of the entry can be posted automatically to the accounts receivable subsidiary ledger as well as to the general ledger.

A simple journal entry is used to write off a specific accounts receivable when it is deemed uncollectible. Therefore, no end-of-the-period adjusting entry is required. Figure 4–31 gives an example of a general journal entry needed to write off a bad debt loss.

FIGURE 4–31
Write-off of Bad Debt Loss Using the Direct Write-Off Method

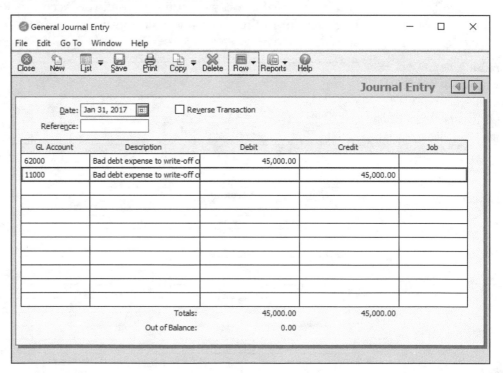

Assume that Running Water Tile has owed $4,000 to Superior Carpet and Tile for six months. Superior has been unsuccessful in its efforts to collect this overdue balance. On January 31, 2017, Superior receives a legal notice that Running Water Tile has gone bankrupt.

Superior uses the direct write-off method for recording uncollectible accounts. Therefore, on January 31, 2017, its accountant made a journal entry to record the bad debt loss for the sale that occurred in 2015. Now you must write off the account of Running Water Tile as of January 31, 2017.

Step 1:

Open Chp. 4 – Superior Carpet and Tile.

Step 2:

Open the Chart of Accounts, add the account *Uncollectible Accounts Expense* to it using the information below, and then click Save and Close.

Account ID:	**515**
Description:	**Uncollectible Accounts Expense**
Account Type:	**Expenses**

Step 3:

Click Tasks and then click *Receive Money*. The Receive Money window will appear. (See Figure 4–32.)

FIGURE 4–32
Receive Money Window

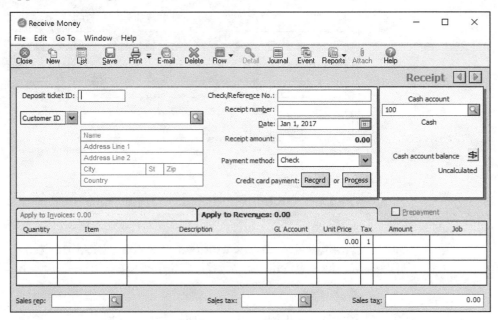

Step 4:

Key **01/31/17** in the *Deposit ticket ID* field.

Step 5:

Click the *magnifying glass* icon and then click *Running Water Tile* in the drop-down list of customer IDs.

Step 6:

Key **Bankruptcy** in the *Check/Reference No.* field.

Step 7:

Click the Journal button on the Receive Money window toolbar. You will now see the Accounting Behind the Screens window.

Step 8:

Click the *magnifying glass* icon in the *Account No.* field and then click *515 Uncollectible Accounts Expense* in the drop-down list of accounts. Normally, there is a default of Cash in the Receive Money window because Cash is the account debited to record an amount received from a customer. However, because a customer's account is being written off, you must go "behind the screens" to ensure that Uncollectible Accounts Expense will be debited. (See Figure 4–33.)

FIGURE 4–33
Uncollectible Accounts
Expense Selected

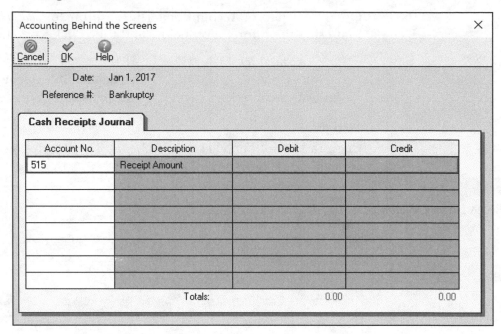

Step 9:

Click the <u>O</u>K button to confirm your choice of the account to be debited.

Step 10:

The Receive Money window will reappear. At the *Date* field, click the *calendar* icon to choose *Jan 31, 2017,* as the date.

Step 11:

Key **Write-off** in the *Payment Method* field.

Step 12:

Click the Apply to I<u>n</u>voices tab.

Step 13:

Key **Bad debt loss** in the *Description* field.

Step 14:

Key **4,000.00** in the *Amount Paid* field.

Step 15:

Tab to the *Pay* field and notice that a check mark appears there.

Step 16:

Click the Journal button on the Receive Money window toolbar. Compare the Accounting Behind the Screens window with Figure 4–34, and then click the OK button.

FIGURE 4–34
Accounting Behind the Screens Window

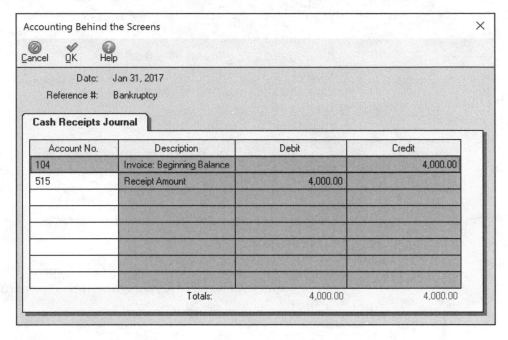

Step 17:

Compare your entries for the write-off with the completed Receive Money window shown in Figure 4–35. Do not continue until the Cash Account drop-down box displays account 515-Uncollectible Accounts Expense.

FIGURE 4–35
Completed Receive Money Window with Write-off

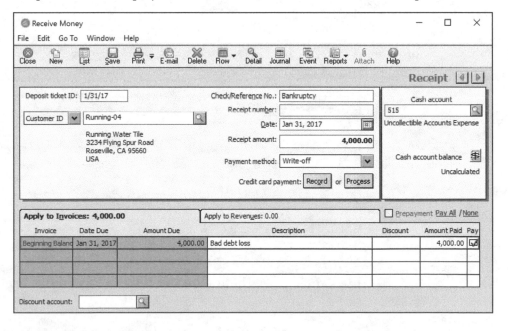

Step 18:

Click the Save button and then the Close button. Select Yes if the Cash Account Warning appears.

Displaying Accounts Receivable Reports

Sage 50 can produce several accounts receivable reports, including:

- Aged Receivables
- Cash Receipts Journal
- Customer Ledgers
- Customer List
- Customer Management Detail
- Customer Master File List
- Customer Transaction History
- Invoice Register
- Items Sold to Customers

Assume that the management of Superior Carpet and Tile wants to print two of these reports: the Customer List and Customer Ledgers.

Step 1:

Click Reports & Forms and then click *Accounts Receivable.*

Step 2:

The Select a Report or Form dialog box will appear. Click *Customer List* in the Accounts Receivable: Customers and Sales section, as shown in Figure 4–36.

FIGURE 4–36
Customer List Chosen from Select a Report or Form Dialog Box

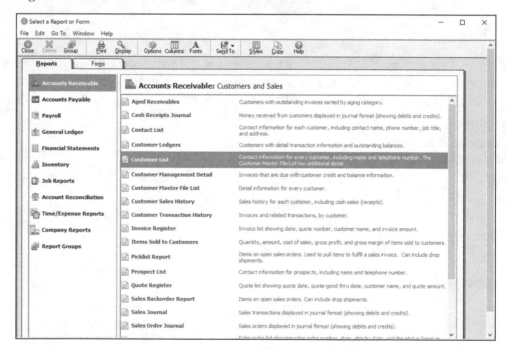

Step 3:

Click the Options button on the Select a Report or Form toolbar.

Step 4:

Click *Customer ID,* if it is not already selected, in the *Select a filter* scroll-down list and select *All* in the *Select an option* section, as shown in Figure 4–37.

FIGURE 4–37
Customer ID Selected from Select a Filter Scroll-Down List

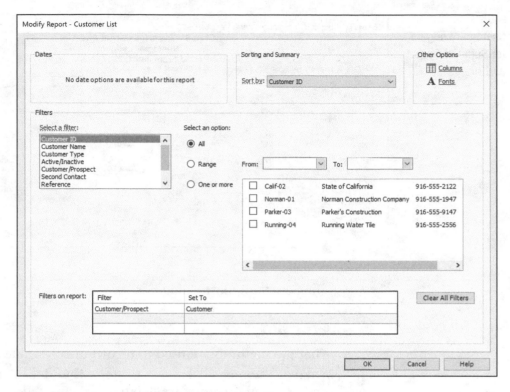

Step 5:
Click OK.

Step 6:
Compare your Customer List report with the one shown in Figure 4–38.

FIGURE 4–38
Customer List for Superior Carpet and Tile

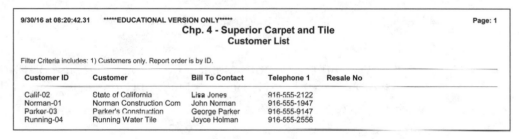

Step 7:
Close the Customer List window. Use steps 2–5 to display the Customer Ledgers. (In step 2, select *Customer Ledgers* in the Accounts Receivable: Customers and Sales section and select *Jan. 1, 2017* to *Jan. 31, 2017* as the range date.) Compare your display with the one shown in Figure 4–39.

FIGURE 4–39
Customer Ledgers
for Superior Carpet
and Tile

Chp. 4 - Superior Carpet and Tile
Customer Ledgers
For the Period From Jan 1, 2017 to Jan 31, 2017

Filter Criteria includes: Report order is by ID. Report is printed in Detail Format.

Customer ID Customer	Date	Trans No	Type	Debit Amt	Credit Amt	Balance
Calif-02 State of California	1/1/17	Begining Balan	SJ	4,000.00		4,000.00
Norman-01 Norman Construction Co	1/1/17 1/4/17	Beginning Bala 1001	SJ SJ	5,000.00 1,250.00		5,000.00 6,250.00
Parker-03 Parker's Construction	1/1/17 1/14/17 1/14/17	Beginning Bala 1002 1002	SJ SJ CRJ	2,000.00 5,000.00	2,500.00	2,000.00 7,000.00 4,500.00
Running-04 Running Water Tile	1/1/17 1/31/17	Beginning Bala Bankruptcy	SJ CRJ	4,000.00	4,000.00	4,000.00 0.00
Report Total				**21,250.00**	**6,500.00**	**14,750.00**

Step 8:

Close the Select a Report dialog box.

Checkpoint 4–5

1. What two methods are used to record uncollectible accounts?
2. When a customer's balance is written off under the direct write-off method, what accounts are debited and credited?

Objective 4–5 Practice

Step 1:

Open Chp. 4 – Meadowland Healthcare Services.

Step 2:

Write off the Doctor's Medical Center account (use Bad Debt Expense) as of January 31, 2017. Doctor's Medical Center has gone bankrupt. It owes $12,000 for Invoice 1101.

Step 3:

Print a copy of the Customer List report. Compare your report to the report shown in Figure 4–40.

FIGURE 4–40
Customer List for Meadowland Healthcare Services

9/11/16 at 08:19:20.54 *****EDUCATIONAL VERSION ONLY*****				Page: 1
	Chp. 4 - Meadowland Healthcare Services			
	Customer List			

Filter Criteria includes: 1) Customers only. Report order is by ID.

Customer ID	Customer	Bill To Contact	Telephone 1	Resale No
Doctor's-10	Doctor's Medical Center	Jim Conway, MD	916-555-4934	
Good-20	Good Samaritan Hospital	Jane Campbell, RN	916-555-6780	
Rapid-30	Rapid Medical Response	Kim Smith, RN	916-555-4719	
Valley-40	Valley Response	Robert Romero, PA	916-555-5678	

Step 4:

Print a copy of the Customer Ledgers report. Compare your report to the report shown in Figure 4–41.

FIGURE 4–41
Customer Ledgers for Meadowland Healthcare Services

9/11/16 at 08:20:07.83 *****EDUCATIONAL VERSION*****						Page: 1
	Chp. 4 - Meadowland Healthcare Services					
	Customer Ledgers					
	For the Period From Jan 1, 2017 to Jan 31, 2017					

Filter Criteria includes: Report order is by ID. Report is printed in Detail Format.

Customer ID Customer	Date	Trans No	Type	Debit Amt	Credit Amt	Balance
Doctor's-10	1/2/17	1101	SJ	12,000.00		12,000.00
Doctor's Medical Center	1/31/17	Bankruptcy	CRJ		12,000.00	0.00
Good-20	1/8/17	1102	SJ	2,420.00		2,420.00
Good Samaritan Hospital						
Rapid-30	1/19/17	1103	SJ	5,760.00		5,760.00
Rapid Medical Response						
Valley-40	1/29/17	1104	SJ	1,650.00		1,650.00
Valley Response	1/29/17	1104	CRJ		825.00	825.00
Report Total				**21,830.00**	**12,825.00**	**9,005.00**

Step 5:

Close the Select a Report or Form dialog box.

Chapter Review and Assessment

Software Command Summary

Create Customer Accounts	Maintain, Customers/Prospects, General Tab, Sales Info Tab, Payment & Credit Tab, Enter Beginning Balances
Accounts Receivable and Sales Transactions	Tasks, Sales/Invoicing
Adjusting Accounts Receivables	Tasks, Receive Money
Action Items and Event Log Options	Tasks, Action Items, Options, Action Items and Event Log Options
Create Action Items/Alerts	Tasks, Action Items, To Do, Event Toolbar Icon, Alert Toolbar Icon

Checkpoint Answers

Checkpoint 4–1

1. An accounts receivable subsidiary ledger provides detailed information about the transactions with credit customers and shows the balances they owe.
2. Accounts Receivable is debited and the appropriate revenue account is credited when a firm makes a sale on credit.

Checkpoint 4–2

1. The accounts in the subsidiary ledger provide detailed information about transactions with customers and show the current balances owed by the individual customers.
2. The Accounts Receivable controlling account is a link between the general ledger and the subsidiary ledger because its balance is equal to the total of the balances in the subsidiary ledger.

Checkpoint 4–3

1. The Customer Ledgers report lists all transactions with credit customers and the balances owed by the customers.
2. The Sales/Invoicing function of Sage 50 is used to record credit sales and partial payment at time of sale.

Checkpoint 4–4

1. The action item and event log options allow you to create a list of actions to be taken and program the system to display alerts before these events occur.
2. The alert function allows you to select certain conditions for notification.

Study Quizzes

Take the study quiz online to check your understanding of chapter concepts. The quiz can be taken multiple times.

Content Check

Multiple Choice: Choose only one response for each question.

1. When a business sells goods or services on credit, it records the amounts owed by the customers as
   A. accounts receivable.
   B. accounts payable.
   C. prepaid expenses.
   D. unearned revenue.
   E. None of the above

2. From a seller's perspective, sales on credit to customers affect
   A. assets and expenses.
   B. assets and revenue.
   C. liabilities and expenses.
   D. liabilities and revenue.
   E. None of the above

3. When a business makes a sale on credit, what function of Sage 50 is used to record the transaction?
   A. Action Items
   B. Purchases/Receive Inventory
   C. Receive Money
   D. Sales/Invoicing
   E. None of the above

4. Which accounts receivable report shows the beginning balances of the customer accounts, all transactions with the customers during a period, and the ending balances?
   A. Aged Receivables
   B. Customer Ledgers
   C. Invoice Register
   D. Sales Journal
   E. None of the above

5. Which general ledger accounts are involved in the direct write-off of a specific customer's account?
   A. Accounts Receivable and Sales
   B. Uncollectible Accounts Expense and Accounts Receivable
   C. Allowance for Doubtful Accounts and Accounts Receivable
   D. Uncollectible Accounts Expense and Allowance for Doubtful Accounts
   E. None of the above

Short Essay Response

Provide a detailed answer for each question.

1. What are the advantages and disadvantages to a business when it sells on credit?
2. What is the purpose of the accounts receivable subsidiary ledger?
3. Under what circumstance will a resale number be required when an account is set up for a new customer?
4. Why is a default for a credit limit established when customer accounts are set up?
5. How can the Alert function be used to aid a business in collecting its accounts receivable?
6. Explain the difference between the direct write-off method and the allowance method of recording uncollectible accounts.

Cooperative Learning

1. Form groups of three or four students, and assume that you are the managers of a business that sells on credit. Discuss the criteria necessary to decide whether to grant credit to a new customer.
2. As a group, prepare a list of Sage 50 features that help a business to monitor its accounts receivable and locate problems that may lead to uncollectible accounts.

Writing and Decision Making

Assume that the company for which you work has always had a policy of selling for cash. The owner, Susan Nicholson, is now considering whether to provide credit to customers. She has asked you to suggest measures that the company can take to organize, manage, and collect its accounts receivable. She has also asked that you explain to her how the controlling account in the general ledger relates to the customer accounts in the subsidiary ledger. Prepare a memo that provides Ms. Nicholson with the information she has requested.

Case Problems

Demonstrate your knowledge of the Sage 50 Accounting features discussed in this chapter by completing the following case problems.

Case Problem 4–1A

Open Tracy Accounting Solutions from the student data files.

The following are customers who purchase services on credit.

Customer

Customer ID:	**JM-1**
Name:	**Johnson Manufacturing**

General Tab

Account Number:	**120501**
Billing Address:	**4731 Eaton Avenue**
City, ST, Zip:	**Stockton, CA 95210**
Country:	**USA**
Customer Type:	**General**
Telephone 1:	**209-555-4178**
Fax:	**209-555-4180**

Contacts Tab

Contact:	**Randy Johnson**

Sales Info Tab

GL Sales Account:	**40000**
Ship Via:	**Fed-EX**
Pricing Level:	**Default**
Form Delivery Options:	**Default**

Payment & Credit Tab

Terms and Credit:	**Default**

History Tab

Beginning Balance:	**400.00**

Customer

Customer ID:	**CE-2**
Name:	**Computer Expertise**

General Tab

Account Number:	**120502**
Billing Address:	**475 West Lincoln Boulevard**
City, ST, Zip:	**Tracy, CA 95376**
Country:	**USA**
Customer Type:	**General**
Telephone 1:	**209-555-3820**
Fax:	**209-555-3840**

Contacts Tab

Contact:	**Marie Jameson**

Sales Info Tab

GL Sales Account:	40000
Ship Via:	Fed-EX
Pricing Level:	Default
Form Delivery Options:	Default

Payment & Credit Tab

Terms and Credit:	Default

History Tab

Beginning Balance:	320.00

Customer

Customer ID:	SC-3
Name:	Stephanie's Catering

General Tab

Account Number:	120503
Billing Address:	4837 6th Street
City, ST, Zip:	Watsonville, CA 95760
Country:	USA
Customer Type:	General
Telephone 1:	209-555-2864
Fax:	209-555-2875

Contacts Tab

Contact:	Stephanie Barron

Sales Info Tab

GL Sales Account:	40000
Ship Via:	Fed-EX
Pricing Level:	Default
Form Delivery Options:	Default

Payment & Credit Tab

Terms and Credit:	Default

History Tab

Beginning Balance:	180.00

HINT

Enter all performances of service on credit using the Sales/Invoicing function. Enter cash sales and all other transactions using the General Journal Entry function. Use Account 10200, Regular Checking Account for all cash sales transactions.

The following cash sales and credit sales occurred during January 2017:

Date	Transaction
Jan. 3	Performed accounting services for $1,400 on credit for Johnson Manufacturing. Issued Invoice 1001.
4	Performed tax preparation services for $850 in cash.
6	Performed accounting services for $650 on credit for Computer Expertise. Issued Invoice 1002.
14	Performed accounting services for $350 on credit for Stephanie's Catering. Issued Invoice 1003. The customer paid $100 to be applied against the invoice.
15	Performed consulting services for $220 in cash.

24   Performed consulting services for $725 on credit for Johnson Manufacturing. Issued Invoice 1004. The customer paid $200 to be applied against the invoice.

27   Performed accounting services for $245 on credit for Computer Expertise. Issued Invoice 1005. The customer paid $120 to be applied against the invoice.

1. Create a subsidiary ledger account for each credit customer and enter their beginning balance as of January 1, 2017.

2. Enter each of the transactions for January. Use the appropriate option on the Tasks menu: Sales/Invoicing or General Journal Entry. Note that this business has three different types of revenue: accounting fees, tax preparation fees, and consulting fees. Therefore, be sure that you select the number of the correct revenue account in the *GL Account* field of the Sales/Invoicing window. (The customer accounts have been set up with a GL Sales Account default to Account 40000, Accounting Fees.)

3. Print the following reports for January: Customer Ledgers, Sales Journal, General Journal, and Income Statement.

Case Problem 4–2A

Open Tracy Accounting Solutions from the student data files.

1. Record the following events as action items on the To Do list.
 • On January 3, 2017, call Computer Expertise to discuss accounting services schedule.
 • On January 15, 2017, meet with Infinite Graphics to discuss company logo.
 • On January 17, 2017, call Johnson Manufacturing to discuss pricing policy.
 • On January 24, 2017, meet with Stephanic's Catering to set up a new accounting services schedule.

2. Create the following alert.
 • Notify you when the current balance owed by any of the customers reaches or exceeds $2,500.

Case Problem 4–1B

Open Infinite Graphics from the student data files.

The following are customers who purchase services on credit.

Customer
  Customer ID: **JP-1**
  Name: **Jackson Photography**

General Tab

Account Number:	**510**
Billing Address:	**1374 West Bessie Avenue**
City, ST, Zip:	**Stockton, CA 95210**
Country:	**USA**
Customer Type:	**General**
Telephone 1:	**209-555-1478**
Fax:	**209-555-1485**

Contacts Tab

Contact:	**Sarah Bautista**

Sales Info Tab

GL Sales Account:	**40000**
Ship Via:	**Fed-EX**
Pricing Level:	**Default**
Form Delivery Options:	**Default**

Payment & Credit Tab

Terms and Credit:	**Default**

History Tab

Beginning Balance:	**400.00**

Customer

Customer ID:	**CC-2**
Name:	**Computer Creations**

General Tab

Account Number:	**520**
Billing Address:	**733 Madison Boulevard**
City, ST, Zip:	**Tracy, CA 95376**
Country:	**USA**
Customer Type:	**General**
Telephone 1:	**209-555-4710**
Fax:	**209-555-4730**

Contacts Tab

Contact:	**Lee Chang**

Sales Info Tab

GL Sales Account:	**40000**
Ship Via:	**Fed-EX**
Pricing Level:	**Default**
Form Delivery Options:	**Default**

Payment & Credit Tab

Terms and Credit:	**Default**

History Tab

Beginning Balance:	**0**

Customer

Customer ID:	FD-3
Name:	First Designs

General Tab

Account Number:	530
Billing Address:	1385 12th Street
City, ST, Zip:	Stockton, CA 95210
Country:	USA
Customer Type:	General
Telephone 1:	209-555-6842
Fax:	209-555-6846

Contacts Tab

Contact:	Richard Thompson

Sales Info Tab

GL Sales Account:	40000
Ship Via:	Fed-EX
Pricing Level:	Default
Form Delivery Options:	Default

Payment & Credit Tab

Terms and Credit:	Default

History Tab

Beginning Balance:	1,000.00

The following cash sales and credit sales occurred during January 2017:

> **HINT**
>
> Enter all performances of service on credit using the Sales/Invoicing function. Enter cash sales and all other transactions using the General Journal Entry function. Use Account 10200, Regular Checking Account for all cash sales transactions.

Date	Transaction
Jan. 3	Performed graphic design services for $875 on credit for Jackson Photography. Issued Invoice 1001.
4	Performed graphic design services for $950 in cash.
6	Performed graphic design services for $560 on credit for Computer Creations. Issued Invoice 1002.
12	Performed retouching services for $1,050 in cash.
15	Performed graphic design services for $1,350 on credit for Jackson Photography. Issued Invoice 1003. The customer paid $350 to be applied against the invoice.
15	Performed drafting services for $320 in cash.
20	Purchased graphing supplies for $120 in cash. (Because this business is on the accrual basis, it records purchases of supplies in an asset account.)
25	Performed graphic design services for $1,325 on credit for First Designs. Issued Invoice 1004. The customer paid $725 to be applied against the invoice.
26	Performed retouching services for $460 on credit for Jackson Photography. Issued Invoice 1005. The customer paid $360 to be applied against the invoice.
27	Performed graphic design services for $750 on credit for Computer Creations. Issued Invoice 1006.

1. Create a subsidiary ledger account for each credit customer and enter their beginning balances as of January 1, 2017.

2. Enter each of the transactions for January. Use the appropriate option on the Tasks menu: Sales/Invoicing or General Journal Entry. Note that this business has three different types of revenue: graphic design income, retouching income, and drafting income. Therefore, be sure that you select the number of the correct revenue account in the *GL Account* field of the Sales/Invoicing window. (The customer accounts have been set up with a GL Sales Account default to Account 40000, Graphic Design Income.)

3. Print the following reports for January: Customer Ledgers, Sales Journal, General Journal, and Income Statement.

Case Problem 4–2B

Open Infinite Graphics from the student data files.

1. Record the following events as action items on the To Do list.
    *   On January 4, 2017, call Computer Creations to discuss pricing policy.
    *   On January 13, 2017, meet with Jackson Photography to discuss graphic design work.
    *   On January 20, 2017, meet with First Designs to discuss subcontracting work.
    *   On January 27, 2017, call GJ Professional Accounting to discuss accounting services offered.

2. Create the following alert.
    *   Notify you when the current balance owed by any of the customers reaches or exceeds $2,300.

CHAPTER 5

Accounts Payable and Purchases for a Service Business

Objectives

5-1 Review recording accounts payable

5-2 Create subsidiary ledger accounts for vendors and enter the beginning balances

5-3 Process accounts payable and purchase transactions

5-4 Print accounts payable reports

Software Features

- Maintain Vendor toolbar buttons

- Vendor defaults

- Purchases/Receive Inventory toolbar

Company Files

Before beginning chapter work, access the links menu to download company files.

Most businesses use credit to buy the goods and services they need in their operations. Credit helps a firm to grow and to handle its resources efficiently. Paying cash for all purchases would make it much more difficult to expand operations and take advantage of new opportunities.

OBJECTIVE 5–1

Review Recording Accounts Payable

The amounts that a firm owes for goods or services purchased on credit are called *accounts payable*. The businesses or individuals to whom these amounts are owed are known as *vendors*, *creditors*, or *suppliers*.

Accounts payable are short-term debts that usually extend for 30 or 60 days, depending on the credit terms offered by the vendor. Many vendors also allow a discount if payment is made within a specified short discount period. For example, a vendor might offer terms of 2% 10 days, net 30 days. This means that the buyer can pay in 10 days and receive a 2% discount from the total due or pay the full amount in 30 days.

As you learned in Chapter 2, businesses that buy on credit set up a liability account called Accounts Payable in the general ledger. This account is credited for purchases of goods or services. The account debited depends on the nature of the purchase. A purchase of an asset such as office supplies or equipment is debited to the appropriate asset account. A purchase of a service is usually debited to an expense account. For example, a bill for electricity would be debited to Utilities Expense. A purchase of merchandise for resale is debited to a cost account called Purchases or debited to the Inventory account directly.

When a bill for a purchase on credit becomes due, a check is issued to the vendor. The payment is debited to Accounts Payable and credited to Cash.

The Accounts Payable Subsidiary Ledger

In addition to the Accounts Payable account in the general ledger, most businesses that buy on credit maintain a subsidiary ledger with individual accounts for their vendors. This subsidiary ledger is known as the *accounts payable ledger* or *vendors ledger*.

Remember that subsidiary ledgers supplement the information in the general ledger. For example, the accounts payable ledger provides detailed information about all transactions with vendors and shows the balances owed to them. Sage 50 updates the vendor accounts automatically when accounts payable transactions are recorded and posted.

The Controlling Account in the General Ledger

When an accounts payable subsidiary ledger is used, the Accounts Payable account in the general ledger becomes a controlling account. It provides a link between the general ledger and the accounts payable ledger because

accounts payable Amounts that a firm owes for goods or services purchased on credit.

vendors The businesses or individuals to whom accounts payable are owed. Also called creditors or suppliers.

accounts payable ledger A subsidiary ledger that contains accounts for vendors. Also called the vendors ledger.

its balance is equal to the total of all the balances of the individual accounts in the subsidiary ledger. This is similar in function to how the accounts receivable subsidiary ledger is used as described in Chapter 4.

Managing Accounts Payable

If credit is used properly, it can be helpful to a business. However, credit can also present a danger. Some firms take on too much debt, find that their cash flow is not adequate to pay bills as they become due, and eventually go bankrupt.

Every firm that buys on credit should have procedures in place to ensure that it:

- Pays vendors on time to maintain a good credit reputation.
- Takes advantage of discounts whenever they are offered.
- Keeps the total amount owed to vendors from becoming too high in relation to the firm's resources.

Sage 50 assists firms in managing their accounts payable by providing a means of quickly and efficiently recording purchases and cash payments and by generating accounts payable reports. Sage 50 produces 16 reports to closely monitor the status of the accounts payable. Another helpful feature is the Action Items function, which can be programmed to alert you to actions that must be taken in connection with vendor accounts.

Checkpoint 5–1

1. What is another name for the accounts payable ledger?
2. Why should every firm that buys on credit have procedures in place?

OBJECTIVE 5–2

Create Subsidiary Ledger Accounts for Vendors and Enter the Beginning Balances

In Chapters 2 and 3, you learned how to set up general ledger accounts and enter the beginning balances. The procedure for establishing vendor accounts in the accounts payable ledger is similar. In this chapter, you will use Sage 50 to handle the accounts payable of Superior Carpet and Tile.

Superior is a small service business that operates on the accrual basis. In Chapter 4, you established customer accounts for this firm and recorded its credit sales.

Information Needed to Create the Vendor Accounts

In Sage 50, certain information is needed to create an account for each vendor in the accounts payable subsidiary ledger. This information is entered in the Maintain Vendors window, as shown in Figure 5–1, and is outlined on the next pages.

FIGURE 5–1
Maintain Vendors Blank
Window with General
Folder Tab Selected

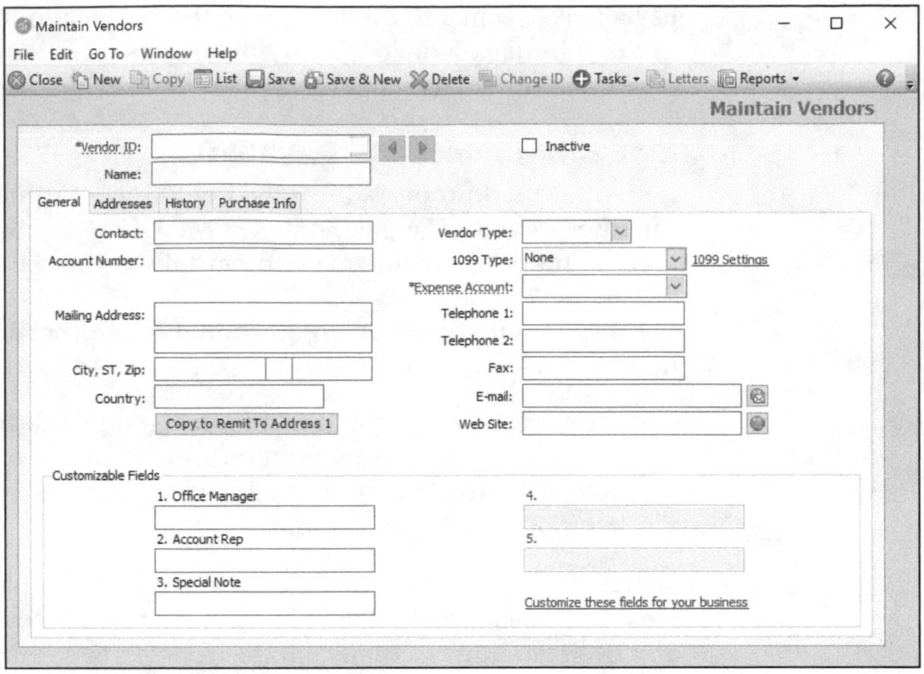

- **Vendor ID**

  Sage 50 requires an alphanumeric identifier for each vendor's account. For example, Superior Carpet and Tile uses JCM-001 as the identifier for the first account in its accounts payable subsidiary ledger. This account is for John Charles Management.

- **Name**

  The name given to a vendor's account may be the name of a business, such as John Charles Management, or the name of an individual.

- **Inactive**

  Sometimes a company stops doing business with a vendor. A check mark is entered in the *Inactive* box to indicate this type of vendor. Sage 50 automatically removes the accounts of inactive vendors when the fiscal year is closed.

General Tab

- **Contact**

  The contact is the person whom the business calls or writes in connection with questions about orders.

- **Account Number**

  The account number is the numeric identifier the vendor has issued to the company.

- **Mailing Address**

  The address entered in the account is the one where the vendor receives checks and correspondence.

- **Vendor Type**

  Sage 50 allows you to classify vendors by type. For example, many companies have vendors that provide services and vendors that provide goods. Superior uses Expense as the type for vendors that provide services and Supplier as the type for vendors that provide goods and supplies.

- **1099 Type**

  It is necessary to issue Form 1099, a tax form, to certain types of vendors. For example, some vendors are individuals who provide their services on a project-by-project basis. These individuals are considered independent contractors rather than part-time employees. By January 31 of each year, the Internal Revenue Service requires that a company issue a Form 1099 to each independent contractor for tax reasons. This form shows the amount paid to the independent contractor during the previous year. A copy of Form 1099 goes to the IRS. (If the company pays less than $600 to an independent contractor, it need not issue a Form 1099.)

- **Expense Account**

  The Expense Account is the account in the general ledger that is debited when a purchase is made from a particular vendor. As noted previously, a purchase of a service such as electricity is debited to an expense account. A purchase of an asset such as office supplies is debited to an asset account. A purchase of goods for resale is debited to a cost account called Purchases or debited directly to an Inventory account. The number of the appropriate general ledger account is entered in each vendor's account.

- **Telephone/Fax Numbers**

  Sage 50 provides space for recording two telephone numbers and a fax number in each vendor's account.

- **Email**

  Enter the customer's email address in this field for correspondence. Email can be sent by clicking the E-mail button to the right of the *E-mail* field.

- **Web Site**

  Enter the customer's web address in this field. The customer's website can be displayed by clicking the Internet button to the right of the *Web Site* field.

Customizable Fields

- **Office Manager**

  In some cases, a business will want to enter the name of the vendor's office manager as a second contact person.

- **Account Rep**

  Some vendors assign a sales representative to each of their customers. The name of the sales representative is entered in the vendor's account.

- **Special Note**

  Any additional information about the vendor that is needed can be entered in the *Special Note* field.

Addresses Tab

- Default addresses are selected using the Address Defaults drop-down boxes. Specific addresses can be selected for Payments, Purchase Orders, and Shipments.

History Tab

- **Vendor Since**
  Some businesses enter the date of the first order issued to the vendor.
- **Last Invoice Date**
  Some businesses enter the date of the last invoice received from the vendor.
- **Last Invoice Amount**
  Some businesses enter the amount of the last invoice received from the vendor.
- **Last Payment Date**
  Some businesses enter the date of the last payment made to the vendor.
- **Last Payment Amount**
  Some businesses enter the amount of the last payment made to the vendor.
- **Period, Purchases, Payments Grid**
  This section gives the user running totals of purchases and payments.
- **Vendor Beginning Balances**
  When a business creates accounts for its vendors, there may be some outstanding (unpaid) invoices. Information about these invoices is needed to enter the beginning balances in the accounts.

Purchase Info Tab

- **Purchase Rep**
  The Purchase Rep is used to select the purchaser's representative to the vendor.
- **Tax ID Number**
  The tax identification number is the number of the resale certificate (the sales tax exemption certificate) that the vendor may have. This number is entered in the vendor's account. It is also the number used to identify a vendor on a Form 1099.
- **Ship Via**
  The vendor may have a preferred method of shipping. The method chosen should be entered in the vendor's account.
- **Terms and Credit**
  Each vendor specifies certain credit terms. For example, one vendor might offer terms of 2% 10 days, net 30 days. Another vendor might offer terms of net EOM, which means that the full amount of a bill is due at the end of the month in which the bill is issued. The terms are entered in the vendor's account. (Standard vendor terms can be established as a default when a company is set up in Sage 50. These terms can be changed as necessary for individual vendors.)
- **Form Options**
  The Form Option allows the user to deliver paper or email forms. Email can be carbon copied (CC) to the purchase rep.

Creating Subsidiary Ledger Accounts for Vendors

In this section, you will create subsidiary ledger accounts for four vendors of Superior Carpet and Tile. Start Sage 50 and then open Superior Carpet and Tile (Chp. 5 – Superior Carpet and Tile if student data files are used).

Then follow the steps outlined below to create a subsidiary ledger account for John Charles Management.

Step 1:

Click Maintain and then click *Vendors*.

Step 2:

Click the General folder tab in the Maintain Vendors window. Set up the account information for John Charles Management, the first vendor of Superior Carpet and Tile, by taking the following steps:

Step 3:

Key **JCM-001** in the *Vendor ID* field.

Step 4:

Click the OK button at the bottom of the Vendor ID drop-down list, as shown in Figure 5–2.

FIGURE 5–2
Vendor ID Drop-Down List with JCM-001 Entered

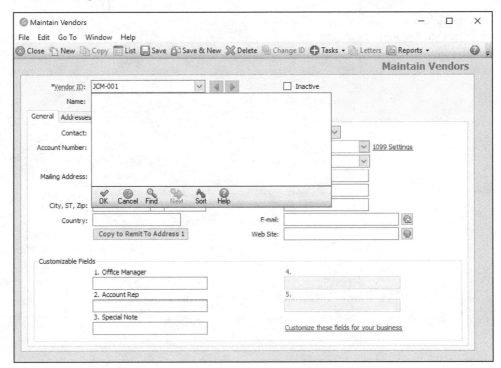

Step 5:

Key **John Charles Management** in the *Name* field.

Step 6:

If there is a check mark in the *Inactive* box, remove it. John Charles Management is an active vendor.

Step 7:

Key **John Charles** in the *Contact* field.

Step 8:

Key **2800** in the *Account Number* field.

Step 9:

Key **1320 Washington Street** in the *Mailing Address* field.

Step 10:

Key **Sacramento, CA 95760** in the *City, ST, Zip* field, key **USA** in the *Country* field, and click the Copy to Remit To Address 1 button.

Step 11:

Key **Expense** in the *Vendor Type* field.

Step 12:

At the 1099 Type drop-down list, click *None.*

Step 13:

At the Expense Account drop-down list, select *500, Rent Expense,* as shown in Figure 5–3.

FIGURE 5–3
Expense Account Drop-Down List with Account 500 Selected

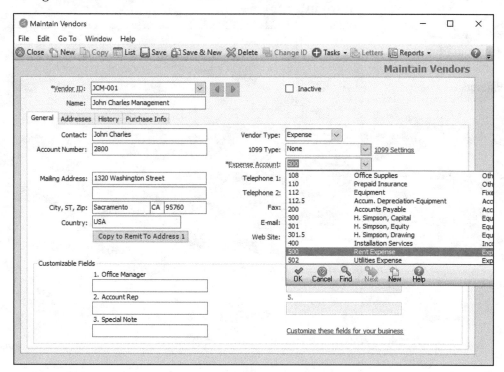

Step 14:

Key **916-555-2456** in the *Telephone 1* field.

Step 15:

Key **916-555-7890** in the *Telephone 2* field.

Step 16:

Key **916-555-3846** in the *Fax* field.

Step 17:

Compare your completed window with Figure 5–4. Make any necessary corrections by selecting the erroneous items and entering the correct information.

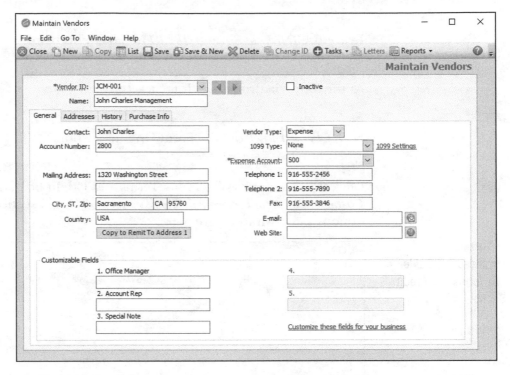

Purchase Info Tab
The purchase defaults must be established whenever a vendor's account is created.

Step 1:
Click the Purchase Info folder tab, as shown in Figure 5–5.

FIGURE 5–5
Maintain Vendors
Window with Purchase
Info Tab Selected

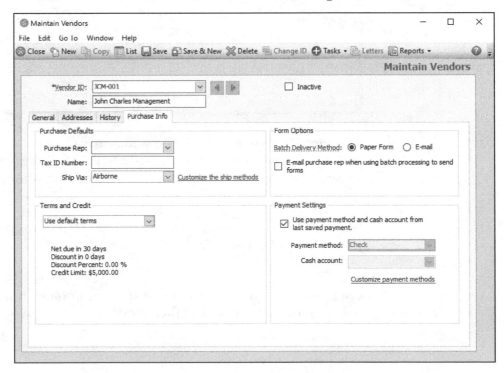

Step 2:

Leave the *Purchase Rep* and *Tax ID Number* fields blank.

Step 3:

At the Ship Via drop-down list, click *US Mail.*

Step 4:

Select *Paper Form* from the Form Options section.

Step 5:

Click the down arrow key in the Terms and Credit box and then select *Customize terms for this vendor.* The Terms and Credit section displays more options as shown in Figure 5–6.

FIGURE 5–6
Purchase Info Folder Tab Terms and Credit Section

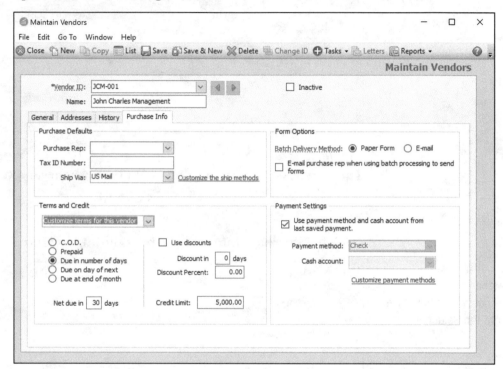

As noted previously, credit terms may vary from vendor to vendor. In addition, each vendor may set a credit limit. The Terms and Credit section is used to change the credit terms and credit limit whenever necessary.

Step 6:

Click the button next to *Due at end of month.* These are the terms offered by John Charles Management.

Step 7:

Click to remove the check mark next to *Use discounts* if necessary. Generally, only vendors of supplies or other goods allow a discount.

Step 8:

Compare your entry with the completed Terms and Credit section in Figure 5–7.

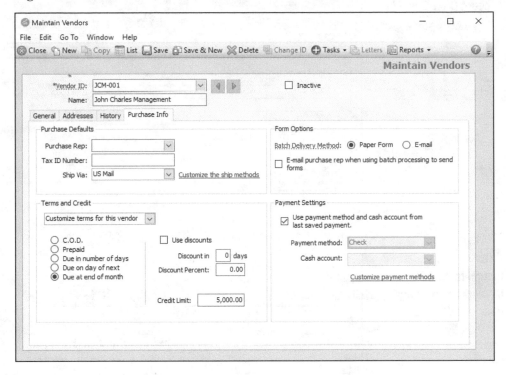

Step 9:

Click the Save button to accept the changes to the vendor terms.

Beginning Balances

Step 1:

Click the History folder tab in the Maintain Vendors window.

Step 2:

Click the Vendor Beginning Balances button at the bottom of the window.

Step 3:

Click the Purchases from: JCM-001 John Charles Management folder tab. Then key **Beginning Balance** in the *Invoice Number* field.

Step 4:

Key **01/01/17** in the *Date* field.

Step 5:

Key **900.00** in the *Amount* field.

Step 6:

Select *200 Accounts Payable* from the A/P Account drop-down list, as shown in Figure 5–8.

FIGURE 5–8
Accounts Payable
Selected from the A/P
Account Drop-Down List

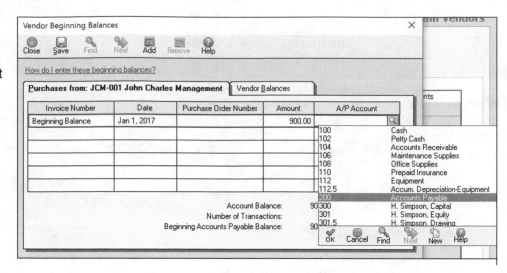

Step 7:

Compare your entries with those in Figure 5–9.

FIGURE 5–9
Completed Entries
in Vendor Beginning
Balances Window

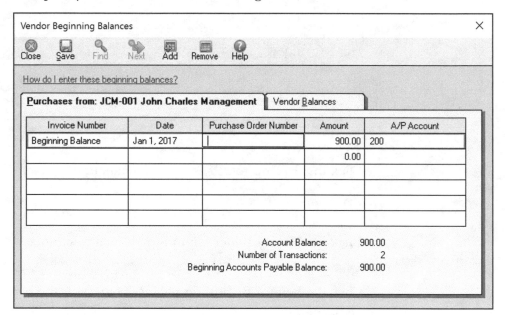

Step 8:

Click the Save button and then click the Close button.

Step 9:

Click the History folder tab to view the current balance for the selected vendor, as shown in Figure 5–10.

FIGURE 5–10
History Folder Tab
in Maintain Vendors
Window

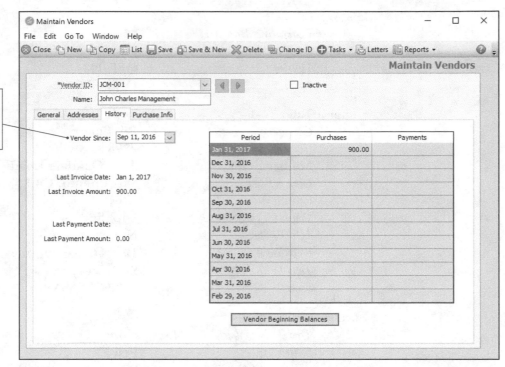

Your screen will display the current date in this location.

Create the following three vendor accounts for Superior Carpet and Tile using the information given below and enter their beginning balances as of January 1, 2017. Use the steps that you followed for the account of John Charles Management. When you complete your work, close the Maintain Vendors window.

Vendor

Vendor ID:	**MID-002**
Name:	**MID Midtown Irrigation District**

General Tab

Contact:	**Harvey Bliss**
Account Number:	**3548**
Mailing Address:	**2356 Orangethorpe Street**
City, ST, Zip:	**Sacramento, CA 95506**
Country:	**USA**
Vendor Type:	**Expense**
1099 Type:	**None**
Expense Account:	**502 (Utilities Expense)**
Telephone 1:	**916-555-6675**
Fax:	**916-555-9008**

Purchase Info Tab

Tax ID Number:	**None**
Ship Via:	**US Mail**
Terms and Credit:	**Net 30 days (Use default terms)**
Form Options:	**Default**

History Tab

Beginning Balance:	450.00

Vendor

Vendor ID:	OFF-003
Name:	Office Max

General Tab

Contact:	Bill Baker
Account Number:	2778
Mailing Address:	2532 Oakdale Road
City, ST, Zip:	Sacramento, CA 95306
Country:	USA
Vendor Type:	Supplier
1099 Type:	None
Expense Account:	108 (Office Supplies)
Telephone 1:	916-555-1978
Fax:	916-555-2334

Purchase Info Tab

Tax ID Number:	None
Ship Via:	Fed-EX
Terms and Credit:	2% 10 days, net 30 days
Form Options:	Default

History Tab

Beginning Balance:	450.00

Vendor

Vendor ID:	PAC-004
Name:	Pacific Bell

General Tab

Contact:	Customer Service
Account Number:	2379
Mailing Address:	3234 Airport Road
City, ST, Zip:	Sacramento, CA 95670
Country:	USA
Vendor Type:	Expense
1099 Type:	None
Expense Account:	514 (Miscellaneous Expense)
Telephone 1:	916-555-2556
Fax:	916-555-9998

Purchase Info Tab

Tax ID Number:	None
Ship Via:	US Mail
Terms and Credit:	Net 30 days (Use default terms)
Form Options:	Default

History Tab

Beginning Balance:	500.00

Checkpoint 5–2

1. What is the purpose of the vendor accounts in the accounts payable subsidiary ledger?
2. Why is the Accounts Payable account in the general ledger known as a controlling account?

Objective 5–2 Practice

Create subsidiary ledger accounts for the vendors of Meadowland Healthcare Services.

Step 1:

Open Meadowland Healthcare Services (Chp. 5 – Meadowland Healthcare Services if student data files are used).

Step 2:

Create the following vendor accounts and enter the beginning balances.

Vendor

Vendor ID:	**ALT-001**
Name:	**Alta Vista Business Park**

General Tab

Contact:	**Alicia Marquez**
Account Number:	**3900**
Mailing Address:	**1325 Smith Road**
City, ST, Zip:	**Lodi, CA 95355**
Country:	**USA**
Vendor Type:	**Expense**
1099 Type:	**None**
Expense Account:	**76000 (Rent or Lease Expense)**
Telephone 1:	**209-555-4256**
Fax:	**209-555-8346**

Purchase Info Tab

Tax ID Number:	**None**
Ship Via:	**US Mail**
Terms and Credit:	**Net 30 days (Use default terms)**
Form Options:	**Default**

History Tab

Beginning Balance:	**0**

Vendor

Vendor ID:	**PGE-002**
Name:	**Pacific Gas & Electric**

General Tab

Contact:	**George House**
Account Number:	**345566**
Mailing Address:	**3423 Mission Street**
City, ST, Zip:	**Sacramento, CA 95655**
Country:	**USA**
Vendor Type:	**Expense**
1099 Type:	**None**
Expense Account:	**78500 (Utilities Expense)**
Telephone 1:	**916-555-9905**
Fax:	**916-555-0008**

Purchase Info Tab

Tax ID Number:	**None**
Ship Via:	**US Mail**
Terms and Credit:	**Net 30 days (Use default terms)**
Form Options:	**Default**

History Tab

Beginning Balance:	**0**

Vendor

Vendor ID:	**OFD-003**
Name:	**Office Depot**

General Tab

Contact:	**Jim Nielson**
Account Number:	**3465**
Mailing Address:	**125 Oak Road**
City, ST, Zip:	**Sacramento, CA 95655**
Country:	**USA**
Vendor Type:	**Supplier**
1099 Type:	**None**
Expense Account:	**14000 (Office Supplies)**
Telephone 1:	**916-555-9178**
Fax:	**916-555-3234**

Purchase Info Tab

Tax ID Number:	**None**
Ship Via:	**Fed-EX**
Terms and Credit:	**2% 10 days, net 30 days**
Form Options:	**Default**

History Tab

Beginning Balance:	**0**

Vendor

Vendor ID:	**GTE-004**
Name:	**General Telephone**

General Tab

Contact:	**Customer Service**
Account Number:	**391345**
Mailing Address:	**32133 Tuolumne Road**
City, ST, Zip:	**Sacramento, CA 95655**
Country:	**USA**
Vendor Type:	**Expense**
1099 Type:	**None**
Expense Account:	**78000 (Telephone Expense)**
Telephone 1:	**916-555-2545**
Fax:	**916-555-9945**

Purchase Info Tab

Tax ID Number:	**None**
Ship Via:	**US Mail**
Terms and Credit:	**Net 30 days (Use default terms)**
Form Options:	**Default**

History Tab

Beginning Balance:	**0**

Step 3:
Close the Maintain Vendors window.

OBJECTIVE 5–3

Process Accounts Payable and Purchase Transactions

Once the vendor accounts have been established, Sage 50 can be used to record purchases on credit and post them automatically to the accounts payable subsidiary ledger. Remember that each purchase is credited to Accounts Payable. The account debited may be an asset account, an expense account, or a cost account, depending on the nature of the purchase. When the bill for a purchase becomes due, the payment is debited to Accounts Payable and credited to Cash.

If there is an accounts payable ledger, each purchase requires a credit to both the Accounts Payable controlling account in the general ledger and the vendor's account in the subsidiary ledger. Similarly, each payment to a vendor requires a debit to both the Accounts Payable controlling account in the general ledger and the vendor's account in the subsidiary ledger.

It is possible to record purchases of goods and services on credit in the general journal. However, the general journal function of Sage 50 does not permit the automatic posting of entries to the vendor accounts. Therefore, in this chapter, you will use the purchases function of Sage 50 to record purchases of goods and services. This function, which is called *Purchases/ Receive Inventory*, allows automatic posting to both the general ledger and the accounts payable subsidiary ledger.

Recording Purchases on Credit

During January 2017, Superior Carpet and Tile conducted three trans-actions that involved the purchase of services and one transaction that involved the purchase of supplies.

- On January 3, 2017, Superior received a bill (Invoice 2621) from John Charles Management for its monthly rent of $2,100. The bill is payable at the end of the month.

The accountant's analysis of this transaction reveals that an expense (Rent Expense) has increased by $2,100 and a liability (Accounts Payable) has increased by $2,100. The account for John Charles Management has also increased by $2,100. The accountant records this transaction by debiting Rent Expense for $2,100 and crediting Accounts Payable for $2,100.

When you post this transaction, you must post the credit part of the entry to both the Accounts Payable controlling account in the general ledger and the vendor's account in the accounts payable subsidiary ledger.

Use the steps outlined below to record this purchase on credit made by Superior Carpet and Tile during January 2017.

Step 1:

Open Chp. 5 – Superior Carpet and Tile, which you updated previously in the chapter, and close the Action Items window, if open.

Step 2:

Click Tasks and then click *Purchases/Receive Inventory.*

The Purchases/Receive Inventory window will appear, as shown in Figure 5–11. Enter the data for the purchase on credit that occurred on January 3, 2017.

FIGURE 5–11
Blank Purchases/Receive Inventory Window

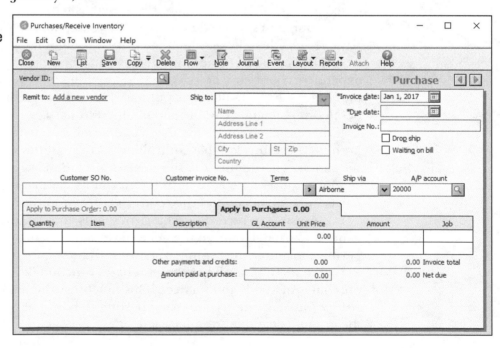

Step 3:

Click the *magnifying glass* icon next to the *Vendor ID* field.

Step 4:

Highlight *JCM-001* in the drop-down list of vendors, as shown in Figure 5–12.

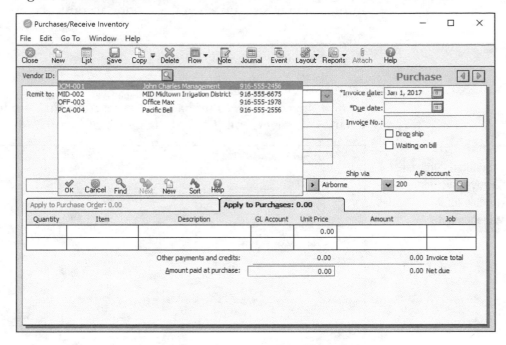

Step 5:

Click OK at the bottom of the drop-down list of vendors to accept JCM-001. Sage 50 enters the name and address automatically.

Step 6:

Click the *calendar* icon to the right of the *Invoice date* field and select *Jan 3, 2017*.

Step 7:

Key **2621** in the *Invoice No.* field.

Step 8:

The credit terms are selected when the vendor accounts are originally created. To view the terms for John Charles Management, click the right arrow key in the *Terms* field. You will then see the Terms Information dialog box, as shown in Figure 5–13. Click OK after viewing the terms.

Step 9:

Key **Monthly Rent** in the *Description* field.

Step 10:

Select *500 (Rent Expense)* from the drop-down list of general ledger accounts. The GL Account information should already be completed. This information was set up when the vendor account was created.

Step 11:

Key **2,100.00** in the *Amount* field.

Step 12:

Review the completed Purchases/Receive Inventory window for John Charles Management, JCM-001, as shown in Figure 5–14.

FIGURE 5–14
Completed Purchases/
Receive Inventory
Window for John Charles
Management

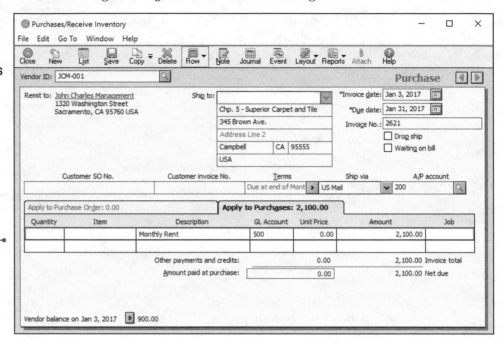

HINT
When there is no quantity and unit price, leave those fields blank and simply enter the total of the vendor's bill in the *Amount* field.

Step 13:

Click the <u>S</u>ave button to save the entry of the purchase on credit.

Step 14:

Repeat steps 3–13 to enter the following three purchases that Superior Carpet and Tile made during January 2017.

- On January 10, 2017, Superior received a bill (Invoice 4763) of $226.65 from MID Midtown Irrigation District for its monthly usage of electricity. The bill is payable net 30 days.

The accountant's analysis of this transaction reveals that an expense (Utilities Expense) has increased by $226.65 and a liability (Accounts Payable) has increased by $226.65. The account for MID Midtown Irrigation District has also increased by $226.65. The accountant records this transaction by debiting Utilities Expense for $226.65 and crediting Accounts Payable for $226.65.

- On January 12, 2017, Superior received a bill (Invoice 2867) of $265.39 from Pacific Bell for special repair services. The bill is payable net 30 days.

The accountant's analysis of this transaction reveals that an expense (Miscellaneous Expense) has increased by $265.39 and a liability (Accounts Payable) has increased by $265.39. The account for Pacific Bell has also increased by $265.39. The accountant records this transaction by debiting Miscellaneous Expense for $265.39 and crediting Accounts Payable for $265.39.

- On January 29, 2017, Superior received a bill (Invoice 3556) from Office Max for $1,400 of office supplies. The bill has terms of 2% 10 days, net 30 days.

The accountant's analysis of this transaction reveals that an asset (Office Supplies) has increased by $1,400 and a liability (Accounts Payable) has increased by $1,400. The account for Office Max has also increased by $1,400. The accountant records this transaction by debiting Office Supplies for $1,400 and crediting Accounts Payable for $1,400.

Editing Accounts Payable Transactions

Accounts payable transactions can be edited as necessary after they are entered. Follow the steps outlined below to edit a particular transaction.

Step 1:

Click List on the toolbar at the top of the Purchases/Receive Inventory window.

Step 2:

At the Date Range drop-down list, click *All Transactions*.

Step 3:

Select the entry for John Charles Management, as shown in Figure 5–15. (Notice that the window contains a *Status* column, which shows that the four bills recorded in January are unpaid.) Click Open on the Purchase List toolbar.

FIGURE 5–15
Purchase List Window with John Charles Management Selected

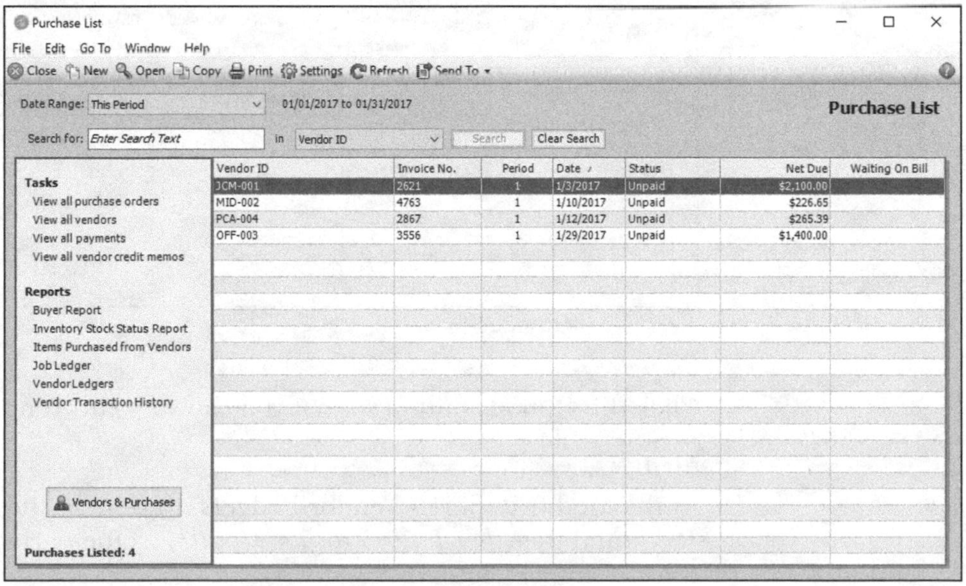

Step 4:

The entry appears in the Purchases/Receive Inventory window and can be edited if necessary. For example, if there is an error in the date, invoice number, or amount, you can change it now. When your work is complete, click Save. Then close the Purchases/Receive Inventory window.

Step 5:

Close the Purchase List window.

Printing and Displaying the Vendor Ledgers Report

Sage 50 produces a wide variety of accounts payable reports. All of these reports will be covered to some extent throughout this text. The Vendor Ledgers report is probably the most important of the accounts payable reports. This report shows all transactions with the vendors and the balances owed to them. Use the following steps to view and print the Vendor Ledgers report.

Step 1:

Click Reports & Forms and then click *Accounts Payable.*

Step 2:

At the Select a Report or Form dialog box, in the Accounts Payable: Vendor and Purchases section, click *Vendor Ledgers,* as shown in Figure 5–16.

FIGURE 5–16
Accounts Payable: Vendors and Purchases Report List with Vendor Ledgers Selected

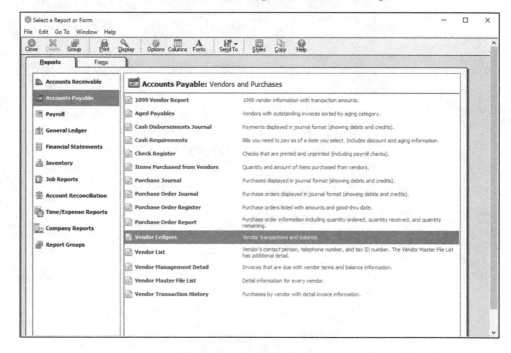

Step 3:

Click the Options button so that you can view the Vendor Ledgers report.

Step 4:

At the Modify Report – Vendor Ledgers window, in the *Date* field, click *Range* and then *Jan 1, 2017* to *Jan 31, 2017* as the period to be covered. Click OK. (See Figure 5–17.)

FIGURE 5–17

FIGURE 5–17
Modify Report – Vendor Ledgers Window

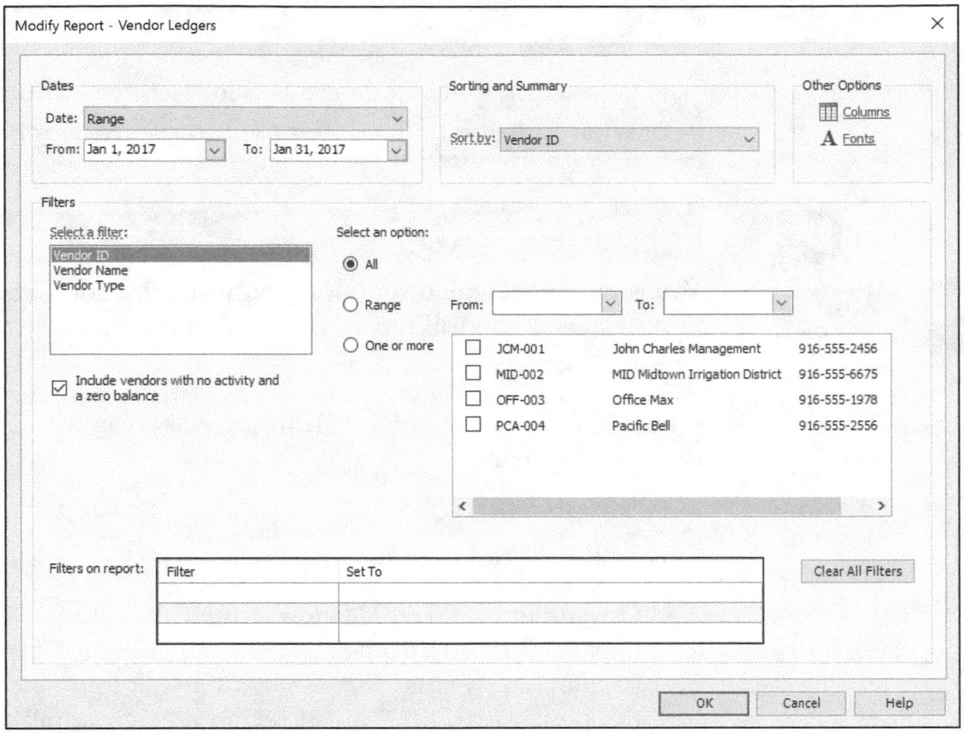

Step 5:

Examine the Vendor Ledgers report, as shown in Figure 5–18. Use the scroll bar to make sure that the four purchases recorded in January appear in the report. (The abbreviation PJ in the report stands for *purchases journal*.)

FIGURE 5–18
Vendor Ledgers Report

9/11/16 at 13:25:48.87 *****EDUCATIONAL VERSION ONLY***** Page: 1

Chp. 5 - Superior Carpet and Tile
Vendor Ledgers
For the Period From Jan 1, 2017 to Jan 31, 2017

Filter Criteria includes. Report order is by ID.

Vendor ID Vendor	Date	Trans No	Type	Paid	Debit Amt	Credit Amt	Balance
JCM-001	1/1/17	Beginning Bala	PJ			900.00	900.00
John Charles Managomo	1/3/17	2621	PJ			2,100.00	3,000.00
MID-002	1/1/17	Beginning Bala	PJ			450.00	450.00
MID Midtown Irrigation Di	1/10/17	4763	PJ			226.65	676.65
OFF-003	1/1/17	Beginning Bala	PJ			450.00	450.00
Office Max	1/29/17	3556	PJ			1,400.00	1,850.00
PCA-004	1/1/17	Beginning Bala	PJ			500.00	500.00
Pacific Bell	1/12/17	2867	PJ			265.39	765.39
Report Total						6,292.04	6,292.04

Step 6:

Click **P**rint to print a copy of the Vendor Ledgers report, if required.

Objective 5–3 Practice

You previously created vendor accounts for Meadowland Healthcare Services. Now you will record purchases on credit for this firm.

Step 1:

Open Chp. 5 – Meadowland Healthcare Services, which you updated previously in the chapter.

Step 2:

Record the following transactions:

- On January 2, 2017, Meadowland Healthcare Services received a bill (Invoice 012301) from Alta Vista Business Park for its monthly rent of $1,200.
- On January 10, 2017, Meadowland received a bill (Invoice 98345) of $345.89 from Pacific Gas & Electric for its monthly usage of electricity.
- On January 18, 2017, Meadowland received a bill (Invoice 55665) from Office Depot for $890 of office supplies.
- On January 27, 2017, Meadowland Healthcare Services received a bill (Invoice 645935) of $265.98 from General Telephone for its monthly usage of telephone service (Telephone Expense).

Step 3:

Print the Vendor Ledgers report for the month of January 2017. Check the accuracy of your work by comparing your report to the report shown in Figure 5–19.

FIGURE 5–19
Vendor Ledgers Report for Meadowland Healthcare Services

9/11/16 at 13:31:00.41	*****EDUCATIONAL VERSION ONLY*****						Page: 1
			Chp. 5 - Meadowland Healthcare Services				
			Vendor Ledgers				
			For the Period From Jan 1, 2017 to Jan 31, 2017				
Filter Criteria includes: Report order is by ID.							
Vendor ID **Vendor**	**Date**	**Trans No**	**Type**	**Paid**	**Debit Amt**	**Credit Amt**	**Balance**
ALT-001 Alta Vista Business Park	1/2/17	012301	PJ			1,200.00	1,200.00
GTE-004 General Telephone	1/27/17	645935	PJ			265.98	265.98
OFD-003 Office Depot	1/18/17	55665	PJ			890.00	890.00
PGE-002 Pacific Gas & Electric	1/10/17	98345	PJ			345.89	345.89
Report Total						2,701.87	2,701.87

Step 4:

Close the Select a Report dialog box.

OBJECTIVE 5-4

Print Accounts Payable Reports

Sage 50 can produce the following accounts payable reports and many others.

- Vendor List
- Vendor Master File List
- Vendor Ledgers
- Purchase Order Report

- Purchase Journal
- Aged Payables
- 1099 Vendor Report

Assume that the management of Superior Carpet and Tile wants to print two of these reports: the Vendor List and the Vendor Ledgers.

Step 1:

Open Superior Carpet and Tile (Chp. 5 – Superior Carpet and Tile if student data files are used).

Step 2:

Click Reports & Forms and then click *Accounts Payable.*

Step 3:

The Select a Report or Form dialog box will appear. At the Accounts Payable: Vendors and Purchases section, click *Vendor List,* as shown in Figure 5–20.

FIGURE 5–20
Accounts Payable:
Vendors and Purchases
List with Vendor List
Selected

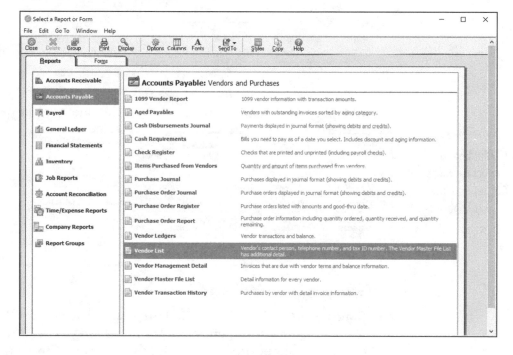

Step 4:

Click the Options button on the Select a Report or Form toolbar.

Step 5:

At the Modify Report – Vendor List window, in the Select a filter scroll-down list, click *Vendor ID*, as shown in Figure 5–21, and then click OK.

FIGURE 5–21
Vendor ID Selected
from Select a Filter
Scroll-Down List

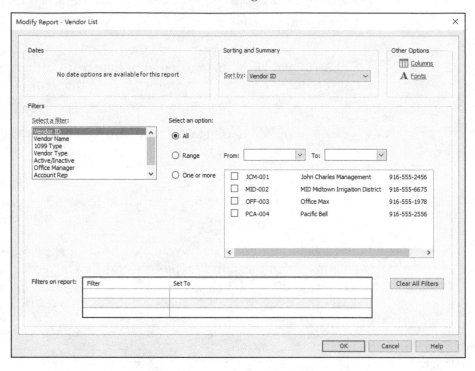

Step 6:

Compare your Vendor List report with the one shown in Figure 5–22.

FIGURE 5–22
Partial Vendor List
Report for Superior
Carpet and Tile

9/11/16 at 13:36:42.82   *****EDUCATIONAL VERSION ONLY*****   Page: 1
Chp. 5 - Superior Carpet and Tile
Vendor List

Filter Criteria includes: Report order is by ID.

Vendor ID	Vendor	Contact	Telephone 1	Tax Id No
JCM-001	John Charles Management	John Charles	916-555-2456	
MID-002	MID Midtown Irrigation Distr	Harvey Bliss	916-555-6675	
OFF-003	Office Max	Bill Baker	916-555-1978	
PCA-004	Pacific Bell	Customer Service	916-555-2556	

Step 7:

Repeat steps 1–5 to display the Purchase Journal report. In step 2, click *Purchase Journal* and then select *Jan 1, 2017* to *Jan 31, 2017* as the range. Compare your printed report with the one shown in Figure 5–23.

FIGURE 5–23
Purchase Journal Report for Superior Carpet and Tile

Chp. 5 - Superior Carpet and Tile
Purchase Journal
For the Period From Jan 1, 2017 to Jan 31, 2017
Filter Criteria includes: 1) Includes Drop Shipments. Report order is by Date. Report is printed in Detail Format.

Date	Account ID Account Description	Invoice/CM #	Line Description	Debit Amount	Credit Amount
1/1/17	500 Rent Expense	Beginning Balance	Beginning Balances	900.00	
	200 Accounts Payable		John Charles Management		900.00
1/1/17	502 Utilities Expense	Beginning Balance	Beginning Balances	450.00	
	200 Accounts Payable		MID Midtown Irrigation District		450.00
1/1/17	108 Office Supplies	Beginning Balance	Beginning Balances	450.00	
	200 Accounts Payable		Office Max		450.00

Step 8:

Close the Select a Report or Form dialog box.

Checkpoint 5–4

1. What is the purpose of the Vendor List?
2. What is the purpose of the Purchase Journal report?

Objective 5–4 Practice

You previously established vendor accounts for Meadowland Healthcare Services and recorded purchases. Now you will set action items and print reports.

Step 1:

Open Chp. 5 – Meadowland Healthcare Services and enter the following action items related to vendors:

- On January 14, 2017, call General Telephone about its new rate plan.
- On January 15, 2017, call to set up a meeting with Alicia Marquez of Alta Vista Business Park.
- On January 18, 2017, call Office Depot to check the price of a new computer.

Remember, action items require 2 days before telephone calls and 1 day before meetings.

Step 2:

Display the Vendor List report. (See Figure 5–24.)

FIGURE 5–24
Vendor List Report for Meadowland Healthcare Services

Chp. 5 - Meadowland Healthcare Services
Vendor List

Filter Criteria includes: Report order is by ID.

Vendor ID	Vendor	Contact	Telephone 1	Tax Id No
ALT-001	Alta Vista Business Park	Alicia Marquez	209-555-4256	
GTE-004	General Telephone	Customer Service	916-555-2545	
OFD-003	Office Depot	Jim Nielson	916-555-9178	
PGE-002	Pacific Gas & Electric	George House	916-555-9905	

Step 3:

Display the Vendor Ledgers report. (See Figure 5–25.)

FIGURE 5–25
Vendor Ledgers
Report for
Meadowland
Healthcare Services

9/11/16 at 13:34:46.75   *****EDUCATIONAL VERSION ONLY*****   Page: 1

Chp. 5 - Meadowland Healthcare Services
Vendor Ledgers
For the Period From Jan 1, 2017 to Jan 31, 2017

Filter Criteria includes: Report order is by ID.

Vendor ID Vendor	Date	Trans No	Type	Paid	Debit Amt	Credit Amt	Balance
ALT-001 Alta Vista Business Park	1/2/17	012301	PJ			1,200.00	1,200.00
GTE-004 General Telephone	1/27/17	645935	PJ			265.98	265.98
OFD-003 Office Depot	1/18/17	55665	PJ			890.00	890.00
PGE-002 Pacific Gas & Electric	1/10/17	98345	PJ			345.89	345.89
Report Total						**2,701.87**	**2,701.87**

Step 4:

Close the Select a Report or Form dialog box.

Chapter Review and Assessment

Software Command Summary

Create Vendor Accounts	Maintain, Vendors, General Tab, Purchase Info Tab, History Tab, Enter Beginning Balances
Accounts Payable and Purchases Transactions	Tasks, Purchases/Receive Inventory

Checkpoint Answers

Checkpoint 5–1

1. The accounts payable ledger is also known as the vendors ledger.
2. Every firm that buys on credit should have procedures in place to ensure that it pays vendors on time, takes advantage of discounts, and keeps the total amount owed to vendors from becoming too high.

Checkpoint 5–2

1. The vendor accounts in the accounts payable subsidiary ledger provide detailed information about transactions with vendors and show the current balances owed to the vendors.
2. The Accounts Payable account is a link between the general ledger and the subsidiary ledger because its balance is equal to the total of the balances in the subsidiary ledger.

Checkpoint 5–3

1. The Vendor Ledgers report lists all transactions with vendors and the balances owed to them.
2. The Purchases/Receive Inventory function of Sage 50 is used to record purchases on credit.

Checkpoint 5–4

1. The Vendor List lists all active and inactive vendors.
2. The Purchase Journal report displays all purchases in journal format.

Study Quizzes

Take the study quiz online to check your understanding of chapter concepts. The quiz can be taken multiple times.

Content Check

Multiple Choice: Choose only one response for each question.

1. Purchases made on credit are entered in the accounting records as
   A. accounts receivable.
   B. accounts payable.
   C. prepaid expense.
   D. unearned revenue.
   E. None of the above

2. When a business purchases a service such as utilities on credit, the two types of accounts affected from the buyer's perspective are
   A. an asset account and an expense account.
   B. an asset account and a revenue account.
   C. a liability account and an expense account.
   D. a liability account and a revenue account.
   E. None of the above

3. Which function of Sage 50 is used when a business buys goods or services on credit and must enter the transaction?
   A. Action Items
   B. Purchases/Receive Inventory
   C. Receive Money
   D. Sales/Invoicing
   E. None of the above

4. Which accounts payable report contains information about all transactions with vendors and the balances owed to them?
   A. Vendor List
   B. Check Register
   C. Customer Ledgers
   D. Vendor Ledgers
   E. None of the above

5. Which general ledger account is credited to record a company's purchases on credit?
   A. Cash
   B. Accounts Payable
   C. Accounts Receivable
   D. Purchases
   E. None of the above

Short Essay Response

Provide a detailed answer for each question.

1. What are the advantages and disadvantages to a business when it purchases goods and services on credit?
2. What is the purpose of the accounts payable subsidiary ledger?
3. How does the Accounts Payable controlling account in the general ledger relate to the accounts payable subsidiary ledger?

4. Why should a business closely monitor its accounts payable?
5. Briefly explain how a purchase can be edited after it has been posted.

Cooperative Learning

1. Form into groups of three or four students, and discuss what a business can do to maintain a good credit reputation. Why is a good credit reputation important?
2. As a group, research the Small Business Administration, a government entity that helps businesses obtain the capital they need to start or expand operations. What methods does it use to assist businesses? What are its requirements to receive assistance?

Writing and Decision Making

Assume that the company for which you work currently makes all purchases with cash. However, the owner, Susan Nicholson, has decided to obtain credit from vendors. She has therefore asked you to suggest measures that the company can take to organize and manage its accounts payable. She has also asked that you explain to her how the controlling account in the general ledger relates to the vendor accounts in the subsidiary ledger. Prepare a memo with the information that has been requested.

 ## Case Problems

Demonstrate your knowledge of the Sage 50 features discussed in this chapter by completing the following case problems.

Case Problem 5–1A

Open Professional Accounting Concepts from the student data files. The owner has decided to set up vendor accounts and purchase goods and services on credit.

1. Create a subsidiary ledger account for the following vendors dated 1/1/17.

   Vendor
Vendor ID:	**JMC-01**
Name:	**JMC Management Group**

   General Tab
Contact:	**Annette Bradley**
Account Number:	**1178**
Mailing Address:	**4137 Lincoln Boulevard**
City, ST, Zip:	**Stockton, CA 95210**
Country:	**USA**
Vendor Type:	**Expense**
1099 Type:	**None**
Expense Account:	**75000 (Rent or Lease Expense)**
Telephone 1:	**209-555-3349**
Fax:	**209-555-3352**

Purchase Info Tab

Tax ID Number:	None
Ship Via:	US Mail
Terms and Credit:	Net 30 days
Form Options:	Default

History Tab

Beginning Balance:	1,100.00

Vendor

Vendor ID:	SW-02
Name:	Stockton Water District

General Tab

Contact:	Robert Henderson
Account Number:	95845
Mailing Address:	3159 Madison Avenue
City, ST, Zip:	Stockton, CA 95210
Country:	USA
Vendor Type:	Expense
1099 Type:	None
Expense Account:	78500 (Utilities Expense)
Telephone 1:	209-555-4738
Fax:	209-555-4750

Purchase Info Tab

Tax ID Number:	None
Ship Via:	US Mail
Terms and Credit:	Net 30 days
Form Options:	Default

History Tab

Beginning Balance:	820.00

Vendor

Vendor ID:	OFFMAX-03
Name:	Office Max

General Tab

Contact:	Joshua Baker
Account Number:	61345
Mailing Address:	3915 Webber Lane
City, ST, Zip:	Stockton, CA 95207
Country:	USA
Vendor Type:	Supplier
1099 Type:	None
Expense Account:	12000 (Office Supplies)
Telephone 1:	209-555-7981
Fax:	209-555-7988

Purchase Info Tab

Tax ID Number:	**None**
Ship Via:	**Fed-EX**
Terms and Credit:	**2% 10 days, net 30 days**
Form Options:	**Default**

History Tab

Beginning Balance:	**2,400.00**

Vendor

Vendor ID:	**PACBELL-04**
Name:	**Pacific Bell**

General Tab

Contact:	**Barbara Sinclair**
Account Number:	**127648**
Mailing Address:	**6581 East Montgomery Avenue**
City, ST, Zip:	**Stockton, CA 95207**
Country:	**USA**
Vendor Type:	**Expense**
1099 Type:	**None**
Expense Account:	**79000 (Telephone Expense)**
Telephone 1:	**209-555-7890**
Fax:	**209-555-7900**

Purchase Info Tab

Tax ID Number:	**None**
Ship Via:	**US Mail**
Terms and Credit:	**Net 30 days**
Form Options:	**Default**

History Tab

Beginning Balance:	**600.00**

HINT

To change accounting period:
- Click Tasks
- Click System
- Change Accounting Period
- Select *02-Feb 01, 2017* to *Feb 28, 2017*
- Click OK
- Select No to query

2. Change the accounting period to *Feb 1, 2017* to *Feb 28, 2017*.

3. Enter each of the following transactions for February 2017. Note that this business has three different sources of revenue: accounting fees, tax preparation fees, and consulting fees. Therefore, be sure that you select the number of the correct revenue account in the *GL Account* field in the Sales/Invoicing window. (The customer accounts have been set up with a GL Sales Account default to Account 40000, Accounting Fees.) Services performed on account will be entered in the Sales/Invoicing window, and purchases on account in the Purchases/Receive Inventory window.

Date	Transaction
Feb. 3	Received a bill (Invoice 16475) of $1580 for monthly rent from JMC Management Group.
4	Received a bill (Invoice 62351) of $65 for monthly usage of water from Stockton Water District.

5	Performed accounting services for $620 on credit for Johnson Manufacturing. Issued Invoice 1006.
5	Received a bill (Invoice 51956) of $125 for monthly usage of telephone service from Pacific Bell.
8	Performed accounting services for $450 on credit for Computer Expertise. Issued Invoice 1007.
10	Purchased office supplies for $340 on credit from Office Max. Received Invoice 4891.
14	Performed accounting services for $650 on credit for Stephanie's Catering. Issued Invoice 1008. Received Check No. 461 for $325 from the customer.
17	Purchased office supplies for $234 on credit from Office Max. Received Invoice 5216.
24	Performed consulting services for $800 on credit, for Johnson Manufacturing. Issued Invoice 1009. Received Check No. 11964 for $350 from the customer.
27	Performed accounting services for $245 on credit for Computer Expertise. Issued Invoice 1010. Received Check No. 9865 for $100 from the customer.

4. Print the following reports for February: Vendor Ledgers, Customer Ledgers, and Cash Receipts Journal.

Case Problem 5–2A

Open CC Advertising, which is located in the student data files. The owner has decided to set up vendor accounts and purchase goods and services on credit.

1. Create a subsidiary ledger account for each of the following new vendors. Enter the beginning balances as of March 1, 2017.

Vendor

Vendor ID:	**JMG-01**
Name:	**J. Madison Graphing**

General Tab

Contact:	**John Madison**
Account Number:	**2180**
Mailing Address:	**6529 West Highland Avenue**
City, ST, Zip:	**Tracy, CA 95376**
Country:	**USA**
Vendor Type:	**Expense**
1099 Type:	**None**
Expense Account:	**516 (Advertising Expense)**
Telephone 1:	**209-555-3349**
Fax:	**209-555-3352**

Purchase Info Tab

Tax ID Number:	**None**
Ship Via:	**US Mail**
Terms and Credit:	**Net 30 days**
Form Options:	**Default**

History Tab

    Beginning Balance: **640.00**

Vendor

    Vendor ID: **OD-02**
    Name: **Office Depot**

General Tab

    Contact: **Brian Gentry**
    Account Number: **32181**
    Mailing Address: **6529 Harding Avenue**
    City, ST, Zip: **Tracy, CA 95376**
    Country: **USA**
    Vendor Type: **Supplier**
    1099 Type: **None**
    Expense Account: **108 (Office Supplies)**
    Telephone 1:   **209-555-6459**
    Fax: **209-555-6467**

Purchase Info Tab

    Tax ID Number: **None**
    Ship Via: **UPS Ground**
    Terms and Credit: **2% 10 days, net 30 days**
    Form Options: **Default**

History Tab

    Beginning Balance: **1,200.00**

2. Print a Vendor Ledgers report for March 2017.

Case Problem 5–1B

Open Alpha Zeta Graphics from the student data files. The owner has decided to set up vendor accounts and purchase goods and services on credit.

1. Create a subsidiary ledger account for each vendor dated 1/1/17.

Vendor

    Vendor ID: **JPS-01**
    Name: **Johnson Photography**

General Tab

    Contact: **Matthew Rosario**
    Account Number: **3194**
    Mailing Address: **1371 West Bessie Avenue**
    City, ST, Zip: **Stockton, CA 95210**
    Country: **USA**
    Vendor Type: **Expense**
    1099 Type: **None**
    Expense Account: **76000 (Printing and Copying Expense)**
    Telephone 1:   **209-555-4651**
    Fax: **209-555-4658**

Purchase Info Tab

Tax ID Number:	**None**
Ship Via:	**Fed-EX**
Terms and Credit:	**Net 30 days**
Form Options:	**Default**

History Tab

Beginning Balance:	**370.00**

Vendor

Vendor ID:	**SD-02**
Name:	**Stockton Water District**

General Tab

Contact:	**Robert Henderson**
Account Number:	**40381**
Mailing Address:	**3159 Madison Avenue**
City, ST, Zip:	**Stockton, CA 95210**
Country:	**USA**
Vendor Type:	**Expense**
1099 Type:	**None**
Expense Account:	**81500 (Utilities Expense)**
Telephone 1:	**209-555-4738**
Fax:	**209-555-4750**

Purchase Info Tab

Tax ID Number:	**None**
Ship Via:	**US Mail**
Terms and Credit:	**Net 30 days**
Form Options:	**Default**

History Tab

Beginning Balance:	**420.00**

Vendor

Vendor ID:	**OFFMAX-03**
Name:	**Office Max**

General Tab

Contact:	**Kevin Randall**
Account Number:	**395481**
Mailing Address:	**3915 Webber Lane**
City, ST, Zip:	**Stockton, CA 95207**
Country:	**USA**
Vendor Type:	**Supplier**
1099 Type:	**None**
Expense Account:	**12000 (Graphing Supplies)**
Telephone 1:	**209-555-7981**
Fax:	**209-555-7988**

Purchase Info Tab

Tax ID Number:	None
Ship Via:	Fed-EX
Terms and Credit:	2% 10 days, net 30 days
Form Options:	Default

History Tab

Beginning Balance:	2,200.00

Vendor

Vendor ID:	SJR-04
Name:	San Joaquin Rentals

General Tab

Contact:	Peter Ramirez
Account Number:	94612
Mailing Address:	9462 Lowell Avenue
City, ST, Zip:	Stockton, CA 95207
Country:	USA
Vendor Type:	Expense
1099 Type:	None
Expense Account:	78500 (Rent-Office)
Telephone 1:	209-555-6454
Fax:	209-555-6460

Purchase Info Tab

Tax ID Number:	None
Ship Via:	US Mail
Terms and Credit:	Net 30 days
Form Options:	Default

History Tab

Beginning Balance:	0

Vendor

Vendor ID:	PACBELL-05
Name:	Pacific Bell

General Tab

Contact:	Barbara Sinclair
Account Number:	32348
Mailing Address:	6581 East Montgomery Avenue
City, ST, Zip:	Stockton, CA 95207
Country:	USA
Vendor Type:	Expense
1099 Type:	None
Expense Account:	80000 (Telephone Expense)
Telephone 1:	209-555-7890
Fax:	209-555-7900

Purchase Info Tab

Tax ID Number:	**None**
Ship Via:	**US Mail**
Terms and Credit:	**Net 30 days**
Form Options:	**Default**

History Tab

Beginning Balance:	**300.00**

HINT

To change accounting period:
- Click Tasks
- Click System
- Change Accounting Period
- Select *02-Feb 01, 2017* to *Feb 28, 2017*
- Click OK
- Select No to query

2. Change the accounting period to *Feb 1, 2017* to *Feb 28, 2017*.

3. Enter each of the following transactions for February 2017. Note that this business has three different types of revenue: graphic design income, retouching income, and drafting income. Therefore, be sure that you select the number of the correct revenue account in the *GL Account* field in the Sales/Invoicing window. (The customer accounts have been set up with a GL Sales Account default to Account 40000, Graphic Design Income.) Services performed on account will be entered in the Sales/Invoicing window, and purchases on account in the Purchases/Receive Inventory window.

Date	Transaction
Feb. 2	Performed graphic design services for $575 on credit for Jackson Photography. Issued Invoice 1007.
3	Received a bill (Invoice 4952) of $695 for the monthly rent from San Joaquin Rentals.
4	Received a bill of $120 (Invoice 13795) for monthly usage of telephone service from Pacific Bell.
4	Received a bill (Invoice 65429) of $134 for monthly usage of water from Stockton Water District.
5	Purchased graphing supplies for $335 on credit from Office Max. Received Invoice 4620.
8	Performed graphic design services for $620 on credit for Computer Creations. Issued Invoice 1008.
12	Purchased printing services for $550 on credit from Johnson Photography. Received Invoice 2615.
15	Performed graphic design services for $1,250 on credit for Jackson Photography. Issued Invoice 1009. Received Check No. 4504 for $400 from the customer.
19	Purchased graphing supplies for $235 on credit from Office Max. Received Invoice 5229.
25	Performed graphic design services for $1,125 on credit for First Designs. Issued Invoice 1010. Received Check No. 3271 for $350 from the customer.
26	Performed retouching services for $460 on credit for Jackson Photography. Issued Invoice 1011.
27	Performed graphic design services for $750 on credit for Computer Creations. Issued Invoice 1012.

4. Print the following reports for February: Vendor Ledgers, Customer Ledgers, and Cash Receipts Journal.

Case Problem 5–2B

Open Ritter Insurance, which is located in the student data files. This firm plans to purchase goods and services on credit.

1. Create a subsidiary ledger account for each of the following new vendors. Enter the beginning balances as of March 1, 2017.

Vendor

Vendor ID:	**OFFMAX-01**
Name:	**Office Max**

General Tab

Contact:	**Kevin Randall**
Account Number:	**4150**
Mailing Address:	**3915 Webber Lane**
City, ST, Zip:	**Stockton, CA 95207**
Country:	**USA**
Vendor Type:	**Supplier**
1099 Type:	**None**
Expense Account:	**108 (Office Supplies)**
Telephone 1:	**209-555-7981**
Fax:	**209-555-7988**

Purchase Info Tab

Tax ID Number:	**None**
Ship Via:	**Fed-EX**
Terms and Credit:	**2% 10 days, net 30 days**
Form Options:	**Default**

History Tab

Beginning Balance:	**840.00**

Vendor

Vendor ID:	**GJPA-02**
Name:	**GJ Professional Accounting**

General Tab

Contact:	**Jim Tyler**
Account Number:	**491502**
Mailing Address:	**1506 East March Lane**
City, ST, Zip:	**Stockton, CA 95207**
Country:	**USA**
Vendor Type:	**Expense**
1099 Type:	**None**
Expense Account:	**516 (Accounting Expense)**
Telephone 1:	**209-555-2112**
Fax:	**209-555-1221**

Purchase Info Tab

Tax ID Number:	**None**
Ship Via:	**US Mail**
Terms and Credit:	**Net 30 days**
Form Options:	**Default**

History Tab

Beginning Balance:	**720.00**

2. Print a Vendor Ledgers report for March 2017.

CHAPTER 6

Cash Payments and Cash Receipts

Objectives

6–1 Review recording and managing cash

6–2 Process cash payments using the cash payments module

6–3 Process cash receipts using the cash receipts module

6–4 Prepare a reconciliation of the checking account

Software Features

- Receive money toolbar buttons

- Payments toolbar buttons

- Account reconciliation toolbar

Company Files

Before beginning chapter work, access the links menu to download company files.

Cash is the most essential of all assets. Without an adequate cash flow, no business can operate for long. Because cash is so important, every firm should have efficient procedures for managing its cash receipts and cash payments.

OBJECTIVE 6–1

Review Recording and Managing Cash

cash The funds that a business has on hand and on deposit in banks.

Remember that *cash* consists of the funds that a business has on hand and the funds that it has on deposit in banks. The funds on hand may include not only currency and coin but also cash equivalents such as checks and money orders received from customers.

Some firms maintain a single cash account in their general ledger. Other firms have a variety of cash accounts such as Cash on Hand, Petty Cash, Regular Checking Account, Payroll Checking Account, and Money Market Savings. If there is a single account called Cash, this account is debited whenever cash is received and credited whenever cash is paid.

You may choose to record all cash transactions in the general journal as you did in Chapter 3. However, many businesses prefer to use special journals for cash receipts and cash payments. Sage 50 provides such journals.

Cash is the asset that is most easily stolen, lost, or misused. Therefore, accountants recommend that businesses follow certain procedures to protect their cash. Some of these procedures are outlined below:

- Make all payments by check except for small expenditures from a petty cash fund.
- Avoid keeping large amounts of cash on the premises. Make frequent bank deposits of cash receipts.
- Use a locked safe or cash drawer to protect any cash that is on hand.
- Record cash transactions promptly.
- Reconcile the monthly bank statement with the firm's internal cash records.
- Divide responsibility. If possible, have different employees handle cash, record cash, and reconcile the bank statement.

Sage 50 allows you to quickly and efficiently issue checks, record cash receipts and cash payments, and carry out the bank reconciliation process.

> ### Checkpoint 6–1
>
> 1. What do the funds that a business has on hand include?
> 2. What are some procedures that businesses can follow to protect their cash?

OBJECTIVE 6–2

Process Cash Payments Using the Cash Payments Module

During January 2017, Superior Carpet and Tile received several bills from vendors. In Chapter 5, you learned how these purchases of goods and services were recorded. Now you will see how the business uses the cash payments module of Sage 50 to issue checks to the vendors and record the payments.

Paying an Invoice with a Discount

On January 29, 2017, Superior Carpet and Tile received Invoice 3556 from Office Max for a purchase of office supplies. The total of the invoice was $1,400 and the terms were 2% 10 days, net 30 days (2/10, net 30). On January 31, Superior's accountant paid bills and issued a check to Office Max. Because the invoice is being paid within the discount period, Superior is entitled to take the 2% discount offered by the vendor.

Step 1:

Open Superior Carpet and Tile (Chp. 6 – Superior Carpet and Tile if student data files are used).

Step 2:

Click Tasks and then select *Payments.*

Step 3:

At the Select a Cash Account dialog box, select *Cash* from the drop-down list, as shown in Figure 6–1.

FIGURE 6–1
Select a Cash Account
Dialog Box with Cash
Selected

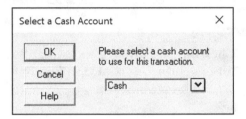

Step 4:

Click OK. The Payments window will appear, as shown in Figure 6–2.

FIGURE 6–2
Blank Payments Window

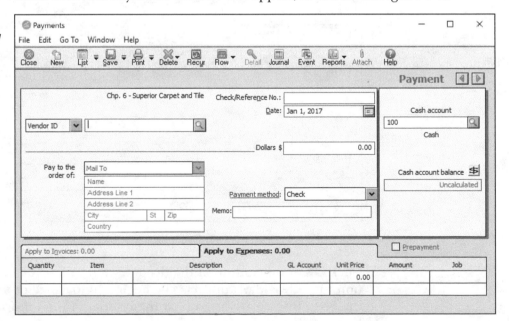

Step 5:

If it is not already selected, click the down arrow in the first box on the left, and then select *Vendor ID* from the drop-down list, as shown in Figure 6–3.

FIGURE 6–3
Vendor ID Selected from
Drop-Down List

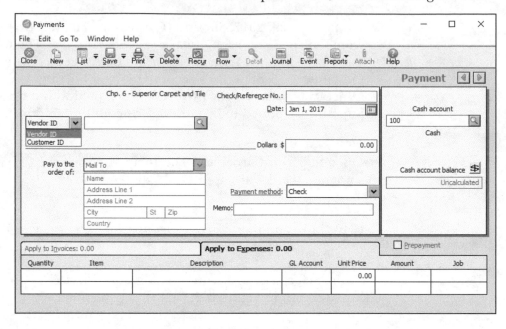

Step 6:

Click the *magnifying glass* icon and then select *OFF-003* from the drop-down list of vendors, as shown in Figure 6–4.

FIGURE 6–4
OFF-003 Selected from
Drop-Down List of
Vendors

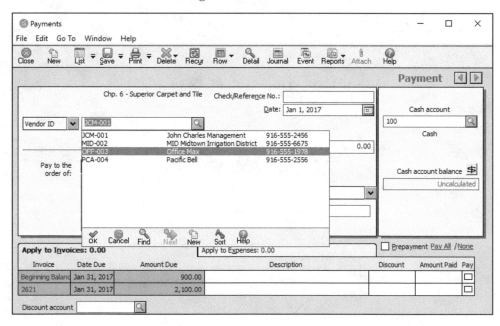

Step 7:

Click OK at the bottom of the drop-down list of vendors. The information for Office Max appears. The beginning balance of its account and the open invoice are listed near the bottom of the window, as shown in Figure 6–5.

FIGURE 6–5
Account Information for Office Max Displayed

FIGURE 6–5
Account Information for Office Max Displayed

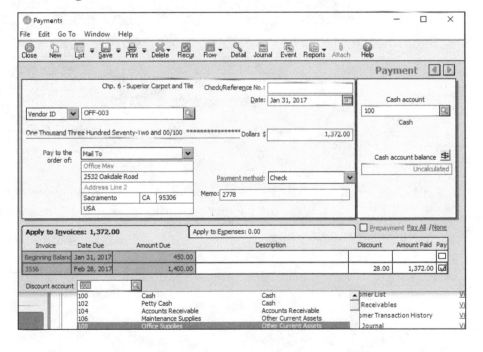

HINT

The *Apply to Invoices* folder tab is highlighted because there are open (unpaid) invoices for the selected vendor.

Step 8:

Choose *Jan 31, 2017* in the *Date* field using the *calendar* icon.

Step 9:

Click the *magnifying glass* icon next to the *Discount Account* field, which is at the lower left side of the Payments window. Click *108, Office Supplies*, as shown in Figure 6–6.

FIGURE 6–6
Office Supplies Selected from Discount Account Drop-Down List

Step 10:

Click to add a check mark in the *Pay* field on the line where Invoice 3556 appears. When the check mark is entered, Sage 50 will automatically calculate the amount to be paid by deducting any discount from the total of the invoice. For example, Invoice 3556 from Office Max is for $1,400.

However, because Superior is paying within the discount period, it can take a 2% discount ($28), which reduces the amount it owes to $1,372.

Step 11:

Click the Journal button on the Payments toolbar.

Step 12:

Review the Accounting Behind the Screens window that appears to see how the discount was treated, as shown in Figure 6–7. Notice that the Office Supplies account (108) is credited for $28, the amount of the discount. This is a logical approach because the cost of the office supplies is less than the amount originally recorded ($1,400). Remember that when the purchase was made, Office Supplies was debited for $1,400. The credit of $28 reduces the recorded cost of the purchase to $1,372, the amount actually paid. Click OK.

FIGURE 6–7
Accounting Behind the Screens Window

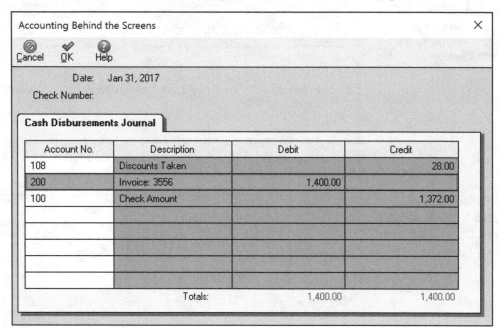

Account No.	Description	Debit	Credit
108	Discounts Taken		28.00
200	Invoice: 3556	1,400.00	
100	Check Amount		1,372.00
	Totals:	1,400.00	1,400.00

Accounting Behind the Screens

Cancel   OK   Help

Date: Jan 31, 2017
Check Number:

Cash Disbursements Journal

Step 13:

Review the Payments window, as shown in Figure 6–8. Make sure that your entries for the payment to Office Max match the ones shown here.

FIGURE 6–8
Payments Window with Entries for Office Max

FIGURE 6–8
Payments Window with Entries for Office Max

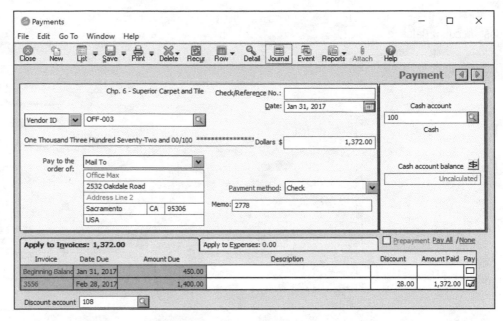

Do not key anything in the *Check/Reference No.* field. Sage 50 will automatically record the check number when the check is printed. If the payment were to be made in cash rather than by check, you would key **CASH**. (In some rare circumstances, you may want to bypass the automatic check preparation feature and write a check manually. In such a case, you must key in the check number.)

Step 14:

If the number of the Cash account (100) is not already selected, click the *magnifying glass* icon next to the *Cash Account* field, and then click *100*, as shown in Figure 6–9.

FIGURE 6–9
Payments Dialog Box with Cash Account 100 Selected

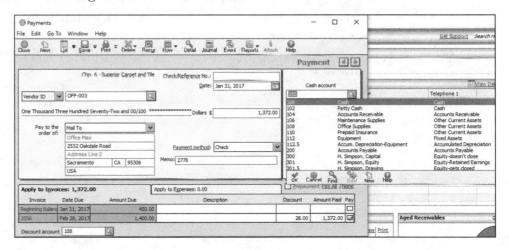

Step 15:

Sage 50 maintains a running balance in the Cash account. This balance can be viewed in the *Cash account balance* field. However, the *Cash account balance* field will sometimes contain only ??????????? or *Uncalculated*. To reveal the balance, click the Recalculate button ($) next to the *Cash account balance* field and the updated Cash account balance will appear in the *Cash account balance* field, as shown in Figure 6–10.

FIGURE 6–10
Cash Account Balance
Field Showing Current
Cash Balance

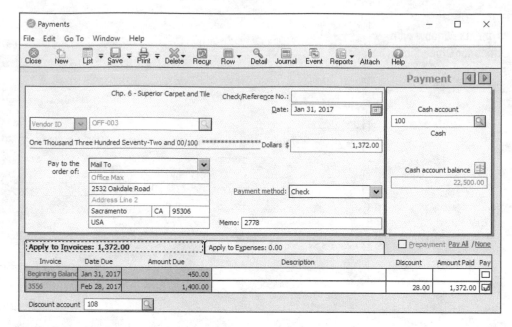

Step 16:

Click the Save button on the Payments toolbar to post the payment.

Paying an Invoice and a Previous Balance

On January 3, 2017, Superior Carpet and Tile received Invoice 2621 for its monthly rent of $2,100. The invoice is due at the end of the month. On January 31, the accountant decides to issue a check that will cover both Invoice 2621 and a balance of $900 owed from the previous month.

Step 1:

Use the steps outlined in the last section to pay the monthly rent and the outstanding balance owed to John Charles Management. However, in this case, enter check marks in the *Pay* field on the lines for both the beginning balance and Invoice 2621. Also, keep in mind that there is no discount involved in this payment.

Step 2:

Compare your entries with those shown in Figure 6–11. Then click Save.

FIGURE 6–11
Completed Payments Window with Entries for John Charles Management

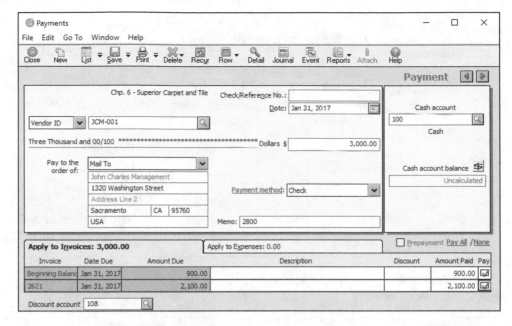

During January 2017, Superior Carpet and Tile received two bills. One came from MID Midtown Irrigation District (Invoice Number 4763), and the other came from Pacific Bell (Invoice Number 2867).

Step 3:

Pay MID Midtown Irrigation District for its monthly bill and a previous balance that Superior owes. When you complete your work, compare your entries with those shown in Figure 6–12.

Vendor ID:	**MID-002**
Date:	**Jan 31, 2017**
Cash Account:	**100**
Discount Account:	**None**
Pay:	**The beginning balance ($450) and the monthly bill ($226.65)**

FIGURE 6–12
Completed Payments Window with Entries for MID Midtown Irrigation District

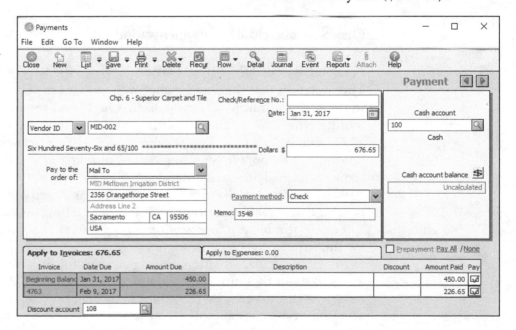

Step 4:

Click Save to post the payment.

Step 5:

Pay Pacific Bell for its monthly bill and a previous balance that Superior owes. When you complete your work, compare your entries with those shown in Figure 6–13.

Vendor ID:	**PAC-004**
Date:	**Jan 31, 2017**
Cash Account:	**100**
Discount Account:	**None**
Pay:	**The beginning balance ($500) and the monthly bill ($265.39)**

FIGURE 6–13
Completed Payments Window with Entries for Pacific Bell

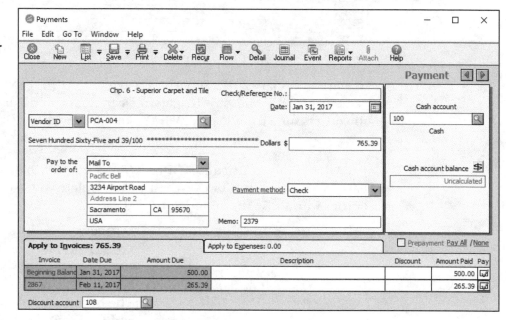

Step 6:

Click Save and close the Payments window.

Paying a Bill for a Purchase Not Previously Recorded

The four bills that the accountant for Superior Carpet and Tile has paid so far were for purchases on credit that had been recorded earlier in the month. Now assume that on January 31, 2017, the accountant is handed a bill from Apex Floor Care Service for $250. This firm has just finished polishing the floors in Superior's office building. The bill from Apex requests immediate payment.

When a situation like this occurs, it is not necessary to first record the purchase and then record the cash payment. However, if the firm that submitted the bill is a new vendor, it is necessary to set up a vendor account for the firm.

In this particular situation, the accountant for Superior Carpet and Tile wants to debit the purchase to Maintenance Expense. However, the business does not have such an account in its general ledger. Therefore, the accountant must create this account before recording the purchase.

Use the steps outlined below to create the Maintenance Expense account, set up the vendor account, record the purchase, and record the cash payment.

Step 1:

Click Tasks on the Menu bar and *Write Checks* in the drop-down list, as shown in Figure 6–14.

FIGURE 6–14
Write Checks Selected from the Tasks Drop-Down List

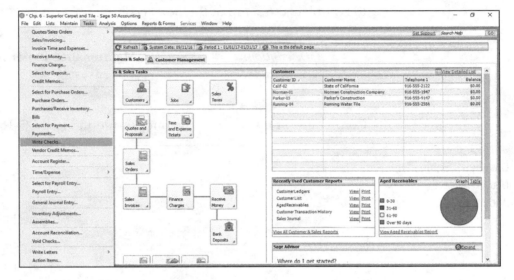

Step 2:

Click the *magnifying glass* icon next to the Expense account box located in the lower left corner of the screen. A drop-down list appears, as shown in Figure 6–15.

FIGURE 6–15
Expense Account Drop-Down List

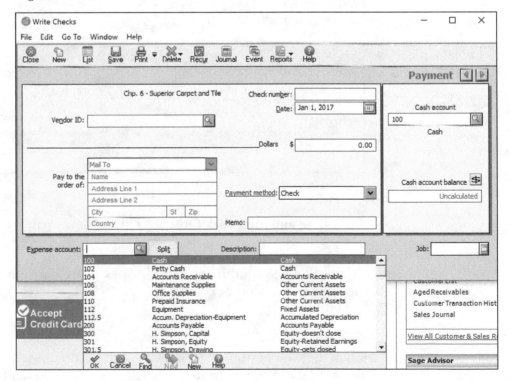

Step 3:

Click the New button at the bottom of the drop-down list of general ledger accounts.

Step 4:

At the Maintain Chart of Accounts window, key the following information to complete the setup of the new account:

Account ID:	**518**
Description:	**Maintenance Expense**
Account Type:	**Expenses**

Step 5:

Compare your entries with the ones shown in Figure 6–16.

FIGURE 6–16
Completed Entries for
Maintenance Expense
Account

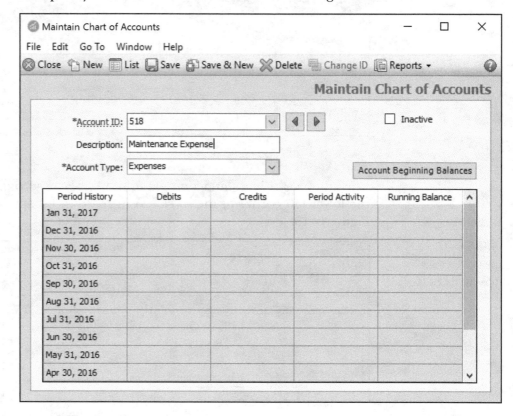

Step 6:

Click Save and then click Close to return to the Write Checks window.

Step 7:

To set up a new vendor account for Apex Floor Care Service, click the *magnifying glass* icon next to the *Vendor ID* box to reveal the drop-down list of vendors.

Step 8:

Click the New button at the bottom of the drop-down list of vendors. At the Maintain Vendors window, click in the *Vendor ID* field as shown in Figure 6–17.

FIGURE 6–17
Vendor ID Field Selected
in the Maintain Vendors
Window

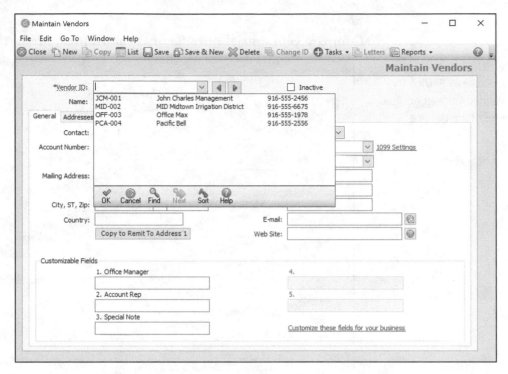

Step 9:

Use the following information to complete the setup of a new vendor account for Apex Floor Care Service:

Vendor

Vendor ID:	**APX-005**
Name:	**Apex Floor Care Service**

General Tab

Contact:	**Tarin Land**
Account Number:	**334223**
Mailing Address:	**2310 Windham Avenue**
City, ST, Zip:	**Sacramento, CA 95670**
Country:	**USA**
Vendor Type:	**Expense**
1099 Type:	**None**
Expense Account:	**518 (Maintenance Expense)**
Telephone 1:	**408-555-5634**
Fax:	**408-555-4638**

Purchase Info Tab

Tax ID Number:	**None**
Ship Via:	**US Mail**
Terms and Credit:	**Due in 30 days, 0.00 Discount**
Form Options:	**Paper Form**

History Tab

Beginning Balance:	**0**

Step 10:

Compare your entries with the ones shown in Figure 6–18.

FIGURE 6–18

Completed Entries for Vendor Account for Apex Floor Care Service

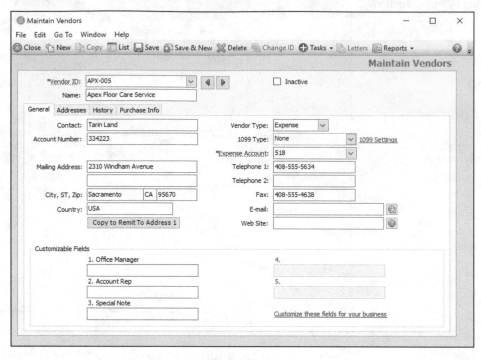

Step 11:

Click Save and then Close to return to the Write Checks window.

Step 12:

To write the check, select *APX-005* from the drop-down list of vendors. The information for Apex Floor Care Service appears, as shown in Figure 6–19.

FIGURE 6–19

Write Checks Window Showing Apex Floor Care Service Information

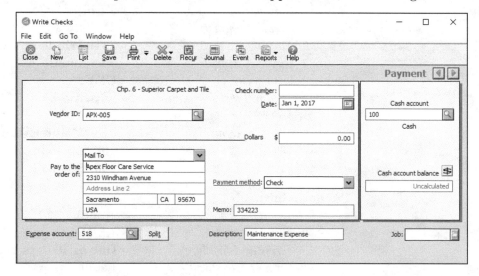

Step 13:

Click the *calendar* icon and then choose *Jan 31, 2017* in the *Date* field.

Step 14:

Key **250.00** in the *Dollars* field.

Step 15:

Click the *magnifying glass* icon and then click the number of the Cash account (*100*) in the *Cash Account* field.

Step 16:

Click account *518, Maintenance Expense* from the drop-down list of general ledger accounts in the *Expense Account* field, if not already complete.

Step 17:

Key **Floor Care** in the *Description* field. You may need to overwrite the existing description of "Maintenance Expense."

Step 18:

Compare your entries with the ones shown in Figure 6–20.

FIGURE 6–20
Completed Write Checks Window for Apex Floor Care Service

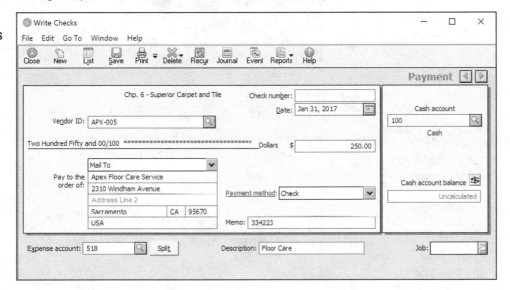

Printing Individual Checks

As noted previously, Sage 50 allows you the option of either preparing checks automatically or preparing them manually. If you select automatic check preparation, the system will enter the check numbers in the *Check Number* field of the Payments window. With manual check preparation, you must key in the check numbers.

Superior Carpet and Tile uses automatic check preparation. Follow the steps outlined below to issue a check for the bill owed to Apex Floor Care Service.

Step 1:

Click the Print button on the Write Checks toolbar. The Print Forms: Disbursement Checks dialog box appears, as shown in Figure 6–21.

FIGURE 6–21
Print Forms:
Disbursement Checks
Dialog Box

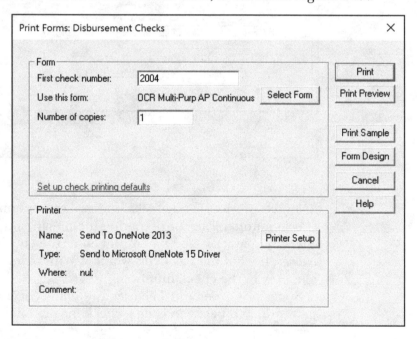

Step 2:

Key **2004** in the *First check number* field, as shown in Figure 6–22.

FIGURE 6–22
First Check Number Field
with 2004 Entered

Step 3:

Click the Print button to print the check. The check will print out on a blank sheet of paper because no check form was placed in the printer paper tray. Compare your check with the one shown in Figure 6–23. It is not necessary to save. The entries are saved when the check is printed.

FIGURE 6–23
Sample of Printed Check
for Apex Floor Care
Service

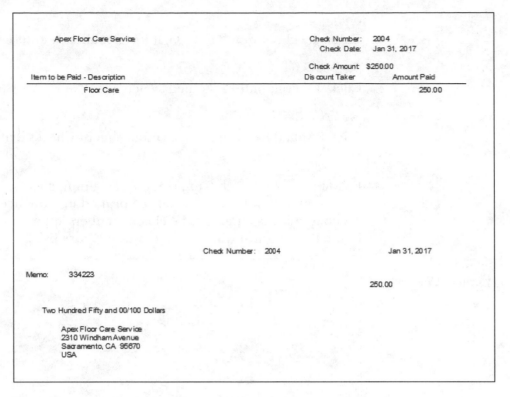

Step 4:

Close the Write Checks window.

Printing Checks Previously Marked for Payment

Superior Carpet and Tile needs the following checks marked for payment in January.

- Office Max, Check 2005
- John Charles Management, Check 2006
- Pacific Bell, Check 2007
- MID Midtown Irrigation District, Check 2008

Step 1:

Click Tasks on the Menu bar and *Payments* in the drop-down list.

Step 2:

Click the List button on the Payments toolbar.

Step 3:

Select *OFF-003(Office Max)* in the Payment List window and then click Open.

Step 4:

Enter the check number, 2005, if it is not already entered.

Step 5:

Click the Print button on the Payments toolbar.

Step 6:

Click Print at the Print Forms: Disbursement Checks dialog box.

Step 7:

Follow steps 2 through 6 to print the remaining checks. Notice that the check numbers will automatically be printed in sequence after the first check number is entered. The check numbers appear in the *Check No.* field in the Payment List window, as shown in Figure 6–24.

FIGURE 6–24
Payment List Window

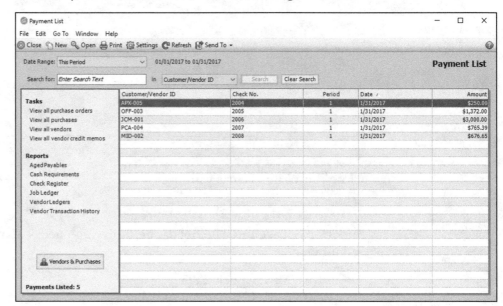

Step 8:

Close the Payment List window.

Checkpoint 6–2

1. What is the cash payments module of Sage 50 used for?
2. Why is it not necessary to key anything in the *Check/Reference No.* field when Sage 50 is used to issue checks?

In Chapter 5, you created vendor accounts for Meadowland Healthcare Services and recorded its purchases on credit. In this chapter, you will record payments to the vendors.

Step 1:

Open Meadowland Healthcare Services (Chp. 6 – Meadowland Healthcare Services if student data files are used).

Step 2:

Record the following payments using 10200 (Regular Checking Account) as the Cash Account and print the checks.

- On January 27, 2017, paid Invoice 55665 for $890, less a discount, owed to Office Depot, Check 700. (Use Office Supplies as the Discount account.)
- On January 31, 2017, paid Invoice 012301 for $1,200 owed to Alta Vista Business Park, Check 701.
- On January 31, 2017, paid a bill of $345.89 owed to Pacific Gas & Electric, Check 702.
- On January 31, 2017, paid a bill of $265.98 owed to General Telephone, Check 703.

Step 3:

On January 31, 2017, Meadowland received Invoice 33223 for $650 from Merry Maids, a new vendor. Meadowland does not have an expense account for housekeeping services. Create the necessary general ledger account.

Account ID:	**67250**
Description:	**Housekeeping Expense**
Account Type:	**Expenses**

Step 4:

Create the necessary vendor account for Merry Maids.

Vendor

Vendor ID:	**MER-005**
Name:	**Merry Maids**

General Tab

Contact:	**David Lee**
Account Number:	**88997**
Mailing Address:	**3211 Williams Avenue**
City, ST, Zip:	**Fresno, CA 96330**
Country:	**USA**
Vendor Type:	**Expense**
1099 Type:	**None**
Expense Account:	**67250 (Housekeeping Expense)**
Telephone 1:	**209-555-6534**
Fax:	**209-555-8364**

Purchase Info Tab

Tax ID Number:	**None**
Ship Via:	**US Mail**
Terms and Credit:	**Due EOM, 0.00 Discount**
Form Options:	**Default**

History Tab

Beginning Balance:	**0**

Step 5:

Using the Write Checks feature, record the immediate payment of Invoice 33223 for $650 owed to Merry Maids, Check 704.

Step 6:

Select List from the Payments window and review the checks and check numbers for correctness against Figure 6–25.

FIGURE 6–25
Payment List Window

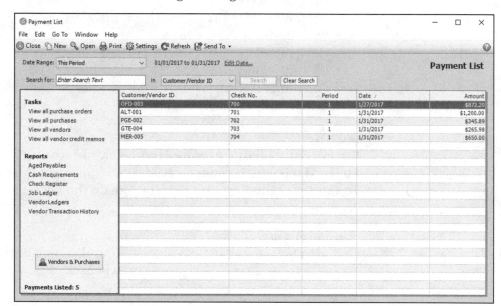

Step 7:

Close the Payment List and Payments windows.

OBJECTIVE 6–3

Process Cash Receipts Using the Cash Receipts Module

During January 2017, Superior Carpet and Tile sold services on credit to several customers. In Chapter 4, you learned how these sales were recorded. Now you will see how the business uses the cash receipts module of Sage 50 to issue invoices and record the amounts collected from customers.

Issuing Invoices

If a business wants to collect the amounts owed by customers on time, it must issue invoices promptly. Remember that an *invoice* is a bill for the goods or services sold to a customer. The invoice shows the amount that the customer owes and the credit terms as well as other information about the sale.

Sage 50 allows for quick preparation of invoices. It also provides flexibility in what information is presented on invoices. For example, on January 14, 2017, Superior Carpet and Tile did a job for Parker's Construction for a fixed fee of $5,000. Parker agreed to pay one-half of the total due ($2,500) as soon as the job was completed. Therefore, when Superior issues Invoice 1002 for this job, the invoice must include both the total of $5,000 and the partial collection of $2,500.

Step 1:

Open Chp. 6 – Superior Carpet and Tile, which you updated previously in the chapter. Click Tasks and then click *Sales/Invoicing*.

Step 2:

Click the List button on the Sales/Invoicing toolbar.

Step 3:

Click *Parker's Construction* at the Sales Invoice List window, as shown in Figure 6–26.

FIGURE 6–26
Parker's Construction Selected at Sales Invoice List Window

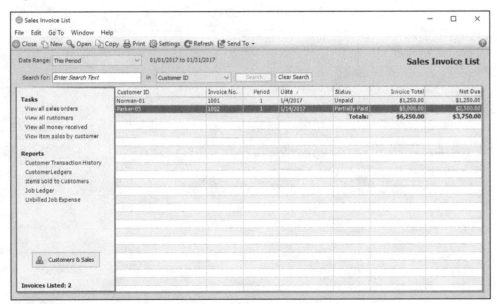

Step 4:

Click Open. The invoice for Parker's Construction appears, as shown in Figure 6–27.

FIGURE 6–27

Invoice 1002 for Parker's
Construction

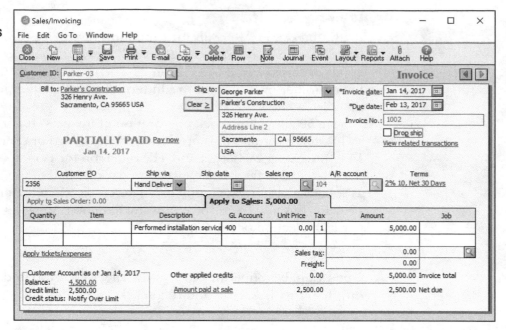

Step 5:

Click the Print button on the Sales/Invoicing toolbar.

Step 6:

The Print Forms: Invoices dialog box appears, as shown in Figure 6–28. Click the Print button.

FIGURE 6–28

Print Forms: Invoices
Dialog Box

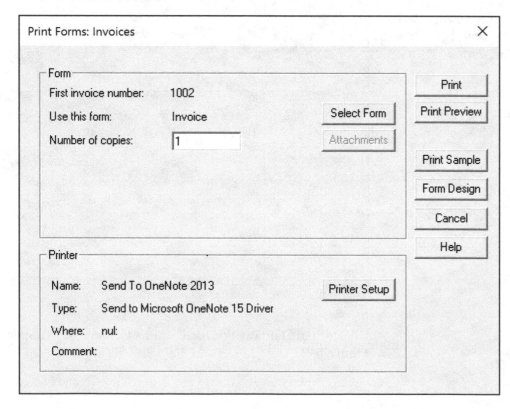

Step 7:

Compare your invoice with the one shown in Figure 6–29.

FIGURE 6–29
Invoice 1002 for Parker's
Construction

Chp. 6 - Superior Carpet and Tile
345 Brown Ave.
Campbell, CA 95555
USA

Voice: 408-555-4444
Fax: 408-555-4445

INVOICE

Invoice Number: 1002
Invoice Date: Jan 14, 2017
Page: 1

Duplicate

Bill To:	Ship to:
Parker's Construction 326 Henry Ave. Sacramento, CA 95665 USA	Parker's Construction 326 Henry Ave. Sacramento, CA 95665 USA

Customer ID	Customer PO	Payment Terms	
Parker-03	2356	2% 10, Net 30 Days	
Sales Rep ID	**Shipping Method**	**Ship Date**	**Due Date**
	Hand Deliver		2/13/17

Quantity	Item	Description	Unit Price	Amount
		Performed installation services		5,000.00

Subtotal	5,000.00
Sales Tax	
Total Invoice Amount	5,000.00
Payment/Credit Applied	2,500.00
TOTAL	**2,500.00**

Check/Credit Memo No. 1002

Step 8:

Close the Sales/Invoicing window and the Sales Invoice List window.

Recording Cash Receipts

On January 23, 2017, Superior Carpet and Tile received a check for $2,400 from Parker's Construction. This check represents the balance owed on Invoice 1002 ($2,500) less a 2% discount on the total of the invoice ($5,000 × .02 = $100). Remember that Superior billed Parker for $5,000 and received $2,500 immediately. Because the invoice is dated January 14, Parker has now paid the full amount due within the 10-day discount period. Thus, it is entitled to the 2% discount on the total of the invoice.

HINT
Invoices can be printed at any time. They can be printed when a job is completed or at a future date such as the end of the month. Each firm has its own billing policy.

Discounts on sales are debited to an account called Sales Discount. This account is known as a *contra income account* because its debit balance is contrary to the normal credit balance of an income account. Superior Carpet and Tile does not yet have such an account in its general ledger. Therefore, use the following information to create this account using Maintain, Chart of Accounts.

Account ID:	**401**
Account Description:	**Sales Discount**
Account Type:	**Income**

After you have created the new account, you will then process a receipt of cash on account using the following steps:

Step 1:

Click Tasks and then click *Receive Money*.

Step 2:

Key **01/23/17** in the *Deposit ticket ID* field.

Step 3:

In the box below the *Deposit ticket ID* field, click the down arrow and then click *Customer ID* if necessary.

Step 4:

In the box to the right of *Customer ID*, click the *magnifying glass* icon and then click *Parker-03* in the drop-down list of customers, as shown in Figure 6–30.

FIGURE 6–30
Parker-03 Selected from Drop-Down List of Customers

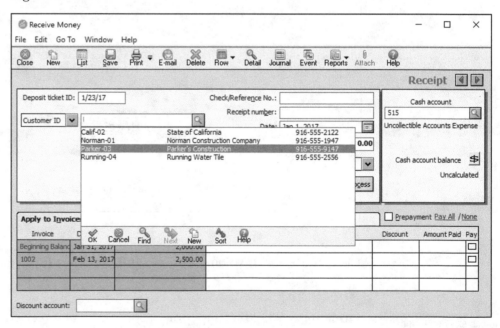

Step 5:

Key **1080** (the check number) in the *Check/Reference No.* field.

Step 6:

Click the *calendar* icon and choose *Jan 23, 2017* in the *Date* field.

Step 7:

Click *Check* in the *Payment Method* field and *Cash (100)* in the *Cash Account* field.

*Note: If you do not see available account numbers in the Cash Account field or the Discount Account field at the bottom of the window, click Options on the Menu bar, and then **Global** in the drop-down list. With the Accounting tab selected, remove the check mark in front of Accounts Receivable (Quotes, Sales Orders, Invoicing, Credit Memos, Receipts).*

Step 8:

Key **100.00** in the *Discount* field aligned with Invoice 1002. Press the Enter key.

Step 9:

The amount of 2,400.00 will appear in the *Amount Paid* field. Press the Enter key. A check mark will appear in the *Pay* field, as shown in Figure 6–31.

FIGURE 6–31
Pay Field Selected for Invoice 1002

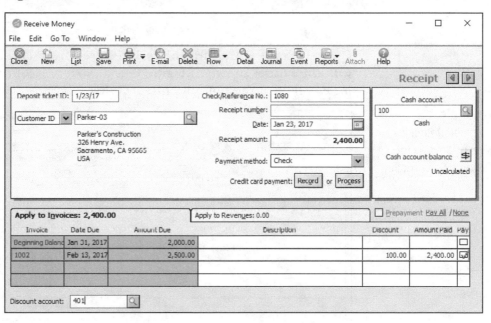

HINT

Remember that if you click the Recalculate button ($), the new cash balance will appear in the *Cash account balance* field.

Step 10:

Click the Journal button on the Receive Money toolbar.

Step 11:

Click in the *Account No.* field, click the *magnifying glass* icon, and then click *401*. This is the account that is used for recording sales discounts. Your screen should look like Figure 6–32.

FIGURE 6–32
Accounting Behind the Screens Window with Sales Discount Account (401) Entered

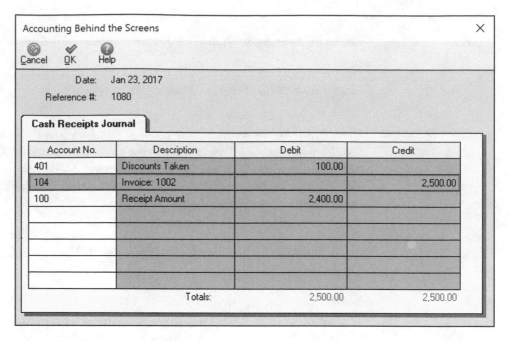

Step 12:
Click OK.

Step 13:
Compare your entries for the cash received from Parker's Construction with the entries shown in Figure 6–33. Make note of *401* in the *Discount account* field at the bottom of the window.

FIGURE 6–33
Completed Receive Money Window for Parker's Construction

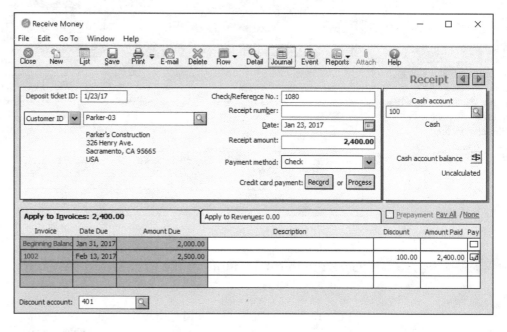

Step 14:
Click Save.

Step 15:

Click the List button on the Receive Money toolbar to view the Receipt List dialog box, and then select *This Period* in the *Date Range* field. Compare your screen with Figure 6–34. If any corrections are needed, you can select and then edit the transaction.

FIGURE 6–34
Receipt List Dialog Box

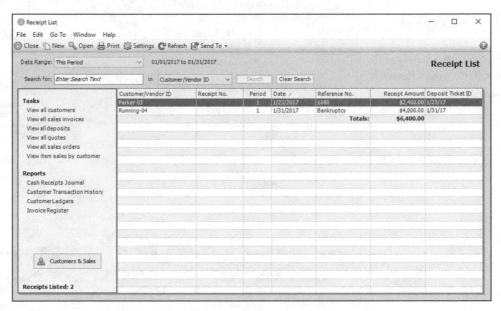

Step 16:

Click Close if no corrections are required.

Step 17:

Close the Receive Money window.

Checkpoint 6–3

1. What is an invoice?
2. The cash receipts module of Sage 50 is used for what task?

Objective 6–3 Practice

In Chapter 4, you created customer accounts for Meadowland Healthcare Services. In this chapter, you will issue invoices and record cash received from a customer.

Step 1:

Open Chp. 6 – Meadowland Healthcare Services, which you updated previously in the chapter.

Step 2:

Print invoices for the following customers:

- Good Samaritan Hospital, Invoice 1102
- Rapid Medical Response, Invoice 1103
- Valley Response, Invoice 1104

Your printouts should look like Figures 6–35, 6–36, and 6–37.

FIGURE 6–35

Good Samaritan Hospital, Invoice 1102

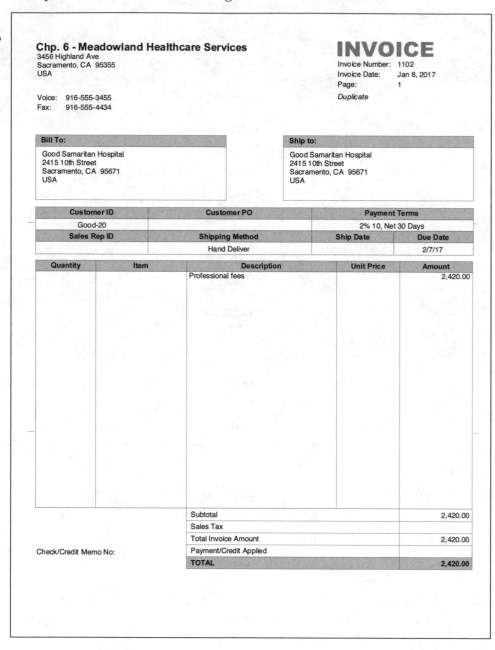

FIGURE 6–36
Rapid Medical Response,
Invoice 1103

Chp. 6 - Meadowland Healthcare Services
3456 Highland Ave
Sacramento, CA 95355
USA

Voice: 916-555-3455
Fax: 916-555-4434

INVOICE

Invoice Number: 1103
Invoice Date: Jan 19, 2017
Page: 1

Duplicate

Bill To:	Ship to:
Rapid Medical Response 2516 Main Street Sacramento, CA 95671 USA	Rapid Medical Response 2516 Main Street Sacramento, CA 95671 USA

Customer ID	Customer PO	Payment Terms	
Rapid-30		2% 10, Net 30 Days	
Sales Rep ID	**Shipping Method**	**Ship Date**	**Due Date**
	US Mail		2/18/17

Quantity	Item	Description	Unit Price	Amount
48.00		Professional fees	120.00	5,760.00
		Subtotal		5,760.00
		Sales Tax		
		Total Invoice Amount		5,760.00
Check/Credit Memo No:		Payment/Credit Applied		
		TOTAL		**5,760.00**

FIGURE 6–37

Valley Response, Invoice
1104

Chp. 6 - Meadowland Healthcare Services
3456 Highland Ave
Sacramento, CA 95355
USA

INVOICE

Invoice Number:	1104
Invoice Date:	Jan 29, 2017
Page:	1

Duplicate

Voice: 916-555-3455
Fax: 916-555-4434

Bill To:	Ship to:
Valley Response 3211 Main Street Sacramento, CA 95761 USA	Valley Response 3211 Main Street Sacramento, CA 95761 USA

Customer ID	Customer PO	Payment Terms	
Valley-40		2% 10, Net 30 Days	
Sales Rep ID	**Shipping Method**	**Ship Date**	**Due Date**
	Hand Deliver		2/28/17

Quantity	Item	Description	Unit Price	Amount
		Monthly professional fees		1,650.00

Subtotal		1,650.00
Sales Tax		
Total Invoice Amount		1,650.00
Payment/Credit Applied		825.00
TOTAL		**825.00**

Check/Credit Memo No: 1104

Step 3:

Meadowland Healthcare Services does not have a Sales Discount account. Use the following information to create this general ledger account:

Account ID:	**40100**
Description:	**Sales Discount**
Account Type:	**Income**

Step 4:

On January 28, 2017, received $5,644.80 from Rapid Medical Response, Check 3240. This check is for Invoice 1103 ($5,760) less a 2% discount ($115.20). Record the transaction. (Remember to enter the sales discount account that you created in Step 3.) Make sure that *Check* and *10200* are selected in the *Payment Method* and *Cash Account* fields, respectively.

Step 5:

Print the Customer Ledgers report. Your printout should look like Figure 6–38.

9/11/16 at 17:40:49.10	*****EDUCATIONAL VERSION ONLY*****					Page: 1

Chp. 6 - Meadowland Healthcare Services
Customer Ledgers
For the Period From Jan 1, 2017 to Jan 31, 2017
Filter Criteria includes: Report order is by ID. Report is printed in Detail Format.

Customer ID Customer	Date	Trans No	Type	Debit Amt	Credit Amt	Balance
Doctor's-10	1/2/17	1101	SJ	12,000.00		12,000.00
Doctor's Medical Center	1/31/17	Bankruptcy	CRJ		12,000.00	0.00
Good-20	1/8/17	1102	SJ	2,420.00		2,420.00
Good Samaritan Hospital						
Rapid-30	1/19/17	1103	SJ	5,760.00		5,760.00
Rapid Medical Response	1/28/17	1103	CRJ	115.20	115.20	5,760.00
	1/28/17	1103	CRJ		5,760.00	0.00
Valley-40	1/29/17	1104	SJ	1,650.00		1,650.00
Valley Response	1/29/17	1104	CRJ		825.00	825.00
Report Total				**21,945.20**	**18,700.20**	**3,245.00**

Step 6:

Close the Select a Report or Form dialog box.

OBJECTIVE 6–4

Prepare a Reconciliation of the Checking Account

Every month, a business receives a ***bank statement*** that shows all transactions that occurred in connection with its checking account. The bank statement lists the following information:

bank statement
A listing of all transactions that occurred in a checking account during a month and the beginning and ending balances.

- The beginning balance for the period
- All deposits received by the bank and added to the balance
- Other items added to the balance such as the proceeds from promissory notes collected for the business by the bank
- All checks paid by the bank and deducted from the balance
- Other items deducted from the balance such as bank service charges
- The ending balance for the period

A business that has efficient cash control procedures will promptly reconcile the bank statement with its own cash records, known as a ***bank reconciliation.***

bank reconciliation
Bringing the ending balances of the bank statement and the firm's own cash records into agreement.

The ending balance on the bank statement will almost always differ from the ending balance in the firm's checkbook and Cash account. The reconciliation process involves finding the factors that are causing the difference and bringing the balances into agreement.

Some of the factors that may cause a difference between the ending bank statement balance and the ending balance in a firm's cash records are as follows:

- Deposits in transit—deposits made by the firm and listed in its cash records that do not appear on the bank statement.
- Outstanding checks—checks issued by the firm and listed in its cash records that have not yet been paid by the bank.

- ATM deposits and withdrawals—deposits and withdrawals made by automatic teller machines that appear on the bank statement but may not yet be listed in the firm's cash records.
- Bank fees—service charges and other bank fees that appear on the bank statement but may not yet be listed in the firm's cash records.
- NSF checks—customer checks that were deposited but have been returned by the bank because of insufficient funds. (NSF means "non-sufficient funds.")
- Errors—errors made by the bank that appear on the bank statement or errors made by the firm in its cash records.

The accountant must examine the bank statement and the firm's cash records to find the factors causing the difference between the two ending balances. The accountant then prepares a bank reconciliation statement such as the one shown below.

ACME Computer Repair
Bank Reconciliation Statement

Ending Bank Statement Balance		$36,800
Add:		
Deposits in Transit	$ 2,000	
Bank Errors	100	2,100
		$38,900
Deduct:		
Outstanding Checks	$ 4,400	
Bank Errors	200	4,600
Adjusted Bank Statement Balance		$34,300
Ending Cash Account/Checkbook Balance		$31,500
Add:		
Bank Collections	$ 5,000	
ATM Deposits	1,000	
Errors	300	6,300
		$37,800
Deduct:		
NSF Checks	$ 400	
Errors	150	
ATM Withdrawals	2,900	
Bank Fees	50	3,500
Adjusted Cash Account/Checkbook Balance		$34,300

Sage 50 allows you to automate this task of preparing a bank reconciliation statement. To prepare for the bank reconciliation process for Superior Carpet and Tile, use the Report function of Sage 50 to obtain information about the firm's cash receipts/bank deposits and checks issued.

Reviewing/Printing the Cash Receipts Journal

Step 1:

Open Chp. 6 – Superior Carpet and Tile, which you updated previously in the chapter. Click Reports & Forms and then click *Accounts Receivable.*

Step 2:

The Select a Report or Form dialog box will appear. At the Accounts Receivable: Customer and Sales section, click *Cash Receipts Journal,* as shown in Figure 6–39.

FIGURE 6–39
Accounts Receivable: Customers and Sales Section with Cash Receipts Journal Chosen

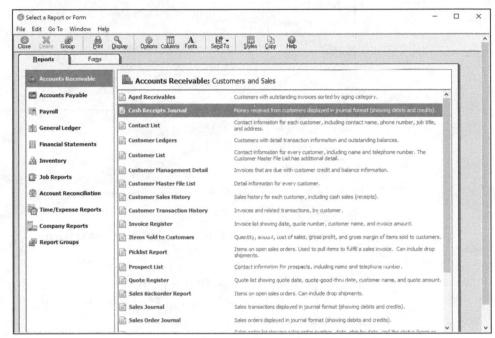

Step 3:

Click the <u>P</u>rint button on the Select a Report or Form toolbar.

Step 4:

Click *Check Date* from the drop-down list in the *Sort by* field.

Step 5:

Select *Cash Account ID* from the *Select a filter* list.

Step 6:

Select the *Equal to* button and click *100, Cash* from the drop-down list of chart of accounts.

Step 7:

Click *Range* in the *Date* field, *Jan 1, 2017* in the *From* field, and *Jan 31, 2017* in the *To* field. Compare your Modify Report – Cash Receipts Journal dialog box with Figure 6–40. Make any changes as necessary.

FIGURE 6–40

Modify Report – Cash
Receipts Journal Dialog
Box

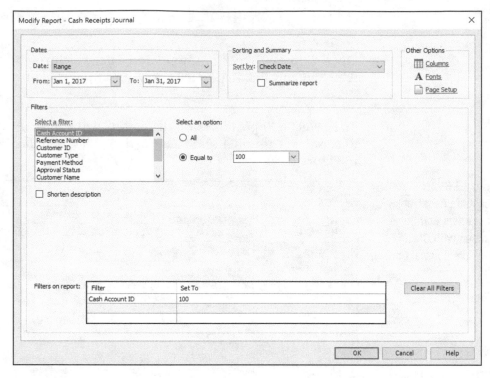

Step 8:

Click OK. Then click OK again at the Print screen.

Step 9:

Compare your printout of the Cash Receipts Journal for Superior Carpet
and Tile with the one shown in Figure 6–41.

FIGURE 6–41

Printout of Cash
Receipts Journal

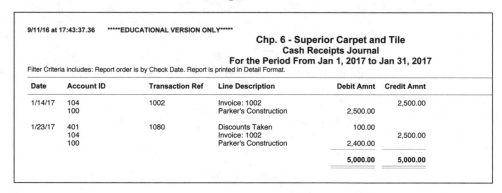

Reviewing/Printing the Check Register

Step 1:

At the Select a Report or Form dialog box, in the Reports tab list, click
Accounts Payable.

Step 2:

At the Accounts Payable: Vendors and Purchases section, click *Check
Register,* as shown in Figure 6–42.

FIGURE 6–42

Accounts Payable: Vendors and Purchases Section with Check Register Chosen

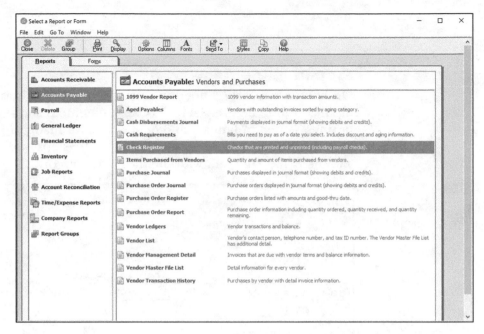

Step 3:
Click the Options button on the Select a Report or Form toolbar.

Step 4:
At the Modify Report – Check Register window, select the following:

Sort by:	**Check Number**
Select a Filter:	**Cash Account ID**
Equal to:	**Account 100, Cash**
Date:	**Range**
From:	**Jan 1, 2017**
To:	**Jan 31, 2017**

Step 5:
Click OK. Then click Print on the Check Register toolbar.

Step 6:
Compare your printout of the Check Register for Superior Carpet and Tile with the one shown in Figure 6–43.

FIGURE 6–43

Printout of Check Register

9/11/16 at 17:45:37.98   *****EDUCATIONAL VERSION ONLY*****   Page: 1

Chp. 6 - Superior Carpet and Tile
Check Register
For the Period From Jan 1, 2017 to Jan 31, 2017

Filter Criteria includes: Report order is by Check Number.

Check #	Date	Payee	Cash Account	Amount
2004	1/31/17	Apex Floor Care Serv	100	250.00
2005	1/31/17	Office Max	100	1,372.00
2006	1/31/17	John Charles Manag	100	3,000.00
2007	1/31/17	Pacific Bell	100	765.39
2008	1/31/17	MID Midtown Irrigatio	100	676.65
Total				**6,064.04**

Step 7:

Close the Select a Report or Form dialog box.

Preparing the Account Reconciliation

On February 8, 2017, Superior Carpet and Tile received the bank statement shown in Figure 6–44. This bank statement shows checks that the business issued in January and deposits that it made in January. The bank paid the checks early in February. Follow the steps outlined below to reconcile the bank statement with the firm's cash records.

FIGURE 6–44
Bank Statement for Superior Carpet and Tile

Bank of California 2346 Center Way Fresno, CA 94534					

Superior Carpet and Tile
Acct: 2341121

REGULAR CHECKING

Previous Balance	$ 20,000.00	**Statement Date: January 31, 2017**
2 Deposits (+)	4,900.00	
4 Checks (-)	5,298.65	
2 Other Deductions (-)	150.00	
Service (-)	20.00	
Ending Balance	19,431.35	

DEPOSITS

January 14, 2017	$ 2,500.00				
January 23, 2017	2,400.00				

CHECKS (Asterisk* indicates break in check number sequence)

January 31, 2017	2005	$ 1,372.00			
January 31, 2017	2006	3,000.00			
January 31, 2017	2008	676.65			
January 31, 2017	2004*	250.00			
January 31, 2017	Bank Fees	20.00			

OTHER DEDUCTIONS (ATM's)

January 16, 2017	ATM	$ 50.00			
January 21, 2017	ATM	100.00			

Step 1:

Click Tasks and then click *Account Reconciliation*.

Step 2:

Click the *magnifying glass* icon next to the *Account to Reconcile* field and then click *100* (the number of the Cash account) in the drop-down list.

Step 3:

At the *Statement Date* field, choose *Jan 31, 2017*.

Step 4:

Click in the *Status* field for each check that is listed on Superior's bank statement to display a blue check mark, which designates that the check has cleared. (See Figure 6–45.) Remember to check off only the cleared checks (the checks paid by the bank).

Step 5:

Compare your work with Figure 6–45. Check 2007 should not be check marked because it did not clear the bank.

Step 6:

Click to insert a blue check mark in the *Status* field for each of the deposits listed on the bank statement.

FIGURE 6–45
Account Reconciliation Window – Cleared Checks

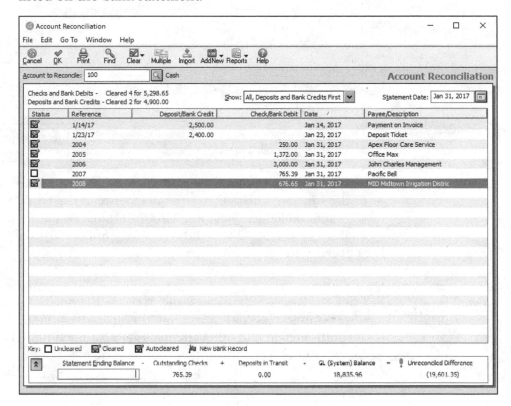

Step 7:

Key **19,431.35** in the *Statement Ending Balance* field, as shown in Figure 6–46, and then press the Enter key.

FIGURE 6–46
Account Reconciliation
Window – Statement
Ending Balance

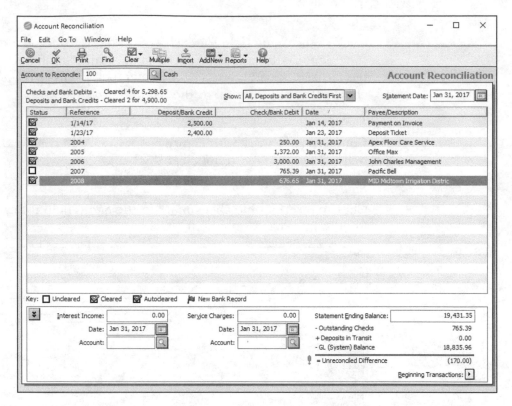

There is an unreconciled difference of (170.00) listed at the bottom of the window. This is the difference between the bank balance and the GL (general ledger) balance. This difference results from a bank service charge ($20) and ATM withdrawals ($50 and $100) that Superior has not yet recorded in its cash records.

Step 8:

Click the AddNew button on the Account Reconciliation toolbar and select General Journal Entry from the drop-down menu to create the new account needed and enter the necessary transactions. The General Journal Entry window will appear, as shown in Figure 6–47.

FIGURE 6–47
General Journal Entry
Window

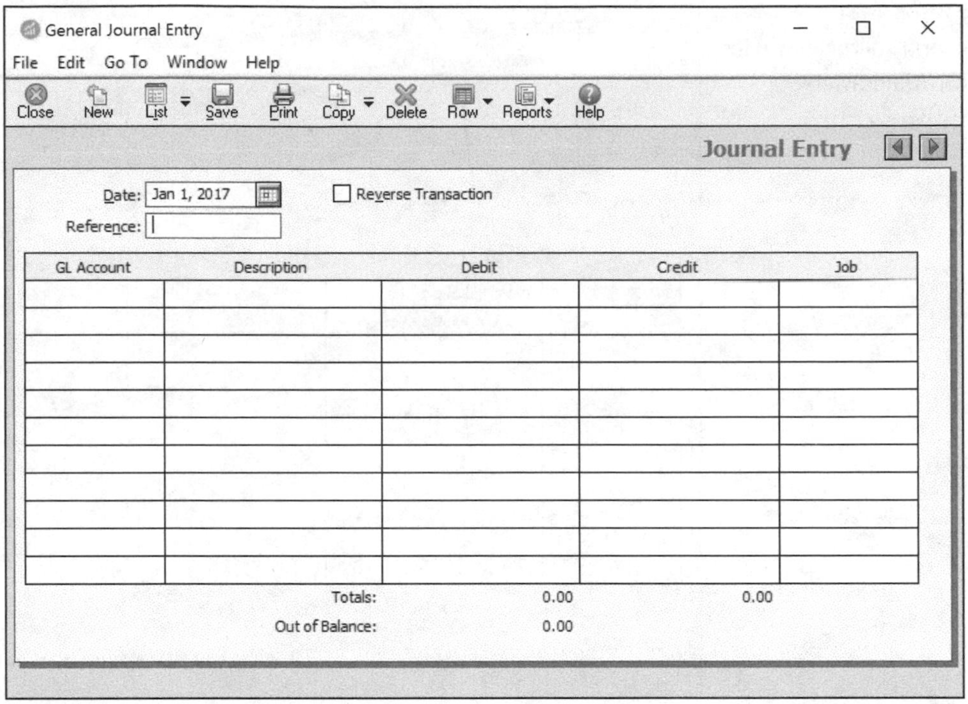

Step 9:

Key **01/16/17** in the *Date* field.

Step 10:

Key **Stmnt 1/31** in the *Reference* field.

Step 11:

Key **301.5 (Drawing)** in the *GL Account* field.

Step 12:

Key **ATM Withdrawals** in the *Description* field.

Step 13:

Key **50.00** in the *Debit* field. This represents the personal withdrawal from the ATM.

Step 14:

Key **100 (Cash)** in the next *GL Account* field. The system should automatically add "ATM Withdrawals" on each description line until the entire entry is saved.

Step 15:

Key **50.00** in the *Credit* field.

Step 16:

Compare your entries with the one shown in Figure 6–48.

FIGURE 6–48
General Journal Entry for
ATM Withdrawals

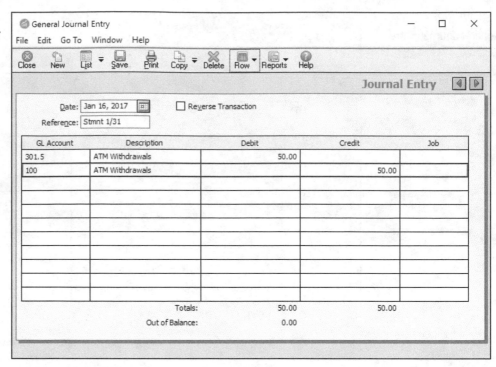

Step 17:
Click Save on the General Journal Entry toolbar.

Step 18:
Key **01/21/17** in the *Date* field and **Stmnt 1/31** in the *Reference* field.

Step 19:
Key **301.5 (Drawing)** in the *GL Account* field.

Step 20:
Key **ATM Withdrawals** in the *Description* field.

Step 21:
Key **100.00** in the *Debit* field. This represents the second personal withdrawal from the ATM.

Step 22:
Key **100 (Cash)** in the next *GL Account* field. The system should automatically add "ATM Withdrawals" on each description line until the entire entry is saved.

Step 23:
Key **100.00** in the *Credit* field.

Step 24:
Click Save and then close the General Journal Entry window.

Step 25:
Click the *Status* field to enter a blue check mark next to the ATM Withdrawals of $50.00 and $100.00 listed in the Account Reconciliation window.

Step 26:

Key **20.00** in the *Service Charges* field at the bottom of the screen.

Step 27:

Click Maintain and then Chart of Accounts on the Menu bar to create the following account:

Account ID:	**520**
Description:	**Bank Fee Expense**
Account Type:	**Expenses**

Click Save and then close the Maintain Chart of Accounts dialog box.

Step 28:

Click *Account 520, Bank Fee Expense,* after clicking the *magnifying glass* icon next to the *Account* field.

Step 29:

After checking off the ATM withdrawals and entering the service charge and the account number, review Figure 6–49 for accuracy.

FIGURE 6–49
Account Reconciliation Window with Adjustments Cleared

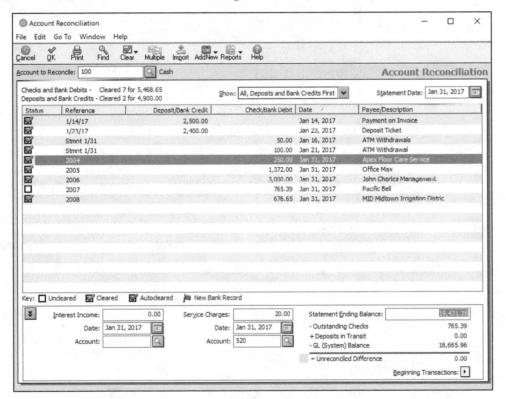

The account reconciliation is now in balance. The unreconciled difference at the bottom of the window is 0.00.

Step 30:

Click OK.

Printing the Account Reconciliation

It is good policy to print a copy of the account reconciliation and keep it on file with the bank statement.

Step 1:

Click Reports & Forms and then click *Account Reconciliation*.

Step 2:

At the Select a Report or Form dialog box, in the Account Reconciliation: Banking Transactions section, click *Account Reconciliation,* as shown in Figure 6–50.

FIGURE 6–50
Account Reconciliation: Banking Transactions Section with Account Reconciliation Chosen

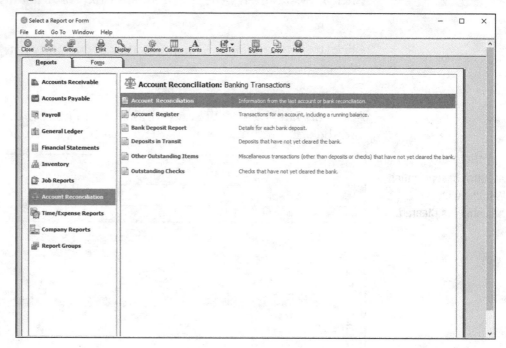

Step 3:

Click the Print button on the Select a Report or Form toolbar.

Step 4:

Select the following filter information:

GL Account ID:	**100**
As of:	**Period 1, (1/31/17)**

Step 5:

Click OK. Then click OK again at the Print window.

Step 6:

Compare your printout with the one shown in Figure 6–51.

FIGURE 6–51
Account Reconciliation for Superior Carpet and Tile

```
9/11/16 at 17:56:38.35    *****EDUCATIONAL VERSION ONLY*****                              Page: 1
                            Chp. 6 - Superior Carpet and Tile
                                 Account Reconciliation
                                   As of Jan 31, 2017
                                      100 - Cash
                          Bank Statement Date: January 31, 2017
Filter Criteria includes: Report is printed in Detail Format.
```

Beginning GL Balance			
Add: Cash Receipts		4,900.00	
Less: Cash Disbursements		(6,064.04)	
Add (Less) Other		19,830.00	
Ending GL Balance		18,665.96	
Ending Bank Balance		19,431.35	
Add back deposits in transit			
Total deposits in transit			
(Less) outstanding checks	Jan 31, 2017 2007	(765.39)	
Total outstanding checks		(765.39)	
Add (Less) Other			
Total other			
Unreconciled difference		0.00	
Ending GL Balance		18,665.96	

Step 7:

Close the Select a Report or Form dialog box.

Checkpoint 6–4

1. What is the purpose of the bank reconciliation process?
2. Name six factors that can cause a difference between the bank statement balance and the Cash account/checkbook balance.

Objective 6–4 Practice

Meadowland Healthcare Services received the bank statement shown in Figure 6–52 for the month ended January 31, 2017. Use the following steps to prepare a bank reconciliation.

FIGURE 6–52
Bank Statement for
Meadowland Healthcare
Services

Bank of California
2121 Market Street
San Francisco, CA 95434

Meadowland Healthcare Services
    Acct: 20000897

REGULAR CHECKING

Previous Balance	$ 25,000.00	Statement Date: January 31, 2017
2 Deposits (+)	6,469.80	
3 Checks (-)	2,338.18	
2 Other Deductions (-)	150.00	
Service (-)	35.00	
Ending Balance	28,946.62	

DEPOSITS

January 28, 2017	$ 5,644.80				
January 29, 2017	825.00				

CHECKS (Asterisk* indicates break in check number sequence)

January 27, 2017	700	$ 872.20				
January 31, 2017	701	1,200.00				
January 31, 2017	703*	265.98				
January 31, 2017	Bank Fees	35.00				

OTHER DEDUCTIONS (ATM's)

January 16, 2017	ATM	$ 50.00			
January 21, 2017	ATM	100.00			

Step 1:

Open Chp. 6 – Meadowland Healthcare Services, which you updated previously in the chapter.

Step 2:

Print the Check Register. Your printout should look like Figure 6–53.

FIGURE 6–53
Check Register
for Meadowland
Healthcare Services

9/11/16 at 17:58:08.67   *****EDUCATIONAL VERSION ONLY*****   Page: 1
Chp. 6 - Meadowland Healthcare Services
Check Register
For the Period From Jan 1, 2017 to Jan 31, 2017
Filter Criteria includes: Report order is by Date.

Check #	Date	Payee	Cash Account	Amount
700	1/27/17	Office Depot	10200	872.20
701	1/31/17	Alta Vista Business P	10200	1,200.00
702	1/31/17	Pacific Gas & Electric	10200	345.89
703	1/31/17	General Telephone	10200	265.98
704	1/31/17	Merry Maids	10200	650.00
Total				3,334.07

Step 3:

Print the Cash Receipts Journal. Your printout should look like Figure 6–54.

FIGURE 6–54
FIGURE 6–54
Cash Receipts Journal for Meadowland Healthcare Services

Date	Account ID	Transaction Ref	Line Description	Debit Amnt	Credit Amnt
1/28/17	40100	1103	Discounts Taken	115.20	
	11000		Invoice: 1103		5,760.00
	10200		Rapid Medical Response	5,644.80	
1/29/17	11000	1104	Invoice: 1104		825.00
	10200		Valley Response	825.00	
1/31/17	11000	Bankruptcy	Invoice: 1101		12,000.00
	62000		Doctor's Medical Center	12,000.00	
				18,585.00	18,585.00

9/11/16 at 17:58:41.40 *****EDUCATIONAL VERSION ONLY***** Page: 1
Chp. 6 - Meadowland Healthcare Services
Cash Receipts Journal
For the Period From Jan 1, 2017 to Jan 31, 2017
Filter Criteria includes: Report order is by Check Date. Report is printed in Detail Format.

Step 4:

Prepare the account reconciliation of *10200 (Regular Checking Account)*. Use the information from the check register, the cash receipts journal, and the bank statement.

Step 5:

Print the Account Reconciliation report. Your report should look like Figure 6–55.

FIGURE 6–55
Account Reconciliation for Meadowland Healthcare Services

9/11/16 at 18:04:00.13 *****EDUCATIONAL VERSION ONLY***** Page: 1
Chp. 6 - Meadowland Healthcare Services
Account Reconciliation
As of Jan 31, 2017
10200 - Regular Checking Account
Bank Statement Date: January 31, 2017
Filter Criteria includes: Report is printed in Detail Format.

Beginning GL Balance				
Add: Cash Receipts				6,469.80
Less: Cash Disbursements				(3,334.07)
Add (Less) Other				24,815.00
Ending GL Balance				27,950.73
Ending Bank Balance				28,946.62
Add back deposits in transit				
Total deposits in transit				
(Less) outstanding checks	Jan 31, 2017	702	(345.89)	
	Jan 31, 2017	704	(650.00)	
Total outstanding checks				(995.89)
Add (Less) Other				
Total other				
Unreconciled difference				0.00
Ending GL Balance				27,950.73

Step 6:

Close the Select a Report or Form dialog box.

Chapter Review and Assessment

Software Command Summary

Cash Payments on Account	Tasks, Payments, Vendor ID, Apply to Invoices
Cash Payments without Invoice	Tasks, Payments, Vendor ID, Apply to Expenses
Cash Receipts on Account	Tasks, Receive Money, Customer ID, Apply to Invoices
Cash Receipts without Invoice	Tasks, Receive Money, Customer ID, Apply to Revenues
Prepare an Account Reconciliation	Print Cash Receipts Journal, Print Check Register, Tasks, Account Reconciliation, AddNew

Checkpoint Answers

Checkpoint 6–1

1. The funds on hand may include not only currency and coin but also cash equivalents such as checks and money orders.
2. To protect their cash, businesses can make all payments by check, avoid keeping large amounts of cash on the premises, use a locked safe or cash drawer, record cash transactions promptly, reconcile the monthly bank statement with the firm's internal cash records, and divide responsibility.

Checkpoint 6–2

1. The cash payments module of Sage 50 is used to record payments to vendors and issue the necessary checks.
2. Sage 50 automatically enters a check number for the check being printed and all subsequent checks.

Checkpoint 6–3

1. An invoice is a bill for goods or services sold to a customer.
2. The cash receipts module is used to record amounts received from customers.

Checkpoint 6–4

1. The purpose of the bank reconciliation process is to bring the ending bank statement balance and the ending Cash account/ checkbook balance into agreement.
2. Six factors that can cause a difference between the balances are deposits in transit, outstanding checks, unrecorded ATM deposits and withdrawals, bank fees, NSF checks, and errors.

Study Quizzes

Take the study quiz online to check your understanding of chapter concepts. The quiz can be taken multiple times.

Content Check

Multiple Choice: Choose only one response for each question.

1. What button within the Receive Money window is used to compute the new balance of the Cash account?
   A. Open
   B. Row
   C. Journal
   D. Recalculate
   E. Save

2. To verify that the correct accounts have been debited and credited, what toolbar button would you use to view the Accounting Behind the Screens window?
   A. Open
   B. Event
   C. Journal
   D. Row
   E. Save

3. Which of the following would provide the most useful information needed for the cash account reconciliation?
   A. Aged Payables
   B. Sales Journal
   C. Check Register
   D. Purchases Journal
   E. Vendor List

4. What toolbar button in the Account Reconciliation dialog box is used to enter withdrawals and other items that must be recorded to update the balance of the firm's Cash account?
   A. Range
   B. AddNew
   C. Multiple
   D. Import
   E. Recur

5. When a business provides a service on credit to a customer, what function of Sage 50 is used to record the transaction?
   A. General Journal Entry
   B. Payments
   C. Purchases/Receive Inventory
   D. Receive Money
   E. Sales/Invoicing

Short Essay Response

Provide a detailed answer for each question.

1. What are some of the procedures that a business should use to protect its cash?
2. What is the purpose of an account reconciliation?
3. What is the purpose of the Accounting Behind the Screens window?
4. What information appears on the bank statement?
5. Why do the ending balance of the bank statement and the ending balance in a firm's cash records usually differ?
6. What information from a firm's records is needed for the account reconciliation?

Cooperative Learning

1. Form a group of three or four students. As a group, examine the Cash Flow Manager and Collection Manager features of Sage 50. These features can be located by accessing Analysis on the Menu bar. Discuss how these features can be used to help a business meet its financial obligations and increase its collection of accounts receivable.
2. As a group, select a local business that you are familiar with, such as a fast-food restaurant, a supermarket, or a department store. What type of cash control problems might this business have? What procedures could this business use to protect its cash?

Writing and Decision Making

Assume that you work for a small company that has a substantial volume of cash receipts from credit customers and cash payments to vendors. The owner, Jesse Ramirez, is thinking about buying Sage 50 for her accounting system. Because you have had experience with Sage 50 in a college course, she asks you to provide her with information about the Sage 50 procedures for the tasks listed below. Write a memo that provides information on the following tasks:

1. Setting up customer accounts and vendor accounts
2. Recording credit sales and credit purchases
3. Recording cash receipts and cash payments on account

Case Problems

Demonstrate your knowledge of the Sage 50 features discussed in this chapter by completing the following case problems.

Case Problem 6–1A

Open Transnational Management Group (TMG), a business consulting firm, which is located in the student data files.

1. TMG plans to make credit purchases from four new vendors. Create new vendor accounts for the businesses listed below.

Vendor

Vendor ID:	**OPS-01**
Name:	**O'Neal Payroll Services**

General Tab

Contact:	**Annette O'Neal**
Account Number:	**846357**
Mailing Address:	**7314 Sycamore Avenue**
City, ST, Zip:	**Stockton, CA 95210**
Country:	**USA**
Vendor Type:	**Expense**
1099 Type:	**None**
Expense Account:	**78500 (Payroll Services Expense)**
Telephone 1:	**209-555-7821**
Fax:	**209-555-7823**

Purchase Info Tab

Tax ID Number:	**None**
Ship Via:	**US Mail**
Terms and Credit:	**Due EOM, 0.00 Discount**

History Tab

Beginning Balance:	**0**

Vendor

Vendor ID:	**GR-02**
Name:	**Grupe Associates**

General Tab

Contact:	**Gary Robertson**
Account Number:	**164325**
Mailing Address:	**4189 Holly Lane**
City, ST, Zip:	**Stockton, CA 95210**
Country:	**USA**
Vendor Type:	**Expense**
1099 Type:	**None**
Expense Account:	**74000 (Rent or Lease Expense)**
Telephone 1:	**209-555-7321**
Fax:	**209-555-7325**

Purchase Info Tab

Tax ID Number:	**None**
Ship Via:	**US Mail**
Terms and Credit:	**Due EOM, 0.00 Discount**

History Tab

Beginning Balance:	**0**

Vendor

Vendor ID:	**OFFMAX-03**
Name:	**Office Max**

General Tab

Contact:	**Joshua Baker**
Account Number:	**154913**
Mailing Address:	**3915 Webber Lane**
City, ST, Zip:	**Stockton, CA 95207**
Country:	**USA**
Vendor Type:	**Supplier**
1099 Type:	**None**
Expense Account:	**12000 (Office Supplies)**
Telephone 1:	**209-555-7981**
Fax:	**209-555-7988**

Purchase Info Tab

Tax ID Number:	**None**
Ship Via:	**Fed-EX**
Terms and Credit:	**2% 10 days, net 30 days**

History Tab

Beginning Balance:	**0**

Vendor

Vendor ID:	**ATT-04**
Name:	**AT&T**

General Tab

Contact:	**George Sanchez**
Account Number:	**198526**
Mailing Address:	**6185 West Montgomery Avenue**
City, ST, Zip:	**Stockton, CA 95207**
Country:	**USA**
Vendor Type:	**Expense**
1099 Type:	**None**
Expense Account:	**76000 (Telephone Expense)**
Telephone 1:	**209-555-5461**
Fax:	**209-555-5463**

Purchase Info Tab

Tax ID Number:	**None**
Ship Via:	**US Mail**
Terms and Credit:	**Due EOM, 0.00 Discount**

History Tab

Beginning Balance:	**0**

2. TMG plans to sell its services on credit to the following three new customers. Create new customer accounts for each.

Customer

Customer ID:	**LM-01**
Name:	**Lee Manufacturing**

General Tab

Account Number:	**1731**
Billing Address:	**4639 Lincoln Boulevard**
City, ST, Zip:	**Stockton, CA 95210**
Country:	**USA**
Customer Type:	**General**
Telephone 1:	**209-555-1320**
Fax:	**209-555-1330**

Contacts Tab

Contact:	**Robert Lee**

Sales Info Tab

GL Sales Account:	**40000**
Ship Via:	**Fed-EX**
Pricing Level:	**Price Level 1**
Form Options:	**Default**

Payment & Credit Tab

Terms and Credit:	**2% 10 days, net 30 days**

History Tab

Beginning Balance:	**0**

Customer

Customer ID:	**CD-02**
Name:	**Computer Designs**

General Tab

Account Number:	**1450**
Billing Address:	**4819 East Powell**
City, ST, Zip:	**Tracy, CA 95376**
Country:	**USA**
Customer Type:	**General**
Telephone 1:	**209-555-2083**
Fax:	**209-555-2085**

Contacts Tab

    Contact: Sylvia Harrison

Sales Info Tab

    GL Sales Account: 40000
    Ship Via: Fed-EX
    Pricing Level: Price Level 1
    Form Options: Default

Payment & Credit Tab

    Terms and Credit: 2% 10 days, net 30 days

History Tab

    Beginning Balance: 0

Customer

    Customer ID: BAS-03
    Name: Barron's Accounting Services

General Tab

    Account Number: 1426
    Billing Address: 4413 21st Street
    City, ST, Zip: Watsonville, CA 95760
    Country: USA
    Customer Type: General
    Telephone 1:   209-555-3621
    Fax: 209-555-3635

Contacts Tab

    Contact: Armando Barron

Sales Info Tab

    GL Sales Account: 40000
    Ship Via: Fed-EX
    Pricing Level: Price Level 1
    Form Options: Default

Payment & Credit Tab

    Terms and Credit: 2% 10 days, net 30 days

History Tab

    Beginning Balance: 0

3. Enter each of the transactions listed below for April 2017. Choose the appropriate option on the Tasks menu: Sales/Invoicing, Purchases/ Receive Inventory, Receive Money, or Payments. Use Account 49000, Fee Discounts for any discounts taken by customers.

Date	Transaction
Apr. 4	Received a bill (Invoice 9582) of $1,780 for monthly rent from Grupe Associates.
5	Performed consulting services for $1,600 on credit for Lee Manufacturing. Issued Invoice 3001.
6	Received a bill (Invoice 12852) of $275 for monthly usage of telephone service from AT&T.
6	Purchased office supplies for $350 on credit from Office Max. Received Invoice 6640.
9	Performed consulting services for $980 on credit for Barron's Accounting Services. Issued Invoice 3002.
9	Performed consulting services for Computer Designs for $1,800 in cash, Check No. 1215.
14	Received the amount due for Invoice 3001 from Lee Manufacturing, less a 2% discount, Check No. 3291.
15	Paid the amount due for Invoice 6640 to Office Max, less a 2% discount. Issued Check No. 1020. (Use Account 12000, Office Supplies as the discount account.)
18	Purchased payroll services for $650 on credit from O'Neal Payroll Services. Received Invoice 1593.
24	Received the full amount due for Invoice 3002 from Barron's Accounting Services, Check No. 3145.
25	Performed consulting services for $785 on credit for Computer Designs. Issued Invoice 3003. Received check for $225 from the customer (Check No. 1230).
30	Paid $1,780 on account to Grupe Associates. Issued Check No. 1021.
30	Paid $275 on account to AT&T. Issued Check No. 1022.
30	Received the balance due (Check No. 1265) for Invoice 3003 from Computer Designs less a 2% discount on the total of the invoice ($785 × 0.02 = $15.70).

4. Print the following reports for April: Customer Ledgers, Cash Receipts Journal, Vendor Ledgers, Cash Disbursements Journal, and General Ledger Trial Balance.

Case Problem 6–2A

Open Chao and Associates, an engineering company, which is located in the student data files.

This firm received the following bank statement for the month ended June 30, 2017:

1. Prepare an account reconciliation. Bring the ending balances of the firm's bank statement and regular checking account into agreement.
2. Print an Account Reconciliation report.

		Bank of San Joaquin
		2876 Main Street
		Tracy, CA 95376
Chao and Associates		
Account No: 87942331		
REGULAR CHECKING		
Beginning Balance	$24,900.00	**Statement Date: June 30, 2017**
2 Deposits (+)	9,900.00	
4 Checks (-)	9,257.50	
2 Other Deductions (-)	300.00	
Service Charges (-)	40.00	
Ending Balance	25,202.50	
DEPOSITS		
June 14, 2017	$5,000.00	
June 23, 2017	4,900.00	
CHECKS AND BANK FEES (Asterisk* indicates break in check number sequence)					
June 20, 2017	2000	$2,744.00			
June 24, 2017	2001	4,200.00			
June 28, 2017	2002	1,813.50			
June 30, 2017	2004*	500.00			
June 30, 2017	Bank Fees	40.00			
OTHER DEDUCTIONS (ATMs)					
June 16, 2017	ATM	$ 100.00			
June 21, 2017	ATM	200.00			

Case Problem 6–1B

Open Abelar Designs, an architectural firm, which is located in the student data files.

1. Create new vendor accounts for the four new vendors listed below.

Vendor

Vendor ID:	**GPS-01**
Name:	**Gentry Payroll Services**

General Tab

Contact:	**Greg Gentry**
Account Number:	**659412**
Mailing Address:	**9137 Corral Drive**
City, ST, Zip:	**Stockton, CA 95210**
Country:	**USA**
Vendor Type:	**Expense**
1099 Type:	**None**
Expense Account:	**78500 (Payroll Services Expense)**
Telephone 1:	**209-555-9865**
Fax:	**209-555-9890**

Purchase Info Tab

Tax ID Number:	**None**
Ship Via:	**US Mail**
Terms and Credit:	**Due EOM, 0.00 Discount**

History Tab

Beginning Balance:	**0**

Vendor

Vendor ID:	**GR-02**
Name:	**Grupe Associates**

General Tab

Contact:	**Gary Robertson**
Account Number:	**654976**
Mailing Address:	**4189 Holly Lane**
City, ST, Zip:	**Stockton, CA 95210**
Country:	**USA**
Vendor Type:	**Expense**
1099 Type:	**None**
Expense Account:	**79000 (Rent or Lease Expense)**
Telephone 1:	**209-555-7321**
Fax:	**209-555-7325**

Purchase Info Tab

Tax ID Number:	**None**
Ship Via:	**US Mail**
Terms and Credit:	**Due EOM, 0.00 Discount**

History Tab
    Beginning Balance: 0

Vendor
    Vendor ID: **OFFMAX-03**
    Name: **Office Max**

General Tab
    Contact: **Heather Brannon**
    Account Number: **496782**
    Mailing Address: **3915 Webber Lane**
    City, ST, Zip: **Stockton, CA 95207**
    Country: **USA**
    Vendor Type: **Supplier**
    1099 Type: **None**
    Expense Account: **12000 (Office Supplies)**
    Telephone 1:   **209-555-7981**
    Fax: **209-555-7988**

Purchase Info Tab
    Tax ID Number: **None**
    Ship Via: **Fed-EX**
    Terms and Credit: **2% 10 days, net 30 days**

History Tab
    Beginning Balance: 0

Vendor
    Vendor ID: **PB-04**
    Name: **Pacific Bell**

General Tab
    Contact: **Monica Volbrecht**
    Account Number: **965329**
    Mailing Address: **6291 South Street**
    City, ST, Zip: **Stockton, CA 95207**
    Country: **USA**
    Vendor Type: **Expense**
    1099 Type: **None**
    Expense Account: **80500 (Telephone Expense)**
    Telephone 1:   **209-555-7834**
    Fax: **209-555-7840**

Purchase Info Tab
    Tax ID Number: **None**
    Ship Via: **US Mail**
    Terms and Credit: **Due EOM, 0.00 Discount**

History Tab

    Beginning Balance: **0**

2. Create new customer accounts for the three customers listed below.

Customer

Customer ID:	**AR-01**
Name:	**Artistic Renovations**

General Tab

Account Number:	**1465**
Billing Address:	**9551 Tracy Boulevard**
City, ST, Zip:	**Stockton, CA 95210**
Country:	**USA**
Customer Type:	**General**
Telephone 1:	**209-555-6497**
Fax:	**209-555-6400**

Contacts Tab

Contact:	**Francisco Moreno**

Sales Info Tab

GL Sales Account:	**40600**
Ship Via:	**Fed-EX**
Pricing Level:	**Price Level 1**
Form Options:	**Default**

Payment & Credit Tab

Terms and Credit:	**2% 10 days, net 30 days**

History Tab

Beginning Balance:	**0**

Customer

Customer ID:	**KCB-02**
Name:	**Kim's Custom Builders**

General Tab

Account Number:	**1398**
Billing Address:	**6432 West Howard Lane**
City, ST, Zip:	**Tracy, CA 95376**
Country:	**USA**
Customer Type:	**General**
Telephone 1:	**209-555-2265**
Fax:	**209-555-2266**

Contacts Tab

Contact:	**Paul Kim**

Sales Info Tab

GL Sales Account:	**40200**
Ship Via:	**Fed-EX**
Pricing Level:	**Price Level 1**
Form Options:	**Default**

Payment & Credit Tab

Terms and Credit:	**2% 10 days, net 30 days**

History Tab

Beginning Balance:	**0**

Customer

Customer ID:	**WC-03**
Name:	**Walsh Construction**

General Tab

Account Number:	**1080**
Billing Address:	**4321 23rd Street**
City, ST, Zip:	**Manteca, CA 95301**
Country:	**USA**
Customer Type:	**General**
Telephone 1:	**209-555-2136**
Fax:	**209-555-2140**

Contacts Tab

Contact:	**Martha Walsh**

Sales Info Tab

GL Sales Account:	**40600**
Ship Via:	**Fed-EX**
Pricing Level:	**Price Level 1**
Form Options:	**Default**

Payment & Credit Tab

Terms and Credit:	**2% 10 days, net 30 days**

History Tab

Beginning Balance:	**0**

3. Enter each of the following transactions for May 2017. Choose the appropriate option on the Tasks menu: Sales/Invoicing, Purchases/Receive Inventory, Receive Money, or Payments. Use Account 49000, Fee Discount for any discounts taken by customers.

Date	Transaction
May 5	Received a bill (Invoice 10115) of $1,300 for monthly rent from Grupe Associates.
6	Performed architectural design services for $825 on credit for Artistic Renovations. Issued Invoice 4001.
7	Received a bill (Invoice 26591) of $170 for monthly usage of telephone service from Pacific Bell.
7	Purchased office supplies for $125 on credit from Office Max. Received Invoice 7281.
10	Performed consulting services for $980 on credit for Kim's Custom Builders. Issued Invoice 4002.
15	Received the amount due for Invoice 4001 from Artistic Renovations, less a 2% discount, Check No. 4521.
16	Paid the amount due for Invoice 7281 to Office Max, less a 2% discount. Issued Check No. 231. (Use Account 12000, Office Supplies as the discount account.)
18	Purchased payroll services for $450 on credit from Gentry Payroll Services. Received Invoice 8972.
25	Performed architectural design services for $2,340 on credit for Walsh Construction. Issued Invoice 4003.
25	Received the full amount due for Invoice 4002 from Kim's Custom Builders, Check No. 3238.
26	Performed architectural design services for $1,480 on credit for Artistic Renovations. Issued Invoice 4004. Received check for $480 from the customer (Check No. 4525).
30	Paid $1,300 on account to Grupe Associates. Issued Check No. 232.
30	Paid $170 on account to Pacific Bell. Issued Check No. 233.
31	Received the balance due (Check No. 4527) for Invoice 4004 from Artistic Renovations, less a 2% discount on the total of the invoice ($1,480 × 0.02 = $29.60).

4. Print the following reports for May: Customer Ledgers, Cash Receipts Journal, Vendor Ledgers, Cash Disbursements Journal, and General Ledger Trial Balance.

Case Problem 6–2B

Open Hendricks' Construction, a home building company, which is located in the student data files.

The firm received the following bank statement for the month ended June 30, 2017:

1. Prepare an account reconciliation. Bring the ending balances of the firm's bank statement and regular checking account into agreement.
2. Print an Account Reconciliation report.

		Bank of Stanislaus			
		18132 West 11th Street			
		Tracy, CA 95376			
Hendricks' Construction					
Account No: 649575321					
REGULAR CHECKING					
Beginning Balance	$32,800.00	**Statement Date: June 30, 2017**			
2 Deposits (+)	14,850.00				
4 Checks (-)	13,886.25				
2 Other Deductions (-)	450.00				
Service Charges (-)	60.00				
Ending Balance	33,253.75				
DEPOSITS					
June 14, 2017	$7,500.00				
June 23, 2017	$7,350.00				
CHECKS AND BANK FEES (Asterisk* indicates break in check number sequence)					
June 20, 2017	2000	$4,116.00			
June 24, 2017	2001	6,300.00			
June 28, 2017	2002	2,720.25			
June 30, 2017	2004*	750.00			
June 30, 2017	Bank Fees	60.00			
OTHER DEDUCTIONS (ATMs)					
June 16, 2017	ATM	$150.00			
June 21, 2017	ATM	300.00			

CHAPTER 7

Preparing the Financial Statements

Objectives

7–1 Journalize the adjusting entries

7–2 Prepare and print financial statements

7–3 Change the accounting period

Software Features

- Print and Filter feature

- Copying Financial Statement Format feature

- Designing Reports feature, including text formatting

- Changing the Accounting Period feature

Company Files

Before beginning chapter work, access the links menu to download company files.

Every accounting system must keep a detailed record of the financial transactions that take place within a business. However, the ultimate purpose of an accounting system is to provide timely, reliable information that the owners and managers can use to make decisions. Much of this information comes from financial statements.

How much profit did we earn? Do we have enough cash to meet our operating needs? How much do we owe to vendors? How much can we expect to receive from credit customers? The financial statements provide the answers to questions such as these.

One of the great benefits of a computerized accounting system like Sage 50 is the ease with which you can produce financial statements. In manual accounting, the process of taking a trial balance of the general ledger accounts, recording adjustments, calculating the adjusted account balances, and then preparing the financial statements can be difficult and time consuming. In Sage 50, much of this work is done by the system itself.

Once adjusting entries have been recorded, Sage 50 can automatically produce an income statement, a balance sheet, a statement of changes in financial position, and a statement of cash flow.

OBJECTIVE 7-1

Journalize the Adjusting Entries

Before the financial statements are prepared at the end of a period, it is necessary to make *adjusting entries*. These types of entries are used to bring the general ledger accounts up to date so that they include previously unrecorded items that relate to the period.

adjusting entries
Entries that are used to bring the general ledger accounts up to date so that they include previously unrecorded items that relate to the period.

In accrual accounting, all revenue must be recorded when earned and all expenses must be recorded when incurred. However, in most businesses, certain items are not recorded during a period. For example, as of January 31, 2017, Superior Carpet and Tile has not yet recorded the expenses for supplies used, depreciation of equipment, and unpaid salaries. Adjusting entries must be made for these items. Adjusting entries affect one balance sheet account and one income statement account.

Recording the Adjusting Entry for Supplies Used

During any accounting period, the employees of a firm constantly use paper clips, computer paper, staples, and other office supplies. Obviously, it is not practical to record the expense for supplies used on a day-to-day basis. Instead, businesses make an adjusting entry for supplies used at the end of the period.

Remember that when Superior Carpet and Tile purchases office supplies, it records their cost in the asset account Office Supplies. On January 31, 2017, this account has a balance of $1,962. However, when the firm takes an inventory of the office supplies on hand, it finds that they total $1,062. Thus, the firm has used $900 of office supplies during January.

On January 31, 2017, Superior must make an adjusting entry to record the expense for the $900 of office supplies used in January. This entry appears in the general journal. It consists of a debit of $900 to Office Supplies Expense and a credit of $900 to Office Supplies.

One effect of this adjusting entry is to establish the expense for office supplies for the period. The other effect is to reduce the balance of the asset account Office Supplies to $1,062, the amount of supplies actually on hand.

Recording the Adjusting Entry for Depreciation

depreciation The process of allocating the cost of a fixed asset to operations during its useful life.

Every fixed asset except land is subject to depreciation. Remember that *depreciation* is the process of allocating the cost of a fixed asset to operations during its useful life. An adjusting entry must be made to record the depreciation expense for each type of fixed asset that a business owns. Various methods are available for calculating depreciation. Some of these methods will be discussed in a later chapter.

Superior Carpet and Tile owns one type of fixed asset—equipment. It depreciates the equipment at the rate of $1,000 a month. Therefore, on January 31, 2017, Superior makes an adjusting entry to record $1,000 of depreciation expense for January. This entry consists of a debit to Depreciation Expense–Equipment and a credit to Accumulated Depreciation–Equipment.

Remember that Accumulated Depreciation–Equipment is a contra asset account. It has a credit balance, which is contrary to the normal debit balance of an asset account. Accumulated Depreciation–Equipment is used to show the total amount of depreciation taken on the equipment during its useful life.

Recording the Adjusting Entry for Unpaid Salaries

Often, when an accounting period ends, a business owes salaries to its employees. This situation occurs because the end of the accounting period falls in the midst of a payroll period. For example, suppose that a firm has a weekly payroll period that extends from Monday to Friday, and the employees receive their paychecks on Friday. If the accounting period ends on a Wednesday, the firm will owe unpaid salaries for three days—Monday, Tuesday, and Wednesday.

On January 31, 2017, Superior Carpet and Tile owes $800 of unpaid salaries. An adjusting entry must be made to record the expense for unpaid salaries. This entry consists of a debit of $800 to Wages and Salaries Expense and a credit of $800 to Wages and Salaries Payable.

The firm has a liability for the salaries owed to its employees. Therefore, the account credited in the adjusting entry is the liability account Wages and Salaries Payable.

Using Sage 50 to Record Sample Adjusting Entries

Follow the steps outlined below to make adjusting entries for Superior Carpet and Tile as of January 31, 2017. All of these entries should appear in the general journal.

Step 1:

Open Superior Carpet and Tile (Chp. 7 – Superior Carpet and Tile if student files are used). Close the Action Items log.

Step 2:

The first adjusting entry is for $900 of office supplies used during January. Click *General Journal Entry* in the More Shortcuts section at the side of the basic Sage 50 window, as shown in Figure 7–1.

FIGURE 7–1
General Journal Entry
Selected from the
Shortcuts Section

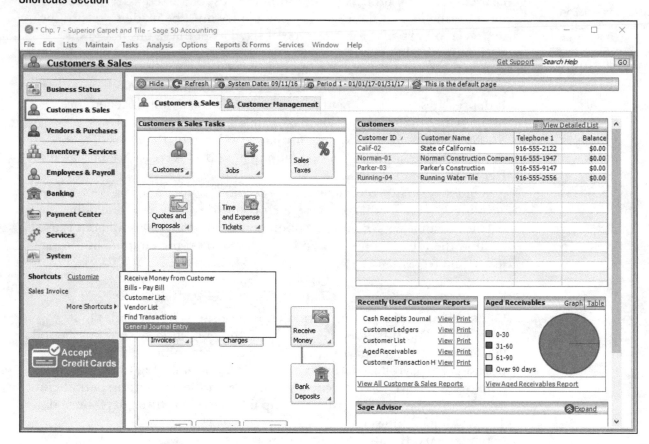

Step 3:

The General Journal Entry window will appear. Change the date to *Jan 31, 2017* and key **Adjusting Entry 1** in the *Reference* field.

Step 4:

Key **506** (Office Supplies Expense) in the *GL Account* field.

Step 5:

Key **Office supplies used** in the *Description* field.

Step 6:

Key **900.00** as the amount in the *Debit* field, and tab to the next row.

Step 7:

Key **108** (Office Supplies) in the *GL Account* field.

Step 8:

Key **900.00** in the *Credit* field.

Step 9:

Compare your work with the completed entry shown in Figure 7–2. Make any necessary changes.

FIGURE 7–2
Completed Adjusting Entry for Office Supplies Used

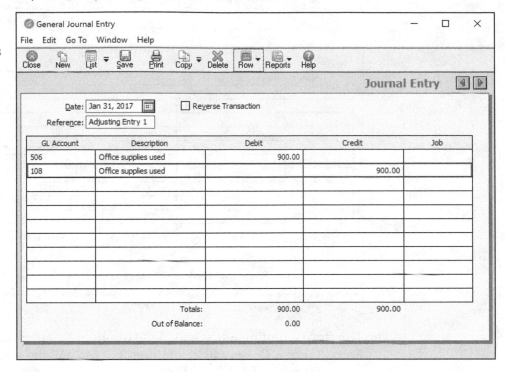

Step 10:

Click <u>S</u>ave.

Note: Although there are additional blank lines on which to record other adjusting entries, it is good practice to enter them separately.

Step 11:

The second adjusting entry is for $1,000 of depreciation on Superior's equipment during January. Key **Adjusting Entry 2** in the *Reference* field and then key **510** (Depreciation Expense–Equipment) in the *GL Account* field.

Step 12:

Key **Equipment depreciation expense** in the *Description* field.

Step 13:

Key **1,000.00** in the *Debit* field, and tab to the next row.

Step 14:

Key **112.5** (Accum. Depreciation–Equipment) in the *GL Account* field.

Step 15:

Key **1,000.00** as the amount in the *Credit* field.

Step 16:

Check your work for accuracy by comparing it with Figure 7–3. Then click <u>S</u>ave.

FIGURE 7–3
Completed Adjusting
Entry for Depreciation

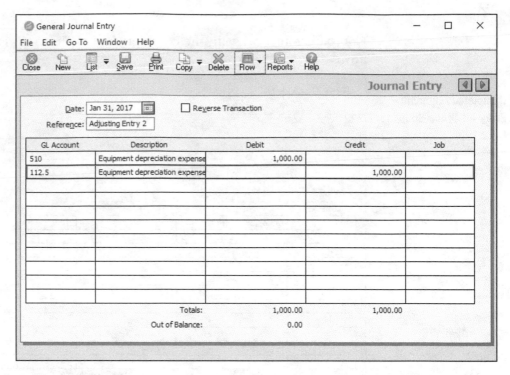

Step 17:

The third adjusting entry is for $800 of unpaid salaries. Key **Adjusting Entry 3** in the *Reference* field and then key **512** (Wages and Salaries Expense) in the *GL Account* field.

Step 18:

Key **Wages and salaries owed** in the *Description* field.

Step 19:

Key **800.00** in the *Debit* field, and tab to the next row.

Step 20:

Superior does not have a Wages and Salaries Payable account. Therefore, use the following information to create this account.

Account ID:	**210**
Description:	**Wages and Salaries Payable**
Account Type:	**Other Current Liabilities**

Step 21:

Key **210** in the *GL Account* field.

Step 22:

Key **800.00** in the *Credit* field.

Step 23:

Check your work for accuracy by comparing it with Figure 7–4. Then click Save and close the General Journal Entry window.

FIGURE 7–4
Completed Adjusting Entry for Unpaid Salaries

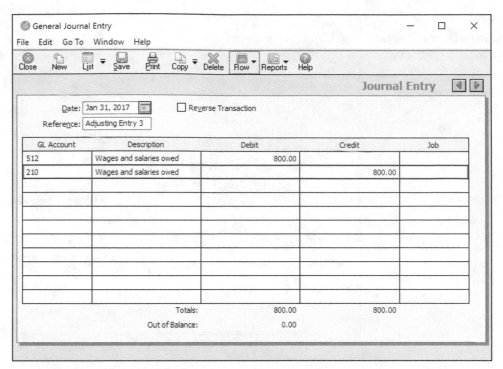

Reviewing the Adjusting Entries

It is a good practice to review the adjusting entries after they have been recorded. To review the adjusting entries made for Superior Carpet and Tile, follow these steps:

Step 1:

Click the *Business Status* icon on the Navigation Aids toolbar at the left side of the basic Sage 50 window.

Step 2:

Select *General Ledger* at the Category drop-down list in the Find a Report section, as shown in Figure 7–5.

FIGURE 7–5
General Ledger Selected from the Category Drop-Down List in the Find a Report Section

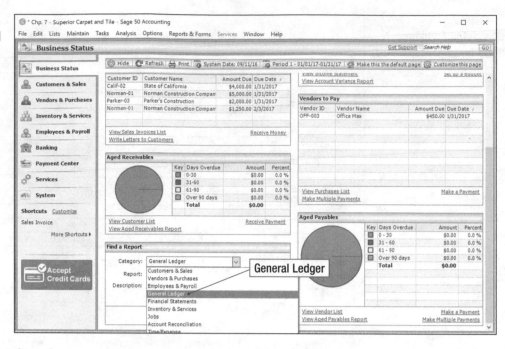

Step 3:

Select *General Journal* at the Report drop-down list in the Find a Report section, as shown in Figure 7–6.

FIGURE 7–6
General Journal Selected from the Report Drop-Down List in the Find a Report Section

HINT
Select Reports & Forms from the Menu bar if you wish to narrow the focus of the report.

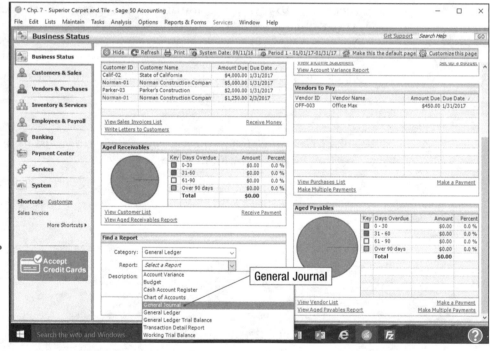

Step 4:
Click Display.

Step 5:

Compare your adjusting entries with the ones shown in Figure 7–7. Make any necessary changes. Note that entries from previous chapters are also included in the General Journal report of January 31, 2017.

FIGURE 7-7

Completed Adjusting Entries in General Journal

Chp. 7 - Superior Carpet and Tile
General Journal
For the Period From Jan 1, 2017 to Jan 31, 2017
Filter Criteria includes: Report order is by Date. Report is printed with Accounts having Zero Amounts and with shortened descriptions and in Detail Format.

Date	Account ID	Reference	Trans Description	Debit Amt	Credit Amt
1/1/17	100	BEGBAL		20,000.00	
	102			450.00	
	112			14,000.00	
	112.5				2,000.00
	300				32,450.00
	301				
1/16/17	301.5	Stmnt 1/31	ATM Withdrawals	50.00	
	100		ATM Withdrawals		50.00
1/21/17	301.5	Stmnt 1/31	ATM Withdrawal	100.00	
	100		ATM Withdrawal		100.00
1/31/17	100	01/31/17	Service Charge		20.00
	520		Service Charge	20.00	
1/31/17	506	Adjusting Entr	Office supplies used	900.00	
	108		Office supplies used		900.00
1/31/17	510	Adjusting Entr	Equipment depreciation expense	1,000.00	
	112.5		Equipment depreciation expense		1,000.00
1/31/17	512	Adjusting Entr	Wages and salaries owed	800.00	
	210		Wages and salaries owed		800.00
			Total	37,320.00	37,320.00

Step 6:

Close the General Journal window.

Checkpoint 7-1

1. What three types of adjusting entries are made by Superior Carpet and Tile?
2. Why does a firm make adjusting entries at the end of an accounting period?

Objective 7-1 Practice

Step 1:

Open Meadowland Healthcare Services (Chp. 7 – Meadowland Healthcare Services if student data files are used), and make the following adjusting entries for the firm for January 31, 2017:

> **HINT**
> The ledger accounts and the balance sheet will provide the necessary information.

1. Record the office supplies used during January. An inventory showed office supplies of $370 on hand on January 31. Subtract this amount from the balance of the Office Supplies account to find the amount of the adjustment.
2. Record the unpaid salaries of $3,400 on January 31. There is no account for Wages and Salaries Payable. Create this account, using 21000 as the Account ID. Remember, this account is of type Other Current Liabilities.
3. Record depreciation of $750 on the medical equipment for the month of January.

Note: Students will use the Office Expense (73500) account.

Step 2:

Compare your adjusting entries with Figure 7–8.

FIGURE 7–8
Completed Adjusting Entries in General Journal

10/7/16 at 14:06:24.00	*****EDUCATIONAL VERSION ONLY*****				Page: 1

Chp. 7 - Meadowland Healthcare Services
General Journal
For the Period From Jan 1, 2017 to Jan 31, 2017
Filter Criteria includes: Report order is by Date. Report is printed with shortened descriptions and in Detail Format.

Date	Account ID	Reference	Trans Description	Debit Amt	Credit Amt
1/1/17	10000	BEGBAL		250.00	
	10200			25,000.00	
	15100			12,000.00	
	17100				750.00
	39005				36,500.00
1/16/17	39007	Stmnt 12/31	ATM Withdrawals	50.00	
	10200		ATM Withdrawals		50.00
1/21/17	39007	Stmnt 1/31	ATM Withdrawals	100.00	
	10200		ATM Withdrawals		100.00
1/31/17	10200	01/31/17	Service Charge		35.00
	62500		Service Charge	35.00	
1/31/17	73500	Adjusting Entr	Office supplies used	502.20	
	14000		Office supplies used		502.20
1/31/17	77000	Adjusting Entr	Wages and salaries owed	3,400.00	
	21000		Wages and salaries owed		3,400.00
1/31/17	64500	Adjusting Entr	Medical equipment depreciation	750.00	
	17100		Medical equipment depreciation.		750.00
			Total	42,087.20	42,087.20

Step 3:

Close the General Journal window.

OBJECTIVE 7–2

Prepare and Print Financial Statements

After the adjusting entries are journalized and posted, Sage 50 can be used to produce the following financial statements: the income statement, the statement of changes in financial position, the balance sheet, and the statement of cash flow. You have already printed some of these reports in Chapter 3; in this chapter you will learn more about how these reports are used in business, as well as how to customize the reports.

The *income statement* reports the results of operations for a period of time. It shows the revenue, expenses, and net income or net loss for the period. The *net income* or *net loss* is the difference between the revenue and expenses. Some people refer to the income statement as the "profit and loss statement."

The *statement of changes in financial position* reports the sources and uses of a firm's working capital for a period of time. *Working capital* is the excess of current assets over current liabilities. Working capital is a measure of a firm's ability to pay its short-term debts as they become due.

The *balance sheet* shows the financial condition of a business as of a specific date. It lists the assets, liabilities, and owner's equity of a business. The balance sheet is a detailed version of the basic accounting equation: Assets = Liabilities + Owner's Equity.

The *statement of cash flow* reports the inflows and outflows of cash from operating activities, investing activities, and financing activities that a business had during a period of time. This statement also shows the net increase or net decrease in cash for the period.

income statement A report of a firm's revenue, expenses, and net income or net loss for a period.

net income or net loss The difference between revenue and expenses.

statement of changes in financial position A report of a firm's sources and uses of working capital for a period.

working capital The excess of current assets over current liabilities.

balance sheet A report of a firm's assets, liabilities, and owner's equity as of a specific date.

statement of cash flow A report of the inflows and outflows of cash from operating activities, investing activities, and financing activities for a period.

Printing the Income Statement

Step 1:

Open Chp. 7 – Superior Carpet and Tile, which you previously updated, and close the Action Items log.

Step 2:

Click Reports & Forms on the Menu bar.

Step 3:

Click *Financial Statements* in the Reports & Forms drop-down list, as shown in Figure 7–9.

FIGURE 7–9
Financial Statements Selected in the Reports & Forms Drop-Down List

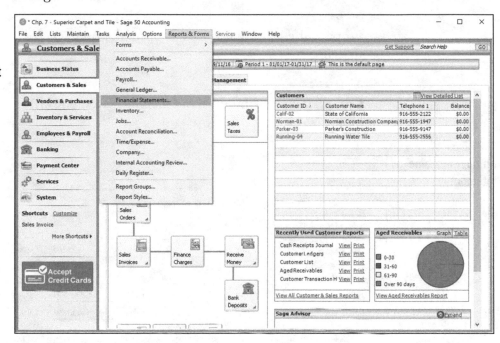

Step 4:

The Select a Report or Form dialog box will appear. Click *<Standard> Income Stmnt* in the Financial Statements: Balance Sheets and Income Statements section, as shown in Figure 7–10.

FIGURE 7–10
<Standard> Income Stmnt Chosen from Reports List

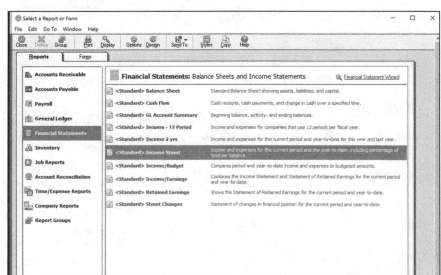

Step 5:

Click the Print button on the toolbar.

Step 6:

Click *Current Period* in the *Time Frame* field on the Options folder tab.

Step 7:

Click *Show Zero Amounts* to deselect it.

Step 8:

Click OK to print.

Step 9:

Prepare the Print dialog box as needed, and click OK when you are ready to print.

Step 10:

Compare your printout of the income statement with the one shown in Figure 7–11.

FIGURE 7–11
Printout of Income Statement

	Current Month			Year to Date	
					Page: 1
Chp. 7 - Superior Carpet and Tile					
Income Statement					
For the One Month Ending January 31, 2017					
Revenues					
Installation Services	$ 6,250.00	101.63	$	6,250.00	101.63
Sales Discount	(100.00)	(1.63)		(100.00)	(1.63)
Total Revenues	6,150.00	100.00		6,150.00	100.00
Cost of Sales					
Total Cost of Sales	0.00	0.00		0.00	0.00
Gross Profit	6,150.00	100.00		6,150.00	100.00
Expenses					
Rent Expense	2,100.00	34.15		2,100.00	34.15
Utilities Expense	226.65	3.69		226.65	3.69
Office Supplies Expense	900.00	14.63		900.00	14.63
Depreciation Expense-Equipment	1,000.00	16.26		1,000.00	16.26
Wages and Salaries Expense	800.00	13.01		800.00	13.01
Miscellaneous Expense	265.39	4.32		265.39	4.32
Uncollectible Accounts Expense	4,000.00	65.04		4,000.00	65.04
Maintenance Expense	250.00	4.07		250.00	4.07
Bank Fee Expense	20.00	0.33		20.00	0.33
Total Expenses	9,562.04	155.48		9,562.04	155.48
Net Income	$ (3,412.04)	(55.48)	$	(3,412.04)	(55.48)

Printing the Statement of Changes in Financial Position

Step 1:

Click *<Standard> Stmnt Changes* in the Reports list section of the Select a Report or Form dialog box, as shown in Figure 7–12.

FIGURE 7–12

<Standard> Stmnt
Changes Chosen from
Reports List

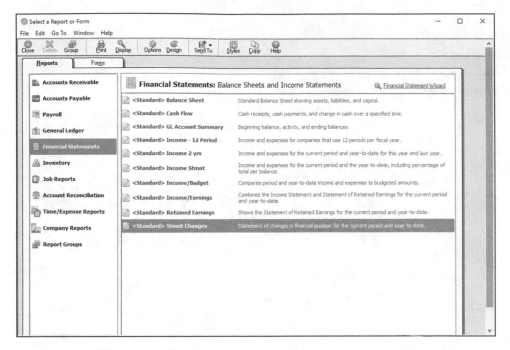

Step 2:

Click the Print button on the toolbar.

Step 3:

Click *Current Period* in the *Time Frame* field on the Options folder tab.

Step 4:

Click *Show Zero Amounts* to deselect it.

Step 5:

Click OK to print.

Step 6:

Prepare the Print dialog box as needed, and click OK when you are ready
to print.

Step 7:

Compare your printout of the statement of changes in financial position
with the one shown in Figure 7–13.

FIGURE 7–13
Printout of
Statement of
Changes in
Financial Position

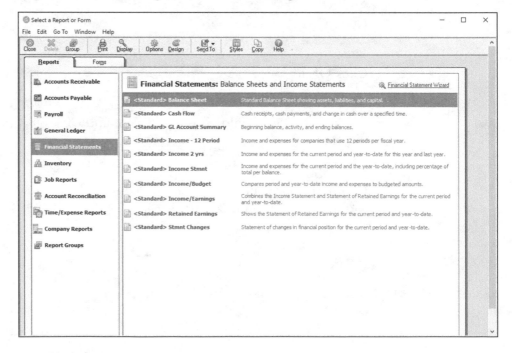

Page: 1

Chp. 7 - Superior Carpet and Tile
Statement of Changes in Financial Position
For the one month ended January 31, 2017

	Current Month	Year To Date
Sources of Working Capital		
Net Income	$ (3,412.04)	$ (3,412.04)
Add back items not requiring working capital		
Accum. Depreciation-Equipment	3,000.00	3,000.00
Working capital from operations	(412.04)	(412.04)
Other sources		
H. Simpson, Capital	32,450.00	32,450.00
Total sources	32,037.96	32,037.96
Uses of working capital		
Equipment	(14,000.00)	(14,000.00)
Total uses	(14,000.00)	(14,000.00)
Net change	$ 18,037.96	$ 18,037.96
Analysis of componants of changes		
Increase <Decrease> in Current Assets		
Cash	$ 18,665.96	$ 18,665.96
Petty Cash	450.00	450.00
Accounts Receivable	(2,750.00)	(2,750.00)
Office Supplies	472.00	472.00
<Increase> Decrease in Current Liabilities		
Accounts Payable	1,850.00	1,850.00
Wages and Salaries Payable	(800.00)	(800.00)
Net change	$ 17,887.96	$ 17,887.96

Printing the Balance Sheet

Step 1:

Click *<Standard> Balance Sheet* in the Reports list section of the Select a
Report or Form dialog box, as shown in Figure 7–14.

FIGURE 7–14
<Standard> Balance
Sheet Chosen from
Reports List

Step 2:

Click the Print button on the toolbar.

Step 3:

Click *Current Period* in the *Time Frame* field on the Options folder tab.

Step 4:

Click *Show Zero Amounts* to deselect it, if necessary.

Step 5:

Click OK to print.

Step 6:

Prepare the Print dialog box as needed, and click OK when you are ready to print.

Step 7:

Compare your printout of the balance sheet with the one shown in Figure 7–15.

FIGURE 7–15
Printout of Balance Sheet

Chp. 7 - Superior Carpet and Tile
Balance Sheet
January 31, 2017

ASSETS

Current Assets		
Cash	$ 18,665.96	
Petty Cash	450.00	
Accounts Receivable	(2,750.00)	
Office Supplies	472.00	
Total Current Assets		16,837.96
Property and Equipment		
Equipment	14,000.00	
Accum. Depreciation-Equipment	(3,000.00)	
Total Property and Equipment		11,000.00
Other Assets		
Total Other Assets		0.00
Total Assets	$	27,837.96

LIABILITIES AND CAPITAL

Current Liabilities		
Accounts Payable	$ (1,850.00)	
Wages and Salaries Payable	800.00	
Total Current Liabilities		(1,050.00)
Long-Term Liabilities		
Total Long-Term Liabilities		0.00
Total Liabilities		(1,050.00)
Capital		
H. Simpson, Capital	32,450.00	
H. Simpson, Drawing	(150.00)	
Net Income	(3,412.04)	
Total Capital		28,887.96
Total Liabilities & Capital	$	27,837.96

Printing the Statement of Cash Flow

Step 1:

Click *<Standard> Cash Flow* in the Reports list section of the Select a Report or Form dialog box, as shown in Figure 7–16.

FIGURE 7–16

<Standard> Cash Flow
Chosen from Reports List

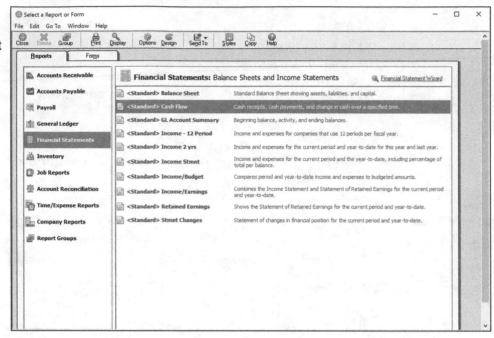

Step 2:

Click the Print button on the toolbar.

Step 3:

Click *Current Period* in the *Time Frame* field on the Options folder tab.

Step 4:

Click *Show Zero Amounts* to deselect it.

Step 5:

Click OK to print.

Step 6:

Prepare the Print dialog box as needed, and click OK when you are ready to print.

Step 7:

Compare your printout of the statement of cash flow with the one shown in Figure 7–17.

FIGURE 7–17
Printout of
Statement of
Cash Flow

Page: 1

Chp. 7 - Superior Carpet and Tile
Statement of Cash Flow
For the one Month Ended January 31, 2017

	Current Month	Year to Date
Cash Flows from operating activities		
Net Income	$ (3,412.04)	$ (3,412.04)
Adjustments to reconcile net income to net cash provided by operating activities		
Accum. Depreciation-Equipment	3,000.00	3,000.00
Accounts Receivable	2,750.00	2,750.00
Office Supplies	(472.00)	(472.00)
Accounts Payable	(1,850.00)	(1,850.00)
Wages and Salaries Payable	800.00	800.00
Total Adjustments	4,228.00	4,228.00
Net Cash provided by Operations	815.96	815.96
Cash Flows from investing activities		
Used For		
Equipment	(14,000.00)	(14,000.00)
Net cash used in investing	(14,000.00)	(14,000.00)
Cash Flows from financing activities		
Proceeds From		
H. Simpson, Capital	32,450.00	32,450.00
Used For		
H. Simpson, Drawing	(150.00)	(150.00)
Net cash used in financing	32,300.00	32,300.00
Net increase <decrease> in cash	$ 19,115.96	$ 19,115.96
Summary		
Cash Balance at End of Period	$ 19,115.96	$ 19,115.96
Cash Balance at Beg of Period	0.00	0.00
Net Increase <Decrease> in Cash	$ 19,115.96	$ 19,115.96

Step 8:

Close the Select a Report or Form dialog box.

Copying One Company's Financial Statement Format for Use by Another

All of the financial statements printed thus far have been selected from the standard list. However, it is possible to use the financial statement format of another company previously set up using Sage 50. For example, suppose a service company likes the format used by another similar company. Sage 50 can transfer that format. Follow the steps outlined below to use another company's financial statement format.

Step 1:

Click Reports & Forms on the Menu bar.

Step 2:

Click *Financial Statements* at the Reports & Forms drop-down list.

Step 3:

Click *<Standard> Balance Sheet* in the R̲eports list section of the Select a Report or Form dialog box.

Step 4:

Click the C̲opy button on the Select a Report or Form toolbar.

Step 5:

The Copy Reports, Financial Statements & Letter Templates dialog box will appear. Click the down arrow at the Select a Company to Copy from field, and then click *Chp. 7 - Meadowland Healthcare Services* at the drop-down list.

Note: You may need to use the Browse feature to locate the company file.

Step 6:

Click the box next to *Include Standard Financial Statements* located at the bottom of the window to select it.

Step 7:

Click *<Standard> Balance Sheet.*

Step 8:

Key **Practice Balance Sheet** in the *New Name* field.

Step 9:

Compare your work with Figure 7–18. Then click C̲opy on the Copy Reports, Financial Statements & Letter Templates toolbar.

FIGURE 7–18
Copy Reports, Financial Statements & Letter Templates Dialog Box

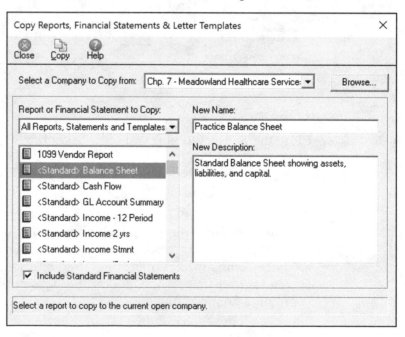

Step 10:

Click Close.

The balance sheet format of Meadowland Healthcare Services is now available for use by Superior Carpet and Tile. The new Practice Balance Sheet is among the financial statement choices appearing in the <u>R</u>eports list section of the Select a Report or Form dialog box, as shown in Figure 7–19. Any financial statement can be copied and used in the same manner as the balance sheet discussed here.

FIGURE 7–19
Practice Balance Sheet Chosen from Report List

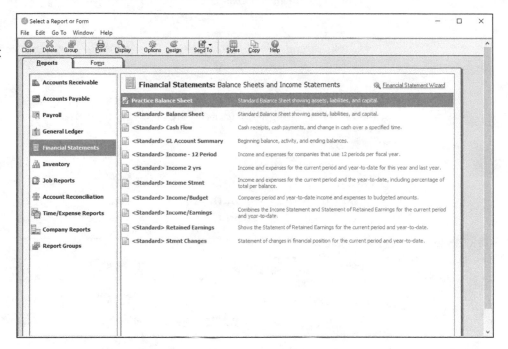

Step 11:
Close the Select a Report or Form dialog box.

Designing Financial Statements

Sage 50 provides a standard, or default, financial statement format for all statements. However, some companies want to make changes to this format. Such changes may be subtle. For example, a company may want to change the font size or the typeface. The changes in format may also be substantial. Sage 50 can accommodate a variety of changes.

You can make changes within each row of the financial statements. A row can have:

- Text Header
- Column Description
- Text Body
- Line Description
- Total Level
- Total Grand Total
- Text Footer

Assume that Superior Carpet and Tile wants to make several changes in the format of its financial statements. Follow the directions given on the next pages to make these changes.

Changing the Text Fonts

Step 1:

Click Reports & Forms on the Menu bar.

Step 2:

Click *Financial Statements* at the drop-down list.

Step 3:

Click *<Standard> Balance Sheet* in the Reports list section of the Select a Report or Form window.

Step 4:

Click the Design button on the Select a Report or Form toolbar.

Step 5:

The <Standard> Balance Sheet window will appear. Click the first Text - Header button, as shown in Figure 7–20. This button is aligned with the first line of text in the balance sheet. Notice that each line of text has a corresponding button type.

FIGURE 7–20
Text - Header Button for First Line of Text

Text - Header button

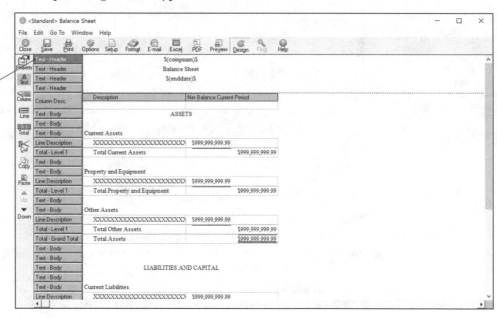

Step 6:

Click the *right* mouse button to reveal the drop-down list with text change options, as shown in Figure 7–21.

FIGURE 7–21
Drop-Down List with Text Change Options

Step 7:

At the drop-down list, click the *left* mouse button to select *Font*.

Step 8:

At the Font dialog box, click *Arial* in the Font list and Bold in the Font style list.

Step 9:

Click *11* in the Size list, as shown in Figure 7–22.

FIGURE 7–22
Font Dialog Box

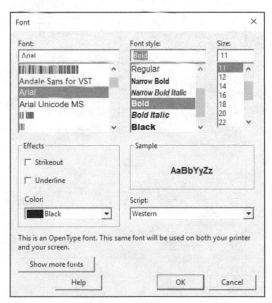

Step 10:

Click OK and then click No at the Sage 50 Query warning. If you click Yes, all fonts on the statement will be changed. If you click No, only the font of the specific line will be changed. Notice the change in the first line of the balance sheet shown in Figure 7–23.

FIGURE 7–23
Font Style Change in
First Line of Balance
Sheet

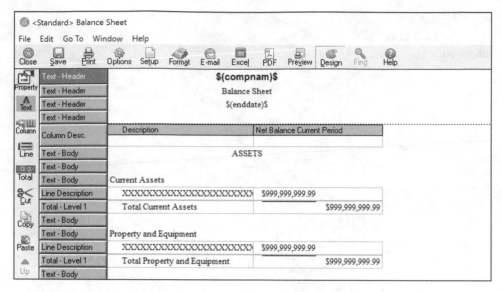

Changing the Text

Assume that Superior Carpet and Tile would like its balance sheet to have the title of *Special Balance Sheet*. Any change can be made in the wording of the title.

Step 1:

Click the second Text - Header button, which is aligned with the words *Balance Sheet*.

Step 2:

Click the Text button on the left side of the window to reveal the drop-down list with text change options, as shown in Figure 7–24.

FIGURE 7–24
Text Drop-Down List with
Text Change Options

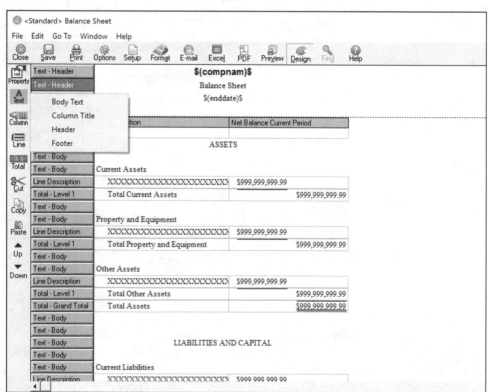

Step 3:

Click *Header.*

Step 4:

The Text dialog box will appear. Key **Special Balance Sheet** in the *Text to Print* field.

Step 5:

Click the down arrow at the *Alignment* field, and then click *Center of Column,* as shown in Figure 7–25.

FIGURE 7–25
Completed Text Dialog Box

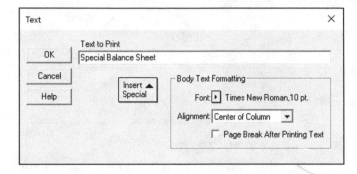

Step 6:

Click OK. Notice that the new header *Special Balance Sheet* was inserted above the header *Balance Sheet.*

Step 7:

Click the third Text - Header button aligned with the words *Balance Sheet.*

Step 8:

Click the *right* mouse button to reveal the drop-down list with text change options.

Step 9:

Click *Delete.*

Step 10:

Review the balance sheet format shown in Figure 7–26. Notice the change in the header.

FIGURE 7–26
Balance Sheet Format
with Change in Header

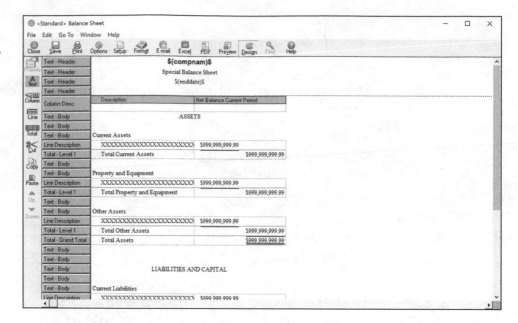

Copying a Line

A line can be copied from one place to another. Copy the header *Special Balance Sheet* to the line below.

Step 1:

Click the second Text - Header button, which is aligned with the words *Special Balance Sheet.*

Step 2:

Click the *right* mouse button to reveal the drop-down list with text change options.

Step 3:

Click *Copy.*

Step 4:

Click the third Text - Header button, and then click the *right* mouse button.

Step 5:

Click *Paste,* and a new line will appear with the words *Special Balance Sheet,* as shown in Figure 7–27.

FIGURE 7–27
Copied Line

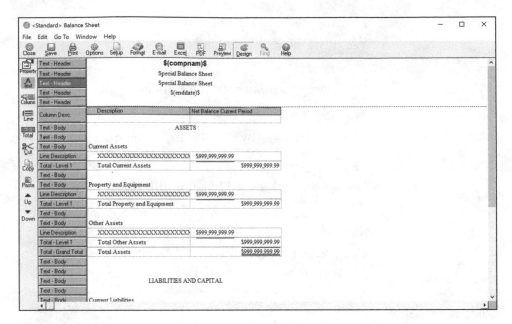

Deleting a Line

Obviously, Superior does not need two lines that say *Special Balance Sheet*. To delete the second line, follow the steps outlined below.

Step 1:

Click the third Text - Header button, which is aligned with the second *Special Balance Sheet* header.

Step 2:

Click the *right* mouse button to reveal the drop-down list with text change options.

Step 3:

Click *Delete*, as shown in Figure 7–28.

FIGURE 7–28
Delete Selected from Text
Change Options

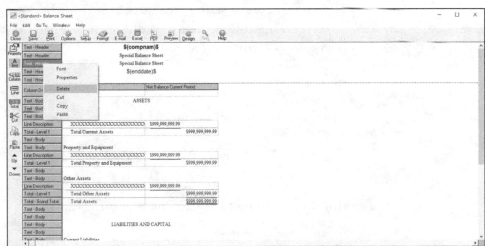

Moving rows and changing column titles can also be accomplished by using the procedures outlined above.

Step 4:

Close the <Standard> Balance Sheet window.

Step 5:

Save the changes by clicking Yes at the query box.

Step 6:

Key **Modified Balance Sheet** in the *Report name* box at the Save As dialog box.

Step 7:

Key **Font Change** in the *Report description* box, as shown in Figure 7–29. Then click Save.

FIGURE 7–29
Modified Balance Sheet
Save As Dialog Box

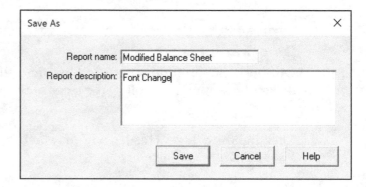

Step 8:

Close the Select a Report or Form dialog box.

Checkpoint 7–2

1. What financial statements does Sage 50 produce?
2. Which button on the Select a Report or Form toolbar is used to customize financial statements?

Objective 7-2 Practice

Step 1:

Open Chp. 7 – Meadowland Healthcare Services.

Step 2:

Print the following financial statements for the month of January 2017:

- Income statement
- Statement of changes in financial position

- Balance sheet
- Statement of cash flow

Your printouts should look like Figures 7–30, 7–31, 7–32, and 7–33.

FIGURE 7–30
Meadowland Healthcare Services Income Statement

Chp. 7 - Meadowland Healthcare Services
Income Statement
For the One Month Ending January 31, 2017

	Current Month		Year to Date	
Revenues				
Professional Fees	$ 21,830.00	100.53	$ 21,830.00	100.53
Sales Discount	(115.20)	(0.53)	(115.20)	(0.53)
Total Revenues	21,714.80	100.00	21,714.80	100.00
Cost of Sales				
Total Cost of Sales	0.00	0.00	0.00	0.00
Gross Profit	21,714.80	100.00	21,714.80	100.00
Expenses				
Bad Debt Expense	12,000.00	55.26	12,000.00	55.26
Bank Charges	35.00	0.16	35.00	0.16
Depreciation Expense	750.00	3.45	750.00	3.45
Housekeeping Expense	650.00	2.99	650.00	2.99
Office Expense	502.20	2.31	502.20	2.31
Rent or Lease Expense	1,200.00	5.53	1,200.00	5.53
Salaries Expense	3,400.00	15.66	3,400.00	15.66
Telephone Expense	265.98	1.22	265.98	1.22
Utilities Expense	345.89	1.59	345.89	1.59
Total Expenses	19,149.07	88.18	19,149.07	88.18
Net Income	$ 2,565.73	11.82	$ 2,565.73	11.82

FIGURE 7–31
Meadowland Healthcare Services Statement of Changes in Financial Position

Chp. 7 - Meadowland Healthcare Services
Statement of Changes in Financial Position
For the one month ended January 31, 2017

	Current Month	Year To Date
Sources of Working Capital		
Net Income	$ 2,565.73	$ 2,565.73
Add back items not requiring working capital		
Accum. Depr-Medical Equipment	1,500.00	1,500.00
Working capital from operations	4,065.73	4,065.73
Other sources		
Total sources	4,065.73	4,065.73
Uses of working capital		
Medical Equipment	(12,000.00)	(12,000.00)
Total uses	(12,000.00)	(12,000.00)
Net change	$ (7,934.27)	$ (7,934.27)
Analysis of componants of changes		
Increase <Decrease> in Current Assets		
Petty Cash	$ 250.00	$ 250.00
Regular Checking Account	27,950.73	27,950.73
Accounts Receivable	3,245.00	3,245.00
Office Supplies	370.00	370.00
<Increase> Decrease in Current Liabilities		
Wages and Salaries Payable	(3,400.00)	(3,400.00)
Net change	$ 28,415.73	$ 28,415.73

FIGURE 7–32
Meadowland
Healthcare Services
Balance Sheet

Chp. 7 - Meadowland Healthcare Services
Balance Sheet
January 31, 2017

ASSETS

Current Assets		
Petty Cash	$ 250.00	
Regular Checking Account	27,950.73	
Accounts Receivable	3,245.00	
Office Supplies	370.00	
Total Current Assets		31,815.73
Property and Equipment		
Medical Equipment	12,000.00	
Accum. Depr-Medical Equipment	(1,500.00)	
Total Property and Equipment		10,500.00
Other Assets		
Total Other Assets		0.00
Total Assets	$	42,315.73

LIABILITIES AND CAPITAL

Current Liabilities		
Wages and Salaries Payable	$ 3,400.00	
Total Current Liabilities		3,400.00
Long-Term Liabilities		
Total Long-Term Liabilities		0.00
Total Liabilities		3,400.00
Capital		
Retained Earnings	36,500.00	
Owner's Draw	(150.00)	
Net Income	2,565.73	
Total Capital		38,915.73
Total Liabilities & Capital	$	42,315.73

FIGURE 7–33
Meadowland
Healthcare Services
Statement of Cash
Flow

Page: 1

Chp. 7 - Meadowland Healthcare Services
Statement of Cash Flow
For the one Month Ended January 31, 2017

	Current Month	Year to Date
Cash Flows from operating activities		
Net Income	$ 2,565.73	$ 2,565.73
Adjustments to reconcile net income to net cash provided by operating activities		
Accum. Depr-Medical Equipment	1,500.00	1,500.00
Accounts Receivable	(3,245.00)	(3,245.00)
Office Supplies	(370.00)	(370.00)
Wages and Salaries Payable	3,400.00	3,400.00
Total Adjustments	1,285.00	1,285.00
Net Cash provided by Operations	3,850.73	3,850.73
Cash Flows from investing activities		
Used For		
Medical Equipment	(12,000.00)	(12,000.00)
Net cash used in investing	(12,000.00)	(12,000.00)
Cash Flows from financing activities		
Proceeds From		
Used For		
Owner's Draw	(150.00)	(150.00)
Net cash used in financing	(150.00)	(150.00)
Net increase <decrease> in cash	$ (8,299.27)	$ (8,299.27)
Summary		
Cash Balance at End of Period	$ 28,200.73	$ 28,200.73
Cash Balance at Beg of Period	0.00	0.00
Net Increase <Decrease> in Cash	$ 28,200.73	$ 28,200.73

Step 3:

Make the following changes to the balance sheet:

- Change the font type of the header *Meadowland Healthcare Services* to Arial.
- Change the font size of the header *Meadowland Healthcare Services* to 12.
- Add a row below the header *Balance Sheet* that will include the words *Customized Version* centered in the column.
- Save as Customized Balance Sheet.
- Print a new balance sheet with the changes made. Your printout should look like the partial balance sheet in Figure 7–34.

FIGURE 7–34
Revised Meadowland
Healthcare Services
Balance Sheet
(Partial View)

Chp. 7 - Meadowland Healthcare Services
Balance Sheet
Customized Version
January 31, 2017

ASSETS

Current Assets		
Petty Cash	$ 250.00	
Regular Checking Account	27,950.73	
Accounts Receivable	3,245.00	
Office Supplies	370.00	
Total Current Assets		31,815.73
Property and Equipment		
Medical Equipment	12,000.00	
Accum. Depr-Medical Equipment	(1,500.00)	
Total Property and Equipment		10,500.00
Other Assets		
Total Other Assets		0.00
Total Assets		$ 42,315.73

LIABILITIES AND CAPITAL

Current Liabilities		
Wages and Salaries Payable	$ 3,400.00	
Total Current Liabilities		3,400.00
Long-Term Liabilities		
Total Long-Term Liabilities		0.00
Total Liabilities		3,400.00
Capital		
Retained Earnings	36,500.00	
Owner's Draw	(150.00)	
Net Income	2,565.73	
Total Capital		38,915.73
Total Liabilities & Capital		$ 42,315.73

Step 4:

Close the Select a Report or Form dialog box.

OBJECTIVE 7-3

Change the Accounting Period

Sage 50 allows you to go from month to month without closing the fiscal year by changing the accounting period. This feature makes it possible to produce interim financial statements. You do not have to record the end-of-year closing entries until the fiscal year actually closes. Thus, the balances of the revenue and expense accounts continue to grow after the accounting period is changed. The same is true for the balance of the owner's drawing account.

As you saw, Superior Carpet and Tile has made its adjusting entries and printed its interim financial statements for January 2017. It is now time to get ready for the February entries.

Changing the Accounting Period

Take the following steps to change the accounting period for Superior Carpet and Tile:

Step 1:

Open Chp. 7 – Superior Carpet and Tile and close the Action Items log.

Step 2:

Click Tasks on the Menu bar, and then *System* and *Change Accounting Period* at the drop-down lists.

Step 3:

At the Change Accounting Period dialog box, click *02 - Feb 01, 2017 to Feb 28, 2017*, as shown in Figure 7–35.

FIGURE 7–35
Feb 01, 2017 to Feb 28, 2017 Selected in Change Accounting Period Dialog Box

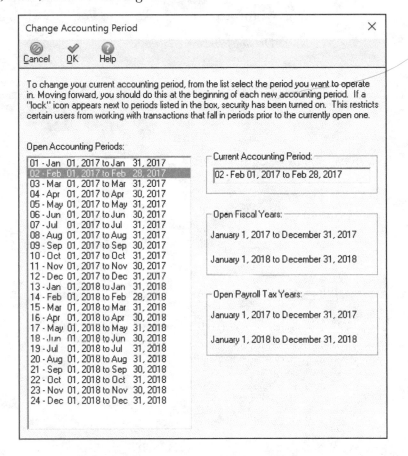

Step 4:

Click OK.

Step 5:

Click No in response to the question "Would you like to print your reports before continuing?" You printed the adjusting entries and the financial statements previously. No further entries or financial statements are needed for January 2017. Click No in response to the question "Would you like to run an Internal Accounting Review?" Superior Carpet and Tile is therefore ready to enter transactions for its second accounting period of the fiscal year—the month of February 2017.

Checkpoint 7-3

1. What feature of Sage 50 allows interim financial statements to be prepared?
2. Do you have to back up a company file when changing an accounting period?

Objective 7-3 Practice

Step 1:

Open Chp. 7 – Meadowland Healthcare Services.

Step 2:

Change the accounting period to Period 2 (Feb 01, 2017 to Feb 28, 2017).

Note: Do not print any reports.

Chapter Review and Assessment

Software Command Summary

Adjusting Entries	Tasks, General Journal Entry
Customizing Financial Statements	Reports & Forms, Financial Statements, Design
Copying Report Formats	Reports & Forms, Financial Statements, Copy
Changing the Accounting Period	Tasks, System, Change Accounting Period

Checkpoint Answers

Checkpoint 7–1
1. Superior Carpet and Tile makes adjusting entries for supplies used, depreciation, and unpaid salaries.
2. Adjusting entries are made to bring the general ledger accounts up to date so that they include previously unrecorded items that relate to the period.

Checkpoint 7–2
1. The financial statements produced by Sage 50 include the income statement, the statement of changes in financial position, the balance sheet, and the statement of cash flow.
2. The Design button is used to customize financial statements.

Checkpoint 7–3
1. The Change Accounting Period feature allows the preparation of interim financial statements.
2. No, Sage 50 maintains 24 accounting periods at any given time. Therefore, it is not necessary to back up each accounting period.

Study Quizzes

Take the study quiz online to check your understanding of chapter concepts. The quiz can be taken multiple times.

Content Check

Multiple Choice: Choose only one response for each question.

1. Which of the following is the basic accounting equation?
   A. Assets + Liabilities = Owner's Equity
   B. Assets = Liabilities + Owner's Equity
   C. Assets = Liabilities – Owner's Equity
   D. Assets – Owner's Equity = Liabilities
   E. None of the above

2. The financial statement that is a detailed version of the accounting equation is the
   A. income statement.
   B. statement of changes in financial position.
   C. balance sheet.
   D. statement of cash flow.
   E. None of the above

3. If the Office Supplies account has a balance of $2,000 at the beginning of the period and $1,200 at the end of the period, the adjusting entry would include
   A. a debit to Office Supplies and a credit to Office Supplies Expense for $1,200.
   B. a debit to Office Supplies Expense and a credit to Office Supplies for $2,000.
   C. a debit to Office Supplies Expense and a credit to Office Supplies for $800.
   D. a debit to Office Supplies and a credit to Office Supplies Expense for $800.
   E. None of the above

4. The adjusting entry for depreciation expense would include
   A. a debit to Accumulated Depreciation and a credit to Depreciation Expense.
   B. a debit to Depreciation Expense and a credit to Accumulated Depreciation.
   C. a debit to Depreciation Expense and a credit to Revenue.
   D. a debit to Revenue and a credit to Depreciation Expense.
   E. None of the above

5. What are the two types of accounts that appear on the income statement?
   A. expenses and liabilities
   B. expenses and capital
   C. revenue and liabilities
   D. revenue and expenses
   E. None of the above

Short Essay Response

Provide a detailed answer for each question.

1. What information appears on the income statement?
2. What is working capital?
3. Define balance sheet.
4. Why must businesses depreciate fixed assets such as equipment?
5. Why is it necessary to make an adjustment for supplies used at the end of an accounting period?
6. What information appears on the statement of cash flow?

Cooperative Learning

1. Form a group of three or four students. As a group discuss what effects there would be on the income statement and the balance sheet if a business did not make adjustments for supplies used, depreciation, and unpaid salaries. Would expenses be overstated or understated? Net income? Assets? Liabilities?
2. As a group, open any three of the companies you have saved and customize the income statement and balance sheet to the group's liking.

Writing and Decision Making

List the different financial statements that Sage 50 produces and state what information each provides. Also explain how these statements can be used to help management make wise financial decisions.

Case Problems

Demonstrate your knowledge of the Sage 50 Accounting features discussed in this chapter by completing the following case problems.

Case Problem 7–1A

Open Premier Management Group, which is located in the student data files.

1. Make the following adjusting entries for April 30, 2017:
   • Office supplies on hand on April 30, 2017: $180. Use Supplies Expense as the account to be debited.
   • Wages earned, but unpaid, as of April 30, 2017: $1,340.
   • Depreciation on the equipment amounted to $100.

2. Print the General Journal and General Ledger Trial Balance reports for April 30, 2017.

Case Problem 7–2A

Open Professional Accounting Services from the student data files.

1. Print the following financial statements for the period 2/1/17 to 2/28/17:
   • Income Statement
   • Statement of Changes in Financial Position
   • Balance Sheet
   • Statement of Cash Flow

HINT

At the Font dialog box, select Arial from the Font options, scroll through the Font styles options, and select Black.

2. Make the following changes to the Income Statement:
   - Change the Font Type of the first header "Professional Accounting Services" to Arial Black.
   - Change the Font Size of the first and second headers to 11.
   - Add a row below the header "Income Statement" to include the words *For Management Purposes Only* in the center of the column.
   - Delete the Text – Footer row.
   - Save as Modified Income Statement.

3. Print a new Income Statement when the changes are complete.

4. Change the accounting period to March 2017.

Case Problem 7–1B

Open Cindy's Interior Designs, which is located in the student data files.

1. Make the following adjusting entries for May 31, 2017:
   - Office supplies on hand on May 31, 2017: $125. Use Supplies Expense as the account to be debited.
   - Wages earned, but unpaid, as of May 31, 2017: $740.
   - Depreciation on the equipment amounted to $150.

2. Print the General Journal and General Ledger Trial Balance reports for May 31, 2017.

Case Problem 7–2B

Open Advanced Graphics from the student data files.

1. Print the following financial statements for the period 2/1/17 to 2/28/17:
   - Income Statement
   - Statement of Changes in Financial Position
   - Balance Sheet
   - Statement of Cash Flow

HINT

At the Font dialog box, select Arial from the Font options, scroll through the Font styles options, and select Black.

2. Make the following changes to the Income Statement:
   - Change the Font Type of the first header "Advanced Graphics" to Arial Black.
   - Change the Font Size of the first and second headers to 12.
   - Add a row below the header "Income Statement" to include the words *For Internal Use Only* in the center of the column.
   - Delete the Text – Footer row.
   - Save as Modified Income Statement.

3. Print a new Income Statement when the changes are complete.

4. Change the accounting period to March 2017.

Comprehensive Problem One

Demonstrate your knowledge of the Sage 50 Accounting features discussed in Chapters 1–7 by completing Comprehensive Problem One. Access the links menu to download the instructions for Comprehensive Problem One.

CHAPTER 8

Purchases of Inventory in a Merchandise Business

Objectives

8–1 Review the two basic inventory systems

8–2 Explore the most common inventory costing methods and create the inventory account

8–3 Establish subsidiary ledger accounts for inventory items

8–4 Establish records for sales representatives

8–5 Process inventory transactions

Software Features

- Maintain inventory items
- Display the Item List
- Maintain sales rep records
- Enter purchases/inventory transactions
- Print the Inventory Valuation Report

Company Files

Before beginning chapter work, access the links menu to download company files.

Chapters 2 through 7 focused on the accounting procedures of service businesses. In this chapter and succeeding chapters, the focus will be on the accounting procedures of merchandising businesses. Remember that *merchandising businesses* buy goods from manufacturers or wholesalers and resell them for a profit to consumers. Examples of merchandising businesses are department stores, grocery stores, and furniture stores.

One of the assets of a merchandising business is the stock of goods that it has on hand for resale to consumers. This stock of goods is called *inventory* or *merchandise inventory.*

OBJECTIVE 8–1

Review the Two Basic Inventory Systems

Two basic systems are used to keep track of inventory: the periodic inventory system and the perpetual inventory system. In the *periodic inventory system*, a count of all items in a firm's inventory is made at regular intervals, such as at the end of each accounting period, to determine ending inventory amounts. In the *perpetual inventory system*, the firm maintains a running balance for all inventory items.

The perpetual inventory system involves the use of inventory records that are updated throughout an accounting period as goods are purchased and sold. The periodic inventory system does not include such records. Sage 50 uses the perpetual inventory system.

Note: Both systems require a physical inventory count to determine discrepancies in inventory amounts.

Methods for Costing Inventory

The periodic and perpetual inventory systems keep track of the number of items of each type that a business has in its inventory. In addition to knowing what inventory is on hand, a business also needs to determine the dollar value of its inventory at the end of each accounting period. Various *inventory costing methods* are used for this purpose.

The three most common inventory costing methods are the average cost method, the last-in, first-out (LIFO) method, and the first-in, first-out (FIFO) method. Sage 50 supports all of these inventory costing methods.

Sales and Inventory Transactions

Sage 50 saves a great deal of time and effort for a merchandising business because it can be used to simultaneously update all records affected by a sale of goods. It increases the Sales, Sales Tax Payable, and Cost of Goods Sold accounts and decreases the Inventory account. Sage 50 also adjusts the sales records for individual customers, salespeople, and inventory records for individual items of inventory.

The Relationship between Inventory and Cost of Goods Sold

The income statement of a merchandising business contains a section called Cost of Goods Sold. This section shows the cost of the merchandise that the firm sold during the accounting period. Cost of goods sold is used to determine the gross profit from sales for the period.

When the periodic inventory system is used, the calculation of cost of goods sold on the income statement involves both the beginning and ending inventory, as shown below.

Beginning Inventory
+ Net Purchases
= Goods Available for Sale
− Ending Inventory
= Cost of Goods Sold

When the perpetual inventory system is used, there is a single Cost of Goods Sold account that includes all merchandise costs.

Inventory Systems

We will now take a closer look at the two basic inventory systems used by merchandising businesses—the periodic inventory system and the perpetual inventory system.

Periodic Inventory System

Traditionally, firms that sell a wide variety of low-cost items have used the periodic inventory system. Drugstores, hardware stores, office supply stores, and grocery stores are examples of such businesses.

With the periodic inventory system, a firm does not keep a continuous record of the changes in its inventory during the accounting period. All purchases of goods are debited to the Purchases account and all sales of goods are credited to the Sales account, but no entries are made in the Inventory account. Therefore, the firm has no precise way of calculating its cost of goods sold during an accounting period.

At the end of the period, a count is made of the goods on hand. The balance of the Inventory account is then updated to show the dollar value of the ending inventory.

The periodic inventory system has several drawbacks. One drawback has already been mentioned—the lack of information about the current dollar value of the inventory during the accounting period. However, an even more serious drawback is the lack of information about the availability of any single inventory item unless a separate tracking system is used.

For example, suppose that an office supply store has a balance of 400 boxes of file folders at the beginning of a period. The store purchases another 700 boxes of file folders during the period, but this amount will not show up in the inventory count until the end of the period. Thus, if a customer orders 500 boxes of file folders, the store will not know for sure whether it has enough stock on hand to fill the order.

Today, the periodic inventory system is less widely used than it was in the past. Modern technology has made the perpetual inventory system feasible and cost efficient for businesses with a large stock of low-priced items. Computerized inventory programs, optical scanners, and the Universal Product Code (UPC) printed on packages allow such firms to maintain a continuous record of inventory transactions.

Perpetual Inventory System

Inventory represents a major investment for a merchandising business. In fact, inventory is often the largest asset that such a firm owns.

The success of a merchandising business depends in part on careful management of its inventory. A firm wants to have an ample supply of fast-selling items available for customers, and it wants to keep its supply of slow-selling items to a minimum. Poor inventory decisions can result in lost sales because of a shortage of needed goods or because of markdowns on surplus goods that customers will buy only at reduced prices.

Because the perpetual inventory system maintains a running balance for all inventory items, it provides the information needed to effectively manage a firm's inventory. In the past, many firms considered the perpetual inventory system too time-consuming and costly. However, computerized accounting programs like Sage 50 have made it possible for even small businesses with limited staff and resources to use the perpetual inventory system.

The perpetual inventory system in Sage 50 has the following advantages:

- It keeps detailed records for all inventory items and updates these records throughout the accounting period as transactions occur.
- It updates the Inventory and Cost of Goods Sold accounts in the general ledger throughout the accounting period. Thus, there is no need to adjust the Inventory account at the end of the period.
- The costs for inventory items are always known, and selling prices can be changed at any time. The firm can raise selling prices on items with rising costs if it wishes. It can also cut selling prices on items with weak demand.

Checkpoint 8–1

1. What are the two basic systems for keeping track of inventory?
2. Which of the two basic inventory systems does Sage 50 use?

OBJECTIVE 8–2

Explore the Most Common Inventory Costing Methods and Create the Inventory Account

The inventory costing method selected by a business depends on the nature of its merchandise and other factors. Each method will produce a slightly different dollar value for the ending inventory and the cost of goods sold. As noted previously, Sage 50 supports three common inventory costing methods: the average cost method; the last-in, first-out (LIFO) method; and the first-in, first-out (FIFO) method.

Average Cost Method

average cost method
Inventory costing method in which the value of the ending inventory is based on a single cost (the average cost) assigned to all units available for sale.

The *average cost method* assigns a single cost (the average cost) to all units of an inventory item. This cost is found by dividing the total cost of the units available for sale during a period by the number of those units. The resulting figure—the average cost—is then multiplied by the number of units in the ending inventory to find the dollar value of the ending inventory.

For example, suppose that a firm had 1,090 units of a certain inventory item available for sale during a period. These units were acquired at three different prices. The total cost of the units available for sale was $12,920. The average cost was $11.85.

Beginning inventory	500 units	@	$11	=	$ 5,500
First purchase	250 units	@	$12	=	3,000
Second purchase	340 units	@	$13	=	4,420
	1,090 units				$12,920

Average cost = $12,920 ÷ 1,090 = $11.85

During the period, the firm sold 560 units of this item. Therefore, its ending inventory consists of 530 units (1,090 units – 560 units). The dollar value of the ending inventory is $6,280.50.

Ending inventory: 530 units × $11.85 (average cost) = $6,280.50

The cost of goods sold is $6,639.50.

Cost of goods available for sale	$12,920.00
Less ending inventory	6,280.50
Cost of goods sold	$ 6,639.50

Last-In, First-Out (LIFO) Method

LIFO method Inventory costing method in which the value of the ending inventory is based on the assumption that the last items purchased are the first ones sold.

The *last-in, first-out (LIFO) method* assumes that the last inventory items purchased are the first ones sold. This pattern may not match the actual flow of inventory items. However, the LIFO method is used for accounting purposes to value the ending inventory and need not be consistent with the physical flow of goods in a business.

Again, suppose that a firm had 1,090 units of a certain inventory item available for sale during a period. It sold 560 units, leaving 530 units in its ending inventory. Also assume the following prices for the beginning inventory and later purchases during the period.

Beginning inventory	500 units	@	$11	=	$ 5,500
First purchase	250 units	@	$12	=	3,000
Second purchase	340 units	@	$13	=	4,420
	1,090 units				$12,920

With the LIFO method, the ending inventory consists of the earliest goods because it is assumed that the first goods sold are the last ones purchased. The value of the ending inventory is therefore $5,860, as shown below. The cost of goods sold is $7,060.

Beginning inventory (earliest goods)	500 units	@	$11	=	$ 5,500
First purchase (next to earliest goods)	30 units	@	$12	=	360
	530 units				$5,860

Cost of goods available for sale	$12,920
Less ending inventory	5,860
Cost of goods sold	$ 7,060

First-In, First-Out (FIFO) Method

The *first-in, first-out (FIFO) method* assumes that the first inventory items purchased are the first ones sold. This pattern may or may not match the actual flow of inventory items in a business. However, keep in mind that an inventory costing method is selected for accounting purposes to value the ending inventory, not as a means to literally track when particular goods are purchased and sold.

Again, suppose that a firm had 1,090 units of a certain inventory item available for sale during a period, sold 560 units, and had 530 units in its ending inventory. Also assume the following prices for the beginning inventory and later purchases during the period.

Beginning inventory	500 units	@	$11	=	$ 5,500
First purchase	250 units	@	$12	=	3,000
Second purchase	340 units	@	$13	=	4,420
	1,090 units				$12,920

With the FIFO method, the ending inventory consists of the latest goods because it is assumed that the first goods sold are the first ones purchased. The value of the ending inventory is therefore $6,700, as shown below. The cost of goods sold is $6,220.

Second purchase (latest goods)	340 units	@ $13	=	$4,420
First purchase (next to latest goods)	190 units	@ $12	=	2,280
	530 units			$6,700

Cost of goods available for sale	$12,920
Less ending inventory	6,700
Cost of goods sold	$ 6,220

A Comparison of the Inventory Costing Methods

Table 8–1 provides a summary of the results of the three inventory costing methods discussed above. In a period of rising prices, the FIFO method will produce the highest dollar value for the ending inventory and the lowest cost of goods sold. The LIFO method will produce the lowest dollar value for the ending inventory and the highest cost of goods sold. The average cost method will produce results that fall between those of FIFO and LIFO.

TABLE 8–1
Inventory Costing Methods

	FIFO Method	Average Cost Method	LIFO Method
1. Cost of goods available for sale	$12,920.00	$12,920.00	$12,920.00
2. Less ending inventory	6,700.00	6,280.50	5,860.00
3. Cost of goods sold	$ 6,220.00	$ 6,639.50	$ 7,060.00

Keep in mind that the higher the cost of goods sold, the lower the net income. Thus, in a period of rising prices, LIFO provides a tax advantage for a business because it results in less taxable income.

Creating the Inventory Account

To use the inventory features of Sage 50 you must create an Inventory account in the general ledger and also create subsidiary ledger accounts for the various inventory items. For example, suppose that Superior Carpet and Tile, which is a service business, decides to add a merchandising operation. It will sell items such as a carpet cleaning compound, tile and carpet storage racks, and ceramic tile to its customers.

The first step for Superior Carpet and Tile is to create the asset account Inventory and the revenue account Carpet and Tile Sales in its general ledger. The Inventory account will serve as the controlling account for subsidiary ledger accounts that will provide detailed records of the various inventory items, and the revenue account will keep track of the sales. Remember that a controlling account links the general ledger to a subsidiary ledger. The balance of the controlling account represents the total of all the individual balances in the subsidiary ledger.

Step 1:

Open Superior Carpet and Tile (Chp. 8 – Superior Carpet and Tile if student files are used) and close the Action Items log.

Step 2:

Click Maintain on the Menu bar at the top of the basic Sage 50 window.

Step 3:

Click *Chart of Accounts*, as shown in Figure 8–1, and click the New button.

FIGURE 8–1
Chart of Accounts
Selected from Maintain
Drop-Down List

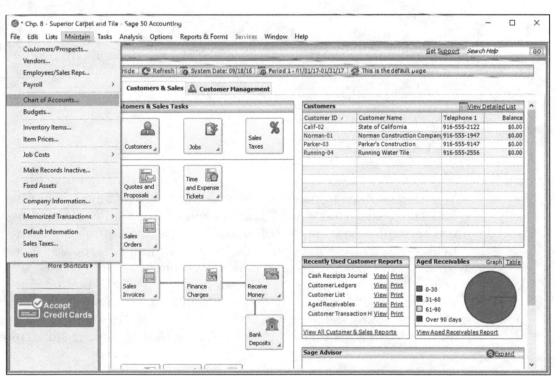

Step 4:

At the *Account ID* field, key **105**, and then click OK.

Step 5:

Key **Inventory** in the *Description* field.

Step 6:

At the *Account Type* field, click the down arrow key, and then click *Inventory*.

Step 7:

Compare your work with the completed information for the Inventory account, as shown in Figure 8–2.

FIGURE 8–2
Completed Information for Inventory Account

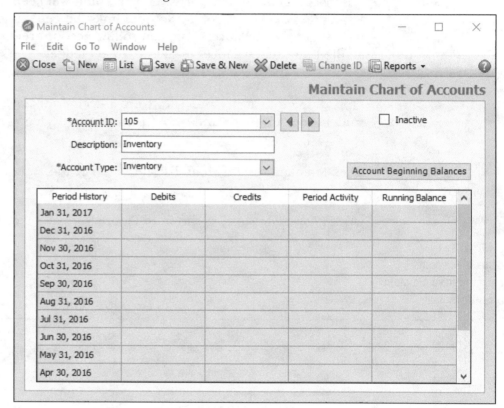

Step 8:

Click Save.

Step 9:

You will also need to create a Cost of Goods Sold account and a Carpet and Tile Sales account. According to standard accounting convention, this account should appear before the expense accounts on the chart of accounts. For example, cost of sales account numbers should begin with 500 and expense account numbers should begin with 600. However, keep in mind that this business began strictly as a service business and expense accounts were set up to begin with an account number of 500. Only recently has Superior Carpet and Tile decided to sell merchandise and keep inventory on hand. Therefore, the Cost of Goods Sold account number will be 503, the first available account number within the 500 range. This will have no adverse effect on any of the financial statements as long as Cost of Sales is chosen as the account type.

Create both the Cost of Goods Sold account and the Carpet and Tile Sales account in the general ledger.

Account ID:	**503**
Description:	**Cost of Goods Sold**
Account Type:	**Cost of Sales**

Account ID:	**400.5**
Description:	**Carpet and Tile Sales**
Account Type:	**Income**

Step 10:

After you have entered and checked the information for the two new accounts, click Close.

Checkpoint 8–2

1. What are the three most common inventory costing methods?
2. What type of account is the Inventory account in the general ledger and what is its function?

Objective 8–2 Practice

Step 1:

Open Meadowland Healthcare Services (Chp. 8 – Meadowland Healthcare Services if student files are used).

Step 2:

Review the Inventory account for this firm and make changes, if necessary.

Account ID:	**12000**
Description:	**Inventory**
Account Type:	**Inventory**

Step 3:

Review the Cost of Goods Sold account for this firm and make changes, if necessary.

Account ID:	**50000**
Description:	**Cost of Goods Sold**
Account Type:	**Cost of Sales**

Step 4:

Close the Maintain Chart of Accounts window.

OBJECTIVE 8-3
Establish Subsidiary Ledger Accounts for Inventory Items

In the perpetual inventory system used by Sage 50, you must set up a subsidiary ledger account for each inventory item. This account contains detailed information about the item and allows the business to keep track of its quantity and cost. Whenever goods are purchased or sold, the subsidiary ledger accounts for the inventory items are updated.

Superior Carpet and Tile will start its merchandising operation with three items: a carpet cleaning compound, tile and carpet storage racks, and ceramic tile. These items will be purchased from two suppliers.

Follow the steps outlined below to establish inventory defaults and to establish subsidiary ledger accounts for the three inventory items that Superior will initially stock.

Step 1:

Open Chp. 8 – Superior Carpet and Tile, which you previously updated in the chapter, and close the Action Items log.

Step 2:

Click Maintain and then click *Default Information* at the drop-down list, as shown in Figure 8–3.

FIGURE 8–3
**Default Information Selected
in Maintain Drop-Down List**

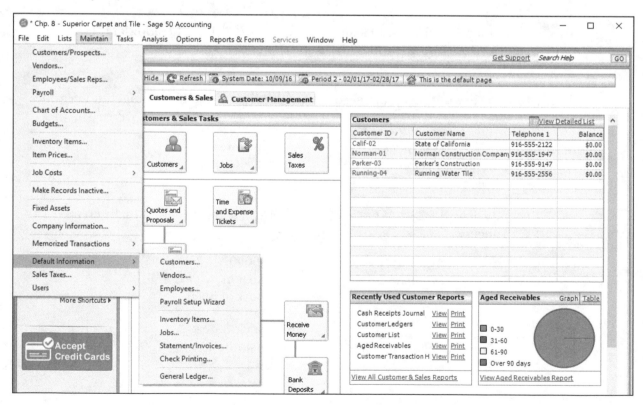

Step 3:

Click *Inventory Items* at the drop-down list and the Inventory Item Defaults window appears, as shown in Figure 8–4.

FIGURE 8–4
Inventory Item Defaults Window

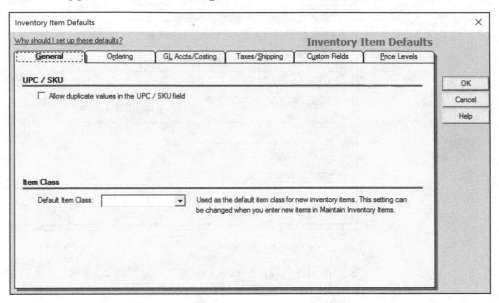

Step 4:

Select the GL Accts/Costing tab in the Inventory Item Defaults window.

Step 5:

Select account *400.5, Carpet and Tile Sales,* in the *GL Sales/Inc* account box aligned with Stock item.

Step 6:

Select account *105, Inventory,* in the *GL Invtry/Wage* account box aligned with Stock item.

Step 7:

Select account *503, Cost of Goods Sold,* in the *GL Cost Sales* account box aligned with Stock item.

Step 8:

Accept the FIFO Costing default.

Step 9:

Enter account *105, Inventory,* in the *GL Freight Account* box located at the bottom of the window. Superior adds the freight cost to inventory.

Step 10:

Review Figure 8–5 for accuracy, making any necessary changes.

FIGURE 8–5
Completed GL Accts/
Costing Tab

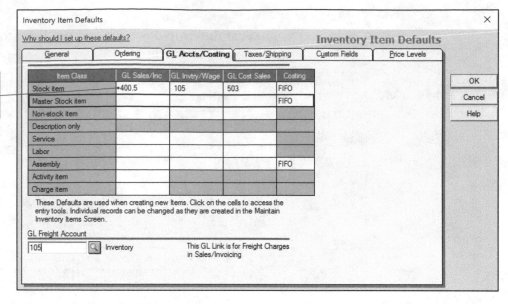

Enter your default data in the first row.

Step 11:

Select the Price Levels tab.

Step 12:

Key **Full Price** in the *Level Name* field aligned with Level 1.

Step 13:

Insert a check mark in the Enabled box in the cell aligned with Level 1 (if there is not already a check mark). Remove all other enabled check marks, if present, as shown in Figure 8–6.

FIGURE 8–6
Completed Price
Levels Tab

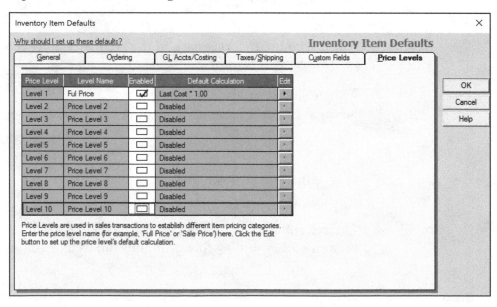

Step 14:

Click the Edit button aligned with Level 1.

Step 15:

Select *Last Cost* from the Use drop-down list.

Step 16:

Accept the default *Increase by Percent* and leave the (%) *0.*

Step 17:

Select *No Rounding* at the Round Price drop-down list, if needed.

Step 18:

Review for accuracy, make any necessary changes, and click OK.

Step 19:

Click OK to establish the pricing defaults.

Step 20:

Click Maintain and then click *Inventory Items.* The Maintain Inventory Items window will appear.

Step 21:

Key **CC-1** in the *Item ID* field and then click OK.

Step 22:

Key **Carpet Care** in the *Description* field.

Step 23:

At the *Item Class* field, click the down arrow key, and then click *Stock item,* if needed.

Step 24:

Click the right arrow key to the right of the Full Price box.

Step 25:

Key **22.50** in the *Price* box aligned with Full Price, as shown in Figure 8–7.

FIGURE 8–7
Multiple Price Levels
Window Completed

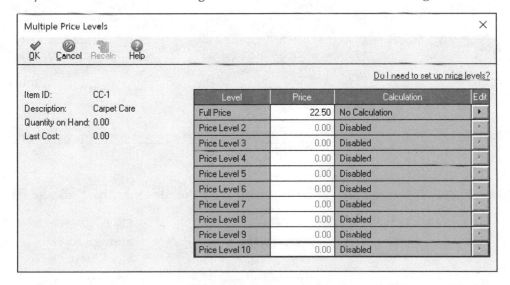

Step 26:

Click OK to exit the Multiple Price Levels window.

Step 27:

In the Maintain Inventory Items window, key **10.00** in the *Last Unit Cost* field.

Step 28:

Key **8877665543** in the *UPC/SKU* field and **Retail** in the *Item Type* field.

Note: UPC/SKU stands for Universal Product Code/Stock Keeping Units. These numbers are used for bar coding and computerized tracking of inventory items.

Step 29:

Key **Each** in the *Stocking U/M* field.

Note: U/M stands for Units of Measure.

Step 30:

At the *Preferred Vendor ID* field, click the *magnifying glass* icon, and then click *APX-005*.

Step 31:

Compare your completed Maintain Inventory Items window with Figure 8–8. Click Save and then New.

FIGURE 8–8
Completed Maintain Inventory Items Window

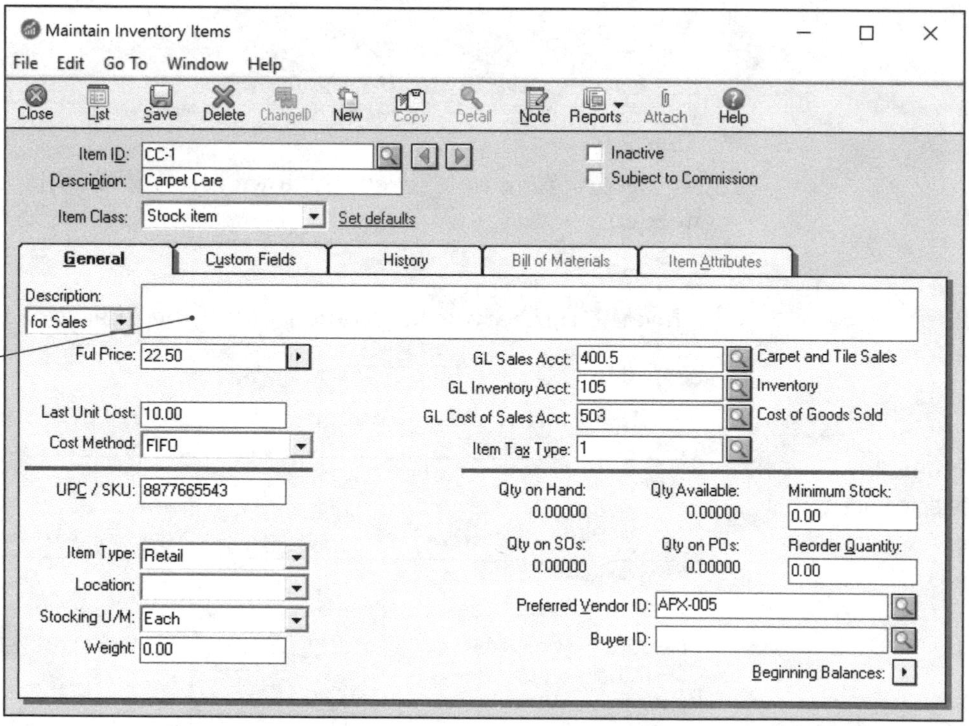

An additional description or comment can be added here if desired.

Step 32:

Enter the information for the tile and carpet storage racks:

Item ID:	**SK-2**
Description:	**Storage Rack**
Item Class:	**Stock item**
Description:	**for Sales**
Full Price:	**125.00**
Last Unit Cost:	**52.50**
Cost Method:	**FIFO**

UPC/SKU:	**1234543456**
Item Type:	**Retail**
Stocking U/M:	**Each**
GL Sales Acct:	**400.5**
GL Inventory Acct:	**105**
GL Cost of Sales Acct:	**503**
Item Tax Type:	**1**
Preferred Vendor ID:	**None**

Step 33:

Click Save and then New.

Step 34:

Enter the information for the ceramic tile:

Item ID:	**CT-3**
Description:	**Ceramic Tile**
Item Class:	**Stock item**
Description:	**for Sales**
Full Price:	**225.00**
Last Unit Cost:	**100.00**
Cost Method:	**FIFO**
UPC/SKU:	**9987655645**
Item Type:	**Retail**
Stocking U/M:	**Each**
GL Sales Acct:	**400.5**
GL Inventory Acct:	**105**
GL Cost of Sales Acct:	**503**
Item Tax Type:	**1**
Preferred Vendor ID:	**None**

Step 35:

Click Save and then Close.

Displaying the Item List

Sage 50 provides a number of different inventory reports. One of these reports—the Item List—shows the quantity on hand and other information about all inventory items. Follow the steps outlined below to display the Item List.

Step 1:

Click Reports & Forms on the Menu bar and then click *Inventory*.

Step 2:

In the Inventory: Items and Services You Buy and Sell section, click *Item List* as shown in Figure 8-9.

FIGURE 8–9

Item List Selected

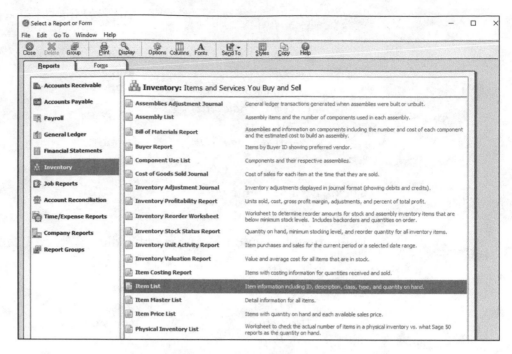

Step 3:

Click the Display button on the Select a Report or Form toolbar.

Step 4:

Review the Item List report shown in Figure 8–10. The *Qty on Hand* field is blank because the firm has not yet received any goods.

FIGURE 8–10

Item List

| 9/18/16 at 05:20:45.03 | *****EDUCATIONAL VERSION ONLY***** | | | | Page: 1 |

Chp. 8 - Superior Carpet and Tile
Item List

Filter Criteria includes: Report order is by ID.

Item ID	Item Description	Item Class	Active?	Item Type	Qty on Hand
CC-1	Carpet Care	Stock item	Active	Retail	
CT-3	Ceramic Tile	Stock item	Active	Retail	
SK-2	Storage Rack	Stock item	Active	Retail	

Step 5:

Click Close. Then close the Select a Report or Form dialog box.

Checkpoint 8–3

1. What is the purpose of the subsidiary ledger account for each inventory item?
2. What inventory report produced by Sage 50 shows the quantity on hand for all inventory items?

Meadowland Healthcare Services has decided to sell some goods to patients. It will sell syringes, roller bandages, and medical scales.

Step 1:

Open Chp. 8 – Meadowland Healthcare Services, which you updated previously in the chapter.

Step 2:

Create the Inventory Defaults, if necessary, using the information given below:

GL Accts/Costing

GL Sales/Inc	**40000**
GL Invtry/Wage	**12000**
GL Cost Sales	**50000**
Costing	**FIFO**
GL Freight Account	**12000**

Price Levels

Level Name, Level 1	**Full Price**
Use	**Last Cost**

Step 3:

Create subsidiary ledger accounts for the following inventory items:

Item 1

Item ID:	**SY-1**
Description:	**Syringes**
Item Class:	**Stock item**
Description:	**for Sales**
Full Price:	**12.00**
Last Unit Cost:	**5.00**
Cost Method:	**FIFO**
UPC/SKU:	**3344234564**
Item Type:	**Retail**
Stocking U/M:	**Package**
GL Sales Acct:	**40000**
GL Inventory Acct:	**12000**
GL Cost of Sales Acct:	**50000**
Item Tax Type:	**1**
Preferred Vendor ID:	**None**

Item 2

Item ID:	**RB-2**
Description:	**Roller Bandages**
Item Class:	**Stock item**
Description:	**for Sales**
Full Price:	**75.00**
Last Unit Cost:	**30.00**
Cost Method:	**FIFO**
UPC/SKU:	**4534543457**
Item Type:	**Retail**
Stocking U/M:	**Case**

GL Sales Acct:	**40000**
GL Inventory Acct:	**12000**
GL Cost of Sales Acct:	**50000**
Item Ta̲x Type:	**1**
Preferred V̲endor ID:	**None**

Item 3

Item I̲D:	**MS-3**
Description:	**Medical Scale**
Item Class:	**Stock item**
Description:	**for Sales**
Full Price:	**325.00**
Last Unit Cost:	**130.00**
Cost Method:	**FIFO**
UP̲C/SKU:	**6234543459**
Item Type:	**Retail**
Stocking U/M:	**Each**
GL Sales Acct:	**40000**
GL Inventory Acct:	**12000**
GL Cost of Sales Acct:	**50000**
Item Ta̲x Type:	**1**
Preferred V̲endor ID:	**None**

Step 4:

Preview the Item List report and compare it with Figure 8–11.

FIGURE 8–11
Item List

9/18/16 at 05:28:14.50	*****EDUCATIONAL VERSION ONLY*****					Page: 1
	Chp. 8 - Meadowland Healthcare Services					
	Item List					

Filter Criteria includes: Report order is by ID.

Item ID	Item Description	Item Class	Active?	Item Type	Qty on Hand
MS-3	Medical Scale	Stock item	Active	Retail	
RB-2	Roller Bandages	Stock item	Active	Retail	
SY-1	Syringes	Stock item	Active	Retail	

Step 5:

Close the Select a Report or Form dialog box.

OBJECTIVE 8-4

Establish Records for Sales Representatives

Many merchandising businesses use sales representatives to market their goods. These sales representatives may be employees or independent contractors. Sage 50 allows a firm to keep track of the sales made by its sales representatives. However, you must first set up a record for each sales representative.

Superior Carpet and Tile has two sales representatives, Ernesto Garcia and Maria Davis, who are independent contractors. Use the steps outlined below to establish records for these sales representatives. The creation of payroll records for sales representatives who are employees will be discussed in a later chapter.

Step 1:

Open Chp. 8 – Superior Carpet and Tile and close the Action Items log.

Step 2:

Click Maintain, and then click *Employees/Sales Reps.* Click No at the Setup Payroll Wizard query. The Maintain Employees & Sales Reps window will appear. Enter the following information for Ernesto Garcia, a sales representative.

Step 3:

Key **EGA-01** in the *Employee ID* field.

Step 4:

Key **Ernesto J. Garcia** in the *Name* field.

Step 5:

Click the *Sales Rep* option.

Step 6:

Key **2335 Wilson Way** in the *Address* field.

Step 7:

Key **Modesto, CA 95355** in the *City, ST, Zip* fields. Key **USA** in the *Country* field.

Step 8:

Key **209-555-1234** in the *Home phone* field.

Step 9:

Key **887-09-9989** in the *Social Security Number* field.

Step 10:

Key **Independ** for independent contractor in the *Type* field.

Step 11:

Compare your entries with the ones shown in Figure 8–12.

FIGURE 8–12
Completed Maintain
Employees & Sales Reps
Window

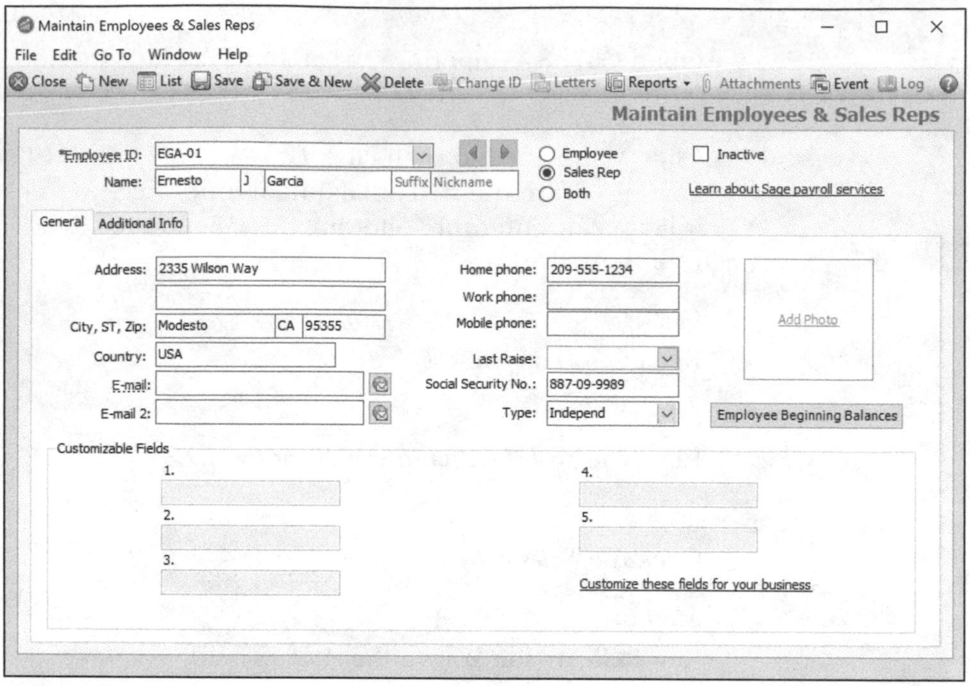

Step 12:

Click Save & New.

Step 13:

Enter the following information for the second sales representative of
Superior Carpet and Tile.

Employee ID:	**MDA-02**
Name:	**Maria P. Davis**
Address:	**778 Kemp Road**
City, ST, Zip:	**Stockton, CA 95250**
Country:	**USA**
Home Phone:	**209-555-2468**
Social Security Number:	**662-04-4434**
Type:	**Independ**

Step 14:

Click Save and then Close.

Checkpoint 8–4

1. Why would a user of Sage 50 want to set up records for its sales
   representatives?
2. What are the two types of sales representatives?

Meadowland Healthcare Services has hired two sales representatives: Julie Hernandez and Isadora Duncan.

Step 1:

Open Chp. 8 – Meadowland Healthcare Services.

Step 2:

Establish a record for each sales representative.

Employee ID:	**JHE-01**
Name:	**Julie Q. Hernandez**
Address:	**1223 Westin Road**
City, ST, Zip:	**Stockton, CA 95250**
Country:	**USA**
Home Phone:	**209-555-4556**
Social Security Number:	**533-45-8743**
Type:	**Independ**

Employee ID:	**IDU-02**
Name:	**Isadora X. Duncan**
Address:	**2389 Alexandria Drive**
City, ST, Zip:	**Modesto, CA 95355**
Country:	**USA**
Home Phone:	**209-555-9008**
Social Security Number:	**332-09-8743**
Type:	**Independ**

OBJECTIVE 8-5

Process Inventory Transactions

One of the advantages of using Sage 50 for a merchandising business is the ease of processing inventory transactions. Sage 50 can be used to quickly and efficiently set up vendor accounts, issue purchase orders, record the receipt of inventory items, pay vendors for the items, and keep track of the quantity and cost of inventory items.

Creating Vendor Accounts with Discounts

The procedure for creating vendor accounts was covered in Chapter 5. However, most of the vendors discussed there did not offer discounts. Many vendors who provide goods to merchandising businesses allow discounts for payment within a short period.

For example, Superior Carpet and Tile will buy its storage racks from BMC Supply Company. BMC offers credit terms of 2/10, n/30. This means that Superior can take a 2% discount if it pays within 10 days. Otherwise, it has 30 days to pay the net (full) amount of the invoice.

Use the steps outlined below to create a vendor account for the BMC Supply Company.

Step 1:

Open Chp. 8 – Superior Carpet and Tile.

Step 2:

Click Maintain and then click *Vendors*.

Step 3:

The Maintain Vendors dialog box will appear. Key **BMC-007** in the *Vendor ID* field.

Step 4:

Key **BMC Supply Company** in the *Name* field.

Step 5:

At the General folder tab, key **Jerome Jones** in the *Contact* field.

Step 6:

Key **00789** in the *Account Number* field.

Step 7:

Key **2150 First Street** in the *Mailing Address* field.

Step 8:

Key **Modesto, CA 95355** in the *City, ST, Zip* field. Key **USA** in the *Country* field.

Step 9:

Key **Supplier** in the *Vendor Type* field and select *None* from the 1099 Type drop-down list (if necessary).

Step 10:

Key **105** (Inventory) in the *Expense Account* field.

Step 11:

Key **209-555-4444** in the *Telephone 1* field. Then check your work for accuracy by comparing it with Figure 8–13.

FIGURE 8–13
Completed Entries under General Folder Tab

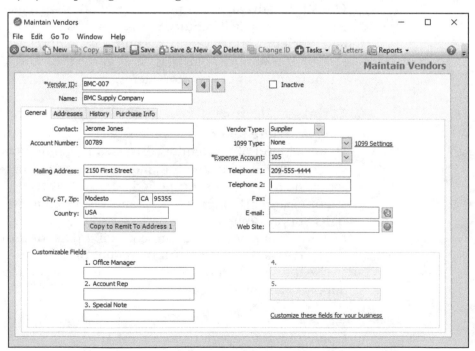

Step 12:

Click the Purchase Info folder tab.

Step 13:

Key **09-667755** in the *Tax ID Number* field.

Step 14:

Click *UPS Ground* in the *Ship Via* field.

Step 15:

Click the drop-down list arrow in the Terms and Credit box and then select *Customize terms for this vendor*. The dialog box that appears is used to change the credit terms offered by a vendor.

Step 16:

The default terms for vendors were set up when the company was created in Sage 50. Change the standard terms to 2/10, n/30.

Step 17:

Accept the default, *Paper Form*, at the Form Options box, and Use payment method and cash account from last saved period, at the payments setting box.

Step 18:

Compare your work with the completed Purchase Info folder tab shown in Figure 8–14.

FIGURE 8–14
Completed Entries on
Purchase Info Folder Tab

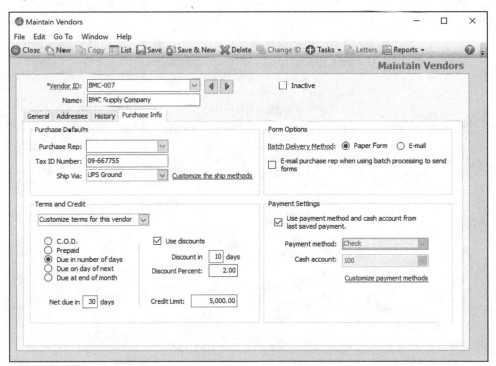

Step 19:

Click Save and then Close.

Purchasing Goods without a Purchase Order

Some businesses issue a purchase order to vendors whenever they want to buy goods. Other businesses buy goods without a purchase order. Sage 50 supports either method of purchasing goods.

For example, on February 3, 2017, Superior Carpet and Tile ordered 23 storage racks on credit from the BMC Supply Company. Superior placed the order over the telephone and did not issue a written purchase order. BMC will send Invoice 3244 to bill Superior for the goods.

Follow the steps outlined below to record this purchase without a purchase order.

Step 1:

Click Tasks, and then click *Purchases/Receive Inventory*.

Step 2:

At the Purchases/Receive Inventory window, click the *magnifying glass* icon at the *Vendor ID* field and then click *BMC-007*.

Step 3:

Change the *Invoice date* field to *Feb. 3, 2017*.

Step 4:

Key **3244** in the *Invoice No.* field.

HINT

Remember to enter a decimal when entering amounts.

Step 5:

Key **23.00** in the *Quantity* field.

Step 6:

Click the *magnifying glass* icon at the *Item* field and then click *SK-2*. Notice that the window is automatically completed.

Step 7:

Compare your entries with the completed Purchases/Receive Inventory window shown in Figure 8–15.

FIGURE 8–15
Completed Purchases/
Receive Inventory
Window

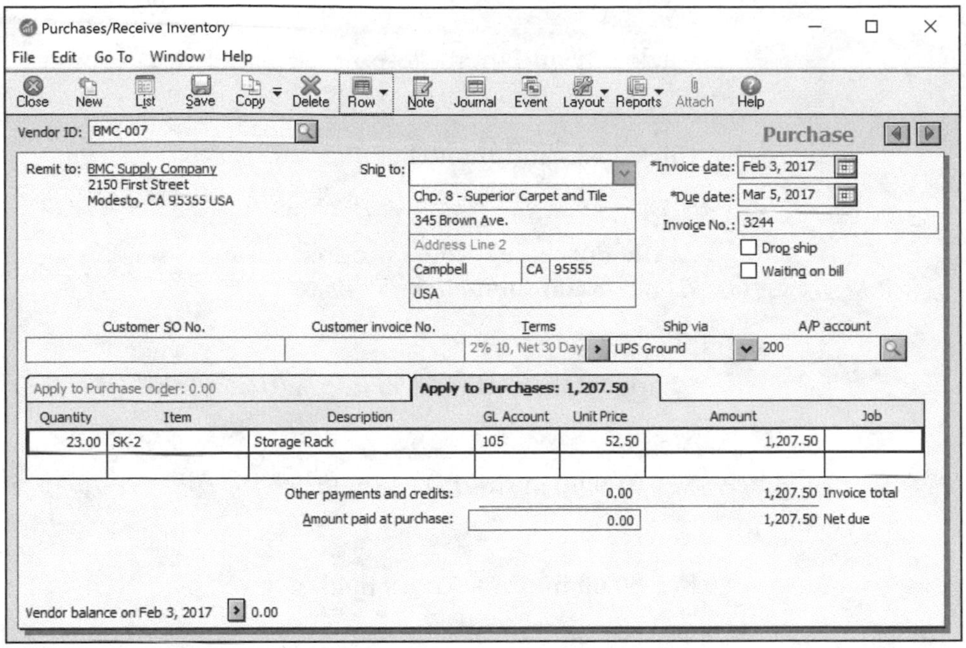

Step 8:

Click Save and then Close.

Purchasing Goods with a Purchase Order

Some businesses have a policy of issuing purchase orders to vendors for all purchases of goods and supplies. This policy helps guard against unauthorized purchases.

Suppose that Superior Carpet and Tile adopts such a policy. On February 5, 2017, it decides to issue Purchase Order 010500 to the JS West Company for 30 cases of ceramic tile. Follow the steps outlined below to create the necessary purchase order.

Step 1:

Set up a vendor account for the JS West Company.

Vendor ID:	**JSW-008**
Name:	**JS West Company**
Contact:	**Harry West**
Account Number:	**010589**
Mailing Address:	**2121 Third Street**
City, ST, Zip:	**Modesto, CA 95355**
Country:	**USA**
Vendor Type:	**Supplier**
1099 Type:	**None**
Expense Account:	**105**
Telephone 1:	**209-555-2222**
Tax ID Number:	**09-557766**
Ship Via:	**UPS Ground**
Terms and Credit:	**2/10, n/30**
Form Options:	**Default**

Step 2:

Click Save and then Close.

Step 3:

Click Tasks and then click *Purchase Orders.*

Step 4:

At the Purchase Orders window, click the *magnifying glass* icon at the *Vendor ID* field, and then click *JSW-008.*

Step 5:

Change the *Date* field to *Feb. 5, 2017* and the *Good thru* field to *Mar 7, 2017.*

Step 6:

Key **010500** in the *PO No.* field.

Step 7:

Key **30.00** in the *Quantity* field.

Step 8:

At the *Item* field, click the *magnifying glass* icon and then click *CT-3.*

Step 9:

Compare your work with Figure 8–16.

FIGURE 8–16
Completed Purchase Orders Window

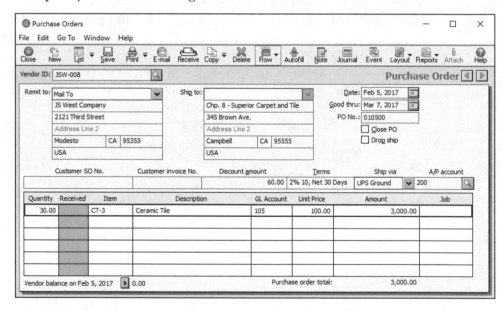

Step 10:

Click Save and then Close.

Receiving Goods Purchased with a Purchase Order

Remember that Superior Carpet and Tile issued Purchase Order 010500 to buy 30 cases of ceramic tile from JS West Company. On February 10, 2017, Superior received the goods along with Invoice 998778. Follow the steps outlined below to record the receipt of these inventory items.

Step 1:

Click Tasks and then click *Purchases/Receive Inventory*.

Step 2:

At the *Vendor ID* field, click the *magnifying glass* icon and then click *JSW-008*.

Step 3:

Change the *Invoice date* field to *Feb. 10, 2017*.

Step 4:

Key **998778** in the *Invoice No.* field.

Step 5:

Click the down arrow key to the right of the folder tab labeled *Apply to Purchase Order No.*, and then click *010500*, as shown in Figure 8–17.

FIGURE 8–17
Purchase Order
Number Selected

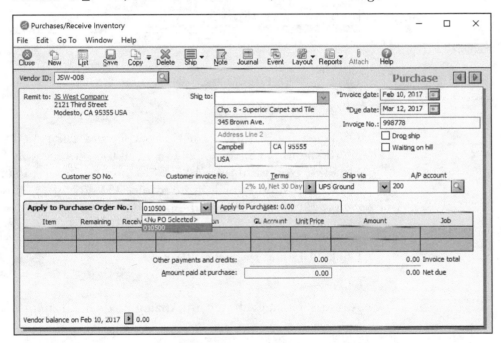

Step 6:

Key **30.00** in the *Received* field. This indicates that all the cases of ceramic tile that the business ordered were received.

Step 7:

Compare your completed Purchases/Receive Inventory window with Figure 8–18.

FIGURE 8–18
Completed Purchases/
Receive Inventory
Window

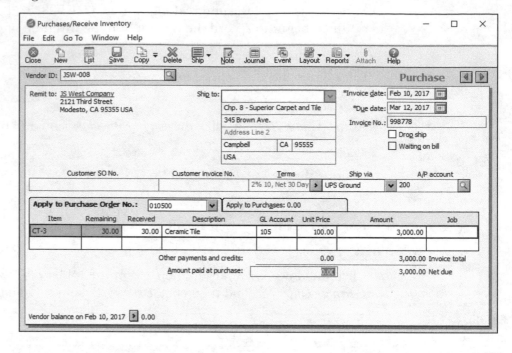

Step 8:

Click Save and then Close.

Paying an Invoice with a Discount

On February 10, 2017, Superior Carpet and Tile issued a check for $1,183.35 to pay Invoice 3244 owed to the BMC Supply Company. Because Superior paid within the 10-day discount period, it took a 2% discount ($24.15) from the total of the invoice ($1,207.50). Follow the steps outlined below to record the payment of Invoice 3244.

Step 1:

Click Tasks and then click *Payments*.

Step 2:

At the Select a Cash Account dialog box, click *Cash Account, 100*, if needed.

Step 3:

At the Payments window, click the *magnifying glass* icon in the box to the right of the *Vendor ID* field, and then click *BMC-007*.

Step 4:

Key **105** in the *Check/Reference No.* field.

Step 5:

Change the *Date* field to *Feb. 10, 2017*.

Step 6:

Click the *Apply to Invoices* folder tab, if needed.

Step 7:

Click the check box in the *Pay* field and a red check mark will appear. Notice that the discount amount is automatically calculated.

Step 8:

Key **105** in the *Discount account* field at the bottom of the window.

Step 9:

Compare your completed entries with those shown in Figure 8–19.

FIGURE 8–19
Completed Payments
Window

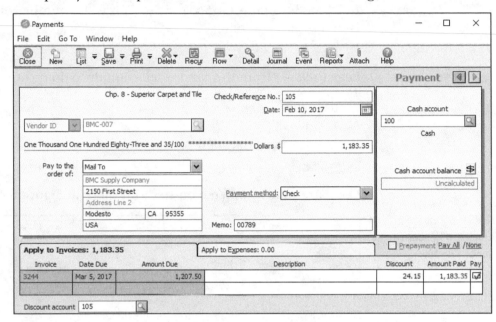

Step 10:

Click Save and Close.

Step 11:

Open the payment you just created and click the $ icon on the right side of the payment window next to the *Cash account balance* field to update the balance. The new balance should be $17,482.61.

Step 12:

Click Close.

Returning Goods

Sometimes a business receives damaged goods or incorrect goods from a vendor. For example, assume that after Superior Carpet and Tile records the receipt of the 30 cases of ceramic tile purchased from JS West Company, it discovers that 2 of the cases are damaged. It therefore returns these items to the vendor. JS West Company issues a vendor credit memo for the returned goods. Take the following steps to record the vendor credit memo.

Step 1:

Click Tasks and then click *Vendor Credit Memos.*

Step 2:

At the Vendor Credit Memos window, click the *magnifying glass* icon next to the *Vendor ID* field, and then click *JSW-008*.

Step 3:

Click the *calendar* icon next to the *Credit date* field and select *Feb. 10, 2017* as the date.

Step 4:

Key **CM3390** in the *Credit No.* field. This is the number of the credit memo issued by the vendor.

Step 5:

Select *998778* from the invoice selection drop-down list next to *Apply to Invoice No.*

Step 6:

Key **2.00** in the *Returned* field.

Step 7:

Compare your completed entries with those in Figure 8–20.

FIGURE 8–20
Completed Vendor Credit Memos Window

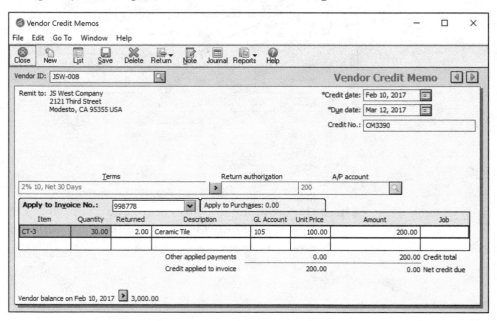

Step 8:

Click Save and then Close.

Printing the Inventory Valuation Report

One of the inventory reports that Sage 50 produces shows the quantity on hand, the cost of each inventory item, and the total cost of the firm's inventory. This report is called the *Inventory Valuation Report*. Follow the steps outlined below to print the Inventory Valuation Report.

Step 1:

Click Reports & Forms and then click *Inventory*.

Step 2:

At the Select a Report or Form dialog box, in the Inventory: Items and Services You Buy and Sell section, click *Inventory Valuation Report.*

Step 3:

Click <u>P</u>rint on the Select a Report or Form toolbar.

Step 4:

Click OK at the Modify Report – Inventory Valuation Report, and then OK again at the Print dialog box.

Step 5:

Compare your printout to the Inventory Valuation Report shown in Figure 8–21.

FIGURE 8–21
Inventory Valuation Report

9/18/16 at 05:58:34.63	*****EDUCATIONAL VERSION ONLY*****					Page: 1
		Chp. 8 - Superior Carpet and Tile				
		Inventory Valuation Report				
		As of Feb 28, 2017				
Filter Criteria includes: 1) Stock/Assembly. Report order is by ID. Report is printed with shortened descriptions.						

Item ID Item Class	Item Description	Stocking U/M	Cost Method	Qty on Han	Item Value	Avg Cost	% of Inv Value
CC-1 Stock item	Carpet Care	Each	FIFO				
CT-3 Stock item	Ceramic Tile	Each	FIFO	28.00	2,800.00		69.87
SK-2 Stock item	Storage Rack	Each	FIFO	23.00	1,207.50		30.13
					4,007.50		**100.00**

Step 6:

Click Close.

Checkpoint 8–5

1. What do the terms 2/10, n/30 on an invoice mean?
2. What does the Inventory Valuation Report show?

Objective 8-5 Practice

Meadowland Healthcare Services buys its roller bandages from General Medical Services and its syringes from LK Surgical Supply Co.

Step 1:

Open Chp. 8 – Meadowland Healthcare Services.

Step 2:

Create the following vendor accounts using the information provided below. Be careful to adjust vendor terms as given.

Vendor ID:	**GMS-006**
Name:	**General Medical Services**
Contact:	**Stan Sherman**
Account Number:	**09088676**
Mailing Address:	**3450 Orangeburg Drive**
City, ST, Zip:	**Modesto, CA 95357**
Country:	**USA**
Vendor Type:	**Supplier**
1099 Type:	**None**
Expense Acct:	**12000**
Telephone 1:	**209-555-8894**
Tax ID Number:	**09-754345**
Ship Via:	**UPS Ground**
Terms and Credit:	**1/10, n/45**
Form Options:	**Default**
Payment Settings:	**Default**

Vendor ID:	**LKS-007**
Name:	**LK Surgical Supply Co.**
Contact:	**Lou Kim**
Account Number:	**1000345**
Mailing Address:	**1245 Arrow Smith Road**
City, ST, Zip:	**Modesto, CA 95353**
Country:	**USA**
Vendor Type:	**Supplier**
1099 Type:	**None**
Expense Acct:	**12000**
Telephone 1:	**209-555-8445**
Tax ID Number:	**09-777998**
Ship Via:	**UPS Ground**
Terms and Credit:	**3/15, n/60**
Form Options:	**Default**
Payment Settings:	**Default**

Step 3:

Record the following transactions:

- On February 2, 2017, Meadowland Healthcare Services purchased 230 roller bandages (RB-2) on credit from General Medical Services. Meadowland received Invoice 4556.
- On February 4, 2017, Meadowland ordered 100 packages of syringes (SY-1) on credit from LK Surgical Supply Co. Meadowland issued Purchase Order 010402.
- On February 10, 2017, Meadowland received 100 packages of syringes ordered on Purchase Order 010402 from LK Surgical Supply Co. Enclosed with the syringes was Invoice 558990.

- On February 11, 2017, Meadowland returned 10 cases of roller bandages purchased from General Medical Services. Meadowland received Vendor Credit Memo 890 (CM890). The original invoice was 4556.
- On February 11, 2017, Meadowland paid Invoice 558990, less discount, to LK Surgical Supply Co., Check No. 705.

Note: The Discount Account field should read 12000.

Step 4:

Print the Inventory Valuation Report. Your printout should look like Figure 8–22.

FIGURE 8–22
Inventory Valuation Report for Meadowland Healthcare Services

9/18/16 at 06:16:43.01	*****EDUCATIONAL VERSION ONLY*****						Page: 1
		Chp. 8 - Meadowland Healthcare Services					
		Inventory Valuation Report					
		As of Feb 28, 2017					
Filter Criteria includes: 1) Stock/Assembly. Report order is by ID. Report is printed with shortened descriptions.							

Item ID Item Class	Item Description	Stocking U/M	Cost Method	Qty on Han	Item Value	Avg Cost	% of Inv Value
MS-3 Stock item	Medical Scale	Each	FIFO				
RB-2 Stock item	Roller Bandages	Case	FIFO	220.00	6,600.00		92.96
SY-1 Stock item	Syringes	Package	FIFO	100.00	500.00		7.04
					7,100.00		**100.00**

Chapter Review and Assessment

Software Command Summary

Create Inventory Item	Maintain, Inventory Items
Display Item List	Reports & Forms, Inventory, Select Item List
Create Salesperson Record	Maintain, Employees/Sales Reps
Create Vendor Account	Maintain, Vendors
Enter Purchase without Purchase Order	Tasks, Purchases/Receive Inventory
Create Purchase Order	Tasks, Purchase Orders
Pay Invoice	Tasks, Payments
Return Goods	Tasks, Vendor Credit Memos

Checkpoint Answers

Checkpoint 8–1

1. The periodic inventory system and the perpetual inventory system are the two basic systems for keeping track of inventory.
2. Sage 50 uses the perpetual inventory system.

Checkpoint 8–2

1. The three most common inventory costing methods are the average cost, LIFO, and FIFO methods.
2. The Inventory account in the general ledger is an asset account. It serves as the controlling account for the subsidiary ledger accounts kept for the various inventory items.

Checkpoint 8–3

1. The subsidiary ledger account for each inventory item is used to keep track of the quantity and cost of the item.
2. The Item List shows the quantity on hand for all inventory items.

Checkpoint 8–4

1. By setting up records for its sales representatives, a user of Sage 50 can keep track of each representative's sales.
2. Some sales representatives are employees, and others are independent contractors.

Study Quizzes

Take the study quiz online to check your understanding of chapter concepts. The quiz can be taken multiple times.

Content Check

Multiple Choice: Choose only one response for each question.

1. Sage 50 supports which of the following inventory costing methods?
   A. average cost
   B. LIFO
   C. FIFO
   D. All of the above

2. Credit terms of 1/10, n/30 mean
   A. a 1% discount is allowed if the invoice is paid within 10 days, or the entire net amount is due within 30 days.
   B. a 1% discount is allowed if the invoice is paid within 30 days.
   C. a 10% discount is allowed if the bill is paid within 1 day of receipt, or the entire amount is due within 30 days.
   D. None of the above

3. The perpetual inventory system involves
   A. counting goods at regular intervals.
   B. estimating the number of goods on hand.
   C. maintaining a running balance for all inventory items.
   D. estimating the cost of the goods on hand.

4. In a period of rising prices, which inventory costing method will result in the highest cost of goods sold?
   A. average cost
   B. LIFO
   C. FIFO
   D. perpetual

5. What function of Sage 50 will a firm use to record the return of damaged goods to a vendor?
   A. Sales/Invoicing
   B. Receive Money
   C. Vendor Credit Memos
   D. Payments

Short Essay Response

Provide a detailed answer for each question.

1. What is the difference between the perpetual inventory system and the periodic inventory system?
2. Explain each of the three most common inventory costing methods: average cost, LIFO, and FIFO.
3. Sage 50 will automatically update which accounts when an inventory item is sold? Will these accounts increase or decrease?
4. Explain the steps necessary to create a new vendor account.
5. List two inventory reports that Sage 50 produces. What information does each of these reports contain?
6. What advantages might a business gain by switching from the periodic inventory system to the perpetual inventory system?

Cooperative Learning

1. Form groups of three or four students and discuss how each of the inventory costing methods will affect taxable income in periods when prices are rising.
2. As a group, choose a local business such as a clothing store, a sporting goods store, or a drugstore. What inventory control problems might this business have?

Writing and Decision Making

Assume that you work for a small merchandising business that does not yet use computerized inventory procedures. The owner, Marie Ramirez, has asked you to provide information on how Sage 50 can help her manage the firm's inventory. She has specifically asked you to explain the steps necessary to set up Sage 50's inventory system, what tasks the system can handle, and what records and reports it produces. Prepare a memo providing the information that has been requested.

 ## Case Problems

Demonstrate your knowledge of the Sage 50 Accounting features discussed in this chapter by completing the following case problems.

Case Problem 8–1A

Open Kathleen's Designs, an interior decorating business, which is located in the student data files.

1. Create the Inventory account for this business.

Account ID:	**105**
Description:	**Inventory**
Account Type:	**Inventory**

2. Create the Cost of Sales account.

Account ID:	**503**
Description:	**Cost of Goods Sold**
Account Type:	**Cost of Sales**

3. Create the following vendor accounts:

Vendor ID:	**SHGS-01**
Name:	**Sanders Home and Garden Supply**
Contact:	**Robert Sanders**
Account Number:	**1691**
Mailing Address:	**2345 Main Street**
City, ST, Zip:	**Modesto, CA 95355**
Country:	**USA**
Vendor Type:	**Supplier**
1099 Type:	**None**
Expense Acct:	**105**
Telephone 1:	**209-555-9756**
Tax ID Number:	**09-999378**
Ship Via:	**Fed-EX**
Terms and Credit:	**2/10, n/30**

Vendor ID:	**MHS-02**
Name:	**Martin's Hobby Store**
Contact:	**Luke Martin**
Account Number:	**1239**
Mailing Address:	**2348 West Lane**
City, ST, Zip:	**Modesto, CA 95355**
Country:	**USA**
Vendor Type:	**Supplier**
1099 Type:	**None**
Expense Acct:	**105**
Telephone 1:	**209-555-5623**
Tax ID Number:	**09-999465**
Ship Via:	**Fed-EX**
Terms and Credit:	**5/10, n/30**

4. Create the following subsidiary ledger accounts for inventory items:

Item ID:	**STENCILS-01**
Description:	**Flower Stencils**
Item Class:	**Stock item**
Description:	**for Sales**
Price Level 1:	**15.00**
Last Unit Cost:	**5.50**
Cost Method:	**FIFO**
GL Sales Acct:	**401**
GL Inventory Acct:	**105**
GL Cost of Sales Acct:	**503**
Item Tax Type:	**1**
UPC/SKU:	**1722839894**

Item Type:	Retail
Stocking U/M:	Each
Preferred Vendor ID:	MHS-02

Item ID:	PILLOWS-02
Description:	12-inch Pillows
Item Class:	Stock item
Description:	for Sales
Price Level 1:	35.00
Last Unit Cost:	12.50
Cost Method:	FIFO
GL Sales Acct:	401
GL Inventory Acct:	105
GL Cost of Sales Acct:	503
Item Tax Type:	1
UPC/SKU:	7930093271
Item Type:	Retail
Stocking U/M:	Each
Preferred Vendor ID:	SHGS-01

5. Record the following transactions, which occurred in January 2017.

Jan. 6	Ordered 15 flower stencils from Martin's Hobby Store, using Purchase Order 100.
8	Ordered 20 pillows from Sanders Home and Garden Supply, using Purchase Order 101.
10	Received the stencils ordered, Invoice 3264.
11	Received 16 of the pillows ordered, Invoice 16425.
11	Returned 2 of the stencils, and received VCM15 from the vendor.
20	Paid the balance owed to Sanders Home and Garden Supply, less discount, Check 125. (Use 105 as the Discount Account.)
20	Paid the balance owed to Martin's Hobby Store, less discount, Check 126.

HINT

Because the vendor credit memo is received before payment, enter the return of inventory using the Apply to Purchases tab of the Vendor Credit Memos screen.

6. Print the Inventory Valuation Report, Vendor Ledgers, and Cash Disbursements Journal reports.

Case Problem 8–2A

Open Kathleen's Designs, which you updated in 1A.

1. Create records for the following sales representatives:

Employee ID:	ACHANG-01
Name:	Annette Chang
Address:	2984 Monte Vista Lane
City, ST, Zip:	Modesto, CA 95355
Country:	USA
Mobile phone:	209-555-6565
Social Security Number:	888-55-5555
Type:	Independ

Employee ID:	**TWILSON-02**
Name:	**Thomas Wilson**
Address:	**2154 Holly Drive**
City, ST, Zip:	**Modesto, CA 95355**
Country:	**USA**
Mobile phone:	**209-555-9564**
Social Security Number:	**555-88-8888**
Type:	**Independ**

2. Print the Employee List.

Case Problem 8–1B

Open Ana's Creations, a beauty salon, which is located in the student data files.

1. Create the Inventory account for this business.

Account ID:	**105**
Description:	**Inventory**
Account Type:	**Inventory**

2. Create the Cost of Sales account.

Account ID:	**503**
Description:	**Cost of Goods Sold**
Account Type:	**Cost of Sales**

3. Create the following vendor account:

Vendor ID:	**BP-01**
Name:	**Beauty Products**
Contact:	**Maxine Williams**
Account Number:	**1653**
Mailing Address:	**2951 Corral Hollow Road**
City, ST, Zip:	**Tracy, CA 95376**
Country:	**USA**
Vendor Type:	**Supplier**
1099 Type:	**None**
Expense Acct:	**105**
Telephone 1:	**209-555-4612**
Tax ID Number:	**09-912348**
Ship Via:	**Fed-EX**
Terms and Credit:	**2/10, n/30**

4. Create the following ledger accounts for inventory items:

Item ID:	**EXSHAMPOO-01**
Description:	**Ecstasy Shampoo**
Item Class:	**Stock item**
Description:	**for Sales**
Price Level 1:	**22.00**
Last Unit Cost:	**13.50**
Cost Method:	**FIFO**

GL Sales Acct:	**401**
GL Inventory Acct:	**105**
GL Cost of Sales Acct:	**503**
Item Tax Type:	**1**
UPC/SKU:	**1209234291**
Item Type:	**Retail**
Stocking U/M:	**Each**
Preferred Vendor ID:	**BP-01**

Item ID:	**EXCONDITIONER-02**
Description:	**Ecstasy Conditioner**
Item Class:	**Stock item**
Description:	**for Sales**
Price Level 1:	**18.00**
Last Unit Cost:	**9.50**
Cost Method:	**FIFO**
GL Sales Acct:	**401**
GL Inventory Acct:	**105**
GL Cost of Sales Acct:	**503**
Item Tax Type:	**1**
UPC/SKU:	**3948909812**
Item Type:	**Retail**
Stocking U/M:	**Each**
Preferred Vendor ID:	**BP-01**

Item ID:	**HAIRGEL-03**
Description:	**Ecstasy Hair Gel**
Item Class:	**Stock item**
Description:	**for Sales**
Price Level 1:	**12.00**
Last Unit Cost:	**5.50**
Cost Method:	**FIFO**
GL Sales Acct:	**401**
GL Inventory Acct:	**105**
GL Cost of Sales Acct:	**503**
Item Tax Type:	**1**
UPC/SKU:	**8127673219**
Item Type:	**Retail**
Stocking U/M:	**Each**
Preferred Vendor ID:	**BP-01**

5. Record the following transactions with Beauty Products, which occurred in June 2017.

HINT

Because the vendor credit memo is received before payment, enter the return of inventory using the Apply to Purchases tab of the Vendor Credit Memos screen.

June 10	Ordered 22 bottles of shampoo and 8 bottles of conditioner, using Purchase Order 200.
13	Ordered 15 bottles of hair gel, using Purchase Order 201.
13	Received 22 bottles of shampoo and 6 of the bottles of conditioner that were ordered, Invoice 1864.
15	Received 15 bottles of hair gel, Invoice 1925.
18	Returned 2 bottles of hair gel, and received VCM10 from the vendor.
23	Paid Invoices 1864 and 1925, less discounts, Check 450. (Use 105 as the Discount Account.)

6. Print the Inventory Valuation Report, Vendor Ledgers, and Cash Disbursements Journal reports.

Case Problem 8–2B

Open Ana's Creations, which you updated in Problem 1B.

1. Create records for the following hairstylists who are independent contractors:

Employee ID:	**MANDERSON-01**
Name:	**Melody Anderson**
Address:	**1997 West Pershing Avenue**
City, ST, Zip:	**Tracy, CA 95376**
Country:	**USA**
Mobile phone:	**209-555-6936**
Social Security Number:	**645-55-5555**
Type:	**Independ**

Employee ID:	**WKINCAID-02**
Name:	**William Kincaid**
Address:	**6543 Angelica Court**
City, ST, Zip:	**Modesto, CA 95355**
Country:	**USA**
Mobile phone:	**209-555-9564**
Social Security Number:	**544-55-9999**
Type:	**Independ**

2. Print the Employee List.

CHAPTER 9

Sales of Inventory in a Merchandise Business

Objectives

9–1 Review inventory sales concepts

9–2 Create sales tax accounts and codes

9–3 Process sales transactions and create invoices

9–4 Create sales orders and invoices from quotations

9–5 Record finance charges on overdue customer balances

9–6 Print inventory and sales reports

Software Features

- Sales Invoices

- Credit Memos

- Sales Quotations and Orders

- Sales Taxes

- Finance Charges

Company Files

Before beginning chapter work, access the links menu to download company files.

Chapter 8 focused on establishing a perpetual inventory system for a merchandising business and recording the initial purchases of goods. In this chapter, you will see how a merchandising business processes sales of inventory, sales tax, sales returns and allowances, sales discounts, and finance charges on overdue customer balances.

OBJECTIVE 9-1

Review Inventory Sales Concepts

Some merchandising businesses sell goods "over the counter" and record their sales transactions on a cash register. Examples of such businesses are supermarkets, drugstores, and department stores. Increasingly, these businesses are using optical scanners and electronic cash registers that transfer information about their sales to a computerized accounting system and a computerized inventory system.

Other merchandising businesses sell their goods through sales representatives who visit customers, through catalogs sent to customers, over the telephone, or through websites. When businesses sell through these types of channels, they usually issue invoices to their customers. Remember that an invoice is a bill for goods or services. It lists the items sold, the prices, the total owed, the credit terms, and other information about the sale. The invoice is sent to the customer with the goods or mailed after the goods are shipped.

These businesses may also issue sales quotations, sales orders, and credit memos:

- Sometimes a potential customer will ask a business to provide a form showing the prices it will charge for specified goods. In response, the business will issue a *sales quotation*.
- When a customer orders goods, a business may prepare a form that shows the items involved, the quantities, the name of the sales representative, and other information about the order. This form is called a *sales order*.
- If a customer returns damaged or incorrect goods, the business provides credit for the return. It issues a *credit memo* to the customer to show the amount of credit granted.

Sage 50 allows a merchandising business to quickly and efficiently prepare invoices, sales quotations, sales orders, and credit memos. It also helps a merchandising business by automatically calculating sales tax, sales discount, and finance charges.

Accounting for Sales under the Perpetual Inventory System

Suppose that a business sells goods for $500 on credit to a customer. The business must collect a 7% sales tax on all of its sales. The cost of the items sold was $300. Because the business uses the perpetual inventory system, it must make two sets of entries to record this sale.

- The business must debit Accounts Receivable for $535 (the total amount owed by the customer), credit the appropriate revenue account for $500 (the amount of revenue earned by the business), and credit Sales Tax Payable for $35 (the amount of sales tax owed).

sales quotation
A form that shows the prices a business will charge for specified goods.

sales order A form that a business may prepare to record the details of a customer's order.

credit memo A form issued to a customer to show the credit granted for a return of goods.

- The business must debit Cost of Goods Sold for $300 and credit Inventory for $300. This amount is the cost of the items sold to the customer.

One of the advantages of Sage 50 is that it can update all of these general ledger accounts simultaneously when you enter a sale on credit. It can also update the subsidiary ledger accounts for the customer and for the inventory items sold.

Checkpoint 9-1

1. Name four types of forms that many merchandising businesses prepare when they sell their goods.
2. A merchandising business that uses the perpetual inventory system makes a sale for $1,000. The goods have a cost of $600. What entry is made in the Cost of Goods Sold account and the Inventory account?

OBJECTIVE 9-2

Create Sales Tax Accounts and Codes

Most states and some cities and counties impose a sales tax on goods that are sold to consumers. The retail businesses that make the sales are responsible for collecting the tax and sending it to the sales tax authority at regular intervals—usually monthly or quarterly.

When a sale is recorded, the amount of sales tax owed is credited to a liability account called Sales Tax Payable. Later, when the business remits the sales tax owed for a period to the sales tax authority, it debits the Sales Tax Payable account.

Sales Tax Payable is a current liability (a short-term debt) for a business. In the Sage 50 system of account classification, this account appears after Accounts Payable and is part of the group of accounts called Other Current Liabilities.

Creating the Sales Tax Account and a Vendor Account

Superior Carpet and Tile must charge a 7% sales tax on the inventory that it sells. In California, where Superior is located, there are several local sales tax authorities and a state sales tax authority. Superior is under the jurisdiction of an agency called the Board of Equalization and will send the amounts of sales tax it owes to this agency.

Superior must now create the Sales Tax Payable account in its general ledger and a vendor account for the Board of Equalization in its accounts payable ledger. Follow the steps outlined on the next page to accomplish these tasks.

Step 1:

Open Superior Carpet and Tile (Chp. 9 – Superior Carpet and Tile if student data files are used).

Step 2:

Create the Sales Tax Payable account in the general ledger. Use the following information:

Account ID:	**212**
Description:	**Sales Tax Payable**
Account Type:	**Other Current Liabilities**

Step 3:

Compare your work with Figure 9–1, then click Save and Close.

FIGURE 9–1
Completed Entries for Sales Tax Payable Account

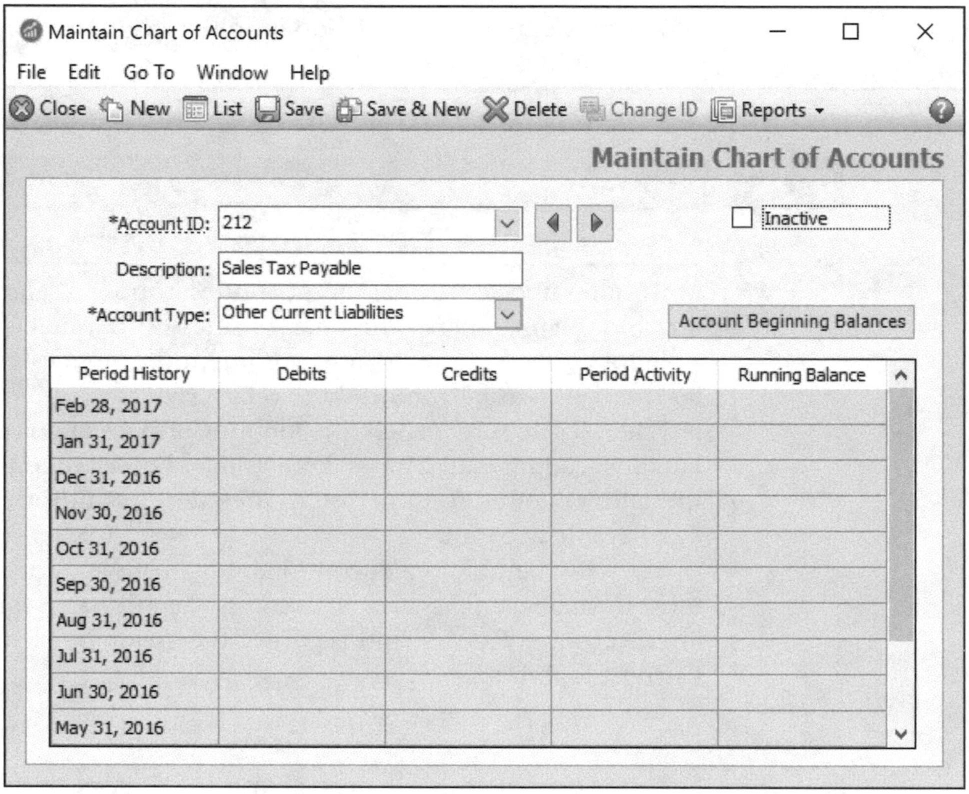

Step 4:

Create a vendor account for the Board of Equalization.

Vendor ID:	**BRE-006**
Name:	**Board of Equalization**
Expense Account:	**212**
Tax ID Number:	**None**
Ship Via:	**US Mail**
Terms and Credit:	**Net due in 30 days, 0.00 Discount**
Form Options:	**Default**

Step 5:

Compare your work with Figure 9–2, then click Save and Close.

FIGURE 9–2
Completed Vendor
Account for Board of
Equalization

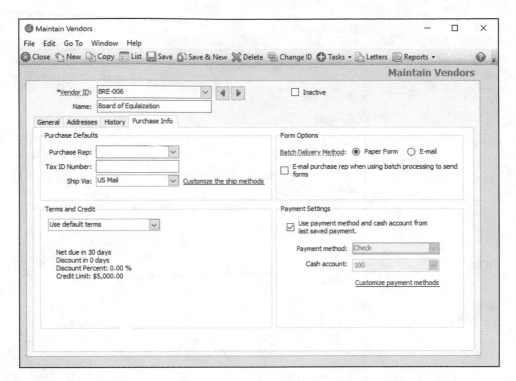

Step 6:

Click Maintain, then *Sales Taxes*, and then click the button next to *Set up a new sales tax* in the Sales Taxes window.

Step 7:

Click Next to continue setting up the new sales tax.

Step 8:

Key **7.00** in the *What is the total rate that you will charge?* field.

Step 9:

Select *1* from the How many individual rates make up this total rate? drop-down list. Then click Next to continue.

Step 10:

Key **CA** in the *Sales tax agency ID* field and key **Board of Equalization** in the *Sales tax agency name* field.

Step 11:

Select *BRE-006 (Board of Equalization)* from the Which vendor do you send the taxes you've collected to? drop-down list.

Step 12:

Select *by single rate* in the next drop-down list, if necessary.

Step 13:

Key **7.00** in the *Rate* field, and select *212 (Sales Tax Payable)* from the Select an account to track sales taxes drop-down list. Compare your entries with Figure 9–3. Click Next.

FIGURE 9–3
Completed Add Sales Tax
Agency Window

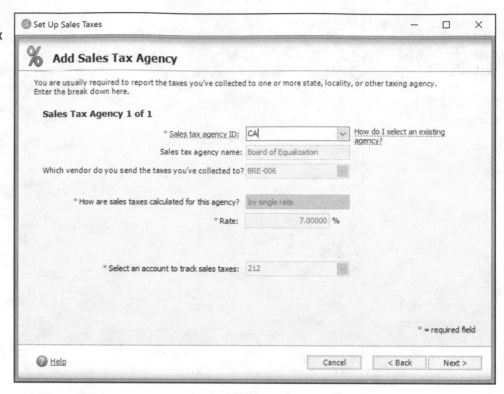

Step 14:

Key **CAL** in the *Sales tax ID* field of the Sales Tax Entered window.

Step 15:

Key **California Sales Tax** in the *Sales tax name* field, and select *No* from the Do you charge sales taxes on freight? drop-down list. Compare your work with Figure 9–4.

FIGURE 9–4
Completed Sales Tax
Entered Window

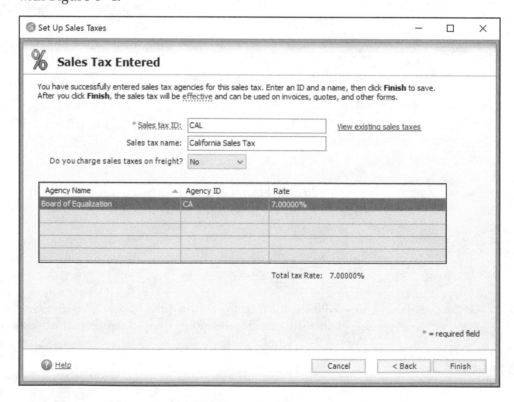

Step 16:

Click Finish. Click the button next to *Close the sales tax wizard* and then click Finish.

Checkpoint 9–2

1. Who is responsible for collecting sales tax from consumers?
2. What type of account is Sales Tax Payable?

Objective 9–2 Practice

Meadowland Healthcare Services must revise its general ledger accounts so that it can record sales of goods and sales tax.

Step 1:

Open Meadowland Healthcare Services (Chp. 9 – Meadowland Healthcare Services if student data files are used).

Step 2:

Create the new income account needed to record sales of goods.

Account ID:	**40000.5**
Account Description:	**Medical Sales Revenue**
Account Type:	**Income**

Step 3:

Because you now have two separate income accounts, change the *GL Sales Acct* field for each of your current inventory items from *40000 (Revenue)* to *40000.5 (Medical Sales Revenue)*.

Step 4:

Create a new vendor account for the Board of Equalization.

Vendor ID:	**BRE-008**
Name:	**Board of Equalization**
Expense Account:	**23100**
Tax ID Number:	**None**
Ship Via:	**US Mail**
Terms and Credit:	**Net due in 30 days, 0.00 Discount**
Form Options:	**Default**
Payment Setting:	**Default**

Step 5:

Enter the information about the sales tax agency.

Total Tax Rate:	**7.00**
Sales Tax Agency ID:	**CA**
Sales Tax Agency Name:	**Board of Equalization**
Vendor:	**BRE-008**
Taxes Calculated:	**by single rate**
Tax Rate:	**7.00**
Account to Track Sales Tax:	**23100**
Sales Tax ID:	**CATAX**
Sales Tax Name:	**California Sales Tax**
Sales Tax on Freight:	**No**

Step 6:

To view the Sales Tax Payable account, display the chart of accounts and compare it to Figure 9–5.

FIGURE 9–5
Chart of Accounts for Meadowland Healthcare Services

Chp. 9 - Meadowland Healthcare Services
Chart of Accounts
As of Feb 28, 2017

Filter Criteria includes: Report order is by ID. Report is printed with Accounts having Zero Amounts and in Detail Format.

Account ID	Account Description	Active?	Account Type
16900	Land	Yes	Fixed Assets
17000	Accum. Depreciation - Furn	Yes	Accumulated Depreciation
17100	Accum. Depr-Medical Equi	Yes	Accumulated Depreciation
17200	Accum. Depreciation - Auto	Yes	Accumulated Depreciation
17300	Accum. Depreciation - Oth	Yes	Accumulated Depreciation
17400	Accum. Depreciation - Lea	Yes	Accumulated Depreciation
17500	Accum. Depreciation - Buil	Yes	Accumulated Depreciation
17600	Accum. Depreciation - Bldg	Yes	Accumulated Depreciation
19000	Deposits	Yes	Other Assets
19100	Organization Costs	Yes	Other Assets
19150	Accum. Amortiz. - Org. Cost	Yes	Other Assets
19200	Note Receivable-Noncurre	Yes	Other Assets
19900	Other Noncurrent Assets	Yes	Other Assets
20000	Accounts Payable	Yes	Accounts Payable
21000	Wages and Salaries Paya	Yes	Other Current Liabilities
23000	Accrued Expenses	Yes	Other Current Liabilities
23100	Sales Tax Payable	Yes	Other Current Liabilities
23200	Wages Payable	Yes	Other Current Liabilities
23300	Deductions Payable	Yes	Other Current Liabilities
23400	Federal Payroll Taxes Paya	Yes	Other Current Liabilities
23500	FUTA Tax Payable	Yes	Other Current Liabilities
23600	State Payroll Taxes Payabl	Yes	Other Current Liabilities
23700	SUTA Payable	Yes	Other Current Liabilities
23800	Local Payroll Taxes Payabl	Yes	Other Current Liabilities
23900	Income Taxes Payable	Yes	Other Current Liabilities

OBJECTIVE 9–3

Process Sales Transactions and Create Invoices

When a merchandising business receives an order from a customer, it selects and packs the necessary goods and issues an invoice to bill the customer. The invoice may be enclosed with the goods when they are shipped to the customer, or it may be mailed separately.

Occasionally, a merchandising business will send incorrect goods to a customer or the goods will arrive in damaged condition. The customer will then return the goods and request credit or agree to keep the goods if an allowance is offered. (An allowance is a reduction in the selling price of goods.) To provide evidence of the credit granted for a return or allowance, the business issues a credit memo to the customer.

Sage 50 allows a merchandising business to efficiently make accounting entries for sales on credit and sales returns and allowances and also generate the necessary invoices and credit memos.

Recording a Sale on Credit and Creating the Invoice

Suppose that on February 7, 2017, Superior Carpet and Tile sells storage racks on credit to Jim Green, who operates his own business. The terms of the sale are 2/10, n/30.

Because Green is a new customer, it is necessary to create a customer account for him before recording the sale and issuing Invoice 1003.

Step 1:

Open Chp. 9 – Superior Carpet and Tile, which you updated previously in the chapter.

Step 2:

Create a new customer account for Jim Green. Use the following information.

Customer

Customer ID:	**Green-11**
Name:	**Jim Green**

General Tab

Account Number:	**1821**
Billing Address:	**12 Onyx Road**
City, ST, Zip:	**Modesto, CA 95355**
Country:	**USA**
Sales Tax:	**CAL**
Customer Type:	**Retail**
Telephone 1:	**209-555-4845**

Contacts Tab

Contact:	**Jim Green**

Sales Info Tab

GL Sales Account:	**400.5**
Ship Via:	**UPS Ground**
Pricing Level:	**Full Price (Price Level 1)**
Form Options:	**Default**

Payment & Credit Tab

Terms and Credit:	**2% 10 days, net 30 days**

History Tab

Beginning Balance:	**0**

Now record the credit sale to Jim Green and create Invoice 1003.

Step 3:

Click Tasks and then click *Sales/Invoicing*.

Step 4:

The Sales/Invoicing window now appears. At the *Customer ID* field, click the *magnifying glass* icon and then click *Green-11*.

Step 5:

Key **02/07/17** in the *Date* field.

Step 6:

Key **1003** in the *Invoice No.* field.

Step 7:

Key **6.00** in the *Quantity* field.

Step 8:

At the *Item* field, click the *magnifying glass* icon and then click *SK-2*.

Step 9:

Compare your completed work with Figure 9–6.

FIGURE 9–6
Completed Sales/Invoicing Window

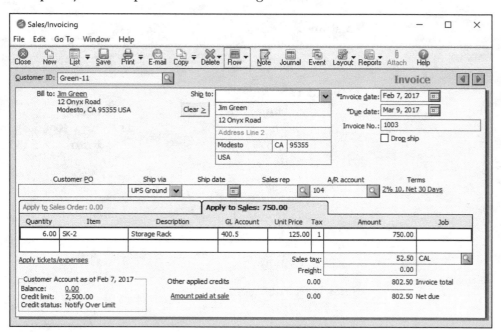

Step 10:

Click <u>S</u>ave and then click Close.

Printing the Invoice

The sale on credit made to Jim Green has now been posted to the general ledger and the appropriate subsidiary ledgers. In the general ledger, Accounts Receivable has been debited for $802.50, Sales Revenue has been credited for $750, and Sales Tax Payable has been credited for $52.50. Also in the general ledger, Cost of Goods Sold has been debited for $315 and

Inventory has been credited for $315. This amount is the cost of the six storage racks. Finally, the account for Jim Green in the accounts receivable subsidiary ledger has been debited for $802.50 and the account for the storage racks in the inventory subsidiary ledger has been credited for $315.

The next task for Superior Carpet and Tile is to print Invoice 1003 and send it to Jim Green. Superior has a policy of mailing an invoice on the day the goods are shipped to the customer. Follow the steps outlined below to print Invoice 1003.

Step 1:
Click Tasks and then click *Sales/Invoicing*.

Step 2:
Click the List button at the top of the Sales/Invoicing window.

Step 3:
The Sales Invoice List window will appear. Click the sale to Jim Green (Invoice 1003), as shown in Figure 9–7.

FIGURE 9–7
Invoice Chosen at
Sales Invoice List
Window

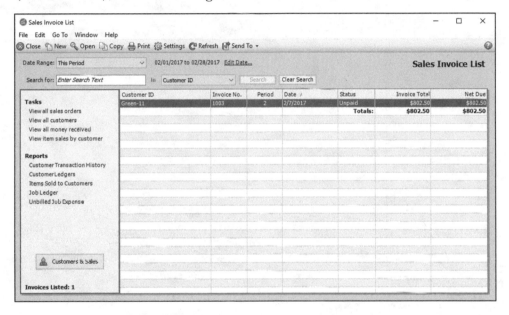

Step 4:
Click Open.

Step 5:
Click the Print button on the Sales/Invoicing toolbar.

Step 6:
Click Print at the Print Forms: Invoices dialog box. Compare your completed invoice with Figure 9–8.

FIGURE 9–8
Invoice 1003

Chp. 9 - Superior Carpet and Tile
345 Brown Ave.
Campbell, CA 95555
USA

Voice: 408-555-4444
Fax: 408-555-4445

INVOICE

Invoice Number: 1003
Invoice Date: Feb 7, 2017
Page: 1

Duplicate

Bill To:	Ship to:
Jim Green 12 Onyx Road Modesto, CA 95355 USA	Jim Green 12 Onyx Road Modesto, CA 95355 USA

Customer ID	Customer PO	Payment Terms	
Green-11		2% 10, Net 30 Days	
Sales Rep ID	**Shipping Method**	**Ship Date**	**Due Date**
	UPS Ground		3/9/17

Quantity	Item	Description	Unit Price	Amount
6.00	SK-2	Storage Rack	125.00	750.00
		Subtotal		750.00
		Sales Tax		52.50
		Total Invoice Amount		802.50
Check/Credit Memo No:		Payment/Credit Applied		
		TOTAL		802.50

Step 7:

Close the Sales/Invoicing window and the Sales Invoice List window.

Recording a Sales Return and Creating the Credit Memo

Suppose that on February 8, 2017, Jim Green receives the six storage racks shipped by Superior Carpet and Tile on February 7. Green finds that one storage rack is damaged and notifies Superior that he intends to return the storage rack. Superior agrees to give him a credit of $133.75 for the return. This amount includes the selling price of $125 and sales tax of $8.75.

Superior must now record the sales return and create a credit memo. The return requires a debit of $125 to Sales Returns and Allowances, a debit of $8.75 to Sales Tax Payable, and a credit of $133.75 to Accounts Receivable. It is also necessary to record a credit of $133.75 in the subsidiary ledger account for Jim Green.

Sales returns and allowances reduce the revenue of a business. These transactions can be recorded by debiting them to the Sales Revenue account if desired. Most businesses, however, prefer to have a separate record of these transactions and therefore use a Sales Returns and Allowances account.

Follow the steps outlined below to record the storage rack returned by Jim Green and create the necessary credit memo.

Step 1:
Click Tasks and then click *Credit Memos.*

Step 2:
At the *Customer ID* field, click the *magnifying glass* icon and then click *Green-11.*

Step 3:
At the *Date* field, click the *calendar* icon and choose *Feb 8, 2017.*

Step 4:
Key **CM012** (the credit memo number) in the *Credit No.* field.

Step 5:
Select Invoice *1003* from the drop-down list next to the *Apply to Invoice No.* tab.

Step 6:
Key **1.00** in the *Returned* field.

Step 7:
Key **Storage Rack** in the *Description* field, if needed.

Step 8:
Click the Journal button on the Credit Memos toolbar. The Accounting Behind the Screens window will appear, as shown in Figure 9–9.

FIGURE 9–9
Accounting Behind the Screens Window

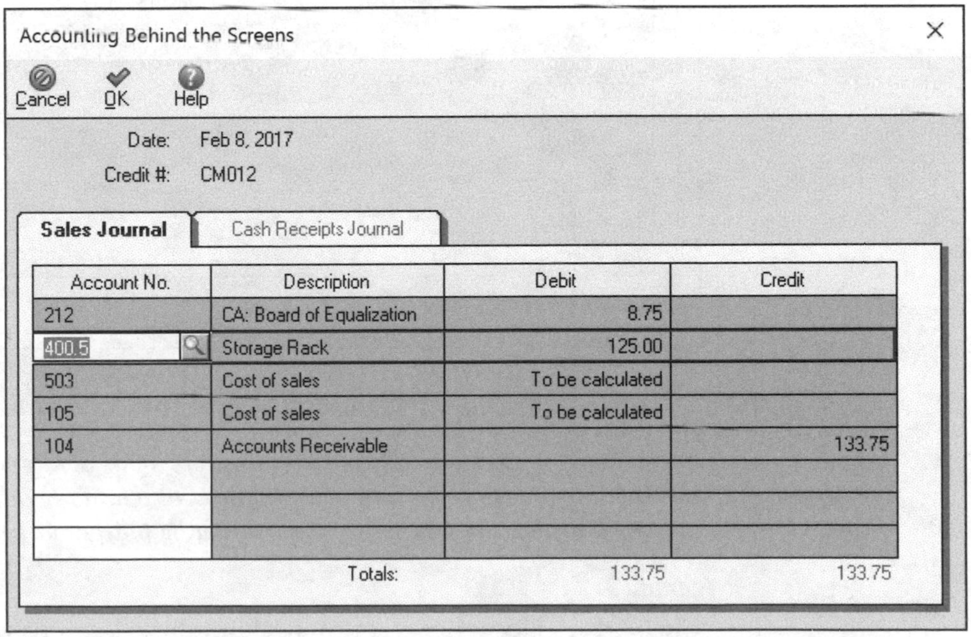

Accounting Behind the Screens
Cancel
OK
Help
Date: Feb 8, 2017
Credit #: CM012
Sales Journal
Cash Receipts Journal
Account No.
Description
Debit
Credit
212
CA: Board of Equalization
8.75
400.5
Storage Rack
125.00
503
Cost of sales
To be calculated
105
Cost of sales
To be calculated
104
Accounts Receivable
133.75
Totals:
133.75
133.75

Because Superior does not yet have a Sales Returns and Allowances account, this window shows that the Sales Revenue account (400.5) is being decreased to record the return. It is therefore necessary to create a Sales Returns and Allowances account in Superior's general ledger.

Step 9:

Click the *magnifying glass* icon in the second row of the *Account No.* field, and then click the New button at the bottom of the window.

Step 10:

Use the following information to create the Sales Returns and Allowances account:

Account ID:	**404**
Description:	**Sales Returns and Allowances**
Account Type:	**Income**

Step 11:

Compare your work with Figure 9–10. Click Save and then Close.

FIGURE 9–10
Account 404 Added
to Maintain Chart of
Accounts Window

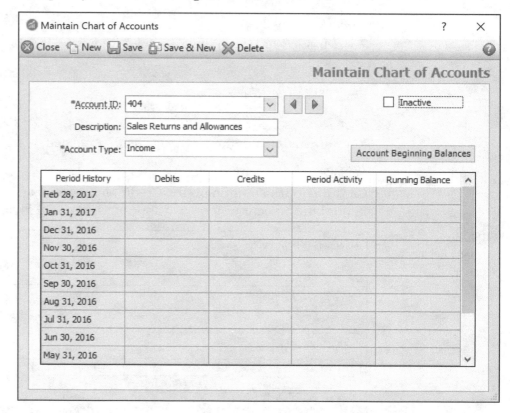

Notice that account 404 will now appear in the *Account No.* field.

Note: Sage 50 automatically updates Cost of Goods Sold and Inventory for returned items. However, you may still need to manually adjust for the cost of damaged or defective inventory that cannot be placed back in stock.

Step 12:

Click <u>O</u>K to close the Accounting Behind the Screens window.

Printing the Credit Memo

Follow the steps outlined below to print the credit memo that Superior Carpet and Tile must send to Jim Green.

Step 1:

Click the Print button on the Credit Memos toolbar.

Step 2:

At the Print Forms: Credit Memos dialog box, click Print, as shown in Figure 9–11.

FIGURE 9–11
Print Forms: Credit Memos Dialog Box

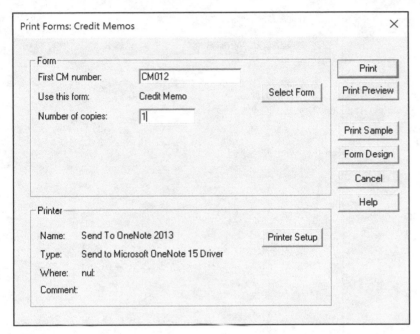

Step 3:

Compare your completed credit memo with Figure 9–12.

FIGURE 9–12
Credit Memo

Chp. 9 - Superior Carpet and Tile
345 Brown Ave.
Campbell, CA 95555
USA

Voice: 408-555-4444
Fax: 408-555-4445

CREDIT MEMO

Credit Memo Number: CM012
Credit Date: Feb 8, 2017
Page: 1
Duplicate

Credit To:

Jim Green
12 Onyx Road
Modesto, CA 95355
USA

Customer ID	Customer PO	Sales Rep ID
Green-11		

Quantity	Item	Description	Unit Price	Amount
-1.00	SK-2	Storage Rack	125.00	-125.00
		Subtotal		-125.00
		Sales Tax		-8.75
		Freight		
Invoice No: 1003		**TOTAL**		**-133.75**

Step 4:

Click Save and Close to close the Credit Memos window.

Recording a Cash Receipt When a Customer Pays an Invoice

Suppose that on February 20, 2017, Superior Carpet and Tile receives a check for $668.75 from Jim Green. This check is in payment of Invoice 1003 ($802.50) less Credit Memo 012 ($133.75).

When Superior Carpet and Tile receives the check from Jim Green, it must debit Cash for $668.75 (the amount received), and credit Accounts Receivable for $668.75 (the total amount owed by the customer).

Follow the steps outlined below to record the payment Superior has received from Jim Green for Invoice 1003 less Credit Memo 012.

Step 1:

Click Tasks and then click *Receive Money.*

Step 2:

Select *Check* from the Payment Method drop-down list and *100 (Cash)* from the Cash account drop-down list.

Step 3:

In the *Deposit Ticket ID* field, key **02/20/17**.

Step 4:

At the *Customer ID* field in the Receive Money window, click the *magnifying glass* icon, and then click *Green-11*, as shown in Figure 9–13.

FIGURE 9–13
Green-11 (Jim Green)
Selected from Customer
ID Field Drop-Down List

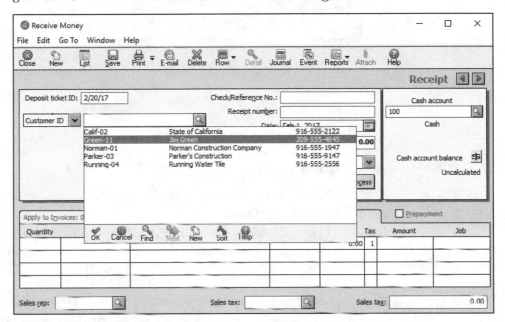

Step 5:

Key **1328** (the check number) in the *Check/Reference No.* field.

Step 6:

At the *Date* field, click the *calendar* icon and choose *Feb 20, 2017.*

Step 7:

Click the check box in the *Pay* field for the invoice, as shown in Figure 9–14. Notice that the *Receipt amount* field indicates that the amount paid is $668.75.

FIGURE 9–14

Pay Check Box Selected

Receive Money

File   Edit   Go To   Window   Help

Close   New   List   Save   Print   E-mail   Delete   Row   Detail   Journal   Event   Reports   Attach   Help

Receipt

Deposit ticket ID: 2/20/17	Check/Reference No.: 1328
Customer ID ▾ Green-11	Receipt number:
Jim Green	Date: Feb 20, 2017
12 Onyx Road	Receipt amount: 668.75
Modesto, CA 95355	
USA	Payment method: Check ▾
	Credit card payment: Record or Process

Cash account

100

Cash

Cash account balance

Uncalculated

Apply to Invoices: 668.75   Apply to Revenues: 0.00   ☐ Prepayment Pay All /None

Invoice	Date Due	Amount Due	Description	Discount	Amount Paid	Pay
1003	Mar 9, 2017	668.75			668.75	☑

Discount account: 401

Step 8:

Click Save.

Step 9:

Close the Receive Money window.

Checkpoint 9–3

1. What document does a business issue in connection with a sales return or allowance?

2. When entering a sales return using the Credit Memo, is the number entered in the *Returned* field as a positive or negative number?

Objective 9–3 Practice

On February 11, 2017, Meadowland Healthcare Services sold 20 packages of syringes on credit to Dr. George Johnson, a new customer. Meadowland issued Invoice 1105 with credit terms of 3/10, n/30.

Step 1:

Open Chp. 9 – Meadowland Healthcare Services, which you updated previously in the chapter.

Step 2:

Create a new customer account for George Johnson. Use the following information.

Customer

Customer ID:	**Johnson-50**
Name:	**Dr. George Johnson**

General Tab

Account Number:	**1290**
Billing Address:	**1342 Rose Marie Lane**
City, ST, Zip:	**Modesto, CA 95355**
Country:	**USA**
Sales Tax:	**CATAX**
Customer Type:	**Retail**
Telephone 1:	**209-555-4982**

Contacts Tab

Contact:	**Dr. George Johnson**

Sales Info Tab

GL Sales Account:	**40000.5**
Ship Via:	**UPS Ground**
Pricing Level:	**Price Level 1**
Form Options:	**Default**

Payment & Credit Tab

Terms and Credit:	**3% 10 days, net 30 days**

History Tab

Beginning Balance:	**0**

Step 3:

Use the Sales/Invoicing feature to record the sale and create Invoice 1105.

Step 4:

Print the invoice. Your invoice should look like Figure 9–15.

FIGURE 9–15
Invoice 1105

Chp. 9 - Meadowland Healthcare Services
3456 Highland Ave
Sacramento, CA 95355
USA

Voice: 916-555-3455
Fax: 916-555-4434

INVOICE

Invoice Number: 1105
Invoice Date: Feb 11, 2017
Page: 1

Duplicate

Bill To:	Ship to:
Dr. George Johnson 1342 Rose Marie Lane Modesto, CA 95355 USA	Dr. George Johnson 1342 Rose Marie Lane Modesto, CA 95355 USA

Customer ID	Customer PO	Payment Terms	
Johnson-50		3% 10, Net 30 Days	
Sales Rep ID	**Shipping Method**	**Ship Date**	**Due Date**
	UPS Ground		3/13/17

Quantity	Item	Description	Unit Price	Amount
20.00	SY-1	Syringes	12.00	240.00

Subtotal		240.00
Sales Tax		16.80
Total Invoice Amount		256.80
Payment/Credit Applied		25.68
TOTAL		**231.12**

Check/Credit Memo No: CM201

Step 5:

On February 12, 2017, Dr. Johnson returned two packages of syringes. Meadowland issued Credit Memo 201 (CM201).

Create the Sales Returns and Allowances account. Use the following information:

Account ID:	**40050**
Description:	**Sales Returns and Allowances**
Account Type:	**Income**

Step 6:

Create and then print the credit memo. Your credit memo should look like Figure 9–16.

FIGURE 9–16
Credit Memo CM201

Chp. 9 - Meadowland Healthcare
3456 Highland Ave
Sacramento, CA 95355
USA

Voice: 916-555-3455
Fax: 916-555-4434

CREDIT MEMO

Credit Memo Number: CM201
Credit Date: Feb 12, 2017
Page: 1
Duplicate

Credit To:

Dr. George Johnson
1342 Rose Marie Lane
Modesto, CA 95355
USA

Customer ID	Customer PO	Sales Rep ID
Johnson-50		

Quantity	Item	Description	Unit Price	Amount
-2.00	SY-1	Syringes	12.00	-24.00
		Subtotal		-24.00
		Sales Tax		-1.68
		Freight		
Invoice No: 1105		**TOTAL**		**-25.68**

OBJECTIVE 9–4

Create Sales Orders and Invoices from Quotations

Some businesses have a policy of requesting a price quotation or bid before they buy goods from a new supplier. Usually, these businesses obtain quotations from several competing suppliers and then compare the prices and credit terms offered.

Sage 50 allows you to easily create quotations for potential customers. It also permits you to maintain a list of potential customers who have requested quotations and to convert quotations into sales orders or invoices if the potential customers end up placing orders.

Creating the Quotation

Suppose that Maria Davis, one of the sales representatives for Superior Carpet and Tile, visits Parker's Construction. She finds that the management of this firm is interested in buying 10 cases of ceramic tile but wants a price quotation. Thus, on February 10, 2017, Superior issues Quotation 2345. The prices quoted are good until February 25, 2017.

Follow the steps outlined below to create the quotation for Parker's Construction.

Step 1:

Open Chp. 9 – Superior Carpet and Tile and close the Action Items log.

Step 2:

Click Tasks, click *Quotes/Sales Orders*, and then click *Quotes*.

Step 3:

At the Quotes window, in the *Customer ID* field, click the *magnifying glass* icon, and then click *Parker-03*.

Step 4:

At the *Date* field, click the *calendar* icon and then choose *Feb 10, 2017*.

Step 5:

At the *Good Thru* field, click the *calendar* icon and choose *Feb 25, 2017*.

Step 6:

Key **2345** in the *Quote No.* field.

Step 7:

At the *Sales Rep* field, click the *magnifying glass* icon and then click *MDA-02*.

Step 8:

Key **10.00** in the *Quantity* field.

Step 9:

Click in the *Item* field, click the *magnifying glass* icon, and then click *CT-3*.

Step 10:

At the *Sales tax* field at the bottom of the Quotes screen, click the *magnifying glass* icon and then click *CAL*. Compare your work with Figure 9–17.

FIGURE 9–17
Completed Quotes
Dialog Box

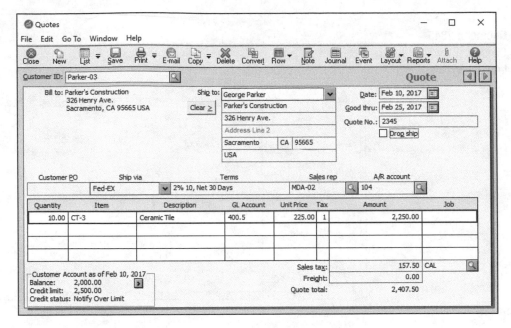

Step 11:

Click Save and then click Close.

Step 12:

If a warning window appears indicating that the transaction will cause the customer's balance to go over the credit limit, click Yes.

Converting a Quotation into a Sales Order or an Invoice

If a customer places an order after a quotation is issued, Sage 50 makes it possible to quickly convert the quotation into a sales order or an invoice. Some firms need a sales order because they use it for the internal processing of the customer's order—the removal of the necessary goods from inventory and the packing and shipping of the goods. When the goods are sent to the customer, the sales order is converted into an invoice.

Other firms do not use a sales order and immediately convert the quotation into an invoice. Superior Carpet and Tile follows this policy.

Suppose that on February 15, 2017, Parker's Construction accepts Quotation 2345. Superior must now use the quotation to create an invoice. Follow the steps outlined below to accomplish this task.

Step 1:

Click Tasks, click *Quotes/Sales Orders*, and then click *Quotes*.

Step 2:

The Quotes window appears. Click the List button on the Quotes toolbar.

Step 3:

The Quote List dialog box will appear. Click the quotation *2345* issued to Parker's Construction, as shown in Figure 9–18.

FIGURE 9–18

Quotation 2345
Chosen at the Quote
List Dialog Box

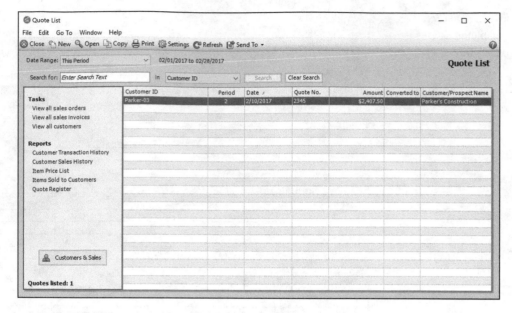

Step 4:

Click Open and Quotation 2345 will appear in the active Quotes window.

Step 5:

At the *Date* field, click the *calendar* icon and choose *Feb 15, 2017.*

Step 6:

Click the Conver*t* button on the Quotes toolbar.

Step 7:

Click the Sale/Invoice radio button in the Convert Quote dialog box.

Step 8:

Key **1004** in the *Invoice* # field, as shown in Figure 9–19.

FIGURE 9–19

Convert Quote Dialog Box

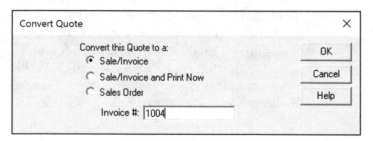

Step 9:

Click OK.

Step 10:

Click Yes to override the customer's credit limit. The quotation has now been converted to an invoice. The invoice can be printed or edited by using the Sales/Invoicing function.

Step 11:

Close the Quotes window.

> ### Checkpoint 9–4
>
> 1. What is the purpose of a quotation?
> 2. What is the purpose of a sales order?

Objective 9–4 Practice

On February 2, 2017, Isadora Duncan, a sales representative for Meadowland Healthcare Services, gave Quotation 5432 for 120 roller bandages to Rapid Medical Response. This firm intends to use the roller bandages and not resell them. Therefore, sales tax must be collected. The quotation was good until February 15, 2017. Rapid Medical Response accepted the quotation on February 4, 2017.

Step 1:

Open Chp. 9 – Meadowland Healthcare Services.

Step 2:

Create Quotation 5432 for Rapid Medical Response.

Step 3:

Convert the quotation into Invoice 1106 on February 4, 2017.

Step 4:

Print the invoice. Your invoice should look like Figure 9–20.

FIGURE 9–20
Invoice 1106

Chp. 9 - Meadowland Healthcare Services
3456 Highland Ave
Sacramento, CA 95355
USA

Voice: 916-555-3455
Fax: 916-555-4434

INVOICE

Invoice Number: 1106
Invoice Date: Feb 4, 2017
Page: 1

Duplicate

Bill To:	Ship to:
Rapid Medical Response 2516 Main Street Sacramento, CA 95671 USA	Rapid Medical Response 2516 Main Street Sacramento, CA 95671 USA

Customer ID	Customer PO	Payment Terms	
Rapid-30		2% 10, Net 30 Days	
Sales Rep ID	**Shipping Method**	**Ship Date**	**Due Date**
	Fed-EX		3/6/17

Quantity	Item	Description	Unit Price	Amount
120.00	RB-2	Roller Bandages	75.00	9,000.00

	Subtotal	9,000.00
	Sales Tax	630.00
	Total Invoice Amount	9,630.00
Check/Credit Memo No:	Payment/Credit Applied	
	TOTAL	**9,630.00**

OBJECTIVE 9-5

Record Finance Charges on Overdue Customer Balances

statement of account A form that a business sends each month to show all transactions with a customer and the balance owed by the customer.

In addition to issuing invoices whenever goods are sold to a customer, many firms send a monthly *statement of account* to the customer. This statement lists all transactions with the customer during the period—sales on credit, returns, and cash received on account. Most important, this statement shows the balance owed at the end of the period.

Some businesses have a policy of imposing a finance charge when customers do not pay their bills within a specified period of time. This policy is intended to discourage customers from allowing their balances to become overdue. If the firm has a policy of adding a finance charge to overdue balances, the finance charge appears on the statement of account.

Sage 50 allows you to set defaults for a finance charge so that the charge is automatically calculated and recorded whenever customer accounts have overdue balances.

Creating the Defaults for Finance Charges

Remember that Superior Carpet and Tile offers credit terms of 2/10, n/30 to its customers. Suppose that Superior decides to add an 8% finance charge to invoices that are more than 30 days overdue. Superior must create the necessary defaults, as outlined below. However, before that, Superior must establish an Interest Income account in its general ledger. This account will be used to record the income received from finance charges. Interest Income will be credited for all finance charges.

Step 1:

Open Chp. 9 – Superior Carpet and Tile, which you updated previously in the chapter.

Step 2:

Create the following account in the general ledger:

Account ID:	**450**
Description:	**Interest Revenue**
Account Type:	**Income**

Step 3:

Click Maintain, click *Default Information*, and then click *Customers.*

Step 4:

Click the Finance Charges tab from the Customer Defaults dialog box.

Step 5:

Click the box next to *Charge finance charges* to insert a check mark.

Step 6:

Key **30** in the *On invoices…days overdue* field.

Step 7:

Key **10,000.00** in the *up to* field.

Step 8:

Key **8.00** in the *Annual interest rate* field.

Step 9:

Click the box next to *Charge interest on finance charges* to insert a check mark. This indicates that the system should calculate interest on any accumulated finance charges.

Step 10:

Key **450** in the *Finance Charge GL Account* field. Compare your work with Figure 9–21.

FIGURE 9–21 Completed Finance Charges Entries in Customer Defaults Dialog Box

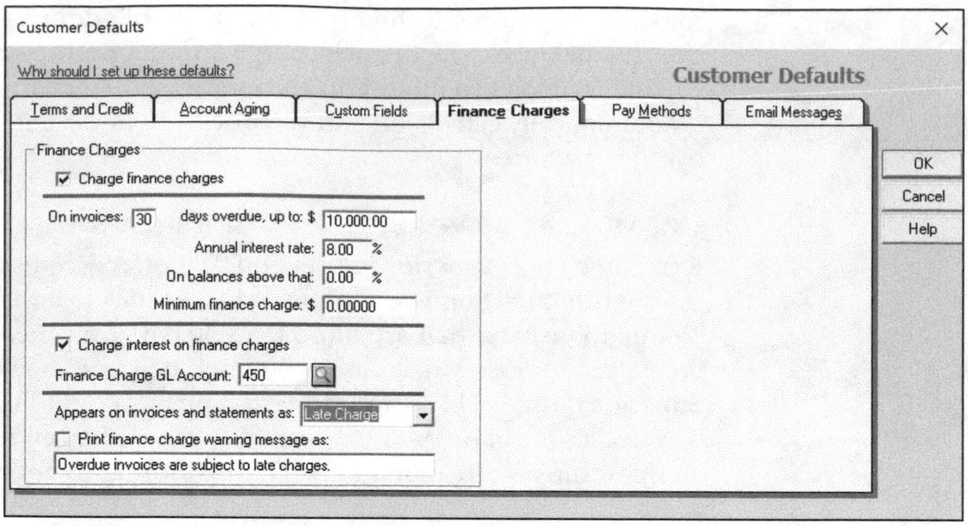

Step 11:

Click OK to accept the finance charge defaults.

Creating the Finance Charge Report

Suppose that Superior Carpet and Tile has one overdue account on March 31, 2017. A report can be generated showing the finance charges imposed on the customer's account. This report can be printed or viewed on the screen. Follow the steps outlined below to view the finance charge report for Parker's Construction.

Step 1:

Click *Customer/Prospects* in the Maintain drop-down list on the Menu bar.

Step 2:

Click the drop-down arrow next to the *Customer ID* field, and then click *Parker-03*.

Step 3:

Select the Payment & Credit Tab and click the box next to *Charge Finance Charges* to insert a check mark. Click Save and then Close.

Step 4:

Click Tasks and then click *Finance Charge.*

Step 5:

The Calculate Finance Charges dialog box appears. At the *Starting Customer* field, click the *magnifying glass* icon and then click *Parker-03.*

Step 6:

At the *Ending Customer* field, click the *magnifying glass* icon and then click *Parker-03.*

Step 7:

At the *Date* field, click the *calendar* icon and then choose *Mar 31, 2017.*
Compare your work with Figure 9–22.

FIGURE 9–22
Calculate Finance
Charges Window

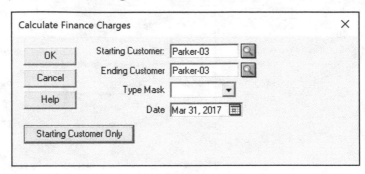

Step 8:

Click OK.

Step 9:

The Apply Finance Charges dialog box now appears. Click the No radio
button in the Apply Finance Charges section. (You would click Yes if
adding finance charges to a statement of account.)

Step 10:

Click the Screen radio button in the Report Destination section.

Step 11:

Click the No radio button in the Print Calculation Sheet section. Compare
your work with Figure 9–23.

FIGURE 9–23
Completed Apply Finance
Charges Window

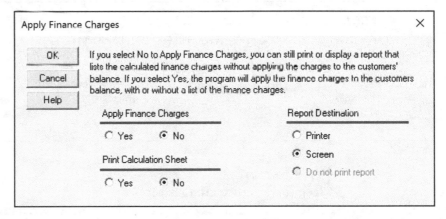

Step 12:

Click OK.

Step 13:

The Finance Charge Report Selection dialog box now appears. Click the
Detail radio button in the Report Style section.

Step 14:

Click the By Id radio button in the Report Order section. Compare your work with Figure 9–24.

FIGURE 9–24
Completed Finance
Charge Report Selection
Window

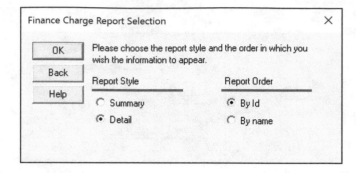

Step 15:

Click OK.

Step 16:

Compare the report on your screen with Figure 9–25.

FIGURE 9–25
Completed Finance
Charges Report

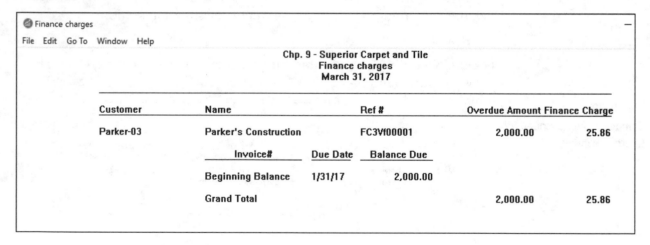

Step 17:

Close the Finance charges report.

> **Checkpoint 9–5**
>
> 1. Why do some businesses impose finance charges on customer accounts?
> 2. What account is used to record finance charges?

Meadowland Healthcare Services wants to add a finance charge to all customer balances that are more than 45 days overdue. The interest rate will be 9.5% on invoices up to $15,000. Interest will also be calculated on finance charges.

Step 1:

Open Chp. 9 – Meadowland Healthcare Services, which you updated previously in the chapter.

Step 2:

Create the following account in the general ledger, if not already created:

Account ID:	**45400**
Description:	**Finance Charge Revenue**
Account Type:	**Income**

Step 3:

Create the customer finance charge defaults.

Step 4:

Print a report showing the finance charges on the open invoices for Rapid Medical Response as of April 30, 2017. Your report should look like Figure 9–26.

FIGURE 9–26
Finance Charges
Report for Rapid
Medical Response

Finance charges

File Edit Go To Window Help

Chp. 9 - Meadowland Healthcare Services
Finance charges
April 30, 2017

Customer	Name		Ref #	Overdue Amount	Finance Charge
Rapid-30	Rapid Medical Response		FC4Uf00001	9,630.00	137.85
	Invoice#	**Due Date**	**Balance Due**		
	1106	3/6/17	9,630.00		
	Grand Total			9,630.00	137.85

Sage 50 provides a variety of inventory and sales reports for merchandising businesses. The information from these reports can help management answer the following types of questions: What items are selling well and what items are selling poorly? Do we have too much stock of the slow-selling items? If we want to close out some of the slow-selling items, how much can we reduce the prices for those items and still make a profit?

Creating Inventory Reports

Sage 50 offers the following inventory reports to merchandising businesses. These reports offer a wide range of information that can be used to plan and control inventory.

- The *Inventory Valuation Report* shows the value (cost) of the current inventory.
- The *Inventory Adjustment Journal* lists all inventory adjustments that were made.
- The *Item Costing Report* lists the cost, receipts, and sales for each inventory item.
- The *Cost of Goods Sold Journal* shows the cost of all inventory items sold during a period.
- The *Item Master List* gives detailed information about all inventory items.
- The *Item Price List* gives the various prices and the quantity on hand of all inventory items.
- The *Physical Inventory List* is used to compare the actual inventory on hand with the reported inventory.
- The *Inventory Profitability Report* shows the units sold and profitability of inventory items.

Superior Carpet and Tile wants to see the Cost of Goods Sold Journal for the month of February 2017. Follow the steps outlined below to generate this inventory report.

Step 1:

Open Chp. 9 – Superior Carpet and Tile and close the Action Items log.

Step 2:

Click Reports & Forms and then click *Inventory*.

Step 3:

At the Inventory: Items and Services You Buy and Sell section, select *Cost of Goods Sold Journal*.

Step 4:

Click the Display button on the Select a Report or Form toolbar.

Step 5:

Compare your journal with the one shown in Figure 9–27.

FIGURE 9–27
Cost of Goods Sold Journal

9/18/16 at 09:06:03.43 *****EDUCATIONAL VERSION ONLY***** Page: 1

Chp. 9 - Superior Carpet and Tile
Cost of Goods Sold Journal
For the Period From Feb 1, 2017 to Feb 28, 2017

Filter Criteria includes: Report order is by Date. Report is printed in Detail Format and with shortened descriptions.

Date	GL Acct ID	Reference	Qty	Line Description	Debit Amount	Credit Amount
2/7/17	105	1003	6.00	Storage Rack		315.00
	503		6.00	Storage Rack	315.00	
2/8/17	105	CM012	-1.00	Storage Rack	52.50	
	503		-1.00	Storage Rack		52.50
2/15/17	105	1004	10.00	Ceramic Tile		1,000.00
	503		10.00	Ceramic Tile	1,000.00	
		Total			**1,367.50**	**1,367.50**

Step 6:

Click Close.

Creating Sales Reports

As we have discussed, Sage 50 helps a merchandising business by making it easy to produce a variety of sales-related documents that are needed in the firm's operations:

- Quotations for potential customers
- Sales orders
- Invoices
- Credit memos
- Statements of account
- Collection letters for overdue accounts

Sage 50 also provides many different sales reports for merchandising businesses. Some of these reports are described below.

- The *Customer List* shows the names and contact information of all customers.
- The *Prospect List* shows the names and contact information of all prospects.
- The *Invoice Register* is a list of all invoices that have been issued to customers.
- The *Quote Register* is a list of all outstanding price quotations.
- The *Sales Journal* shows all sales on credit made during a period.
- The *Sales Rep Reports* is a list of sales made by each sales representative.
- The *Customer Ledgers* include the accounts for all credit customers.
- The *Sales Taxes* is a list of all sales tax codes used by the business.
- The *Sales Order Register, Journal,* and *Report* show information about all sales orders issued.
- The *Customer Sales History* is a list of the transactions with each customer.

Superior Carpet and Tile wants to see the Sales Journal for the month of February 2017. Follow the steps outlined on the following page to create this report.

Step 1:

At the Select a Report or Form dialog box, in the <u>R</u>eports section, click *Accounts Receivable.*

Step 2:

In the Accounts Receivable: Customer and Sales section, select *Sales Journal.*

Step 3:

Click the <u>D</u>isplay button on the Select a Report or Form toolbar.

Step 4:

Compare your journal with the one shown in Figure 9–28.

FIGURE 9–28
Sales Journal

9/18/16 at 09:06:57.22   *****EDUCATIONAL VERSION ONLY*****   Page: 1

Chp. 9 - Superior Carpet and Tile
Sales Journal
For the Period From Feb 1, 2017 to Feb 28, 2017

Filter Criteria includes: Report order is by Invoice/CM Date. Report is printed in Detail Format.

Date	Account ID	Invoice/CM #	Line Description	Debit Amnt	Credit Amnt
2/7/17	212	1003	CA: Board of Equalization		52.50
	400.5		Storage Rack		750.00
	503		Cost of sales	315.00	
	105		Cost of sales		315.00
	104		Jim Green	802.50	
2/8/17	212	CM012	CA: Board of Equalization	8.75	
	404		Storage Rack	125.00	
	503		Cost of sales		52.50
	105		Cost of sales	52.50	
	104		Jim Green		133.75
2/15/17	212	1004	CA: Board of Equalization		157.50
	400.5		Ceramic Tile		2,250.00
	503		Cost of sales	1,000.00	
	105		Cost of sales		1,000.00
	104		Parker's Construction	2,407.50	
2/15/17	212	2345	CA: Board of Equalization		157.50
	400.5		Ceramic Tile		2,250.00
	104		Parker's Construction	2,407.50	
	Total			**7,118.75**	**7,118.75**

Step 5:

Click Close, then close the Select a Report or Form dialog box.

Checkpoint 9–6

1. What does the Cost of Goods Sold Journal show?
2. What does the Sales Journal show?

Step 1:

Open Chp. 9 – Meadowland Healthcare Services.

Step 2:

Print the Sales Journal and the Cost of Goods Sold Journal for the month of February and compare them with Figures 9-29 and 9-30, respectively.

FIGURE 9–29

Sales Journal for
Meadowland
Healthcare Services

9/18/16 at 09:04:08.81	*****EDUCATIONAL VERSION ONLY*****				Page: 1
		Chp. 9 - Meadowland Healthcare Services			
		Sales Journal			
		For the Period From Feb 1, 2017 to Feb 28, 2017			

Filter Criteria includes: Report order is by Invoice/CM Date. Report is printed in Detail Format.

Date	Account ID	Invoice/CM #	Line Description	Debit Amnt	Credit Amnt
2/2/17	23100	5432	CA: Board of Equalization		630.00
	40000.5		Roller Bandages		9,000.00
	11000		Rapid Medical Response	9,630.00	
2/4/17	23100	1106	CA: Board of Equalization		630.00
	40000.5		Roller Bandages		9,000.00
	50000		Cost of sales	3,600.00	
	12000		Cost of sales		3,600.00
	11000		Rapid Medical Response	9,630.00	
2/11/17	23100	1105	CA: Board of Equalization		16.80
	40000.5		Syringes		240.00
	50000		Cost of sales	100.00	
	12000		Cost of sales		100.00
	11000		Dr. George Johnson	256.80	
2/12/17	23100	CM201	CA: Board of Equalization	1.68	
	40050		Syringes	24.00	
	50000		Cost of sales		10.00
	12000		Cost of sales	10.00	
	11000		Dr. George Johnson		25.68
		Total		**23,252.48**	**23,252.48**

FIGURE 9–30

Cost of Goods Sold
Journal for Meadowland
Healthcare Services

9/18/16 at 09:05:00.54	*****EDUCATIONAL VERSION ONLY*****					Page: 1
		Chp. 9 - Meadowland Healthcare Services				
		Cost of Goods Sold Journal				
		For the Period From Feb 1, 2017 to Feb 28, 2017				

Filter Criteria includes: Report order is by Date. Report is printed in Detail Format and with shortened descriptions.

Date	GL Acct ID	Reference	Qty	Line Description	Debit Amount	Credit Amount
2/4/17	12000	1106	120.00	Roller Bandages		3,600.00
	50000		120.00	Roller Bandages	3,600.00	
2/11/17	12000	1105	20.00	Syringes		100.00
	50000		20.00	Syringes	100.00	
2/12/17	12000	CM201	-2.00	Syringes	10.00	
	50000		-2.00	Syringes		10.00
		Total			**3,710.00**	**3,710.00**

Chapter Review and Assessment

Software Command Summary

Create Sales Tax Agency and Sales Tax	Maintain, Sales Taxes
Create Sales Invoice	Tasks, Sales/Invoicing
Print Sales Invoice	Tasks, Sales/Invoicing, Print
Create a Credit Memo	Tasks, Credit Memos
Collect on an Invoice	Tasks, Receive Money, Apply to Invoices
Create a Quotation	Tasks, Quotes/Sales Orders, Quotes
Convert a Quotation to a Sales Order or Invoice	Tasks, Quotes/Sales Orders, Quotes, Convert
Create Finance Charge Defaults	Maintain, Default Information, Customers, Finance Charges
Create a Finance Charge Report	Tasks, Finance Charge
Create Inventory Reports	Reports & Forms, Inventory, Select a Report from the List
Create Sales Reports	Reports & Forms, Accounts Receivable, Select a Report from the List

Checkpoint Answers

Checkpoint 9–1
1. The four types of forms that many merchandising businesses prepare are the invoice, sales quotation, sales order, and credit memo.
2. The Cost of Goods Sold account is debited for $600 and the Inventory account is credited for $600.

Checkpoint 9-2
1. The businesses that sell goods to consumers are responsible for collecting sales tax from them.
2. Sales Tax Payable is a current liability account.

Checkpoint 9–3
1. A business issues a credit memo as evidence that it is granting credit to a customer for a sales return or allowance.
2. You must enter a positive number in the *Returned* field for a sales return.

Study Quizzes

Take the study quiz online to check your understanding of chapter concepts. The quiz can be taken multiple times.

Content Check

Multiple Choice: Choose only one response for each question.

1. The Sales Revenue account is what type of account?
   A. Cost of Sales
   B. Income
   C. Inventory
   D. Asset

2. A business that uses the perpetual inventory system sells goods for $450. The goods cost $200. When recording the sale, the business must
   A. debit Inventory and credit Cost of Goods Sold for $450.
   B. debit Cost of Goods Sold and credit Inventory for $450.
   C. debit Inventory and credit Cost of Goods Sold for $200.
   D. debit Cost of Goods Sold and credit Inventory for $200.

3. When a customer returns damaged goods, what form must be prepared for sales returns and allowances?
   A. Sales Invoice
   B. Sales Order
   C. Credit Memo
   D. Sales Quote

4. Which inventory report lists the quantity on hand and sales price for each inventory item?
   A. Inventory Adjustment Journal
   B. Inventory Profitability Report
   C. Inventory Valuation Report
   D. Item Price List

5. What type of account is Sales Tax Payable?
   A. Inventory
   B. Income
   C. Expense
   D. Liability

Short Essay Response

Provide a detailed answer for each question.

1. Why would a business want to keep separate accounts for recording sales of services and sales of goods?
2. What is the purpose of each of the following: the sales quotation, the invoice, and the statement of account?
3. Why would a business establish a separate account for recording sales returns and allowances rather than just debiting them to the Sales Revenue account?
4. Why do some businesses impose a finance charge when customers do not pay their invoices on time?
5. How is a finance charge entered in a firm's accounting records?
6. What effect does a sale on credit have on the following accounts: Accounts Receivable, Sales Revenue, Cost of Goods Sold, and Inventory? (Does each account increase or decrease?)

Cooperative Learning

1. Form groups of three or four students and determine the factors to be taken into consideration when establishing credit terms for each customer.
2. As a group, discuss what factors a business should consider when deciding whether to impose a finance charge on customers who do not pay invoices on time.

Writing and Decision Making

Assume that the owner of the company for which you work, Marie Ramirez, is concerned about the increasing level of sales returns that she has noticed on the financial statements during the last six months. She has asked you for reasons why this may be occurring and for ideas about how the level of sales returns can be reduced. She would also like to know how the inventory reports could be used to investigate the problem. Prepare a memo with the information that has been requested.

Case Problems

Demonstrate your knowledge of the Sage 50 Accounting features discussed in this chapter by completing the following case problems.

Case Problem 9–1A

Open Frederica's Designs, an interior decorating business, which is located in the student data files.

1. Create the following general ledger accounts:

Account ID:	**212**
Description:	**Sales Tax Payable**
Account Type:	**Other Current Liabilities**

Account ID:	**404**
Description:	**Sales Returns and Allowances**
Account Type:	**Income**

Account ID:	**406**
Description:	**Sales Discount**
Account Type:	**Income**

2. Create a new vendor account for the Board of Equalization.

Vendor ID:	**BE-10**
Name:	**Board of Equalization**
Expense Account:	**212**
Tax ID Number:	**None**
Ship Via:	**US Mail**
Terms and Credit:	**Net due in 30 days, 0.00 Discount**
Form Options:	**Default**
Payment Settings:	**Default**

3. Enter the following information about the sales tax authorities:

Total Tax Rate:	**7.00**
Sales Tax Agency ID:	**CA**
Sales Tax Agency Name:	**Board of Equalization**
Vendor:	**BE-10**
Taxes Calculated:	**by single rate**
Tax Rate:	**7.00**
Account to Track Sales Tax:	**212**
Sales Tax ID:	**CATAX**
Sales Tax Name:	**California Sales Tax**
Sales Tax on Freight:	**No**

4. Create the following new customer accounts:

    Customer
Customer ID:	**RM-01**
Name:	**Richard Marquez**

General Tab

Account Number:	1020
Billing Address:	1785 Thornton Road
City, ST, Zip:	Modesto, CA 95355
Country:	USA
Sales Tax:	CATAX
Customer Type:	Retail
Telephone 1:	209-555-3692

Contacts Tab

Contact:	Richard Marquez

Sales Info Tab

GL Sales Account:	401
Ship Via:	Fed-EX
Pricing Level:	Price Level 1
Form Options:	Default

Payment & Credit Tab

Terms and Credit:	3.5% 10 days, net 30 days

History Tab

Beginning Balance:	0

Customer

Customer ID:	SM-02
Name:	Sandra McGuire

General Tab

Account Number:	1030
Billing Address:	1495 Lower Stockton Road
City, ST, Zip:	Modesto, CA 95355
Country:	USA
Sales Tax:	CATAX
Customer Type:	Retail
Telephone 1:	209-555-8462

Contacts Tab

Contact:	Sandra McGuire

Sales Info Tab

GL Sales Account:	401
Ship Via:	Fed-EX
Pricing Level:	Price Level 1
Form Options:	Default

Payment & Credit Tab

Terms and Credit:	3% 10 days, net 30 days

History Tab

Beginning Balance:	0

Customer

    Customer ID: **LA-03**

    Name: **Luis Abelar**

General Tab

    Account Number: **1040**

    Billing Address: **2465 Eaton Avenue**

    City, ST, Zip: **Stockton, CA 95210**

    Country: **USA**

    Sales Tax: **CATAX**

    Customer Type: **Retail**

    Telephone 1:   **209-555-5217**

Contacts Tab

    Contact: **Luis Abelar**

Sales Info Tab

    GL Sales Account: **401**

    Ship Via: **Fed-EX**

    Pricing Level: **Price Level 1**

    Form Options: **Default**

Payment & Credit Tab

    Terms and Credit: **3% 10 days, net 30 days**

History Tab

    Beginning Balance: **0**

5. Record the following transactions for the month of January 2017:

Jan. 11	Sold 8 flower stencils and 4 pillows on credit to Richard Marquez, Invoice 649. (Note that all customers pay sales tax on purchases.)
12	Sold 3 pillows on credit to Sandra McGuire, Invoice 650.
14	Sandra McGuire returned 1 of the pillows. Issued Credit Memo 011 (CM011) to her.
15	Sold 4 flower stencils and 6 pillows on credit to Luis Abelar, Invoice 651.
18	Richard Marquez paid Invoice 649, less discount, Check No. 1473.
20	Luis Abelar paid Invoice 651, less discount, Check No. 2003.
21	Sandra McGuire paid Invoice 650, less discount, Check No. 1146.

6. Print the Customer Ledgers and Cost of Goods Sold Journal.

HINT

Click the Journal button to review the Accounting Behind the Screens window. Make sure Sales Returns and Allowances, account 404, is debited for the return amount.

HINT

Click the Journal button to review the Accounting Behind the Screens window. Make sure Sales Discount, account 406, is debited for the discount amount.

Case Problem 9-2A

Executive Consultants, a business consulting company, prepared the following quotations for two prospective clients during the month of June 2017. The prices were negotiated by the firm's sales representatives: Annette Johnson and Thomas Watson.

1. Open Executive Consultants from the student data files.

2. Create the following general ledger account:

Account ID:	**212**
Description:	**Sales Tax Payable**
Account Type:	**Other Current Liabilities**

3. Create a new vendor account for the Board of Equalization.

Vendor ID:	**BE-30**
Name:	**Board of Equalization**
Expense Account:	**212**
Tax ID Number:	**None**
Ship Via:	**US Mail**
Terms and Credit:	**Net due in 30 days, 0.00 Discount**
Form Options:	**Default**
Payment Settings:	**Default**

4. Enter the following information about the sales tax authorities:

Total Tax Rate:	**7.00**
Sales Tax Agency ID:	**CA**
Sales Tax Agency Name:	**Board of Equalization**
Vendor:	**BE-30**
Taxes Calculated:	**by single rate**
Tax Rate:	**7.00**
Account to Track Sales Tax:	**212**
Sales Tax ID:	**CATAX**
Sales Tax Name:	**California Sales Tax**
Sales Tax on Freight:	**No**

5. Create the new following customer accounts:

Customer

Customer ID:	**KD-01**
Name:	**Kathleen's Designs**

General Tab

Account Number:	**10**
Billing Address:	**1748 West Fair Oaks**
City, ST, Zip:	**Modesto, CA 95355**
Country:	**USA**
Sales Tax:	**None**
Customer Type:	**Retail**
Telephone 1:	**209-555-6925**

Contacts Tab

Contact: **Kathleen Rosario**

Sales Info Tab

GL Sales Account: **401**
Ship Via: **Fed-EX**
Pricing Level: **Price Level 1**
Form Options: **Default**

Payment & Credit Tab

Terms and Credit: **3% 10 days, net 30 days**

History Tab

Beginning Balance: **0**

Customer

Customer ID: **HD-02**
Name: **Hendricks' Construction**

General Tab

Account Number: **20**
Billing Address: **2469 Rose Marie Lane**
City, ST, Zip: **Stockton, CA 95207**
Country: **USA**
Sales Tax: **None**
Customer Type: **Retail**
Telephone 1:   **209-555-6523**

Contacts Tab

Contact: **Randy Hendricks**

Sales Info Tab

GL Sales Account: **402**
Ship Via: **Fed-EX**
Pricing Level: **Price Level 1**
Form Options: **Default**

Payment & Credit Tab

Terms and Credit: **3% 10 days, net 30 days**

History Tab

Beginning Balance: **0**

6. Create the following quotations as of the dates specified:

HINT

As these are non-inventory items, enter the number of hours in the *Quantity* field and the hourly rate in the *Unit Price* field.

June 1   Annette Johnson gave Quotation 103 for 7 hours of training at $90 per hour to Kathleen's Designs. The quotation was good until June 10, 2017.

5   Thomas Watson gave Quotation 104 for 5 hours of consulting service at $75 per hour to Hendricks' Construction. The quotation was good until June 18, 2017.

7. Convert both quotations to invoices as of the dates specified:

> June 9   Kathleen's Designs has accepted the quotation. Issued Invoice 302.
>
> 18   Hendricks' Construction has accepted 4 of the 5 hours for which the quotation was prepared. Issued Invoice 314.

8. Print the Sales Journal and Customer Ledgers.

Case Problem 9–1B

Open Monica's, a beauty salon, which is located in the student data files.

1. Create the following general ledger accounts:

Account ID:	**212**
Description:	**Sales Tax Payable**
Account Type:	**Other Current Liabilities**

Account ID:	**404**
Description:	**Sales Returns and Allowances**
Account Type:	**Income**

Account ID:	**406**
Description:	**Sales Discount**
Account Type:	**Income**

2. Create a new vendor account for the Board of Equalization.

Vendor ID:	**BE-20**
Name:	**Board of Equalization**
Expense Account:	**212**
Tax ID Number:	**None**
Ship Via:	**US Mail**
Terms and Credit:	**Net due in 30 days, 0.00 Discount**
Form Options:	**Default**
Payment Settings:	**Default**

3. Enter the following information about the sales tax authorities:

Total Tax Rate:	**7.00**
Sales Tax Agency ID:	**CA**
Sales Tax Agency Name:	**Board of Equalization**
Vendor:	**BE-20**
Taxes Calculated:	**by single rate**
Tax Rate:	**7.00**
Account to Track Sales Tax:	**212**
Sales Tax ID:	**CATAX**
Sales Tax Name:	**California Sales Tax**
Sales Tax on Freight:	**No**

4. Create the following new customer accounts:

Customer

Customer ID:	**NJ-01**
Name:	**Natalie Jones**

General Tab

Account Number:	**100**
Billing Address:	**1654 Lower Sacramento Road**
City, ST, Zip:	**Stockton, CA 95207**
Country:	**USA**
Sales Tax:	**CATAX**
Customer Type:	**Retail**
Telephone 1:	**209-555-6493**

Contacts Tab

Contact:	**Natalie Jones**

Sales Info Tab

GL Sales Account:	**401**
Ship Via:	**Fed-EX**
Pricing Level:	**Price Level 1**
Form Options:	**Default**

Payment & Credit Tab

Terms and Credit:	**2% 10 days, net 30 days**

History Tab

Beginning Balance:	**0**

Customer

Customer ID:	**RG-02**
Name:	**Raquel Gannon**

General Tab

Account Number:	**200**
Billing Address:	**2610 Country Club**
City, ST, Zip:	**Modesto, CA 95355**
Country:	**USA**
Sales Tax:	**CATAX**
Customer Type:	**Retail**
Telephone 1:	**209-555-5915**

Contacts Tab

Contact:	**Raquel Gannon**

Sales Info Tab

GL Sales Account:	**401**
Ship Via:	**Fed-EX**
Pricing Level:	**Price Level 1**
Form Options:	**Default**

Payment & Credit Tab

Terms and Credit:	**2% 10 days, net 30 days**

History Tab

Beginning Balance:	**0**

Customer

Customer ID:	RC-03
Name:	Richard Chang

General Tab

Account Number:	300
Billing Address:	1518 West Schulte Road
City, ST, Zip:	Modesto, CA 95355
Country:	USA
Sales Tax:	CATAX
Customer Type:	Retail
Telephone 1:	209-555-5639

Contacts Tab

Contact:	Richard Chang

Sales Info Tab

GL Sales Account:	401
Ship Via:	Fed-EX
Pricing Level:	Price Level 1
Form Options:	Default

Payment & Credit Tab

Terms and Credit:	2% 10 days, net 30 days

History Tab

Beginning Balance:	0

> **HINT**
> Click the Journal button to review the Accounting Behind the Screens window. Make sure Sales Discount, account 406, is debited for the discount amount.

> **HINT**
> Click the Journal button to review the Accounting Behind the Screens window. Make sure Sales Returns and Allowances, account 404, is debited for the return amount.

5. Record the following transactions for the month of June 2017:

June 13	Sold 2 bottles of shampoo and 1 bottle of conditioner on credit to Natalie Jones, Invoice 964. (Note that all customers pay sales tax on purchases.)
15	Sold 2 bottles of shampoo and 2 bottles of hair gel on credit to Raquel Gannon, Invoice 965.
17	Natalie Jones paid Invoice 964, less discount, Check No. 7906.
18	Raquel Gannon returned 1 bottle of hair gel. Issued Credit Memo 014 (CM014) to her.
21	Sold 2 bottles of shampoo and 1 bottle of hair gel on credit to Richard Chang, Invoice 966.
24	Raquel Gannon paid Invoice 965, less discount, Check No. 1321.
30	Richard Chang paid Invoice 966, less discount, Check No. 4320.

6. Print the Customer Ledgers and Cost of Goods Sold Journal.

Case Problem 9–2B

VP Computer Systems, a computer programming services company, prepared the following quotations for two of its prospective clients during the month of April 2017. The prices were negotiated by the firm's sales representatives: Stacey Anderson and William London.

1. Open VP Computer Systems from the student data files.

2. Create the following general ledger account:

Account ID:	**212**
Description:	**Sales Tax Payable**
Account Type:	**Other Current Liabilities**

3. Create a new vendor account for the Board of Equalization.

Vendor ID:	**BE-40**
Name:	**Board of Equalization**
Expense Account:	**212**
Tax ID Number:	**None**
Ship Via:	**US Mail**
Terms and Credit:	**Net due in 30 days, 0.00 Discount**
Form Options:	**Default**

4. Enter the following information about the sales tax authorities:

Total Tax Rate:	**7.00**
Sales Tax Agency ID:	**CA**
Sales Tax Agency Name:	**Board of Equalization**
Vendor:	**BE-40**
Taxes Calculated:	**by single rate**
Tax Rate:	**7.00**
Account to Track Sales Tax:	**212**
Sales Tax ID:	**CATAX**
Sales Tax Name:	**California Sales Tax**
Sales Tax on Freight:	**No**

5. Create the following new customer accounts:

Customer

Customer ID:	**KD-01**
Name:	**Kathleen's Designs**

General Tab

Account Number:	**100**
Billing Address:	**1748 West Fair Oaks**
City, ST, Zip:	**Modesto, CA 95355**
Country:	**USA**
Sales Tax:	**None**
Customer Type:	**Retail**
Telephone 1:	**209-555-6925**

Contacts Tab

Contact:	**Kathleen Rosario**

Sales Info Tab

GL Sales Account:	**401**
Ship Via:	**Fed-EX**
Pricing Level:	**Price Level 1**
Form Options:	**Default**

Payment & Credit Tab

Terms and Credit: 3% 10 days, net 30 days

History Tab

Beginning Balance: 0

Customer

Customer ID: GJ-02
Name: GJ Marketing Group

General Tab

Account Number: 200
Billing Address: 1510 East March Lane
City, ST, Zip: Stockton, CA 95207
Country: USA
Sales Tax: None
Customer Type: Retail
Telephone 1:   209-555-7685

Contacts Tab

Contact: Cynthia Flores

Sales Info Tab

GL Sales Account: 402
Ship Via: Fed-EX
Pricing Level: Price Level 1
Form Options: Default

Payment & Credit Tab

Terms and Credit: 3% 10 days, net 30 days

History Tab

Beginning Balance: 0

6. Create the quotations as of the dates specified.

HINT

As these are non-inventory items, enter the number of hours in the *Quantity* field and the hourly rate in the *Unit Price* field.

    April 10   Stacey Anderson gave Quotation 150 for 12 hours of design services at $65 per hour to Kathleen's Designs. The quotation was good until April 20, 2017.
    15   William London gave Quotation 151 for 6 hours of computer services at $90 per hour to GJ Marketing Group. The quotation was good until April 25, 2017.

7. Convert both quotations to invoices as of the dates specified.

    April 18   Kathleen's Designs has accepted the quotation. Issued Invoice 164.
    25   GJ Marketing Group has accepted the quotation. Issued Invoice 175.

8. Print the Sales Journal and Customer Ledgers.

Payroll

Objectives

Software Features

- Establish a Payroll System

- Set Employee Defaults

- Prepare a Payroll

- Print Payroll Checks

- Print Payroll Reports

Company Files

Before beginning chapter work, access the links menu to download company files.

People are aware of payroll because of the checks they receive from their employers. However, issuing payroll checks is just one part of the payroll work that a business must do. For even a small firm with just a few employees, managing a payroll can be difficult and time-consuming.

The payroll activities of a business fall into six basic areas:

- Calculating the earnings and deductions of employees and issuing payroll checks
- Keeping records of the time that employees work and their earnings and deductions
- Calculating the payroll taxes owed by the employer
- Depositing the taxes deducted from employee earnings and the payroll taxes owed by the employer
- Preparing payroll tax returns that must be sent to federal, state, and sometimes local tax agencies
- Making entries for payroll in the accounting records

Obviously, it is important that payroll calculations, records, and tax returns be prepared with great accuracy. It is also important to do all the necessary work on time. Employees expect to receive their payroll checks promptly, and government agencies require that tax deposits and tax returns be submitted according to strict schedules. Failure to meet these schedules can result in financial penalties.

Sage 50 allows a business to handle its payroll work quickly and efficiently. Once the payroll system is set up, most operations are done automatically when the information for a payroll period is entered.

OBJECTIVE 10–1

Review General Payroll Concepts

Preparing a payroll can be a complex process because many laws and government regulations affect it. Federal, state, and local tax agencies publish annual guides for employers that specify the requirements for keeping payroll records, withholding taxes from employee earnings, calculating the employer's payroll taxes, depositing all taxes owed, and filing tax returns.

Payroll Periods

payroll period The time period for which earnings and deductions are calculated.

Every business must establish a payroll period. The **payroll period** is the time period for which earnings and deductions are calculated. This period may be weekly, biweekly (every other week), semimonthly (on the 15th and the last day of each month), or monthly. Some large businesses use different payroll periods for different types of employees. For example, they may pay their factory workers on a weekly basis but pay their office staff on a monthly basis.

Pay Plans

pay plan The method used to calculate an employee's earnings.

Employees are paid according to various pay plans. The **pay plan** is the method used to calculate an employee's earnings. The most common pay plans are the hourly rate plan, the salary plan, the commission plan, the salary-commission plan, and the piece-rate plan.

- With the *hourly rate* plan, an employee receives a fixed amount for each hour worked, such as $9 an hour.

- With the *salary* plan, an employee receives a fixed amount for the payroll period, such as $500 a week.
- With the *commission* plan, an employee involved with sales receives a percentage of his or her sales, such as 5% of sales.
- With the *salary-commission* plan, an employee receives a fixed amount for the payroll period plus a percentage of his or her sales, such as $400 a week plus 2% of sales.
- With the *piece-rate* plan, an employee receives a fixed amount for each item produced, such as $2 for each circuit board assembled. This plan is used in some factories.

Payroll Laws and Regulations

Many laws and regulations govern payroll work. The most important of these laws and regulations are briefly described below.

- The *Fair Labor Standards Act* is a federal law that covers many employers. This law requires that employers pay at least the federal minimum wage and pay overtime to most employees when they work more than 40 hours in a workweek. The overtime rate must be at least 1½ times the regular hourly rate. Managerial and supervisory employees may be exempt from the overtime pay requirement.
- Some states and cities have their own *minimum wage laws*, which may set a higher minimum wage than the federal government.
- The *Current Tax Payment Act* requires employers to withhold federal income tax from the earnings of their employees.
- The *Federal Insurance Contributions Act (FICA)* requires employers to withhold Social Security tax and Medicare tax from the earnings of their employees and pay a matching amount themselves.
- The *Federal Unemployment Tax Act (FUTA)* requires employers to pay a tax that is intended to provide jobless benefits to employees who are temporarily out of work.
- Each state has its own *State Unemployment Tax Act (SUTA)*. In most cases, these laws impose a tax on just the employer. However, a few states also require a contribution from employees.
- Many states and some cities and counties have their own *income tax laws* and require employers to withhold this tax from employee earnings.
- Some states have *disability insurance laws*. For example, California requires employers to withhold a state disability insurance (SDI) tax from employee earnings. This tax is used to pay benefits to employees who temporarily cannot work because of illness or injury.

Federal and State Tax Returns

The federal government requires employers to file a variety of tax returns. Some of the most important of these returns are as follows.

- *Form 941*, Employer's Quarterly Federal Tax Return, is prepared after the end of each quarter. It shows the wages paid during the quarter and the federal income tax and FICA taxes owed.
- *Form 940*, Employer's Annual Federal Unemployment Tax Return, is prepared after the end of each year. It shows the wages paid during the year and the FUTA tax liability for the year.

- *Form W-2*, Wage and Tax Statement, is prepared for each employee after the end of each year. This multiple-copy form shows the wages earned by the employee during the year and the federal and state taxes withheld. Copies of this form go to the employee and to federal and state tax agencies.
- *Form W-3*, Transmittal of Wage and Tax Statements, is prepared after the end of each year. This form shows the total wages paid to employees during the year and the federal and state taxes withheld from employee earnings.
- *Form 1099* is prepared for each independent contractor after the end of each year. This multiple-copy form shows the fees paid to the independent contractor during the year. Copies of Form 1099 go to the independent contractor and to federal and some state tax agencies. Remember that an independent contractor does work for a business on a project-by-project basis and is not an employee. As a result, the business does not withhold taxes from the fees paid to an independent contractor. This person is responsible for paying his or her taxes directly to federal and state tax agencies.
- *Form 8109*, Federal Tax Deposit Coupon, is prepared when a deposit of federal taxes is made by check in a bank or other depositary institution. This form shows the amount being deposited. If a business makes deposits by means of electronic funds transfer, Form 8109 is not used. The schedule for making federal tax deposits depends on the amounts owed. *Note: This form is not currently included in the Sage 50 software.*

You can prepare and print all of the federal payroll reports and statements mentioned above (except Form 8109) by clicking Reports & Forms and then *Payroll.*

State tax agencies also require employers to file tax returns. These forms vary from state to state, as do the schedules for filing the forms and making tax deposits.

Required and Voluntary Deductions

As you have seen, federal, state, and sometimes local laws require that employers deduct certain taxes from employee earnings. For example, Wardwood Construction Company, which is located in California, must withhold the following taxes from the earnings of its employees: federal income, Social Security, Medicare, state income, and State Disability Insurance (SDI).

In addition to these required deductions, some businesses allow voluntary deductions for items such as medical insurance, life insurance, and a retirement savings plan (a 401(k) plan).

Accounting Entries for Payroll

Businesses use a number of liability and expense accounts to record payroll transactions. Taxes withheld from employee earnings and taxes owed by the employer are debts of a business until they are deposited. Therefore, they are recorded in current liability accounts.

- When the payroll is calculated, the total of the employee earnings is debited to Wages and Salaries Expense and the amounts withheld for the various taxes are credited to individual liability accounts such as

Federal Income Tax Payable, FICA—Social Security Tax Payable, FICA—Medicare Tax Payable, State Income Tax Payable, and SDI Tax Payable.

- When the employer's payroll taxes are calculated, the total of the taxes is debited to Payroll Taxes Expense and the amounts of the various taxes owed are credited to individual liability accounts such as FICA—Social Security Tax Payable, FICA—Medicare Tax Payable, FUTA Tax Payable, and SUTA Tax Payable.
- When a business pays the taxes it owes, it debits the appropriate liability accounts and credits Cash.

Features of the Sage 50 Payroll System

The Sage 50 payroll system allows a business to set up and maintain an earnings record for each employee, calculate earnings and deductions, calculate the employer's payroll taxes, prepare payroll tax returns for government agencies, prepare payroll reports for management, and make the necessary accounting entries for payroll.

Sage 50 Accounting 2017 has a special feature called the Payroll Setup Wizard, which will help you establish the payroll system. Version 2017 also has enhanced Internet access to federal and state tax publications and tax forms. This feature helps employers stay informed about changes in tax rates, schedules for making deposits, and schedules for filing tax returns.

Checkpoint 10–1

1. What are the different types of payroll periods?
2. What three federal taxes must employers withhold from employee earnings?

OBJECTIVE 10–2

Create a Payroll System Using the Sage 50 Payroll Setup Wizard

The Payroll Setup Wizard in Sage 50 Accounting 2017 provides you with step-by-step guidance for establishing your payroll system. At the start of this process, you must select the appropriate payroll tax percentages and create several new general ledger accounts.

Assume that the Wardwood Construction Company decides to establish a payroll system using Sage 50 as of February 1, 2017. Follow the steps outlined below to create the new payroll system.

Step 1:

Open Chp. 10 – Wardwood Construction Company and close the Action Items log.

Step 2:

Click Options on the Menu bar and then *Default Information* and *Payroll Setup Wizard* at the drop-down lists.

HINT

You can also access the Payroll Setup Wizard by clicking Maintain, *Default Information*, and *Payroll Setup Wizard*.

Step 3:

Click Next at the Payroll Setup Wizard window, as shown in Figure 10–1.

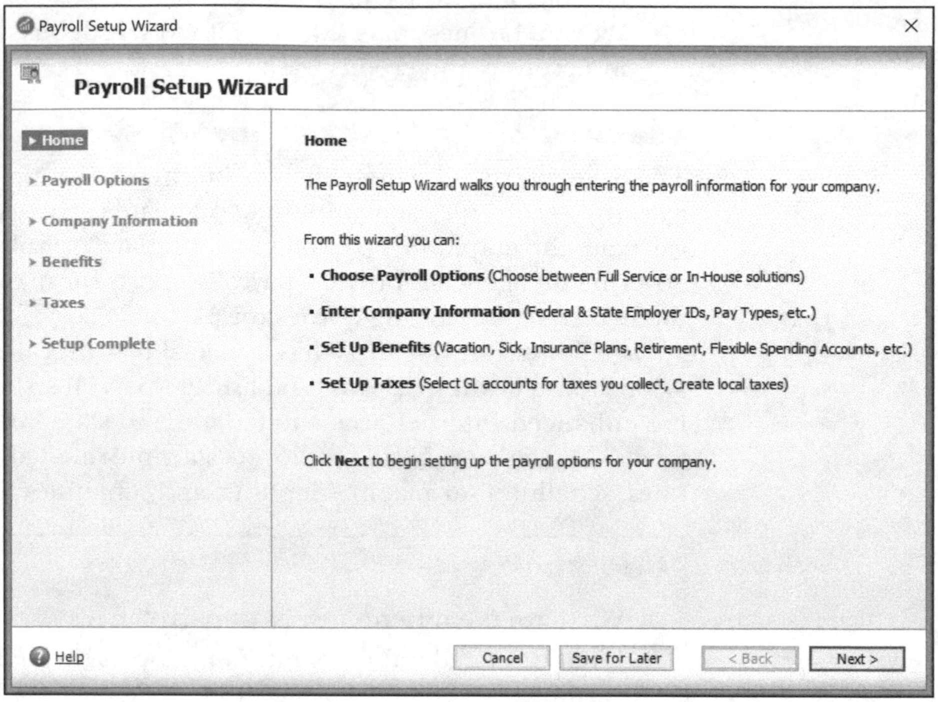

FIGURE 10–1
Sage 50 Payroll Setup Wizard Window

Step 4:

Click Next at the Payroll Setup Wizard – Other Payroll Options window, as shown in Figure 10–2.

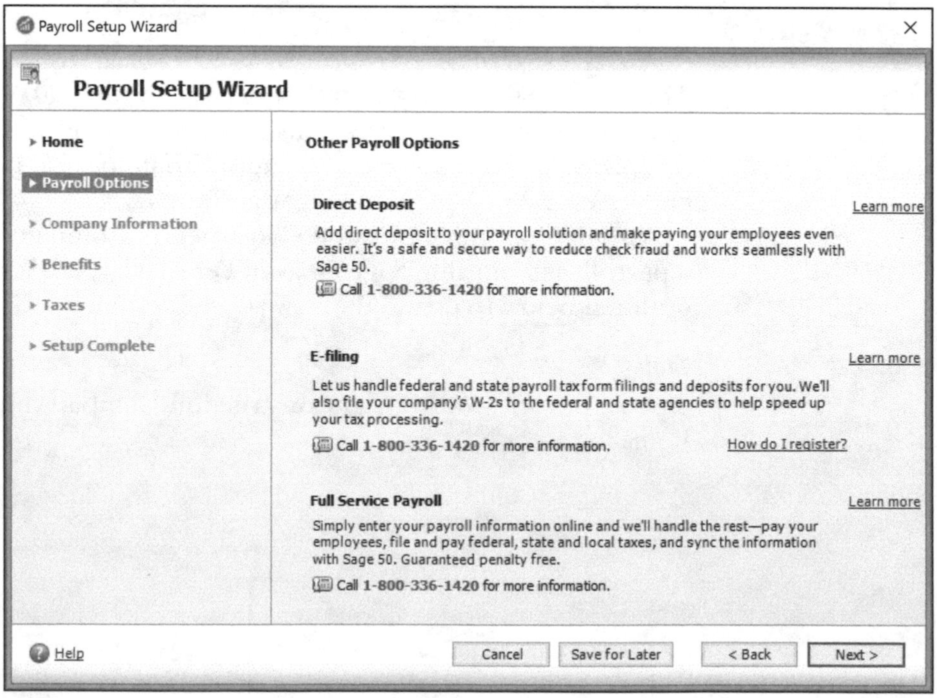

FIGURE 10–2
Payroll Setup Wizard Screen

Step 5:

Click *CA* at the drop-down list in the *State* field. (*CA* stands for California, the state where Wardwood is located.) Key **5.00** in the *State Unemployment Rate* field. If the screen looks like Figure 10–3, click the Next button.

FIGURE 10–3
Payroll Setup Wizard –
Company Information
Dialog Box

HINT
The tax tables change periodically and must be updated. Go to the Sage 50 website, http://sage.com, for updated information.

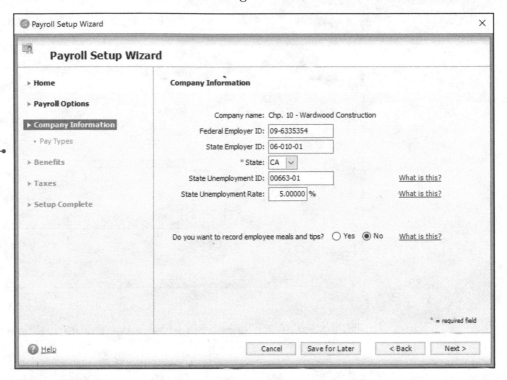

Step 6:

At the Payroll Setup Wizard – Pay Types window, click the drop-down arrow at the *Hourly – Regular* field and scroll to account *#512 – Wages and Salaries Expense*. Repeat this process for the *Hourly – Overtime* and *Salary – Salary* sections.

Step 7:

Compare your completed work with Figure 10–4 and click Next.

FIGURE 10–4

Completed Payroll Setup
Wizard – Pay Types
Dialog Box

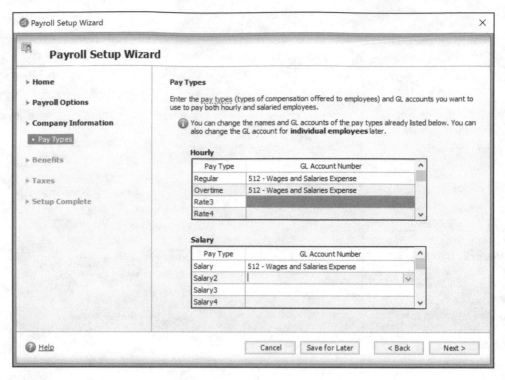

Step 8:

Click Next at the Payroll Setup Wizard – Benefits window.

Step 9:

At the *Tax liability acct. no.* field, click the *downward arrow*, click the New
button, and create the following general ledger account.

Account ID:	**218**
Description:	**Payroll Taxes Payable**
Account Type:	**Other Current Liabilities**

a. Click the Save button and then close the Maintain Chart of Accounts
window.
b. In the *Tax Liability account no.* field, choose Account #218, Payroll
Taxes Payable.

Step 10:

At the *Tax expense acct. no.* field, click the *downward arrow*, click the New
button, and then create the following general ledger account.

Account ID:	**513**
Description:	**Payroll Tax Expense**
Account Type:	**Expenses**

a. Click the Save button and then close the Maintain Chart of Accounts
window.
b. In the *Tax Expense account no.* field, choose Account #513, Payroll Tax
Expense.

Compare your screen with Figure 10–5 and make any necessary corrections. Then click Next to continue.

FIGURE 10–5
Payroll Setup Wizard –
Payroll Taxes Dialog Box

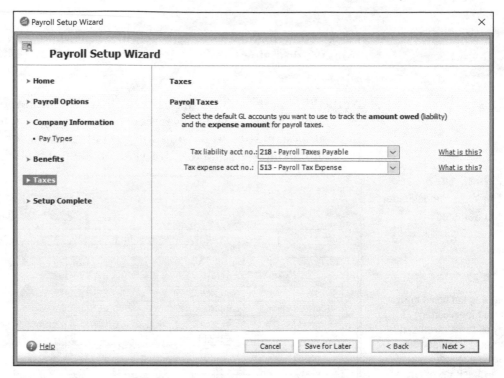

Step 11:

At the Payroll Setup Wizard – Setup Complete screen, click Finish, as shown in Figure 10–6.

FIGURE 10–6
Payroll Setup Wizard –
Setup Complete Dialog Box

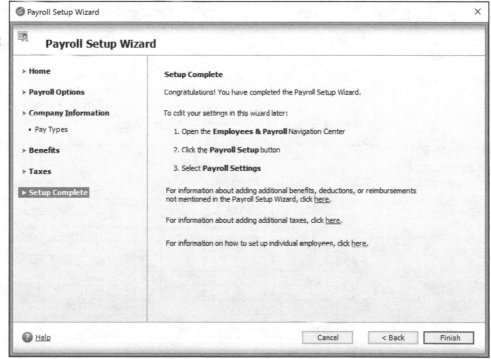

It is necessary to set up the employee and employer individual payroll accounts before Sage 50 can be used to complete a payroll. This requires using the general ledger accounts for gross pay and deductions, including required federal and state tax deductions for each individual employee. The same is true for creating the employer general ledger accounts.

Step 12:

Click Maintain and *Default Information* on the Menu bar. Select *Employees* from the drop-down list.

Step 13:

At the Employee Defaults dialog box, click the Employee Fields folder tab, as shown in Figure 10–7. This screen shows the general ledger accounts that were established as defaults for recording employee earnings (gross pay) and deductions, notably 218 (Payroll Taxes Payable).

FIGURE 10–7
Employee Fields Folder Tab Selected

HINT

The liability account that was set up as the default for recording payroll taxes owed (Account 218) may be changed to more accurately track the different liabilities. An individual liability account for each type of tax can be established. This process will be demonstrated later in the chapter.

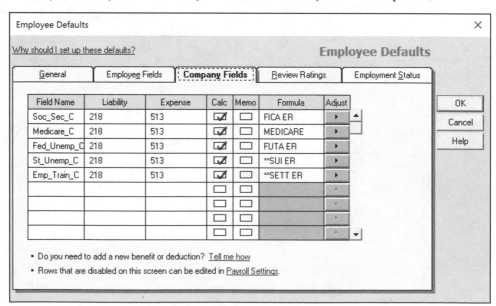

Step 14:

Click the Company Fields folder tab in the Employee Defaults dialog box, as shown in Figure 10–8. This screen shows the general ledger accounts that were established as defaults for recording the employer's payroll taxes, notably 218 (Payroll Taxes Payable) and 513 (Payroll Tax Expense).

FIGURE 10–8
Company Fields Folder Tab Selected

Step 15:

Click OK to accept the Employee Defaults.

    This concludes the payroll setup process. Note that changes can be made to the payroll defaults at any time by clicking Maintain on the Menu bar, clicking *Default Information*, and then clicking *Employees*.

Checkpoint 10–2

1. Where can Sage 50 users find updated tax tables?
2. What account will be used to record gross pay?

Objective 10–2 Practice

Step 1:

Open Chp. 10 – Blufrog Maintenance Company.

Step 2:

Use the Payroll Setup Wizard to establish the payroll system for Blufrog.

Step 3:

Use the following information to set up the payroll system.

State:	**CA**
Unemployment Rate:	**5.00**
Gross Pay Acct:	**512**

Step 4:

Create the following general ledger accounts for recording payroll taxes.

Account ID:	**218**
Description:	**Payroll Taxes Payable**
Account Type:	**Other Current Liabilities**

Account ID:	**513**
Description:	**Payroll Taxes Expense**
Account Type:	**Expenses**

Step 5:

Accept all remaining defaults, and then click Finish.

OBJECTIVE 10–3

Maintain the Payroll System

Maintaining the payroll system usually involves updating accounts and updating employee information. Let us look first at the procedures for changing accounts that have been established as defaults.

Creating Additional Default Accounts

Suppose that Wardwood Construction Company is not happy with the default accounts that it established with the Payroll Setup Wizard. Instead of having a single liability account called *Payroll Taxes Payable*, Wardwood wants to create separate liability accounts to keep track of the different types of employee withholding taxes and employer payroll taxes.

Step 1:

Open Chp. 10 – Wardwood Construction Company, which you updated previously in the chapter, and close the Action Items log.

Step 2:

Click Maintain, click *Default Information*, and then click *Employees*.

Step 3:

At the Employee Defaults window, click the Employee Fields folder tab, as shown in Figure 10–9.

FIGURE 10–9
Employee Defaults Window with Employee Fields Folder Tab Selected

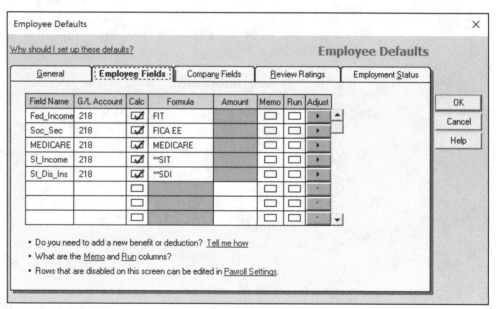

Step 4:

Up to this point, Payroll Taxes Payable (Account 218) was Wardwood's default account for all the employee withholding taxes. Click in the *Fed_Income* row of the *G/L Account* column and then click the *magnifying glass* icon to create new accounts as the defaults in the following fields. Note that all of these accounts are considered "Other Current Liabilities."

HINT
After you click on the magnifying glass, you need to click the New button at the bottom of the chart of accounts pop-up screen.

a. In the *Fed_Income* field, change Account 218 to:

Account ID:	**220**
Description:	**Federal Income Taxes Payable**
Account Type:	**Other Current Liabilities**

b. In the *Soc_Sec* field, change Account 218 to:

Account ID:	**222**
Description:	**Social Security Taxes Payable**
Account Type:	**Other Current Liabilities**

c. In the *MEDICARE* field, change Account 218 to:

Account ID:	**224**
Description:	**Medicare Taxes Payable**
Account Type:	**Other Current Liabilities**

d. In the *St_Income* field, change Account 218 to:

Account ID:	**226**
Description:	**State Income Taxes Payable**
Account Type:	**Other Current Liabilities**

e. In the *St_Dis_Ins* field, change Account 218 to:

Account ID:	**228**
Description:	**SDI Taxes Payable**
Account Type:	**Other Current Liabilities**

Step 5:

Review the new defaults in the Employee Fields folder tab, as shown in Figure 10–10. Make any necessary changes.

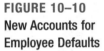

FIGURE 10–10
New Accounts for
Employee Defaults

Employee Defaults

Why should I set up these defaults?   **Employee Defaults**

| General | Employee Fields | Company Fields | Review Ratings | Employment Status |

Field Name	G/L Account	Calc	Formula	Amount	Memo	Run	Adjust
Fed_Income	220	☑	FIT		☐	☐	▸
Soc_Sec	222	☑	FICA EE		☐	☐	▸
MEDICARE	224	☑	MEDICARE		☐	☐	▸
St_Income	226	☑	**SIT		☐	☐	▸
St_Dis_Ins	228	☑	**SDI		☐	☐	▸
		☐			☐	☐	▸
		☐			☐	☐	▸
		☐			☐	☐	▸

OK
Cancel
Help

• Do you need to add a new benefit or deduction? Tell me how
• What are the Memo and Run columns?
• Rows that are disabled on this screen can be edited in Payroll Settings.

Step 6:

Click the Company Fields folder tab.

Step 7:

Change the defaults for the liability accounts to be used in recording the employer's payroll taxes. Create new accounts as follows.

a. In the *Soc_Sec_C* field, change Account 218 to 222.

HINT

After you click on the magnifying glass, you need to click the New button at the bottom of the chart of accounts pop-up screen.

b. In the *Medicare_C* field, change Account 218 to 224.

c. In the *Fed_Unemp_C* field, change Account 218 to:

Account ID:	**230**
Description:	**FUTA Taxes Payable**
Account Type:	**Other Current Liabilities**

d. In the *St_Unemp_C* field, change Account 218 to:

Account ID:	**232**
Description:	**SUTA Taxes Payable**
Account Type:	**Other Current Liabilities**

Note: The educational version of Sage 50 may include the field **Emp_Train_C.** *Remove the check mark in the* **Calc** *field aligned with* **Emp_Train_C.**

Step 8:

Compare your entries with Figure 10–11, and make any necessary changes.

FIGURE 10–11
New Accounts for
Company Defaults

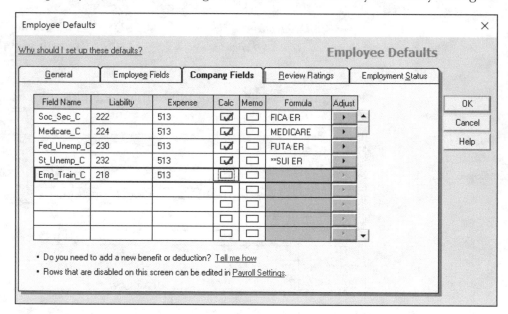

Step 9:

Click OK to accept the new defaults.

The general ledger accounts that were entered as defaults are now the accounts that Sage 50 will use during the payroll process. Two of these accounts, Social Security Tax Payable and Medicare Tax Payable, are used to record both employee taxes and employer payroll taxes. That is why they were listed in the employee and employer fields. (Remember that the Federal Insurance Contributions Act requires employers to match the Social Security tax and Medicare tax paid by their employees.)

Creating the Employee Records

In the Sage 50 payroll system, an individual record must be set up for each employee. This record includes general information, withholding information, and pay information for the employee. The withholding information is needed to calculate the federal, state, and local income tax owed by the employee. The pay information specifies the payroll period (frequency), the pay plan (pay method) used for the employee, and the employee's pay rate.

Follow the steps outlined below to establish employee records for the four employees of Wardwood Construction Company. This firm has a weekly payroll period and uses the hourly rate plan and the salary plan. The hourly employees have a 40-hour workweek.

Step 1:
Click Maintain and then click *Employees/Sales Reps.*

Step 2:
The Maintain Employees & Sales Reps window will appear, as shown in Figure 10–12.

FIGURE 10–12
Maintain Employees & Sales Reps Window

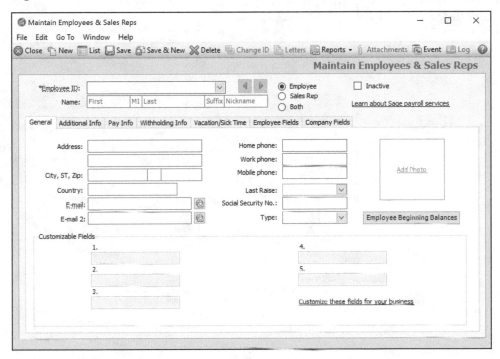

Enter the information for the first employee—George Clark.

Employee ID:	**GCL-03**
Name:	**George Clark**

General Tab

Address:	**126 New Castle Road**
City, ST, Zip:	**Modesto, CA 95355**
Country:	**USA**
Home Phone:	**209-555-0332**
Last Raise:	**Jan 31, 2011**
Social Security No.	**559-30-6523**
Type:	**Salaried**

Step 3:

Click the Withholding Info tab and enter the following information:

Withholding Info Tab

Federal:	**Single**	*Allowances:* **2**	*Addl Withholding:* **0.00**
State:	**Single**	*Allowances:* **2**	*Addl Withholding:* **0.00**
State/Locality: **CA**			
Local:	**Single**		

Step 4:

Compare your completed Maintain Employees & Sales Reps window Withholding Info folder tab to the one shown in Figure 10–13 and make any necessary corrections.

FIGURE 10–13
Completed Withholding Info Tab

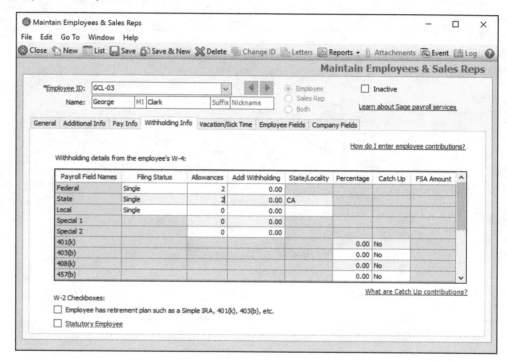

Step 5:

Click the Pay Info folder tab, and then enter the following information:

Pay Info Tab

Pay Method:	**Salary**
Pay Frequency:	**Weekly**
Hours Per Pay Period:	**40**
Rate Used To Bill	
Customer:	**25.00**
Salary Pay Rate:	**1,000.00**

Step 6:

Compare your Pay Info folder tab to the one shown in Figure 10–14 and make any necessary corrections. Then click Save to save the new employee information for George Clark.

FIGURE 10–14
Completed Pay Info Tab

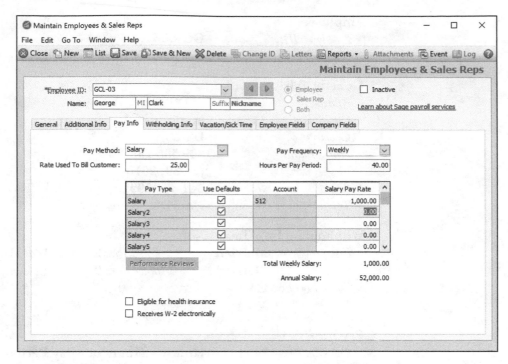

Step 7:

Enter the information for the remaining three employees of Wardwood Construction Company.

Employee

Employee ID:	**SJO-04**
Name:	**Samuel P. Jones**

General Tab

Address:	**413 Mill River Drive**
City, ST, Zip:	**Modesto, CA 95351**
Country:	**USA**
Home Phone:	**209-555-3032**
Social Security No:	**562-90-9866**
Type:	**Hourly**

Withholding Info Tab

Federal:	**Married**	*Allowances:* **2**	*Addl Withholding:* **0.00**
State:	**Married**	*Allowances:* **2**	*Addl Withholding:* **0.00**
State/Locality: **CA**			
Local:	**Married**		

Pay Info Tab

Pay Method:	**Hourly—Hours per Pay Period**
Pay Frequency:	**Weekly**
Hours Per Pay Period:	**40.00**
Rate Used To Bill Customer:	**24.00**
Regular:	**15.00**
Overtime:	**22.50**

Employee

Employee ID:	**GGR-05**
Name:	**Ginger Z. Griggs**

General Tab

Address:	**11121 Ceres Avenue**
City, ST, Zip:	**Modesto, CA 95351**
Country:	**USA**
Home Phone:	**209-555-2334**
Last Raise:	**Jan 30, 2010**
Social Security No:	**544-87-9099**
Type:	**Hourly**

Withholding Info Tab

Federal:	**Married**	*Allowances:* **2**	*Addl Withholding:* **0.00**
State:	**Married**	*Allowances:* **2**	*Addl Withholding:* **0.00**
State/Locality: **CA**			
Local:	**Married**		

Pay Info Tab

Pay Method:	**Hourly—Hours per Pay Period**
Pay Frequency:	**Weekly**
Hours Per Pay Period:	**40.00**
Rate Used To Bill	
Customer:	**24.50**
Regular:	**14.50**
Overtime:	**21.75**

Employee

Employee ID:	**SBR-06**
Name:	**Steven Brown**

General Tab

Address:	**554 Boston Way**
City, ST, Zip:	**Modesto, CA 95351**
Country:	**USA**
Home Phone:	**209-555-2344**
Last Raise:	**Jan 30, 2015**
Social Security No:	**545-09-0009**
Type:	**Salaried**

Withholding Info Tab

Federal:	**Single**	*Allowances:* **0**	*Addl Withholding:* **0.00**
State:	**Single**	*Allowances:* **0**	*Addl Withholding:* **0.00**
State/Locality: **CA**			
Local:	**Single**		

Pay Info Tab

Pay Method:	**Salary**
Pay Frequency:	**Weekly**
Hours Per Pay Period:	**40**
Rate Used To Bill	
Customer:	**60.00**
Salary:	**1,200.00**

Step 8:

Click Save, and then close the Maintain Employees & Sales Reps window.

Checkpoint 10–3

1. What three types of information are entered when establishing an employee record?
2. Why does a firm need withholding information for each employee?

Objective 10–3 Practice

Step 1:

Open Chp. 10 – Blufrog Maintenance Company, which you updated previously in the chapter.

Step 2:

Make the following changes in the employee and employer defaults. Create new accounts as necessary.

Employee Fields

In the *Fed_Income* field, change Account 218 to:

Account ID:	**220**
Description:	**Federal Income Taxes Payable**
Account Type:	**Other Current Liabilities**

In the *Soc_Sec* field, change Account 218 to:

Account ID:	**222**
Description:	**Social Security Taxes Payable**
Account Type:	**Other Current Liabilities**

In the *MEDICARE* field, change Account 218 to:

Account ID:	**224**
Description:	**Medicare Taxes Payable**
Account Type:	**Other Current Liabilities**

In the *St_Income* field, change Account 218 to:

Account ID:	**226**
Description:	**State Income Taxes Payable**
Account Type:	**Other Current Liabilities**

In the *St_Dis_Ins* field, change Account 218 to:

Account ID:	**228**
Description:	**SDI Taxes Payable**
Account Type:	**Other Current Liabilities**

Company Fields

In the *Soc_Sec_C* field, change Account 218 to Account 222.

In the *Medicare_C* field, change Account 218 to Account 224.

In the *Fed_Unemp_C* field, change Account 218 to:

Account ID:	**230**
Description:	**FUTA Taxes Payable**
Account Type:	**Other Current Liabilities**

In the *St_Unemp_C* field, change Account 218 to:

Account ID:	**232**
Description:	**SUTA Taxes Payable**
Account Type:	**Other Current Liabilities**

Note: The educational version of Sage 50 may include the field **Emp_Train_C.** *Remove the check mark in the* **Calc** *field aligned with* **Emp_Train_C.**

Step 3:

Set up employee records for the following three employees:

Employee

Employee ID:	**HCA-03**
Name:	**Henry Carver**

General Tab

Address:	**2799 Rodeo Drive**
City, ST, Zip:	**Stockton, CA 95501**
Country:	**USA**
Home Phone:	**209-555-0098**
Social Security No:	**344-58-9088**
Type:	**Hourly**

Withholding Info Tab

Federal:	**Single**	*Allowances:* 1	*Addl Withholding:* **0.00**
State:	**Single**	*Allowances:* 1	*Addl Withholding:* **0.00**
State/Locality:	**CA**		
Local:	**Single**		

Pay Info Tab

Pay Method:	**Hourly—Hours per Pay Period**
Pay Frequency:	**Weekly**
Hours Per Pay Period:	**40.00**
Rate Used To Bill	
Customer:	**20.00**
Regular:	**12.00**
Overtime:	**18.00**

Employee

Employee ID:	**JST-04**
Name:	**James Stewart**

General Tab

Address:	**1221 Grant Avenue**
City, ST, Zip:	**Lodi, CA 95331**
Country:	**USA**
Home Phone:	**209-555-9867**
Last Raise:	**Jan 30, 2015**
Social Security No:	**599-09-3343**
Type:	**Hourly**

Withholding Info Tab

Federal:	**Married**	*Allowances:* **2**	*Addl Withholding:* **0.00**
State:	**Married**	*Allowances:* **2**	*Addl Withholding:* **0.00**
State/Locality:	**CA**		
Local:	**Married**		

Pay Info Tab

Pay Method:	**Hourly—Hours per Pay Period**
Pay Frequency:	**Weekly**
Hours Per Pay Period:	**40.00**
Rate Used To Bill	
Customer:	**22.00**
Regular:	**11.50**
Overtime:	**16.75**

Employee

Employee ID:	**SSM-05**
Name:	**Stanley Smith**

General Tab

Address:	**5233 Ireland Way**
City, ST, Zip:	**Galt, CA 95001**
Country:	**USA**
Home Phone:	**209-555-3422**
Last Raise:	**Jan 30, 2005**
Social Security No:	**523-88-7654**
Type:	**Salaried**

Withholding Information Tab

Federal:	**Single**	*Allowances:* **2**	*Addl Withholding:* **0.00**
State:	**Single**	*Allowances:* **2**	*Addl Withholding:* **0.00**
State/Locality: **CA**			
Local:	**Single**		

Pay Info Tab

Pay Method:	**Salary**
Pay Frequency:	**Weekly**
Hours Per Pay Period:	**40**
Rate Used To Bill	
Customer:	**80.00**
Salary Rate:	**1,600.00**

Step 4:

Click the Save button and close the Maintain Employees & Sales Reps window.

OBJECTIVE 10–4

Prepare a Payroll and Print Payroll Checks

Once you have set up the Sage 50 payroll system and established a record for each employee, it is possible to prepare the payroll. Usually, this process requires entry of the hours worked by employees who are on the hourly rate plan and entry of the overtime earned by any employee.

After you have entered the necessary information about hours worked and overtime, Sage 50 will calculate the earnings and deductions of each employee for the payroll period and print a payroll check. The total amount earned by the employee is his or her gross pay. The amount remaining after all deductions is the employee's *net pay*. This is the amount that will appear on the employee's payroll check.

net pay The amount received by employees after deductions are made from their gross pay.

Payroll Tax Tables

When Sage 50 is initially installed, a generic tax table is also installed. In most cases, Sage 50 will not be able to calculate automatically or accurately federal, state, and most local payroll taxes during the payroll process using this generic table. To calculate actual and accurate payroll tax amounts, you should subscribe to the Sage 50 Payroll Tax Service and install the most current Tax Service update. Information pertaining to Sage 50 Payroll Tax Service can be obtained from the Sage website.

For educational purposes, a modified tax table has been created that will allow you to complete the payroll process. Remember that this tax table should be used for educational purposes only.

Preparing the Payroll with No Overtime

Suppose that there was no overtime for the employees of Wardwood Construction Company during the weekly payroll period ended January 30, 2017. Follow the steps outlined below to prepare this payroll.

Step 1:

Open Chp. 10 – Wardwood Construction Company and close the Action Items log.

Step 2:

Click the Employees & Payroll tab on the Navigation Aids toolbar at the left side of the opening window.

Step 3:

Click the *Pay Employees* icon and then *Enter Payroll for Multiple Employees,* as shown in Figure 10–15. Select OK from the Sage 50 Payroll query window.

FIGURE 10–15

Enter Payroll for Multiple Employees Option at Pay Employees Icon

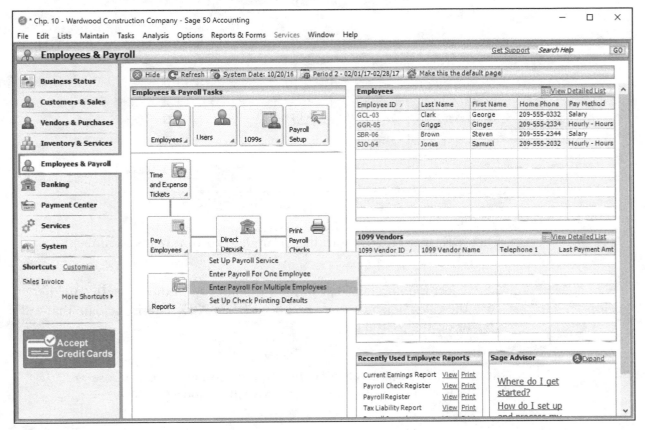

Step 4:

The Select Employees – Filter Selection dialog box will appear. At the *Pay End Date* field, click the *calendar* icon, and then choose the date *Jan. 30, 2017.*

Step 5:

In the Include Pay Frequencies section, click *Weekly* only and deselect the other frequency options.

Step 6:

In the Include Pay Methods section, click *Hourly* and *Salary,* if needed.

Step 7:

In the Include Employees section, choose *All* from the Employees drop-down list and *All* from the Type drop-down list. Your completed dialog box should look like Figure 10–16.

FIGURE 10–16
Completed Select
Employees – Filter
Selection Dialog Box

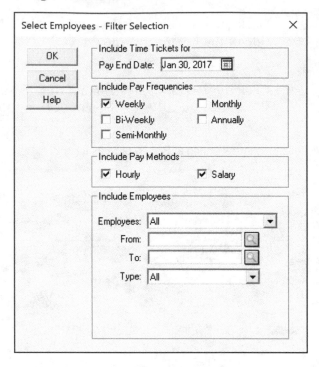

Step 8:

Click OK. (Select *OK* at warning to "update current year's formulae.")

Step 9:

The Select Employees to Pay window will appear. In the *Check Date* field, click the *calendar* icon and then choose *Feb 1, 2017.* This is the date that will appear on the payroll checks.

Step 10:

At the *Pay End Date* field, click the *calendar* icon and then choose *Jan 30, 2017.* This is the ending date of the payroll period.

Step 11:

At the *Cash Acct* field, click the *magnifying glass* icon, and then click *100,* if needed.

Step 12:

Review the Select Employees to Pay window to be sure that all employees for Wardwood Construction Company are included in the payroll. Compare your work with Figure 10–17.

FIGURE 10–17
Completed Select Employees to Pay Window

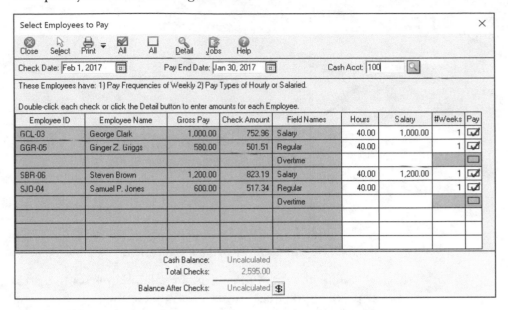

Printing the Payroll Checks

Before you attempt to print the payroll checks, be sure that there are check marks in all the *Pay* boxes at the right of the Select Employees to Pay window. If a particular individual is not to be paid for the payroll period, no check mark should appear in the *Pay* field for that employee. Follow these steps to print checks.

Step 1:

Click Print on the toolbar at the top of the Select Employees to Pay window.

Step 2:

At the Print Forms: Payroll Checks dialog box, in the *First check number* field, key **2005**, as shown in Figure 10–18.

FIGURE 10–18

Print Forms: Payroll
Checks Dialog Box

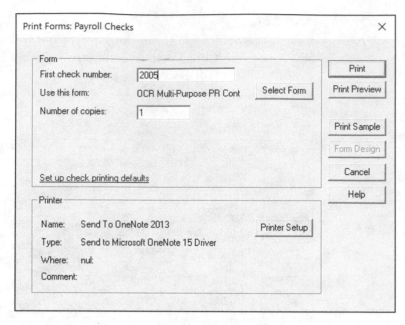

FIGURE 10–19

**Check for George
Clark of Wardwood
Construction Company**

Note: Be sure that the printer is attached and turned on.

The checks will print on any plain paper in the printer. Several types of preprinted check forms are available through Sage 50. Refer to the Sage website to locate a source for preprinted check forms.

Step 3:

Click Print.

Step 4:

Review your checks. The first one should look like Figure 10–19. If there are errors, click No at the Sage 50 query screen and repeat the printing process from step 1 above. Go to step 5 if your checks are correct.

George Clark	This Check	Year to Date		Employee ID: GCL-03
				Social Sec# xxx-xx-6523
Gross	1,000.00	1,000.00		Total
Fed Income	-121.51	-121.51	Salary	1,000.00
Soc_Sec	-62.00	-62.00		
MEDICARE	-14.50	-14.50		
St_Income	-39.03	-39.03		
St Dis Ins	-10.00	-10.00		

Net Check: $752.96   Total   1,000.00

Pay Period Beginning: 1/24/17   Check Date: 2/1/17
Pay Period Ending: 1/30/17   Weeks in Pay Period: 1

Check Number: 2005   Feb 1, 2017

752.96

Seven Hundred Fifty-Two and 96/100 Dollars

George Clark
126 New Castle Road
Modesto, CA 95355
USA

Step 5:

Click Yes at the Sage 50 query screen and the check numbers (2005–2008) will be assigned. The payroll is then posted.

Preparing the Payroll with Overtime

During the weekly payroll period ended January 30, 2017, none of the employees of Wardwood Construction Company worked overtime. However, during the payroll period ended February 6, 2017, Ginger Griggs worked 50 hours rather than the normal 40 hours. She is paid according to the hourly rate plan.

Follow the steps outlined below to prepare the February 6 payroll for Wardwood Construction Company.

Step 1:

Click Employees & Payroll on the Navigation Aids toolbar, if needed.

Step 2:

Click the *Pay Employees* icon in the Employees & Payroll Tasks section and then select *Enter Payroll For One Employee*, as shown in Figure 10–20.

FIGURE 10–20
Payroll Entry Selected from Pay Employees Icon

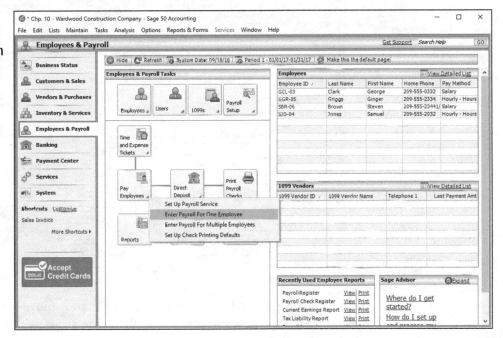

Step 3:

Click OK to acknowledge the Sage 50 payroll tax registration information, if necessary.

Step 4:

At the Payroll Entry window, at the *Date* field, click the *calendar* icon and choose *Feb 8, 2017*.

Step 5:

At the *Employee ID* field, click the *magnifying glass* icon, and then click *GGR-05*. The *Hours Worked* and *Taxes-Benefits-Liabilities* fields should display their data.

Step 6:

At the *Pay Period Ends* field, click the *calendar* icon and choose *Feb 6, 2017*.

Step 7:

Key **1** in the *Weeks in Pay Period* field, if needed.

Step 8:

In the Hours Worked section, key **40.00** in the *Regular* field, if needed, and **10.00** in the *Overtime* field. Compare your completed entry with the one shown in Figure 10–21. Then click <u>S</u>ave. (Do not print a check unless your instructor tells you to do so.)

FIGURE 10–21
Completed Payroll Entry for Ginger Z. Griggs

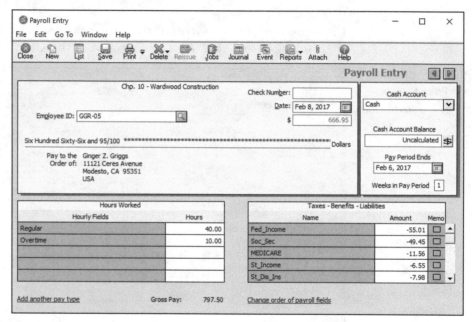

Step 9:

Prepare the payroll for the remainder of the employees listed below for the pay period ending February 6. Use the same steps as you did for Ginger Z. Griggs, excluding overtime. (Do not print checks.)

- George Clark
- Samuel Jones
- Steven Brown

HINT

If you make an error, use the List function on the toolbar to retrieve the entry. Make any necessary corrections and post when it is complete.

Step 10:

Close the Payroll Entry window.

Printing Payroll Checks at a Later Date

Sometimes payroll checks are printed after the payroll is prepared. Use the following procedure to print the checks for the pay period ending February 6, 2017 of Wardwood Construction Company. The date on the checks will be February 8, 2017.

Step 1:

Click Tasks on the Menu bar, if needed.

Step 2:

Click *Payroll Entry* at the drop-down list.

Step 3:

Click OK to acknowledge the Sage 50 payroll tax registration information, if necessary.

Step 4:

Click List on the Payroll Entry toolbar.

Step 5:

At the Paycheck List window, click the down arrow at the *Date Range* field and then click *Prd 2: 2/1/17 – 2/28/17.*

Step 6:

Click *Ginger Z. Griggs* (Employee ID GGR-05), as shown in Figure 10–22.

FIGURE 10–22
Ginger Z. Griggs
Selected from the
Paycheck List Window

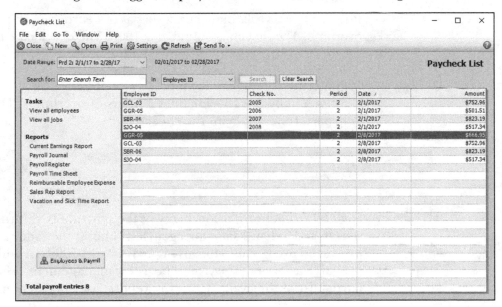

Step 7:

Click Open.

Step 8:

Click Print on the Payroll Entry toolbar.

Step 9:

Click Print in the Print Forms: Payroll Checks dialog box. The first check number should be 2009.

Step 10:

Repeat steps 4 through 9 to print checks for the remaining employees who have not been assigned a check number.

Step 11:

Close the Paycheck List window and the Payroll Entry window.

Checkpoint 10–4

1. What is net pay?
2. Is it necessary to print payroll checks when the payroll is prepared?

Objective 10–4 Practice

Step 1:

Open Chp. 10 – Blufrog Maintenance Company.

Step 2:

Prepare the payroll for all employees as of February 8, 2017. There was no overtime. The first check number is 1000. The check date is February 9, 2017.

Step 3:

Prepare the payroll for all employees as of February 15, 2017. Henry Carver worked 45 hours. (This includes 5 hours of overtime). The check date is February 16, 2017. Print the checks.

OBJECTIVE 10–5

Print Payroll Reports

Sage 50 Accounting prints many of the payroll tax returns that must be sent to federal and state tax agencies. Among the federal tax returns produced are Forms 940, 941, W-2, W-3, and 1099. In addition, Sage 50 prepares a variety of payroll reports for management. The following is a partial list of the available payroll reports for management.

- The *Current Earnings Report* lists each employee's earnings and deductions.
- The *Payroll Journal* lists payroll transactions in a journal format.
- The *Payroll Tax Report* lists the payroll deductions.
- The *Quarterly Earnings Report* lists the quarterly earnings of all employees.
- The *Tax Liability Report* lists the employer's liabilities for payroll taxes.
- The *Yearly Earnings Report* lists the annual earnings of all employees.

Follow the steps outlined on the next page to print the *Current Earnings Report*.

Step 1:

Open Chp. 10 – Wardwood Construction Company and close the Action Items log.

Step 2:

Click Reports & Forms and then click *Payroll.*

Step 3:

At the Payroll: Employee Information and Earnings section, click *Current Earnings Report.*

Step 4:

Click <u>P</u>rint on the Select a Report or Form toolbar.

Step 5:

At the Modify Report – Current Earnings Report window, click *Range* in the *Date* field.

Step 6:

At the *From* field, click the drop-down arrow to choose *Jan 1, 2017.* At the *To* field, choose *Feb 28, 2017,* as shown in Figure 10–23.

FIGURE 10–23
Modify Report – Current
Earnings Report Window

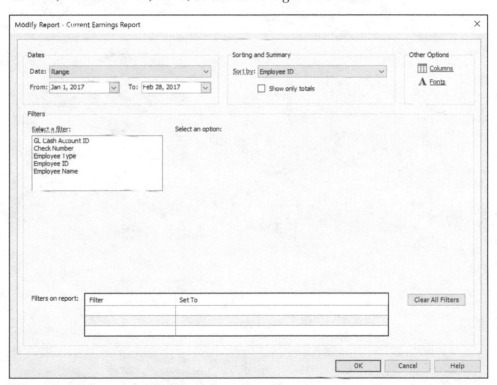

HINT
The tax amounts shown in the Current Earnings Report will vary depending on the tax tables that were loaded. This payroll was prepared with the modified tax table that is included in the student data files.

Step 7:

Click OK and then OK again at the Print dialog box.

Step 8:

Review the Current Earnings Report shown in Figure 10–24. Notice that this report shows the gross pay, deductions, and net pay for the first three employees as this is a partial view of the report.

FIGURE 10-24
Current Earnings
Report (Partial View)

Chp. 10 - Wardwood Construction Company
Current Earnings Report
For the Period From Jan 1, 2017 to Feb 28, 2017

Filter Criteria includes: Report order is by Employee ID. Report is printed in Detail Format.

Employee ID Employee Masked SS No	Date Reference	Amount	Gross St_Income Fed_Unemp_	Fed_Income St_Dis_Ins St_Unemp_C	Soc_Sec Soc_Sec_C Emp_Train_C	MEDICARE Medicare_C
GCL-03 George Clark XXX-XX-6523	2/1/17 2005	752.96	1,000.00 -39.03 -6.00	-121.51 -10.00 -50.00	-62.00 -62.00	-14.50 -14.50
GCL-03 George Clark XXX-XX-6523	2/8/17 2010	752.96	1,000.00 -39.03 -6.00	-121.51 -10.00 -50.00	-62.00 -62.00	-14.50 -14.50
Total 1/1/17 thru 2/28/17		1,505.92	2,000.00 -78.06 -12.00	-243.02 -20.00 -100.00	-124.00 -124.00	-29.00 -29.00
Report Date Total for George Clark		1,505.92	2,000.00 -78.06 -12.00	-243.02 -20.00 -100.00	-124.00 -124.00	-29.00 -29.00
YTD Total for George Clark		1,505.92	2,000.00 -78.06 -12.00	-243.02 -20.00 -100.00	-124.00 -124.00	-29.00 -29.00
GGR-05 Ginger Z. Griggs XXX-XX-9099	2/1/17 2006	501.51	580.00 -1.76 -3.48	-26.56 -5.80 -29.00	-35.96 -35.96	-8.41 -8.41
GGR-05 Ginger Z. Griggs XXX-XX-9099	2/8/17 2009	666.95	797.50 -6.55 -4.79	-55.01 -7.98 -39.88	-49.45 -49.45	-11.56 -11.56
Total 1/1/17 thru 2/28/17		1,168.46	1,377.50 -8.31 -8.27	-81.57 -13.78 -68.88	-85.41 -85.41	-19.97 -19.97
Report Date Total for Ginger Z. Griggs		1,168.46	1,377.50 -8.31 -8.27	-81.57 -13.78 -68.88	-85.41 -85.41	-19.97 -19.97
YTD Total for Ginger Z. Griggs		1,168.46	1,377.50 -8.31 -8.27	-81.57 -13.78 -68.88	-85.41 -85.41	-19.97 -19.97
SBR-06 Steven Brown XXX-XX-0009	2/1/17 2007	823.19	1,200.00 -63.51 -7.20	-209.50 -12.00 -60.00	-74.40 -74.40	-17.40 -17.40
SBR-06 Steven Brown XXX-XX-0009	2/8/17 2011	823.19	1,200.00 -63.51 -7.20	-209.50 -12.00 -60.00	-74.40 -74.40	-17.40 -17.40
Total 1/1/17 thru 2/28/17		1,646.38	2,400.00 -127.02 -14.40	-419.00 -24.00 -120.00	-148.80 -148.80	-34.80 -34.80
Report Date Total for Steven Brown		1,646.38	2,400.00 -127.02	-419.00 -24.00	-148.80 -148.80	-34.80 -34.80

Step 9:

Close the Select a Report or Form dialog box and then close Wardwood
Construction Company.

Checkpoint 10–5

1. Name five types of federal tax returns that Sage 50 can produce.
2. What information is shown in the Current Earnings Report?

Objective 10–5 Practice

Step 1:

Open Chp. 10 – Blufrog Maintenance Company.

Step 2:

Print the Current Earnings Report for January 1, 2017 through
February 28, 2017. Your printout should look like Figure 10–25.

9/18/16 at 13:57:49.31   *****EDUCATIONAL VERSION ONLY*****   Page: 1

Chp. 10 - Blufrog Maintenance Company
Current Earnings Report
For the Period From Jan 1, 2017 to Feb 28, 2017

Filter Criteria includes: Report order is by Employee ID. Report is printed in Detail Format.

Employee ID / Employee / Masked SS No	Date / Reference	Amount	Gross / St_Income / Fed_Unemp_	Fed_Income / St_Dis_Ins / St_Unemp_C	Soc_Sec / Soc_Sec_C / Emp_Train_C	MEDICARE / Medicare_C
HCA-03 Henry Carver XXX-XX-9088	2/9/17 1000	386.73	480.00 -6.36 -2.88	-45.39 -4.80 -24.00	-29.76 -29.76	-6.96 -6.96
HCA-03 Henry Carver XXX-XX-9088	2/16/17 1003	451.48	570.00 -10.32 -3.42	-58.89 -5.70 -28.50	-35.34 -35.34	-8.27 -8.27
Total 1/1/17 thru 2/28/17		838.21	1,050.00 -16.68 -6.30	-104.28 -10.50 -52.50	-65.10 -65.10	-15.23 -15.23
Report Date Total for Henry Carver		838.21	1,050.00 -16.68 -6.30	-104.28 -10.50 -52.50	-65.10 -65.10	-15.23 -15.23
YTD Total for Henry Carver		838.21	1,050.00 -16.68 -6.30	-104.28 -10.50 -52.50	-65.10 -65.10	-15.23 -15.23
JST-04 James Stewart XXX-XX-3433	2/9/17 1001	405.65	460.00 -2.76	-14.56 -4.60 -23.00	-28.52 -28.52	-6.67 -6.67
JST-04 James Stewart XXX-XX-3433	2/16/17 1004	405.65	460.00 -2.76	-14.56 -4.60 -23.00	-28.52 -28.52	-6.67 -6.67
Total 1/1/17 thru 2/28/17		811.30	920.00 -5.52	-29.12 -9.20 -46.00	-57.04 -57.04	-13.34 -13.34
Report Date Total for James Stewart		811.30	920.00 -5.52	-29.12 -9.20 -46.00	-57.04 -57.04	-13.34 -13.34
YTD Total for James Stewart		811.30	920.00 -5.52	-29.12 -9.20 -46.00	-57.04 -57.04	-13.34 -13.34
SSM-05 Stanley Smith XXX-XX-7654	2/9/17 1002	1,090.14	1,600.00 -99.95 -9.60	-271.51 -16.00 -80.00	-99.20 -99.20	-23.20 -23.20
SSM-05 Stanley Smith XXX-XX-7654	2/16/17 1005	1,090.14	1,600.00 -99.95 -9.60	-271.51 -16.00 -80.00	-99.20 -99.20	-23.20 -23.20
Total 1/1/17 thru 2/28/17		2,180.28	3,200.00 -199.90 -19.20	-543.02 -32.00 -160.00	-198.40 -198.40	-46.40 -46.40
Report Date Total for Stanley Smith		2,180.28	3,200.00 -199.90	-543.02 -32.00	-198.40 -198.40	-46.40 -46.40

Step 3:

Close Blufrog Maintenance Company.

Chapter Review and Assessment

Software Command Summary

Establish a Payroll	Maintain, Default Information, Payroll Setup Wizard
Set Employee Defaults	Maintain, Default Information, Employees
Create an Employee Record	Maintain, Employees/Sales Reps
Prepare a Payroll (Group)	Tasks, Select for Payroll Entry
Prepare a Payroll (Individual)	Tasks, Payroll Entry
Preview/Print Payroll Reports	Reports & Forms, Payroll, Select a Report or Form

Checkpoint Answers

Checkpoint 10–1
1. Payroll periods may be weekly, biweekly, semimonthly, or monthly.
2. The three federal taxes that employers must withhold are federal income tax, Social Security tax, and Medicare tax.

Checkpoint 10–2
1. Updated tax tables are available from Sage 50's website at http://sage.com.
2. Wages and Salaries Expense will be used to record gross pay.

Checkpoint 10–3
1. The three types of information used to establish employee records are general information, withholding information, and pay information.
2. Withholding information is needed to calculate the income tax owed by each employee.

Checkpoint 10–4
1. Net pay is the amount remaining after deductions are made from an employee's gross pay.
2. No, payroll checks can be printed at a later date.

Checkpoint 10–5

1. Forms 940, 941, W-2, W-3, and 1099 are among the federal tax forms that Sage 50 can produce.
2. The Current Earnings Report shows the gross pay, deductions, and net pay for each employee.

Study Quizzes

Take the study quiz online to check your understanding of chapter concepts. The quiz can be taken multiple times.

Content Check

Multiple Choice: Choose only one response for each question.

1. The act that requires that employers pay the federal minimum wage and overtime to most employees when they work more than 40 hours a workweek is the
   A. Current Tax Payment Act.
   B. Fair Labor Standards Act.
   C. Federal Insurance Contributions Act.
   D. Federal Unemployment Tax Act.

2. Which form is prepared at the end of the year to show the total earnings by independent contractors?
   A. Form 941
   B. Form W-2
   C. Form W-3
   D. Form 1099

3. Payroll taxes deducted from an employee's earnings are recorded in what type of account?
   A. Assets
   B. Accounts Payable
   C. Long Term Liabilities
   D. Other Current Liabilities

4. FICA – Social Security Tax and FICA – Medicare Tax are paid by the
   A. employee.
   B. employer.
   C. both the employee and employer.
   D. local taxing authority.

5. The payroll report that lists each employee's earnings and deductions is the
   A. Current Earnings Report.
   B. Payroll Journal.
   C. Payroll Tax Report.
   D. Tax Liability Report.

Short Essay Response

Provide a detailed answer for each question.

1. What are the six basic areas of payroll activities?
2. List and explain the five various pay plans.
3. List and explain the payroll reports available through Sage 50.
4. What are the six federal tax returns that employers are required to file?
5. What are the various required and voluntary deductions to be withheld from employees' earnings?
6. What is the purpose of the Payroll Setup Wizard?

Cooperative Learning

1. Form groups of three or four students and research the available job market in your area. Determine the factors that are taken into consideration when determining wages and salaries for particular positions.
2. As a group, research jobs that will be in high demand in the future. What skills and training will be required for the jobs of the future? Are you currently acquiring these skills?

Writing and Decision Making

Assume that the owner of the company for which you work, Steve Randolph, is deciding whether to stop outsourcing payroll and prepare it internally using Sage 50. One of the concerns he has is the time that will be required to both initially set up the payroll system, and then prepare the periodic payroll. He also wants to know about the costs and benefits of using Sage 50 to prepare the payroll. Prepare a memo with the information that has been requested.

Case Problems

Demonstrate your knowledge of the Sage 50 features discussed in this chapter by completing the following case problems.

Case Problem 10–1A

Open Rico's Coffee House, a coffee house known for its exotic coffees, from the student data files.

1. Use the Payroll Setup Wizard to establish the payroll system for Rico's Coffee House.

   Use the following information to set up the payroll system:

Federal Employer ID:	**15-8110392**
State Employer ID:	**123-9567-8**
State:	**CA**
State Unemployment ID:	**123-9567-8**
State Unemployment Rate:	**5.00**

Hourly (Reg. and Over.):	**512**
Salary:	**512**

Create and then enter the following general ledger accounts for recording payroll taxes:

Account ID:	**218**
Description:	**Payroll Taxes Payable**
Account Type:	**Other Current Liabilities**

Account ID:	**513**
Description:	**Payroll Taxes Expense**
Account Type:	**Expenses**

2. Make the following changes in the employee and employer defaults. Create new accounts as necessary.

Employee Fields
In the *Fed_Income* field, change Account 218 to:

Account ID:	**220**
Description:	**Federal Income Taxes Payable**
Account Type:	**Other Current Liabilities**

In the *Soc_Sec* field, change Account 218 to:

Account ID:	**222**
Description:	**Social Security Taxes Payable**
Account Type:	**Other Current Liabilities**

In the *MEDICARE* field, change Account 218 to:

Account ID:	**224**
Description:	**Medicare Taxes Payable**
Account Type:	**Other Current Liabilities**

In the *St_Income* field, change Account 218 to:

Account ID:	**226**
Description:	**State Income Taxes Payable**
Account Type:	**Other Current Liabilities**

In the *St_Dis_Ins* field, change Account 218 to:

Account ID:	**228**
Description:	**SDI Taxes Payable**
Account Type:	**Other Current Liabilities**

Company Fields
In the *Soc_Sec_C* field, change Account 218 to Account 222.
In the *Medicare_C* field, change Account 218 to Account 224.
In the *Fed_Unemp_C* field, change Account 218 to:

Account ID:	**230**
Description:	**FUTA Taxes Payable**
Account Type:	**Other Current Liabilities**

In the *St_Unemp_C* field, change Account 218 to:

Account ID:	**232**
Description:	**SUTA Taxes Payable**
Account Type:	**Other Current Liabilities**

Note: The educational version of Sage 50 may include the field Emp_Train_C. *Remove the check mark in the* Calc *field aligned with* Emp_Train_C.

3. Set up employee records for the following three employees:

Employee

Employee ID:	**BCA-01**
Name:	**Benjamin Carter**

General Tab

Address:	**2982 West Chrisman Boulevard**
City, ST, Zip:	**Stockton, CA 95207**
Country:	**USA**
Home Phone:	**209-555-0251**
Social Security No:	**654-46-2509**
Type:	**Hourly**

Withholding Info Tab

Federal:	**Single**
Allowances: **1**	*Addl Withholding:* **0.00**
State:	**Single**
Allowances: **1**	*Addl Withholding:* **0.00**
State/Locality:	**CA**
Local:	**Single**

Pay Info Tab

Pay Method:	**Hourly—Hours per Pay Period**
Rate Used To Bill Customer:	**20.00**
Pay Frequency:	**Weekly**
Hours Per Pay Period:	**40.00**
Regular Rate:	**10.00**
Overtime:	**15.00**

Employee

Employee ID:	**CSO-02**
Name:	**Cynthia Solario**

General Tab

Address:	**1651 Central Avenue**
City, ST, Zip:	**Tracy, CA 95376**
Country:	**USA**
Home Phone:	**209-555-4852**
Social Security No:	**568-16-2137**
Type:	**Hourly**

Withholding Info Tab

Federal:	**Married**
Allowances: **2**	*Addl Withholding:* **0.00**
State:	**Married**
Allowances: **2**	*Addl Withholding:* **0.00**
State/Locality:	**CA**
Local:	**Married**

Pay Info Tab

Pay Method:	**Hourly—Hours per Pay Period**
Rate Used To Bill Customer:	**22.50**
Pay Frequency:	**Weekly**
Hours Per Pay Period:	**40.00**
Regular Rate:	**12.00**
Overtime:	**18.00**

Employee

Employee ID:	**VMO-03**
Name:	**Victor Moreno**

General Tab

Address:	**5549 Ramona Drive**
City, ST, Zip:	**Tracy, CA 95376**
Country:	**USA**
Home Phone:	**209-555-4652**
Social Security No:	**558-91-4852**
Type:	**Salary**

Withholding Info Tab

Federal:	**Single**
Allowances: **1**	*Addl Withholding:* **0.00**
State:	**Single**
Allowances: **1**	*Addl Withholding:* **0.00**
State/Locality:	**CA**
Local:	**Single**

Pay Info Tab

Pay Method:	**Salary**
Rate Used To Bill Customer:	**50.00**
Pay Frequency:	**Weekly**
Salary Rate:	**1,600.00**

4. Print the Chart of Accounts and Employee List.

5. Close Rico's Coffee House.

Case Problem 10–2A

Open Rico's Coffee House, which you updated in Problem 10-1A.

1. Prepare the payroll for all employees as of March 6, 2017. There was no overtime. The first check number is 1500. The check date is March 7, 2017.

2. Prepare the payroll for all employees as of March 13, 2017. Cynthia Solario worked 46 hours (6 hours overtime) this pay period. The check date is March 14, 2017.

3. Print the Current Earnings Report and Payroll Register.

4. Close Rico's Coffee House.

Case Problem 10–1B

Open Barista's, a coffee house known for good friends and great coffee, from the student data files.

1. Use the Payroll Setup Wizard to establish the payroll system for Barista's.

   Use the following information to set up the payroll system:

Federal Employer ID:	**15-8110478**
State Employer ID:	**123-5734-7**
State:	**CA**
State Unemployment ID:	**123-5734-7**
State Unemployment Rate:	**5.00**
Hourly (Reg. and Over.):	**512**
Salary:	**512**

   Create and then enter the following general ledger accounts for recording payroll taxes:

Account ID:	**218**
Description:	**Payroll Taxes Payable**
Account Type:	**Other Current Liabilities**

Account ID:	**513**
Description:	**Payroll Taxes Expense**
Account Type:	**Expenses**

2. Make the following changes to the employee and employer defaults. Create new accounts as necessary.

   Employee Fields
   In the *Fed_Income* field, change Account 218 to:

Account ID:	**220**
Description:	**Federal Income Taxes Payable**
Account Type:	**Other Current Liabilities**

   In the *Soc_Sec* field, change Account 218 to:

Account ID:	**222**
Description:	**Social Security Taxes Payable**
Account Type:	**Other Current Liabilities**

In the *MEDICARE* field, change Account 218 to:

Account ID:	**224**
Description:	**Medicare Taxes Payable**
Account Type:	**Other Current Liabilities**

In the *St_Income* field, change Account 218 to:

Account ID:	**226**
Description:	**State Income Taxes Payable**
Account Type:	**Other Current Liabilities**

In the *St_Dis_Ins* field, change Account 218 to:

Account ID:	**228**
Description:	**SDI Taxes Payable**
Account Type:	**Other Current Liabilities**

Company Fields
In the *Soc_Sec_C* field, change Account 218 to Account 222.
In the *Medicare_C* field, change Account 218 to Account 224.
In the *Fed_Unemp_C* field, change Account 218 to:

Account ID:	**230**
Description:	**FUTA Taxes Payable**
Account Type:	**Other Current Liabilities**

In the *St_Unemp_C* field, change Account 218 to:

Account ID:	**232**
Description:	**SUTA Taxes Payable**
Account Type:	**Other Current Liabilities**

Note: The educational version of Sage 50 may include the field **Emp_Train_C.**
Remove the check mark in the **Calc** *field aligned with Emp_Train_C.*

3. Set up employee records for the following three employees:

Employee

Employee ID:	**MCA-01**
Name:	**Marie Case**

General Tab

Address:	**2256 East Madison Way**
City, ST, Zip:	**Stockton, CA 95210**
Country:	**USA**
Home Phone:	**209-555-9526**
Social Security No:	**665-58-4259**
Type:	**Hourly**

Withholding Info Tab

Federal:	**Single**
Allowances: **2**	*Addl Withholding:* **0.00**
State:	**Single**

Allowances: **2**	*Addl Withholding:* **0.00**
State/Locality:	**CA**
Local:	**Single**

Pay Info Tab

Pay Method:	**Hourly—Hours per Pay Period**
Rate Used To Bill Customer:	**30.00**
Pay Frequency:	**Weekly**
Hours Per Pay Period:	**40.00**
Regular Rate:	**10.00**
Overtime:	**15.00**

Employee

Employee ID:	**JWH-02**
Name:	**Jonathan White**

General Tab

Address:	**5219 South Grant Line**
City, ST, Zip:	**Stockton, CA 95207**
Country:	**USA**
Home Phone:	**209-555-9635**
Social Security No:	**559-52-4825**
Type:	**Hourly**

Withholding Info Tab

Federal:	**Married**
Allowances: **2**	*Addl Withholding:* **0.00**
State:	**Married**
Allowances: **2**	*Addl Withholding:* **0.00**
State/Locality:	**CA**
Local:	**Married**

Pay Info Tab

Pay Method:	**Hourly—Hours per Pay Period**
Rate Used To Bill Customer:	**24.00**
Pay Frequency:	**Weekly**
Hours Per Pay Period:	**40.00**
Regular Rate:	**14.00**
Overtime:	**21.00**

Employee

Employee ID:	**ACH-03**
Name:	**Albert Chavez**

General Tab

Address:	**425 East Main Street**
City, ST, Zip:	**Tracy, CA 95376**
Country:	**USA**
Home Phone:	**209-555-5236**
Social Security No:	**559-64-8745**
Type:	**Salary**

Withholding Info Tab

Federal:	**Married**
Allowances: **5**	*Addl Withholding:* **0.00**
State:	**Married**
Allowances: **5**	*Addl Withholding:* **0.00**
State/Locality:	**CA**
Local:	**Married**

Pay Info Tab

Pay Method:	**Salary**
Rate Used To Bill Customer:	**50.00**
Pay Frequency:	**Weekly**
Salary Rate:	**1,500.00**

4. Print the Chart of Accounts and Employee List.

5. Close Barista's.

Case Problem 10–2B

Open Barista's, which you updated in Problem 10-1B.

1. Prepare the payroll for all employees as of February 6, 2017. There was no overtime. The first check number is 2200. The check date is February 7, 2017.

2. Prepare the payroll for all employees as of February 13, 2017. Marie Case worked 44 hours (4 hours of overtime) this pay period. The check date is February 14, 2017.

3. Print the Current Earnings Report and Payroll Register.

4. Close Barista's.

CHAPTER 11

Job Costing

Objectives

11–1 Review the general concepts of job costing

11–2 Set up a project for job costing

11–3 Create phase codes and cost codes, and enter estimated revenue and expenses

11–4 Use the job costing system to record purchases, payroll, and sales

11–5 Create and print job cost reports

Software Features

- Set Up Jobs

- Enter Estimated Expenses and Revenue

- Create Phase Codes and Cost Codes

- Maintain Jobs

- Enter the Costs of Materials and Labor

- Enter Revenue

- Print Job Cost Reports

Company Files

Before beginning chapter work, access the links menu to download company files.

The work of some manufacturing businesses and service businesses is divided into a series of separate jobs (projects). For example, a printing firm may produce 5,000 catalogs for one customer and 20,000 sales brochures for another customer. A computer-consulting firm may design a website for one customer and plan an internal network for another customer.

For businesses such as these, it is important to be able to determine all the costs associated with completing a job. Otherwise, it is difficult to price the job properly and earn a satisfactory profit.

Having detailed information about job costs also helps management assess the efficiency of the firm's operations. Keeping job costs under control is a necessity if a firm is to be able to offer competitive prices and obtain new business.

OBJECTIVE 11-1

Review the General Concepts of Job Costing

job costs The costs of the materials, labor, and other items required for completion of a job.

job costing Tracking all costs associated with a job and totaling those costs at the end of the project.

Job costs are the costs of the materials, labor, and other items required for completion of a particular job. The process of *job costing* involves tracking all costs associated with a project and totaling these costs at the end of the project.

Job Costing Procedures

When planning jobs, many businesses break them into a series of phases. Each phase represents a different stage of the project. For example, the first phase of a construction job might be preparing blueprints. The second phase might be excavating the site and putting in the foundation. Often, such jobs are covered by a contract with the customer, and payments are tied to the completion of each phase.

In some cases, however, a job is small and will last for only a short period of time. Therefore, the job is not divided into phases.

If a job does consist of phases, businesses will need to record the costs for each phase. When a phase is completed, the business can bill the customer for any revenue earned.

The Sage 50 Job Costing System

Sage 50 allows you to assign a job identifier to each project and track the revenue and expenses of many projects at the same time. For example, Wardwood Construction Company usually has several jobs in production simultaneously and must be able to record financial information for each job. In this way, management can evaluate the expenses incurred and the revenue received as each job moves through the production process.

Sage 50 supports three methods of job costing:

1. The Jobs Only Method is used for projects that are not divided into phases and do not require cost codes. The jobs that fall into this category are usually small jobs.
2. The Jobs with Phases Method is used for projects that will be completed in phases.
3. The Jobs with Phases and Cost Codes Method is used for projects that are divided into phases and require cost codes.

The method chosen depends on the types of jobs that a business has as well as the amount of information that management wants about each job.

OBJECTIVE 11-2

Set Up a Project for Job Costing

Suppose that Smith's Monument Shop hires Wardwood Construction Company to build a fence around its parking area. Wardwood estimates that its revenue from this project will be $5,240 and its expenses will be $3,150. Because this is a small project, Wardwood will use Sage 50's Jobs Only Method to track the costs of materials and labor and record the revenue. Use the following steps to track the costs of this job.

Step 1:

Open Wardwood Construction Company (Chp. 11 – Wardwood Construction Company if student data files are used) and close the Action Items log.

Step 2:

Click Maintain, click *Job Costs*, and then click *Jobs*.

Step 3:

The Maintain Jobs window will appear. Key **Smith Fence-Job 1** in the *Job ID* field. Then click OK.

Step 4:

Key **Smith Fence Job** in the *Description* field.

Step 5:

Click the General folder tab and key **George Clark** in the *Supervisor* field.

Step 6:

At the *For Customer* field, click the drop-down arrow, and then click *Smith-02*, as shown in Figure 11–1.

FIGURE 11–1
Smith-02 Selected from
For Customer Drop-Down
List

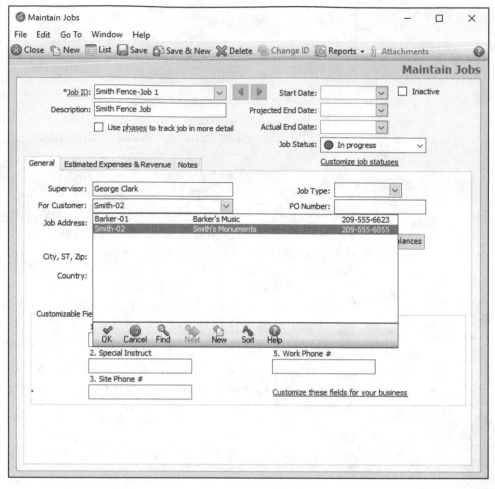

Step 7:

At the *Start Date* field, key **2/20/17**.

Step 8:

At the *Projected End Date* field, key **3/5/17**. (This is the estimated date of completion.)

Step 9:

Key **Fence** in the *Job Type* field.

Step 10:

Key **0** in the *Percent Complete* field, if needed.

Step 11:

Compare your work with Figure 11–2. Make any necessary corrections. Then click Save.

FIGURE 11–2
Completed Maintain
Jobs Window

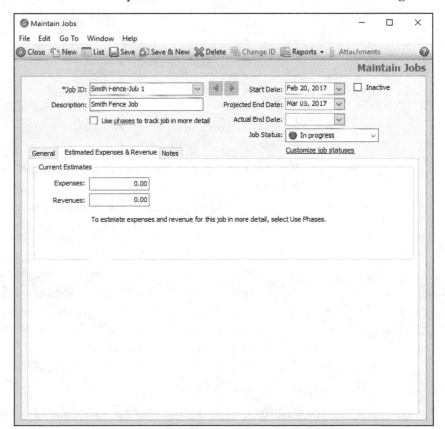

Step 12:

Click the Estimated Expenses & Revenue folder tab, as shown in Figure 11–3.

FIGURE 11–3
Estimated Expenses
& Revenue Folder Tab
Selected

Step 13:

Key **3,150.00** in the *Expenses* field and **5,240.00** in the *Revenues* field, as shown in Figure 11–4.

FIGURE 11–4
Entries for Estimated Expenses and Revenues

Step 14:

Click Save and then Close.

Checkpoint 11–2

1. What menu options do you click to start the process of setting up a project for job costing?
2. What dollar amounts are entered when a project is set up for job costing?

Objective 11–2 Practice

Assume that Blufrog Maintenance Company accepts a job from Tim Conway of Honda Center to clean a building that suffered some fire damage. Blufrog wants to use the Jobs Only Method to keep track of the revenue and expenses associated with the project.

Step 1:

Open Blufrog Maintenance Company (Chp. 11 – Blufrog Maintenance Company if student data files are used).

Step 2:

Set up the project of Honda Center for job costing. The revenue is expected to be $15,000, and the expenses are expected to be $8,900. The job identifier is Honda Fire-Job 1. The estimated starting date is February 10, 2017, and the estimated ending date is March 2, 2017. The job type is Clean Up and the percentage of completion is zero (0). Stanley Smith will supervise the project. Make sure to choose Honda Center-01 as the customer.

OBJECTIVE 11–3

Create Phase Codes and Cost Codes, and Enter Estimated Revenue and Expenses

In many cases, it is not possible to track the costs of a job effectively unless the job is divided into phases. Each phase should represent a significant stage of the project. This approach provides management with useful information throughout the life of a project. If there are cost overruns at any stage, management can take action immediately.

However, in planning the phases of a job, it is important not to create too many small steps. Otherwise, management may be overwhelmed with too much information. Having too many details about a job actually makes it difficult to keep a close watch on its progress.

Suppose that Wardwood Construction Company accepts a job from Barker's Music to build more office space for the firm. Wardwood decides to divide this project into four phases: planning/permits, excavation, building, and landscaping.

The identifier for the job is Barker Office-Job 2. The revenue is expected to be $500,000, and the expenses are expected to be $225,000. The estimated starting date is February 15, 2017, and the estimated ending date is December 30, 2017.

The first task for Wardwood is to set up the project for job costing. Then it must create phase codes and cost codes. Finally, Wardwood must enter the estimated revenue and expenses for each phase of the job.

Setting Up a Project for Job Costing

Follow the steps outlined below to set up the project to build new office space for Barker's Music in the job costing system of Wardwood Construction Company.

Step 1:

Open Chp. 11 – Wardwood Construction Company, which you updated previously in the chapter.

Step 2:

Click Maintain, click *Job Costs*, and then click *Jobs*.

Step 3:

Key **Barker Office-Job 2** in the *Job ID* field. Then click OK.

Step 4:

Key **Barker Office Job** in the *Description* field.

Step 5:

Click the General folder tab and key **George Clark** in the *Supervisor* field.

Step 6:

At the *For Customer* field, click the drop-down arrow, and then click *Barker-01*.

Step 7:

At the *Start Date* field, click the drop-down arrow and select *Feb 15, 2017*.

Step 8:

At the *Projected End Date* field, click the drop-down arrow and select *Dec 30, 2017*.

Step 9:

Click to insert a check mark in the box next to *Use phases to track job in more detail*, as shown in Figure 11–5.

FIGURE 11–5
Maintain Jobs
Window with Use
Phases Selected

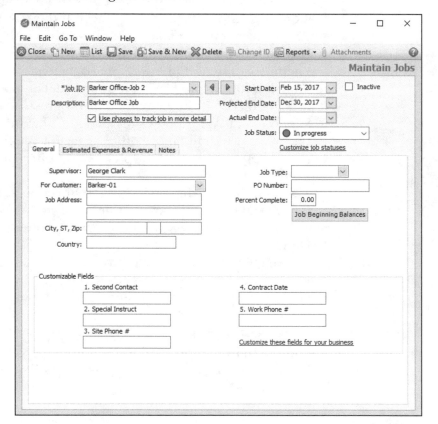

Step 10:

Key **Const** in the *Job Type* field.

Step 11:

Key **0** in the *Percent Complete* field, if needed.

Step 12:

Click Save and then Close.

Creating the Phase Codes for a Job

The next task for Wardwood Construction Company is to establish the phases and phase codes for the job that it will do for Barker's Music.

Step 1:

Click Maintain, click *Job Costs*, and then click *Phases*.

Step 2:

The Maintain Phases window will appear. Key **Plan-01** in the *Phase ID* field.

Step 3:

Key **Planning and Permits** in the *Description* field.

Step 4:

Sage 50 supports five different cost types:

- Labor
- Materials
- Equipment
- Subcontractors
- Other

Click the drop-down arrow and then select *Other* as the cost type shown for Plan-01, the first phase of the job for Barker's Music. (See Figure 11–6.)

FIGURE 11–6
Other Selected as Cost Type

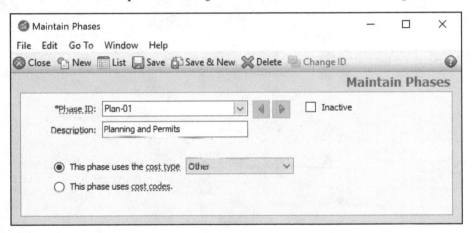

Step 5:

Click Save.

Step 6:

Create the following additional phases for the job for Barker's Music. (The building phase will be established in the next section.)

Phase ID	Description	Cost Type
Excav–02	Excavation	Subcontractors
Lands–04	Landscaping	Subcontractors

Step 7:

Review your work, make any necessary corrections, then resave each entry. Then click Close.

Creating the Cost Codes for a Job

The cost codes provide additional information for management. These codes help management track several cost areas for any phase of a job. For example, in the building phase of the project that Wardwood Construction Company is doing for Barker's Music, management wants to track the cost of materials and the cost of labor. Follow the steps outlined below to create the necessary cost codes.

Step 1:

Click Maintain, click *Job Costs*, and then click *Phases*.

Step 2:

Key **Build–03** in the *Phase ID* field. Then click OK.

Step 3:

Key **Building** in the *Description* field.

Step 4:

Click the radial button next to *This phase uses cost codes*, as shown in Figure 11–7.

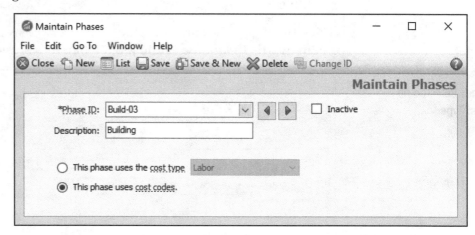

Step 5:

Click Save and then Close.

Step 6:

Click Maintain, click *Job Costs*, and then click *Cost Codes*.

Wardwood Construction Company will use Buildlab-10 as the identifier for the labor costs in the building phase and Buildmat-11 as the identifier for the materials costs.

Step 7:

At the Maintain Cost Codes window, key **Buildlab-10** in the *Cost Code ID* field.

Step 8:

Key **Building Labor** in the *Description* field.

Step 9:

Click the drop-down arrow at the *This cost code uses the cost type* field, and then click *Labor*, if necessary, as shown in Figure 11–8.

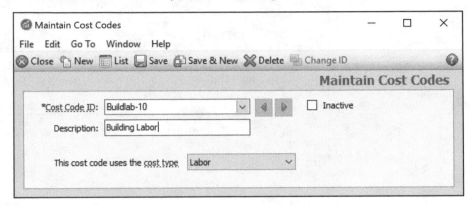

Step 10:

Click Save.

Step 11:

Create the remaining cost code for the building phase of the job for Barker's Music. Use the following information:

Cost ID	Description	Cost Type
Buildmat-11	Building Materials	Materials

Step 12:

Click Save and then Close.

Entering Estimated Revenue and Expenses for Each Phase

Sage 50 allows you to enter the estimated expenses and revenue for a specific phase of a job into the job costing system. For example, Wardwood Construction Company will enter expense and revenue amounts for each phase of the project that it is doing for Barker's Music.

Step 1:

Click Maintain, click *Job Costs*, and then click *Jobs*.

Step 2:

The Maintain Jobs window will appear. At the *Job ID* field, click the drop-down arrow, and then click *Barker Office-Job 2*.

Step 3:

Click the Estimated Expenses & Revenue folder tab.

Step 4:

Click in the *Phase ID* field, click the drop-down arrow, and then click *Plan-01*, as shown in Figure 11–9.

FIGURE 11–9
Plan-01 Selected in
Phase ID Field

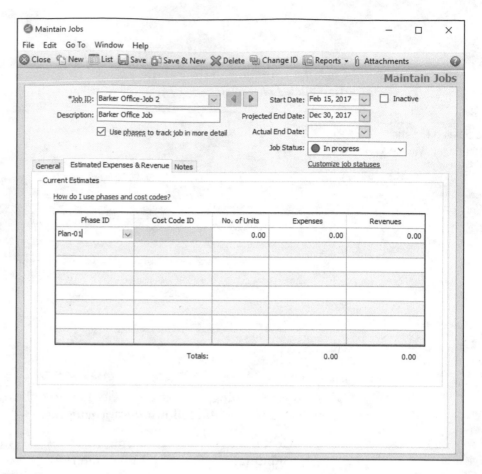

Step 5:

Key **5,000.00** in the *Expenses* field and **12,000.00** in the *Revenues* field.

Step 6:

In the second row of the *Phase ID* field, click the drop-down arrow, and then click *Excav-02*.

HINT
The *Cost Code ID* field is disabled because these phases do not use cost codes.

Step 7:

Key **33,000.00** in the *Expenses* field and **55,000.00** in the *Revenues* field.

Step 8:

In the third row of the *Phase ID* field, click the drop-down arrow, and then click *Lands-04*.

Step 9:

Key **20,000.00** in the *Expenses* field and **40,000.00** in the *Revenues* field.

Step 10:

In the fourth row of the *Phase ID* field, click the drop-down arrow, and then click *Build-03*. Tab to the next field and notice that the *Cost Code ID* field is now enabled.

Step 11:

At the *Cost Code ID* field, click the drop-down arrow, and then click *Buildlab-10*.

Step 12:

Key **100,000.00** in the *Expenses* field and **203,000.00** in the *Revenues* field.

Step 13:

In the fifth row of the *Phase ID* field, click the drop-down arrow and then click *Build-03.*

Step 14:

At the *Cost Code ID* field, click the drop-down arrow, and then click *Buildmat-11.*

Step 15:

Key **70,000.00** in the *Expenses* field and **190,000.00** in the *Revenues* field.

Step 16:

Compare your completed entries with the ones shown in Figure 11–10. Make any necessary changes.

FIGURE 11–10
Completed Entries for Estimated Expenses and Revenues

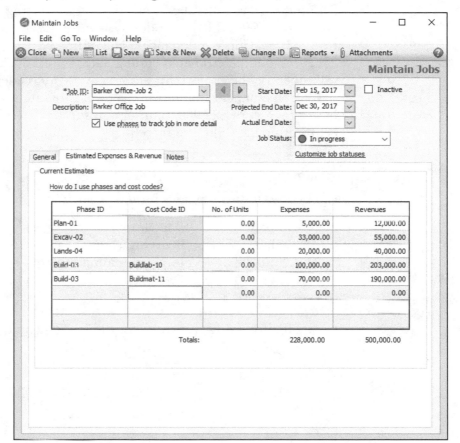

Step 17:

Click Save and then Close.

Step 18:

Close Wardwood Construction Company.

> ## Checkpoint 11–3
> 1. What are the five cost types supported by Sage 50?
> 2. What is the purpose of the cost codes?

Objective 11–3 Practice

Assume that Blufrog Maintenance Company accepts a job from Valley Mercedes to develop a maintenance system that can be used at five other Mercedes dealerships throughout the area.

Step 1:

Open Chp. 11 – Blufrog Maintenance Company, which you updated previously in the chapter.

Step 2:

Set up the project of Valley Mercedes for job costing. The job identifier is *Valley System-Job 2*, the description is *Mercedes Maintenance Job*, and the job type is *Maint* (for Maintenance). The estimated starting date is February 20, 2017, and the estimated ending date is April 30, 2017. Stanley Smith will supervise the project. Be sure to choose Mercedes-02 as the customer.

Blufrog estimates that this project will generate revenue of $45,500 and have expenses of $22,000. Blufrog wants to track the costs of the project by using the following three phases: Planning, Implementation, and Feedback.

Step 3:

Create the following phases for the project:

Phase ID	Description	Cost Type
Plan-01	Planning	Other
Impl-02	Implementation	Use cost codes (shown below)
Feed-03	Feedback	Subcontractors

Step 4:

Create the following cost codes for the implementation phase (Impl-02):

Cost ID	Description	Cost Type
Impllab-10	Implementation Labor	Labor
Implmat-11	Implementation Materials	Materials

Step 5:

HINT
Use Maintain, *Job Costs*, *Jobs*.

Enter the estimated revenue and expenses for each phase of the project:

Phase	Expenses	Revenue
Planning	$ 2,000	$ 4,000
Feedback	2,500	5,000
Implementation Labor	8,000	25,000
Implementation Materials	9,500	11,500
Totals	$22,000	$45,500

Step 6:

Compare your work with the Maintain Jobs window shown in Figure 11–11. Make any necessary changes. Notice the totals at the bottom of your screen.

FIGURE 11–11
Completed Maintain Jobs Window

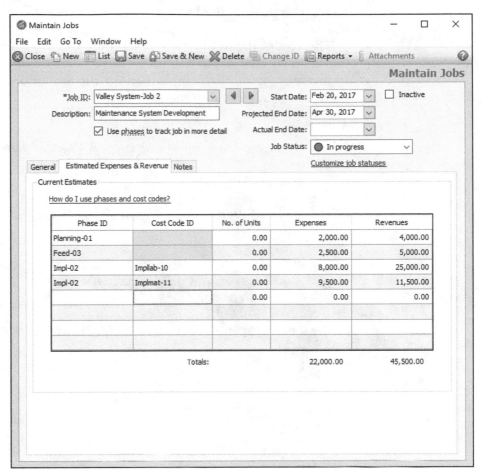

Step 7:
Click Save and Close.

OBJECTIVE 11-4

Use the Job Costing System to Record Purchases, Payroll, and Sales

The Sage 50 job costing system allows you to record the actual expenses incurred and the actual revenue received as a project moves through production. Remember that the estimated expenses and revenue are entered at the beginning of the project. Management is therefore able to compare estimated and actual amounts for every phase of the project.

Labor costs can easily be allocated to jobs if employees keep track of the hours that they spend on each job. Similarly, the costs of materials and other items purchased specifically for jobs can easily be allocated. However, it is more difficult to allocate the costs of materials and other items that are purchased for the firm's inventory and later used for jobs.

Recording the Cost of Purchases

Suppose that Wardwood Construction Company receives Invoice 1009 from the BMC Supply Company on February 21, 2017. This invoice is for 5,000 feet of lumber to be used in the fence being built for Smith's Monument Shop. The price of the lumber is $0.50 per foot. In addition, Wardwood will use 40 gallons of white paint from the firm's inventory.

The cost of the lumber, which will be used only for the Smith job, is immediately charged to that job. However, the cost of the paint is charged to inventory when the paint is used for the Smith job. The cost of that paint will be allocated to the job.

Step 1:

Open Chp. 11 – Wardwood Construction Company and close the Action Items log.

Step 2:

Click Tasks and then click *Purchases/Receive Inventory*.

Step 3:

At the Purchases/Receive Inventory window, in the *Vendor ID* field, click the *magnifying glass* icon, and then click *BMC-007*.

Step 4:

At the *Invoice Date* field, click the *calendar* icon and select *Feb 21, 2017*.

Step 5:

Key **1009** in the *Invoice No.* field.

Step 6:

Key **5,000.00** in the *Quantity* field.

Step 7:

At the *Item* field, click the *magnifying glass* icon, and then click *New* at the bottom of the drop-down list.

Step 8:

Create the following inventory item. Click <u>S</u>ave after the item is entered.

Non-stock Item (purchased for a job)

Item ID:	**BOARD-4**
Description:	**Lumber**
Item Class:	**Non-stock item**
Full Price:	**1.50**
Last Unit Cost:	**0.50**
GL Sales Acct:	**400.5**
GL Salary/Wages Acct:	**512**
GL Cost of Sales Acct:	**503**
Item Tax Type:	**2 (Exempt)**
Stocking U/M:	**Foot**
Preferred Vendor ID:	**BMC-07**

Step 9:

Click Close to return to the Purchases/Receive Inventory window.

Step 10:

At the *Item* field in the Purchases/Receive Inventory window, click the *magnifying glass* icon, and then click *BOARD-4*.

Step 11:

At the *GL Account* field, click *105*.

Step 12:

Key **0.50** in the *Unit Price* field.

Step 13:

At the *Job* field, click the drop-down arrow, and then select *Smith Fence-Job 1*, as shown in Figure 11–12.

FIGURE 11–12
Smith Fence-Job 1
Selected from Job
Field Drop-Down List

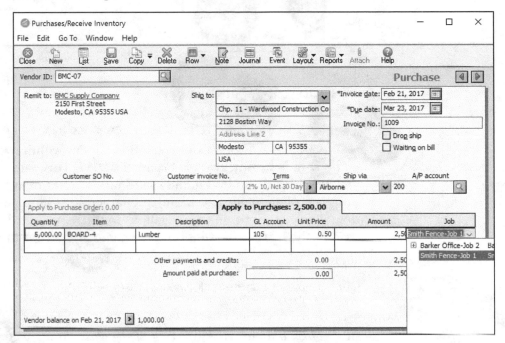

Step 14:

Review the Completed Purchases/Receive Inventory window. Compare your entries with those shown in Figure 11–13.

FIGURE 11–13
Completed Purchases/
Receive Inventory
Window

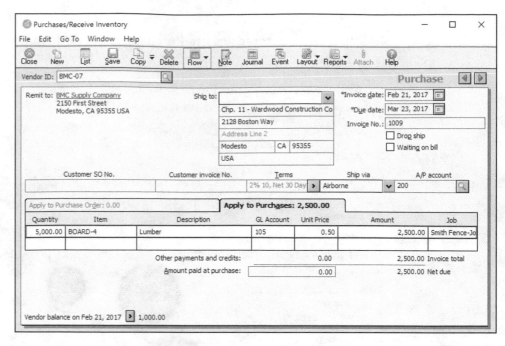

Step 15:

Click Save and then Close.

Allocating the Cost of Inventory Items to Jobs

Assume that Wardwood Construction Company withdraws 40 gallons of white paint from its inventory on February 23, 2017. This paint will be used for the fence that Wardwood is building for Smith's Monument Shop. Because the purchase of the paint was originally charged to Inventory, Wardwood must now allocate the cost of the 40 gallons to the Smith job. Like the lumber used in the fence, this paint is part of the materials for the job.

Step 1:

Click Tasks and then click *Inventory Adjustments.*

Step 2:

At the *Item ID* field, click the *magnifying glass* icon, and then click *PAINTWH-5.*

Step 3:

Key **2/23/17** in the *Date* field.

Step 4:

At the *Job* field, click the *folder* icon, and then click *Smith Fence-Job 1.*

Step 5:

At the *GL Source Acct* field, key **105**.

Step 6:

Key **–40.00** in the *Adjust Quantity By* field. (Be sure to key this amount as a negative number.)

Step 7:

Key **Used for Smith Fence Job** in the *Reason to adjust* field. Compare your completed entries with those shown in Figure 11–14.

FIGURE 11–14
Completed Inventory Adjustments Window

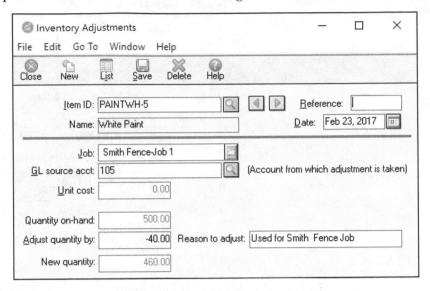

Step 8:

Click **S**ave and then Close.

Allocating Labor Costs to Jobs

On February 28, 2017, Wardwood Construction Company records the labor costs related to the job it is doing for Smith's Monument Shop. These labor costs consist of one week of salary for George Clark ($1,000) and 40 hours of wages for Samuel Jones at $15 per hour ($15 × 40 = $600). Make note that you had processed the payroll for this period in Chapter 10.

Step 1:

Click Tasks and then click *Payroll Entry*.

Step 2:

The Payroll Entry window will now appear. Click the L**i**st button on the Payroll Entry toolbar.

Step 3:

Select *All Transactions* from the *Date Range* drop-down list in the Paycheck List window.

Step 4:

Double-click *GCL-03, Check 2005*. George Clark's payroll data for the week of Jan 30, 2017, will now appear in the Payroll Entry window.

Step 5:

Click the Jobs button on the Payroll Entry toolbar. The Labor Distribution to Jobs dialog box will appear, as shown in Figure 11–15.

FIGURE 11–15
Labor Distribution to
Jobs Dialog Box

Step 6:

In the *Job* field, click the drop-down arrow and then select *Smith Fence-Job 1*.

Step 7:

Key **1,000.00** in the *Amount* field and then press Enter. All of George Clark's salary has now been allocated to the Smith job. Compare your completed entries with those shown in Figure 11–16.

FIGURE 11–16
Salary Allocated to
Smith Job

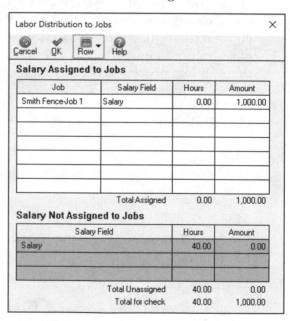

Step 8:

Click <u>O</u>K to save, and then <u>S</u>ave again at the Payroll Entry window.

Step 9:

Click the L<u>i</u>st button on the Payroll Entry toolbar.

Step 10:

Double-click *SJO-04, Check 2008.* Samuel Jones's payroll data for the week of Jan 30, 2017, will now appear in the Payroll Entry window.

Step 11:

Click the Jobs button on the Payroll Entry toolbar. The Labor Distribution to Jobs dialog box will appear.

Step 12:

In the *Job* field, click the drop-down arrow and then select *Smith Fence-Job 1.*

Step 13:

Key **40.00** in the *Hours* field and then press Enter. Note that the total amount of *$600.00* is automatically entered ($15 per hour × 40 hours).

Step 14:

Click OK. Close the Paycheck List window.

Step 15:

At the Payroll Entry window, click Save and then Close.

Recording the Revenue Received from Jobs

Suppose that Wardwood Construction Company completes the fence that it is building for Smith's Monument Shop on February 28, 2017. Wardwood receives a check for $5,240 from Smith.

The effect of this transaction is to increase the revenue earned from construction services and to increase the asset Cash. Therefore, Wardwood must debit Cash and credit Construction Revenue. You make this entry using the Receive Money function of Sage 50.

Step 1:

Click Tasks, click *Receive Money*, and then after ensuring *Cash* is selected from the drop-down list, click OK at the Select a Cash Account window.

Step 2:

At the Receive Money window, key **02/28/17** in the *Deposit Ticket ID* field.

Step 3:

At the *Customer ID* field, click the *magnifying glass* icon, and then click *Smith-02.*

Step 4:

Key **Fence Job** in the *Check/Reference No.* field.

Step 5:

At the *Date* field, click the *calendar* icon and select *Feb 28, 2017.*

Step 6:

Select *Check* from the Payment Method drop-down list, if needed.

Step 7:

Click the Apply to Revenues folder tab.

Step 8:

Key **Fence Job** in the *Description* field.

Step 9:

At the *GL Account* field, key **400.5**.

Step 10:

Key **5,240.00** in the *Amount* field.

Step 11:

At the *Job* field, click the drop-down arrow and then click *Smith Fence-Job 1*, as shown in Figure 11–17.

FIGURE 11–17
Smith Fence-Job 1
Selected

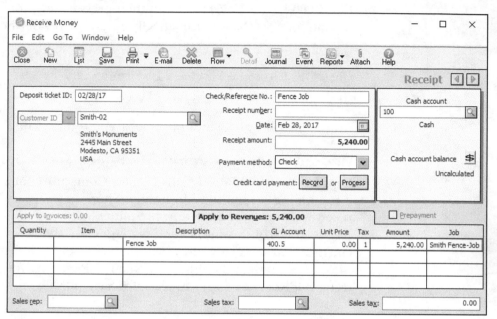

HINT

If the *GL Account* field does not display on the Apply to Revenues tab, click Options on the Menu bar, and then click *Global.* The Maintain Global Options dialog box will appear. Deselect the box that is checked next to *Accounts Receivable (Quotes, Sales Orders, Invoicing, Credit Memos, Receipts),* then click OK. Close and then reopen the Receive Money window.

Step 12:

Click Save and then Close.

Tracking Costs and Revenue for Job Phases

The job that Wardwood Construction Company did for Smith's Monument Shop was a simple one. However, the job for Barker's Music is more complex and was therefore divided into four phases: planning/permits, excavation, building, and landscaping. The building phase was further divided by assigning cost codes for materials and labor.

One of the advantages of the Sage 50 job costing system is that you can use it to track costs and revenue for each phase of a project as the project moves through production. The phase codes and cost codes make this possible.

Suppose that Wardwood Construction Company wants to access the phase codes and cost codes for the Barker job. We will use the Purchases function to accomplish this task, but it is also possible to use the Payroll and Sales functions.

Step 1:

Click Tasks and then click *Purchases/Receive Inventory.*

Step 2:

At the Purchases/Receive Inventory window, click in the *Job* field, and then click the drop-down arrow.

Step 3:

Click the + icon next to *Barker Office-Job* icon to view the phases available for cost allocation, as shown in Figure 11–18.

FIGURE 11–18
Phases Available for Barker Office Job

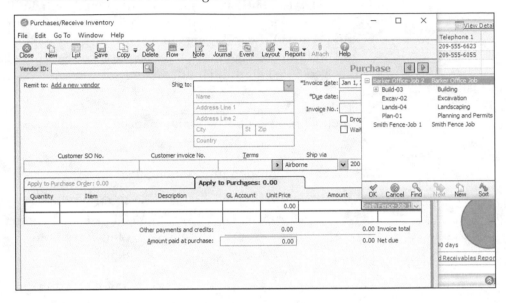

Step 4:

Click the + icon next to *Build-03* to reveal the cost codes for the building phase of the Barker job, as shown in Figure 11–19.

FIGURE 11–19
Cost Codes Available for Barker Office Job

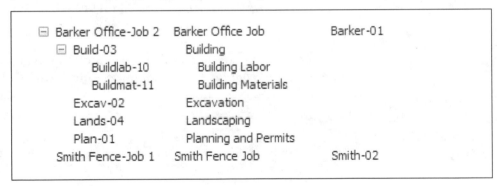

Step 5:

Do *not* click Save. Click Close to exit the Purchases/Receive Inventory window.

Checkpoint 11–4

1. When inventory items are used for a job, what must happen to the cost of those items?

2. Why must employees keep track of the hours they spend on each job?

On February 12, 2017, Blufrog Maintenance Company began the fire cleanup job for Honda Center. It purchased 1,400 gallons of a floor care product on credit from Lou's Janitorial Supply Company at a cost of $4.56 per gallon (Invoice 596781). This product will be used only for the Honda Center job. In addition, Blufrog will use 20 gallons of carpet shampoo, CPTSHAM-1. The carpet shampoo will be taken from Blufrog's inventory.

On February 22, 2017, Blufrog completed the job for Honda Center and recorded the following labor costs: one week's salary for Stanley Smith and 40 hours of wages for James Stewart. On February 28, 2017, Blufrog received $15,000 from Honda Center for the job.

Step 1:

Open Chp. 11 – Blufrog Maintenance Company.

Step 2:

Create the following inventory item:

Item ID:	**FLOCARE-4**
Description:	**Floor Care Product**
Item Class:	**Non-stock item**
Full Price:	**9.50**
Last Unit Cost:	**4.56**
GL Sales Acct:	**400.5**
GL Salary/Wages Acct:	**512**
GL Cost of Sales Acct:	**503**
Item Tax Type:	**2 (Exempt)**
Stocking U/M:	**Gallon**
Preferred Vendor ID:	**LOU-01**

Step 3:

Enter the purchase of the floor care product. Key **105** at the *GL Account* field and **4.56** at the *Unit Price* field. Compare your entries with Figure 11–20.

FIGURE 11–20
Completed
Purchases/Receive
Inventory Window

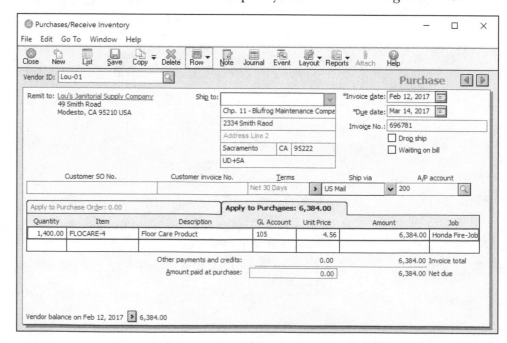

Step 4:

Make the necessary inventory adjustment for the carpet shampoo and allocate its cost to the Honda Center job. Compare your Inventory Adjustments window with Figure 11–21.

FIGURE 11–21
Completed Inventory Adjustments Window

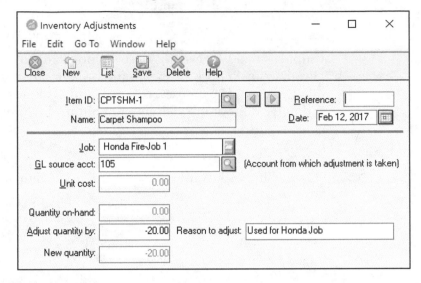

Step 5:

Allocate the labor costs to the Honda Center job. Note that the weekly payroll for the week ending February 22, 2017, has not yet been processed; therefore, create the payroll entries for all three employees and assign the labor costs of Stanley Smith and James Stewart to the Honda job. (The pay period ends February 22 and the date of the check is February 23. Print the checks.)

Step 6:

Enter the service revenue received from the Honda Center job, Reference Fire Cleanup, GL Account 400.5.

Step 7:

Close the active window.

OBJECTIVE 11–5

Create and Print Job Cost Reports

The Sage 50 job costing system produces many reports. Management can use the information in these reports to review estimated expenses and revenue for jobs, compare these amounts to the actual expenses and revenue, monitor profitability, and keep track of the progress of each job. Among the reports available from the Sage 50 job costing system are the following:

- Cost Code List
- Estimated Job Expenses
- Estimated Job Revenue
- Job Costs by Type
- Job Estimates
- Job Ledger
- Job List

- Job Master File List
- Job Profitability Report
- Job Register
- Phase List
- Unbilled Job Expense

Preparing the Job Profitability Report

Suppose that Wardwood Construction Company wants to create the Job Profitability Report for the month of February 2017. This report will show the actual expenses, revenue, and profit for the job that Wardwood completed for Smith's Monument Shop—building a fence around a parking area.

Step 1:

Open Chp. 11 – Wardwood Construction Company, which you updated previously in the chapter.

Step 2:

Click Reports & Forms and then click *Jobs.*

Step 3:

The Select a Report or Form dialog box will appear. Click *Job Profitability Report* from the Job Reports: Project Information section.

Step 4:

Click Options on the Select a Report or Form toolbar.

Step 5:

In the *Time Frame* field of the Modify Report – Job Profitability Report window, click *Range.* In the *From* field, select *Feb 1, 2017,* and in the *To* field, select *Feb 28, 2017.*

Step 6:

Click OK at the bottom of the window.

Step 7:

Review the Job Profitability Report and compare it to the one shown in Figure 11–22.

FIGURE 11–22
Job Profitability
Report

10/20/16 at 06:24:05.11   *****EDUCATIONAL VERSION ONLY*****   Page: 1

Chp. 11 - Wardwood Construction Company
Job Profitability Report
For the Period From Feb 1, 2017 to Feb 28, 2017
Filter Criteria includes: Report order is by ID. Report is printed including Balance Forward.

Job ID	Phase ID	Cost Code ID	GL Acct ID	Actual Rev.	Actual Exp.	Profit $	Profit %
Smith Fence			105		2,500.00		
					80.00		
			400	5,240.00			
			512		1,000.00		
					600.00		
				5,240.00	4,180.00		
Smith Fenc	Total			5,240.00	4,180.00	1,060.00	20.23
Report	Total			5,240.00	4,180.00	1,060.00	20.23

Step 8:

Click Close.

Preparing the Estimated Job Expenses Report

Suppose that Wardwood Construction Company now wants to create the Estimated Job Expenses report for the month of February 2017. This report will show the estimated expenses for current and completed jobs.

Step 1:

At the Select a Report or Form dialog box, click *Estimated Job Expenses* in the Job Reports: Project Information section.

Step 2:

Click Options on the Select a Report or Form toolbar.

Step 3:

In the *Date* field, click *Exact Date*, and in the *As of* field, select *Feb 28, 2017.*

Step 4:

Click OK in the Modify Report – Estimated Job Expenses window.

Step 5:

Review the Estimated Job Expenses report and compare it to the report shown in Figure 11–23.

FIGURE 11–23
Estimated Job
Expenses Report

9/24/16 at 21:00:07.53   *****EDUCATIONAL VERSION ONLY*****   Page: 1
Chp. 11 - Wardwood Construction Company
Estimated Job Expenses
As of Feb 28, 2017
Filter Criteria includes: Report order is by ID.

Job ID	Phase ID	Cost Code ID	Est. Exp. Units	Act. Exp. Units	Diff. Exp. Units	Est. Expense	Act. Expense	Diff. Expenses
Barker Office-J	Build-03	Buildlab-10				100,000.00		-100,000.00
		Buildmat-11				70,000.00		-70,000.00
	Excav-02					33,000.00		-33,000.00
	Lands-04					20,000.00		-20,000.00
	Plan-01					5,000.00		-5,000.00
Barker Office-	Total					228,000.00		-228,000.00
Smith Fence-J				5,080.00	5,080.00	3,150.00	4,180.00	1,030.00
Smith Fence-J	Total			5,080.00	5,080.00	3,150.00	4,180.00	1,030.00
Report	Total			5,080.00	5,080.00	231,150.00	4,180.00	-226,970.00

Step 6:

Close Wardwood Construction Company.

> ## Checkpoint 11–5
>
> 1. Name two reports available from the Sage 50 job costing system.
> 2. What information about a job is shown in the Job Profitability Report?

Blufrog Maintenance Company wants to prepare two job cost reports for the month of February 2017.

Step 1:

Open Chp. 11 – Blufrog Maintenance Company, which you updated previously in the chapter.

Step 2:

Prepare and print the Job Profitability Report and Estimated Job Expenses report. Your printouts should look like Figures 11–24 and 11–25, respectively.

FIGURE 11–24
Job Profitability
Report – Blufrog
Maintenance
Company

10/20/16 at 06:27:44.29   *****EDUCATIONAL VERSION ONLY*****   Page: 1

Chp. 11 - Blufrog Maintenance Company
Job Profitability Report
For the Period From Feb 1, 2017 to Feb 28, 2017
Filter Criteria includes: Report order is by ID. Report is printed including Balance Forward.

Job ID	Phase ID	Cost Code ID	GL Acct ID	Actual Rev.	Actual Exp.	Profit $	Profit %
Honda Fire-			105		6,384.00		
					480.00		
			400.5	15,000.00			
			512		460.00		
					1,600.00		
				15,000.00	8,924.00		
Honda Fire-	Total			15,000.00	8,924.00	6,076.00	40.51
Report	Total			15,000.00	8,924.00	6,076.00	40.51

FIGURE 11–25
Estimated Job
Expenses Report –
Blufrog Maintenance
Company

9/24/16 at 21:31:07.80   *****EDUCATIONAL VERSION ONLY*****   Page: 1

Chp. 11 - Blufrog Maintenance Company
Estimated Job Expenses
As of Feb 28, 2017
Filter Criteria includes: Report order is by ID.

Job ID	Phase ID	Cost Code ID	Est. Exp. Units	Act. Exp. Units	Diff. Exp. Units	Est. Expense	Act. Expense	Diff. Expenses
Honda Fire-Jo				1,460.00	1,460.00	8,900.00	8,924.00	24.00
Honda Fire-Jo	Total			1,460.00	1,460.00	8,900.00	8,924.00	24.00
Valley System-	Feed-03					2,500.00		-2,500.00
	Impl-02	Impllab-10				8,000.00		-8,000.00
		Implmat-11				9,500.00		-9,500.00
	Planning-01					2,000.00		-2,000.00
Valley System	Total					22,000.00		-22,000.00
Report	Total			1,460.00	1,460.00	30,900.00	8,924.00	-21,976.00

Chapter Review and Assessment

Software Command Summary

Set Up a Job for Costing	Maintain, Job Costs, Jobs, Enter Job Information
Estimated Expenses and Revenue	Same as Set Up a Job for Costing, then Estimated Expenses & Revenue Tab and Enter Data
Create Phase Codes	Maintain, Job Costs, Phases, Enter Information, Select the Cost Type
Create Cost Codes	Maintain, Job Costs, Cost Codes, Enter Information, Select the Cost Type
Enter Purchases	Tasks, Purchases/Receive Inventory, Job, Select a Job, a Phase, and a Cost Code
Allocate the Cost of Inventory Items	Tasks, Inventory Adjustments, Item ID, Adjust Quantity By
Allocate the Cost of Labor to Jobs	Tasks, Payroll Entry, Employee ID, Jobs, Select a Job, a Phase, and a Cost Code, Enter the Salary/ Hourly Information
Enter the Revenue from Jobs	Tasks, Receive Money, Job, Select a Job, a Phase, and a Cost Code
Print Job Cost Reports	Reports & Forms, Jobs, Select a Report from the Report List, Print

Checkpoint Answers

Checkpoint 11–1
1. Job costs are the costs of materials, labor, and other items required for completion of a particular job.
2. The three methods are the Jobs Only Method, the Jobs with Phases Method, and the Jobs with Phases and Cost Codes Method.

Checkpoint 11–2
1. The menu options to click are Maintain, Job Costs, and Jobs.
2. The estimated expenses and estimated revenues are entered.

Checkpoint 11–3
1. The five cost types are Labor, Materials, Equipment, Subcontractors, and Other.
2. The cost codes help management track several cost areas for any phase of a job.

> ### Checkpoint 11–4
> 1. The cost of inventory items that are used for a job must be allocated to the job.
> 2. Keeping track of the hours spent on each job makes it possible to allocate labor costs.
>
> ### Checkpoint 11–5
> 1. Answers will vary.
> 2. This report shows the actual expenses, revenue, and profit for a job.

Study Quizzes

Take the study quiz online to check your understanding of chapter concepts. The quiz can be taken multiple times.

Content Check

Multiple Choice: Choose only one response for each question.

1. Which of the following methods for tracking job costs does Sage 50 support?
   A. Jobs Only
   B. Jobs with Phases
   C. Jobs with Phases and Cost Codes
   D. All of the above

2. When managers want maximum detail in their cost reports, they should use
   A. Phases.
   B. Cost Types.
   C. Cost Codes.
   D. All of the above

3. What are job costs?
   A. The costs incurred in operating a business
   B. The revenue and expenses connected with inventory adjustments
   C. The materials, labor, and other items required to complete a job
   D. None of the above

4. The Sage 50 job costing system tracks
   A. the estimated revenue and expenses for each job.
   B. the actual revenue and expenses for each job.
   C. the profit for each job.
   D. All of the above

5. Which of the following job cost reports would management consult to see how much profit the business made from a completed job?
   A. Estimated Job Expenses
   B. Job Profitability Report
   C. Estimated Job Revenue
   D. Job Register

Short Essay Response

Provide a detailed answer for each question.

1. What is the purpose of job costing? Why would the information from a job costing system help managers make decisions?
2. Sage 50 supports several levels of detail for job costing. Name two situations in which it would be helpful for management to have cost information for the various phases of a job.
3. Suppose a construction company will complete a job over several months. What factors would management consider when deciding whether to divide this job into phases?
4. Why is the Job Profitability Report helpful to a user of Sage 50?
5. What are the steps necessary to set up a project for job costing?
6. List and explain the five different cost types used in Sage 50.

Cooperative Learning

1. Form groups of three or four students and contact a local construction company to discuss its use of job costing. If possible, determine the level of detail the managers would like to see in the job cost information. For example, do they want to see the information broken down by phase and cost type?
2. In groups of three or four students, visit a meeting of the local chapter of the Institute of Management Accountants (IMA). Find out what types of jobs are available to management accountants in the area. Also find out what courses are necessary for students who want to become management accountants. Visit www.imanet.org to gain information about the IMA.

Writing and Decision Making

Assume that you work for a construction company and have been given the job of project manager for a $20 million shopping mall. Your supervisor wants some insight about how a job costing system operates. In memo format, briefly explain the possible ways that costs can be broken down so that you can closely monitor them throughout the job, recognize revenue and expenses in a timely manner, and determine the profitability of the project.

Case Problems

Demonstrate your knowledge of the Sage 50 features discussed in this chapter by completing the following case problems.

Case Problem 11–1A

Robertson Construction Company accepted a job from Jerome Parks of the Parkview Apartments to repair an apartment that had been damaged by renters. Robertson wants to use the Jobs Only Method to keep track of the revenue and expenses associated with the project. The revenue is expected to be $30,000, and the expenses are expected to be $20,000. The job identifier is Park Repair-Job 1. The estimated starting date is January 10, 2017, and the estimated ending date is January 30, 2017. The percentage of completion is zero (0). Barbara Williams will supervise the project.

1. Open Robertson Construction Company from the student data files.

2. Create a customer account for Parkview Apartments.

Customer ID:	**Park-10**
Name:	**Parkview Apartments**

General Tab

Account Number:	**230**
Billing Address:	**3455 Mission Street**
City, ST, Zip:	**Modesto, CA 95355**
Country:	**USA**
Sales Tax:	**None**
Customer Type:	**Building**
Telephone 1:	**209-555-1234**

Contacts Tab

Contact:	**Jerome Parks**

Sales Info Tab

GL Sales Account:	**400**
Ship Via:	**Fed-EX**
Pricing Level:	**Price Level 1**
Form Options:	**Default**

Payment & Credit Tab

Terms and Credit:	**2% 10 Days, Net 30 Days**

History Tab

Beginning Balance:	**0**

3. Set up the project for job costing.

4. On January 10, 2017, Robertson Construction Company purchased the following stock items for its inventory: 1,000 feet of lumber, one sink, and 2,400 feet of vinyl flooring. All items were purchased on credit from Steve's Supply Warehouse (Invoice 1220). Use the following information to create inventory records for the items.

Stock Item

Item ID:	**BOARD-5**
Description:	**Lumber**
Item Class:	**Stock item**
Price Level 1:	**2.50**
Last Unit Cost:	**1.50**
Cost Method:	**Average**
GL Sales Acct:	**400**
GL Inventory Acct:	**105**
GL Cost of Sales Acct:	**503**
Item Tax Type:	**2 (Exempt)**
Stocking U/M:	**Foot**
Preferred Vendor ID:	**STEVES-01**

Stock Item

Item ID:	**SINK-12**
Description:	**Sink**
Item Class:	**Stock item**
Price Level 1:	**425.00**
Last Unit Cost:	**250.00**
Cost Method:	**Average**
GL Sales Acct:	**400**
GL Inventory Acct:	**105**
GL Cost of Sales Acct:	**503**
Item Tax Type:	**2 (Exempt)**
Stocking U/M:	**Each**
Preferred Vendor ID:	**Steves-01**

Stock Item

Item ID:	**VFLOOR-15**
Description:	**Vinyl Flooring**
Item Class:	**Stock item**
Price Level 1:	**7.50**
Last Unit Cost:	**4.50**
Cost Method:	**Average**
GL Sales Acct:	**400**
GL Inventory Acct:	**105**
GL Cost of Sales Acct:	**503**
Item Tax Type:	**2 (Exempt)**
Stocking U/M:	**Foot**
Preferred Vendor ID:	**STEVES-01**

5. Enter the purchases.

6. Robertson used 250 feet of the lumber, the sink, and 500 square feet of vinyl flooring for the Parkview job. Allocate the cost of these inventory items by making an inventory adjustment as of January 15, 2017. (Use 105 as the GL Source Acct when entering the inventory adjustment.)

7. Barbara Williams worked 40 hours on the Parkview job, and Michael Anderson worked 40 hours. Allocate these employees' labor costs ending January 23, 2017, to the job. The check number is 2215 and the check date is January 24, 2017.

8. Parkview Apartments made a partial payment (Check No. 1285) of $10,000 on January 26, 2017.

9. Print the following reports for the month of January 2017: Job Ledger and Job Profitability Report.

Case Problem 11–2A

Robertson Construction Company accepted a job from Palmdale Offices to build a new office building. The estimated starting date is February 1, 2017, and the estimated ending date is June 1, 2017. Michael Anderson will supervise the project. The job identifier is Palm Offices-Job 2. The percentage complete is zero.

Robertson has decided to create phases and cost codes to better track the revenue and expenses associated with this project. It has decided on the following phases and cost types.

Phases:

Phase ID	Description	Cost Type
Plan-01	Planning	Other
Land-03	Landscaping	Labor
Building-02	Building	Use cost codes shown below

Cost Codes:

Cost ID	Description	Cost Type
BUILDMAT-111	Building Materials	Materials
BUILDLAB-110	Building Labor	Labor

1. Open Robertson Construction Company, which you updated in Problem 11–1A.

2. Create a customer account for Palmdale Offices.

Customer ID:	**Palm-15**
Name:	**Palmdale Offices**

General Tab

Account Number:	**250**
Billing Address:	**4315 South First Street**
City, ST, Zip:	**Modesto, CA 95355**
Country:	**USA**
Sales Tax:	**None**
Customer Type:	**Building**
Telephone 1:	**209-555-2143**

Contacts Tab

Contact:	**Janet Bromberg**

Sales Info Tab

GL Sales Account:	**400**
Ship Via:	**Fed-EX**
Pricing Level:	**Price Level 1**
Form Options:	**Default**

Payment & Credit Tab

Terms and Credit:	**2% 10 Days, Net 30 Days**

History Tab

Beginning Balance:	**0**

3. Set up the project for job costing.

4. Create the phases and cost codes.

5. Print the following reports: Phase List, Cost Code List, and General Ledger Trial Balance.

Case Problem 11-1B

Abelar Construction Company accepted a job from the City of Lodi to repair a storm drain that had been damaged by heavy rains. Abelar wants to use the Jobs Only Method to keep track of the revenue and expenses associated with the project. The revenue is expected to be $15,000, and the expenses are expected to be $8,000. The job identifier is Lodi Drain-Job 1. The estimated starting date is January 5, 2017, and the estimated ending date is January 31, 2017. The percentage of completion is zero (0). Alfred Martinez will supervise the project.

1. Open Abelar Construction Company from the student data files.

2. Create a customer account for the City of Lodi.

Customer ID:	**Lodi-89**
Name:	**City of Lodi**

General Tab

Account Number:	**2130**
Billing Address:	**34 Main Street**
City, ST, Zip:	**Lodi, CA 95290**
Country:	**USA**
Sales Tax:	**None**
Customer Type:	**Repair**
Telephone 1:	**209-555-3423**

Contacts Tab

Contact:	**James Wright**

Sales Info Tab

GL Sales Account:	**400**
Ship Via:	**Fed-EX**
Pricing Level:	**Price Level 1**
Form Options:	**Default**

Payment & Credit Tab

Terms and Credit:	**2% 10 Days, Net 30 Days**

History Tab

Beginning Balance:	**0**

3. Set up the project for job costing.

4. On January 10, 2017, Abelar Construction Company purchased the following stock items for its inventory: 400 feet of 24-inch culvert pipe, one drain assembly, and 400 feet of copper pipe. All items were purchased on credit from Construction Supply Warehouse (Invoice 2009). Use the following information to create inventory records for the items.

Stock Item

Item ID:	**CULVERT-9**
Description:	**24-Inch Culvert Pipe**
Item Class:	**Stock item**

Price Level 1:	**25.00**
Last Unit Cost:	**15.00**
Cost Method:	**Average**
GL Sales Acct:	**400**
GL Inventory Acct:	**105**
GL Cost of Sales Acct:	**503**
Item Tax Type:	**2 (Exempt)**
Stocking U/M:	**Foot**
Preferred Vendor ID:	**CSW-01**

Stock Item

Item ID:	**DRAIN-16**
Description:	**Drain Assembly**
Item Class:	**Stock item**
Price Level 1:	**950.00**
Last Unit Cost:	**500.00**
Cost Method:	**Average**
GL Sales Acct:	**400**
GL Inventory Acct:	**105**
GL Cost of Sales Acct:	**503**
Item Tax Type:	**2 (Exempt)**
Stocking U/M:	**Each**
Preferred Vendor ID:	**CSW-01**

Stock Item

Item ID:	**COPPERPIPE-20**
Description:	**1-Inch Copper Pipe**
Item Class:	**Stock item**
Price Level 1:	**2.00**
Last Unit Cost:	**0.75**
Cost Method:	**Average**
GL Sales Acct:	**400**
GL Inventory Acct:	**105**
GL Cost of Sales Acct:	**503**
Item Tax Type:	**2 (Exempt)**
Stocking U/M:	**Foot**
Preferred Vendor ID:	**CSW-01**

5. Enter the purchases.

6. Abelar used 350 feet of the culvert pipe, the drain assembly, and 200 feet of the copper pipe for the Lodi job. Allocate the cost of these inventory items by making an inventory adjustment as of January 15, 2017. (Use 105 as the GL Source Acct when entering the inventory adjustment.)

7. Alfred Martinez worked 40 hours on the Lodi job, and Peter Monroe worked 40 hours. Allocate these employees' labor costs ending January 16, 2017, to the job. The check number is 4713 and the check date is January 17, 2017.

8. City of Lodi made a partial payment (Check No. 4510) of $8,000 on January 20, 2017.

9. Print the following reports for the month of January 2017: Job Ledger and Job Profitability Report.

Case Problem 11–2B

Abelar Construction Company accepted a job from Jeremy Lyons to build a new septic tank for a house he is renovating. The estimated starting date is January 11, 2017, and the estimated ending date is February 28, 2017. Alfred Martinez will supervise the project. The job identifier is Lyons Tank-Job 2. The percentage of the job completed is zero.

Abelar has decided to create phases and cost codes to better track the revenue and expenses associated with this project. It has decided on the following phases and cost types:

Phases:

Phase ID	Description	Cost Type
Plan-01	Planning/Permits	Other
Excav-02	Excavation	Labor
Build-03	Building	Use the cost codes shown below

Cost Codes:

Cost ID	Description	Cost Type
BUILDMAT-111	Building Materials	Materials
BUILDLAB-110	Building Labor	Labor

1. Open Abelar Construction Company, which you updated in Problem 11-1B.

2. Create a customer account for Lyons Renovation.

Customer ID:	**Lyons-90**
Name:	**Lyons Renovation**

General Tab

Account Number:	**2150**
Billing Address:	**1278 Boston Street**
City, ST, Zip:	**Modesto, CA 95357**
Country:	**USA**
Sales Tax:	**None**
Customer Type:	**Constr**
Telephone 1:	**209-555-4312**

Contacts Tab

Contact:	**Jeremy Lyons**

Sales Info Tab

GL Sales Account:	**400**
Ship Via:	**Fed-EX**
Pricing Level:	**Price Level 1**
Form Options:	**Default**

Payment & Credit Tab

Terms and Credit:	**2% 10 Days, Net 30 Days**

History Tab
    Beginning Balance: **0**

3. Set up the project for job costing.

4. Create the phases and cost codes.

5. Print the following reports: Phase List, Cost Code List, and General Ledger Trial Balance.

Comprehensive Problem Two

Demonstrate your knowledge of the Sage 50 Accounting features discussed in Chapters 8–11 by completing Comprehensive Problem Two. Access the links menu to download the instructions and company files for Comprehensive Problem Two.

CHAPTER 12

Partnerships and Corporations

Objectives

12–1 Review partnerships and corporations

12–2 Create partnership accounts and enter partnership transactions

12–3 Create corporate accounts and enter corporate transactions

12–4 Print partnership and corporate reports

Software Features

- Select or Change Organization Type

- Create General Ledger Accounts

- Edit General Ledger Accounts

- Print Financial Statements

Company Files

Before beginning chapter work, access the links menu to download company files.

Remember that there are three basic types of business organizations: the sole proprietorship, the partnership, and the corporation. A *sole proprietorship* is a business owned by one person. A *partnership* is a business owned by two or more people. A *corporation* is a business owned by stockholders or shareholders. A small corporation may have just a few stockholders, but large corporations have thousands of stockholders.

Up to now, the businesses that we have discussed in this book have all been sole proprietorships. Because sole proprietorships are simple to form and operate, they are the most common type of business organization in the United States. However, the vast majority of sole proprietorships are small firms with limited resources. Larger businesses are usually partnerships or corporations.

The accounting procedures of sole proprietorships, partnerships, and corporations are similar. The main differences involve owners' equity accounts, transactions, and financial statements. You can use Sage 50 to support all three types of business organization.

sole proprietorship A business owned by one person.

partnership A business owned by two or more people.

corporation A business owned by stockholders or shareholders.

OBJECTIVE 12–1

Review Partnerships and Corporations

In this chapter, you will see how Sage 50 is used to create owners' equity accounts, record owners' equity transactions, and prepare financial statements for partnerships and corporations. However, it is first necessary to understand the basic characteristics of partnerships and corporations.

Characteristics of Partnerships

A partnership is formed when two or more people enter into a business arrangement for the purpose of making a profit.

Partnerships carry a variety of advantages. Like a sole proprietorship, a partnership is easy to form. In most areas, all that is required to form a partnership is to obtain a business license for the firm. No written contract between the partners is necessary. However, lawyers advise that such a contract, called a *partnership agreement*, be drawn up to avoid later disputes. The partnership agreement specifies the beginning investment of each partner, the responsibilities of the partners, the method of dividing profits and losses, the method of admitting new partners, the method of dissolving the partnership, and other important matters. If there is no partnership agreement, by law, all profits and losses are divided equally.

The management of a partnership usually has a greater amount of expertise than the management of a sole proprietorship. Each partner brings additional knowledge, skills, and experience to the business. For example, suppose that a software engineer, a sales manager, and an accountant become partners in a new software company. Each will be able to contribute expertise in a different area of the business: product development, marketing, and financial management. The contributions of the different partners can have a synergistic effect. Together, the blend of talents may produce more successful results than the individual partners would be able to achieve on their own.

It is difficult to run a business successfully without sufficient capital. This is especially true for new businesses, which may have a weak cash flow in their early years. A partnership has a greater potential for obtaining capital than a sole proprietorship. In a partnership, two or more people are able

partnership agreement A written contract that specifies the terms of a partnership such as the division of profits and losses.

to pool their resources. If they need additional capital, they may have a better chance of borrowing the required sum than a single individual does.

Partnerships are subject to less government regulation than corporations. Also, unlike corporations, partnerships do not pay an income tax on their earnings. Partnerships file information returns with federal and state tax agencies, but they are not liable for any income tax. Instead, each partner pays income tax on his or her share of the firm's earnings.

There are also disadvantages to organizing a business as a partnership. Like the owner of a sole proprietorship, partners have *unlimited liability* for the debts of the business. If the business is unable to pay its debts, the creditors can sue to obtain the personal assets of the partners to satisfy the outstanding debts.

Although the blend of management talent can be beneficial to a partnership, disputes about management decisions can be harmful. If there are serious, ongoing disagreements about business policy, a partnership may eventually have to dissolve. Because of the divided management control, successful operation of a partnership requires a willingness to consider different viewpoints and make compromises.

Partnerships operate under the *mutual agency rule*. This means that any partner can enter into a contractual agreement on behalf of the partnership. All other partners must honor the agreement, even if they were not consulted in advance and they do not approve of the agreement. The mutual agency rule points out the need to select business partners wisely.

Partnerships have a *limited life*. A partnership ends whenever an existing partner dies or withdraws or when a new partner is admitted. In each of these cases, a new partnership must be formed to continue the business.

unlimited liability
Personal responsibility for the debts of a business by a sole proprietor or partner.

mutual agency rule A rule that allows a single partner to enter into a contract that is binding on all other partners with or without their consent.

limited life A partnership ends when an existing partner dies or withdraws or when a new partner is admitted.

Accounting for Partnerships

A partnership must have a separate capital account and a separate drawing account for each partner. When a partnership is formed, the investment of each partner is credited to his or her capital account. For example, suppose that Julie Smith and Anna Ramos form a partnership on January 1, 2017. Each invests $75,000 in cash.

January 1, 2017
Cash	150,000	
J. Smith, Capital		75,000
A. Ramos, Capital		75,000

At the end of each accounting period, the profit or loss of the partnership for the period is calculated. If there was a profit during the period, each capital account is credited for the partner's share. If there was a loss, each capital account is debited for the partner's share. Remember that the division of profits and losses in a partnership is specified in the partnership agreement. If there is no partnership agreement, then, by law, profits and losses must be divided equally among the partners. The following entry is for a year-end profit of $60,000 divided equally.

December 31, 2017
Income Summary	60,000	
J. Smith, Capital		30,000
A. Ramos, Capital		30,000

When a partner withdraws cash or other assets for personal use, the amounts are debited to the partner's drawing account. Many partners withdraw cash at regular intervals to have funds available to pay their personal living expenses. This amount is often referred to as a *salary*, but it is actually a withdrawal of expected future profits and is therefore debited to the partner's drawing account rather than to the Salaries Expense account. In a sole proprietorship and a partnership, only the earnings of employees can be recorded in the Salaries Expense account. The following entry is for a monthly withdrawal of $2,000 in cash by each of the two partners.

January 31, 2017		
J. Smith, Drawing	2,000	
A. Ramos, Drawing	2,000	
Cash		4,000

At the end of each accounting period, the balances of the partners' drawing accounts are closed into their capital accounts, as shown in the following year-end general journal entry.

December 31, 2017		
J. Smith, Capital	24,000	
A. Ramos, Capital	24,000	
J. Smith, Drawing		24,000
A. Ramos, Drawing		24,000

The balances of the partners' capital accounts are reported on the balance sheet. Some businesses also prepare a separate statement showing all changes in the partners' capital during the accounting period.

	J. Smith	A. Ramos	Total
Capital, Jan. 1, 2017	$ 75,000	$ 75,000	$150,000
Net income for year	30,000	30,000	60,000
Totals	$105,000	$105,000	$210,000
Less: Withdrawals	24,000	24,000	48,000
Capital, Dec. 31, 2017	$ 81,000	$ 81,000	$162,000

Characteristics of Corporations

The ownership of a corporation is divided into shares of stock. The owners are therefore known as *stockholders* or *shareholders*. Unlike a sole proprietorship or a partnership, a corporation is a legal entity that is separate from its owners.

A corporation may be small and have just a few stockholders, perhaps family members or a group of managers. This type of corporation is known as a *closely held corporation*. However, the corporations that most of us are familiar with—corporations such as IBM, Microsoft, Dell, Walmart, and General Motors—are large and have thousands of stockholders. A corporation of this kind is known as a *publicly held corporation* because the public, usually through a stock exchange, can purchase its stock.

Although there are more sole proprietorships and partnerships than corporations in the United States, corporations produce two-thirds of all business revenue. The reason for this disparity in revenue is that the largest businesses are most often organized as corporations.

stockholders or shareholders The owners of a corporation.

closely held corporation A corporation owned by just a few stockholders.

publicly held corporation A corporation with stock that can be purchased by the public.

Like a sole proprietorship and a partnership, a corporation has both advantages and disadvantages. The ability of a sole proprietorship or partnership to obtain capital depends mostly on the personal resources and personal credit reputation of the owners. A corporation, on the other hand, can raise funds by selling stock or issuing bonds. A corporation that has good prospects for growth can obtain funding from a large pool of potential investors.

Unlike the owners of sole proprietorships and partnerships, the stockholders of a corporation have *limited liability*. They are not personally liable for the debts of the business. If the corporation is unable to pay its debts, creditors cannot sue to obtain the personal assets of the stockholders. Therefore, the maximum amount that stockholders can lose in a failing corporation is the amount of their investment.

Because a corporation is a legal entity that is separate from its owners, it has a *continuous life*. Its life is not affected by changes in ownership, that is, by sales and purchases of shares by stockholders. A corporation can theoretically exist forever unless it is dissolved.

The mutual agency rule mentioned earlier does not apply to corporations. No contractual agreement made by an ordinary stockholder is legally binding on the firm. Only officers of the corporation are able to make binding commitments on its behalf.

When a corporation is formed, the stockholders elect a *board of directors* to look after their interests. The board of directors establishes policies for the firm and hires managers to carry out the policies. This separation of ownership and management allows the corporation to obtain the services of professional managers who have appropriate business training and experience.

Stockholders can vote in periodic elections for the board of directors but do not participate in the day-to-day operations of the corporation unless they are members of management.

The corporation structure has some disadvantages. Corporations require a *charter* from a state to operate. The state granting the charter is usually the one in which the corporation will have its headquarters. The process of applying for a charter, organizing the corporation, and issuing stock involves the work of lawyers and accountants. Therefore, the cost of forming a corporation can be substantial.

Organizing a corporation also involves much time and effort. For example, the organizers must establish a set of *bylaws*—the rules by which the corporation will operate. They must also establish corporate records such as the stockholders' ledger.

Corporations are more heavily regulated than sole proprietorships and partnerships. For example, the state and federal governments require that corporations file many different types of reports. Publicly held corporations must also meet accounting and financial reporting standards established by the Securities and Exchange Commission (a federal agency) and by the stock exchange (examples include NASDAQ and NYSE) on which their shares trade. These organizations require that publicly held corporations issue quarterly and annual financial statements.

Because a corporation is a legal entity that is separate from its owners, it pays an income tax on its earnings to the federal and state governments. When it distributes part of its earnings to stockholders in the form of

---

limited liability The stockholders of a corporation are not personally liable for the debts of the business.

continuous life A corporation can exist forever. Its life is not affected by changes in ownership.

board of directors Individuals elected by stockholders to establish policies for a corporation and hire managers.

charter A legal document issued by a state that permits a corporation to operate.

bylaws A set of rules by which a corporation will operate.

dividends, the individual stockholders must pay income tax on the amounts they receive. This situation is referred to as *double taxation*.

Accounting for Corporations

The corporate charter specifies the types of stock that can be issued and the maximum number of shares of each type. The two basic types of stock are *common stock* and *preferred stock*. Common stock provides various rights such as the right to vote for the board of directors and the right to receive dividends if the board of directors declares them. Preferred stock usually does not carry the right to vote but does provide a fixed dividend. Many corporations issue just one type of stock—common stock.

Some states require that stock be issued with a par value. The *par value* is an arbitrary amount that a corporation assigns to each share of its stock for legal and accounting purposes. This amount is printed on the stock certificate. The par value of a stock has nothing to do with its *market value*—the amount that a buyer is willing to pay for the stock at any given time.

The maximum number of shares of stock permitted by the corporate charter is known as the *authorized stock*. However, the number of shares actually sold is called *issued stock*. As the corporation sells more shares to investors, the amount of issued stock changes. Sometimes, a corporation will buy back shares from investors in the form of *treasury stock*. When treasury stock exists, *outstanding stock* refers to the number of shares that are actually held by investors. For example, if a corporation issues 100,000 shares and then buys back 10,000 shares, the number of issued shares is still 100,000; however, the number of outstanding shares is now 90,000. Dividends are paid only on outstanding shares. The earnings per share (EPS) ratio is also based on the number of outstanding shares.

Paid-in Capital and Retained Earnings

When a corporation issues common stock at par value for cash, it debits the amount received to Cash and credits a stockholder's equity account called Common Stock. If the stock is issued above par value, the corporation still credits the par-value amount to the Common Stock account. However, it must credit the amount that is above par value to another stockholders' equity account called Paid-in Capital in Excess of Par—Common. For example, suppose that a corporation sells 1,000 shares of $10 par-value common stock at $15 per share. It receives $15,000 in cash. The journal entry appears below.

January 6, 2017

Cash	15,000	
Common Stock		10,000
Paid-in Capital in Excess of Par—Common		5,000

If a corporation has par-value preferred stock, it will use stockholders' equity accounts called Preferred Stock and Paid-in Capital in Excess of Par—Preferred to record transactions involving the preferred stock.

At the end of each accounting period, the corporation's profit or loss for the period is transferred from the Income Summary account to a stockholders' equity account called Retained Earnings. This account shows the accumulated earnings of the corporation that have not been distributed

double taxation As a legal entity, a corporation pays income tax on its earnings. When the stockholders receive part of the earnings in the form of dividends, they also pay income tax.

common stock Stock that provides the right to vote and to receive dividends if the board of directors declares them.

preferred stock Stock that usually does not carry the right to vote but provides a fixed dividend.

par value An arbitrary amount that some states require corporations to assign to each share of stock for legal and accounting purposes.

market value The amount that a buyer is willing to pay for stock.

authorized stock The maximum number of shares of stock permitted by the corporate charter.

issued stock The number of shares of stock actually sold by a corporation.

treasury stock The shares a corporation buys back from its investors.

outstanding stock The number of shares that are actually held by investors.

to stockholders in the form of dividends. For example, suppose that a corporation has a profit (net income) of $130,000 for the year 2017. This amount is credited to Retained Earnings.

December 31, 2017

Income Summary	130,000	
Retained Earnings		130,000

The Stockholders' Equity Section of the Balance Sheet

The balance sheet of a corporation has a Stockholders' Equity section, which contains the type of information shown below. Notice that the total stockholders' equity consists of paid-in capital and retained earnings.

paid-in capital The amount of capital received from stockholders through their purchases of stock.

Paid-in capital is the amount of capital received from stockholders through their purchases of stock. *Retained earnings* are accumulated profits less dividends from past operations. The term *earned capital* is often used to describe retained earnings.

retained earnings The accumulated profits of a corporation less dividends from past operations.

earned capital A term often used to describe retained earnings.

Stockholders' Equity

Paid-in Capital:		
Preferred Stock	$200,000	
Paid-in Capital in Excess of Par—Preferred	40,000	$240,000
Common Stock	$450,000	
Paid-in Capital in Excess of Par—Common	80,000	530,000
Total Paid-in Capital		$770,000
Retained Earnings		180,000
Total Stockholders' Equity		$950,000

Dividends

Stockholders expect to receive a return on their investments. This return can come from an increase in the market value of their stock and/or from dividends paid by the corporation to its stockholders. When the market value of a stock increases, stockholders can sell their shares and realize the monetary gain if they wish.

dividend A distribution of part of a corporation's earnings to stockholders.

A *dividend* is a distribution of part of a corporation's earnings to stockholders. Some corporations have a policy of paying dividends on a regular basis, such as every quarter. Other corporations, especially newer corporations in high-growth industries such as software and computers, might not pay dividends because they want to use their accumulated earnings to expand operations.

The board of directors is responsible for declaring dividends. For example, suppose that on January 31, 2017, the board of directors of a corporation declares a dividend of $1 per share to be paid on February 28 to "stockholders of record" (stockholders whose names appear in the corporation's records) as of February 15.

Dividends are usually paid in cash, but they may be paid in stock. On the date when a cash dividend is declared, the total amount is debited to Cash Dividends and credited to Cash Dividends Payable. Cash Dividends is a contra stockholders' equity account—a stockholders' equity account with a debit balance. Cash Dividends Payable is a liability account. On the date when the dividend is paid, Cash Dividends Payable is debited and Cash is credited. Note that no journal entry is made on the date of record.

January 31, 2017		
Cash Dividends	20,000	
Cash Dividends Payable		20,000

February 28, 2017		
Cash Dividends Payable	20,000	
Cash		20,000

Cash Dividends is a temporary account. When closing entries are made at the end of an accounting period, its balance is transferred to Retained Earnings. For example, suppose that the corporation discussed in this section pays only $20,000 in cash dividends during 2017. On December 31, it makes the entry shown below. The effects of this entry are to close the Cash Dividends account and to decrease the Retained Earnings account by $20,000, the amount paid out of retained earnings for the dividends.

December 31, 2017		
Retained Earnings	20,000	
Cash Dividends		20,000

The Statement of Retained Earnings

statement of retained earnings A financial statement that shows the changes in a corporation's retained earnings during an accounting period.

Many corporations prepare a *statement of retained earnings* at the end of each accounting period. This statement shows the beginning balances of the Retained Earnings account, an addition for net income or a deduction for a net loss, a deduction for dividends paid, and the ending balance of the Retained Earnings account. An example is shown below.

Retained Earnings, Jan. 1, 2017	$ 70,000
Add: Net Income	130,000
	$200,000
Less: Dividends	20,000
Retained Earnings, Dec. 31, 2017	$180,000

Checkpoint 12–1

1. What is a partnership?
2. Name five advantages of a corporation.

OBJECTIVE 12–2

Create Partnership Accounts and Enter Partnership Transactions

When a partnership is formed, it is necessary to establish a capital account for each partner and a drawing account for each partner. All other general ledger accounts are the same as those used for a sole proprietorship.

Billings Financial Services has operated as a sole proprietorship. However, John Billings, the owner, wants to expand operations and has decided to form a partnership with Molly Stone and Marjorie Brown. Both Stone and Brown have experience as financial managers and will provide additional capital.

According to the partnership agreement, Billings will contribute the assets of his sole proprietorship business as of January 2, 2018. Stone will contribute $20,000 in cash. Brown will contribute $15,000 in cash and $5,000 in office supplies. The partnership will assume the liabilities of Billings' sole proprietorship business. The starting date for the partnership is January 2, 2018.

Because Billings is contributing more capital than the other partners and because they will benefit from his prior work in establishing the business, profits will be shared unequally. The partnership agreement they establish specifies that Billings will receive 80% of the profits, Stone will receive 10%, and Brown will receive 10%. Losses will be shared in the same way.

Follow the steps outlined below to convert Billings Financial Services from a sole proprietorship to a partnership and set up the necessary capital and drawing accounts. Note that the individual (monthly) fiscal year should be closed before converting Billings Financial Services to a partnership.

Closing the Fiscal Year

The closing process is similar to the process for changing the accounting period. However, when the fiscal year is closed, the records are generally purged and the company information must be backed up to save the data for future use. Once the fiscal year is closed, it is difficult to access that information. Although it is not the end of Billings' fiscal year, the closing process will be conducted to make a logical progression to the partnership formation.

Step 1:

Open Chp. 12 – Billings Financial Services. Close the Action Items window if necessary.

Step 2:

Click Tasks, *System*, and then *Year-End Wizard*.

Step 3:

Click Yes at the opening query, "Do you still want to open the Year-End Wizard?" if asked.

Step 4:

At the Year-End Wizard – Welcome dialog box, click Next, as shown in Figure 12–1.

FIGURE 12–1
Year-End Wizard –
Welcome Dialog Box

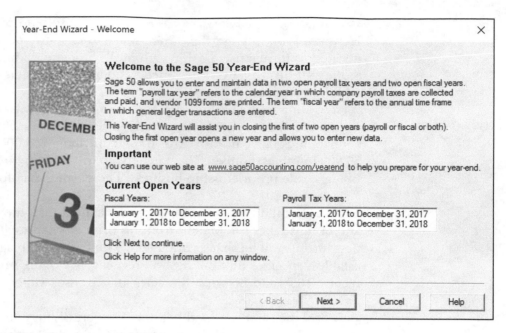

Step 5:

Click Next at the Year-End Wizard – Close Options dialog box to close the Fiscal and Payroll Tax Years, as shown in Figure 12–2.

FIGURE 12–2
Year-End Wizard – Close
Options Dialog Box

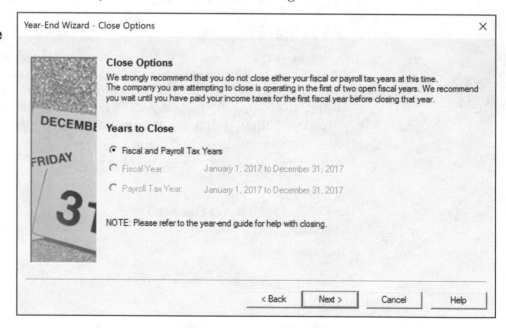

Step 6:

Click Check None and Next at the Year-End Wizard – Reports dialog box.

Step 7:

Click Next at the Year-End Wizard – Internal Accounting Review dialog box.

Step 8:

Click Back Up at the Year-End Wizard – Back Up dialog box. At the Back Up Company dialog box, select *Include company name in the backup file name,* as shown in Figure 12–3, then click Back Up.

FIGURE 12–3
Back Up Company Dialog Box

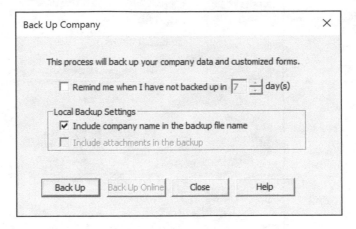

Step 9:

Click Save to accept the default file name and location to save the backup file for Billings Financial Services.

Step 10:

Click OK at the Sage 50 window indicating the size of the required backup file, and then click Next to proceed past the Year-End Wizard Back Up window.

Step 11:

Click Next at the Year-End Wizard – New Open Fiscal Years dialog box, as shown in Figure 12–4.

FIGURE 12–4
New Open Fiscal Years Dialog Box

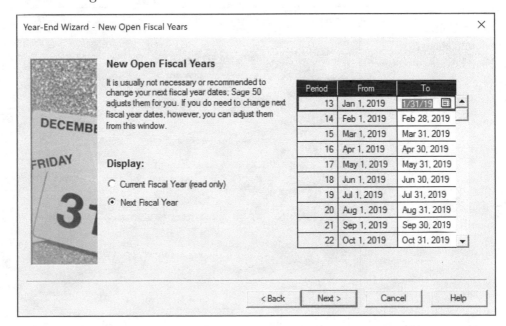

Step 12:

Click Next to confirm the closing of fiscal year 2017 and the opening of fiscal years 2018 and 2019, as shown in Figure 12–5.

FIGURE 12–5
Year-End Wizard –
Confirm Close
Dialog Box

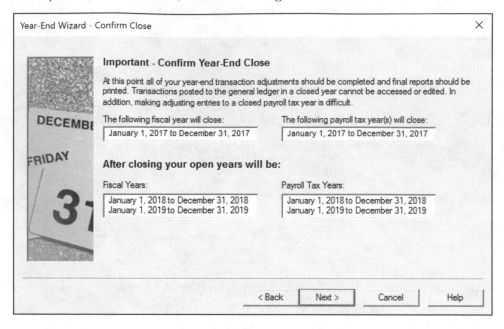

Step 13:

Click Begin Close at the Year-End Wizard – Begin Close dialog box to begin the closing process.

Step 14:

Finally, click Finish at the Year-End Wizard – Congratulations! dialog box, as shown in Figure 12–6.

FIGURE 12–6
Year-End Wizard –
Congratulations!
Dialog Box

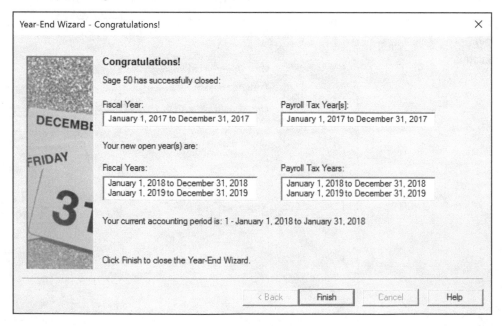

Converting to a Partnership and Creating the Partnership Accounts

Step 1:

Open Chp. 12 – Billings Financial Services, if needed.

Step 2:

Click Maintain and then click *Company Information.*

Step 3:

At the Maintain Company Information window, click the down arrow at the *Form of Business* field, and then click *Partnership,* as shown in Figure 12–7.

FIGURE 12–7
Partnership Selected as the Form of Business

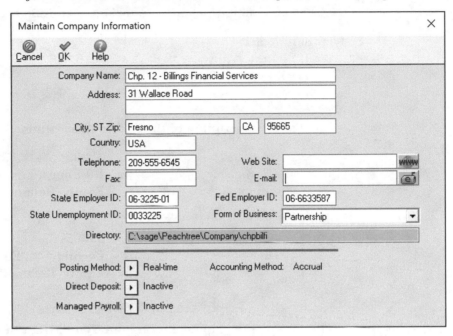

Step 4:

Click OK. The form of business has now been changed from a sole proprietorship to a partnership.

Step 5:

It is necessary to establish a capital account and a drawing account for each of the new partners. Create the following general ledger accounts:

Account ID:	**39026**
Description:	**M. Stone, Capital**
Account Type:	**Equity–doesn't close**
Account ID:	**39027**
Description:	**M. Stone, Drawing**
Account Type:	**Equity–gets closed**
Account ID:	**39046**
Description:	**M. Brown, Capital**
Account Type:	**Equity–doesn't close**

Account ID:	39047
Description:	**M. Brown, Drawing**
Account Type:	**Equity–gets closed**

Note: A balance of $16,546.34 in the J. Billings, Equity Account (39005) will be transferred to the J. Billings, Capital Account (39006) using the general journal entry below.

The $16,546.34 balance is John Billings' beginning capital at the formation of the partnership. This is standard procedure because he had earned this before he admitted partners into the business. It is not necessary to make the journal entry as it has already been made.

The general journal entry to make the transfer was:

January 1, 2018
| J. Billings, Equity | 16,546.34 | |
| J. Billings, Capital | | 16,546.34 |

Step 6:

Change the description of the following account:

Account ID:	39005
Description:	**J. Billings, Equity**
Account Type:	**Equity–Retained Earnings**

to:

Account ID:	39005
Description:	**Partnership, Equity**
Account Type:	**Equity–Retained Earnings**

Recording Partnership Transactions

The new partnership begins on January 1, 2018, when Molly Stone contributes $20,000 in cash and Marjorie Brown contributes $15,000 in cash and $5,000 in office supplies. Follow the steps outlined below to enter these partnership transactions.

Step 1:

Click Tasks and then *Receive Money.*

Step 2:

Select *Regular Checking Account* from the drop-down list at the Select a Cash Account dialog box. Then click OK.

Step 3:

At the Receive Money window, key **1/1/18** in the *Deposit ticket ID* field and key **Cash** in the *Customer ID* field.

Step 4:

Key **Partner** in the *Check/Reference No.* field.

Step 5:

At the *Date* field, click the *calendar* icon, and then select *Jan 1, 2018.*

Step 6:

Key **Partner contribution** in the first row of the *Description* field.

Step 7:

Key **20,000.00** in the *Amount* field, as shown in Figure 12–8.

FIGURE 12–8
Completed Receive Money Window

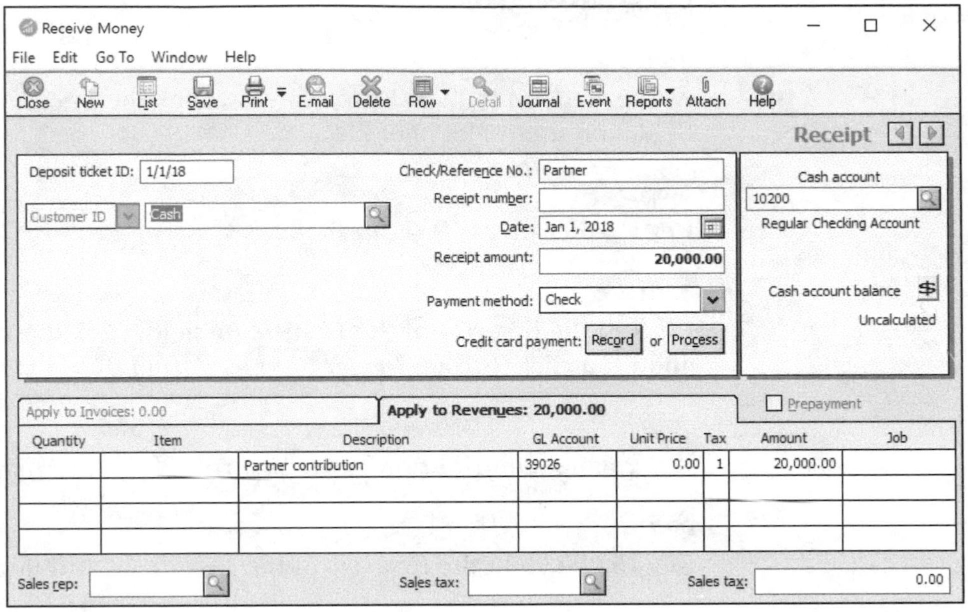

Step 8:

Click Journal on the Receive Money toolbar. The Accounting Behind the Screens window will appear. At the *Account No.* field in the first row, click the *magnifying glass* icon, and then select *39026, M. Stone, Capital.* Compare your screen with Figure 12–9.

FIGURE 12–9
Accounting Behind the Screens Window

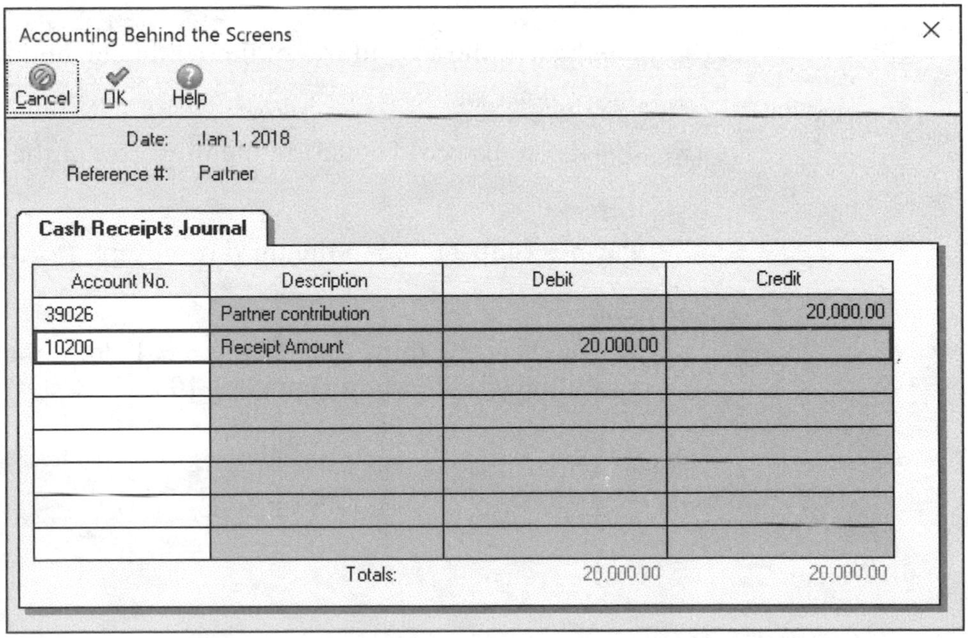

Step 9:

Click <u>O</u>K to close the Accounting Behind the Screens window.

Step 10:

Click <u>S</u>ave to save the entry, and then click Fast Add to create the cash account. Click Close.

Step 11:

Click Tasks and then click *General Journal Entry.*

Step 12:

At the General Journal Entry window, click the *calendar* icon at the <u>D</u>ate field, and then select *Jan 2, 2018.*

Step 13:

Key **Partner** in the *Refere<u>n</u>ce* field.

Step 14:

Click in the first row of the *GL Account* field, click the *magnifying glass* icon, and then click *10200, Regular Checking Account.*

Step 15:

Key **Partner contribution** in the first row of the *Description* field.

Step 16:

Key **15,000.00** in the first row of the *Debit* field, and tab to the next line.

Step 17:

Key **14000** (Prepaid Expenses) in the second row of the *GL Account* field.

Step 18:

Key **Partner contribution** in the second row of the *Description* field, if needed.

Step 19:

Key **5,000.00** in the second row of the *Debit* field, and tab to the next line.

Step 20:

Key **39046** (M. Brown, Capital) in the third row of the *GL Account* field.

Step 21:

Key **Partner contribution** in the third row of the *Description* field.

Step 22:

Key **20,000.00** in the third row of the *Credit* field. Compare your completed entry with the one shown in Figure 12–10.

FIGURE 12–10
Completed
General Journal
Entry for Partner
Contributions

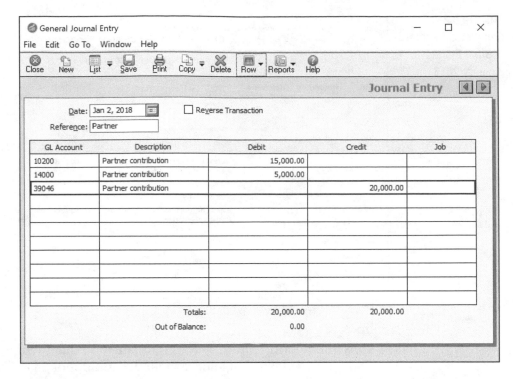

Step 23:

Click Save, and then click Close.

Allocating Partnership Profits and Losses

Billings Financial Services will allocate profits and losses to the partners in the following proportions: 80% to Billings, 10% to Stone, and 10% to Brown. Sage 50 does not automatically distribute profits and losses to the capital accounts of partners. You must make the distribution before the closing process.

Before we can look at how profits and losses are allocated at Billings Financial Services, we have to record the transactions for the month of January 2018.

Step 1:

Record the following transactions for January 2018 in the general journal using Account 10200 for all cash transactions. Then compare your completed entries with the ones shown on the General Journal report in Figure 12–11.

Jan. 10	Received $25,000 for brokerage services provided to customers. (Use Account 40200, Brokerage Fees Earned.)
12	Paid $1,400 for rent.
14	Paid $2,600 for utilities.
20	Molly Stone withdrew $1,500 for personal use.
21	Marjorie Brown withdrew $1,600 for personal use.

FIGURE 12–11

Completed General
Journal Entries
January 2018

Chp. 12 - Billings Financial Services
General Journal
For the Period From Jan 1, 2018 to Jan 31, 2018

Filter Criteria includes: Report order is by Date. Report is printed with Accounts having Zero Amounts and with shortened descriptions and in Detail Format.

Date	Account ID	Reference	Trans Description	Debit Amt	Credit Amt
1/1/18	39005		Transfer to capital	16,546.34	
	39006		Transfer to capital		16,546.34
1/2/18	10200	Partner	Partner contribution	15,000.00	
	14000		Partner contribution	5,000.00	
	39046		Partner contribution		20,000.00
1/10/18	10200		Received brokerage fees	25,000.00	
	40200		Received brokerage fees		25,000.00
1/12/18	74000		Paid monthly rent	1,400.00	
	10200		Paid monthly rent		1,400.00
1/14/18	78000		Paid monthly utilities	2,600.00	
	10200		Paid monthly utilities		2,600.00
1/20/18	39027		Partner draw	1,500.00	
	10200		Partner draw		1,500.00
1/21/18	39047		Partner draw	1,600.00	
	10200		Partner draw		1,600.00
		Total		**68,646.34**	**68,646.34**

Step 2:

Use the Report feature to review the income statement for the month of January 2018. Your income statement should look like the one shown in Figure 12–12.

FIGURE 12–12

Income Statement
for January 2018

Page: 1

Chp. 12 - Billings Financial Services
Income Statement
For the One Month Ending January 31, 2018

	Current Month			Year to Date	
Revenues					
Brokerage Fees Earned	$ 25,000.00	100.00	$	25,000.00	100.00
Total Revenues	25,000.00	100.00		25,000.00	100.00
Cost of Sales					
Total Cost of Sales	0.00	0.00		0.00	0.00
Gross Profit	25,000.00	100.00		25,000.00	100.00
Expenses					
Rent or Lease Expense	1,400.00	5.60		1,400.00	5.60
Utilities Expense	2,600.00	10.40		2,600.00	10.40
Total Expenses	4,000.00	16.00		4,000.00	16.00
Net Income	$ 21,000.00	84.00	$	21,000.00	84.00

Although the allocation of profit or loss from the Partnership Equity Account does not usually occur until the fiscal year is closed, it will be done at the end of January for educational purposes.

Notice that the income statement shows a net income (profit) of $21,000 for the month of January 2018. This net income must be distributed to the capital accounts of the partners as follows: $16,800 (80%) to Billings, $2,100 (10%) to Stone, and $2,100 (10%) to Brown. The entry to distribute the net income involves a debit of $21,000 to Partnership Equity (Account 39005) and a credit to each of the capital accounts for the appropriate amount. Partnership Equity takes the place of Income Summary in Billings' accounting system. Its balance at the end of the accounting period represents the firm's net income or net loss for the period.

Step 3:

Click Tasks and then click *General Journal Entry.*

Step 4:

Record the entry needed to distribute the net income to the capital accounts of each of the partners. Compare your completed entry with the one shown in Figure 12–13.

FIGURE 12–13
Completed Entry for Distribution of Net Income to Partners

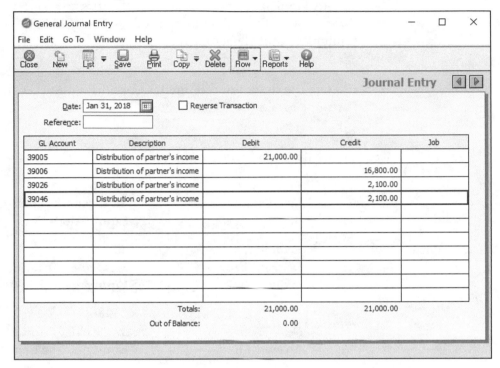

Step 5:

Click Save and then Close.

Checkpoint 12–2

1. What two general ledger accounts are required for each partner?
2. What accounts are credited when net income is distributed to partners?

Objective 12–2 Practice

On January 1, 2018, James Overland of Overland Management Services will form a partnership with Michael Green and Mitchell Norris. Overland will contribute the assets of his business, Green will contribute $30,000 in cash, and Norris will contribute $20,000 in cash and $10,000 in office equipment. The partnership will assume the liabilities of Overland's business. Profits and losses will be allocated in the following proportions: 70% to Overland, 15% to Green, and 15% to Norris.

Step 1:

Open Chp. 12 – Overland Management Services.

Step 2:

Change the form of business to a partnership.

Step 3:

Create a journal entry as of January 2, 2018, to transfer the balance of $10,629.06 in the J. Overland, Equity account (39005) to the J. Overland, Capital account (39006).

Step 4:

Change the description of the J. Overland, Equity account (39005) to the Partnership, Equity account.

Step 5:

Create the following accounts:

Account ID:	**39036**
Description:	**M. Green, Capital**
Account Type:	**Equity–doesn't close**

Account ID:	**39037**
Description:	**M. Green, Drawing**
Account Type:	**Equity–gets closed**

Account ID:	**39046**
Description:	**M. Norris, Capital**
Account Type:	**Equity–doesn't close**

Account ID:	**39047**
Description:	**M. Norris, Drawing**
Account Type:	**Equity–gets closed**

Step 6:

Journalize the contributions of Green and Norris as of January 2, 2018.

Step 7:

Journalize the following transactions that occurred in January 2018 using Account 10200 for all cash transactions.

Jan. 10 Received $50,000 for management services provided to customers. (Credit Account 40000, Consulting Fees.)

12 Paid $3,400 for rent.

14 Paid $4,600 for utilities.

Step 8:

Review the Income Statement for the period ending 1/31/2018.

Step 9:

Journalize the distribution of $42,000 of net income on January 31, 2018. Transfer the partnership equity balance to the capital accounts of the partners according to the allocation agreement regarding profits and losses.

Create Corporate Accounts and Enter Corporate Transactions

Legaleze Law Firm, Inc. has obtained a corporate charter from the State of California and is now ready to begin operations. It will do research and prepare documents for law firms and the legal departments of large companies.

The corporate charter authorizes Legaleze to issue 1 million shares of $1 par-value common stock and 25,000 shares of $100 par-value, 5% noncumulative preferred stock. The preferred stock pays an annual dividend of $5 per share (5% of $100). This stock is called *noncumulative* because unpaid dividends do not accumulate from year to year. If the corporation is not able to pay the dividend one year, it does not have to add the unpaid amount to the next year's dividend.

Setting Up a Corporation in Sage 50

Legaleze plans to use Sage 50 to keep its accounting records. Therefore, its first task is to complete Sage 50's new company setup procedure.

Step 1:

Set up a new company in Sage 50 using the company information found in Figure 12–14.

FIGURE 12–14
Create a New Company –
Company Information
Dialog Box

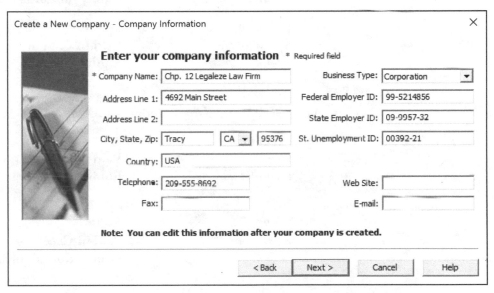

Step 2:
Select Legal Firm as the business type to create a chart of accounts.

Step 3:
Select Accrual as the Accounting Method.

Step 4:
Select Real Time as the Posting Method.

Step 5:
Select 12 Monthly Accounting Periods.

Step 6:

Select January 2018 as the date of the first monthly accounting period.

Step 7:

Accept all other defaults.

Creating Corporate Accounts

Legaleze will use a sample corporate chart of accounts for a legal firm provided by Sage 50. This chart of accounts includes general ledger accounts for common stock. However, because Legaleze plans to issue preferred stock as well as common stock, it must add the following accounts: Preferred Stock and Paid-in Capital in Excess of Par—Preferred.

Remember that when preferred stock is issued for more than its par value, two stockholders' equity accounts are affected. Preferred Stock is used to record the par-value amount of the shares issued. Paid-in Capital in Excess of Par—Preferred is used to record the amount received that is above par value.

Step 1:

Create the following general ledger accounts:

Account ID:	**39000**
Description:	**Preferred Stock**
Account Type:	**Equity–doesn't close**

Account ID:	**39001**
Description:	**Paid-in Capital in Excess-PS**
Account Type:	**Equity–doesn't close**

Step 2:

Change the following general ledger account:

Account ID:	**39004**
Description:	**Paid-in Capital**
Account Type:	**Equity–doesn't close**

to:

Account ID:	**39004**
Description:	**Paid-in Capital in Excess-CS**
Account Type:	**Equity–doesn't close**

Step 3:

View the newly created stock accounts on the firm's chart of accounts. Compare them with the stockholders' equity accounts shown in Figure 12–15. Make any necessary corrections.

FIGURE 12–15
Partial Chart of
Accounts with Newly
Created Accounts

Chp. 12 Legaleze Law Firm
Chart of Accounts
As of Jan 31, 2018
Filter Criteria includes: Report order is by ID. Report is printed with Accounts having Zero Amounts and in Detail Format.

Account ID	Account Description	Active?	Account Type
23400	Federal Payroll Taxes Paya	Yes	Other Current Liabilities
23500	FUTA Tax Payable	Yes	Other Current Liabilities
23600	State Payroll Taxes Payabl	Yes	Other Current Liabilities
23700	SUTA Payable	Yes	Other Current Liabilities
23800	Local Payroll Taxes Payabl	Yes	Other Current Liabilities
23900	Income Taxes Payable	Yes	Other Current Liabilities
24000	Other Taxes Payable	Yes	Other Current Liabilities
24100	Employee Benefits Payabl	Yes	Other Current Liabilities
24200	Current Portion Long-Term	Yes	Other Current Liabilities
24400	Client Escrow Funds	Yes	Other Current Liabilities
24800	Other Current Liabilities	Yes	Other Current Liabilities
24900	Suspense-Clearing Accou	Yes	Other Current Liabilities
27000	Notes Payable-Noncurrent	Yes	Long Term Liabilities
27400	Other Long-Term Liabilitie	Yes	Long Term Liabilities
39000	Preferred Stock	Yes	Equity-doesn't close
39001	Paid-in Capital in Excess-	Yes	Equity-doesn't close
39003	Common Stock	Yes	Equity-doesn't close
39004	Paid-in Capital in Excess-	Yes	Equity-doesn't close
39005	Retained Earnings	Yes	Equity-Retained Earnings
39007	Dividends Paid	Yes	Equity-gets closed
40000	Fee Income-Corporate	Yes	Income
40200	Fee Income-Labor	Yes	Income
40400	Fee Income-Litigation	Yes	Income
40600	Fee Income-Real Estate	Yes	Income
40800	Fee Income-Taxation	Yes	Income

Entering Corporate Transactions—Issuing Common Stock

On January 2, 2018, Legaleze issued 50,000 shares of its $1 par-value common stock for $10 per share. It received $500,000 in cash. The entry for this transaction requires a debit of $500,000 to Cash, a credit of $50,000 to Common Stock (50,000 shares × $1 par value), and a credit of $450,000 to Paid-in Capital in Excess of Par—Common Stock (50,000 shares × $9).

Step 1:
Click Tasks and then click *General Journal Entry.*

Step 2:
At the General Journal Entry window, at the *Date* field, click the *calendar* icon, and then select *Jan 2, 2018.*

Step 3:
At the *GL Account* field, click the *magnifying glass* icon, and then click *Regular Checking Account (10200)* as the account to be debited. (Legaleze uses Regular Checking Account as its main cash account.)

HINT
This entry can also be made in the cash receipts journal by using the Accounting Behind the Screens feature.

Step 4:
Key **Issued 50,000 shares of common stock** in the *Description* field.

Step 5:
Key **500,000.00** in the *Debit* field.

Step 6:

Tab to the next row and click *Common Stock (39003)* as the first account to be credited.

Step 7:

Key **50,000.00** in the *Credit* field. This amount represents the par value of the 50,000 shares issued (50,000 × $1).

Step 8:

Tab to the next row and click *Paid-in Capital in Excess – CS (39004)* as the second account to be credited.

Step 9:

Key **450,000.00** in the *Credit* field. This amount represents the difference between the issue price and the par value of the 50,000 shares ($10 – $1 = $9 × 50,000 = $450,000). Compare your completed entry with the one that appears in Figure 12–16.

FIGURE 12–16
Journal Entry for the Issuance of Common Stock

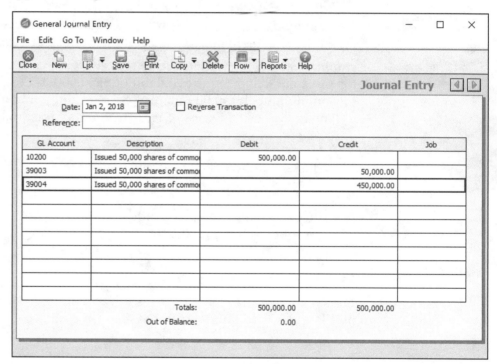

Step 10:

Click **S**ave and Close.

Entering Corporate Transactions—Receiving Donated Capital

Sometimes a state, county, or city will donate an asset such as land or an unused building to a business. This donation is made for the purpose of economic development—so that the business will establish or expand operations in the area and create jobs for local residents.

For example, on January 5, 2018, the City of Tracy donated a parcel of land valued at $150,000 to Legaleze Law Firm, Inc. The firm will use this land to construct a building that will allow it to expand its staff. (The firm is currently renting an office with limited space.)

To record this transaction, it is necessary to debit Land for $150,000 and credit a stockholders' equity account called Donated Capital for $150,000. Donated capital will appear in the Stockholders' Equity section of the balance sheet along with paid-in capital (the capital supplied by investors through their purchases of stock) and retained earnings (the accumulated profits of the firm less dividends paid).

Step 1:

Create a general ledger account for donated capital. (Replace the account that is currently using 39005 as its ID.)

Account ID:	**39005**
Description:	**Donated Capital**
Account Type:	**Equity–doesn't close**

Create a new account for retained earnings, which was previously Account 39005:

Account ID:	**39006**
Description:	**Retained Earnings**
Account Type:	**Equity–Retained Earnings**

Step 2:

Click Save and Close.

Step 3:

Click Tasks and then click *General Journal Entry.*

Step 4:

At the General Journal Entry window, in the *Date* field, click the *calendar* icon and then select *Jan 5, 2018.*

Step 5:

Click in the *GL Account* field, click the *magnifying glass* icon, and then click *Land (16900).*

Step 6:

Key **Received donation of land** in the *Description* field.

Step 7:

Key **150,000.00** in the *Debit* field and tab down to the next row.

Step 8:

Click the *magnifying glass* icon and then *Donated Capital (39005)* in the *GL Account* field.

Step 9:

Key **150,000.00** in the *Credit* field. Compare your completed entry with the one that appears in Figure 12–17.

FIGURE 12–17

Journal Entry for a
Donation of Land

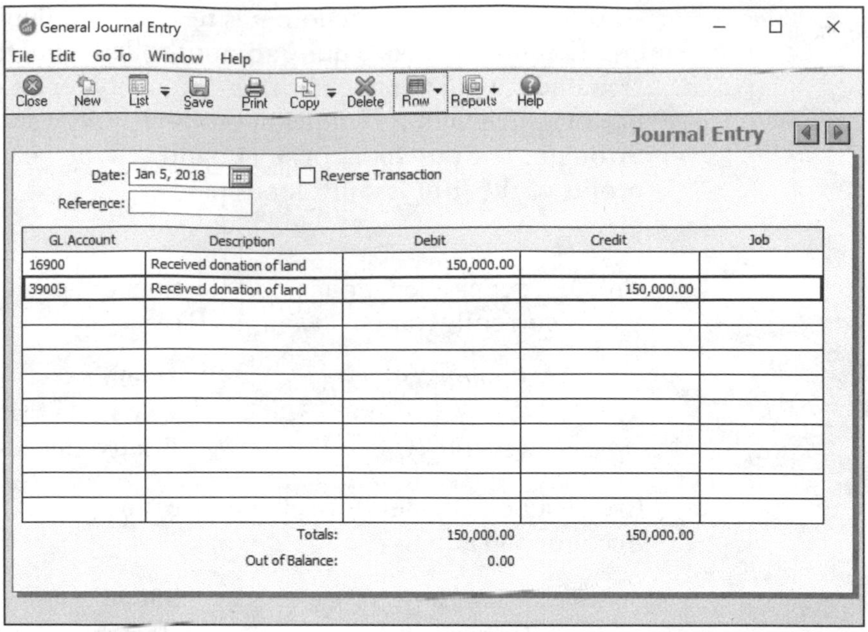

```
General Journal Entry                                    —  □  ×
File  Edit  Go To  Window  Help

  Close   New   List   Save   Print   Copy   Delete   Row   Reports   Help

                                                    Journal Entry   ◄  ►

        Date:  Jan 5, 2018   ▦      ☐ Reverse Transaction
   Reference:

  GL Account      Description          Debit          Credit         Job
  16900      Received donation of land   150,000.00
  39005      Received donation of land                  150,000.00




                        Totals:        150,000.00      150,000.00
                   Out of Balance:           0.00
```

Step 10:

Click Save and Close to save the entry.

Entering Corporate Transactions—General Transactions

Legaleze had the following revenue and expense transactions during the
month of January 2018.

Jan. 10   Received fees of $10,000 in cash for corporate legal
          services performed.
15   Paid $2,500 for rent.
16   Paid $565 for utilities.
20   Paid $1,200 for professional development costs.

Step 1:

Record the transactions in the general journal. Then compare your entries
with Figure 12–18.

FIGURE 12–18

Journal Entries
for Revenue
and Expense
Transactions

```
9/25/16 at 06:19:29.11    *****EDUCATIONAL VERSION ONLY*****                          Page: 1
                              Chp. 12 Legaleze Law Firm
                                  General Journal
                        For the Period From Jan 1, 2018 to Jan 31, 2018
Filter Criteria includes: Report order is by Date. Report is printed with Accounts having Zero Amounts and with shortened descriptions and in Detail Format.
```

Date	Account ID	Reference	Trans Description	Debit Amt	Credit Amt
1/2/18	10200		Issued 50,000 shares of common sto	500,000.00	
	39003		Issued 50,000 shares of common sto		50,000.00
	39004		Issued 50,000 shares of common sto		450,000.00
1/5/18	16900		Received donation of land	150,000.00	
	39005		Received donation of land		150,000.00
1/10/18	10200		Received fees for corporate legal ser	10,000.00	
	40000		Received fees for corporate legal ser		10,000.00
1/15/18	76000		Paid rent	2,500.00	
	10200		Paid rent		2,500.00
1/16/18	79000		Paid utilities	565.00	
	10200		Paid utilities		565.00
1/20/18	74500		Professional development costs	1,200.00	
	10200		Professional development costs		1,200.00
		Total		**664,265.00**	**664,265.00**

Step 2:

Click Close.

Declaring a Cash Dividend

On January 30, 2018, Legaleze declares a cash dividend of $0.10 per share of common stock outstanding. The dividend is payable on February 20, 2018. Because there are 50,000 shares of common stock outstanding, the total amount of the dividend will be $5,000 (50,000 × $0.10 = $5,000).

The declaration of the dividend creates a liability for Legaleze to its stockholders. To record this transaction, the firm must debit Cash Dividends for $5,000 and credit Dividends Payable for $5,000. Remember that Cash Dividends is a contra stockholders' equity account and Dividends Payable is a liability account.

When the dividend is paid, Legaleze will debit Dividends Payable for $5,000 and credit Cash for $5,000. This entry eliminates the liability.

Step 1:

Create the following general ledger account:

Account ID:	**24300**
Description:	**Dividends Payable**
Account Type:	**Other Current Liabilities**

Change the following general ledger account from:

Account ID:	**39007**
Description:	**Dividends Paid**
Account Type:	**Equity–gets closed**

to:

Account ID:	**39007**
Description:	**Cash Dividends**
Account Type:	**Equity–gets closed**

Step 2:

Record the declaration of the cash dividend in the general journal. Then compare your entry with Figure 12–19.

FIGURE 12–19
Journal Entry for
Declaration of a Cash
Dividend

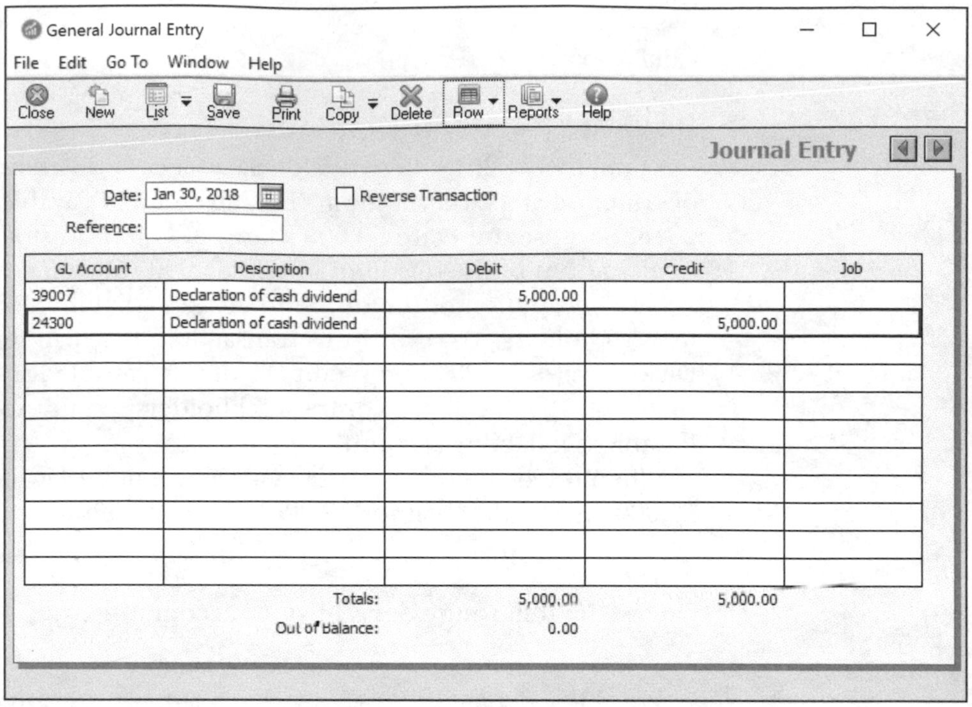

General Journal Entry

File   Edit   Go To   Window   Help

Close   New   List   Save   Print   Copy   Delete   Row   Reports   Help

Journal Entry

Date: Jan 30, 2018   ☐ Reverse Transaction
Reference:

GL Account	Description	Debit	Credit	Job
39007	Declaration of cash dividend	5,000.00		
24300	Declaration of cash dividend		5,000.00	
	Totals:	5,000.00	5,000.00	
	Out of Balance:	0.00		

Step 3:

Click Save and Close to save the entry.

Checkpoint 12–3

1. What two types of stock can a corporation issue?
2. What account is credited when a cash dividend is declared?

Objective 12–3 Practice

Abacus Executive Search, Inc., is a new corporation that will use Sage 50 Accounting 2017. On January 2, 2018, Abacus received its corporate charter. This charter authorizes the firm to issue 450,000 shares of $2 par-value common stock and 20,000 shares of $50 par value, 6% preferred stock.

Step 1:

Complete the new company setup procedure for Abacus. Use the information provided in Figure 12–20.

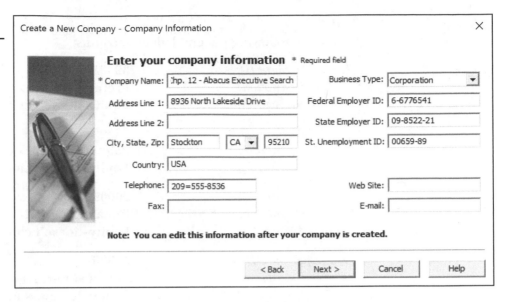

FIGURE 12–21
Create a New
Company – Fiscal
Year Window

Step 2:

Use a sample company Chart of Accounts, and click *Employment Agency* as the type of business.

Step 3:

Use accrual accounting and real-time posting.

Step 4:

Use a fiscal year of 12 monthly accounting periods. Set up the monthly periods as shown in Figure 12–21.

Step 5:

Accept all other defaults.

Step 6:

Create the following general ledger accounts:

Account ID:	**39001**
Description:	**Preferred Stock**
Account Type:	**Equity–doesn't close**

Account ID:	**39002**
Description:	**Paid-in Capital in Excess-PS**
Account Type:	**Equity–doesn't close**

Account ID:	**39005**
Description:	**Donated Capital**
Account Type:	**Equity–doesn't close**

Account ID:	**39006**
Description:	**Retained Earnings**
Account Type:	**Equity–Retained Earnings**

Account ID:	**24300**
Description:	**Dividends Payable**
Account Type:	**Other Current Liabilities**

Change the following general ledger account from:

Account ID:	**39004**
Description:	**Paid-in Capital**
Account Type:	**Equity–doesn't close**

to:

Account ID:	**39004**
Description:	**Paid-in Capital in Excess-CS**
Account Type:	**Equity–doesn't close**

Change the following general ledger account from:

Account ID:	**39007**
Description:	**Dividends Paid**
Account Type:	**Equity–gets closed**

to:

Account ID:	**39007**
Description:	**Cash Dividends**
Account Type:	**Equity–gets closed**

Step 7:

Abacus had the following transactions during the month of January 2018. Record these transactions in the general journal using Account 10200 for all cash transactions.

Jan. 3	Issued 45,000 shares of $2 par-value common stock for $300,000 in cash.
4	Issued 3,000 shares of $50 par-value preferred stock for $200,000 in cash.
5	Received land valued at $54,000 as a donation from the City of Stockton.

10	Received fees of $20,000 in cash for professional placement services performed.
15	Paid rent of $4,500.
16	Paid utilities of $1,565.
20	Paid professional dues of $1,200 (Account 64500, Dues and Subscriptions Exp).
21	Paid license fees of $1,345.
31	Declared a $4,500 cash dividend to all common stockholders. This dividend is payable on Feb. 15 at a rate of $0.10 per share. (The preferred stockholders do not receive a dividend until year-end.)

Step 8:

Review your work and make any necessary corrections. Then save the entries.

OBJECTIVE 12-4

Print Partnership and Corporate Reports

Every business—sole proprietorship, partnership, and corporation—prepares an income statement and a balance sheet at the end of the accounting period. Remember that the *income statement* reports the results of operations for the accounting period—the revenue, expenses, and net income or net loss. The *balance sheet* reports the financial condition of the business as of a specific day of the accounting period—the assets, liabilities, and owner's equity.

These statements are essentially the same for all types of business organizations. The one major difference is the treatment of owner's equity on the balance sheet, as will be seen on the next few pages.

Partnerships and corporations may also prepare certain supplemental statements. For example, a corporation may prepare a statement of retained earnings that shows the changes in its retained earnings during the accounting period.

income statement
A report of a firm's revenue, expenses, and net income or net loss for an accounting period.

balance sheet A report of a firm's assets, liabilities, and owner's equity as of a specific date.

Preparing a Partnership Report

The balance sheet of a partnership shows the capital and cash withdrawals of each partner. A separate statement that explains the changes that took place in the partnership's equity during the accounting period may supplement this information. Such a statement usually includes the beginning balance of each partner's capital account, each partner's share of the net income or net loss for the period, each partner's withdrawals for this period, and the ending balance of each partner's capital account. This report is usually known as a statement of partners' equity.

Follow the steps outlined below to prepare a balance sheet for the partnership of Billings Financial Services. (The income statement for this partnership appeared earlier in Figure 12–12.)

Step 1:

Open Chp. 12 – Billings Financial Services, which you updated previously in the chapter.

Step 2:

Click Reports & Forms and then click *Financial Statements.*

Step 3:

In the Financial Statements: Balance Sheets and Income Statements section, click *<Standard> Balance Sheet.*

Step 4:

Display the balance sheet with a date of January 31, 2018. Examine the Capital section of the balance sheet, which shows the partners' equity. There is a separate capital account for each partner, as shown in Figure 12–22.

**FIGURE 12–22
Partners' Equity on
the Balance Sheet**

Chp. 12 - Billings Financial Services
Balance Sheet
January 31, 2018

ASSETS

Current Assets		
Regular Checking Account	$ 69,446.34	
Prepaid Expenses	5,000.00	
Total Current Assets		74,446.34
Property and Equipment		
Total Property and Equipment		0.00
Other Assets		
Total Other Assets		0.00
Total Assets		$ 74,446.34

LIABILITIES AND CAPITAL

Current Liabilities		
Total Current Liabilities		0.00
Long-Term Liabilities		
Total Long-Term Liabilities		0.00
Total Liabilities		0.00
Capital		
Partnership, Equity	$ (21,000.00)	
J. Billings - Capital	33,346.34	
M. Stone, Capital	22,100.00	
M. Stone, Drawing	(1,500.00)	
M. Brown, Capital	22,100.00	
M. Brown, Drawing	(1,600.00)	
Net Income	21,000.00	
Total Capital		74,446.34
Total Liabilities & Capital		$ 74,446.34

Step 5:

Print the report, if desired. Then close the display window.

Preparing a Corporate Report

As noted previously, the balance sheet of a corporation contains a Stockholders' Equity section. This section shows the various types and amounts of capital that the corporation has as of a specific date. The three basic types of corporate capital are paid-in capital, earned capital, and donated capital.

Remember that paid-in capital is the capital received from stockholders through their purchases of common and preferred stock. Earned capital consists of accumulated earnings from the firm's operations. Donated capital comes from assets that are donated to a corporation by a state, county, or city.

The statement of retained earnings reports the changes that took place in retained earnings during the accounting period. It shows the beginning balance of the Retained Earnings account, an addition for net income or a deduction for a net loss, a deduction for dividends paid, and the ending balance of the Retained Earnings account.

Follow the steps outlined below to prepare a balance sheet for Legaleze Law Firm, Inc.

Step 1:

Open Chp. 12 – Legaleze Law Firm, Inc., which you created previously in the chapter.

Step 2:

Click Reports & Forms and then click *Financial Statements.*

Step 3:

In the Financial Statements: Balance Sheets and Income Statements section, click *<Standard> Balance Sheet.*

Step 4:

Display the balance sheet with a date of January 31, 2018. Examine the Capital section of the balance sheet, which shows the stockholders' equity. It should resemble Figure 12–23.

FIGURE 12–23
Stockholders' Equity on the Balance Sheet

Chp. 12 Legaleze Law Firm		
Balance Sheet		
January 31, 2018		
ASSETS		
Current Assets		
Regular Checking Account	$ 505,735.00	
Total Current Assets		505,735.00
Property and Equipment		
Land	150,000.00	
Total Property and Equipment		150,000.00
Other Assets		
Total Other Assets		0.00
Total Assets		$ 655,735.00
LIABILITIES AND CAPITAL		
Current Liabilities		
Dividends Payable	$ 5,000.00	
Total Current Liabilities		5,000.00
Long-Term Liabilities		
Total Long-Term Liabilities		0.00
Total Liabilities		5,000.00
Capital		
Common Stock	50,000.00	
Paid-in Capital in Excess-CS	450,000.00	
Donated Capital	150,000.00	
Cash Dividends	(5,000.00)	
Net Income	5,735.00	
Total Capital		650,735.00
Total Liabilities & Capital		$ 655,735.00

Step 5:

Close the display window.

1. What accounts appear in the equity section of the balance sheet for a partnership?
2. What are the three basic types of capital for a corporation?

Objective 12–4 Practice

Step 1:

Open Chp. 12 – Abacus Executive Search, Inc., which you created previously in the chapter.

Step 2:

Print the income statement, the balance sheet, and the statement of retained earnings for the month of January 2018. Your printouts should look like Figures 12–24, 12–25, and 12–26, respectively.

FIGURE 12–24
Income Statement for Abacus Executive Search, Inc.

Page: 1

Chp. 12 - Abacus Executive Search
Income Statement
For the One Month Ending January 31, 2018

	Current Month			Year to Date	
Revenues					
Professional placement fees/co	$ 20,000.00	100.00	$	20,000.00	100.00
Total Revenues	20,000.00	100.00		20,000.00	100.00
Cost of Sales					
Total Cost of Sales	0.00	0.00		0.00	0.00
Gross Profit	20,000.00	100.00		20,000.00	100.00
Expenses					
Dues and Subscriptions Exp	1,200.00	6.00		1,200.00	6.00
Licenses Expense	1,345.00	6.73		1,345.00	6.73
Rent or Lease Expense	4,500.00	22.50		4,500.00	22.50
Utilities Expense	1,565.00	7.83		1,565.00	7.83
Total Expenses	8,610.00	43.05		8,610.00	43.05
Net Income	$ 11,390.00	56.95	$	11,390.00	56.95

FIGURE 12–25

Balance Sheet for Abacus Executive Search, Inc.

Chp. 12 - Abacus Executive Search
Balance Sheet
January 31, 2018

ASSETS

Current Assets		
Regular Checking Account	$ 511,390.00	
Total Current Assets		511,390.00
Property and Equipment		
Land	54,000.00	
Total Property and Equipment		54,000.00
Other Assets		
Total Other Assets		0.00
Total Assets		$ 565,390.00

LIABILITIES AND CAPITAL

Current Liabilities		
Dividends Payable	$ 4,500.00	
Total Current Liabilities		4,500.00
Long-Term Liabilities		
Total Long-Term Liabilities		0.00
Total Liabilities		4,500.00
Capital		
Preferred Stock	150,000.00	
Paid-in Capital in Excess-PS	50,000.00	
Common Stock	90,000.00	
Paid-in Capital in Excess-CS	210,000.00	
Donated Capital	54,000.00	
Cash Dividends	(4,500.00)	
Net Income	11,390.00	
Total Capital		560,890.00
Total Liabilities & Capital		$ 565,390.00

FIGURE 12–26

Statement of Retained Earnings for Abacus Executive Search, Inc.

Page: 1

Chp. 12 - Abacus Executive Search
Statement of Retained Earnings
For the One Month Ending January 31, 2018

Beginning Retained Earnings	$ 0.00
Adjustments To Date	0.00
Net Income	11,390.00
Subtotal	11,390.00
Cash Dividends	(4,500.00)
Ending Retained Earnings	$ 6,890.00

Chapter Review and Assessment

Software Command Summary

Change Organization Type	Maintain, Company Information, Change the Form of Business
Edit Account Information	Maintain, Chart of Accounts, Enter the Changes, Save
Print Financial Statements	Reports & Forms, Financial Statements, Select the Report Type

Checkpoint Answers

Checkpoint 12–1

1. A partnership is a business owned by two or more people.
2. Five advantages of a corporation are ease of raising capital, limited liability, continuous life, no mutual agency rule, and professional management.

Checkpoint 12–2

1. A capital account and a drawing account are required for each partner.
2. The capital accounts of the partners are credited (increased) when net income is distributed.

Checkpoint 12–3

1. A corporation can issue common stock and preferred stock.
2. The account credited is Dividends Payable.

Checkpoint 12–4

1. The accounts that appear in the equity section are the capital and drawing accounts of the partners.
2. The three basic types of capital for a corporation are paid-in capital, earned capital, and donated capital.

Study Quizzes

Take the study quiz online to check your understanding of chapter concepts. The quiz can be taken multiple times.

Content Check

Multiple Choice: Choose only one response for each question.

1. The equity section of the balance sheet for a partnership must show the
   A. liabilities.
   B. assets.
   C. capital of each partner.
   D. expenses.

2. Unless otherwise stated, partners share profits and losses
   A. according to their capital balances.
   B. according to the amount of time spent at the firm by each partner.
   C. based on the amount of business each partner generates.
   D. equally.

3. Which of the following is a disadvantage of the partnership form of organization?
   A. Ease of formation
   B. Greater management expertise than a sole proprietorship
   C. Mutual agency rule
   D. Less regulation and taxation than a corporation

4. Which of the following is a disadvantage of a corporation?
   A. Limited liability
   B. Ease of raising capital
   C. Continuous life
   D. Double taxation

5. Which of the following accounts would *not* be found in the equity section of a corporation's balance sheet?
   A. Common Stock
   B. Donated Capital
   C. Preferred Stock
   D. Dividends Payable

Short Essay Response

Provide a detailed answer for each question.

1. What is the par value of stock? What is the market value?
2. What is a partnership? What are the advantages and disadvantages of this type of business organization?
3. What is the difference between authorized and outstanding stock?
4. What is a dividend?
5. What is the paid-in capital of a corporation? What is the earned capital?
6. What information appears on the statement of retained earnings for a corporation?

Cooperative Learning

1. In groups of three or four students, research both the Small Business Administration website at http://sba.gov and the IRS website at http://irs.gov to find information related to starting a business.

2. In groups of three or four students, research the requirements for obtaining a corporate charter in your state. Check the website of your state or the office of your Secretary of State. Prepare a list of the requirements.

Writing and Decision Making

Bruce Cho, the owner of a sole proprietorship software business, would like to expand operations. He needs additional capital to develop new products. He is thinking of forming a corporation. In memo form, briefly explain the advantages and disadvantages of a corporation to Bruce Cho.

Case Problems

Demonstrate your knowledge of the Sage 50 features discussed in this chapter by completing the following case problems.

Case Problem 12–1A

On January 2, 2017, Jim Mathews and Gary Corbett formed a partnership. They will operate a business called ABC Collection Service. Each will contribute $30,000 in cash. Profits and losses will be divided equally.

1. Use the information in Figure 12–27 and the information given below to set up the business in Sage 50.

FIGURE 12–27
Setup Information for ABC Collection Service

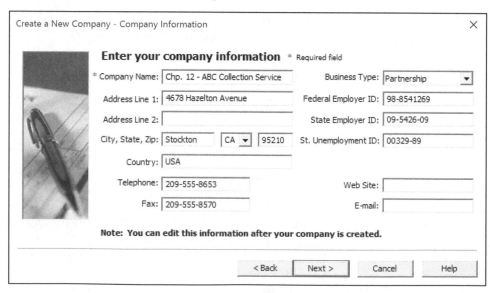

Chart of Accounts:	**(Detailed Type) Service Company**
Accounting Method:	**Accrual**
Posting Method:	**Real Time**
Accounting Periods:	**12 Monthly Accounting Periods**
Fiscal Year to Start:	**January 2017**

2. Establish the capital and drawing accounts needed by the partnership.

Create the following general ledger accounts:

Account ID:	**39008**
Description:	**Gary Corbett, Capital**
Account Type:	**Equity–doesn't close**

Account ID:	**39009**
Description:	**Gary Corbett, Drawing**
Account Type:	**Equity–gets closed**

Change the following general ledger account from:

Account ID:	**39006**
Description:	**Partner's Contribution**
Account Type:	**Equity–gets closed**

to:

Account ID:	**39006**
Description:	**Jim Mathews, Capital**
Account Type:	**Equity–doesn't close**

Change the following general ledger account from:

Account ID:	**39007**
Description:	**Partner's Draw**
Account Type:	**Equity–gets closed**

to:

Account ID:	**39007**
Description:	**Jim Mathews, Drawing**
Account Type:	**Equity–gets closed**

3. Change the accounting period to January 2017.

4. Journalize the following transactions for the month of January. (Use the general journal and Regular Checking Account.)

Jan. 2	Mathews contributed $30,000 in cash, and Corbett contributed $30,000 in cash.
10	Had cash sales of $23,000 for professional fees from customers.
11	Paid rent of $4,500.
15	Paid utilities of $1,500.
20	Mathews withdrew $1,000 in cash, and Corbett withdrew $1,000 in cash.

5. Print the following financial statements as of January 31, 2017: the income statement, balance sheet, and statement of retained earnings.

Case Problem 12–2A

On January 2, 2017, General Consulting, Inc. received its corporate charter, which authorizes it to issue up to 2 million shares of $1 par-value common stock and 50,000 shares of $100 par-value, 6%, cumulative preferred stock.

1. Open General Consulting, Inc. from the student data files.

2. Journalize the following transactions for the month of January 2017. (Use the general journal and Regular Checking Account.)

Jan. 3	Issued 30,000 shares of common stock for $300,000 in cash.
10	Had cash sales of $23,000 for consulting services provided to customers.
11	Paid rent of $6,000.
15	Paid utilities of $600.
31	Declared a cash dividend of $0.20 for each share of common stock outstanding. (Create the Dividends Payable account, Account ID 24300. Change the Dividends Paid account into the Cash Dividends account.)

3. Print the following financial statements as of January 31, 2017: the income statement, balance sheet, and statement of retained earnings.

Case Problem 12–1B

On January 2, 2017, Terry Jones and Carol Smith formed a partnership. They will operate a business called CBA Résumé Service. Each will contribute $25,000 in cash. Profits and losses will be divided equally.

1. Use the information in Figure 12–28 and the information given below to set up the business in Sage 50.

FIGURE 12–28
Setup Information for CBA Résumé Service

Chart of Accounts:	**(Detailed Type) Service Company**	
Accounting Method:	**Accrual**	
Posting Method:	**Real Time**	
Accounting Periods:	**12 Monthly Accounting Periods**	
Fiscal Year to Start:	**January 2017**	

2. Establish the capital and drawing accounts needed by the partnership.

Create the following general ledger accounts:

Account ID:	**39008**
Description:	**Terry Jones, Capital**
Account Type:	**Equity–doesn't close**

Account ID:	**39009**
Description:	**Terry Jones, Drawing**
Account Type:	**Equity–gets closed**

Change the following general ledger account from:

Account ID:	**39006**
Description:	**Partner's Contribution**
Account Type:	**Equity–gets closed**

to:

Account ID:	**39006**
Description:	**Carol Smith, Capital**
Account Type:	**Equity–doesn't close**

Change the following general ledger account from:

Account ID:	**39007**
Description:	**Partner's Draw**
Account Type:	**Equity–gets closed**

to:

Account ID:	**39007**
Description:	**Carol Smith, Drawing**
Account Type:	**Equity–gets closed**

3. Change the accounting period to January 2017.

4. Journalize the following transactions for the month of January. (Use the general journal and Regular Checking Account.)

Jan. 2	Jones contributed $25,000 in cash, and Smith contributed $25,000 in cash.
5	Had cash sales of $13,000 for professional services provided to customers.
11	Paid rent of $2,500.
15	Paid utilities of $1,500.
20	Jones withdrew $1,500 in cash, and Smith withdrew $1,500 in cash.

5. Print the following financial statements as of January 31, 2017: the income statement, balance sheet, and statement of retained earnings.

Case Problem 12–2B

Barker Architectural Services, Inc. received its corporate charter, which authorizes it to issue up to 1 million shares of $2 par-value common stock and 100,000 shares of $50 par-value, 5%, cumulative preferred stock.

1. Open Barker Architectural Services, Inc. from the student data files.

2. Journalize the following transactions for the month of January 2017. (Use the general journal and Regular Checking Account.)

Jan. 3	Issued 20,000 shares of common stock for $200,000 in cash.
10	Had cash sales of $36,000 for design services provided to customers.
11	Paid rent of $11,000.
15	Paid utilities of $700.
31	Declared a cash dividend of $0.60 for each share of common stock outstanding. (Create the Dividends Payable account, Account ID 24300. Change the Dividends Paid account into the Cash Dividends account.)

3. Print the following financial statements as of January 31, 2017: the income statement, balance sheet, and statement of retained earnings.

Fixed Assets

Objectives

A–1 Explore fixed assets and depreciation

A–2 Create ledger accounts for individual fixed assets

A–3 Calculate and record the depreciation of fixed assets

A–4 Make entries to record the disposal of fixed assets

A–5 Prepare and modify reports showing fixed assets and depreciation

Software Features

- Set Up Subsidiary Ledger Records for Fixed Assets
- Select a Depreciation Method
- Calculate and Record Depreciation
- Record the Disposal of Fixed Assets
- Prepare Fixed Asset Reports

Company Files

Before beginning chapter work, access the links menu to download company files.

Note: The Fixed Assets (FAS for Sage 50) Module is not available on the Educational Version of Sage 50 Accounting 2017 that is distributed with this text. Complete the exercises in this Appendix to gain experience with the FAS Module of Sage 50 2017.

Remember that assets are divided into several groups. One group consists of *current assets*: cash, assets that will be turned into cash within one year, and assets that will be used up within one year. Current assets include cash, petty cash, accounts receivable, merchandise inventory, supplies, and prepaid insurance.

Another group consists of *fixed assets*. These assets have the following characteristics:

- They have an expected life of more than one year.
- They are intended for use in the business and not for resale to customers.
- They are tangible, which means that they have a physical substance.

Examples of fixed assets are land, buildings, furniture, office equipment, factory machines, automobiles, and trucks. Fixed assets are also known as *plant assets*, *capital assets*, and *property, plant, and equipment*.

In addition to current assets and fixed assets, some businesses have intangible assets and natural resources. *Intangible assets* are long-term assets that have no physical substance, such as patents, trademarks, copyrights, and franchises. *Natural resources* are long-term assets that are removed from the ground, such as oil, natural gas, coal, and timber.

current assets Cash, assets that will be turned into cash within one year, and assets that will be used up within one year.

fixed assets Assets that have an expected life of more than one year, will be used in the business, and are tangible.

intangible assets Long-term assets that have no physical substance.

natural resources Long-term assets that are removed from the ground.

OBJECTIVE A–1

Explore Fixed Assets and Depreciation

A business must set up a general ledger account for each broad class of fixed assets that it owns. It might have general ledger accounts for land, land improvements, buildings, office furniture, office equipment, factory machines, and trucks. These accounts include all items in a class. For example, the Office Furniture account covers desks, chairs, sofas, file cabinets, and bookshelves. The Office Equipment account covers computers, printers, fax machines, copying machines, and telephone systems.

Because the general ledger accounts for fixed assets involve broad classes, most businesses also maintain records for the individual assets. These records form a subsidiary ledger called the *fixed asset ledger*.

fixed asset ledger A subsidiary ledger that contains records for individual fixed assets.

Recording the Cost of Fixed Assets

When a fixed asset is purchased, the cost is debited to the appropriate general ledger account and entered in the appropriate subsidiary record. The cost of a fixed asset may be greater than the price paid for the asset. For example:

- The cost of land includes not only the price but also any amounts paid for real estate commissions, legal fees, taxes, removal of old structures, draining, and grading.
- Newly acquired land may require improvements such as sidewalks, fences, and outdoor lighting. (The cost of these items is debited to an account called Land Improvements rather than to the Land account.)
- The cost of a new building includes not only the amount paid for construction but also any fees paid for the planning work of architects and engineers, for permits and inspections, and for insurance during construction.
- The cost of machinery and equipment includes not only the price of the item but also any amounts paid for freight, taxes, installation, and insurance during delivery and installation.

Recording Depreciation

depreciation The process of allocating the cost of a fixed asset to operations during its estimated useful life.

Remember that *depreciation* is the process of allocating the cost of a fixed asset to operations during its estimated useful life. Because fixed assets help to produce revenue for a business, their cost must gradually be recorded as an expense while they are being used. This procedure allows the business to match its revenue and expenses.

All fixed assets except land are subject to depreciation. Land is not depreciated because it is considered to have an indefinite useful life. The other fixed assets have limited lives.

Because land is not subject to depreciation, when land and a building are purchased together for one price, this amount must be divided. One portion is debited to the Land account, and the other portion is debited to the Building account. Similarly, land improvements, which are subject to depreciation, are recorded in a separate account, not in the Land account.

Depreciation is an operating expense for a business. It is recorded as part of the adjusting entries for each accounting period. The adjustment for each class of fixed assets consists of a debit to a depreciation expense account and a credit to an accumulated depreciation account. For example, the depreciation for office equipment is recorded by debiting Depreciation Expense–Office Equipment and crediting Accumulated Depreciation–Office Equipment.

Notice that the account used for the credit part of the entry is not the asset account Office Equipment. Instead, it is Accumulated Depreciation–Office Equipment, a contra asset account. As long as the business owns the office equipment, the asset account shows the cost and the contra asset account shows all depreciation taken. On the balance sheet, both amounts are reported and the balance of the contra asset account is subtracted from the balance of the asset account. The difference between the two balances is the *book value* of the fixed asset.

book value The difference between the cost of a fixed asset and its accumulated depreciation.

Cost of Fixed Asset – Accumulated Depreciation = Book Value

Each class of fixed assets has its own depreciation expense account and its own accumulated depreciation account.

Calculating Depreciation

Various methods are used to calculate depreciation. Most of these methods base depreciation on three basic factors: the cost of a fixed asset, its estimated salvage value, and its estimated useful life.

estimated salvage value The amount that a business expects a fixed asset to be worth at the end of its useful life; also known as trade-in value, scrap value, and residual value.

- As noted previously, the cost of a fixed asset is the purchase price plus any amounts that must be spent to prepare the asset for use, such as shipping and installation.
- The *estimated salvage value* is the amount that a business expects a fixed asset to be worth at the end of its useful life. Salvage value is also known as *trade-in value, scrap value,* and *residual value.*
- The *estimated useful life* is the number of years that a business expects a fixed asset to be used in its operations.

estimated useful life The number of years that a business expects a fixed asset to be used in its operations.

Depreciation is calculated on a yearly basis. However, if a business owns a fixed asset for less than a year, it takes depreciation for only the amount of time that the asset was in service during the year. This situation often occurs in the year when a fixed asset was purchased and in the year when it is sold or scrapped.

For financial accounting purposes, the four most commonly used depreciation methods are:

- The straight-line method
- The units-of-production method
- The double declining-balance method
- The sum-of-the-years'-digits method

The Straight-Line Method

straight-line method
A method in which an equal amount of depreciation is taken each year.

The *straight-line method* of depreciation allocates an equal amount of depreciation to each year of an asset's useful life. For example, assume that a business buys a new machine for $42,000 on January 1, 2017. The machine has an estimated salvage value of $2,000 and an estimated useful life of four years. The annual depreciation for the machine is therefore $10,000.

Cost − Salvage Value = Depreciable Cost
$42,000 − $2,000 = $40,000

Depreciable Cost ÷ Useful Life = Annual Depreciation
$40,000 ÷ 4 (years) = $10,000

Table A–1 shows the depreciation expense, accumulated depreciation, and book value of the machine throughout its life when the straight-line method is used. Notice that at the end of the fourth year (2019), the book value is equal to the estimated salvage value ($2,000). No fixed asset can be depreciated below its salvage value.

Table A–1
An Example of
the Straight-Line
Depreciation Method

Year	Cost	Depreciation Expense	Accumulated Depreciation	Book Value End of Year
2017	$42,000	$10,000	$10,000	$32,000
2018	42,000	10,000	20,000	22,000
2019	42,000	10,000	30,000	12,000
2020	42,000	10,000	40,000	2,000

Keep in mind that the book value is simply the depreciated cost of a fixed asset. It does not necessarily represent the market value or even the replacement value of the asset.

The Units-of-Production Method

units-of-production method A method that allocates depreciation on the basis of how much work an asset produces.

The *units-of-production method* allocates depreciation on the basis of how much work the asset produces during each year of its useful life. For a factory machine, the work produced might be expressed in hours of operation. For an automobile or truck, it might be expressed in miles driven.

Consider again the machine purchased for $42,000 on January 1, 2017, which has an estimated salvage value of $2,000. Suppose that management expects the useful life of the machine to be 40,000 hours. The depreciation rate for the machine is $1 per hour.

Cost − Salvage Value = Depreciable Cost
$42,000 − $2,000 = $40,000

Depreciable Cost ÷ Useful Life = Depreciation Rate
$40,000 ÷ 40,000 (hours) = $1 per hour

Assume that the machine is used for 9,000 hours in the first year, 11,000 hours in the second year, 12,000 hours in the third year, and 8,000 hours in the fourth year. The amount of depreciation for the first year will be $9,000.

Usage × Depreciation Rate = Depreciation
9,000 hours × $1 per hour = $9,000

Table A–2 shows the depreciation expense, accumulated depreciation, and book value for the machine through its life when the units-of-production method is used. Again, the book value at the end of the asset's life (40,000 hours) is $2,000, which is the salvage value.

TABLE A–2
An Example of the Units-of-Production Depreciation Method

Year	Cost	Hours	Depreciation Expense	Accumulated Depreciation	Book Value End of Year
2017	$42,000	9,000	$9,000	$9,000	$33,000
2018	42,000	11,000	11,000	20,000	22,000
2019	42,000	12,000	12,000	32,000	10,000
2020	42,000	8,000	8,000	40,000	2,000

The Double Declining-Balance Method

double declining-balance method A method that allocates depreciation at twice the straight-line rate.

accelerated method A method in which more depreciation is taken in the early years of an asset's useful life and less in the later years.

The *double declining-balance method* allocates depreciation at twice the straight-line rate. The doubled rate is applied to the book value of the asset each year. Because the book value decreases from year to year, more depreciation is taken in the early years of the asset's useful life and less depreciation is taken in the later years. Thus, the double declining-balance method is considered an *accelerated method* of depreciation.

Again, assume that a machine is purchased for $42,000 on January 1, 2017, and has an estimated useful life of four years and an estimated salvage value of $2,000. With the double declining-balance method, the salvage value is ignored. The first step in calculating depreciation is to find the straight-line rate and then double it. In this case, the doubled rate is 50%. (The straight-line rate for an asset with a four-year useful life is 25%.)

1/4 = 0.25 × 2 = 0.50 or 50%

When the 50% rate is applied to the first year's book value, the depreciation is $21,000.

Book Value × Depreciation Rate = Depreciation
$42,000 × 0.50 = $21,000

In the second year, the book value is $21,000 and the depreciation is $10,500 ($21,000 × 0.50 = $10,500).

Table A–3 shows the depreciation expense, accumulated depreciation, and book value for the machine throughout its life when the double declining-balance method is used. Notice that in the fourth year, the remaining book value is $2,625, slightly more than the estimated salvage value of $2,000. (Although salvage value is ignored when calculating depreciation with the

Year	Cost	Rate	Depreciation Expense	Accumulated Depreciation	Book Value End of Year
2017	$42,000	50%	$21,000	$21,000	$21,000
2018	42,000	50	10,500	31,500	10,500
2019	42,000	50	5,250	36,750	5,250
2020	42,000	50	2,625	39,375	2,625

double declining-balance method, the asset cannot be depreciated below its salvage value.)

The Sum-of-the-Years'-Digits Method

sum-of-the-years'-digits method A method that allocates depreciation on the basis of a fraction that changes each year.

The *sum-of-the-years'-digits method* allocates depreciation on the basis of a fraction that changes for each year of an asset's useful life. This fraction is applied to the depreciable cost of the asset (the cost less the salvage value). Because the sum-of-the-years'-digits method produces more depreciation in the early years and less depreciation in the later years, it is also considered an accelerated method of depreciation.

The denominator of the fraction (the figure at the bottom of the fraction) remains constant. It is the sum of the digits of the years that make up the useful life of the asset. The numerator of the fraction (the figure at the top of the fraction) changes. It is the number of years that remain in the useful life of the asset.

For example, let us look again at the machine purchased for $42,000 on January 1, 2017. This machine has an estimated useful life of four years and an estimated salvage value of $2,000. The sum of the years' digits for the four years of its useful life is 10 (1 + 2 + 3 + 4 = 10). This is the denominator of the fraction that will be used to calculate depreciation for the asset.

The numerator for the first year will be 4 because there are four years remaining in the useful life of the asset. The numerator for the second year will be 3 because there are only three years remaining in its useful life at that point.

The fraction for the first year is 4/10 while the fraction for the second year is 3/10. Therefore, based on a depreciable cost of $40,000 ($42,000 – $2,000), the depreciation expense for the first two years is calculated as follows:

4/10 of $40,000 = $16,000
3/10 of $40,000 = $12,000

Table A–4 shows the depreciation expense, accumulated depreciation, and book value for the machine throughout its life when the sum-of-the-years'-digits method is used. The book value remaining at the end of the fourth year is always equal to the estimated salvage value.

TABLE A–4
Example of the
Sum-of-the-Years'-Digits
Method

Year	Cost	Fraction	Depreciation Expense	Accumulated Depreciation	Book Value End of Year
2017	$42,000	4/10	$16,000	$16,000	$26,000
2018	42,000	3/10	12,000	28,000	14,000
2019	42,000	2/10	8,000	36,000	6,000
2020	42,000	1/10	4,000	40,000	2,000

Accelerated Cost Recovery Systems

The four depreciation methods that we have discussed so far are used for financial accounting purposes. However, when preparing federal income tax returns, businesses must use either the *accelerated cost recovery system (ACRS)* or the *modified accelerated cost recovery system (MACRS)* to calculate depreciation. The federal government has mandated the use of these two methods to calculate depreciation for most types of fixed assets. ACRS applies to assets placed in service between 1981 and 1986. MACRS applies to assets placed in service after 1986.

The ACRS and MACRS apply to all types of fixed assets except real estate. These methods are intended to encourage businesses to purchase new fixed assets by providing quicker depreciation than the other accelerated methods. Both of these methods operate in a similar way, with just the details differing:

- Each method assigns different types of fixed assets to classes. The classes have specified cost recovery periods rather than useful lives. With the MACRS, the cost recovery periods are 3, 5, 7, 10, 15, and 20 years. For example, automobiles and light trucks have a cost recovery period of 5 years. Office equipment has a cost recovery period of 7 years.
- Each method ignores salvage value. The cost of the asset is fully depreciated.
- Each method uses accelerated depreciation in the early years of the cost recovery period and then switches to straight-line depreciation in the later years.
- Each method uses an approach called the *half-year convention* for the first year. No matter when the asset is placed in service during the first year, the rate for the first year assumes that the asset has been owned for half a year.
- The federal government publishes a table for each method that shows the year-by-year percentage of the cost of an asset that a business can take as depreciation. A portion of the MACRS table is shown in Table A–5. (The percentages after year 6 and for the entire 15-year and 20-year classes have been omitted.)

TABLE A–5
MACRS Depreciation Percentages

Recovery Year	Recovery Period			
	3-Year	5-Year	7-Year	10-Year
1	33.33%	20.00%	14.29%	10.00%
2	44.45	32.00	24.49	18.00
3	14.81	19.20	17.49	14.40
4	7.41	11.52	12.49	11.52
5		11.52	8.93	9.22
6		5.76	8.92	7.37

To see how MACRS works, assume that the machine purchased for $42,000 on January 1, 2017, falls into the class that has a five-year cost recovery period. Because of the half-year convention, the machine is actually depreciated for six years. The first and last years are considered half years. Table A–6 provides an example of depreciation using the MACRS method.

Year	Cost	Rate	Depreciation Expense	Accumulated Depreciation	Book Value End of Year
2017	$42,000	20.00%	$8,400	$8,400	$33,600
2018	42,000	32.00	13,440	21,840	20,160
2019	42,000	19.20	8,064	29,904	12,096
2020	42,000	11.52	4,838	34,742	7,258
2021	42,000	11.52	4,838	39,580	2,420
2022	42,000	5.76	2,420	42,000	—

Checkpoint A–1

1. What is depreciation?
2. Name four financial accounting methods for calculating depreciation.

OBJECTIVE A–2

Create Ledger Accounts for Individual Fixed Assets

Wardwood Construction Company currently owns one piece of equipment—a versatile machine that serves as an excavator, backhoe, and bulldozer. This machine was purchased for $112,000 and recorded in a general ledger account called Equipment. Wardwood's general ledger also contains an Accumulated Depreciation–Equipment account and a Depreciation Expense–Equipment account. These two accounts are used to make adjusting entries for depreciation.

Because of its limited resources, Wardwood currently leases any other fixed assets that it needs, such as a pickup truck to transport materials to jobs. Later, as its finances improve, Wardwood plans to purchase additional fixed assets.

Wardwood Construction wants to use the general journal and the purchases journal to maintain its fixed assets, adjust depreciation expense, and accumulate depreciation for reporting purposes. Its only asset is the machine purchased at a cost of $112,000 and placed into service at the beginning of 2017, when the business was formed.

On February 1, 2017, Wardwood Construction Company purchased a new computer system for $4,500 on account from Office Max (Invoice 33299). Wardwood estimates that the computer system will have a useful life of four years and have no salvage value. Record the purchase in Sage 50 Accounting 2017.

Step 1:

Open Sage 50 Accounting.

Step 2:

Open App. – Wardwood Construction Company.

Step 3:

Create the following ledger accounts:

Account ID:	**109**
Description:	**Computer**
Account Type:	**Fixed Assets**

Account ID:	**109.5**
Description:	**Accum. Depr.–Computer**
Account Type:	**Accumulated Depreciation**

Account ID:	**511**
Description:	**Depr. Expense–Computer**
Account Type:	**Expenses**

Step 4:

Record the purchase of the computer using the Purchases/Receive Inventory window and using 109 as the GL Account.

Step 5:

Key **Purchased computer w/4 year life** in the *Description* field, as shown in Figure A–1.

FIGURE A–1
Computer Purchase Recorded

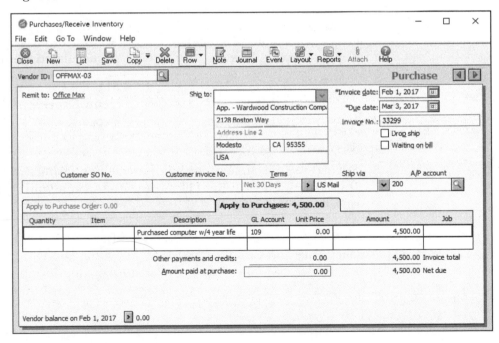

Step 6:

Click <u>S</u>ave and then Close.

Checkpoint A–2

1. What journal is used for fixed asset purchases on account?
2. What is a subsidiary ledger? How might it be used for fixed assets?

Objective A–2 Practice

Blufrog Maintenance Company wants to use Sage 50 to maintain records of its fixed assets and calculate depreciation. Blufrog currently owns only one fixed asset, a truck that appears in the Equipment account (112). This truck cost $42,000, has a salvage value of $2,000, has an expected life of five years, and has accumulated depreciation of $10,000 through January 31, 2017.

On February 23, 2017, Blufrog Maintenance Company purchased a new computer system for $7,500 on credit from Office Depot (Invoice 23998). Blufrog estimates that the computer system will have a salvage value of $500 and a useful life of five years.

Step 1:

Open App. – Blufrog Maintenance Company in Sage 50 Accounting.

Step 2:

Create the following general ledger accounts:

Account ID:	**111**
Description:	**Computer**
Account Type:	**Fixed Assets**
Account ID:	**111.5**
Description:	**Accum. Depr.–Computer**
Account Type:	**Accumulated Depreciation**
Account ID:	**511**
Description:	**Depr. Expense–Computer**
Account Type:	**Expenses**

Step 3:

Record the purchase of the computer system using the Purchases/Receive Inventory window, using 111 as the GL Account, and referring to the purchase data above.

Step 4:

Click $\underline{S}$ave and Close.

Calculate and Record the Depreciation of Fixed Assets

Wardwood Construction Company wants to calculate and record depreciation for the excavator (Account 112) and the computer (Account 109), as of March 31, 2017. It will be necessary to manually calculate the depreciation and enter the amount into the accounting records.

Calculating Depreciation

Wardwood Construction Company wants to calculate two months' worth of depreciation for both assets because no depreciation has been taken for February or March 2017. Follow the steps to manually calculate the total depreciation for the two-month period.

Excavating Equipment

The original cost of the excavator is $112,000, the salvage value is listed at $52,000, its useful life is five years (60 months), and it was placed into service on January 1, 2017. Note that depreciation of $1,000 has already been taken for the period January 1, 2017 to January 31, 2017.

Computer Equipment

The original cost of the computer is $4,500, there is no salvage value, its useful life is four years (48 months), and it was placed into service on January 1, 2017.

Step 1:

Open App. – Wardwood Construction Company, if necessary.

Step 2:

Divide the cost of the excavator minus its salvage value by 60 (Total Life in Months) and multiply that amount by 2. The result is the depreciation for the period.

> (($112,000 – $52,000)/60) = $1,000 per month.
> $1,000 × 2 = $2,000, the depreciation for the two-month period.

Step 3:

Divide the cost of the computer minus its salvage value by 48 (Total Life in Months) and multiply that amount by 2. The result is the depreciation for the period.

> (($4,500 – $0)/48) = $93.75 per month.
> $93.75 × 2 = $187.50, the depreciation for the two-month period.

Entering Depreciation in the General Journal and General Ledger

Once the depreciation has been calculated, it is necessary to enter the amount as an adjusting entry in the general journal. Sage 50 will automatically post the amounts from the general journal to the general ledger. The appropriate accounts have been created previously and are available for use in the general journal. The entries include the following:

March 31, 2017
  Depreciation Expense–Equipment   2,000
      Accumulated Depreciation–Equipment   2,000
      (To record depreciation through Mar. 31, 2017)

March 31, 2017
  Depreciation Expense–Computer   187.50
      Accumulated Depreciation–Computer   187.50
      (To record depreciation through Mar. 31, 2017)

Step 4:

Click Tasks and *General Journal Entry* on the Menu bar, as shown in Figure A–2.

FIGURE A–2
Tasks and General Journal Entry Selected from the Menu Bar

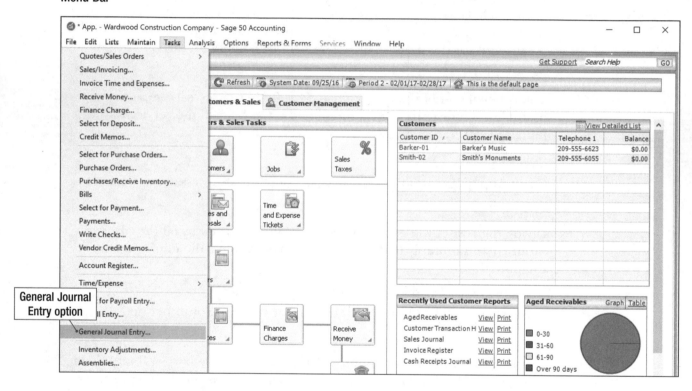

Step 5:
Key **3/31/2017** in the *Date* field.

Step 6:
Key **Adjustment** in the *Reference* field.

Step 7:
Select *510* (Depreciation Expense–Equipment) as the GL Account.

Step 8:
Key **Depreciation Adjustment** in the *Description* field.

Step 9:

Key **2000.00** (Depreciation manually calculated) in the *Debit* field.

Step 10:

Select *112.5* (Accumulated Depreciation–Equipment) as the GL Account in the second row.

Step 11:

Key **Depreciation Adjustment** in the *Description* field, if needed.

Step 12:

Key **2000.00** (Depreciation manually calculated) in the *Credit* field.

Step 13:

Select *511* (Depreciation Expense–Computer) as the GL Account in the third row.

Step 14:

Key **Depreciation Adjustment** in the *Description* field.

Step 15:

Key **187.50** (Depreciation manually calculated) in the *Debit* field.

Step 16:

Select *109.5* (Accumulated Depreciation–Computer) as the GL Account in the fourth row.

Step 17:

Key **Depreciation Adjustment** in the *Description* field.

Step 18:

Key **187.50** (Depreciation manually calculated) in the *Credit* field.

Step 19:

Review your screen against Figure A–3 for accuracy, making any necessary changes.

FIGURE A–3
Completed General
Journal Entry for Fixed
Asset Depreciation

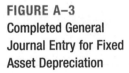

General Journal Entry

File   Edit   Go To   Window   Help

Close   New   List   Save   Print   Copy   Delete   Row   Reports   Help

Journal Entry

Date: Mar 31, 2017   ☐ Reverse Transaction
Reference: Adjustment

GL Account	Description	Debit	Credit	Job
510	Depreciation Adjustment	2,000.00		
112.5	Depreciation Adjustment		2,000.00	
511	Depreciation Adjustment	187.50		
109.5	Depreciation Adjustment		187.50	
	Totals:	2,187.50	2,187.50	
	Out of Balance:	0.00		

Step 20:

Click Save and then close the General Journal Entry window.

> ## Checkpoint A-3
>
> 1. What journal is used to record depreciation?
> 2. What accounts are affected when adjusting for fixed asset depreciation?

 Objective A-3 Practice

Blufrog Maintenance Company wants to calculate and record depreciation from February 1, 2017 through June 30, 2017.

Step 1:

Open the App. – Blufrog Maintenance Company in Sage 50 Accounting.

Step 2:

The manual calculation of the assets are as follows:

Equipment–Truck
($42,000 – $2,000)/60 = $666.67 per month.
$666.67 × 5 = $3333.35, the depreciation for the five-month period.

Computer
($7,500 – $500)/60 = $116.67 per month.
$116.67 × 4 = $466.68, the depreciation for the four-month period.
Notice that the computer was put into service February 23, 2017.
Therefore, there are only four full months of depreciation.

Step 3:

Record the depreciation expense in the general journal and post it to the general ledger. Refer to Figure A–4 for comparison, making any necessary changes.

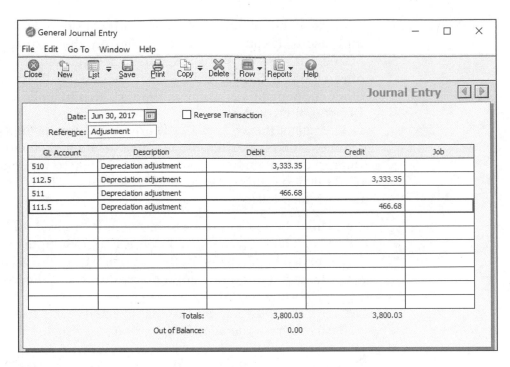

General Journal Entry — □ ✕

File   Edit   Go To   Window   Help

Close   New   List   Save   Print   Copy   Delete   Row   Reports   Help

Journal Entry ◀ ▶

Date: Jun 30, 2017   ☐ Reverse Transaction
Reference: Adjustment

GL Account	Description	Debit	Credit	Job
510	Depreciation adjustment	3,333.35		
112.5	Depreciation adjustment		3,333.35	
511	Depreciation adjustment	466.68		
111.5	Depreciation adjustment		466.68	
	Totals:	3,800.03	3,800.03	
	Out of Balance:	0.00		

Step 4:

Close Blufrog Maintenance Company.

OBJECTIVE A–4

Make Entries to Record the Disposal of Fixed Assets

Remember that all fixed assets except land have limited lives. Eventually, they wear out or become obsolete or their owners want to replace them with newer, more efficient models. When a fixed asset is no longer useful, a business will dispose of the asset by selling it, trading it in for a new asset, or scrapping it if it has no remaining value.

Suppose that Wardwood Construction Company decides to sell the excavator that it owns. On March 31, 2017, it receives $120,000 for the excavator. Wardwood must determine whether there is a gain or loss on this transaction and then record the disposal in its accounting records.

When a firm disposes of a fixed asset, it must bring depreciation on the asset up to date. Then it can find the book value of the asset and determine whether the sale produced a gain or loss.

In the case of the excavator sold by Wardwood Construction Company, the depreciation entry made on March 31, 2017, results in accumulated depreciation of $3,000 and a book value of $109,000. Remember that the book value of a fixed asset is the difference between its cost and its accumulated depreciation. The cost of the excavator was $112,000. The book value is therefore $109,000 ($112,000 – $3,000 = $109,000).

If the selling price of a fixed asset is greater than its book value, there is a gain on the sale. If the selling price of a fixed asset is less than its book value, there is a loss on the sale. Because Wardwood sold its excavator for $120,000 and the book value of the machine is $109,000, the firm has a gain of $11,000.

The gain on the sale of a fixed asset is considered other (nonoperating) income because it does not result from the normal operations of a business. It is therefore recorded in an account called Gain on Disposal of Fixed Assets. Similarly, the loss on the sale of a fixed asset is considered other (nonoperating) expense. It is recorded in an account called Loss on Disposal of Fixed Assets.

The sale of the excavator by Wardwood Construction Company requires a debit of $120,000 to Cash, a debit of $3,000 to Accumulated Depreciation–Equipment, a credit of $112,000 to Equipment, and a credit of $11,000 to Gain on Disposal of Fixed Assets. The effects of this transaction are as follows:

- The debit to Cash records the amount received for the excavator.
- The debit to Accumulated Depreciation–Equipment removes the accumulated depreciation of the excavator from the accounting records.
- The credit to Equipment removes the cost of the excavator from the accounting records.
- The credit to Gain on Disposal of Fixed Assets records the income earned from the sale of the excavator.

Recording the Disposal of a Fixed Asset at a Gain

Wardwood Construction Company does not yet have a Gain on Disposal of Fixed Assets account in its general ledger. Therefore, it must now create this account.

Step 1:

Open App. – Wardwood Construction Company in Sage 50 Accounting.

Step 2:

Create the following general ledger account:

Account ID:	**452**
Description:	**Gain on Disposal of Fxd Assets**
Account Type:	**Income**

Step 3:

Click Tasks and *General Journal Entry* on the Menu bar.

Step 4:

Key **3/31/2017** in *Date* field.

Step 5:

Key **Disposal** in the *Reference* field.

Step 6:

Select *100* (Cash) as the GL Account.

Step 7:

Key **Disposal of Excavator** in the *Description* field.

Step 8:
Key **120,000.00** in the *Debit* field.

Step 9:
Go to the next line and select *112.5* (Accumulated Depreciation–Equipment) as the GL Account.

Step 10:
Key **3,000.00** in the *Debit* field.

Step 11:
Go to the next line and select *112* (Equipment) as the GL Account.

Step 12:
Key **112,000.00** in the *Credit* field.

Step 13:
Go to the next line and select *452* (Gain on Disposal of Fixed Assets) as the GL Account.

Step 14:
Key **11,000.00** in the *Credit* field.

Step 15:
Compare your screen with Figure A–5 for accuracy, making any necessary changes.

FIGURE A–5
General Journal Entry for Disposal of Fixed Asset

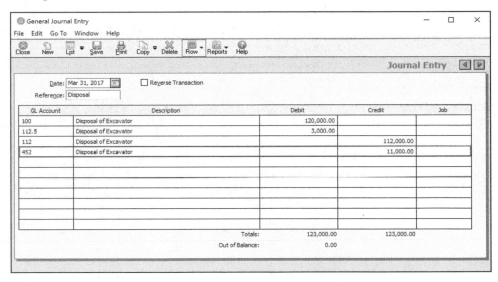

Step 16:
Click Save and then Close.

Objective A-4 Practice

On June 30, 2017, Blufrog Maintenance Company decides to dispose of the truck that it owns to purchase a new model. Blufrog sells the truck for $40,000 in cash. The current book value is $28,666.65.

Step 1:

Open Blufrog Maintenance Company in Sage 50 Accounting.

Step 2:

Create the following general ledger account.

Account ID:	**452**
Description:	**Gain on Disposal of Fxd Assets**
Account Type:	**Income**

Step 3:

Record the disposal of the truck in the general journal and post to the general ledger.

Step 4:

Compare you screen with Figure A-6 for accuracy, make any necessary changes, and then close.

FIGURE A-6
General Journal Entry for Disposal of a Fixed Asset

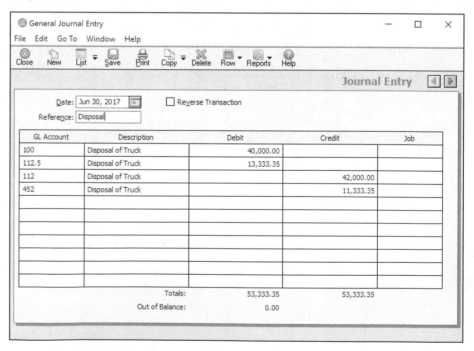

OBJECTIVE A-5

Prepare and Modify Reports Showing Fixed Assets and Depreciation

Management needs to have information on the purchase, depreciation, and disposal of fixed assets so it can develop plans to replace older, less efficient ones. Many businesses set up long-term budgets for the replacement and acquisition of new fixed assets.

On March 31, 2017, Wardwood Construction Company wants to review the depreciation and disposal of fixed assets since March 1, 2017. In addition, it would like to modify the default format of the report.

Step 1:

Open Wardwood Construction Company, if it is not already open.

Step 2:

Click Reports & Forms on the Menu bar and then *General Ledger* at the drop-down list.

Step 3:

Select General Journal from the General Ledger: Account Information window.

Step 4:

Click Options on the Menu bar.

Step 5:

Deselect *Include Accounts with Zero Amounts.*

Step 6:

Select *Range* in the *Date* field.

Step 7:

Select from *Mar 1, 2017* to *Mar 31, 2017.*

Step 8:

Click OK. Compare your screen with Figure A–7.

FIGURE A–7
General Journal Report

| 10/24/16 at 14:00:01.58 | *****EDUCATIONAL VERSION ONLY***** | | | | Page: 1 |

App. - Wardwood Construction Company
General Journal
For the Period From Mar 1, 2017 to Mar 31, 2017

Filter Criteria includes: Report order is by Date. Report is printed with Accounts having Zero Amounts and with shortened descriptions and in Detail Format.

Date	Account ID	Reference	Trans Description	Debit Amt	Credit Amt
3/31/17	510	Adjustment	Depreciation Adjustment	2,000.00	
	112.5		Depreciation Adjustment		2,000.00
	511		Depreciation Adjustment	187.50	
	109.5		Depreciation Adjustment		187.50
3/31/17	100	Disposal	Disposal of Excavator	120,000.00	
	112.5		Disposal of Excavator	3,000.00	
	112		Disposal of Excavator		112,000.00
	452		Disposal of Excavator		11,000.00
		Total		**125,187.50**	**125,187.50**

Management would like to design a new form for this printout to read "Wardwood Construction Company Depreciation and Disposal" in bold type centered on the report.

Step 9:

Click Fonts on the Menu bar.

Step 10:

Key **Depreciation and Disposal** in the *Title 1 Report Label* field, as shown in Figure A–8.

FIGURE A–8
Depreciation and
Disposal Name Change

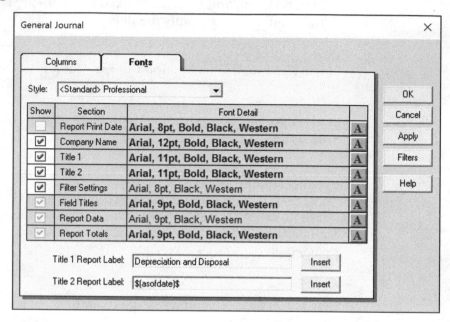

Step 11:

Click Insert, OK, and then OK again.

Step 12:

Click Save on the Menu bar.

Step 13:

Key **Depreciation and Disposal, Mar** in the *Report name* field, as shown in Figure A–9.

FIGURE A–9
File Saved as
Depreciation and
Disposal, Mar

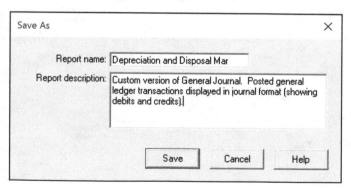

Step 14:

Click Save, and then close or cancel all subsequent queries.

This report is available as a special report in the reports section.

Checkpoint A–5

1. Where can fixed asset depreciation and disposal transactions be found?
2. Can the General Journal Report be modified? If so, how?

Objective A–5 Practice

Blufrog Maintenance Company wants to prepare a report for the period of February 1, 2017, to June 30, 2017.

Step 1:

Open Blufrog Maintenance Company.

Step 2:

Prepare the report using the General Journal Report and modify the report name to Depreciation and Disposal. Your printout should look like Figure A–10.

FIGURE A–10
General Journal Report
February to June 2017

10/24/16 at 09:21:07.34	*****EDUCATIONAL VERSION ONLY*****				Page: 1

App. - Blufrog Maintenance Company
Depreciation and Disposal
For the Period From Feb 1, 2017 to Jun 30, 2017

Filter Criteria includes: Report order is by Date. Report is printed with Accounts having Zero Amounts and with shortened descriptions and in Detail Format.

Date	Account ID	Reference	Trans Description	Debit Amt	Credit Amt
6/30/17	510	Adjustment	Depreciation adjustment	3,333.35	
	112.5		Depreciation adjustment		3,333.35
	511		Depreciation adjustment	466.68	
	111.5		Depreciation adjustment		466.68
6/30/17	100	Disposal	Disposal of Truck	40,000.00	
	112.5		Disposal of Truck	13,333.35	
	112		Disposal of Truck		42,000.00
	452		Disposal of Truck		11,333.35
		Total		57,133.38	57,133.38

Chapter Review and Assessment

Software Command Summary

Create Subsidiary Ledger Records	Maintain, Chart of Accounts, Enter the asset information for Fixed Assets Account
Calculate Depreciation	Tasks, General Journal Entry, Manually calculate depreciation for period
Record the Disposal of Fixed Assets	Tasks, General Journal Entry, Manually calculate gain or loss on disposal of asset
Prepare Reports	Reports & Forms, Select the Report Type, Design, Complete Report Filter

Checkpoint Answers

Checkpoint A–1

1. Depreciation is the process of allocating the cost of a fixed asset to operations during its estimated useful life.
2. Four financial accounting methods for calculating depreciation are the straight-line method, the units-of-production method, the double declining-balance method, and the sum-of-the-years'-digits method.

Checkpoint A–2

1. The Purchase/Receive Inventory journal is used for fixed asset purchases on account.
2. A subsidiary ledger keeps track of individual records, and it can be used to keep track of individual fixed assets.

Checkpoint A–3

1. The general journal is used to record depreciation.
2. Depreciation Expense and Accumulated Depreciation accounts are affected when adjusting for fixed asset depreciation.

Checkpoint A–4

1. The book value of a fixed asset is the difference between its cost and its accumulated depreciation.
2. A gain on the disposal of a fixed asset is considered other (non-operating) income.

Checkpoint A–5

1. Fixed asset depreciation and disposal transactions can be found in the General Journal.
2. The General Journal Report can be modified by selecting Design from the menu.

Study Quizzes

Take the study quiz online to check your understanding of chapter concepts. The quiz can be taken multiple times.

Content Check

Multiple Choice: Choose only one response for each question.

1. Which of the following methods allocates an equal amount of depreciation each year?
   A. Sum-of-the-years'-digits method
   B. Double declining-balance method
   C. Straight-line method
   D. Units-of-production method

2. Which of the following statements about fixed assets is *not* true?
   A. Fixed assets are intended for use in the operations of a business.
   B. Fixed assets have an estimated useful life of more than one year.
   C. Fixed assets are acquired for resale to customers.
   D. Fixed assets are tangible.

3. Depreciation is taken on all fixed assets except
   A. land.
   B. land improvements.
   C. buildings.
   D. equipment and machinery.

4. The difference between the cost of a fixed asset and its accumulated depreciation is the
   A. purchase price.
   B. book value.
   C. salvage value.
   D. selling price.

5. Depreciable cost is
   A. cost – depreciation expense.
   B. cost – accumulated depreciation.
   C. cost – salvage value.
   D. accumulated depreciation – salvage value.

Short Essay Response

Provide a detailed answer for each question.

1. What is depreciation? Why must businesses record depreciation?
2. What is accelerated depreciation? Name two financial accounting methods for calculating depreciation that are accelerated.
3. What is the modified accelerated cost recovery system? When is this method used?
4. How is the sale of a fixed asset at a gain recorded? What general ledger accounts are debited and credited?

5. What is the effect on the income statement and balance sheet if the depreciation expense is not taken for the period?

Cooperative Learning

1. Form groups of three or four students and prepare a list of four possible fixed assets that might be used by a construction company. Estimate the cost, salvage value, useful life, and depreciable cost for each of the four assets. Calculate the annual straight-line depreciation for each of the assets.
2. Research online what portion of businesses use the straight-line method of depreciation for financial accounting purposes.

Writing and Decision Making

Gary Stevens, the newly hired manager of an engineering company, does not understand how the cost of the firm's equipment is expensed. In memo format, explain to him how depreciation provides a means of expensing the cost of the equipment and how it affects both the balance sheet and income statement.

Case Problems

Demonstrate your knowledge of the Sage 50 features discussed in this chapter by completing the following case problems.

Case Problem A–1A

On January 31, 2017, Flores Construction Company's only fixed asset currently on its books is construction equipment. This construction equipment cost $16,000, has an estimated salvage value of $1,000, and has an estimated useful life of four years. The equipment was purchased on January 2, 2017.

On January 31, 2017, Flores Construction Company purchases landscaping equipment on credit from Steve's Supply Warehouse. The cost is $13,000, the estimated salvage value is $1,000, and the estimated useful life is four years (Invoice 555).

1. Open the company file from the student data files and then create the following general ledger accounts.

Account ID:	**109**
Description:	**Landscaping Equipment**
Account Type:	**Fixed Assets**

Account ID:	**109.5**
Description:	**Accum. Depr.–Landscaping Eq.**
Account Type:	**Accumulated Depreciation**

HINT

Change the *GL Account* field to *109*.

2. Use the Purchases/Receive Inventory window to record the purchase of the landscaping equipment.

3. Print the Purchase Journal.

Case Problem A–2A

On June 30, 2017, Flores Construction Company updates the depreciation expense on its fixed assets. Use Sage 50 to do the following:

1. Calculate the depreciation expense of the construction equipment (six months) and the landscaping equipment (five months) as of June 30, 2017.

HINT

Use Account 510 for both depreciation expenses.

2. Record the depreciation expense in the general journal.

   On July 1, 2017, Flores decides to sell the landscaping equipment for $12,900 in cash. Flores wants to purchase a more advanced model.

3. Create the following general ledger account.

Account ID:	**452**
Description:	**Gain on Disposal of Fxd Assets**
Account Type:	**Income**

4. Record the disposal of the landscaping equipment in the general journal.

5. Print the general journal entries for June 30, 2017 to July 1, 2017.

Case Problem A–1B

On January 31, 2017, NorCal Construction Company's only fixed asset currently on its books is an excavator. This excavator cost $26,000, has an estimated salvage value of $5,000, and has an estimated useful life of seven years. The equipment was purchased on January 2, 2017.

On January 31, 2017, NorCal Construction Company purchases digging equipment on credit from Construction Supply Warehouse (Invoice 48537). The cost is $18,500, the estimated salvage value is $2,000, and the estimated useful life is five years.

1. Open the company file from the student data files and then create the following general ledger accounts.

Account ID:	**109**
Description:	**Digging Equipment**
Account Type:	**Fixed Assets**

Account ID:	**109.5**
Description:	**Accum. Depr.–Digging Eq.**
Account Type:	**Accumulated Depreciation**

HINT

Change the *GL Account* field to *109*.

2. Use the Purchases/Receive Inventory window to record the purchase of the digging equipment.

3. Print the Purchase Journal.

Case Problem A–2B

On June 30, 2017, NorCal Construction Company updates the depreciation expense on its fixed assets. Use Sage 50 to do the following:

1. Calculate the depreciation expense of the excavator (six months) and the digging equipment (five months) as of June 30, 2017.

2. Record the depreciation expense in the general journal.

   On July 1, 2017, NorCal decides to sell the digging equipment for $17,550 in cash. NorCal intends to lease a more powerful model.

3. Create the following general ledger account.

Account ID:	**452**
Description:	**Gain on Disposal of Fxd Assets**
Account Type:	**Income**

4. Record the disposal of the digging equipment in the general journal.

5. Print the general journal entries for June 30, 2017 to July 1, 2017.

> **HINT**
> Use Account 510 for both depreciation expenses.

Index